JOURNAL FOR STAR WISDOM 2012

JOURNAL FOR STAR WISDOM

2012

Edited by Robert Powell

SteinerBooks

Steinerbooks/Anthroposophic Press, Inc.

610 Main Street, Suite 1

Great Barrington, MA, 01230

www.steinerbooks.org

Cover and interior: William Jens Jensen

Print: isbn: 978-0-88010-652-8

eBook: isbn: 978-0-88010-653-5

CONTENTS

ASTROSOPHY

The Sophia Foundation was founded and exists to help usher in the new Age of Sophia and the corresponding Sophianic culture, the Rose of the World, prophesied by Daniel Andreev and other spiritual teachers. Part of the work of the Sophia Foundation is the cultivation of a new star wisdom, *Astro-Sophia* (Astrosophy), now arising in our time in response to the descent of Sophia, who is the bearer of Divine Wisdom, just as Christ (the Logos, or the Lamb) is the bearer of Divine Love. Like the star wisdom of antiquity, Astrosophy is sidereal, which means "of the stars." Astrosophy, inspired by Divine Sophia, descending from stellar heights, directs our consciousness toward the glory and majesty of the starry heavens, to encompass the entire celestial sphere of our cosmos and, beyond this, to the galactic realm—the realm that Daniel Andreev referred to as "the heights of our universe"—from which Sophia is descending on her path of approach into our cosmos. Sophia draws our attention not only to the star mysteries of the heights, but also to the cosmic mysteries connected with Christ's deeds of redemption wrought two thousand years ago. To penetrate these mysteries is the purpose of the yearly *Journal for Star Wisdom*.

&

For information about Astrosophy/Choreocosmos/Cosmic Dance workshops
Contact the Sophia Foundation:
525 Gough St. #103, San Francisco, CA 94102
(415) 522-1150; sophia@sophiafoundation.org;
www.sophiafoundation.org

PREFACE

Robert Powell, Ph.D.

This is the third edition of the *Journal for Star Wisdom,* which is intended as a help to all people interested in the new star wisdom of astrosophy and in the cosmic dimension of Christianity, which began with the star of the magi. The calendar comprises an ephemeris page for each month of the year computed with the help of Peter Treadgold's Astrofire computer program, and a monthly commentary by Claudia McLaren Lainson (with Sally Nurney). The monthly commentary relates the geocentric and heliocentric planetary movements to events in the life of Jesus Christ.

Jesus Christ united the levels of the earthly personality (geocentric = Earth-centered) and the higher self (heliocentric = Sun-centered) in so far as he was the most highly evolved earthly personality (Jesus) embodying the Higher Self (Christ) of all existence, the Divine "I AM." To see the life of Jesus Christ in relation to the world of stars opens the door to a profound experience of the cosmos, giving rise to a new star wisdom (astrosophy) that is the spiritual science of Cosmic Christianity.

The *Journal for Star Wisdom* is scientific, resting upon a solid mathematical-astronomical foundation and also upon a secure chronology of the life of Jesus Christ, and at the same time it is spiritual, aspiring to the higher dimension of existence that is expressed outwardly in the world of stars. The scientific and the spiritual come together in the sidereal zodiac that originated with the Babylonians and was used by the three magi who beheld the star of Bethlehem and came to pay homage to Jesus a few months after his birth. In continuity of spirit with the origins of Cosmic Christianity with the three magi, the sidereal zodiac is the frame of reference used for the computation of the geocentric and heliocentric planetary movements which are commented upon in the light of the life of Jesus Christ in the *Journal for Star Wisdom.*

Thus, all zodiacal longitudes indicated in the text and presented in the following calendar are in terms of the sidereal zodiac, which has to be distinguished from the tropical zodiac in widespread use in contemporary astrology in the West. The tropical zodiac was introduced into astrology in the middle of the second century AD by the Greek astronomer Claudius Ptolemy. Prior to this the sidereal zodiac was in use. Such was the influence of Ptolemy upon the Western astrological tradition that the tropical zodiac became substituted for the sidereal zodiac used by the Babylonians, Egyptians, and early Greek astrologers. Yet the astrological tradition in India was not influenced by Ptolemy, and so the sidereal zodiac is still used to this day by Hindu astrologers.

The sidereal zodiac originated with the Babylonians in the sixth to fifth centuries BC and was defined by them in relation to certain bright stars. For example, Aldebaran ("the Bull's eye") is located in the middle of the sidereal sign/constellation of the Bull at 15° Taurus, and Antares ("the Scorpion's heart") is in the middle of the sidereal sign/constellation of the Scorpion at 15° Scorpio. The sidereal signs, each 30° long, coincide closely with the twelve astronomical zodiacal constellations of the same name, whereas the signs of the tropical zodiac, since they are defined in relation to the vernal point, now have little or no relationship to the corresponding zodiacal constellations. This is because the vernal point, the zodiacal location of the sun on March 20/21, shifts slowly backward through the sidereal zodiac at a rate of 1° in seventy-two years ("the precession of the equinoxes").When Ptolemy introduced the tropical zodiac into astrology, there was an almost exact coincidence between the tropical and the sidereal zodiac, as the vernal point, which is defined to be 0° Aries in the tropical zodiac, was at 1° Aries in the sidereal zodiac in the middle of the second century AD. Thus, there was only 1° difference between the two zodiacs. So, it made hardly any difference to Ptolemy or his contemporaries to use the tropical zodiac instead of the sidereal zodiac. But now—the vernal point, on account of precession, having shifted back from 1° Aries to 5° Pisces—there is a 25° difference and so there is virtually no correspondence between the two. Without going into further detail concerning the complex issue of the zodiac, as shown in the *Hermetic Astrology* trilogy, the sidereal zodiac is the zodiac used by the three magi, who were the last representatives of the true star wisdom of antiquity. For this reason the sidereal zodiac is used throughout the *Journal for Star Wisdom*.

Readers interested in exploring the scientific (astronomical and chronological) foundations of Cosmic Christianity are referred to the works listed below under "Literature." The *Chronicle of the Living Christ: Foundations of Cosmic Christianity,* listed on the next page, is an indispensable source of reference (abbreviated *Chron.*) for the *Journal for Star Wisdom*, as, too, are the four Gospels (Matthew = Mt.; Mark = Mk.; Luke = Lk.; John = Jn.). The chronology of the life of Jesus Christ rests upon the description of his daily life by Anne Catherine Emmerich in her four-volume work *The Life of Jesus Christ* (abbreviated *LJC*). Further details concerning the *Journal for Star Wisdom* and how to work with it on a daily basis may be found in the general introduction to the *Christian Star Calendar*. The general introduction explains all the features of the *Journal for Star Wisdom*. The new edition, published 2003, includes sections on the megastars (stars of great luminosity) and on the 36 decans (10° subdivisions of the twelve signs of the zodiac) in relation to their planetary rulers and to the extra-zodiacal constellations, those constellations above or below

the circle of the twelve constellations/signs of the zodiac. Further material on the decans, including examples of historical personalities born in the various decans, and also a wealth of other material on the signs of the sidereal zodiac, is to be found in *Cosmic Dances of the Zodiac*, listed below. Also foundational is *History of the Zodiac*, published by Sophia Academic Press, listed below under "Works by Robert Powell."

LITERATURE

(See also "References" on pages 243–244)

General Introduction to the Christian Star Calendar: A Key to Understanding, 2nd ed. Palo Alto, CA: Sophia Foundation, 2003.

Bento, William, Robert Schiappacasse, and David Tresemer, *Signs in the Heavens: A Message for our Time*. Boulder: StarHouse, 2000.

Emmerich, Anne Catherine, *The Life of Jesus Christ,* 4 vols. Rockford, IL: Tan Books, 2004 (cited hereafter as "*LJC*").

Paul, Lacquanna, and Robert Powell, *Cosmic Dances of the Planets*. San Rafael, CA: Sophia Foundation Press, 2007.

———, *Cosmic Dances of the Zodiac*. San Rafael, CA: Sophia Foundation Press, 2007.

Smith, Edward, *The Burning Bush: An Anthroposophical Commentary on the Bible*. Great Barrington, MA: SteinerBooks, 1997.

Sucher, Willi, *Cosmic Christianity and the Changing Countenance of Cosmology*. Great Barrington, MA: SteinerBooks, 1993. *Isis Sophia* and other works by Willi Sucher are available from the Astrosophy Research Center, PO Box 13, Meadow Vista, CA 95722.

Tidball, Charles S., and Robert Powell, *Jesus, Lazarus, and the Messiah: Unveiling Three Christian Mysteries*. Great Barrington, MA: SteinerBooks, 2005.This book offers a penetrating study of the Christ mysteries against the background of *Chronicle of the Living Christ* and contains two chapters by Robert Powell on the Apostle John and John the Evangelist (Lazarus).

Tresemer, David (with Robert Schiappacasse), *Star Wisdom & Rudolf Steiner: A Life Seen Through the Oracle of the Solar Cross*. Great Barrington. MA: SteinerBooks, 2007.

ASTROSOPHIC WORKS BY ROBERT POWELL, PH.D.

Starcrafts (formerly Astro Communication Services, or ACS):
  History of the Houses (1997).
  History of the Planets (1989).
  The Zodiac: A Historical Survey (1984).
  www.acspublications.com

www.astrocom.com

Business Address:

Starcrafts Publishing

334 Calef Hwy.

Epping, NH 03042

Phone: 603-734-4300

Fax: 603-734-4311

Contact maria@starcraftseast.com

SteinerBooks:

Orders: (703) 661-1594; www.steinerbooks.org; PO Box 960, Herndon, VA 20172.

The Astrological Revolution: Unveiling the Science of the Stars as a Science of Reincarnation and Karma, coauthor Kevin Dann (Great Barrington, MA: SteinerBooks, 2010). After reestablishing the sidereal zodiac as a basis for astrology that penetrates the mystery of the stars' relationship to human destiny, the reader is invited to discover the astrological significance of the totality of the vast sphere of stars surrounding the Earth. This book points to the astrological significance of the entire celestial sphere, including all the stars and constellations beyond the twelve zodiacal signs. This discovery is revealed by the study of megastars, illustrating how they show up in an extraordinary way in Christ's healing miracles by aligning with the Sun at the time of those events. This book offers a spiritual, yet scientific, path toward a new relationship to the stars.

Christian Hermetic Astrology: The Star of the Magi and the Life of Christ (Great Barrington, MA: SteinerBooks, 1998). Twenty-five discourses set in the "Temple of the Sun," where Hermes and his pupils gather to meditate on the Birth, the Miracles, and the Passion of Jesus Christ. The discourses offer a series of meditative contemplations on the deeds of Christ in relation to the mysteries of the cosmos. They are an expression of the age-old hermetic mystery wisdom of the ancient Egyptian sage, Hermes Trismegistus. This book offers a meditative approach to the cosmic correspondences between major events in the life of Christ and the heavenly configurations at that time 2,000 years ago.

Chronicle of the Living Christ: Foundations of Cosmic Christianity (Great Barrington, MA: SteinerBooks, 1996). An account of the life of Christ, day by day, throughout most of the 3½ years of his ministry, including the horoscopes of conception, birth, and death of Jesus, Mary and John the Baptist, together with a wealth of material relating to a new star wisdom focused on the life of Christ. This work provides the chronological basis for *Christian Hermetic Astrology* and the *Journal for Star Wisdom*.

Elijah Come Again. A Prophet for our Time: A Scientific Approach to Reincarnation (Great Barrington, MA: Steiner Books, 2009). By way of horoscope comparisons from conception–birth–death in one incarnation to conception–birth–death in the next, this work establishes scientifically two basic astrosophical research findings. These are: the importance 1) of the sidereal zodiac and 2) of the heliocentric positions of the planets. Also, for the first time, the identity of the "saintly nun" is revealed, of whom Rudolf Steiner spoke in a conversation with Marie von Sivers about tracing Novalis's karmic background. The focus throughout the book is on the Elijah individuality in his various incarnations, and is based solidly on Rudolf Steiner's indications. It also can be read as a karmic biography by anyone who chooses to omit the astrosophical material.

Journal for Star Wisdom (Great Barrington, MA: SteinerBooks, annual). Edited by Robert Powell and others in the StarFire research group: A guide to the correspondences of Christ in the stellar and etheric world. Includes articles of interest, a complete sidereal ephemeris and aspectarian, geocentric and heliocentric. Published yearly in November for the coming year. According to Rudolf Steiner, every step taken by Christ during his ministry between the baptism in the Jordan and the resurrection was in harmony with, and an expression of, the cosmos. The journal is concerned with these heavenly correspondences during the life of Christ. It is intended to help provide a foundation for Cosmic Christianity, the cosmic dimension of Christianity. It is this dimension that has been missing from Christianity in its 2,000-year history. A starting point is to contemplate the movements of the Sun, Moon, and planets against the background of the zodiacal constellations (sidereal signs) today in relation to corresponding stellar events during the life of Christ. This opens the possibility of attuning to the life of Christ in the etheric cosmos in a living way.

Sophia Foundation Press and Sophia Academic Press Publications

PO Box 151011, San Rafael, CA 94915; (707) 789-9062; JamesWetmore@mac.com.

History of the Zodiac (San Rafael, CA: Sophia Academic Press, 2007). Book version of Robert Powell's Ph.D. thesis on the history of the zodiac. This penetrating study of the history of the zodiac restores the sidereal zodiac to its rightful place as the original zodiac, tracing it back to fifth-century B.C. Babylonians. Available in paperback and hard cover.

Hermetic Astrology: Volume 1, Astrology and Reincarnation (San Rafael, CA: Sophia Foundation Press, 2007). This book seeks to give the ancient science of the stars a scientific basis. This new foundation for astrology based on research into reincarnation and karma (destiny) is the primary focus. It includes numerous reincarnation examples, the study of which reveals the existence of certain astrological "laws" of reincarnation, on the basis of which it is evident that the ancient sidereal zodiac is the authentic astrological zodiac, and that the heliocentric movements of the planets are of great significance. Foundational for the new star wisdom of astrosophy.

Hermetic Astrology: Volume 2, Astrological Biography (San Rafael, CA: Sophia Foundation Press, 2007). Concerned with karmic relationships and the unfolding of destiny in seven-year periods through one's life. The seven-year rhythm underlies the human being's astrological biography, which can be studied in relation to the movements of the Sun, Moon, and planets around the sidereal zodiac between conception and birth. The "rule of Hermes" is used to determine the moment of conception.

Sign of the Son of Man in the Heavens: Sophia and the New Star Wisdom (San Rafael, CA: Sophia Foundation Press, 2008). Revised and expanded with new material, this edition deals with a new wisdom of stars in the light of Divine Sophia. It is intended as a help in our time, when we are called on to be extremely wakeful during the period leading up to the end of the Mayan calendar in 2012.

Cosmic Dances of the Zodiac (San Rafael, CA: Sophia Foundation Press, 2007) coauthor Lacquanna Paul. Study material describing the twelve signs of the zodiac and their forms and gestures in cosmic dance, with diagrams, including a wealth of information on the twelve signs and the 36 decans (the subdivision of the signs into decans, or 10° sectors, corresponding to constellations above and below the zodiac).

Cosmic Dances of the Planets (San Rafael, CA: Sophia Foundation Press, 2007), coauthor Lacquanna Paul. Study material describing the seven classical planets and their forms and gestures in cosmic dance, with diagrams, including much information on the planets.

American Federation of Astrologers (AFA) Publications

PO Box 22040, Tempe, AZ 85285.

The Sidereal Zodiac, coauthor Peter Treadgold (Tempe, AZ: AFA, 1985). A history of the zodiac (sidereal, tropical, Hindu, astronomical) and a formal definition of the sidereal zodiac with the star Aldebaran ("the Bull's Eye") at 15° Taurus. This is an abbreviated version of *History of the Zodiac*.

Rudolf Steiner College Press Publications

9200 Fair Oaks Blvd., Fair Oaks, CA 95628

The Christ Mystery: Reflections on the Second Coming (Fair Oaks, CA: Rudolf Steiner College Press, 1999). The fruit of many years of reflecting on the Second Coming and its cosmological aspects. Looks at the approaching trial of humanity and the challenges of living in apocalyptic times, against the background of "great signs in the heavens."

The Sophia Foundation

525 Gough St. #103, San Francisco, CA 94102; distributes many of the books listed here and other works by Robert Powell.
Tel: (415) 522-1150
sophia@sophiafoundation.org
www.sophiafoundation.org

Computer Program for Charts and Ephemerides, with grateful acknowledgment to Peter Treadgold, who wrote the computer program *Astrofire* (with research module, star catalog of over 4,000 stars, and database of birth and death charts of historical personalities), capable of printing geocentric and heliocentric/hermetic sidereal charts and ephemerides throughout history. The hermetic charts, based on the astronomical system of the Danish astronomer Tycho Brahe, are called "Tychonic" charts in the program. This program can:

- compute birth charts in a large variety of systems (tropical, sidereal, geocentric, heliocentric, hermetic);
- calculate conception charts using the hermetic rule, in turn applying it for correction of the birth time;
- produce charts for the period between conception and birth;
- print out an "astrological biography" for the whole of lifework with the geocentric, heliocentric (and even lemniscatory) planetary system;
- work with the sidereal zodiac according to the definition of your choice (Babylonian sidereal, Indian sidereal, unequal-division astronomical, etc.);
- work with planetary aspects with orbs of your choice.

The program includes eight house systems and a variety of chart formats. The program also includes an ephemeris program with a search facility. The geocentric/heliocentric sidereal ephemeris pages in the yearly *Journal for Star Wisdom* are produced by *Astrofire*. This program runs under Microsoft Windows. Those interested in *Astrofire* may contact:

The Sophia Foundation
525 Gough St. #103, San Francisco, CA 94102
Tel: (415) 522-1150
sophia@sophiafoundation.org
www.sophiafoundation.org

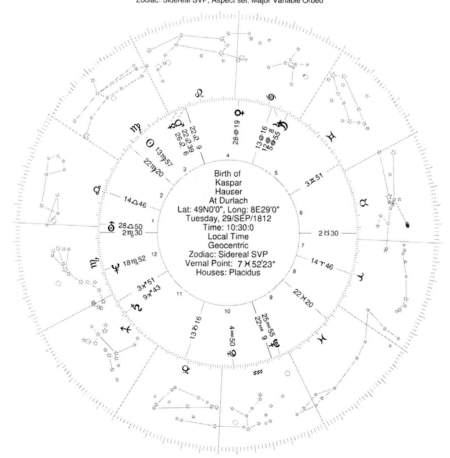

A horoscope generated by the Astrofire program

THE ROSE OF THE WORLD (*ROSA MIRA*)
Daniel Andreev

By warning about the coming Antichrist, and pointing him out and unmasking him when he appears, by cultivating unshakable faith within human hearts and a grasp of the meta-historical perspectives and global spiritual prospects within human minds...[we help Sophia bring to birth the new culture of love and wisdom called by Daniel Andreev the "Rose of the World."]...[Sophia's] birth in one of the *zatomis* will be mirrored not only by the Rose of the World; feminine power and its role in contemporary life are increasing everywhere. It is that circumstance, above all, that is giving rise to worldwide peace movements, an abhorrence of bloodshed, disillusion over coercive methods of change, an increase in woman's role in society proper, an ever-growing tenderness and concern for children, and a burning hunger for beauty and love. We are entering an age when the female soul will become ever purer and broader, when an ever-greater number of women will become profound inspirers, sensitive mothers, wise counselors, and far-sighted leaders. It will be an age when the feminine in humanity will manifest with unprecedented strength, striking a perfect balance with masculine impulses. See, you who have eyes.[1]

[These words are those of Daniel Andreev (1906–1959), the great prophet of the coming Age of Sophia and the corresponding Sophianic culture he called the "Rose of the World." In this quote, *zatomis* refers to a heavenly realm within the Earth's etheric aura. Andreev refers to Sophia as *Zventa-Sventana*, "Holiest of the Holy."]

A mysterious event is taking place in the meta-history of contemporary times: new divine-creative energy is emanating into our cosmos. Since ancient times the loftiest hearts and most subtle minds have anticipated this event that is now taking place. The first link in the chain of events—events so important that they can only be compared to the incarnation of the Logos—occurred at the turn of the nineteenth century. This was an emanation of the energy of the Virgin Mother, an emanation that was not amorphous, as it had been before in human history [at Pentecost, when there was an emanation of Sophia into the Virgin Mary], but incomparably intensified by the personal aspect it assumed. A great God-born monad descended from the heights of the universe into our cosmos (ibid., p. 356).

[The words of the great Russian seer, Daniel Andreev, are prophetic. As indicated in *The Most Holy Trinosophia*,[2] he points to the descent of Sophia and the resulting Sophianic world culture, the Rose of the World, in a most inspiring way.]

She is to be born in a body of enlightened ether....There She is, our hope and joy, Light and Divine Beauty! For Her birth will be mirrored in our history as something that our grandchildren and great-grandchildren will witness: the founding of the Rose of the World, its spread throughout the world, and...the assumption by the Rose of the World of supreme authority over the entire Earth (ibid., p. 357).

[The Sophia Foundation was founded and exists to help usher in the new Age of Sophia and the corresponding Sophianic culture, the Rose of the World, prophesied by Daniel Andreev and other spiritual teachers.

As quoted at the beginning, "Warning about the coming Antichrist, and pointing him out

---

1 Daniel Andreev, *The Rose of the World*, p. 358. Words in brackets [ ] here and in the following text are added by Robert Powell.

2 Robert Powell, *The Most Holy Trinosophia: The New Revelation of the Divine Feminine*.

and unmasking him when he appears" is important. As discussed in the article "In Memory of Willi Sucher" (*Journal for Star Wisdom 2010*).

Humanity's encounter with the Antichrist is part of the initiation trial of humanity as a whole crossing the threshold. The external aspect of this initiation trial is the meeting with the Antichrist as the embodiment of the sum-total of humanity's negative karma, *the double of humankind as a whole*. The inner aspect is the encounter with Christ or the Archangel Michael as the Guardian of the Threshold. The result of successfully passing through this initiation trial is the opening up of conscious awareness of the angelic realm. This is one aspect of the great event at the culmination of the process of humankind as a whole crossing the threshold. Another aspect of this culmination is depicted in the article on World Pentecost.[3]

More than anyone else, Daniel Andreev, as prophet of the coming Sophia culture, the Rose of the World, had a visionary experience of the coming of the Antichrist. His words concerning this are not in the English edition of the *Rose of the World*. Because of the importance of Daniel Andreev's vision of the coming of the Antichrist, his words about this appeared for the first time in English in this journal.

The German translation of Daniel Andreev's book *Rosa Mira: Rose of the World*, in three volumes, comprises a translation of the *whole* original Russian text, whereas the English edition corresponds to volume 1 of the three German volumes.[4]]

THE PREPARATION OF HUMAN BEINGS FOR THE COMING ANTILOGOS

Certainly, humanity has not lacked warnings. Not only the *New Testament* but also the *Qur'an* and even the *Mahabharata* have warned us in the distant past. Have spiritual seers in the East and in the West not proclaimed the Antichrist as an unavoidable evil? All leaders of the Rose of the World will concentrate their forces upon the work of warning about this monster.... This bearer of a dark

mission will probably not truly grasp whom he serves and for whom he prepares the way. With all his intellectual genius, his mind will be completely closed to anything of a mystical nature....He will be greeted enthusiastically: "There he is! The one for whom we have been waiting!" He will show his true force only much later, when the "savior" holds the entire power in his hands....

Is it a matter of a human being? Yes and no. On several occasions [in *Rosa Mira*] I have indicated that this individual was incarnated as a Roman emperor and how, over the centuries and from life to life, he became enveloped in demonic substance. Concerning this monad, whom Gagtungr [Ahriman, or Satan] himself has kidnapped...enough has been said about his previous incarnation [as Stalin] in Russia....[In that incarnation,] the forces of providence hindered [Satan's attempt] to make of him a dark, universal genius.

[Now, in 1958, he is being prepared] for the successful fulfillment of the historic role of the Antichrist. Stalin's tyrannical genius and his ability to control hypnotically the will of others is well known.... [When he reincarnates as the Antichrist,] he will have at his disposal an enormous capacity for work and a multitude of talents....He will be uniquely and terribly beautiful. From his facial characteristics, it will be difficult to place him in any particular race or nation. Rather, he will be seen as a representative of the collective of humanity.... [At a certain point in his life, he will undergo a transformation.] His transformation will be noticed by people immediately, yet they will be unable to recognize the meaning or the "how" [of this transformation]. The external appearance of the transformed one will remain virtually unchanged. However, a terrible and frightening energy will proceed from him...Anyone who touches him will receive an electric shock. An invincible hypnotic force [will proceed from him]....The disturbing influence [on spiritually striving human beings] and upon the entire population set in motion by the transformation of the Antilogos will be extraordinary....

After a rigged vote, he—the miracle worker—will crown himself....Humanity will be divided [into

---

3 See Robert Powell, *Prophecy-Phenomena-Hope*.
4 The following translation from German into English is by RP.

those who accept him as world ruler] and those who refuse to acknowledge the usurper....Of course, force will be used against anyone who refuses to follow the Antichrist. Dark miracles will increasingly occur, shattering the consciousness of people to the very roots of their being. For many, Christ's miracles will pale into insignificance. Crazy enthusiasm will roll in waves across the world....Eventually, the Antilogos will hold the sole rulership of the planet in his hands. Yet, the true and highest leaders will not subject themselves to this usurper. This will also be the case for millions, perhaps hundreds of millions, of people in every country of the world.

The age of persecution commences. From year to year, they become increasingly extensive, methodical, [and] cruel. Here, the cunning Gagtungr [Ahriman/Satan] even makes use of the heroic protest of the masses. The candidate for the Antichrist who had failed...who had taken his life at the end of World War II,[5] advances now to become the self-appointed leader of the rebels in the struggle against the world ruler....His thoroughly dark movement will draw the hearts of many into a spiral of raging wickedness and senseless hatred....Christ's significance will continually be weakened. Then his name will be denied—and finally enveloped in silence....

Shock and terror will take hold of many. Millions of those who had previously distanced themselves from religious matters, who occupied themselves primarily with concerns in their own little world or with artistic pursuits or scientific research, will sense that an irrevocable and very dangerous choice confronts them. In the face of this, even torture and execution pale....Countless people will turn away from this offspring of hell...from the dark miracles and the charm of the superman, as well as from his immeasurable intelligence and frighteningly cynical wickedness....The majority

of people will fall away from God and allow themselves to be led astray by Gagtungr's protégée....

Stalin wanted not only to be feared; he also wanted to be loved. The Antichrist, however, has need of only one thing: the conviction that everyone [should hold] without exception, [to] believe in his superiority and [to] subject themselves to him without hesitation....

When [during the reign of the Antichrist] the machine civilization begins its total assault on Nature, the entire landscape of the Earth's surface will be transformed into a complete Anti-Nature....Nature, having become inwardly empty and outwardly crippled, will no longer awaken aesthetic or pantheistic feelings....

Certainly, too, during the complete rule of the tyrant, there will be many whose innermost life will rebel against the senseless existence under the Antichrist. However, psychic control will stifle such thoughts as they arise, and only a few will succeed in acquiring a system of psychic self-defense to protect them from being physically destroyed....

All written or other testimonies that could be dangerous for the Antichrist will be destroyed....

[The suffering of human beings gives nourishment (gavvach) to the demons.]...No world wars, revolutions, or repressions, no mass spilling of blood, could have produced gavvach in such amounts....In fact, even humanity in its demonized aspect will not satisfy the Antichrist. He needs humanity as his source of gavvach....[However] even in the most sinful soul, an inextinguishable spark of conscience gleams. However, despair, increasing ignorance, and sheer boredom with life will also take hold of many people, and this will lead to their rejection by the Antichrist. Of what use to him is the intellectual paralysis that sets in after such excesses of despair? Such people are hardly suited to the further development of demonic science and technology or to the conquest of the cosmos or the satanizing of the world....

[After the Antichrist's death] the world state will rapidly collapse, and only drastic measures will hinder anarchy in various parts of the world...."And there appears a great sign in

---

5 Daniel Andreev depicts the two main candidates for the Antichrist in their twentieth-century incarnations: Adolf Hitler and Joseph Stalin. In those incarnations, they competed with each other to become the most evil. In the following incarnation, the most evil one would become the vessel for the incarnation of the Antichrist. According to Daniel Andreev, Joseph Stalin outdid Adolf Hitler to become the chosen one, the prince of darkness. —R. POWELL

heaven: a woman clothed with the Sun" [Revelation 12:1]. Who is the *woman clothed with the Sun*? It is *Sventa-Sventana* [Sophia], embraced by the planetary Logos and chosen to give birth to the Great Spirit of the Second Aeon. The reflection of this event in world history is the Rose of the World, whose utmost striving before, during, and after the time of the Antichrist prepares humanity to become a vessel for the Great Spirit.... An unimaginable jubilation will take hold of this and other worlds as humanity passes through a great, light-filled transformation.

The prince of darkness will terrify human beings.... Christ, however, will take on as many forms as there are conscious beings on Earth to behold him. He will adapt himself to everyone and will converse with all. His forms will simultaneously yield an image in an unimaginable way: *One who appears in heaven surrounded by unspeakable glory.* There will not be a single being on Earth who will not see the Son of God and hear his Word.[6]

[These words by Daniel Andreev are prophetic. They were written shortly before his death in 1959. Now, more than fifty years later, not only is the encounter with the Son of God possible, but also the possibility of hearing his Word. Today, we can experience this meeting with the Son of God in the realm of life forces, also known as the *etheric realm*. This is the most important event that anyone in earthly existence can experience. This spiritual event is the initiatory aspect of human encounters with the Antichrist and the initiation trial for humanity as a whole crossing the threshold.

An example of this spiritual event is related in an account of a young woman of her initiatory experience in meeting Christ as the Greater Guardian of the threshold. She prefers to remain anonymous. This description of her meeting with Christ in the etheric realm—with the Etheric Christ, to use Rudolf Steiner's expression—can be a source of inspiration to everyone. She describes how she came to this experience of the Etheric Christ through meditating on Christ's experiences during the night prior to the Mystery of Golgotha, the night in the Garden of Gethsemane.]

My focus was again turned to Gethsemane. I entered the light of his deed in the garden and a state of ecstasy—an ineffable, unutterable ecstasy. The light of Christ in Gethsemane enveloped the Earth. Up to that point, I had never merged with such light. My heart soared in ecstasy, lifted into another realm of spirit. I exclaimed, *"This is Life! This is Life eternal, the Life of the world. This is Love! This is eternal Love, which knows no boundaries, for it has penetrated everything in the Earth. It lives within the Earth as an eternal promise of redemption. His love is eternal; His love is free for all who will accept it!"*

Christ then gave me a message for all: *"Love one another and love the Earth. Send your love to your fellow beings and into the Earth that the Earth may be lifted up on wings of peace. There is a body of the Earth, which is a body of love; this is My body that I gave to the Earth. You become one with the body of love by doing works of love, by cultivating feelings of love and by thinking thoughts of love. I invite all to become one with Me in this body of love. I call you home; My arms are around you. Return to love. Remember love. For where love is there am I; and because I desire to have you in My heart, I ask you to love one another, that I may be in you and you in Me. Look for Me to come to you for I am coming and shall gather you to myself and you shall be safely folded in Me because you are precious in My sight; and My sight is ever upon you. Return to Me."*

I then gazed upon him, embracing all of the cosmos. With his arms outstretched across the expanse of Heaven, his voice penetrating the depths of my heart with these words: "I AM eternally here!"

6 Daniil Andrejew, *Rosa Mira: Die Weltrose*, vol. 3, pp. 202–226.

EDITORIAL FOREWORD

William Bento, Ph.D.

As we move into the calendar year 2012, a mood of expectant dramatic change fills the air. Changes in the current state of the world have already become an undeniable concern in the lives of millions of people. No sphere of human activity seems stable. Economic, political and cultural realms have become so unpredictable that the idea of a world in collapse has become common topic among pundits. These events of uncertainty are intensified by an unprecedented number of natural catastrophes around the world. Statistics and expert analyses of global situations are now being augmented with reference to ancient prophecies. As a result an inordinate amount of anticipation about the Mayan prophecy has been placed front and center in so many mediums of communication—books, newspapers, journals, radio, television, video segments, lectures and workshops, etc. (see also the article "World Pentecost" by Robert Powell in the *Journal for Star Wisdom 2010*—an article that focuses upon the significance of the 2012 date for the end of the Mayan Calendar). It has been nearly impossible to avoid hearing something about prophecies whether it relates to the Mayan Calendar, Jeane Dixon's prophecy of the "Antichrist," Nostradamus's implications of World War III, the dread of an Apocalypse or the anticipation of the Rapture.

Although not always a welcome message, prophecy opens the soul's eyes to a horizon of possible futures. The fault of so many advocates who espouse a single prophetic scenario is their tendency to accept the future as an irrefutable given. Such shortsightedness misses the opportunity to prepare for a more ideal future. Instead it unwittingly incites fear and gives dire prophetic messages a greater power to become fulfilled. Prophecies are calls to vigilance, not hopeless submission to adversary powers greater than oneself. Knowing how to discern the validity of a prophecy and how it may be fruitfully worked with is a lost art (in this connection see William Bento, "Prophecy: A Cauldron of Controversy," *Journal for Star Wisdom 2011*). The first step in regaining this capacity is in acknowledging the need to read the signs of the time with an objective critical eye.

Phenomena are there for us to read. They reveal open secrets within the course of evolution. Reading phenomena as signs on a road map to how we have arrived in the current circumstances not only helps us orient, but also gives clues to how we might chart a different course into the future. Prophecy is but one among many signs, albeit a sign of deep importance. Looking at the wide variety of unheralded events that have unfolded since the outset of the twenty-first century can only give rise to the most serious concerns of human existence. With these concerns there is an implicit mandate to become more awake, more conscientious, more compassionate, and more responsible for how we think, feel, and act with one another in our common journey through these decisive times.

Hope is a power that must emerge in times like these, for without it the demon of fear, doubt and hatred is liable to sweep through our lives. Hope is not that something you wish for will turn out as you desired, but is that no matter what the future brings you will be able to find meaningfulness in it. Vaclav Havel redefined hope in just this manner as he spoke for the Czech people who rose up against the established communist regime in 1989. "Truth and love must prevail over lies and hatred." The meaningfulness we must seek in our time rests upon a faith in the divine course of evolution and a love for humanity's development within that arc of evolution. Hope is then an outcome of a renewed *Pistis Sophia*, a renewed faith in wisdom. The *Journal for Star Wisdom* intends to offer a basis for a renewed faith in Star Wisdom. The editors and authors have entered deep conversation and contemplation to find the source of love that binds them to this pioneering work so as to infuse the articles with that intimate quality of loving that kindles hope in all of us. Such is the sharing in written form before you as reader.

As the editorial board entered its third year of publishing the *Journal for Star Wisdom* a vision of its mission emerged among them. It is expressed in the qualitative content of the articles and commentaries in the journal. Three fundamental aims have arisen as core ideals of the mission of the journal:

1. To educate the readership about the emerging discipline of Star Wisdom;
2. To impart research findings relevant to reading the signs of the time in which we are living;
3. To offer practical ways to work with the elements of Star Wisdom.

The first article *Prophecy, Phenomena and Hope* by Robert Powell sets the tone of the year before us. He draws upon his vast breadth of spiritual scientific knowledge to address two of the most important prophecies given by the great Christian initiate, Rudolf Steiner. His scholarly research establishes a clear basis and rationale for the need to introduce contemplative, prayerful, and meditative practices that are designed to realign our soul life with the light of the spirit. In addition, Robert's keen and awakened intuitive faculty is evident in his own articulation of key points throughout the article. He takes seriously the warnings of prophecy, yet exemplifies the courage to hold the darkness up to the light; and in that spirit the marvels of white magic may be seen.

In the article *Ensouling Star Wisdom* by William Bento we find an imaginative rendering of an educational journey to the temple of Star Wisdom. His hope is explicitly stated in the phrase "there needs to be an 'Ark of Salvation' for the sake of humanity's future." In the article he lays out an educational framework for the study of Star Wisdom. His conviction is that "Star Wisdom, when ensouled, can provide a compass for navigating the rough and turbulent waters of this stage in humanity's evolution." Meditative verses guide the reader to enter into deeper contemplations of what lies at the root of Star Wisdom. It is both an informative and inspirational offering for anyone who wishes to take up the study of Star Wisdom.

David Tresemer's article *The Venus Eclipse of the Sun 2012* highlights what many consider to be the key astrological event of the year. His years of devoted research into the starry configurations of the life of the Cosmic Christ on Earth shine through in his interpretative skills of this rare astrological event. By highlighting key images associated with the zodiacal degree of the Venus eclipse of the Sun, historically drawn from the Persian epoch, Tresemer weaves moving stories both pertinent and urgent for our time. His view on the immoral and moral uses of technology strikes at one of the most disturbing phenomena of the twenty-first century. He, too, sounds a note of hope for us in citing "Star Brothers and Star Sisters," historical events resonating into this particular time through the Venus/Sun eclipse, and the call to be more mindful of hearts that inspire hands to do the redemptive deeds the world is calling for now.

The horoscopes of Joan of Arc and Kaspar Hauser in Wain Farrants's articles honor two significant figures in the struggle to bring the flame of esoteric Christianity into the mainstream of European culture. These anniversaries in the year 2012 of the births of these two important personages can be a call to vigilance for us. 2012 is the year of the six-hundredth anniversary of the birth of Joan of Arc, who was such a mighty Michaelic soul for freedom, and it is also the two-hundredth anniversary of the birth of Kasper Hauser, whose mysterious life and death left Europe stunned as it was hoped he would be the leader of Christendom. Robert Powell states the issue well in his article,

"Abducted after his birth and then hidden away in a secret dungeon through the machinations of dark occult forces, Kasper Hauser, known as the *child of Europe*, was not allowed to unfold his destiny and bring his gifts to the world." These charts provide a focus for remembrance as we seek for the inspirations of light for 2012.

The editorial board is pleased to reprint an extract of a much larger article from Richard Tarnas. *World Transits 2000–2020: An Overview* gives an insightful perspective on the historical dynamics at play in our time. Tarnas brings a thoughtful transpersonal approach into the examination of planetary cycles and aspects that activate universal themes significant for the evolution of consciousness. Although his orbs for aspects are much greater than the orbs used by most other authors in the journal, the periods discussed by Tarnas are unequivocally relevant and informative. His views on the current great T-square aspect of Saturn in opposition to Uranus and squared to Pluto identifies a primary hue in the many-colored tensions of world affairs. By unveiling the archetypal powers within these three outer planets Tarnas is able to describe and give meaning to the world situations in culture, politics, economics, and natural disasters.

My Path to Astrosophy by Robert Schippacasse is the result of having been interviewed in the spring of 2011 by David Tresemer and William Bento. Robert edited extensively and expanded upon his initial responses to questions. The article elaborates on the author's path toward Astrosophy in such a way as to give the reader a sense of the intimate and tender awakenings that occurred along the path. Robert's eyes were set upon the stars within his own being from the very outset, and his journey led him to encounters with others and new and provocative truths. In the end of the article the reader is brought to an appreciation of how Robert was able to find, in freedom, a deep conviction to a way of life illuminated by Star Wisdom.

Brian Gray writes about an approach to reading birth charts from an anthroposophic perspective that is grounded in decades of study and experience.

He contributes an essential cornerstone for the practice of Star Wisdom. Brian addresses the sensitive and ethical issues around reading birth charts, as well as addressing the reactive and misconstrued objections to a practice of astrology within the anthroposophic movement. However, it is his application of spiritual scientific concepts and his formulation of the birth chart that form the heart of his contribution. "The birth chart displays four basic phenomena. Understanding each of these four phenomena is crucially important to finding new ways to consider the birth chart": the zodiac, the moving planets, the relationships between planets, termed aspects, and the astrological houses based on the relationship between the heavens and Earth. Brian's treatment of the houses is by far one of the most comprehensive and elegant renditions on the subject that is in print. We are pleased to share this educational treasure with our readers.

The article "The Two Become One: Possession or Enlightenment," written by Claudia McLaren Lainson, advances a view of the esoteric Christian theme of the year. She brings to our attention a two-millennia anniversary of the mystery of the two Jesus children found in the temple 2,000 years ago. Rudolf Steiner's lecture cycle *The Fifth Gospel* (1910) is the background to understanding the deeper significance of the 2012 theme that Claudia explores in her article. The union of the two Jesus children signifies collaboration on the part of two elevated and enlightened beings, who for the sake of the unification of karmic streams in humanity, enact a sacrificial deed of love. Through this extraordinary event the wisdom of the future was allowed to stream forth, the Anthroposophia! With this great mystery in the foreground Claudia draws upon her years of research working with young children to sound a trumpet of warning. She heeds us to be aware of the impact our technologically infused culture is having upon our children. Claudia implicitly points to the adversarial forces working behind and through this co-opted techno culture to disturb the incarnation process of children today.

The commentaries on the daily planetary aspects referenced to the Christ events are accompanied with a glossary of terms and concepts that may aid the reader to grasp the importance of each day and to share with the reader the esoteric dimensions out of which Claudia McLaren Lainson wrote these commentaries. The ephemerides, with astronomical indications written by Sally Nurney, can serve as a guide for developing a *concentration* on the being of the Stars, or stargazing. The commentaries may be read *contemplatively* by allowing one's soul to associate freely the feelings of one's personal life to the cosmic imaginations that are addressed therein. Knowing the gesture of the planets and how it evokes memories of the great "turning point in time" may give rise to an attitude of *prayer*, whereby we can conduct our lives on a daily basis as a sacrament, making each day sacred. The esoteric content referenced in the commentaries can be a wonderful focus for *meditations* into the wellsprings of Cosmic Christianity. By taking up one or more of these activities, the reader becomes a practitioner of new Star Wisdom and may find the strengthening light for healthy soul life in a time of so much worldly strife.

&

Robert Powell, Ph.D.

The *Journal for Star Wisdom* (formerly *Christian Star Calendar*) has appeared every year since 1991. From the beginning the central feature has been the calendar comprising the monthly ephemeris pages together with commentaries drawing attention to the Christ events remembered by the ongoing cosmic events. The significance of following the Christ events in relation to daily astronomical events is an important foundation for the new star wisdom of astrosophy.[1] This new star

wisdom is arising in our time in response to the second coming of Christ—known as his return in the etheric realm of life forces—as a path of communing with Christ in his life body (ether body). It should also be mentioned that, with the onset of the second coming of Christ during the course of the twentieth century, Christ is now the Lord of Karma, and this is important to take into consideration in the development of a new relationship of humanity to the stars in our time, particularly with respect to the horoscope as an expression of human karma or destiny.

The events of Christ's life lived two thousand years ago are inscribed into his ether body, and to meditate upon these events at times when they are cosmically remembered is a way of drawing near to Christ. The recently updated version of my article "Subnature and the Second Coming"[2] outlines the background to contemporary events as a confrontation between good and evil in relation to Christ's descent at this time through the sub-earthly realms and also gives an overview of the various cosmic rhythms unfolding in relation to his second coming, including the thirty-three-and-one-third-year rhythm of his ether body.

Journal for Star Wisdom encourages the reader to engage in the practice of stargazing as described on my website www.Astrogeographia.org (see "A Modern Path of the Magi" in the section "The Star of the Magi"). Stargazing is fundamental to the development of the new star wisdom of astrosophy. One of the foundations of astrosophy lies in the science of astronomy, providing the new star wisdom with a secure scientific foundation, which moreover, can be brought into the realm of experience through the practice of stargazing. In astrosophy, there is no longer a separation between astronomy and astrology. For example, when in the *Journal for Star Wisdom* it is indicated that currently Mars in the heavens is at 15° Taurus then, assuming that Mars is visible, the red planet

---

1 There are many different approaches to astrosophy and not all use the equal-division sidereal zodiac that forms the basis of the approach followed in the *Journal for Star Wisdom*. All references to the zodiac and to planetary positions in the zodiac in the *Journal for Star Wisdom* are in terms of the sidereal zodiac as defined in my book *History of the Zodiac*. Moreover, in astrosophy there are different chronologies of the life of Christ, and the chronology that forms the basis of the approach followed in the *Journal for Star Wisdom* is set forth in my book *Chronicle of the Living Christ* (Hudson, NY: Anthroposophic Press, 1996). Thus, all references

to planetary positions at the Christ events in the *Journal for Star Wisdom* are in terms of the scientifically established chronology of the life of Christ set forth in my book *Chronicle of the Living Christ*.

2 In P. V. O'Leary (ed.), *The Inner Life of the Earth*, pp. 69–141.

can be seen in conjunction with Aldebaran marking the Bull's eye at the center of the constellation of Taurus, whose longitude, as the central star in this constellation, is 15° Taurus. In astrosophy, the astrological fact of Mars at 15° Taurus is identical with the astronomical reality of Mars's location at the center of the constellation of Taurus. Astrosophy thus relates to sense-perceptible reality and to the Divine "background of existence" (the spiritual hierarchies)[3] underlying this reality, whereas astrology is generally practiced in such a way that there is a split between astrology and astronomy (in this example, modern astrology, which uses the tropical zodiac rather than the equal-division sidereal zodiac used in astrosophy, would say that Mars is "in Gemini"). The historical background as to how this separation between astronomy and astrology arose is described in my book *History of the Zodiac*.

The present issue of *Journal for Star Wisdom* is the twenty-first, but is the third published under the new title, as all previous issues were published under the title *Christian Star Calendar*. By way of explanation concerning the new title, this publication is intended as an outreach from the StarFire research group (an astrosophy group) that meets yearly in Boulder, Colorado, or in Fair Oaks, California. (See the website www.StarWisdom.org. Other related websites concerned with the new star wisdom of astrosophy are www.sophiafoundation.org and www.astrogeographia.org). The *Journal for Star Wisdom* is intended as an organ for the development of the new star wisdom of astrosophy. This was also the purpose of the *Christian Star*

Calendar. However, there the focus, at least initially, was primarily on the calendar—the monthly ephemeris and commentaries. In the course of time, more and more research articles on the new star wisdom of astrosophy came to be published in the *Christian Star Calendar*. A point was reached where it became clear that the publication is more of a journal than a calendar, although the calendar continues to play an important role. It is therefore a natural transition from *Christian Star Calendar* to *Journal for Star Wisdom*.

As referred to in my article in this issue of the *Journal for Star Wisdom*, perhaps the greatest prophecy of our time—one that is little known, but which is the reason for the existence of this journal, and is a source of tremendous spiritual light—is Rudolf Steiner's prophecy from the year 1910, just over one hundred years ago. On January 12, 1910, he prophesied that the second coming of Christ would begin in 1933, an event which he referred to as Christ's appearance in the etheric realm—not a return in a physical body, but in an etheric (life) body, in the realm of life forces. Here with my translation of Marie Steiner's notes from this important, hitherto unpublished lecture:

3000 BC, Kali Yuga commenced and lasted until 1899, a time of great transition.

1933—human beings will appear with clairvoyant faculties, which they will develop naturally. At this time, which we are approaching, the newly beginning clairvoyant faculties have to be satisfied, to experience what they [human beings] should do with them.

I am with you always, even unto the end of the world.

Christ will appear in an etheric form. The physical Christ became the Spirit of the Earth—this was the midpoint, the balance, of Earth evolution.

Fifth Letter of the Ap(ocalypse): I will come again; however, take heed that you do not fail to recognize me.

2,500 years is the time that humanity has to develop again the gifts of clairvoyance. Around 1933, the Gospels must be

---

3 According to Rudolf Steiner, the constellations are the abode of the first hierarchy, called Seraphim, Cherubim, and Thrones. The movement of the planets takes place against the background of the zodiacal constellations, which—considered as the abode of the first hierarchy—form the Divine "background of existence" in the heavens. "Suppose you wanted to point in the direction of certain [group of] Thrones, Cherubim and Seraphim…one denotes them as a particular constellation. The constellations are like signposts; in one direction, over there, are the [group of] Thrones, Cherubim and Seraphim known as Gemini, the Twins; over there [the group of Thrones, Cherubim and Seraphim known as] Leo, the Lion; and so on" (*The Spiritual Hierarchies and the Physical World*, p. 98). Words in brackets [ ] added by RP.

recognized in their spiritual meaning such that they have worked preparing for Christ. Otherwise untold confusion of the soul will result.

Around 1933, there will be some representatives of black magic schools, who will falsely proclaim a physical Christ.

Each time that he becomes perceptible, Christ is perceptible for other faculties.[4]

This was Rudolf Steiner's greatest prophecy: the second coming of Christ, which he referred to as the appearance of Christ in the etheric realm, beginning in 1933. It is this event, the presence of the Etheric Christ, lasting from 1933 for 2,500 years (until 4433), that is considered further in my article in this issue of *Journal for Star Wisdom.*

---

4 Translated from the first page of Marie Steiner's notes, which were recently published in German for the first time in *Der Europäer*, vol. 14, December/January 2009/2010, p. 3.

In conclusion I would like to express gratitude to our publisher, Gene Gollogly of SteinerBooks, and to the able assistance of Jens Jensen of SteinerBooks, for making this third issue of *Journal for Star Wisdom* available, and to all those who have contributed to make this issue possible, in particular to our authors for presenting their research articles as contributions to the foundations of the new star wisdom of astrosophy, and to all our readers who ultimately are the reason for the existence of the *Journal for Star Wisdom.*

Finally, here with a link to Brian Keats' most interesting article about his studies of catastrophic weather events in relation to astronomical factors: www.astro-calendar.com/PDFs /1104Earthquakes%20and%20Floods_Web.pdf.

❦

IN TIMES LIKE THESE

In times like these human hearts weep and lament
With every good reason to do so;
Yet, it is just in times like these
We should learn to open our hearts
And offer love as a sacrament —
For you see, there are more reasons to do this
Than there are reasons not to do it.
Yes, in times like these
We pray for floods of love
To pour into the wounds of human hearts,
And that in this human divine intervention
The bitter salty tears become sweet pearls of wisdom
Settling in the soul and making it once again whole.

—WILLIAM BENTO, October 1997, Amsterdam

WORKING WITH THE
JOURNAL FOR STAR WISDOM

The listing of major planetary events each month is intended as a stimulus toward attunement with the Universal Christ, the Logos, whose being encompasses the entire galaxy. The deeds of the historical Christ wrought two thousand years ago are of eternal significance—inscribed into the cosmos—and they resonate with the movements of the heavenly bodies, especially when certain alignments or planetary configurations occur bearing a resemblance with those prevailing at the time of events in the life of Jesus Christ. With the rare astronomical event of the transit of Venus across the face of the Sun that took place June 8, 2004, at exactly the zodiacal degree (23° Taurus), where the Sun stood at Christ's Ascension, a new impulse was given from divine-spiritual realms for the further unfolding of star wisdom, *Astro-Sophia*.

Toward the end of the journal, the calendar is to be found, comprising ephemeris pages for the twelve months of the year and accompanying monthly commentaries on the astronomical events listed on the ephemeris pages. Indications regarding the similarity of contemporary planetary configurations with those at events in the life of Christ are given in the lower part of the monthly commentaries, and the upper part gives a commentary on the notable astronomical occurrences each month. Unless otherwise stated, all astronomical indications regarding visibility mean "visible to the naked eye." See the note concerning time on the page preceding the monthly commentaries.

With this calendar, astronomy and astrology, which were a unity in the ancient star wisdom of the Egyptians and Babylonians, are reunited and provide a foundation for astrosophy, the all-encompassing star wisdom, *Astro-Sophia*, an expression of Sophia and referred to in the Revelation of John as the "Bride of the Lamb."

2012: PROPHECY PHENOMENA HOPE

Robert Powell
with contributions by Tracy Saucier and Valentin Tomberg
Introduction by Lacquanna Paul

INTRODUCTION

This article builds on the research presented in the 2010 and 2011 issues of the *Journal for Star Wisdom*, wherein various prophecies were considered in relation to what might be of significance relative to December 21, 2012—the date usually indicated as the end of the Maya calendar.

In both the 2011 and 2012 issues of the *Journal for Star Wisdom*, David Tresemer has written extensively about the Venus transit, which is a most significant astronomical event in the year 2012, and in this issue he offers an historical account which presents images recognizable in the challenges faced in the world today as an offering to kindle the moral imagination of the reader. David's historical/artistic/imaginative approach is evidence of a Venus impulse/gesture in the world, bringing art, through the art of storytelling, as a healing medicine for world culture.

In the 2011 issue of the *Journal for Star Wisdom*, William Bento wrote an excellent article concerning the problems inherent in consideration of the phenomena of prophecy. These considerations can serve toward discernment for the consciousness soul when reading this article *Prophecy–Phenomena–Hope*. William Bento, as an educator and psychologist, is a pioneer in the realm of Psychosophy, working toward the healing of the human soul.

In this issue both William Bento and Robert Schiappacasse in their articles bring illuminating insights into the background of the practice of Astrosophy, the wisdom of the stars, and three of the pillars upon which this practice is built.

Brian Gray, a respected figure in the field of anthroposophical education, then takes up this thread, demonstrating through his interpretation of the astrological house system how Rudolf Steiner's spiritual science provides a new foundation for astrology. Brian's work illustrates the importance of forming a positive relationship to the forces of the cosmos as an important activity in the fulfillment of destiny.

Claudia McLaren Lainson follows this thread further by recognizing that the year 2012 remembers the event of the miraculous wisdom demonstrated by the twelve-year-old Jesus in the Temple. Examined in the light of the clairvoyant insights of the Austrian philosopher and educator Rudolf Steiner (1861-1925) concerning the mystery of "the two becoming one," Claudia delves into one of the prevalent challenges she observes in her therapeutic practice with children and young people—the problem of possession—wherein the receptive imagination of young children becomes overwhelmed by the violent and provocative images presented by modern video games, television, and the media in general. Whereas in earlier times nature provided true nourishment for the souls of young people, through the influence of the media resulting in an ever-shorter attention span, children and young people are being robbed of nature's true wisdom. This is an inversion of that which is indicated in Rudolf Steiner's account of the two Jesus children who became united as one.

Through the articles by Wain Farrants, we learn of the anniversaries in the year 2012 of the births of two important personages whose lives were sacrificed for the very principles of consciousness and conscience that we are now called to awaken within ourselves. 2012 is the year of the six-hundredth anniversary of the birth of Joan of Arc, who was such a mighty herald for the call to freedom, and it is also the two-hundredth anniversary of the birth of Kasper Hauser, whose life was hijacked and then cut short at the age of twenty-one, resulting in the loss of the great blessing for humanity which could have resulted from the incarnation of this highly spiritual individuality. Abducted after his birth and then hidden away in a secret dungeon through the machinations of dark occult forces, Kasper Hauser, known as the *child of Europe*, was not allowed to unfold his destiny and bring his gifts to the world. Might this be the fate of our children and youth if they are not shepherded toward a connection with the natural world?

The Venus rhythm lasts 1,199 years (approximately 2 x 600 years). The period of 600 years is referred to by Rudolf Steiner as a "cultural wave."[1] Thus, with the six-hundredth anniversary of the birth of Joan of Arc—contemplating the cultural impulse she brought as a courageous herald for freedom and justice; and now, one cultural wave of 600 years later—there is a noticeable resurgence in the world of women of remarkable courage, coming forward as heralds to expose the evils of our time through investigative journalism and publicly speaking out the truth. In this vein, we also see some modern female mystics coming forward, who are able to shed light on the spiritual significance of our times.

Last, an article is included in this issue of the journal by Richard Tarnas, who offers far-reaching insights into the influence of planetary aspects on world history.

The Second Coming of Christ: the Parousia

This article seeks to shed light on the phenomena of our time through the lens of Christian tradition in relation to two prophecies made by Rudolf Steiner. Above all, the most important and significant prophetic indication that he made is examined: his prophecy concerning the second coming of Christ. (In relation to the second coming, Steiner used the expression *Etheric Christ*, meaning Christ in his etheric body, rather than in a physical body.) This prophecy is a source of great hope, and in this article we shall look at some of the phenomena associated with this central prophecy—a prophecy central to Rudolf Steiner's life work:

Since the commencement of the New Age on September 10, 1899, the 33⅓-year rhythm has begun to play a much more significant role than it did previously. This fact is related to Christ's second coming. Whereas the first incarnation was an event on the physical plane, the second coming is occuring on the etheric plane of existence, in the realm of life forces. Thus, Christ's etheric body is especially active.

Following the Mystery of Golgotha in AD 33, the etheric body of Christ expanded slowly out into cosmic realms, attaining its greatest expansion in AD 966,[2] a year that denoted a point of transition. Then began the slow path of return of Christ's ether body back toward the Earth. With the end of the fifty-sixth 33⅓-year cycle on September 10, 1899, denoting the close of *Kali Yuga*, Christ's ether body began to re-enter the Earth's etheric aura, which attained a certain level of completion 33⅓ years later, on January 8, 1933. This was the birth of the New Age, *Satya Yuga* (the "Age of Light"), whereby 1899 can be likened to the *dawn* and 1933 to the *sunrise* of the New Age. It was precisely during that period, from 1900 to 1925, that Rudolf Steiner's teaching activity unfolded. According to Steiner, Anthroposophy (spiritual science) is preparing the way for the second coming, the approaching advent of which he assigned the

---

1   In Rudolf Steiner's description of spiritual evolution, successive periods of 2,160 years corresponding to the signs of the zodiac unfold historically. He called these periods "cultural epochs." He described the *age of the consciousness soul* as the fifth cultural epoch since the destruction of Atlantis through the great flood and dated this current fifth epoch, corresponding to the Age of Pisces, from the year 1413/1414 to 3573/3574. As described in Robert Powell & Kevin Dann, *The Astrological Revolution* (SteinerBooks, 2010), the Age of Pisces lasts 2,160 years and extends from AD 215 to 2375, and the corresponding cultural epoch, the age of the consciousness soul, began in 1414—after a time-lag of 1,199 years—almost 1,200 after the start of the Age of Pisces, where the time-lag of 1,199 years is an astronomical period associated with the planet Venus, comprising two 600-year cultural waves. According to Rudolf Steiner, a cultural wave lasts for 600, whereas a cultural epoch lasts for 2,160 years.

2   See the diagram of Christ's ascent and descent in my book *The Christ Mystery*, p. iv.

year 1933.[3] In his lectures (around 1910 and the following years), he proclaimed the advent of Christ's second coming as the greatest event of the twentieth century. Steiner acted as a kind of *John the Baptist*, who proclaimed the approaching second coming, just as John the Baptist prepared the way for the first coming nineteen centuries previously.

With the first coming the life of Jesus Christ lasted 33⅓ years, the most important of which were the last 3½ years (the ministry, from the baptism to the Mystery of Golgotha). In contrast, the second coming is an event taking place primarily in the etheric world, which, in accordance with the 33⅓-year rhythm, will last for 2,500 years, or seventy-five 33⅓-year cycles, from September 10, 1899, to May 22, 4399. During these 2,500 years the most important rhythm is the 33⅓-year cycle of Christ's ether body; through comprehension of this rhythm, we are given the possibility of attuning to that ether body. It is the renewed presence of this ether body in the Earth's etheric aura that gave birth to the New Age.[4]

By way of introduction, to readers unfamiliar with the term *Etheric Christ*, this refers to the nonphysical manifestation of Christ in our time—that of the New Age (1899–4399)—as distinct from the physical incarnation of Christ two thousand years ago. *Etheric* refers to the ethereal realm of life forces—the biosphere that surrounds the Earth and interpenetrates the whole of nature. Everything living is immersed in the biosphere, the *etheric realm*.

The *Etheric Christ* was first spoken of by Rudolf Steiner, who indicated the deeper meaning to the prophecies concerning Christ's second coming.

Biblical references to the second coming:

They will see the Son of Man coming on the clouds of heaven with power and great glory. (Matt. 24:30)

He was taken up, and a cloud received him out of their sight. And while they looked steadfastly toward heaven as he went up, behold, two angels appeared to them in white apparel, saying, "Men of Galilee, why do you stand gazing up into heaven? This same Jesus, who was taken up from you into heaven, will so come in like manner as you saw him go into heaven." (Acts 1:9–11)

Behold, he is coming with the clouds; and every eye shall see him . . . (Revelation 1:7)

These prophetic statements from the Bible all refer to the clouds. What does this signify? According to Rudolf Steiner:

Through the Mystery of Golgotha, one is able to experience the whole of Nature morally. If one gazes up at the clouds and sees lightning flashing down from them, one is able to behold Christ in his etheric form. With the clouds—that is to say, with the elements—he appears in spirit form. This vision may be had by everyone sooner or later.[5]

From these words it is clear that the coming of the Etheric Christ—his second coming—is an event that is not only for humanity, but is also for the world of nature, comprising the elements of earth, water, air, and fire (warmth), of which the clouds are an expression, representing for our senses the natural boundary of the extent of nature. It is a new manifestation of Christ—the Etheric Christ—that is indicated in the New Testament by referring to his "coming with the clouds."

In the Greek New Testament, the second coming is expressed by the word *Parousia*, which is usually translated as *Presence*, but which can also be translated as *Coming*, or the "second coming." Rudolf Steiner not only proclaimed the coming of the Etheric Christ, but also said that the second coming would commence during the course of the twentieth century. (See my article "Kashyapa and the Proclamation of Christ in the Etheric."[6]) Steiner called this the *greatest mystery of our time*, ushering in a New Age for humankind.

Rudolf Steiner is not the only one to have spoken of the coming of the Etheric Christ. This was also

---

3 Rudolf Steiner, *The True Nature of the Second Coming*, lecture of January 25, 1910.

4 Robert Powell, "Subnature and the Second Coming," *The Inner Life of the Earth*, pp. 75–76.

5 Rudolf Steiner, *Freemasonry and Ritual Work*, p. 449.

6 Robert Powell, "Kashyapa and the Proclamation of Christ in the Etheric," published in the Easter 2011 issue of *Starlight*, the newsletter of the Sophia Foundation, available as a free download: http://sophiafoundation.org/newsletter/.

spoken of by the Russian spiritual teacher Valentin Tomberg (1900–1973), and an early writing of his, indicating the onset of the second coming in 1932,[7] appears below, at the end of this article. This early writing by Valentin Tomberg brings out the profound significance of Christ's second coming for the whole world of nature.

The work of the *Journal for Star Wisdom* is focused upon helping to promote an understanding of the second coming of Christ: an understanding which is fostered and deepened through Sophia, Divine Wisdom (*Sophia* is the Greek word for *wisdom*): "Christ will appear in spiritual form during the twentieth century [and the twenty-first century] not simply because something happens outwardly, but to the extent that we find the power represented by Holy Sophia."[8]

The foregoing quote by Rudolf Steiner is helpful in order to understand why Karen Rivers and I founded the Sophia Foundation on New Year's Eve 1994/1995. Like *Journal for Star Wisdom*, the Sophia Foundation seeks to foster an understanding of the second coming of Christ by way of deepening an understanding of and a relationship to Sophia. Over and above this goal, the Sophia Foundation exists to assist in bringing to birth a new world culture, inspired by Sophia, known as the *Rose of the World*—a culture based on the one hand on Sophia's Divine Wisdom and on the other hand on the new experience and understanding of Christ as an all-pervading Presence of Divine Love in the etheric realm. Rudolf Steiner referred to this future culture as that of the sixth cultural epoch.

Many others have borne witness to the Etheric Christ in our time. A striking example is provided by the following account, which describes the linking up by a group of seven human beings to Christ's activity in the etheric realm. This description is said to have originated from a group of men incarcerated as political prisoners during the 1950s in a Siberian salt mine. In reading this account, let us bear in mind that the word *Presence* is one of the translations of the Greek word *Parousia*, which is the word used in the Greek New Testament in relation to Christ in his second coming, whose activity extends down to the heart of the Earth, and whose radiance is the protection against radiations from without (radioactivity, electromagnetic radiation, and so on):

> We found that we were overlighted by a Presence—a very great Presence, full of color, who began speaking to us. As He spoke, we found that we were able to see His radiations; they were brilliant beyond belief, so brilliant that we were unable to face them and knelt in our darkened cave overcome with awe and a premonition that we were entering the Kingdom of Heaven…It was some time before we could bear the radiance that proceeded from our Beloved…and we came to gaze upon His beautiful features and to listen to His voice…He told us that…He appeared in many places to give help where it was needed, making Himself known to those who were ready to seek Him…The Brotherhood of Light is composed of those who seek to serve the Christ Light, no matter how devious the way or how great the difficulties encountered. This we discovered only after we beheld the Great Presence and felt His enlightening radiations. The desire or the need for Him invokes His Presence, and His Presence invokes the radiations that become the means of enlightening the world…We have probed into the darkened depths of Earth itself, penetrating them by our radiant beams. We claim such acts not as personal attainments, but rather we acknowledge them once and forever as the reflection of the Christ Mind, the All-Knowing radiation. We draw from the Earth, deep within its heart…Deep within the heart of the Earth itself comes the impulse to a greater growth, a fuller life expression.… Christ and His Kingdom upon the Earth are now being revealed.[9]

Estelle Isaacson, a young woman who has until now contributed anonymously to the *Journal for Star Wisdom*,[10] is an example of a contemporary

---

7 Valentin Tomberg, "Communications concerning the Mystery of the Etheric Christ," reprinted from Appendix 2 of my book *Hermetic Astrology*, vol. 1.

8 Rudolf Steiner, *Isis Mary Sophia*, p. 213. Words in brackets [ ] added by RP.

9 Anonymous, *The Mysterious Story of X7*, pp. 18–80.

10 See also the article by Estelle Isaacson and also the article about Estelle Isaacson published in the Easter 2011 issue of *Starlight*, the newsletter of the Sophia

mystic, who has had numerous experiences of Christ in the etheric realm. For example, Estelle had this vision in the year 2009:

> As I stood before Christ in the Etheric, He lifted me up so that we were hovering just above the Earth. He was like a fire, a purifying fire. He was glowing like the Sun. Upon His chest was a brilliant cross of light, with rays of blue-violet light emanating out from it. He spoke to me: "O child of light, I came to Earth that I might illuminate it with My love, and My love knows no bounds. I love all, and the light of My love shines upon all beings, both good and evil."[11]

I would like to thank Estelle for making her visions available, some of which have been published in the *Starlight* newsletter of the Sophia Foundation, and some in the *Journal for Star Wisdom*. A published edition of Estelle's visions is eagerly awaited—hopefully in the not-too-distant future.

I would also like to take the opportunity to thank all those who have helped the publication of the *Journal for Star Wisdom* to continue this year. To all who have helped in the past, and to all who are helping in the present, enabling us to continue the work dedicated to assisting the emergence of Astrosophy as a new wisdom of the stars...heartfelt gratitude!

In 2009, a book was published that gives some background to what Rudolf Steiner called "a spiritual struggle to which nothing in history is comparable,"[12] and for which we have to be prepared spiritually. According to the research presented in this book, we are fast approaching "the day when [the] evil [one] comes" (Paul's Letter to the Ephesians, 6:13). Since the publication in 2009 of *Christ & the Maya Calendar: 2012 and the Coming of the Antichrist* by Kevin Dann and me, because of the investigative nature of the book, some readers have raised the question as to whether the central prognosis outlined in the book has been/is being/will be fulfilled, and, in the latter case, whether it will be fulfilled in the

near future. Readers may have the question as to why one should devote any attention to a prophecy of such a dark nature. Why not simply focus on the Good, the True, and the Beautiful? This article has been written in the knowledge that Rudolf Steiner forewarned of a possible catastrophe for humanity if the incarnation of Ahriman, which he prophesied would take place shortly after the year 2000,[13] were to go unrecognized. The implication is that on account of a lack of awareness on the part of human beings, the possibility exists that this incarnation might go unnoticed, in which case, according to Rudolf Steiner, a great opportunity for humankind's spiritual evolution would pass by, leading to very serious consequences for humanity and the Earth. This leads us to consider the possibility that *the reason for this dark event is to serve as a spiritual awakening for humanity.* How may this be understood?

The time in which we are presently living is known as the *age of the consciousness soul,*[14] which means the age of awakening consciously to the reality of the Spirit. It is during this time that the Mystery of Evil is being unveiled, just as in the previous age the Mystery of Death was the primary theme.[15] In the previous epoch (747 BC to AD 1414), known as the *age of the mind (or intellectual) soul,* the Mystery of Death was illuminated by Christ's resurrection—by his overcoming of death. This article is written to encourage a connection with the *Parousia,* the presence of Christ in the etheric, the weaving life forces of the Earth, as a protective mantle and guiding light during

---

Foundation, available as a free download: http://sophiafoundation.org/newsletter/.

11 Quoted from my article "In Memory of Willi Sucher (1902–1985)" in the 2010 issue of this journal.

12 Rudolf Steiner, *Freemasonry and Ritual Work,* p. 449.

13 *Ahriman* is the ancient Persian/Zoroastrian designation for the prince of darkness, known as Satan in the Judeo-Christian tradition. Rudolf Steiner preferred to use the name Ahriman. It should be noted that in the Christian tradition, the event referred to by Rudolf Steiner as the *incarnation of Ahriman* is designated as the *coming of the Antichrist.* In the words of Rudolf Steiner: "Before only a part of the third millennium of the post-Christian era has elapsed, there will be in the West an actual incarnation of Ahriman—Ahriman in the flesh." This prophetic statement relating to now was made in a lecture held on November 1, 1919—see Rudolf Steiner, *The Incarnation of Ahriman,* p. 37.

14 See footnote 1.

15 Rudolf Steiner, *From the History & Contents of the First Section of the Esoteric School,* introduction.

these times and the times ahead, during which the Mystery of Evil is becoming unveiled.

The purpose of the unveiling of evil in our time is to awaken consciousness. Both Good and Evil exist. Both are aspects of world existence. The awakening to Good and the awakening to Evil go hand in hand. Mystics have described how the gates of heaven and hell open simultaneously. The higher self ("I") of the human being is able to behold the Mystery of the Good, while at the same time the lower "I" perceives the Mystery of Evil. A spiritual awakening such as that exemplified by Rudolf Steiner signifies beholding with the higher "I" and with the lower "I" simultaneously. In this case, a high degree of spiritual wakefulness is active. It could be added that it is through the strength of the light of beholding the Etheric Christ[16] that one will be able to bear the beholding of the incarnation of Ahriman. The emergence of the Antilogos (to use Daniel Andreev's expression, quoted on page 15 of this journal) is the shadow side of awakening to the *Parousia*, the Presence of Christ in the etheric realm; and cognition of both, as exemplified by Rudolf Steiner, is possible through the beholding of the higher "I" and the lower "I" working together.

There are actually two prophecies under consideration in this article. The one is the momentous event of the second coming of Christ: the return of Christ in the etheric realm as prophesied by Rudolf Steiner. In addition, however, he also prophesied the incarnation of Ahriman into a human being. It is this incarnation of Ahriman into a human being that is generally referred to as the *incarnation of the Antichrist* in the Christian tradition. (However, for Rudolf Steiner the expression *Antichrist* refers to Sorath, who—among other things—prepares the way for Ahriman's incarnation.)[17] Essentially, Rudolf Steiner indicated that the second coming of Christ is an event taking place in the etheric realm of life forces, and is thus a non-physical manifestation of Christ in an ethereal form, the onset of which he prophesied to start in the year 1933, but which at the same time would entail the beginning of a struggle of apocalyptic dimension with *the beast* in the Book of Revelations: "Before the Etheric Christ can be comprehended by human beings in the right way, humanity must first cope with encountering the beast who will rise up in 1933."[18]

The authenticity of Rudolf Steiner's prophecy of this twofold event—that he indicated would begin to be fulfilled in 1933 (some eight years after his death in 1925)—is supported from various perspectives in the book *Christ & the Maya Calendar*. This theme was further elaborated upon in the article "World Pentecost" published in the *Journal for Star Wisdom 2010*, and as appendix 3 in *Prophecy-Phenomena-Hope* (referred to below), in which the end of the Maya calendar was considered possibile for the event of World Pentecost, because of the galactic alignment of the Sun at the winter solstice with the point of intersection of the Milky Way with the ecliptic.

The focus of this article is upon the key prophecy made by Rudolf Steiner concerning the second coming of Christ, in particular that the end of the Maya calendar on December 21, 2012 might be significant as a time when the penetration of the *Parousia* (the Presence of the Etheric Christ) could penetrate more powerfully into human consciousness—in accordance with the possibility of a Christ-filled World Pentecost, beginning at the time of the winter solstice in 2012.

Readers interested in following up on research concerning the second of Rudolf Steiner's prophecies referred to here, the one about the incarnation of Ahriman, are referred to my book, *Prophecy-Phenomena-Hope: The Real Meaning of 2012: Christ & the Maya Calendar—An Update*.[19]

An Experience of the Etheric Christ

The following report is by Tracy Saucier.[20] As Tracy says at the end of her report, something

---

16 See my article "The Mystery of Christ in our Time" for further elucidation concerning the Etheric Christ as the *Parousia*, the Presence of Christ in the etheric realm in our time: https://sophiafoundation.org/articles/.

17 *Christ & the Maya Calendar*, chapters 7 and 8 discuss Sorath.

18 Rudolf Steiner, *The Book of Revelation and the Work of the Priest*, lecture 16, p. 231.

19 Lindisfarne Books, 2011.

20 Tracy Saucier's report describing an experience undergone by participants at the workshop *Sophia*

altogether extraordinary transpired at a workshop she organized: a group experience of Christ in the etheric realm. The Christ experience with which participants were blessed is difficult to express in words, other than to characterize it as being bathed in *solar substance*, in *Light* and *Love*, enveloped in a supernatural *Divine Breath* of *Silence* and *Peace*. Something of this blessing is conveyed by these words:

> It is the profound silence of desires, of preoccupations, of the imagination, of the memory, and of discursive thought. One may say that the entire being becomes like the surface of calm water, reflecting the immense presence of the starry sky and its indescribable harmony. And the waters are deep, they are so deep! And the silence grows, ever-increasing…what silence![21]

It was suggested to participants at the workshop that it would be possible (for those who so wish) each evening at 9 pm to attune to the experience of the Etheric Christ through a *silent minute*. The *silent minute* was an historic movement begun in the United Kingdom by Major Wellesly Tudor Pole in 1940. The idea was developed in Britain during World War II. People were asked to devote one minute of prayer for peace at nine o'clock each evening. Tudor Pole said:

> There is no power on Earth that can withstand the united cooperation on spiritual levels of men and women of goodwill everywhere. It is for this reason that the continued and widespread observance of the Silent Minute is of such vital importance in the interest of human welfare.… [It comes from] an inner request from a high spiritual source that there be a Silent Minute of Prayer for Freedom, at 9 pm each evening.

This invitation, now in our time, to have a silent minute at 9 pm each evening to attune to the Etheric Christ—to bathe in his *solar substance*, in *Light* and *Love*, to become enveloped in his

supernatural *Divine Breath* of *Silence* and *Peace*— is open to everyone.

Report by Tracy Saucier

This weekend (April 8–10, 2011) at Robert Powell's workshop, "Sophia and the Spiritual Hierarchies," at Summerfield Waldorf School and Farm, in Sebastopol, California, something truly remarkable took place. It occurred toward the end of Robert's talk on Saturday afternoon. On Saturday morning, he had spoken of the various kinds of negative radiation coming toward us: for example, electricity, electromagnetism, and atomic power— pointing out that activating our inner radiance is the answer to the increasing radiation from without (radiation that is inimical toward human beings, particularly on an etheric level, but also on other levels).

On Saturday afternoon, Robert made the point that since 9/11 we are living in the period prophetically indicated in chapter 13 of the Book of Revelations, as discussed in the book *Christ & the Maya Calendar*. Then he read from the article "Rose of the World" in the 2011 issue of the *Journal for Star Wisdom* and came to the words where Daniel Andreev indicates that everyone will see the Son of God and hear his Word:

> Christ will take on as many forms as there are consciousnesses on Earth to behold him. He will adapt himself to everyone, and will converse with all. His forms, in an unimaginable way, will simultaneously yield an image: One who appears in heaven surrounded by unspeakable glory. There will not be a single being on Earth who will not see the Son of God and hear his Word.

Robert continued by giving a brief introduction to the last part of this "Rose of the World" article, describing Estelle Isaacson's experience of meeting with the Etheric Christ that came from her contemplation of the scene of Christ's suffering in the Garden of Gethsemane. Robert asked if anyone would like to read a passage from this last part of the article. A young woman, at her first Sophia Foundation workshop (it happened to be her birthday), responded "yes." At Robert's request she

---

and the Spiritual Hierarchies is reprinted from the Easter 2011 issue of *Starlight*, the newsletter of the Sophia Foundation, which is available as a free download from: http://sophiafoundation.org /newsletter/.

21 Anonymous, *Meditations on the Tarot*, p. 10.

then read the following passage from the article, which is a message from Christ to all people:

Love one another and love the Earth. Send your love to your fellow beings and into the Earth that the Earth may be lifted up on wings of peace. There is a body of the Earth, which is a body of love; this is My body that I gave to the Earth. You become one with the body of love by doing works of love, by cultivating feelings of love and by thinking thoughts of love. I invite all to become one with Me in this body of love. I call you home; My arms are around you. Return to love. Remember love. For where love is there am I; and because I desire to have you in My heart, I ask you to love one another, that I may be in you and you in Me. Look for Me to come to you, for I am coming and shall gather you to myself, and you shall be safely folded in Me because you are precious in My sight; and My sight is ever upon you. Return to Me.

When she had read Christ's message and passed the *Journal for Star Wisdom* back to Robert for him to read the last part of the vision, he could hardly speak the closing words to the "Rose of the World" article, as the whole room was by this time filled with the Light and Love of Christ. Everyone present was enveloped in this Light and Love. There was total stillness and silence for about ten minutes as everyone underwent—all together—a group experience of the over-lighting Presence of the Etheric Christ.

Reading Daniel Andreev's words and the words from the message of Christ at the end of the "Rose of the World" article in the 2011 issue of the *Journal for Star Wisdom* had somehow helped to bring about this beautiful and profound experience undergone by all at the workshop. For this blessing, we are all inexpressibly grateful. It was truly an altogether extraordinary workshop. (Tracy Saucier)

❦

May these words concerning the overlighting Presence of the Etheric Christ be a source of inspiration to everyone. The overlighting Presence of the Etheric Christ is needed all the more

now, at this time of crisis for Mother Earth and all her creatures.

In conclusion, as relevant to the foregoing indications relating to the Etheric Christ and the challenges now facing Mother Earth, let us consider these words written down by Valentin Tomberg in 1933, exactly the date indicated by Rudolf Steiner for the onset of Christ's second coming:

Communications concerning the Mystery of the Etheric Christ

It was in 1933 that Valentin Tomberg reached the age of 33. Among his diary notes, the following (written June 3, 1933) expresses something of his intimate experience of the onset of the second coming, the *etheric return*, or Christ's return to Earth in a spiritual—etheric (and not physical)—form. The translator of the following has not had access to the esoteric diaries from which this text stems, but received this extract from a diary entry for June 3, 1933, from someone who did have access and who typed out this particular entry (written in German, with the heading *Mitteilungen über das Geheimnis des ätherischen Christus*: "Communications concerning the Mystery of the Etheric Christ").[22]

The etheric return of Christ has its source of origin in a still higher world sphere than did the descent of Christ prior to the Mystery of Golgotha...Just as the present descent of Christ is beginning in a higher sphere than at that time, so it ends correspondingly DEEPER than it could at that time. Nineteen centuries ago Christ descended as far as the sixth-sub earthly sphere; now he will descend to the ninth sphere....

Since 1932 it is important that the necessary takes place in order that Christ is able to appear in the earthly realm. The line of his descent down to the Earth is vertical. Then his horizontal movement across the Earth's surface begins. This is the CROSS of his second coming. Then his descent down through the nine sub-earthly spheres begins.

The occurrence [of the second coming] in its various stages is as follows: Through Christ's etheric return the Christ-Power is penetrating

---

22 Comments added by the translator (Robert Powell) are in brackets [ ].

nature much more intensively than before [at the time of the Mystery of Golgotha]. At that time it was up to humankind; this time it involves nature also. The Christ-Power will reach right into the root-forces of plants, in which the mystery of the Fall of nature is locked up....

The reappearance of Christ on the Earth will signify the meeting of the whole of humanity with the Lesser Guardian of the Threshold. Usually the etheric return of Christ is imagined as signifying joy and happiness for humankind. But the reality will be quite different. Initially, it will not be joy and happiness which will be felt, but SHAME. A feeling of shame—in an elemental and powerful form—will take hold of human beings. Human beings will become conscious of all their shortcomings, and no one else will be able to comfort them. Human beings will then go out to seek comfort from nature. One will be able to see someone going up to a tree and embracing it—seeking comfort from it—and, standing thus, how they will weep bitterly.

And people will then be right in seeking comfort from dumb creatures, for creatures (the beings of nature) will become transformed through the presence of Christ. At present nature has lost all hope of being redeemed, but will be filled anew with hope through the breath of the presence of Christ. Nature will become good, and will again radiate trust and kindness toward human beings, instead of fear and mistrust as is the case now. Wonderful changes will take place in nature. Springtimes will come that will be different from all other springtimes—with goodness which will be felt in the air and in the breath, in the breathing of the ground, in the buds and green leaves. These springtimes will be filled with a blessing that nature has never experienced before.

Toward autumn nature will bestow her fruits in generous abundance—the sap will be life-giving and seeds will be ripe and full. For Christ will be there for nature. His presence will work in such a way that—even if it takes place only for a moment—all struggle, hate and fear will withdraw from nature.

Extraordinary changes will become noticeable in the atmosphere. There will be regions where the air will be such that many people will be cured—cured of their illnesses through the air they breath in... Changes in the behavior of children will manifest themselves in surprising and mysterious ways. Thus, it will happen that a circle of children playing will become quite still and will stand there motionless and in deep silence for a while.... Even if communism still exists in Russia, remarkable occurrences in the school-life of communist Russia will take place. There, large groups of children will suddenly experience something, concerning which they won't know what to say, but which will place them in a reverent and devout mood.

Christ will move from the West to the East in wave-like lines. He will begin in America and will continue through Europe to the northeast of Europe. From there he will continue eastward as far as China, where the resistance is strongest. His coming is not for all regions of the Earth simultaneously, but progresses step by step. Thereby each further step of his movement will signify a stronger force, a growth in the transmission of the Christ-Power. Only after traversing the whole of the Earth in this way will he appear to individuals in different parts of the world. Clairvoyant esotericists will see him earlier, where he will be present only in the kingdoms of nature, but for many others the first experience of him will be in the human kingdom, after his expansion throughout nature is accomplished.

❦

ENSOULING STAR WISDOM

William Bento, Ph.D.

Standing in an open clearing of the woods, looking upward into a crystal-clear sky, bejeweled with thousands of stars twinkling and pulsating light, I felt my whole being sighing with a silent and deep gratitude. It was a moment of tender intimacy. After a long day of teaching about the correspondences between the cosmos and the human being this moment struck me with a persistent gnawing riddle. How effortless it was for me to breathe in this starry night with a wonder that was simultaneously a peaceful knowing! Yet, it sharply contrasted with my day where I attempted once again to convey in thoughts, words, movements, and visual depictions the immense mysteries of the Hermetic axiom, "What is above is also below." Why is it such an arduous task to express a phenomenal reality that pervades all of our lives?

Sometimes I feel like I am an alien (in a strange land), speaking a foreign and arcane language. Despite this feeling, which is neither enduring nor frequent, I am always willing to engage with others in the exploration of Star Wisdom and its relevancy to soul life. My conception of reality is inseparable from the framework of a spiritual scientific cosmology, wherein Star Wisdom is an expressed manifestation of the ongoing working of the Divine. I dare say I find it inconceivable to understand the meaning of humanity's journey upon the Earth without such a reference. However, putting my own conviction aside, I do realize why the majority of people in our modern Western civilization find such a reference point to anchor reality difficult. The predominant materialistic thinking in today's world is so pervasive that one is rarely exposed to any other alternative. Within this Cartesian materialistic paradigm there is only skepticism and the dismissal of anything that links the human being with the starry world.

Yet, it seems the time is close approaching for a paradigm shift. For many the year 2012 has become a significant landmark in a multitude of convergent planetary cycles. There is an expectant mood of crisis, catharsis, and new revelations in the air. That in an uncanny way engenders great hope in me—hope that a younger generation faced with creating a different kind of future may hunger and thirst for an understanding of how Star Wisdom can provide a light into the life of the soul. We need to craft boats of spirit cognition that care for and transport thirsty souls across the salt waters of materialism into a new world. I believe Star Wisdom, when ensouled, can provide a compass for navigating the rough and turbulent waters of this stage in humanity's evolution.

And furthermore, I hold the optimistic view that the hidden treasures of Soul Wisdom may be illumined through a renewal of the comprehension of the starry world. For indeed, if we are to experience a collapse of the faulty foundations of our modern Western Civilization, then there needs to be an "Ark of Salvation" for the sake of humanity's future.

So little has been written about the meditative path of inner development, which can prepare one to take up the study and practice of a new Star Wisdom. The few who ask the question, "Where can I learn about Star Wisdom?" rarely take the steps to commit to an apprenticeship or to immerse themselves into phenomenological observations. The lack of a 101 primer on *Astrosophy* (literal translation Star Wisdom) tends to be a discouraging barrier for many curious and interested souls to move through. I believe one of the reasons that there is no primer on Astrosophy beyond Willi Sucher's pioneering publications and Robert Powell's *Hermetic Astrology* (volumes 1 to 3) and the recently published book, *The Astrological Revolution,* by Robert Powell and Kevin Dann, is that the essence of preparation for taking up the study of Star Wisdom lies elsewhere.

Within the core fellowship of the StarFire Research Group (William Bento, Brian Gray, Robert Powell, Robert Schiappacasse, and David Tresemer), an agreement about such a preparation exists. It is the view that any aspirant who wishes to take up the study and practice of a new Star Wisdom must fully embrace the *three pillars* before the *Temple of Astro-Sophia.* This means to have more than a familiarity with the three pillars. It means a complete absorption into the disciplines of study belonging to each pillar.

The *first pillar* rests on the knowledge of and language within Astrology that facilitates a capacity for living into the world of images. Such a study encompasses a basic orientation in astronomy and horoscope construction. The search to find Star Wisdom's origin, nature, and purpose is paramount. Identifying one's self with this lineage is an essential part of the preparation for entering into the *Temple of Astro Sophia.*

The *second pillar* is founded on the spiritual scientific principles of Rudolf Steiner. Ideally it entails knowing the essence of anthroposophic cosmology in its entirety, including all the workings of the Divine and the spiritual hierarchies from the beginning to the end of time. Imaginatively grasping the musical score of how the human being came into existence and how he is foreordained to attain the freedom to create a cosmos of love is one of the most awe-filled discoveries one can have in this journey toward a gnosis (a knowing of the full potential of the human being) of Anthropos. As one lives with this understanding it becomes both empowering and inspirational.

The *third pillar* is about a communion with the "Being of Time," as known in the open-yet-secret revelations of esoteric Christianity. The aspirant's aim here is to experience truly the moral intuition that comes as one upholds the truth about the turning point in time. It is a vital aspect of one's preparation. Knowing the Cosmic Christ's life, as he walked upon the Earth disseminating the teachings of love's redemptive power and healing the sickness of sin, forms the foundation for a new Star Wisdom.

THE THREE PILLARS OF STAR WISDOM

ASTROLOGY	ANTHROPOSOPHIC COSMOLOGY	ESOTERIC COSMIC CHRISTIANITY
Knowledge and language of the stars as given in the wisdom of antiquity	Cosmic symphony of creation and the indications for co-creation	The life of the Cosmic Christ and its significance for Future Jerusalem
Seeds of Imaginative Cognition	Seeds of Inspirational Cognition	Seeds of Intuitive Cognition

The First Pillar: Astrology

We can imagine inscribed into the first pillar are the words of the Star Verse given to Marie Steiner by Rudolf Steiner on Christmas day 1922.

> The Stars once spoke to human beings.
> It is World Destiny, they are silent now.
> To be aware of this silence
> Can become pain for Earthly humanity.
> But in the deepening silence
> There grows and ripens
> What human beings speak to the Stars.
> To be aware of this speaking
> Can become strength for spirit body.

Penetrating the first line leads one into the vast esoteric knowledge of how heavenly realms were actively engaged in the creation of the human being. The second line tells the story of evolution. The inevitable event of our parental caregivers (Stars) letting humanity go forward into evolution on its own becomes clear in this second line. Without this cosmic historical event humanity could never attain freedom. Yet, the loss of direct guidance, as exemplified by the silence does have the consequence of feeling abandonment and experiencing pain. It is part of what human beings must endure on Earth if we are to become fully human and attain the soul wisdom that sheds light on the karma and destiny of all.

Once the learning gained from the first four lines written into this pillar of Star Wisdom are integrated and warmed by the open heart, an experiential kind of baptism occurs. Meditations on the ensouled content of this pillar can then lead to a sense of and for conscious dialogue with the starry world. It gives confirmation to the words, *"In the deepening silence there grows and ripens what man speaks to the stars."* Making this a spiritual practice highlights the last two lines to the Star verse by Rudolf Steiner, *"To be aware of this speaking can become strength for spirit body."* The strength referred to here is not about an outward power, but about an inner faith of communion with the starry world. These experiences can occur in times of aloneness, as when in deep meditation one senses a presence amidst the silent contemplation of the meaning of certain starry configurations or in a moment of gazing into the starry vault of the night and experiencing currents of warmth within one's being.

The speech and language of the Stars does not exist merely in the great array of images depicting ancient mythological lore. It also exists in the writing of the glyphs of the zodiac, the symbols of the planets and planetary aspects. There is nothing arbitrary to the shape of glyphs or the form of the planetary symbols. As aspirants learn to read the signs and decipher the occult script written in the astrological code, they will gradually come to appreciate the open secrets these glyphs and symbols convey. All zodiacal glyphs can be found as imprints of the formative life forces that sculpted the human form from Aries in the head, Taurus in the neck and larynx, and so on. All planetary symbols are composed of three elements: the cross, as associated to the body; the crescent arc, as associated to the soul; and the circle, as associated to the spirit. They comprise an imaginative pictorial language written as a continuous script, revealing the interplay between the Cosmos and Earth and all her inhabitants. When this book of Star Wisdom is read in the context of the many themes of human life, a sense of coherence may arise.

Meaningfulness can be restored, even to the most difficult passages in life. In fact, it can be said that the book can become an instruction manual for living one's life in accordance with the cosmos. Moreover, when Star Wisdom is applied seriously to contemplating one's own starry configurations, it becomes possible to understand one's pre-earthly resolves in relationship to life experiences.

This article can only introduce this book of Star Wisdom in its relationship to Soul Wisdom. Yet, I can suggest a way to grasp this mysterious and wondrous correlation. The following table highlights some basic correlations worth noting. It can give the aspirant a starting point to begin the reading of these two glorious books of wisdom given to us out of antiquity, two books that I believe were once essential readings in the ancient Mystery Schools. As the fifteenth-century teacher of the Florentine Platonic Academy, Marsilio Ficino, once said, "A star is a heavenly human being, and the human being is an earthly star."

THE BOOKS OF STAR WISDOM AND SOUL WISDOM

The Great Mysteries	Star Wisdom	Soul Wisdom
Space	Zodiac	The capacity for embodiment as the magic of sensory integration, the management and transformation of urges into the expression of creative will, which distinguishes man from animal
Time	Planetary Rhythms	The capacity to live in the four streams of time: Past, Present, Future and Eternity
Consciousness	Story of Evolution in the Images of the Heavens	The capacities to develop higher faculties of cognition: Imaginative, Inspirational and Intuitive
Being	The Divine and the Spiritual Hierarchies	The capacity to become fully human throughout the series of incarnations leading to the ideal destined place of humanity as the tenth spiritual hierarchy

Out of the substance of the Spirits of Will (Thrones), which was offered up to the process of evolution, the Spirits of Harmony (Cherubim) shaped the warmth exuded from it into the circle of light we now identify as the Zodiac. Imaginatively we can see the twelve zodiacal sectors as streams of light that shaped the three dimensional planes of space (forward and back, above and below, left and right) that we inhabit today. It has been understood in esotericism as the "Cube of Space." Within the Cube of Space is the divine upright form of the human being, wherein we find the light-sculpting forces of the zodiac imprinted into the human body. The glyphs of each zodiacal sign can be seen imprinted into the human physiology and anatomy. For example, the glyph of Aries indicates the down streaming forces of the spirit separating the left and right hemispheres of the brain and the shape of the eyebrow curving down into the bridge of the nose. Its imprint was made upon the external form. Hence every human being inhabits his or her zodiac.

A full sense of embodiment, however, requires an integration of all twelve senses and the management of the twelve instinctual urges. Each zodiacal sign is associated with a sense and by its very nature as part of the "animal circle" (the meaning of the word *zodiac*) associated with an urge. Ancient forms of education were based on the fundamental activities in agriculture, land work, craft, and arts that naturally aided young people in sensory motor integration, as well as providing the opportunity to express a degree of creativity. These innate forms of work ethic set the basis for a higher degree of education as the young person grew into being a full contributor to his or her community. In the iconography of many of the medieval European churches we find the twelve virtues known to esoteric Christianity associated with the zodiac. It was the teaching to instill a conscious effort to embody in one's soul the moral forces for co-creating the world.

Time would not even exist as a concept if it were not for the Earth rotating on its axis (day) and orbiting around the Sun (year). The Sun against the background of the fixed stars gives us a means of tracking our earthly biography as in celebrating our birthday and counting the years of our lives. The movement of the vernal point (now March 21) against the zodiacal signs marks the great ages of humanity. The planetary rhythms are also part of the great celestial clock. They point to various generational themes that characterize the conditions of the times we live through. For instance, the Jupiter/Saturn rhythm of twenty years between conjunctions frames a period of new societal changes based on significant cultural events. By reading such a planetary rhythm we can illumine the past, grasp needs of the present, and envision the future all based on the eternal qualities of these two planets, in this case, Saturn as Memory and Jupiter as Wisdom. Indeed, remembering our history is one form of cultivating wisdom!

There is no greater storybook than reading the mythological dramas spread out before us in the heavenly sky. In the mythology lies the development of human consciousness from the divine to the all-too-human. In the book *Signs in the Heavens: A Message for Our Times* by William Bento, Robert Schiappacasse and David Tresemer, there is a fine example of how reading the myths in the sky can serve as a key to understanding the different stages of consciousness. The authors focused on the myth of Perseus, rescuer of Andromeda, found in the region of the sky between the Fishes and the Ram to depict a form of imaginative consciousness capable of safeguarding the riches of the human soul. Ensouling such myths gives the human being a sense of direction and meaningfulness to all the events that transpire upon the Earth.

Living with Star Wisdom in the above-mentioned ways brings the human soul into a deeper knowing of how all of evolution is the work of spiritual beings. The awe-filled humility arising from this understanding provides a background for right and healthy regard for fathoming the laws of karma and reincarnation. It can give answer to the many riddles that plague us about why humanity struggles with themes such as good and evil, health and illness, life and death. Star Wisdom has been, and can once again be, the beacon of light for understanding the great Mysteries of existence.

The Second Pillar: Anthroposophy

A guide to contemplating the second pillar can be found in the meditative verse by Rudolf Steiner on the evening when the temple that he had created, the Goetheanum, was set on fire—December 31, 1922. The verse he was writing on the blackboard as the flames began to move through the building was the culmination of his lecture series, *Man and the World of Stars: The Spiritual Communion of Mankind.*

> In Earth-activity draws near to me,
> Given to me in substance-imaged form,
> The Heavenly Being of the Stars—
> In WILLING I see them transformed
>   with Love!
> In Watery life stream into me,
> Forming me through with power
>   of substance-force,
> The Heavenly Deeds of the Stars—
> In FEELING I see them transformed
>   with Wisdom.

The correspondence of macrocosmic/microcosmic correspondence is summarized in these brief lines. Historically speaking this verse can be seen as a kind of culmination to lectures he began in November 23, 1922, and concluded on New Year's Eve. This series of lectures was followed in 1923 by *Mystery Knowledge and Mystery Centers* and *World History in the Light of Anthroposophy.* Steiner began by addressing the life of soul and then moved on to describe the development of mystery teachings that were both perennial, and yet focused on the particular evolutionary stages that humanity was undergoing during each cultural age. No stretch of the imagination is needed to see how Steiner was pointing to the esoteric lineage of what he saw the Goetheanum to be. With the teachings of Anthroposophy embedded in the building's artistic sculpting, stained glass windows, and the performances of the Mystery Dramas written for the space and the time of the fifth Post-Atlantean Age, Steiner was clearly offering a renewal of mystery teaching. The mystery knowledge disseminated took the form of spiritual science, Anthroposophy. The Goetheanum stood as

the main mystery center for its time, akin to the Temple of Ephesus in early times.

The first Goetheanum, Dornach, Switzerland

Anthroposophy is not simply a body of esoteric knowledge that can be studied; it is a way of life that challenges and demands every student to reexamine the cultural constructs of a dualistic worldview. There is no easy guide to enlightenment to be found here. The profound truths embedded in it are not always blatant or transparent upon first encounter. The spiritual-scientific principles Rudolf Steiner established were the result of free thinking—thinking directed from within, thinking freed from the limits of sensory perception and thoughts already acquired. He resisted and critiqued the natural scientific dogma of his time, yet made his method accessible to any one who dared to apply disciplined phenomenological methods to the realm of epistemology. *The Philosophy of Freedom,* now published as *Intuitive Thinking as a Spiritual Path* (2006), foreshadows the path of Anthroposophy and gives it its distinctive approach. Steiner's radical departure from traditional Theosophical teachings rests upon his insistence that the principles of spiritual science should not be taken up on the basis of faith, but on the basis of the will to experience the world for oneself.

When Steiner described and elaborated on thinking as a "spiritual activity," it was then, as it is now, a provocative idea. Although many in the philosophical schools of Hegel and Heidegger could receive such an idea with genuine interest, the popular culture could not recognize the potential of following this activity of thinking to its conclusion. Intellectuality had too strong of a hold on the modern mind to allow the notion of spiritual activity that can be experienced in thinking to become a consensual reality. Aside from the contemporary obstacles to understanding the pathway to Anthroposophy, there were enough interested seekers willing to support the research and teachings of Rudolf Steiner during the first quarter of the twentieth century.

Inasmuch as Carl Jung's legacy could be summed up in the phrase "modern humanity's search for the soul," Rudolf Steiner's legacy could be summed up in the phrase "modern humanity's search for the spirit." Through Anthroposophy, the "heavenly beings of the stars" are identified not only by name but also through their specific activities manifested as earthly forms. The elements fire, earth, air and water; the kingdoms of nature and all their species; and the very kinship of the human form are but phenomenal evidence of the spiritual beings' work. They are the "heavenly deeds of the stars." In Steiner's *Outline of Esoteric Science (1909)*, the details of this grand cosmology are painstakingly rendered. There is no way to read this book other than with suspension of one's judgment and to enter the grand thought pictures offered in it. In conjunction with this open-minded attitude, there needs to be a willingness to see the words transform into mighty pictures of a divine process. Although it is difficult to describe the actual experience of grasping these tremendous occult facts of evolution, one could certainly say that one feels wisdom imbued with love.

Steiner referred to this book as a *Grail book*. For the modern individual, *An Outline of Esoteric Science* is a cosmic compass for navigating the dark forests of materialism. On one hand it orients us to the starry world, and on the other it gives instructions for lighting the starry flame within one's inner life. The preceding publications, *How to Know Higher Worlds* (1904) and *Theosophy: An Introduction to the Spiritual Processes in Human Life and in the Cosmos* (1905) offered important guidelines for the quest to the Spirit. The former

equipped the questing individual with meditative exercises for developing soul organs of perception. In the concluding chapter, the reader is led to an understanding of the practice of white magic. *Theosophy* informed the reader of the journey after death, as well as before one's life on Earth. Spiritual landscapes through the regions of the planetary spheres are defined and explored. These three spiritual-scientific books, along with *Intuitive Thinking as a Spiritual Path,* comprise the foundation stones for the pillar of Anthroposophy.

These books are explicated and expanded in the thousands of lectures given throughout Rudolf Steiner's career as an unparalleled esoteric teacher of the modern age. Some of the key lecture cycles for the aspirant of Star Wisdom (but by no means all the key lecture cycles) beyond those mentioned above are: *Man in the Light of Occultism, Theosophy and Philosophy* (1912); *Philosophy, Cosmology and Religion* (1922); *Spiritual Beings in the Heavenly Bodies and in the Kingdoms of Nature* (1912); *The Spiritual Hierarchies and the Physical World* (1909, 1911); *Human and Cosmic Thought* (1914); *Cosmosophy* (two volumes, 1921); *Human Questions and Cosmic Answers: Man and his Relations to the Planets* (1922); *Mystery of the Universe: The Human Being, Model of Creation* (1921); and *The Search for the New Isis, the Divine Sophia* (1918, 1920).

Throughout most of Steiner's lectures are explicit or implicit indications concerning spiritual beings living and working through the zodiac and the planets. I have rarely read a lecture cycle that did not contain such references. I am firmly convinced his efforts in developing the language of Anthroposophy can be understood as a revival of the ancient mystery teachings, wherein Star Wisdom formed the grammar and syntax of esoteric knowledge. By formulating the principles of spiritual science based on phenomenological and epistemological foundations Steiner gave all astrologers a basis for reaffirming the validity and relevancy of astrology in today's world. He gave the impetus for what Elizabeth Vreede and Willi Sucher pioneered as Astrosophy. Both of them wrote letters to members of the Anthroposophical Society in the hope of sharing a promising and new field of inquiry taking place in the newly founded Mathematical–Astronomical research group at the Goetheanum in Dornach, Switzerland. Elizabeth Vreede wrote letters from September 1927 to August 1930, published as *Astronomy and Spiritual Science*. Willi Sucher continued the spirit of Vreede's letters from April 1944 to March 1946, published as *Isis Sophia I: Introducing Astrosophy* (1999). In 1951, Willi Sucher wrote a book entitled, *Isis Sophia II: Outline of a New Star Wisdom*.

The Third Pillar: Esoteric Cosmic Christianity

As we approach this pillar, we may experience one of the most challenging riddles of all. The stains on the history of Christianity as a religion have effectively obscured its deeper mysteries for most of the general populace. Therefore, any mention of a cosmic significance of Christianity can be, and often is, met with great suspicion. Yet, this pillar is not about the Christian religion per se. It is about the "turning point in time" in human evolution on Earth. It rests not upon religious doctrine, but on the spiritual-scientific facts conveyed by Rudolf Steiner and confirmed by other leading twentieth-century individualities. Steiner's exceptional clairvoyant investigations of cosmic history place the "Mystery of Golgotha" (Christ's crucifixion, descent into Hell, and the resurrection on Easter morning) at the apex of all the efforts of the Divine in relation to world evolution. Divinity's intent was, and is, to endow humanity with its capacity for co-creation in the cosmos. Such was the ultimate gift of the Cosmic Christ to humanity. The ripples of the Mystery of Golgotha continue to unfold into our time, and into the future.

The esoteric thesis is that the Cosmic Christ, as the Son of the Divine, inhabited the body of Jesus of Nazareth for three and a half years, and through this inhabitation gave to every human being the sense of the divine "I am," the creator capacity. This sense of the Cosmic Christ was stated most clearly in such articles of faith as found in the prologue to St. John's Gospel, as well as by St. Paul in the New Testament. However, through St. Augustine's emphasis on humanity's guilt and Christ's divine forgiveness, Christian theology of the fourth and fifth centuries—which persisted until the Reformation and into the Age of Reason in the eighteenth century—perpetuated an erosion of the cosmic historical ground into which the incarnation of the Cosmic Christ was placed. Ultimately, this notion devolved into the "simple man of Nazareth," a mythos that reinforces today's materialistic worldview.

For Rudolf Steiner, Valentin Tomberg, Pierre Teilhard de Chardin, and other esoteric Christian initiates, the Cosmic Christ was understood as a fact of cosmic history, not simply a marvelous story, but a fact. Through a path of inner experience, these individuals rediscovered the centrality of Christ's life upon the Earth. They each understood the "Mystery of Golgotha" as the result of a long process of involution. They viewed the event of the "Mystery of Golgotha" as inaugurating the ascending arc of evolution, wherein human beings set out to earn their place among the Spiritual Beings in the Cosmos.

Biased dogmatic views for and against the Christian principles, inclusive of the concept of Christ Jesus as the Son of the Divine, are the first obstacles to entering into the complexity of this great mystery. Intellectual debate about theories and doctrines does little to invite the sacred holy experience of a direct encounter with the presence of the power of Christ. Each of us must find the Christ as a reality for ourselves. In the first lecture given in December 1920 under the title "The Search for the new Isis, the Divine Sophia," Steiner offers the following uplifting thought:

> There is something in the depths of the human heart that speaks of nothing but what is purely human and dissolves all differences. Moreover, it is just within these depths that we find the Christ. There is a wisdom that extends far beyond all that can be discovered concerning single spheres of world existence, wisdom that is able to grasp the world in its unity, even in space and time. And this again is the star wisdom that leads to Christ.[1]

---

1   Rudolf Steiner, *Search for the New Isis, the Divine Sophia*, p. 8.

Is there any more powerful idea for grasping the world in its unity than realizing that the whole of humanity is shaped and guided by the lawful, orderly, wisdom-filled movements of the stars? Regardless of personal sympathies or antipathies, there is no refuting that our very sense of existence is owed to the fact that the starry world has created our sense of space and rhythms of time in which to unfold our consciousness on Earth. In our limited conception of the centrality of this existence, we are led to acknowledge the Sun as the visible source of our sense of warmth, light, movement, and life. All of our ancient myths point to the Sun as the abode of the being who presides over the course of time; thus, it is not arbitrary to consider the Sun the gateway through which the Cosmic Christ descended to the Earth and ascended when his life imprint was completed on the Earth. In this manner, we can see the Cosmic Christ as having given new meaning to Star Wisdom. This is the riddle engraved into the third pillar of Star Wisdom.

In his second lecture, Steiner shares a verse that can easily be imagined as written into this third pillar of Star Wisdom. It conveys the mystery of a deep fundamental change in human consciousness during the epoch of astrology's birth, the Egyptian–Chaldean–Babylonian Age. Couched in the myth of Osiris and Isis are both the historical events of the third post-Atlantean epoch and the task of the current fifth post-Atlantean epoch in which we now live.

> Isis Sophia, Wisdom of God,
> Lucifer has slain her;
> and on the wings of the world-wide forces
> carried her hence into Cosmic Space.
> Christ Will, working in human beings
> shall wrest from Lucifer,
> and on the boats of spirit cognition,
> call to new life in human souls
> Isis Sophia, Wisdom of God.

Further insight is given by Steiner to the phrase "Lucifer has slain her." He describes how Lucifer strives to cut off all moral forces from the modern worldview. His aim is to allow only the laws of nature, the necessary and natural aspect, to be recognized through the lens of modern natural-scientific thinking. "Thus, the impoverished human being of modern times possesses wisdom of the world in which stars move according to a purely mechanical necessity, devoid of morality, so that the moral meaning of the world's order cannot be found in their movements" (Steiner, 1920, page 20). Reclaiming a moral worldview of evolution becomes for the modern individual an important Grail quest. "Christ Will" in this verse is but another way of referring to the Cosmic Christ. In his will lives the Father principle of the Divine. The will of morality, the aim of the outcome of divine creation, the will to do the deed of the good, all this is but the power of the Christ at work in the lives of men and women. As Steiner so aptly puts it: "It is not the Christ we lack, my dear friends, but the knowledge and wisdom of the Christ, the Sophia of the Christ, the Isis of the Christ."[2]

Uniting our will with the will of Christ is the mandate of every soul living in this age. By doing so, we may be able to liberate the divine Sophia from the coffin of a materialistic astronomy and reengage ourselves in the dialogue with the Stars, for they continue to hold the wisdom of our evolution—past, present and future. In this dialogue there is to be found the new mysteries, the mysteries founded upon the Earth by the life, death, and resurrection of the Christ. Herein is the core theme for Star Wisdom of the future.

However, it is imperative for the aspirant of a new Star Wisdom to build a boat of spirit cognition out of the many incredible and deep insights given throughout the many lectures wherein Steiner imparted his direct experiences of the Christ and the spiritual world. Foundational to this crafting of the boat of spirit cognition is the understanding that when Christ is allowed to indwell the human soul the Christ-power will again shine from Earth's aura, like a star, toward those worlds that the Christ left for the salvation of human beings on Earth. Once this is accomplished, the entire cosmos will become permeated by Christ. In the words of Rudolf Steiner, "The

---

2 Ibid., p. 22.

Christ force impresses the spiritual imagination of humankind into the cosmos. It is the Christ force, united with the Earth.... Since the Christ impulse has been living with the Earth, human beings in their self-aware being, are given back to the cosmos. From cosmic being, the human being has become an earthly being. Human beings have the potential to become cosmic beings again when, as earthly beings, they have become themselves."[3] Earth citizenship is to be followed by a restoration of cosmic citizenship.

In Steiner's spiritual-scientific investigations, he asserts that the luciferic powers did not have the opportunity to experience the Christ power on Earth. Nevertheless, a time will come when these powers will experience the Christ power through humankind and be redeemed. Just think of the immensity of this prophetic view. Human beings will redeem Lucifer if they take the Christ power into themselves in the appropriate way. The redemption of astrology, as given by a new Star Wisdom penetrated with anthroposophic cosmology and spiritual practice, is part of Lucifer's redemption. Earlier in Steiner's esoteric career as an initiate of the new mysteries, he conveyed the following:

Only in this way can we grasp the full dignity and importance of humankind among the members of the hierarchies. Looking up to the exalted nature and glory of the higher hierarchies, we can say to ourselves, "However mighty, wise, and good these higher hierarchies may be—and hence unable to err from the true path—it is humanity's great mission to bring freedom into the world and, along with freedom, what we call, in the truest sense of the word, love." For without freedom, love is impossible. Beings who absolutely must obey a particular impulse, merely do so; but for those who can do otherwise, there is only one power that enables them to do so, and that is love. Freedom and love are two poles that belong together. If love is to enter our cosmos, it can do so only through freedom—that is, through Lucifer and the one who conquers Lucifer—the

one who is also the redeemer of human beings—the Christ. This is why the Earth is the cosmos of love and freedom.... In these lectures, we have endeavored to fathom the meaning and significance of humanity by considering the significance of our cosmos.

Calling "to new life in human souls" is the wisdom of God and a calling of remembrance in the highest order. Remembering humanity's place in the cosmos is a sure way to activate one's relationship with the starry world. When this cognition is combined with the wisdom of the Christ, then the new mysteries begin to come to light. We can characterize one aspect of the new mysteries as the wisdom of knowing that the Christ's life was the imprint of the new man, the man who out of freedom lives his life for the furtherance of love. The Christ's life was no ordinary human life. It was a cosmic life fully lived out on the Earth. Steiner articulates this fact in a very moving way in lecture 3 of *The Spiritual Guidance of the Individual and Humanity* (1911):

During the time that Jesus of Nazareth pursued his ministry and journeys as Jesus Christ in Palestine in the last three years (and a half) of his life—from the age of thirty to thirty-three—the entire cosmic Christ-being continued to work in him. In other words, Christ always stood under the influence of the entire cosmos; he did not take a single step without cosmic forces working in him. The events of these three years (and a half) in Jesus' life were a continuous realization of his horoscope, for in every moment during those years there occurred what usually happens only at birth. This was possible because the entire body of the Nathan Jesus had remained susceptible to the influence of the totality of the forces of the cosmic-spiritual hierarchies that guide our Earth.

Now that we know that the whole spirit of the cosmos penetrated Christ Jesus we may ask, Who was the being who went to Capernaum and all the other places Jesus went? The being who walked the Earth in those years certainly looked like any other human being. But the forces working in him were the *cosmic forces* coming from *the sun and the stars*; they directed his body. The total essence of

---

3   Rudolf Steiner, *Anthroposophical Leading Thoughts*, p. 183 (trans. revised).

the cosmos, to which the Earth belongs, determined what Christ Jesus did. This is why the *constellations* are so often alluded to in the gospel descriptions of Jesus' activities."[4]

Willi Sucher, pioneer of Astrosophy, took these words to heart. He dedicated many years of research to discovering the cosmic correspondences to the events of the Christ's life as cited in the Gospels. He knew such a discovery would give to the modern human being a key to working more consciously with the Cosmic Christ's impulse. Not having an exact chronology of the Christ's life, Willi Sucher attempted to correlate the qualities of the planetary rhythms and aspects with certain healing and teaching events in the Gospels. However, shortly after Willi Sucher's death (May 25, 1985), the deciphering of the Jewish calendar, as referred to in Anne Catherine Emmerich's clairvoyant day-by-day account of Jesus' life, made the actual chronology of the Christ a possibility. The Christ events could then be tracked to the planetary aspects from baptism to ascension (September 23, AD 29—April 5, AD 33). Inspired by Willi Sucher's efforts, Robert Powell published the *Chronicle of the Living Christ* with explicit references to Anne Catherine Emmerich's accounts and many horoscopes of significant moments in the life of Christ.

For the past fifteen years, this publication has been the central guiding framework for the collective research of William Bento, Robert Schiappacasee and David Tresemer, taking into account that every degree of the zodiac is now imprinted with a Christ experience that can be contemplated in images derived from the Christ's life on the day the Sun crossed over that particular zodiacal degree.[5] *Chronicle of the Living Christ* is the basis for the *Journal for Star Wisdom* calendar commentaries written by Claudia McLaren Lainson. By taking in the images of the Christ's life through each degree of the zodiac, we not only ensoul the life of Christ within ourselves, but we also

participate in the activity of co-creation. By living with the images of the cosmic drama of humanity's salvation played out on the Earth in the years the Christ lived in the body of the Nathan Jesus one is transforming the "animal circle" into a "divine humanized circle." It is basically a co-creation of the new zodiac containing in it the new mysteries.

Entry to the Temple of Astro-Sophia

When the *three pillars* before the *Temple of Astro-Sophia* are fully appreciated and acknowledged as guiding principles and spiritual texts, the aspirant to new Star Wisdom may enter the temple and practice the art of "speaking to the stars." The baptism of study, indicated by the three pillars of astrology, Anthroposophy, and cosmic Christianity, leads us to a stage of confirmation of the principles of practice within the temple. This practice begins with the faculty of speaking in images, and then moves on to listening to the spirit speaking through the other, and finally to experiencing solemn communion with the cosmos. Ensouling such experiences in the *Temple of Astro-Sophia* provides a fertile inner space for active dialogue and sacred consultation with one's own Guardian Angel.

For the devotee to a new Star Wisdom, awareness on a day-to-day basis of the planets' movements in relation to one another against the background of the zodiac becomes an important form of mindfulness practice. Through this practice, an affirmation of the moral world order implicitly takes place and can help guide one's decisions to be in accord with the cosmos. It allows for a conscious sense of communion with the starry world in our thoughts, feelings, and actions throughout the day. The same diligence toward following the movement of the planets' interrelationship to one another and to the stars should also be given to one's own natal starry configuration. Self-examination focused on evaluating our own pre-earthly resolves and intentions (which can be done by studying of the prenatal epochal progressions from conception to birth) cultivates the possibility of a sacred marriage between one's sense of ego and one's sense of the emergent Spirit Self. The vow in this inner soul ritual is to fulfill one's pre-earthly resolves to make this world a better place

---

4   Rudolf Steiner, *The Spiritual Guidance of the Individual and Humanity*, p. 65.

5   See David Tresemer and Robert Schiappacasse, *Star Wisdom & Rudolf Steiner*.

through having lived in it fully and consciously, as well as having worked for its divinely intended transformation.

With advanced study and practice, aspirants of new Star Wisdom may be able to use the cosmic compass of Astro-Sophia to navigate their vocational life, to carry out their sense of destiny, and to aid their brothers and sisters along the same God-given path toward the Future Jerusalem. In the spirit of the practice of white magic the use of this Star Wisdom should always be to serve toward the manifestation of the good.

Crafting, within one's soul, a boat of spirit cognition to traverse the apocalyptic waters of our times is not an intellectual endeavor. Amassing volumes of esoteric knowledge, although such an endeavor is part of gathering the materials needed for the task, does not translate into building such a boat. The endeavor is much more a demand for an open heart and an open will. Cultivating the ethers of warmth around the heart and allowing the force of compassion to stream out creates the necessary and requisite space for building the boat of spirit-cognition. The actual building of the boat is never a singular affair of the will. It requires the open will of devotion to truth, a moral injunction to follow the will of the heavens in one's own life. The light of the stars shining with the blessed gifts of the Cosmic Christ offers the aspirant of Star Wisdom the same secrets Hiram had access to in building Solomon's Temple. These secrets are becoming more and more open to modern human beings who will to abide by the creed, "Not my will, but Thy will be done on Earth as it is in Heaven."

The solidity of the Earth shall one day give way to fluidity, dissolving into the etheric realms. Just as Noah was instructed to build the ark prior to the flood that destroyed Atlantis, we are poised to do the same. However, this time it is not a salvation of the animal kingdom that is being called for, but a salvation of the human species in all its variations of individuality. No one ark can carry all of humanity. It will require brothers and sisters in an unbounded universal love to help each other craft the boat of spirit cognition that can carry the weight of individual karma. The Star Wisdom emerging in our time is destined to become the compass that will guide boats of spirit cognition into the brave new world of Future Jerusalem.

As we find our way into the future, I would like to offer a prayer, which may be said within the sacred spaces of the *Temple of Astro-Sophia*. They are excerpted words from an Astrosophy mantra compiled and written by Willi Sucher. The seven parts of this verse are given in sequential order from Moon to Mercury to Venus to Sun to Mars to Jupiter to Saturn. Each part of this mantra addresses the human soul's longing to be reunited with the heavenly world.

We lift up our consciousness
    to your Presence in the Universe
Great Isis, Queen of Heaven;
Thus an old humanity experienced you.
We find you again along new ways by the
Christ-Impulse working in the human being.
Divine Soul of the Universe,
Thy wisdom-filled life-will
    carries the spheres of the
Starry world. And Thou lettest us find access to
Living with Thy universe of Spheres.
Within this Thy Cosmos of Wisdom
    is the Christ present
In the Ether-garment and the Astral stature
    of the "Three (and a half) Years."
Thus are the Deeds of Christ
    ever-lasting events for the
Earth and its humanity,
    as well as for the whole Cosmos.
Michael creates of Thy Divine Thoughts
    the Sword of Light.
May it help us to defend ourselves against the
Adversaries and to learn to discern the Truth.
May Thy healing Word permeate us.
May it help us to become true carriers
    of the Will of Christ.
Thou lettest us live in Thy Being, Astro-Sophia
And work in positive ways toward the
Future of the Earth and its humanity.

THE VENUS ECLIPSE OF THE SUN, 2012

David Tresemer, Ph.D.

The most important rare astronomical event of 2012 is not the coincidence of the axis of Earth and Sun with the center of our galaxy (the well-known date December 21, 2012). An alignment of Sun and Earth with a point near the Galactic Center happens twice every year.[1]

Nor is the most important rare event the total solar eclipse that will occur on November 13, 2012, right across Cairns in Australia, as eclipses are not so rare.

The most important rare astronomical event of 2012 is the movement of Venus before the face of the Sun, which occurs in pairs eight years apart with over a hundred years in between the pairs. Venus orbits the Sun every 225 days. From the Earth's point of view, Venus usually crosses the position of the Sun above or below the Sun's bright disc. In 1874 and 1882, Venus went before the Sun's face, and then in 2004. The second of the pair will occur on June 6, 2012. The Venus eclipse of the Sun will not recur until December 2117, in another pair eight years apart.[2] Eclipses are known for their effects after (and also before) they occur. The themes from this one will affect all of 2012 as well as some years afterward and perhaps before as well.

Though termed a "transit" or an "occultation," we can also see Venus before the face of the Sun as a ring-shaped annular eclipse,[3] a small presence against an immense fiery background, thus having an effect disproportionate to its size.[4] Venus can be understood as influences to see and listen deeply, to explore relationship, to find one's soul groups or karmic affiliations.[5] The "eclipse" will stimulate the question, "To what group does my I belong—and what is the purpose or work of that group?"

What is the location—the heavenly address—of this eclipse? The Sun and Venus will stand between 20° and 21° of Taurus. What is the nature of that location? The Oracle of the Solar Cross gives thematic word images for each of the 360° of the zodiac, as in a cosmic dream.[6] The themes that will be stimulated by this celestial event are explored below, as well as personages who were born with the Sun in that degree, as well as world events and deaths that might condition our ability to work with the qualitative themes active there.

People often seek guidance from celestial locations. However, they want it to be practical, relating to the problems that they face in their lives. Magazines offer "six steps to better digestion" or "eight steps to greater intimacy." Another kind of knowing resides in the mythic, symbolic, or poetic, such as is found in the images in the Oracle of the Solar Cross. In a healthy life, the two realms circulate and inform each other. The mythic/poetic pictures of a Solar Cross image are more akin to the language of dreams, information and feeling tones that do not give immediate practical advice, but can inspire with a feeling tone or quality. Each

---

1   Celestial phenomena are explored in Appendix A.

2   See Appendix A for a description of this pattern of recurrence of eclipses.

3   See Appendix A for the meaning of annular eclipse.

4   As in Matt. 7:3, "And why worry about a speck [of sawdust] in your friend's eye when you have a log in your own?" A speck, a mote, can have the effect of a log.

5   From my article, "The Signature of Venus," *Journal for Star Wisdom 2011.* The phrase, "Venus listens," can apply to karmic relationships also; one must learn to listen to karma, or destiny, speaking in one's life.

6   The method is introduced in David Tresemer with Robert Schiappacasse, *Star Wisdom & Rudolf Steiner: A Life Seen Through the Oracle of the Solar Cross* (Great Barrington, MA: SteinerBooks, 2007).

of us has personal dreams that occur within one's personal sphere. An Image for a particular location in the heavens is a cosmic dream in a world sphere that includes my sense of "I"—I live within the dream. Eventually I will find the interaction where I live within the dream and it within me.

Each of the gates in the Oracle of the Solar Cross has a long word image and an abbreviated word image, then commentaries on the image. Here is the longer Image that streams through the Sun at 20–21° of The Bull, Taurus:

> Seven philosophers recall with pride the great king of their lineage, *Jamshid*, who had gifts from heaven: a golden dagger, a flying firebird, a cup of seven circles, and a golden ring with an emblem of power. With the golden dagger, the king measured the land, separating parcel from parcel, and plowed the soil. From the flying firebird he directed fire for all humankind, intense fire to smelt metals from rock, from which could be made many useful things, as well as the transformative fires of cooking. The waters of the cauldron thwarted disease, old age, and death; in the waters he could see whatever was happening anywhere and anytime. The golden ring could imprint the command of divinity. The king prolonged the life of all people and animals in his kingdom. A wise visitor reminds the seven philosophers that there is a greater king, whose tools are kept in the heart. Does he mean Zoroaster, does he mean Melchizedek, does he mean Inanna or Solomon? Or is there a greater king?

The Image develops in parts. Though the end of the Image extols the ability to use fewer divine implements, the beginning is full of them. We need to understand these implements clearly so that we can internalize their functions in our hearts.

THE SEVEN PHILOSOPHERS

This discussion takes place amongst seven philosophers, an echo of the Seven Rishis, or the Seven Sages, who have overseen human development since its inception. We can perhaps feel them in the background overseeing this discussion.

JAMSHID THE GREAT

The seven discuss Jamshid. Zarathustra (later becoming Zoroaster), the author of the ancient text, the Zend Avesta, now the scripture of the Zoroastrian religion, described in that book how he put a question to the prime creator, Ahura Mazda. He asked if Ahura Mazda had spoken to another human being before Zarathustra. The creator answered, "Jamshid."[7] Ahura Mazda had given Jamshid directions to care for the world. Jamshid replied to Ahura Mazda, "Yes! I will make thy worlds thrive, I will make thy worlds increase. Yes! I will nourish, and rule, and watch over thy world. There shall be, while I am king, neither cold wind nor hot wind, neither disease nor death."[8] Ahura Mazda awarded Jamshid with tools to assist him in this task, those that are enumerated in the Image at 20–21° of the Bull, Taurus.

GOLDEN DAGGER

The first tool that Jamshid received from heaven was a dagger. It had various functions, in the elements of air and earth.

The airy function of this special dagger—golden, indicating its origin in the Sun—was its ability to measure the land. Most governments have a bar of metal kept at a cool temperature with two tiny scratches on it to show the definition of the important measures of the land, as in the twelve-inch foot or the meter. Jamshid's knife includes the royal measures and much more. It shows the proportional interrelations of numbers, including the trigonometric functions necessary to determine, through triangulation, the survey of the land. When the Nile flooded each year, all boundaries between the fertile fields of Egypt were lost. In the spring the priests took the royal measure from the king and applied it to the re-measurement of the fields. The ruler of the land holds a ruler. The rod, staff, and scepter of kings always held a measuring function, defining the

---

7 See Appendix B of this article for greater detail on Jamshid, including his many names.

8 Fargard II of the Zend Avesta, part 1, chap. 5 (14).

"sacred foot" or "sacred cubit" or "sacred yard," plus other measures that helped in the trigonometry necessary for surveying the land.[9]

The knife functioned in the element of earth to cut along the boundary lines between plots of land then separate one side from another. Cutting separates. Thus the tool of discernment is often pictured as a knife or sword.[10] It can also be used to stir the soil, to break up the hard earth and dislodge weeds so that crops can be grown. For millennia people had used digging sticks, with fire-hardened points, to pry up roots. The brilliance of the plow was to attach a pointed stick to animal power so that it probed the soil. Discussions about the right way to stir the earth took people's attention for thousands of years. The first recorded theatrical drama has an actor as Hoe challenging the ascendancy of an actor as Plow. Hoe and Plow enumerate their own good qualities and the detriments of the other.[11] In this same tradition, Thomas Jefferson wrote treatises on the best plow design. So you see it wasn't just up to agricultural engineers as it is in our time. These questions belonged to everyone and were hotly debated. The best kind of plowing involves stirring rather than turning it upside down. I have guided a plowing implement with a piece of wood, hardened in the fire, four times the length of my thumb, attached to a framework pulled by two oxen. Back and forth we went, stirring up the field, separating weeds from the earth to make place for plants that we had chosen. One can imagine the golden dagger, indestructible because it comes from divinity, attached to such a framework to cultivate the soil.[12]

Not until groups of humans could create a surplus of food, in the form of stored grain, could they overcome the daily struggle and create civilization, as we know it, with arts and sciences and theater![13]

I worked together with a group in Melbourne to find physical gestures that summarize the capabilities of the golden dagger to measure near and far, to cut, to separate, to plow the earth. Indeed, the golden dagger indicates every extension of the hand, in a word, all technology. Thus the primal gesture is that depicted by Stanley Kubrick in *2001*, the ape who learns to pick up a jawbone of a skeleton, and turns it into a tool…which then becomes a spaceship approaching the Moon. Finding gestures helps to understand this divine gift and its use by human beings.

FIREBIRD

Divinity gifted a firebird. Fire can then be used for creating things. One begins with the low temperatures, with cooking, including baking and drying. Then one can add, in increasing temperatures, the fashioning of wood and small trees through steaming to make them pliable for furniture, the boiling of water to make soap and tea and dyes, the working of copper, the blowing of glass, the smelting of the higher temperature metals such as iron, and the making of steel. I recall visiting a steel factory and seeing the molten steel poured into immense moulds. My guide explained the sparks splashing nearby, "Watch out! Those sparks are not like sparks from a campfire. Those sparks will go right through your pants and your leg, and won't stop until they hit your bone."

Mastering the elements of fire and earth, the king can direct fire wherever he chooses.

Rudolf Steiner observed that birds focus the warmth of the world—the warmth ether—and the

9 Robert Lawlor goes into this in great detail in *Sacred Geometry*, based in part on his translation (with Deborah Lawlor) of Schwaller de Lubicz's great masterpiece, *The Temple of Man* (Rochester, VT: Inner Traditions: 1998), the foundations for sacred geometry emphasized in vol. 1. The film *Prince of Persia* imagined a golden dagger that affected time. We will see the play with time in Jamshid's seven-ringed cauldron. The anthroposophic journal *The Golden Blade* excites these themes.
10 As in Book of Revelation (1:16): "…from his mouth came a sharp, two-edged sword," by which one understands an ability to cut away truth from falsehood, the true meaning of criticism.
11 The script of this oldest of plays are at http://www.hort.purdue.edu/newcrop/history/lecture09/lec09.html.
12 I have sat on a tractor with a moldboard plow attached. The function is the same. The definition of "acre" is the amount of land that one can plow in a day with a plow pulled by oxen. This is another way that the golden dagger as plow relates to the definition of space.
13 Axel Steensberg has made this argument in his works.

process of human thought: "The bird is the flying thought."[14] Focusing attention on something warms the thing. Intense focus acts as a laser and can, in those trained to do so, cause spontaneous combustion. Thought is related to the firebird.

In the group work in Melbourne, we summarized the firebird with the physical gesture of flicking fire to a specific place, as in a focused abracadabra, the laser-like powers of focused attention.

MAGIC CAULDRON

The cauldron had two functions, relieving the people of disease, old age, and death, as its waters had powers of immortality, and permitting the one gazing into the waters to see far and wide, anyplace and anytime. These functions connect with one another. By banishing distance and time in what one experiences with one's senses, one is freed from their constraint. One has a taste of immortality.[15] This is the first television! It permitted one to see far and wide beyond one's immediate surroundings.

One works here with the elements of earth in the substance of the container and the element of water within the container. The king could look into the water of the magic cauldron and see whatever was happening wherever he chose. The water of the cauldron has a reflective quality, as well as a quality of depth. Gazing into water frees you from the immediate stimuli of the senses and permits you to think about something that is not in front of you, that is, to reflect on something you saw at another time and place, or to imagine something that you haven't experienced before, or to become a philosopher, thinking about abstract concepts and what lies beyond concepts. Does one look at the pictures playing across the surface of the water? Or does one peer down into its depths, as did Nostradamus, to see pictures from other times and places?[16]

Seven-ringed may refer to the seven planetary spheres.[17] The cauldron may be as large as the whole heavens. It is creation itself, into which we gaze and are enchanted.

What is the gesture of function and use for the cauldron? In our Melbourne group, we gathered the arms into a circle, a large "O" shape, forming the rim of a cauldron, then stared deeply down past the rim, as into water, deep into the hidden realities of distant times and places, where we could imagine the extension of eyes and ears through space and time.

DIVINE EMBLEM

Jamshid gave freely of the magic cauldron, so that no people or animals died. There was no ostensible disease or death in people and animals. But the world became overpopulated and grossly polluted. The plant and mineral kingdoms were sorely stressed, and the psychological diseases of overcrowding must have been rife. The Image exactly opposite to this one, at 20–21° Scorpio (which we shall see shortly), is full of disease, despair, and death. Anyone born in this particular degree must struggle with this polarity.

After three hundred years, the prime creator Ahura Mazda warned Jamshid that this could not go on, and urged the king that he send a good portion of animals and people to the realm of death, for the imbalance had to be cured. Instead, Jamshid set the divine emblem on the golden ring to the Earth and commanded that the world increase in size. The Earth stretched out into a larger globe, with a larger surface area. He worked actively with the stuff of Earth itself, interesting especially as this Image lies in the earth sign of Taurus.

Jamshid ruled another 600 years, when the Earth had the same problem and Ahura Mazda

---

14 Rudolf Steiner, *Harmony of the Creative Word*, pp. 6, 83. The most fiery bird is the eagle.

15 The four treasures of the Tuatha De Danaan included the Cauldron of Dagda, which had the same powers. Note that Dagda comes from *dhagho-deiwos*, shining divinity, thus the same meaning as *Jamshid*.

16 Rudolf Steiner described Nostradamus in his room

with the cauldron of water (cited by William Bento, "Prophecy: A Cauldron of Controversy," *Journal for Star Wisdom 2011*, pp. 41–48.

17 Giorgio De Santillana and Hertha von Dechend make this claim about Jamshid's cup, in *Hamlet's Mill: An Essay Investigating the Origins of Human Knowledge and its Transmission Through Myth* (Boston: David Godine, 1977), 47. The frontispiece there gives an excellent illustration of a seven-ringed cup, made of the spheres of the heavens.

warned him again that Ahriman needed people and animals in his realm, whose passage there had been denied by the defeat of death. Jamshid again set his ring with its magic emblem to the Earth, and the Earth expanded. He ruled another nine hundred years, and had to expand the Earth again, but then he became too identified with these works as his own works. He lost the favor of Ahura Mazda, and died.

Before he died, sensing a disaster was coming, not only his own death, but the visitation of disease and death on humans and animals, Jamshid did what others have done since his time. He built a great underground facility, two miles long and two miles wide, on many levels, wherein he hoped to house many people. Perhaps they are still there.[18]

The notion of an expanding Earth has recently been presented with much compelling evidence for it.[19] The story of Jamshid may well encode the facts of Earth's evolution, including the diminishing rate of change, at first 300 years, then 600, then 900, showing that the Earth has slowed down in its rate of change.

What is the gesture that we discovered for the operation of the golden ring? You press the symbol into the stuff of creation, and the stuff responds. In this way, it parallels Buddha's "earth-touching gesture," wherein he pressed a finger to the earth as an act of will to exist, after which the demons left him alone. The modern counterpart of projecting one's intention outward would include all symbols, logos, brands, as well as electronics, through which people project out their personal intention many times a day. The gestures summarize Jamshid's powers.

TECHNOLOGY

We thus celebrate technology and its origins! Here are wonderful capacities that we now have, given by divinity. With gratitude, we celebrate our greater ease in living because of these tools.

What does the great king, Jamshid, do with that technology? He serves humanity. He eases the difficulties of life, increases our capacities to make things that ensure our comfort, and he extends our life in this more comfortable world.

Yet there is a shadow side to this better world. As Jeremy Rifkin once remarked, the single word that thrusts humanity to its downfall is "convenience." For greater ease, other things are sacrificed, wasted, or ignored. Who can argue with Jamshid's good intentions when he banished disease, old age, and death? However, he created the same prison that Siddhartha's parents created for their son. As king and queen, they banished from the central city of their kingdom any evidence of toil, disease, old age, and death. All appeared happy for their darling child. Siddhartha had to burst out of that bubble to mature as a human being, to tread the path to becoming the Buddha.[20]

Modern medicine promises youthfulness through cosmetic surgery and increased longevity through organ replacement.[21] After some thousands of years, Jamshid's story has visited human society again. Is this a good development?

Technology is amoral. The same tool can be used in many different ways. Take a knife, for instance. As the folk singer Lead Belly said, "You take a knife, you use it to cut the bread, so you'll have strength to work; you use it to shave, so

---

18 The tale says that Jamshid created the large underground area for 2,000 people. Rudolf Steiner has a helpful view of numbers like this, as in "Feeding of the 5,000," as follows: the thousand means a large number, and the modifier, in this case, 2, tells us about the quality of energy and the age to which this is related, in this case the second age, the Persian Age, that of Zarathustra. We are presently in the fifth age in that system. Rudolf Steiner, *According to Matthew*, lecture 10.

19 James Maxlow, *Terra Non Firma Earth* (Oneoff Publishing.com, 2008), and various internet presentations on his well-researched thesis.

20 Rudolf Steiner saw the same pattern with the Essenes, who banished all temptation and sin to outside their community. They did not transform the difficulties, merely banished them, thus making life outside their community more difficult. Rudolf Steiner, *The Fifth Gospel*.

21 The technology observer Patrick Cox, in a lecture to the Agora Symposium, 2009, has said that advances in stem-cell replacement of organs, especially in the research centers in Russia and Korea, where other scientist's patents are ignored, has brought us "functional immortality." The television series *Torchwood* touches on the dysfunction of widespread immortality in the episode "Miracle Day."

you'll look nice for your lover; on discovering her with another, you use it to cut out her lying heart."[22] With technology, we have to wrestle with the issue of morality.

Zarathustra posited a "perfecting principle" that works unceasingly on the development of human-kind toward the good.[23] Do tools serve the perfecting principle or detract from it? A tool in itself is inert and neutral, but can be used in many ways. Therein lies its danger. It depends on its master to guide its use, for good or ill.

We have to ask if technology assists or detracts from the perfecting principle. Most people feel that we don't have a choice. Human beings will exercise their ingenuity and create new tools. This is an admission of powerlessness, that is, ineffectiveness of will. Yet look at the oldest society on Earth, that of the aborigines of Australia. From communion with spiritual beings, what can be termed the Dreamtime or Dreaming, aborigines learned that complex tools were inappropriate for development. They minimized the tools that they bore in their wanderings through a living landscape. The perfecting principle was practiced in complicated ceremony, and through the expression of beauty.[24]

We can divide human experience into three realms of thinking, feeling, and willing, in the provinces of head, heart, and hand. Normally we are aware of our thinking—concepts built of perceptions—somewhat aware of our feelings, and little aware of our willing, our deeds and actions. Technology relates to deeds, to actions in the world, not to feelings or thoughts. Technology evidences the power of will. When people say that technology is inevitable, they admit that they don't have

control or much awareness of the realm of the will. However, the aborigines demonstrated that they knew their own will when they refused to take up complex technology.

Let's look at a fuller picture with each of the tools mentioned in this Image.

The dagger misused can be destructive. Swords become plowshares, and back again to swords—they are really the same.[25] The dagger becomes a tool that destroys soils, as witness the diminishment of topsoil in every country from over-working the land.[26]

In its role as device of measurement, it can give us the grid system of GPS, Google Earth, and EPIRB, so that one is never lost. One can always be defined as in a particular place determined by a number grid of rectilinear references. Compare this to an indigenous view where one relates to mountain and stream, marsh and sea, through knowing them personally. One is never lost because one relates to the living Earth.

Measuring all the land and dividing it up can divide a community, creating jealousy around possessions, and distance between people. "Good fences make good neighbors" seems an admission of failure of a social network.[27]

The firebird misused can become atom bombs...and arson, napalm, war in general with its emphasis on "firepower," as well as nuclear power plants with their "hot" water and occasional meltdowns.[28] This article was first written

---

22 Cited in David Mamet, *Three Uses of the Knife* (New York: Vintage, 2000), p. 66. Lead Belly spent much of his life in prison for murder and attempted murder, only rescued by the musicologist John Lomax, whom Lead Belly also tried to kill with a knife.

23 Rudolf Steiner emphasized the perfecting principle in his lecture on Zarathustra, in *Turning Points in Spiritual History*, p. 14.

24 Robert Lawlor, *Voices of the First Day: Awakening in the Aboriginal Dreamtime* (Rochester, VT: Inner Traditions, 1991). Japanese in the 17th century rejected guns and gunpowder for a period of two hundred years (http://infowarethics.org/gun.saga.in.1600s.japan.vs.germany.html).

25 Isaiah 2:4 speaks about beating swords into plowshares as a step toward peace. Adam made Cain into a plowman, who used the plow itself as the weapon to murder. Abel William Blake thinks so, as witness the shovel (a version of the plow) next to the dead body in Blake's print about Cain and Abel.

26 David Montgomery, *Dirt: The Erosion of Civilizations* (Los Angeles: University of California, 2008).

27 A medieval proverb used by Robert Frost in his poem, "Mending Wall."

28 The pivotal experiment of the development of nuclear power, in which Leo Szilard and Enrico Fermi supervised the runaway chain-reaction of radioactive materials, thus demonstrating the feasibility of nuclear bombs as well as nuclear power plants, occurred Dec. 2, 1942, in Chicago, with Venus at 20° 6' Scorpio, exactly opposite to the location of Venus at the eclipse of 2012. The pair of Images in Taurus–Scorpio at 20°–21° was active in that pivotal experiment. At the chain-reaction

before the Fukushima melt-downs, which illustrate that the firebird theme, stimulated by this Venus eclipse, is out of control.[29]

The cauldron misused can become enchantment to other places and times, and fascination with false realities—through television, computers, and all the other devices into which we stare and which take us away from our present surroundings.[30] Think of the story of Narcissus, pictured by the Greeks as a young man so infatuated with the reflection of his own image in a pool of water that he could not leave, and so died there, addicted to his own reflection. One might assume he was looking at the reflection of his own face, but perhaps he was seeing all that the waters had held secret, and became enamored of other places and other times revealing themselves to him, so that his consciousness abandoned his physical body, that great vehicle which brings us repeatedly back to the present moment.

The cauldron can also become an instant link to anyplace and anytime that one then assumes reveals all mysteries. "Consult Guru Google," we

are told, or "Go to Wikipedia and you'll get your answer." People have come to expect that all can be known through these means, that there are no mysteries left beyond the magical surface of one's computer screen. The flood of images, facts, and opinions blocks one from self-initiated action, and one becomes atrophied in the will.

The modern cauldron—the television—illustrates an important aspect of technology: Not being human, technology does not sleep. It thus constitutes an attack on sleep. It is also an attack on nutrition because, like Narcissus, many watchers pine away unfed, enchanted by its images. Finally, it steals attention, one could even say sucks attention, leaving the person less full of life energy than before. Observe what happens when you view television (in its various forms, including movie theaters, and what you hold in your hand): Though the content seems to go into you, note what flows out from you to it.

The ring of power misused can become J. R. R. Tolkein's ring, about which he wrote his famous trilogy, a ring indeed with too much power. A ring can become a symbol, as in the Pope's ring, which visitors are expected to kiss.[31] Think of all the emblems used by religions and nations to promote their ideologies, that become much more than wars of words, turning into wars with knives and fire(birds). Genetic modification can be seen as the imposition of a conceptual pattern into nature (thus a function of the ring of power) that has had disastrous consequences.

Consider the widespread use of emblems, logos, and pictures to promote oneself, as in FaceBook, or one's personal website, or one's blog, or Twitter accounts. Magazines and their electronic counterparts now expect authors to write about their opinions and their lives for free because of the lure to "build an audience based on your personal brand."[32] These promise relationship but are not relational. People talk to walls, and not to each

experiment, the Sun lay at Antares, what Robert Schiappacasse and I have termed the "Star of Death and Resurrection."

29 At the initial Fukushima explosion, at the time of the earthquake and tsunami, Venus lay at 17 Capricorn. Saturn lay at 20° Virgo and 40', a trine of 120° to 20–21° of Taurus, showing a resonance with what lives in this Image. Fukushima now looks to outstrip the previous large dysfunctions of the firebird, at Three Mile Island (March 28, 1979) and Chernobyl (April 26, 1986). At Chernobyl, Saturn was at Antares (see previous footnote). At Three Mile Island, Saturn lay exactly square to the Aldebaran/Antares axis. The Royal Stars of Aldebaran (Eye of the Bull) and Antares (Heart of the Scorpion) are described elsewhere, especially in Tresemer, with Schiappacasse, *Star Wisdom & Rudolf Steiner*, chapter 1, and are an additional influence in this dance of the firebird with the cosmos. In an astrological sense, they are "close"—five°—to the 20–21° mark, close enough in the reading of a personal chart, but not close enough for the sharp indications that we seek in this research paper about the Venus eclipse.

30 Television was defined in the *Oxford English Dictionary* in 1907, when it was mostly imagined and not yet realized, as "the action of seeing by means of Hertzian waves or otherwise, what is existing or happening at a place concealed or distant from the observer's eyes," in other words, exactly as one would describe the magic cauldron. "Tele" means far off or distant.

31 The recent movie *Salt* pictures a man who trains obedience in children, who learn to do his bidding, including murder and mayhem, punctuating their deeds with kissing of his ring.

32 David Carr at http://www.nytimes.com/2011/02/14/business/media/14carr.html.

other. Shouting "me, me, me!" does not bring on relationships.

All technology—including the old-fashioned telephone,[33] another version of the magic cauldron taking us across barriers of space and time—seems to take us away from the most important teaching for our soul's development, namely relationships. Thirty SMS texts a day does not assist relationship;[34] this activity undermines relationship, by making it banal, impulsive, narcissistic, isolated. Whenever we leave these messages on any of these media, we are a person speaking to a wall—or to pool of water in a magic cauldron—a monologue pretending as dialogue.

The misuses of these tools and their descendents have served to disembody human beings, at a rate that is becoming epidemic. *World of Warcraft, Call of Duty: Black Ops*, and other electronic games engage the full attention of millions of people at every minute of the day. The semblances, assumed personalities, or agents—arrogantly called "avatars"[35]—of many people appear to be in relationship yet they are not. Little thought goes to the consequences of killing in a bloody manner the agent of another person from some other place on the planet, who watches and hears himself or herself die by the hand of an unidentified but quite real other.

Confession in the Catholic Church can now be made by iPhone to an application (an "app") that responds as if it were a priest, but is not linked to a human being.

Separated from actual bodies, people expect to see instant effects from impulse, a push of a button that appears to operate a rifle, bazooka, magic lightning weapon, or forgiving priest. By making the semblance of a deed seem much more powerful, true will is diminished.

Technology is not, in fact, necessary to perfect one's soul nature. In the eyes of some, it may seem

necessary to world evolution. In the eyes of others, it may indicate degeneration of the nobility of the human being. Yet technology need not be seen as a requirement for an individual. We can create a moral stance toward technology.

The polar opposite to this Image drives up the stakes in this matter, and also shows a way to come to terms with the shadow side of Jamshid's gifts.

HIGH STAKES

Imagine what is held in the exact opposite image, at 20° to 21° of Scorpio, which in an alignment with Earth, Venus, and Sun, will also be stimulated:

> The dark streets are filled with the sick, the bleeding, the weak, the blind, the near-dead. Many were healed before and then relapsed. They wait in line, yearning for another chance. To the relapsed, the healer speaks, "The hands of your heart are withdrawn and locked up, for you are filled with darkness." The healer works in the night, bringing light into darkness, moving down the line along the street. The healer passes over some completely.

Picture how relapse works. One was healthy and then lost that health in a specific way—blindness as a failure of the eyes or bleeding as a failure of the skin—or in a general way—"sick," "weak," "near-dead." Already that challenges us with the enormity of suffering in the world. But "relapse" adds another part of the story. A person was healthy, then sick, sought help, and was healed. Imagine the feeling of being sick, then healthy again. Is there relief? Then something happened that the healer defines, a contraction of the hands of the heart, a withdrawal. The healed one holds on to the healing for himself or herself alone. Trying to lock up the light of health in one's own being, he or she creates only darkness. Illness returns, perhaps the same one, perhaps another form of illness. In a workshop on this pair of Images in Melbourne, we set up the scene whereby the ill were lifted up by a healer and approached the light, but then something happened—some turning point where the healed person's hands were withdrawn from the light of healing, and contracted back into the self, disconnected from the world. The healed person

---

33 *Tele-*, distant, -*phone*, sound, or "sound from a distance."

34 The average now hovers around 100 per day for teenagers, and is rising quickly.

35 Traditionally, *avatar* has meant the incarnation of a divinity from spirit into flesh. An incarnated divinity behaves divinely in the material realm.

turned his or her back to the light of healing, and walked away, until the illness took over again.

Everyone who has been ill knows that the body generously offers a second chance. In the Image, the once-sick and the twice-sick wait in line, yearning for another chance. The healer generously gives another chance. Some are exceptions, those whom the healer passes over completely. Termed "triage" in the First World War, this is where the physician, overwhelmed by the number of injured, chooses who can be saved, and passes by those whom he judges cannot be revived. The sense of despair underlying this Image is tremendous.

We can think of the will as expressed through the hands and feet, arms and legs. The hint from this Image is that, for the greater king, deeds of the will must emanate from the heart, the home of feeling, and that this be done freely with light, to light, and in light.

The darkness referred to—darkness in the heart and corresponding darkness in the streets—describes the world of the narcissist or the losing of oneself in self-reference. Even when around others, these people are closed off, alone, despairing. The rise of social networks provides a measure not of social facility but of narcissism, multiple millions talking to walls or computer screens, not to people.

When inquiring about the use of the will, it helps to think through the use of hands. What do your hands do? Observe yourself objectively, not with judgment. What is your experience when you shake another's hand? How often does that happen? Do you feel the other person—look into his or her eyes? Or is it perfunctory, or even something that you would like to get through quickly? What do your hands touch during your day? What do you imagine heart-originated hands would touch, or what would be the quality of that touch? Do you have someone who touches you, or whom you touch, with ease and familiarity, with warmth and light?

These two Images combined demand that you explore the quality of your relationships, and the quality of your hands touching and doing deeds in the world. Reacquaint yourself with your hands.[36]

---

36 Lila Sophia Tresemer and David Tresemer, in *One*

A MORAL USE OF TECHNE

Techne is the goddess who rules technology, that is, the application of human cleverness and ingenuity to matter in order to create the artificial.[37] In our modern society we expend more and more time and energy making things that are useful and efficient, that promote the picture of kicking back with a drink in hand to relax in front of the television. We expend less and less time making something that is beautiful for its own sake, something that is noble, something that gives pure delight. When an artisan fashions something from raw material, either from mirroring the world or from expressing inner experience, attending to the beauty of the creation rather than to its utility, a deep love is nurtured in the artisan and in all who behold what has been made. As utility increases and art for the sake of beauty decreases, we may find that the technology of efficiency will grow in angry power and will confront our humanity with that anger. We might then discover that our sense of beauty and delight have disappeared. We might find ourselves in the picture of the Scorpio Image, *because of* decisions made in the context of the Taurus Image. Every day that we create something only utilitarian, or even use the technology of convenience without making an effort to balance it with beauty in our own lives, we press toward the Image at Scorpio in our own lives and in all human lives to follow.

How does Jamshid use the powers of technology? He prolongs life, hundreds of years for people and animals. He avoids the end of life by expanding the size of the Earth. He deepens Siddhartha's prison by dispelling old age and death. But how does death function in the world? It quickens; it stresses; it causes us to work the heart, and find the hands of the heart. A caring heart comes from

---

Two ONE, explore ways to empower relationship for personal development, including activity of the will, through many exercises to link hands, hearts, and concepts.

37 *Artificial* comes from *facere* (to make) and the word *art*, which means artisan, and at its root means joining something together. Thus the foundation of art comes from imagination and execution of the joining of two pieces of wood that grew separately, held either by a dovetailed mortise and tenon or by pounded nails.

having had cares. Then the heart is a purified heart. Then the hands can reach out. At death, the hands then can become the wings of the heart.

Recently I spoke with someone who worked closely with those who have been responsible for the very rapid rise of computing technology, taking it from an activity that helped out on the side in the accounting department (computers as faster than abacuses) or gave an evening's entertainment once a week (television), to an activity that today takes up much of most people's time. My client described those in charge of the development of this new technology as having much undeveloped social skills. They could not look at you in the eye; they had little personal warmth or empathy; they shrank from conversation and social encounters; they excelled at a non-personal focus into dazzling lights that blinked and twittered. She summarized her experience of these people by diagnosing them with Asperger's Syndrome, whose symptoms she listed. Asperger's is thought perhaps to be its own syndrome, or perhaps a form of autism, the root *aut-* meaning to oneself, that is, narcissistic.[38] She concluded, "They were unable to play like other children, so wanted to make other children play like them," in other words alone with the flickering firebird playing across the face of the image-creating cauldron, imprinted with the ring of branding.

This caused me for the first time to inquire, "What kind of person was King Jamshid?" I had vaguely assumed that, as king, he had the best in mind for his people. But perhaps he was self-possessed, interested mostly in playing with his magical toys, to the extent that he didn't notice that the world was suffering, and had to be reminded by a divinity that things were not going well. One often assumes that philanthropists are what the term implies: lovers, *philo-*, of humanity, *anthropos*. However, the world abounds with examples of sociopaths and egotists who give money to charities. Perhaps Jamshid was such a character,

and that solves the question of why the Image goes to the next step, a greater king.

KINGS AND QUEENS

A wise visitor reminds the seven that there is a greater king. Beyond Jamshid, the king of great powers, a greater ruler exists. The wise visitor doesn't announce a new king. He reminds, suggesting that the seven already knew this.

The greater king does not rely on external tools. People go through stages when they collect tools—including amulets, talismans, crystals, chalices, swords, lucky coins, all versions of what Jamshid had. Indeed, all jewelry can be considered as magical tools. At a certain point, it all seems so much to care for, to ensure the appropriate use of each, to clean and tend the myriad pieces. Fewer tools mean that one relies on one's own body and being as the tool for one's divine intention. Having one's tools or capacities held in the heart means that they are always ready and always used appropriately.

GREATER KINGS: THE BODHISATTVAS

The seven philosophers wonder about the greater kings. Could it be Zarathustra? Could it be Melchizedek? Could it be Inanna? Could it be Solomon?

This sounds like a list of all the greats. We could include the names of powerful earthly kings, such as Nebuchadnezzar. We could include the names of powerful kings of the spirit, such as Jeshua ben Pandira or Pythagoras or Hermes or Jesus Christ. We could include names of both the spiritual and societal, Solomon or Abraham. We could include queens of societies and of the spirit, Inanna or Deborah or Sheba. We could include the names of Ascended Masters, such as Koot Hoomi or El Morya or the seven rishis. We could add to Zarathustra the names of other bodhisattvas, such as Hermes or Buddha or Scythianos.[39] We seek to find among the leaders of humanity those who exert a

---

38 I am not referring to present discussions on the internet about whether or not these leaders of computing technology actually can be diagnosed as having Asperger's Syndrome. I am relying on the first-hand experience of the one who worked with them daily.

39 The website http://www.cosmochristosophy.org takes up the question of Masters versus bodhisattvas, and examines many individuals critically. T. H. Meyer and Elisabeth Vreede delve into this very deeply in *The Bodhisattva Question* (London: Temple Lodge, 2010).

power of great vision, and who rely less on exterior tools than on their own capacities, held in the heart.

The seminal study of star wisdom and culture, *Hamlet's Mill*, identifies Jamshid with Saturn, both as planet and as Kronos, Lord of Time, Lord of the Golden Age, and, as we might learn from Rudolf Steiner, Lord of Cosmic Memory.[40] All leaders have a streak of Saturn in them. Connected with the Sun, and thus greater powers of heart, as strongly urged in the Image opposite at Scorpio, this Saturn-infused leader becomes great, a great king.

In reading the history of these characters, we realize that we don't have birthdates and we actually know very little about them. Groups have co-opted them for their particular propaganda purposes. We can only truly know them by inner reflection. Let's examine a few.

Zarathustra either lived in the sixth century BC in Babylon, or five thousand years before Troy in the Ancient Persian age, or both, with other incarnations in between.[41] We know of no implements that he used, except perhaps, as the Zoroastrians claim, the baresman or barson, a collection of thirty-five twigs of tamarisk, pomegranate, and other trees, to affirm his gratitude for the natural world.[42] He was the wisest human being alive, and had a personal experience of the beings of the heavens—in the so-called first hierarchy of Thrones, Cherubim, and Seraphim—from which he suggested a map of the heavens, the zodiac as we know it today.[43]

Melchizedek—king or great (*melchi-*) priest or righteous one (*-zedek*)—gave the grail cup to Abraham, who passed it on to Yeshua. Melchizedek was the mysterious desert king and priest combined, who brought the ceremony of bread and wine to Abraham.[44] The Holy Grail can be seen as a kind of magic cauldron, its tradition passed down from Jamshid's time.[45]

Abraham took the ceremonial instruction and the implements and spread them to the world. He was also known for his use of the ritual knife in nearly slitting the throat of his son Isaac on the pyre of sacrifice, before being dissuaded by an angel.[46]

Inanna, Queen of Heaven and Earth, was celebrated by the Sumerian culture from thousands of years ago. Her story has recently been translated from cuneiform tablets found in Iraq.[47] I have co-authored a drama called "The Great Below" that presents her story in relation to modern times.[48] Inanna also received many gifts from the gifting-God Enki.

The grail cup is common to many of those named. Even Solomon had an immense container for sacred water, called the Brazen Sea, that measured ten cubits across and five cubits deep (a cubit being the measure from elbow to outstretched fingers, approximately twenty inches). Its capacity was 24,000 gallons. He also commissioned many sacred vessels for his temple made of orichalcum, an unknown alloy of high value, perhaps a mixture of gold, copper, and silver.

THE TOOLS OF THE BODHISATTVAS

The grail cup of Christian legend has many similarities to Jamshid's Cauldron. Wagner's opera *Parsifal* pictures the Grail cup, brought from the

---

40 Re Jamshid and Saturn, *Hamlet's Mill*, op. cit., pp. 146–147.

41 The names *Zarathustra* or *Zoroaster* or *Zaratos* can be seen as successors in this line, or reincarnations of the same individuality. Andrew Wellburn, *The Book with Fourteen Seals* (London: Rudolf Steiner Press, 1991).

42 Zoroastrians claim that Zoroaster or Zarathustra (or perhaps also Zostrianos, as in the Nag Hammadi library) originated the use of the kushti, a gathering of 72 fine white wool threads that they wrap around the body three times, performing this ceremony several times a day.

43 The equal-length zodiac of twelve beings, each with thirty qualities, making 360 different° in the heavens. These names denote the most developed of the nine ranks of angelic presences, the lower being archangels, and finally angels.

44 Gen. 14:18–20, also Psalm 110:4. Paul's Letter to the Hebrews stated that Jesus was a priest in this line of Melchizedek, 5:6 and 10, 6:20, and all of 7.

45 The myth of the Grail figured prominently in my article on the aspects of Venus referred to in *Journal for Star Wisdom 2011*, op. cit. Venus has a connection with the Grail as an item of perfection, to which one can resonate.

46 Abraham lived approximately from 175 years, some say from 1812 BC to 1637 BC, some claiming his birth was 1946 BC, in either case four millennia before the present, and at the beginning of the Age of Aries (vernal point entering Aries).

47 Diane Wolkstein and Samuel Kramer, *Inanna, Queen of Heaven and Earth: Her Stories and Hymns from Sumer* (New York: Harper, 1983).

48 "The Great Below," DavidAndLilaTresemer.com.

crucifixion to the remote forest where it is protected by the Grail Knights. The Grail cup is the pivot around which the entire drama takes place, the tool that keeps the band of Grail Knights alive, though barely. Parsifal was first performed on July 26, 1882, with Venus at 19° 2' of Leo, thus square to the 20° mark of the Venus eclipse, in the year of the previous Venus eclipse, namely 1882. In *Parsifal*, the lance, paralleling the golden dagger of Jamshid, has been stolen. It had been the weapon that wounded the Fisher King, thus another "use of a knife," technology for good or ill. By extension, one wonders if Jamshid's dagger also has the blood of spirit on it. In Wagner's opera, a firebird as dove of light appears in the opening scene, when the Grail is uncovered.[49]

Trevor Ravenscroft popularized the grail and lance in his books, *The Spear of Destiny* and its sequel, finding that the power of these divine tools—parallels to Jamshid's—was still operative after many centuries.[50]

The little bits known about each of these don't give an entire picture, yet can be used as gateways to come to know them better through inner contacts.

THE MEANING OF A BODHISATTVA

What does a bodhisattva look like? They have an interest and capacity for care for others. They have no tradition. Typically they are empowered in their work past thirty years of age, and are not recognized before that time. They are completely devoted to the spiritual maturation of human beings, and indeed consciousness at all levels, down even to the mineral. Rudolf Steiner's book *Turning Points in Spiritual History* is about such people and their impact on human society. The lives of these human beings are all turning points for human development. Steiner gives a picture of twelve such bodhisattvas, some incarnate

and others not. We can learn from them, even at a distance of space and time. The Venus eclipse Image suggests several, and does not give us certainty about who, in fact, is the greater king. That confusion does not cripple us. Each of the ones named can become the mentor that works with an individual to guide through further development. These individualities, living even though not in body, can guide one through challenging times, such as we now experience in the world.

The beginning of the Image empowered by Venus crossing the face of the Sun lists magical tools. The latter part of the Image lists powerful guides of humanity. Going from the first to the second part marks a process of evolution. And there is a further step.

THE GREATER KING

What rules over the three centers of thinking, feeling, and willing? What rules over the seven energy centers of the human body? The first body or entity to rule over them is the personality. But there is a greater King, the "I AM," the spark of the divine that is not a gift of heaven to humanity, but rather an essence of heaven that *is* humanity. The "I AM" is aware of itself: "I exist!" "I perceive!" "I am aware of the world, and I am aware that I am aware!" No matter what skills one has in any of the above three or seven centers of power, a greater vision spans them all and then some. Thus this Image has in it a grand drama of hierarchy, finding above the more obvious *things*, even if powerful things or spiritual things, a principle or being that rules them all. The personality (the small "ego," the grasping "me-me-me!") seeks physical immortality; the larger "I AM" gazes over lifetimes, and does not avoid death.

While one must rely on the mentoring from elders, including from the great kings mentioned in the Image from Taurus, in the process of personal development, this leads to a sense of one's own sovereignty in close relationship with all of living creation. Sovereignty means realization of the royal self. It does not mean isolation and aloneness, but rather the ultimate insertion of oneself—one's Self—into the divinity that exists at all levels of being right here and right now.

---

49 *Parsifal* is Wagner's spelling of *Parzival*. As detailed later Wagner's birth shows a prominent connection between Venus and the Sun.

50 Trevor Ravenscroft, born April 23, 1921, with Sun (9° Aries) conjunct Venus (8° Aries), thus related to the Sun–Venus connection that we've been following. *The Spear of Destiny* (York Beach, ME: Weiser, 1982) and *The Mark of the Beast* (York Beach, ME: Weiser, 1997).

Thus this Image relates a process of growth, from the egocentricity that comes from owning tools of great power, to devoted discipleship to other authorities, to a sense of the regality of one's own nature.

EXPRESSIONS OF THIS DEGREE: STAR BROTHERS AND STAR SISTERS

Those born in a degree come into the world with their first breath pulsing with the themes of the Image. Looking at a few of them can instruct us as to these main themes.

The eighteenth-century magical genius, *Alessandro Cagliostro*, was born with the Sun in this degree. He was called Grand Master by his admirers. He numbered kings and queens as his clients. He was also hated by powerful people, including Goethe and the Pope. He healed many with magical powers and with magical implements, and had an unending source of wealth that people thought he created with divine help through the magic art of alchemy. Those visiting his "Temple of Egypt" in Paris were first met by two servants clothed as Egyptian slaves, then by Cagliostro dressed in a black silk robe with an Arabian turban made of gold cloth and sparkling with jewels. On a black marble slab was the "Universal Prayer" by Alexander Pope, a man who also drew his first breath on this Solar Day.[51] Cagliostro healed thousands, and attempted to revive the ancient arts of Masonry, which go back at least to Egypt and perhaps also to Iranian times. Here was a king like Jamshid, with powers and magical implements.[52]

Was his magic derived from heavenly sources or from old Atlantean dark sources? We could say that Cagliostro enjoyed the earlier part of his birth Image but did not mature to the latter part of it.

The Inquisition didn't burn him, as burning ended in 1600. But they were happy to imprison people for long periods of time in dank and dark places, creating the kinds of illness that we meet in the Scorpio Image. Cagliostro died in this miserable manner.[53]

Philip II of Spain ruled the largest empire of the world ever assembled, owning large pieces of several continents.[54] The accounts of his life range from the Black Legend to the White Legend. The Black Legend depicts Philip as a terrible monster, destroying all that he met in Europe and the New World, pressing for more and yet more gold from the enslaved miners in the New World, expanding the Inquisition to become a secret police force that imprisoned and killed political dissidents, and sending his men to death in the Armada that was defeated by the English. The White Legend depicts him as a prudent and pious statesman, champion of the arts, leader of Spain at the height of its cultural development. In Philip II we can find an increase in reliance on techne, and the improvement of convenience for all his people, especially the wealthy. We see also the negative, indeed dark, side for others.

Federico Garcia Lorca responded to the entire Image.[55] He relied on fewer and fewer props, eventually summarizing the greatest gift that one could have and use as "duende." Duende cannot be defined, only felt. It includes capacities of spontaneity, great power that rises up from the feet, engulfing the artist and then the entire audience. One could call it charisma, yet it is far more Dionysian, dangerous, and consuming. Lorca learned from his birth Image to eschew tools, and hold in his heart something great and wild. In just a few words, he fired the imagination in a way that needed no tools: "But like love/the archers/are blind." So few words, yet so rich! Lorca is a positive example of the evolution suggested in the Image.

EVENTS

World events can indicate how an Image from the cosmos works into culture. Two occurred on this day, bookends for an immense conflict: Pearl

---

51 Alexander Pope, born May 21, 1688 (Julian calendar).
52 *The Last Alchemist: Count Cagliostro, Master of Magic in the Age of Reason* by Iain McCalman (New York: HarperCollins, 2003). H. P. Blavatsky affirmed that his powers were real. Cagliostro, born June 2, 1743, is considered the author of *The Most Holy Trinisophia.*

53 Cagliostro's Sun Image was in Taurus. His Earth Image (as explained in Tresemer and Schiappacasse, *Star Wisdom & Rudolf Steiner,* op. cit.) was directly opposite, in Scorpio. Thus he was pulled by his Earth Image at the end of his life.
54 Philip II was born on May 21, 1527 (J).
55 Born June 5, 1898.

Harbor and D-Day, exactly opposite. The destruction of the US naval fleet at Pearl Harbor, took place on December 7, 1941, Sun at 21° of Scorpio. The Japanese called it Operation Tora, meaning tiger.[56] D-Day, called Operation Overlord (connecting to the notion of a powerful king) took place on June 6, 1944, Sun at 21° of Taurus. It was the largest sealift in human history.[57] Both of these events are marvels of technology.

This attunes us to power, the kinds of power and how it is used. We have spoken of turning points in people. These are turning points in history. These events hit it home at a societal and world level. Exact opposites are often related and useful in the Oracle of the Solar Cross.

With Venus at 20° of Scorpio, Leo Szilard and Enrico Fermi undertook the great experiment in 1942 that proved an atom bomb possible, in which neutrons were bombarded until there was a runaway chain reaction, which the scientists were then luckily able to bring to a halt.[58] This illustrates our theme about runaway technology, and its uses for good or ill. Characteristic with the human penchant to experiment beyond the limits of control, the scientists attending this experiment did not know if the reaction once started could be stopped, and thus the whole world might have exploded, Jamshid's firebird run amok. What that meeting with the firebird gave us was the atomic age, from which we are suffering now.

With Venus at 21° of Taurus, Neil Armstrong was the first human being to set foot on the Moon,

also an astonishing feat of technology.[59] Did it really happen? If so, how is it that we haven't been able to return forty years later? Or was it the magic of the cauldron, giving the world false pictures of what occurred, for the purposes of political gain?[60] Either way, this event puts us squarely into the question of technology and its uses.

MENTORS AND SPOILERS—THE BODES

Those who die into a degree, lifting up their life's harvest into that place, leave a trace or impression there. I have called them bodes, as they either bode well and become mentors, or they bode ill and become spoilers. Someone entering birth through that same gate, as well as anyone seeking a true connection with the spiritual themes living in that domain of the heavens, can be affected by the patterns existing there in those who have died there.

Usually we're interested in the deaths of powerful individuals, who might leave an impression in the heavens. We're also interested in mass deaths, such as in the two main world events occurring in this degree: Pearl Harbor and D-Day are exactly opposite, June and December, whose many fatalities in the same degree can create a kind of haze obscuring the import of an Image coming from the stars and amplified by the Sun.

Wolfgang Amadeus Mozart died in this degree. In *The Magic Flute*, Mozart gave us the figure of Sarastro, a representative in name and power of Zarathustra. He thus related toward the end of his life to the gate of his last breath. We can gain strength from Mozart's later music, that which was fresh in his mind and heart when he offered his life's deeds as harvest at his death. He can thus become a mentor for working with the themes of this Image of the Solar Cross.[61] Cultivate a relationship with Mozart's music, enjoyed with live

---

56 The planes were launched at 6:05 a.m., when the Sun was at 21°, 16 angular minutes of Scorpio, thus into the next degree, though less than 30 angular minutes from the Venus eclipse. The first strike was at 7:51 a.m. *Angular minutes* refer to a portion of a celestial degree in contrast to clock minutes. The Earth rotates by fifteen angular minutes for every clock minute.

57 When the preliminary airstrikes began, it was just after midnight, with the Sun at 21°, 7 angular minutes of Scorpio. The landing on the beach began at 5:30 a.m. Though this is just into the next degree, it is 17 angular minutes from the Venus eclipse position.

58 The Neutron Chain-Reaction experiment was undertaken by Leo Szilard and Enrico Fermi at the University of Chicago, Dec. 2, 1942, with Venus at 20° 10' of Scorpio.

59 July 20, 1969, Venus at 21° 2' of Taurus.

60 There are many books and DVDs on the Moon landing "hoax," the most interesting being Jay Weidner's "Kubrick's Odyssey" (www.sacredmysteries .com), wherein he demonstrates how Stanley Kubrick might have filmed the Moon landing on a film set.

61 Died Dec. 5, 1791, Sun at the edge of 21° Scorpio, thus possibly in this degree, though the time of death is not known. We use exact opposites when appropriate.

musicians when you can, both before and after the Venus eclipse, as it can give one strength and insight into our times. Music becomes the magic formed from technology—the flute—that takes the young couple through harsh initiations.[62] But more important are the qualifications noticed by the priests: "His heart is bold, and pure his mind."

Two kings died into this degree, *Ronald Reagan* and *King Henry VI of England*.[63] Both were mad toward the end of their lives, Reagan with Alzheimer's whose traces can be seen even while he was still in office, and King Henry VI sometimes catatonic, and sometimes hysterically singing while battles raged close by. The historians tell us that Henry was murdered while at prayer, though Shakespeare had him die in an argument by stabbing.[64] Either way, when we have men and women of power die by murder, it adds disturbances to our ability to feel the pure vibration of the degree.

We can perhaps feel the legacy of Ronald Reagan as a conditioning of our experience of this Image. Recently more facts about his presidency have come to light. Even though he had credible evidence from his own staff that the Soviet military was in decline and had few serious weapons, he revived the cold war, labeling the Soviets the "evil empire" and increasing the fear in the American public to the extent that his weaponization of space ("Star Wars," or Strategic Defense Initiative) almost came to pass. He created evidence for his claims and pressured the Congress to increase mightily the expenditures on military weapons for the US, as well as convincing many other countries to weaponize. This is a president who was

enamored of Jamshid's technologies and their potential uses for war.

Robert Kennedy was shot in this degree. Though he died when the Sun had moved to the next degree, he was shot and descended into a coma when the Sun lay in this degree.[65] Here is a man who championed the voice of the people and their needs, a man who was able to reach out from his heart, murdered in this degree. This disturbance must be acknowledged and then intentionally set aside in order to establish a pure strong connection to the Image.

Eduard von Hartmann died with the Sun in this degree, who earned the label "the philosopher of pessimism."[66] Rudolf Steiner met him before publishing his own book, *The Philosophy of Freedom*, and was disappointed at Hartmann's insistence that thinking could only wander in illusion, and that freedom was merely one of those illusions. One has to encounter and pass through the coloration of Hartmann's pessimism in order to find the true power of this Image.

Tintoretto died here. One could view his last great painting, his *Paradise*, the largest classical painting ever painted, at 74 feet by 30 feet, for inspiration to approach the Image. Or seek out any of his other paintings. Tintoretto can become a mentor on how to achieve hands from the heart.[67]

Carl Gustav Jung died in this degree.[68] He could function as a mentor to understand the true significance of the mythic structures of leadership, and how to learn from them. For example, Jung could well understand the magic cauldron as the collective unconscious, the great well of human possibility and destined future, a bottomless fount of creativity, horror, and love. He further understood that no event or person occurs out of relation with everything else. This viewpoint is a cure for all those who

---

62 The initiation themes of The Magic Flute are well researched in Jacques Chailley, *The Magic Flute Unveiled: Esoteric Symbolism in Mozart's Masonic Opera* (Rochester, VT: Inner Traditions, 1992). A fine guide to using Mozart's music to prepare one for difficult times comes in Don Campbell's *The Mozart Efect: Tapping the Power of Music to Heal the Body, Strengthen the Mind, and Unlock the Creative Spirit* (New York: Quill, 2001).

63 Ronald Reagan died June 5, 2004. King Henry VI of England died May 21, 1471 (J), both with Sun at this degree of Taurus.

64 Shakespeare wrote three plays about Henry VI, and was sympathetic to the challenges that Henry faced.

---

65 Shot on June 5, 1968, died the next day.

66 Eduard von Hartmann, died June 5, 1906.

67 Jacopo Tintoretto died May 31, 1594. Larger paintings have been done since by modern artists using methods that are much more rapid in execution.

68 Jung died on June 6, 1961, time unknown, with Sun at this degree of Taurus. If it was before six in the morning, the death Sun lay between 20° and 21°, otherwise, quite close.

become enamored of technology and think that they can use that technology for their own pleasure privately without any impact on others.

A FEW WHO WERE BORN WITH VENUS CONJUNCT THE SUN

We have looked at Sun and Venus at the twenty-first degree of Taurus–Scorpio, when we can emphasize the Images from the twenty-first degree of Taurus–Scorpio. We can also mention a few people who were born with Venus conjunct the Sun, who have more of a connection to karmic groups, and we find very interesting connections with the themes upon which we have already touched: Leo Szilard, mentioned previously in relation to the Chain-Reaction Experiment, which occurred when Venus was at 20° Scorpio; Richard Wagner, whose *Parsifal* was first performed in the year of the last Venus eclipse of the Sun; the very powerful teacher, The Mother of Auroville Ashram in India; Sai Baba with his large ashram in Puttaparthi; Trevor Ravenscroft, mentioned with *Parsifal* earlier; and Mani, the great philosopher of the third century, who supposedly reincarnated as the real-life ninth-century Parzival.[69]

HANDS OF THE HEART

We are guided by the Image at Taurus and its opposite at Scorpio to develop capacities within rather than without, holding them in our heart. Indeed, we receive the hint that the forces of the will must emanate from the heart, with the light

---

69   Leo Szilard, born Feb. 11, 1898, both Sun and Venus at 29° of Capricorn, superior conjunction (Venus beyond the Sun); Richard Wagner, May 22, 1813, both at 8° Taurus, superior; The Mother (Mirra Alfassa), born Feb. 21, 1878, both at 9° Aquarius, the only inferior conjunction, Venus between the Sun and Earth, though not in front of the Sun; Sai Baba, born Nov. 23, 1926, both at 6° Scorpio, superior; Trevor Ravenscroft, born April 23, 1921, superior conjunction at 8° Aries; Mani, born April 13, 216 (J), both at 23° Aries, superior. The reincarnation of Mani to Parsifal is suggested by Rudolf Steiner (see Sergei O. Prokofieff, *Relating to Rudolf Steiner*, p. 18). Though the painter Raphael has been described as having Sun conjunct Venus at his birth, it is 3° separate, enough to note in a personal reading, but not in an overview such as this, where we use a 1° orb to find patterns.

of one's interior streaming out in deeds to the world. We can respect the wonderful tools and magical implements that exist in the outer world, but learn to depend on the capacities of our own heart. Physically reach out—not just metaphorically but physically—to other people and to the world. Reach out not to your computer, or to your pocketbook to give a donation to a worthy charity—but rather reach out to other human beings.

One feels perhaps the desire to perform big deeds for the world, as Jamshid did. However, the best way to give hands to the heart begins with small deeds. Here is an instance that I observed at an airport recently. The arriving passengers crowded around the baggage claim, spread out along two hundred feet of access. The bags were coming off the conveyor belt very quickly. One bag fell off at a corner, at someone's feet. I watched her shift from a vigil for her own bags to a warm concern for an unknown passenger further down the line. She leaned over and picked up the fallen suitcase and set it back on the conveyor belt. Some people do this automatically. This woman had to become available to the concerns of her heart—understanding the plight of another—and then responding to what she felt. Her heart made the connection, and her hands did the work. She didn't require a tool or a magical tool, but simple hands from her heart.

SUMMARY

We have explored the ramifications of the Image at 20° to 21° of Taurus, finding in the opposite sign of Scorpio hints about the heart, which was less clear in the Taurus Image on its own. Venus's "eclipse" of the Sun in this degree will stimulate all of the themes that we've discussed, stimulate with a sense of the urgency of finding one's karmic group affiliations, those whose common purpose one has a destiny to encounter and further in the world. In Anthroposophy such groups have sometimes been referred to as "streams," such as Grail stream, king stream, shepherd stream, Rosicrucian stream, Templar stream, and so on. In the context of this Image, one could feel the call of a powerful leader, such as Solomon, or Inanna, or Melchizedek. One could feel the call of one's Self. One could focalize around any of the technologies named. One could define oneself by the group that shares a malady—bleeding, blind, near-dead. With what do you identify that is greater than yourself, that involves others now and through history? What is your soul group and are you assisting in fulfilling its gift to humanity?

Your will forces may well be activated by the Venus "eclipse" of June 6, 2012. Venus will excite these themes, and cast them in terms of karmic and soul connections. Each individual and the world as a whole will be challenged by great new technologies that will promise to ease the world from disease, old age, and death. Will this lead to a narcissistic withdrawal each into his or her own heart, clothed in darkness? Or will each find the hands of the heart stretching forth in light, developing the tools of one's own being, the tools within the heart?

From this Venus eclipse, new technologies will arise or be newly energized, and humanity will have to choose. The potential of this Image is that one can discover that the faculties necessary for human development must be found in the human being, in the hands of the heart, not in technology. The cyborg—the human being embedded with machines—devolves the possible human being (the anthropos). The distractions of convenience, technological gadgets that permeate our lives, must be set aside, at least for some period of time on a regular basis. If you cannot stop the intrusion of Jamshid's tools, then at least balance their effect with time in nature, in self-originated imaginations, in the exercise of the heart in the world of relationships.[70] One must have the time to explore the vast realms of one's own heart, in a concerted practice of discovery and expression through simple deeds in the world. Find the capacities in your heart, then let the essence of

your heart move out through your hands to the world and to others. Not conceptually, not even through miracle technological breakthroughs, but through your hands. Your attention is invited, as well as your participation in human relationships with others, beginning now, so you are not taken by surprise by the surge of these themes unleashed by the eclipse.

In order to achieve the most with this event, you can learn from the mentors who hover in this degree and you can press aside the distracting influences of the spoilers who also hover in this degree.

Practice connecting heart to the light of the cosmos, as it expresses through the streams of destiny to which you are personally related—and to which you can come closer in this time. Let that light and power express through your hands. Thereby claim your place in space and time as an expression of that heart-filled light.

&

This article is a shortened version of the recent book, *The Venus Eclipse of the Sun 2012: A Rare Celestial Event: Going to the Heart of Technology* (Lindisfarne Books), available from www.steinerbooks.org.

Appendix A
Celestial Phenomena

Alignment of Sun, Earth, and Galactic Center. An alignment of Sun and Earth to a point near the Galactic Center happens twice every year. As our solar system lies over ten light years above the main disc of the galaxy, and the Sun-Earth plane (the ecliptic) is tilted at 60° from that plane of the galaxy, technically the line between Sun and Earth does not point to the Galactic Center at any time. Pointing nearby could mean either to the point on the great circle perpendicular to the ecliptic which is closest to the Galactic Center (2° Sagittarius) or it could mean the place where the Galactic Equator, the plane of the Milky Way, crosses that of the ecliptic (5° Sagittarius).[71]

---

70 Two decades ago, Waldorf school teachers advised parents against any television for their children or any devices such as mobile phones until high school. They then retreated to advising against these things for the first seven, and now five, years of life. Teachers can point to such studies as Jane Healy's *Endangered Minds* (New York: Simon & Schuster, 1999) or anything by Joseph Chilton Pearce, which detail the dangers of premature encounters with Jamshid's magic devices, but the pressure from the world eager for stimulation proves very powerful.

71 These degrees are from sidereal reckoning, which is their actual astronomical location along the ecliptic (Sun-Earth plane) in a system of twelve equally long

If you add in the coincidence of this alignment at the Earth's solstice (December 21, shortest winter day in the northern hemisphere, longest summer day in the south), the alignment of Sun, Earth, and (near to) the Galactic Center occurs twice a year for a period of over thirty years. The promise of the movie "2012: Doomsday" that there will be five celestial objects in a unique alignment, causing immense earthquakes and upheavals, will not be met in the year 2012. A longer description of the alignment of Earth, Sun, and Galactic Center can be found in "Sun on the Galactic Center," *Journal for Star Wisdom 2010*, with an updated version in the Journal of the International Society for Astrological Research (ISAR), August 2011.

Transits of Venus. The height of the Venus eclipse will be 1:30 AM UT on June 6, 2012, which is 11:30 EST Australia on June 6 (and late on June 5 in the United States). The duration will be 6 hours and 40'.

The time between the pair of transits, what I call eclipses in this paper, is eight years or 2^3 years. The time between the first of the previous pair (as in December 9, 1874, both at 23° and 58' of Scorpio) and the first of the present pair (to June 8, 2004, Sun and Venus at 23° and 2' of Taurus) is $129\frac{1}{2}$ years = $5^3 + 5 - .5$.[72]

Looking at longer stretches of time, the gap of 129.5 years oscillates with a gap of 113.5 years, totaling 243 years, which repeats. $113\frac{1}{2} = 5^3 - 5^2 + (3 \times 5) - (3 \times .5)$. Thus the time between the last of a pair and the first of the next pair alternates between $121\frac{1}{2}$ and $105\frac{1}{2}$ years. $121\frac{1}{2} = 5^3 - 5 + (3 \times .5)$ and $105\frac{1}{2} = 5^3 - 5^2 + 5 + .5$.[73]

The sidereal orbit of Venus around the Sun is 225 days, which is $5^3 + (4 \times 5^2)$, also seen as $5^2 \times 3^2$. Seen both from the points of view of the different cycles of year and day, the number 5—and the powers

of 5, its square and cube, and fraction—plays an important role in the dance of Venus with the Sun. In any eight-year period (2^3), Venus completes a beautiful five-petalled flower from the Earth's point of view, having in that time moved on a small increment through the zodiac.

In contrast, transits of Mercury occur much more frequently. November transits occur at intervals of 7, 13, or 33 years; May transits only occur at intervals of 13 or 33 years. Combined, there might be only three years between a May and a November transit.

Annular eclipses of the Sun. An annular eclipse by the Moon occurs when the Moon is further away from the Earth and does not completely cover the face of the Sun. One observes a fiery ring of Sun around the center darkened by the Moon. Thus the Venus eclipse is a version of an annular eclipse, though the rim of the Sun around the dark dot of Venus is huge. The notion of a seven-ringed cup can also stimulate this imagination, that there are seven rings of increasing size which would not then be the bodies of the seven classical planets, but the rings of their orbits.

Rudolf Steiner referred to the Venus "eclipse," giving hints but little detail: "Very significant things can be observed when Venus is passing in front of the Sun. One can see what the Sun's halo looks like when Venus is passing in front of the Sun. ["Halo" is another way of speaking of an annular eclipse of the Sun by the Moon.] This event brings about great changes."[74] He did not say what those changes might be, though he suggested that the event would influence the weather.

✺

APPENDIX B

JAMSHID IN GREATER DETAIL

Jamshid has been called *Jamshed, Jamshyd, Jambushad, Janbushad,*[75] *Djem, Djemschid, Dschemschid,*[76] *Djemscheed, Gamshed, Dsem-*

---

zodiacal signs. However, the point made here does not require that one embrace a sidereal view of the heavens (vs. the conventional tropical or seasonal view).

72 The same can be said from the second of the previous pair, Dec. 6, 1882 (with Sun and Venus at 21° and 26' Scorpio), and the second of the present pair, June 6, 2012 (Sun and Venus at 20° 51' of Taurus).

73 Looking over many centuries, one occasionally sees that the second of a pair does not occur.

---

74 Rudolf Steiner, *From Sunspots to Strawberries*, pp. 170–173.

75 These two from Giorgio De Santillana and Hertha von Dechend, *Hamlet's Mill*, op. cit.

76 From Walter J. Stein's *The Ninth Century and The*

chid, Djemjid,[77] and *Djemjdid.*[78] In the Avestan language of most ancient Persia, this is the shining aspect (-*shid*) of *Yima.* One can sometimes find *Yama* used instead of *Yima.* I use *Jamshid* for all the different spellings of this ancient name.

One name for Jamshid, *Yama,* recalls the Sanskrit word *Yama,* meaning qualities of character that come from restraint of the bestial temptations of the lower nature of the will. It has five qualities:

1. *Ahimsa*: non-violence; choosing not to commit the violence to which one is drawn;
2. *Satya*: truthfulness; choosing not to deceive, to which one is also pulled;
3. *Asteya*: non-theft; choosing not to steal from others;
4. *Brahmacharya*: moderation in sex, and sometimes abstinence; choosing not to rush into sexual pleasures;
5. *Aparigraha*: non-acquisitiveness; choosing to give away wealth and to ignore desires.

These qualities of *Yama,* which may have been held over from the Indian epoch to the Iranian epoch when Jamshid flourished, may give an idea of the character of this great king, a mastery of the will—which we have said technology expresses.

The name *Jamshid* calls forth the participation of the celestial creators in the "fixed signs" of the zodiac, Taurus and Scorpio, which we have seen, as well as Leo and Aquarius. Working backward in that name, *d* is the gift of Leo; *sh* the gift of Scorpio; and *m* the gift of Aquarius. If one pronounces *j* as in "jump," the sound "j" comes from a combination of the "d" sound (from Leo) and "zh" (from Scorpio). Only Taurus's gift, *r,* is missing in this name. The vowel sound "ee," mediated into our world by Mercury, and "ah," mediated by Venus, become the bearers of the consonants of Leo, Scorpio, and Aquarius into the human realm.[79] One can also feel a similarity in sound

between the core name, *Yama* or *Yima,* and the declaration, "I am!"

Rudolf Steiner affirmed that the gifts to Jamshid came directly from Ahura Mazda, the Father God, who taught Zarathustra 5,000 years before Troy. Steiner referred to Troy because the battle of Troy broke the last vestiges of the ancient Persian culture, making way for the epoch of Greece and Rome.[80] Zarathustra had laid the foundations for the Persian culture in its beginnings.

Steiner spoke of the leadership of Jamshid in the whole Iranian or Persian epoch, the second post-Atlantean Civilization, after ancient India and before the age of Egypt–Chaldea. Through the guidance of Jamshid, the Iranians did not follow the path of their neighbors, the Turanians, who tried to use the decrepit magic of Atlantis to change substance and influence people. Their old spells turned dark and, though they wreaked havoc on their neighbors in wars supported by black magic, the misuse of these powers folded in upon itself, and the Turanians eventually died out.[81] You can see a picture of these two realms in conflict with each other in Tolkein's trilogy *The Lord of the Rings,* and indeed one could see the ring of Jamshid pictured there, too. One can see the contrasts of these ancient tales in the contrast between the pictures of the Scorpio and Taurus Images.

In Jamshid, we see a figure similar to Marduk of the Sumerians and Prometheus of the Greeks, a bearer of fire, how to make it and how to use it for many crafts including metalworking, the fashioning of glass, the arts of agriculture, and intelligence generally. He has the ability to apply intelligence to the Earth, measuring it, dividing it, and cultivating it. The golden dagger becomes that which separates, categorizes, measures, stirs and plows the earth. It is the prototype of all tools

---

Holy Grail (London: Temple Lodge, 2009).

77 Rudolf Steiner, *According to Matthew.*

78 From the explanation of the title of the annual series, *The Golden Blade,* (Edinburgh: Floris Books).

79 With the spelling of *Jamshid* as *Yima,* the only consonant *m* comes from Aquarius, and the rest are the vowels of Mercury and Venus. The association of

sounds with gifts from the zodiac and planets originated with the Hindu understanding of the *matrika* goddesses and was picked up and developed by Rudolf Steiner in the art of eurythmy.

80 The history, and gap of 5,000 years, came from Plutarch's *Isis and Osiris* (46–7), which Steiner affirms by his use of this evaluation of time. Between the time of ancient Persia and the Greek/Roman times came the two thousand years of the Egyptian–Chaldean civilization.

81 Steiner, *According to Matthew,* lecture I.

and inventions of civilization. Separation is the task of the senses. From the blob of color and blob of sound that the infant experiences, we slowly differentiate between one kind of stimulus and another, as we develop our intelligence, exercising the knife of discernment.

A person with a connection to this Image might speak aloud some lines of Jamshid himself, such as those quoted above, where Jamshid speaks to the Creator, Ahura Mazda, "Yes! I will make thy worlds thrive, I will make thy worlds increase. Yes! I will nourish, and rule, and watch over thy world. There shall be, while I am king, neither cold wind nor hot wind, neither disease nor death." Speak it loudly, as a proclamation. Speak it softly and tenderly for Ahura Mazda and the Seven Rishis are also close by, and can hear your words of intent when spoken quietly.

"It became clearer and clearer to me—as the outcome of many years of research—that in our epoch there is really something like a resurrection of the Astrology of the third epoch [the Egyptian–Babylonian period], but permeated now with the Christ Impulse. Today, we must search among the stars in a way different from the old ways. The stellar script must once more become something that speaks to us."

—RUDOLF STEINER (*Christ and the Spiritual World and the Search for the Holy Grail*, p. 106)

"In Palestine during the time that Jesus of Nazareth walked on Earth as Jesus Christ—during the three years of his life, from his thirtieth to his thirty-third year—the entire being of the cosmic Christ was acting uninterruptedly upon him, and was working into him. The Christ stood always under the influence of the entire cosmos; he made no step without this working of the cosmic forces into and in him. . . . It was always in accordance with the collective being of the whole universe with whom the Earth is in harmony, that all which Jesus Christ did took place."

—RUDOLF STEINER (*Spiritual Guidance of Man and Humanity*, p. 66)

JOAN OF ARC: A FORERUNNER OF OUR AGE

Wain Farrants

THE DAWN OF THE CONSCIOUSNESS SOUL EPOCH (1413–3573)

Joan of Arc was born at the start of the age of the Consciousness Soul. Now, in the year 2012, we celebrate the 600-year anniversary of her birth. To begin our contemplation of this heroic figure from the fifteenth century, let us consider the following words of Rudolf Steiner concerning Joan of Arc:

> Medieval society was indoctrinated with Catholicism, which counted upon a certain unconsciousness of the human soul, a susceptibility to suggestionism. Humankind did not yet possess the capacity for independent reflection. However, at the dawn of the fifth post-Atlantean epoch of the consciousness soul, national identity began to be looked upon as something vastly more important than Catholicism and all it represented like the papacy. But the luciferic and ahrimanic adversaries wished to prevent the entry of the Spiritual Soul or Consciousness Soul. An event which reveals the inpouring of the Spiritual into the earthly events in a most clear and radiant way is the appearance and subsequent history of Joan of Arc, the Maid of Orelans. The impulses for what she does lie in the deep, subconscious foundations of her soul. She follows dim inspirations from the spiritual world. On the Earth there is confusion and disorder, through which the age of the Spiritual Soul is to be hindered. Michael has to prepare from the spiritual world for his later mission; this he is able to do where his impulses are received into human souls. Such a soul lives in the Maid of Orleans.[1]

Prior to the epoch of the Consciousness Soul, special individuals could undergo initiation during the Holy Nights. One such individual was Olaf Åsteson, who fell asleep on Christmas Eve, awoke on Epiphany morning and described his experiences to the congregation of his local Church.[2] Perhaps one of the last individuals to undergo this initiation was Joan of Arc, if we consider the possibility that she was initiated during the Holy Nights of 1411–1412 while still in her mother's womb. She was born on Epiphany, January 6, 1412. In fact, Christmas Eve (December 24–25) in German is *Weihenachten,* meaning consecration, or initiation, night. Then there follows the twelve Holy Nights (December 25–26 to January 5–6), ending at sunrise on Epiphany Day.

Most Likely Time of Birth

It has been generally accepted by astrologers that Joan of Arc was born in the late afternoon. But just as Olaf Åsteson awoke on Epiphany morning, it makes sense that Jehanne la Pucelle was born on Epiphany morning. In fact there is well documented evidence that she was:

> Three days after the victory of Patay, Perceval de Boulainvilliers, one of Charles VII's chamberlains and Seneschal of Berri, wrote an excited letter to the Duke of Milan, describing the personage of the moment. He says that she was born on the night of Epiphany, as the peasants celebrated in the fields, and as the cocks began to crow. (Jules Quicherat. *Procès de réhabilitation*)[3]

---

1 Rudolf Steiner, *From Symptom to Reality in Modern History,* lecture 1 (trans. revised); and *Anthroposophical Leading Thoughts,* Dec. 7, 1924.

2 *The Dream Song of Olaf Åsteson: An Ancient Norwegian Folksong of the Holy Nights* (Edinburgh: Floris Books, 2007).

3 Edward Lucie-Smith, *Joan of Arc* (New York: Penguin, 1976). This book refers to Jules Quicherat, *Procès de réhabilitation,* p. 116.

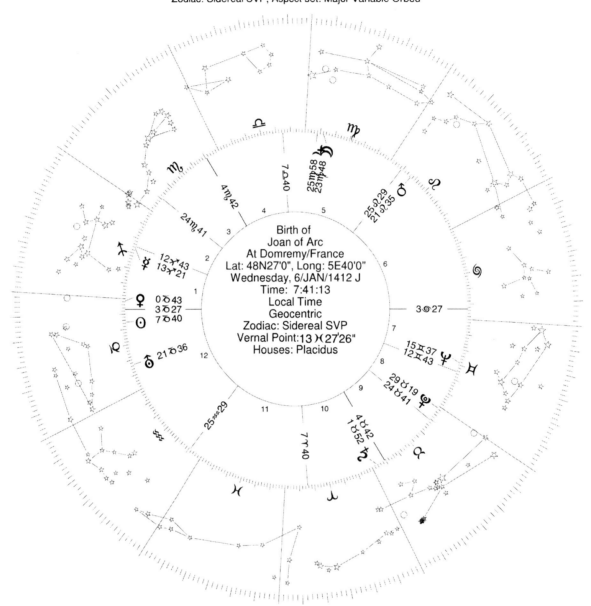

Birth of Joan of Arc - Geocentric
At Domremy/France, Latitude 48N27'0", Longitude 5E40'0"
Date: Wednesday, 6/JAN/1412, Julian
Time: 7:41:13, Local Time
Sidereal Time 15:15:13, Vernal Point 13 ⨯27'26", House System: Placidus
Zodiac: Sidereal SVP, Aspect set: Major Variable Orbed

The dawn chorus occurs in the twilight period before sunrise, which leads us to consider a time of birth before sunrise. I came up with one at 7:41 a.m., just minutes before sunrise.

When I was in my thirteenth year, I heard a voice from God to help me govern my conduct. And the first time I was very much afraid. And came the voice about the hour of noon, in the summertime.... I knew that it was the voice of an angel... but afterward, St. Michael taught me and showed me and proved to me that I must believe firmly that it was him. I knew who he was by his speech and by the language of the angels.[4]

According to Rudolf Steiner, she saw the Virgin Mary and the Archangel Michael in the form of a certain picture... although the Maid of Orleans

4 Joan M. Edmunds, *The Mission of Joan of Arc*, p. 15 (London: Temple Lodge, 2008).

Death of Joan of Arc - Geocentric
At Rouen, France, Latitude 49N25'0", Longitude 1E5'0"
Date: Wednesday, 30/MAY/1431, Julian
Time: 12:0:0, Local Time
Sidereal Time 5: 4: 2, Vernal Point 13 ♓ 11'14", House System: Placidus
Zodiac: Sidereal SVP, Aspect set: Major Variable Orbed

did not see their true form, it did come down toward her.[5]

Joan's first challenge was to lift the siege of Orleans. "She arrived on May 4, 1429. "Even at her first appearance in Orléans, the populace reacted toward her, as the Journal recorded, 'as if they had seen God descend in their midst'. What was felt and experienced in human souls was the tremendous strength and energy of the Christ Impulse, the compelling Christ Force, which radiated from her with powerful effect."[6]

On May 7, 1429, there was fierce fighting all day. When the French were about to withdraw behind the city walls, Joan seized her standard, began to rally the troops, and when they advanced

---

5 Ibid., p. 19.

6 Rudolf Steiner, "The Christ Impulse as Bearer of the Union of the Spiritual and the Bodily," lecture on Feb. 14, 1915 (CW 174; not published in English).

unexpectedly, the English trembled with terror. Later reports circulated that the English had actually seen the Archangel Michael and St Aignan, patron saint of Orléans, riding on horseback in mid-air to the aid of the French![7] On May 8, Joan's forces waited to see what the British would do but they withdrew without any more fighting.

Transiting Planet May 7, 1429	Aspect	Birth Planet
Moon Node 15° Pisces 59'	Opposition	Heliocentric Jupiter 15° Virgo 46'
Heliocentric Mercury 23° Virgo 23'	Conjunction	Moon 23° Virgo 46'

In Reims, On Sunday, July 17, 1429, 9 a.m., when the Dauphin was crowned King Charles VII, France now had a French King. She continued recapturing towns back from the British until on May 23, 1430, she was captured in Compiegne. During the summer and autumn her captors were taking her from place to place. Joan tried to escape by leaping from the tower of Beaurevoir, where she was imprisoned from mid-July to mid-November. "She had no desire to commit suicide—she had only the desire to get away. To fall into English hands was the thing she most dreaded. It was in vain that her voices sought to restrain her. Saint Catherine assured her that she would not be delivered until she had seen the King of England. She had no desire to see him, and said so. Still, the voices would not authorize her to do as she wished. The argument continued daily for some time, Joan beseeching, the voices refusing their permission. Finally she took the law into her own hands, commended herself to God, and threw herself off the top of the castle tower. It is assumed that the height cannot have been less than sixty or seventy feet. . . She seems to have been knocked thoroughly unconscious, perhaps even suffered a slight concussion."[8]

This incident made me think of the second temptation of Christ by Lucifer and Ahriman

combined, to throw himself down from the parapet of the temple and the angels will protect him.[9] Rudolf Steiner also informed us, "Just as a nature such as that of Joan of Arc had actively to confront the luciferic forces, so must people today offer resistance to the forces of Ahriman…must make themselves strong against them…as is right, in the Age of Michael."[10] Once again she demonstrates her lack of faith and courage when she is willing to give in to demands to change her man's clothing for a woman's in order to escape death by fire but quickly changes her mind when she learns that instead she will have to remain imprisoned for the rest of her life.

A Brief Delineation of Her Birth Horoscope

In the *Journal for Star Wisdom 2011*, I gave some sample delineations of the horoscopes of John F. Kennedy, Gandhi, Mozart, and Rudolf Steiner, using the clockwise house system presented by Jacques Dorsan.[11] I will apply the same technique here to Joan's horoscope. In addition, I will consider the placements of a few of the planets in the sidereal zodiac.

Saturn in the clockwise tenth house of childhood, home life and the land describes her humble beginnings. Mercury in the first clockwise house gives an easy self-expression through the spoken word, with rapid repartee while Venus gives a pleasant appearance, an attraction to fine clothing and a magnetic nature. The Sun in the clockwise twelfth house indicates hostile attacks from false friends and other adversaries, which, in an extreme case, could lead to hospital or prison. The Sun here can also give spiritual protection. Her guides assured her she would have a spiritual victory, but did not promise that she would come out alive. Uranus in the twelfth house warns that there is a danger of injury from animals, a fall from a horse, for instance. Joan was finally captured when a soldier pulled her off her horse! Uranus so placed, allows one to exercise

---

7   Joan M. Edmunds, ibid., pp. 52–53.

8   V. Sackville-West, *Saint Joan of Arc* (New York: Sphere, 1990), pp. 254–255.

9   Rudolf Steiner. *The Fifth Gospel*, Oct. 6, 1913.

10 Rudolf Steiner. *Thoughts for the Times*, 12 lectures Berlin, Sept. 1, 1914–July 5, 1915, lecture 5 (manuscript, trans. revised).

11 Jacques Dorsan. *The Clockwise House System*.

occult faculties well beyond the norm. Finally, the greatest dangers will come from hidden enmities against which it is difficult to defend oneself; the native has the gift of being able to dominate her interlocutors (cross-examiners, interviewers), crowds and animals with a single look. On February 21, 1431, the trial began and three days later Beaupère asked her,

> "Do you know if you are in the grace of God?" This cunning question, which was intended to trap Joan, would have been impossible to answer, even by someone well versed in theology. Not to be in a state of grace was to be in mortal sin; but because grace is the gift of God, no one can say that one is in possession of it. Had Joan said yes, she would have committed herself to heresy and presumption. Her sublime and immortal answer was, "If I am not, may God put me there; if I am, may He keep me there." In his testimony [later at the trial of reconciliation], Boisguillaume stated, "Those who were interrogating her were stupefied."[12]

Pluto in the eighth house indicates a strange or tragic death, possibly prematurely. Moon–Jupiter in the fifth house of education, entertainment and children presages how her life would inspire so many books, plays and films. Mars in the sixth house indicates that her success will mainly be dependent upon the quality of her relationships within her working environment...and especially those under her orders. She ought to be careful when manipulating tools, instruments, and machines, in order to avoid injuries or burns. Joan continually had to argue with her fellow military commanders. During the siege of Orléans, Joan was wounded by an arrow between her neck and shoulder. With Neptune in her seventh house, collective events can favor the destiny. Joan's destiny was to expel the English from France, and so she did, even though she paid for it with her martyrdom. According to Rudolf Steiner, Britain's immediate destiny at that time was to orient itself toward far distant lands rather than European conquest or intervention.[13] Isambart de la Pierre described what happened immediately after her death.

> Immediately after the execution, the executioner came to me and my companion, Martin Ladvenu, struck and moved to a marvelous repentance and contrition, all in despair, fearing never to obtain pardon and indulgence from God for what he had done to that saintly woman; and said and affirmed that despite the oil, the sulfur and the charcoal which he had applied, nevertheless he had not by any means been able to consume nor reduce to ashes the heart nor the entrails, at which was he as greatly astonished as by a manifest miracle. He said to us both that he greatly feared he was damned, for he had burnt a saint.[14]

On Mediaeval pictures of the human being, the signs of the zodiac are shown on different parts of the body. For example, Leo is on the heart. Joan's Mars was in sidereal Leo. Moon-Jupiter are in conjunction in sidereal Virgo, the constellation of the civil and military engineer, strategist and tactician.[15] Sun in Capricorn manifests the virtue of courage, which becomes the power of redemption...we can imagine the work of the frugal Goat, who is able to subsist on the most arid of landscapes, capable and agile, able to make leaping leaps and tread gracefully over the most dangerous precipices.[16] When Joan leapt from the tower, she was acting in the character of her Sun sign. The Ascendant, Venus, and Uranus were also in Capricorn.

The Mission of Joan of Arc

Joan of Arc had a mission to introduce the age of the consciousness soul as Steiner indicates below:

> At that time, it was indeed the Christ impulse acting in Joan of Arc through its Michaelic servants that prevented a possible merging of France and England, forcing England back into its island. This achieved two things: first, France continued to have a free hand in

---

12 Joan M. Edmunds, ibid., p. 10.
13 Rudolf Steiner. *The Destinies of Individuals and of Nations*, Jan. 19, 1915.
14 Joan M. Edmunds, ibid., p. 144.
15 Cyril Fagan, *Astrological Origins* (Woodbury, MN: Llewellyn, 1971).
16 Lacquanna Paul and Robert Powell, *Cosmic Dances of the Zodiac*.

Europe.... The second thing that was achieved was that England was given its domain outside the continent of Europe.[17]

I sometimes wonder how Joan of Arc would be received today with her claims of conversing with the Archangel Michael and with saints. Rudolf Steiner foresaw a great crisis at the end of the twentieth century. It appears to be ongoing:

Let the Michael power and the Michael will penetrate the whole of life. The Michael power and the Michael will are none other than the Christ will and the Christ power going before to implant the power of Christ in the right way into the Earth. If this Michael power is able verily to overcome all that is of the demon and the dragon...if you all, who have received the Michael thought in the light, have indeed received it with a true and faithful heart and with tender love, and will endeavor to go forward from the Michael mood of this year, until not the Michael thought has been revealed only in your soul, but now you are able to make the Michael thought live in your actions in all its strength and all its power—if this is so, then will you be true servants of the Michael thought, worthy helpers of what has now to enter earthly evolution through Anthroposophy, and take its place there in the meaning of Michael.[18]

❦

---

17 Rudolf Steiner, ibid., p. 55.

18 Rudolf Steiner, *Karmic Relationships*, vol. 4, "The Last Address," Sept. 28, 1924.

"Every earthly condition during a certain period of time is to be explained as a weaving and interplay of those forces that come into flower and those that die away, those that belong to the rising and those that belong to the falling line—sunrise and sunset—and in between, the zenith at noon, where the two forces unite and become one. Seen from one's horizon, a person beholds the stars in the sky, rising in the east and climbing ever higher until they reach their highest point in the south. From then onward, they sink until they set in the west. And though the stars disappear from sight in the west, one must nevertheless say to oneself: The real place of setting lies in the south and coincides with the zenith, just as the true place of rising is in the north and coincides with the nadir. The rising starts from the nadir. Through that, a circular motion is described that can be divided into two halves by a vertical line running south to north. In the part containing the eastern point, the rising forces are active. In the part containing the western point, the sinking forces are present. The eastern and western points cut the semicircle through the center. They are the two points in which, for our physical eye, vision of the forces begins and ends. They are one's horizon."

—RUDOLF STEINER, *"Freemasonry" and Ritual Work*
(SteinerBooks, 2007), p. 387

KASPAR HAUSER: THE CHILD OF EUROPE

Born in Baden, September 29, 1812–Died in Ansbach, December 17, 1833

Wain Farrants

This year, 2012, we celebrate the two-hundred-year anniversary of the birth of Kaspar Hauser, who was the son of the Grand Duke Karl and his wife Stephanie de Beauharnais, the adopted daughter of Napoleon Bonaparte. In October 1812, Napoleon began his retreat from Russia. Charles Dickens, a novelist with compassion for the downtrodden was born on February 7, Zygmunt Krasinski, Polish romantic author on February 19, Robert Browning, poet, on May 7, I.A. Goncharov, Russian novelist on June 6 (OS), and Joseph Ignatius Kraszewski, Polish novelist on July 28.

Robert Powell states that the birth time was 10:30 am, which he found was not directly given but is indirectly indicated from the timing of an incident that occurred several hours after the birth recounted by Johnannes Mayer,[1] one of his biographers. He was secretly removed within a few days of his birth and in his place was put a sickly child who died shortly thereafter. As a young child, he was taken care of for about three years and then imprisoned in a darkened underground room.

Two other sons born to Stephanie died mysteriously. With no male heirs to the throne, Leopold of Hochberg became the Grand Duke. Why wasn't the firstborn son murdered as well? Rudolf Steiner stated that he would have reincarnated quickly into more favourable circumstances.[2] This was more than a dynastic crime. The evil forces recognized the potentiality this child, when he grew up, would have in revolutionizing the social order for the good.

Eventually the evil forces reckoned that it was safe to release him, expecting that he would remain obscure or be simply mistreated. The jailer taught him to read and write simple texts, and to say a few words. Over a period of several days, he was half carried, half dragged by his jailer to a marketplace in Nuremberg on Whitmonday afternoon when he was fifteen years and eight months old. Being a religious holiday, apparently no one witnessed him being placed there, but he was found shortly thereafter.

On the day of his appearance geocentric Saturn and Neptune were in opposition. At such times, people can be very concerned about human wrongs and looking after the weakest members of society. In addition Mars was in conjunction with Neptune and Venus in conjunction with Saturn. The Mars-Neptune conjunction is related to sensitivity, compassion, imagination and victims of violence, the Venus-Saturn conjunction to denial of affection.[3] Transiting Pluto was approaching opposition to his natal (birth) Sun. In traditional astrology Pluto transit Sun indicates the possibility of a difficult time, metamorphosis or resurrection.

It soon became apparent that Kaspar had amazing sense perceptions. He could even see dark shades of colors in the dark, and small objects at an unusual distance; he had very sensitive senses of smell and also of taste. When it was announced that Kaspar Hauser was writing his autobiography, his former jailer was sent to assassinate him. He tried to cut his throat but instead grazed his forehead.

1 Johannes Meyer and Peter Tradowsky. *Kaspar Hauser.*

2 Peter Tradowsky: "This statement by Rudolf Steiner has not been confirmed up till now, the contents of which, however, can be held to be reliable."

3 Sue Tompkins. *Aspects in Astrology: A Comprehensive Guide to Interpretation* (London: Rider, 2001).

Birth of Kaspar Hauser - Geocentric
At Durlach, Latitude 49N0'0", Longitude 8E29'0"
Date: Tuesday, 29/SEP/1812, Gregorian
Time: 10:30:0, Local Time
Sidereal Time 11: 2: 3, Vernal Point 7✠52'23", House System: Placidus
Zodiac: Sidereal SVP, Aspect set: Major Variable Orbed

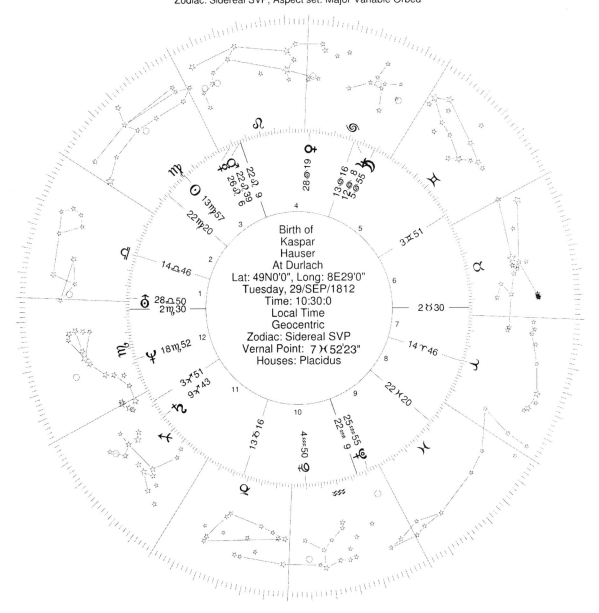

Lord Philip Henry Stanhope visited Kaspar Hauser at the end of May 1831, in an attempt to befriend him, corrupt him, blunt his growing awareness of himself and ultimately get rid of him.

Pastor Fuhrmann confirmed Kaspar Hauser in the Swan Knights' Chapel of St. Gumbertus on May 20, 1833. This was the culmination of Kaspar's introduction to Christianity in a chapel named after the Knights founded by Lohengrin, one of the sons of Parzival.. Even angelic beings born on earth have to learn about heavenly things.

Kaspar Hauser was assassinated on December 14 but miraculously survived until the night of December 17, 1833. It might remind us of Christ's three days from the Last Supper and agony in Gethsemane on Maundy Thursday evening (April 2) to the Resurrection on Easter Sunday morning (April 5). On his deathbed, and in the presence of Pastor Fuhrmann he said, "The monster was

Death of Kaspar Hauser - Geocentric
At Ansbach, Germany, Latitude 49N18'0", Longitude 10E36'0"
Date: Tuesday, 17/DEC/1833, Gregorian
Time: 22:0:0, Local Time
Sidereal Time 3:45: 2, Vernal Point 7♓34'38", House System: Placidus
Zodiac: Sidereal SVP, Aspect set: Major Variable Orbed

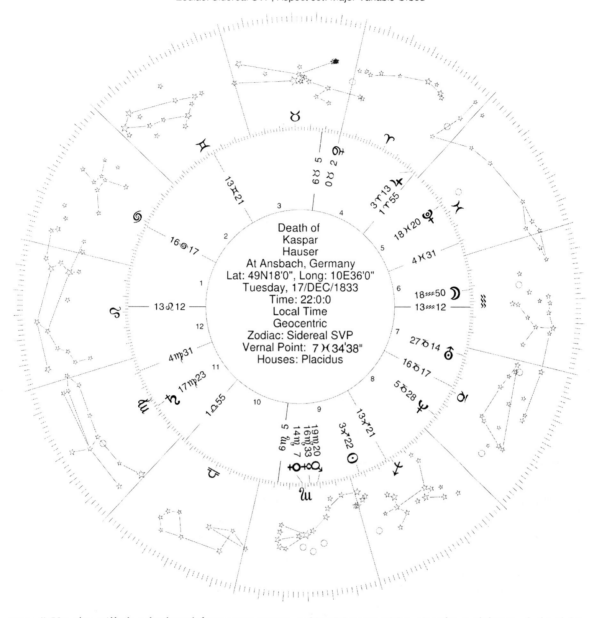

stronger." Yet, he still thanked and forgave every-one, including his murderer.

Delineation of his Horoscope[4]

For the time of 10:30, which I have not recti-fied, Neptune is in the 12th house. This can be a very difficult position, especially with Nep-tune square a Mars-Mercury conjunction above the horizon and square Pluto below the horizon.

Sun-Mercury-Mars in the 3rd house helped him to learn very quickly. He was endowed with an incredible memory for people and everything he observed. Venus in the 4th house gives social suc-cess. Venus square Uranus is an attractive indi-vidual because of his uniquenes. Jupiter and the Moon in the 5th house essentially put him on stage for everyone to see. He became known as "The Child of Europe." Pluto in the 9th house is a very good position for seeking the truth. Chiron

---

4   Jacques Dorsan. *The Clockwise House System.*

in the 10th house, which represents the home, robbed him of his mother and his longing for her lured him to a particular park in Ansbach, where instead of meeting his mother he was murdered. Chiron in the 10th house describes the problems he had in finding a good home. His incarceration in a darkened basement room can hardly be called a room. He sometimes lived with highly sympathetic people and other times with completely antipathetic people, like Teacher Meyer. Saturn in the 11th house warns that he should choose his friends very carefully. In fact, he had hardly any choice. Uranus in the 1st house grants a creative mind and a tendency to abandon the beaten path.

With his Sun in Virgo, he epitomised courtesy and tact. Virgos have excellent powers of observation and are strict followers of the law. In fact he eventually had a boring job working in a court. Mars in Leo protected his heart when the stab wound went through his chest (Cancer) into his liver (Jupiter) and because Jupiter is exalted in Cancer he survived three days.

Where can Kaspar Hauser be placed in relation to the life of Christ? Kaspar Hauser had some astrological connections to the Nathan Jesus in whom Christ incarnated at the Baptism in the Jordan.[5]

KASPAR HAUSER	NATHAN JESUS
Birth Heliocentric Neptune 20 Scorpio 35	Birth Geocentric Neptune 20 Scorpio 0
Birth Geocentric Mars 22 Leo 39	Death Heliocentric Uranus 22 Leo 45
Birth Heliocentric Saturn 15 Sagittarius 25	Death Heliocentric Pluto 15 Sagittarius 44
Birth Heliocentric Saturn 15 Sagittarius 25	Birth Sun 16 Sagittarius 4

It seems the most remarkable connection is the closeness of Neptune. In Orphic cosmology, as related by Robert Powell, ancient Uranus (Ouranos), ancient Neptune (Greek Nyx, Egyptian Nut, Novalis "Night") and ancient Pluto (Phanes) preceded ancient Saturn (Chronos).[6]

---

5   Robert Powell. *Chronicle of the Living Christ*.

6   In his book *Hermetic Astrology*, vol. 2, Robert Powell refers to W. K. C. Guthrie. *Orpheus and Greek Religion* (London, 1952) p. 290.

Kaspar Hauser was said by Rudolf Steiner to be a stray Atlantean,[7] an angelic being[8] who hardly touched solid earth. Neptune in the same position of Scorpio reminds us of a few periods of the fourth Atlantean epoch covering the Age of Scorpio and the Age of Libra when "the human shape gradually constructed itself out of the Bull (physical body) Lion (etheric body) and Scorpio-Eagle (astral body) nature into the full Aquarius Angel-Human form ['I']."[9]

When Adam and Eve underwent the Fall of Man, "certain of the life forces of Adam's etheric body were held back by the leadership of humankind and fostered in the great Mother-Lodge of humanity directed by the sublime Sun Initiate Manu" [Noah–Melchisedek–Titurel].[10] These life forces were in essence Adam's sister-soul, whose first earthly incarnation was the Nathan Jesus. The same soul spoke to Arjuna through the soul of his charioteer when he stood on the battlefield. He was none other than Krishna[11] who appeared in history at the conclusion of the Dvapara Yuga or Bronze Age, which ended in 3102 BC, just before the start of the Kali Yuga.[12]

Neptune returns to this position about every 165 years, and when it does it makes either one loop backward and forward or two loops so it can return to the same place either three or five times. It returned here in 988, and in 989 Vladimir, Prince of Kiev, was baptised and later brought Christianity to Russia. Bernard of Clairvaux, who inspired the Crusades, died on August 21, 1153, with Neptune in 20 Scorpio 0. Raphael Santi was born April 6, 1483, and heliocentric

---

7   Karl Heyer. *Kaspar Hauser und das Schicksal Mitteleuropas im 19 Jahrhundert* (Stuttgart: Kressbroun, 1958).

8   At the gathering of Christian Community Priests for the lecture course *The Book of Revelation: And the Work of the Priest*, though not printed in the text, Steiner stated that Kaspar Hauser was an angelic being.

9   Rudolf Steiner. *Egyptian Myths and Mysteries*, Sept. 10, 1908.

10   Rudolf Steiner. *According to Luke*, Sept. 18, 1909.

11   Rudolf Steiner. *The Bhagavad Gita and the West*, June 3, 1913.

12   Rudolf Steiner. *The Reappearance of Christ in the Etheric*, Jan. 25, 1910.

Neptune was in 20 Scorpio 43. Martin Luther was born November 10, 1483, and when he was probably conceived in February or March 1482, heliocentric Neptune was between 20 and 21 Scorpio. The sons of King Edward were murdered in the Tower of London in 1453, resulting in a change of dynasty in England to the Tudors, also with Neptune in this degree. At the most recent return, medical scientists succeeded in creating a test tube baby, named Louise Brown born July 25, 1978, at 23:47 in Oldham, Lancashire.[13] If we apply the hermetic rule, then it is possible to work out that she was conceived on November 10, 1977, 4:52 a.m., which agrees exactly with the date that her mother, Lesley Brown underwent the IVF procedure. Her epoch geocentric Neptune was 20 Scorpio 7.

Peter Tradowsky relates that Rudolf Steiner once said, "Next to Christian Rosenkreutz, Kaspar Hauser had the greatest feeling for the suffering of Christ."[14] In fact, "the individuality that hid behind the veil of Kaspar Hauser is a being which has worked inspiringly into the Rosicrucian connection from the very start."

John the Evangelist went through many incarnations. About AD 1250, there was an unusual connection between heaven and the earth. Even the most highly developed souls could not maintain a present connection to the spiritual worlds. They only had memories of what they had spiritually achieved in earlier times. A young child who was recognized to be a reincarnation of John was kept isolated from the world and surrounded by "a council of twelve individuals who possessed clairvoyant memory and intellectual wisdom."[15] They initiated the young child and the young child initiated the twelve. He died shortly thereafter and in his next incarnation became known as Christian Rosenkreutz.[16]

Kaspar Hauser was also isolated from the world but with hardly any human contact. Rudolf Steiner once stated: "If Kaspar Hauser had not lived and died as he did, then the contact between the earth and the heavenly world would have been completely severed."[17]

At the time of the French Revolution (late eighteenth century) Christian Rosenkreutz in his incarnation at that time was known as the Count of St. Germain. He died shortly after the Revolution and true to his mission, he was back in incarnation in the nineteenth century, and it would not be at all surprising if at least once Kaspar Hauser met him during the last few years of his life.

There is a remark made by Rudolf Steiner, according to Peter Tradowsky that "South Germany should have become the new Grail Castle of the new Knights of the Grail" in which Kaspar Hauser would have been the Grail King. Tradowsky goes on to say that "Kaspar Hauser would have implanted spiritual impulses into society to prevent the nineteenth century from sinking so deeply into materialism and to prepare for the epoch of light."[18] Like Kaspar Hauser, Julian the Apostate was assassinated by the thrust through the liver by a spear. According to Walter Johannes Stein, Julian was seeking a synthesis between Christianity and the ancient Mystery wisdom, which was to come about through the Grail Mysteries.[19]

My personal connection with Kaspar Hauser has arisen through living in a Camphill Community. The founder, Karl König once had a dream on the morning of Christmas Eve, in which he met some children and coworkers from the Camphill Rudolf Steiner School, who had recently died. At first he did not recognize them. They took him to a house in the forest, which one of them had built with a portrait of Kaspar Hauser on the wall and explained to him that they were forming a Brotherhood in the Land of Life and Truth. "Oh, prepare the Brotherhood, for now I know what you are doing. I cannot describe what I mean, but I feel deeply that you are creating a heart, a heart that

---

13 *Chronicle of the World* and the Internet for Louise's time of birth.

14 Karl Heyer. Ibid.

15 Peter Tradowsky. *Kaspar Hauser*, Appendix I.

16 This popular lecture has been published in a number of places: *Rosicrucian Christianity* (Sept. 27, 1911); *Esoteric Christianity and the Mission of Christian Rosenkreutz*; and *The Secret Stream*, chap. 7.

17 Karl Heyer. Ibid.

18 Peter Tradowsky. *Kaspar Hauser*, p. 83.

19 Walter Johannes Stein. *The Ninth Century*, chap. 5.

pours its strength into the valley through a tenfold coloured window. A heart that allows the blood of Life and Faith to flow from above to below, and from below to above."[20]

Children who are abducted, imprisoned and abused are all undergoing something like a Kaspar Hauser destiny just as much, perhaps even more so than children who are born with special needs or who become handicapped through a sudden accident or illness.

I once helped a friend of a friend to publish a collection of impressions and essays by Kaspar Hauser, as well as comments and notes by Georg Friedrich Daumer.[21]

Another of my friends mentioned a few points made by Paul M. Allen[22] in a talk on Kaspar Hauser. He had said that Kaspar Hauser was born on the day of Michael (September 29), which in Hebrew means "Who is Like God," and died on the day of Lazarus (December 17), which means "Whom God Loved"!

❦

---

20 Karl König. *A Christmas Story.*
21 Kaspar Houser, *Kaspar Hauser Speaks For Himself.*

22 Allmut ffrench, illustrated the cover illustration for the Andrea Damico book referred to in the preceding footnote. She told me a few points she remembered from a lecture given by Paul Marshall Allen on Kaspar Hauser. Paul Marshall Allen is famous for his books, *A Christian Rosenkreutz Anthology, Vladimir Soloviev: Russian Mystic* and others published by Garber (Blauvelt, NY). Lazarus is named on Kaspar Hauser's death date, December 17, in the facsimile edition of Rudolf Steiner's *Calendar of the Soul 1912–1913* (Great Barrington, MA: Steiner Books, 2003).

"A composer works on the basis of compositional theory, which is a sum of all that one needs to know before one can compose. In composing, the laws of composition serve life, serve reality. In just the same way, philosophy is an *art*. All real philosophers have been *artists in concepts*. For them, human ideas have become artistic materials and scientific methods have become artistic technique. Thereby, abstract thinking attains concrete, individual life. Ideas become powers of life. Then we not merely know *about* things, but have made knowing into a real, self-governing organism. Our active, real consciousness has lifted itself above mere passive reception of truths.

"How philosophy as an art relates to human *freedom*, what freedom is, and whether we do, or can, participate in it—this is the principal theme of my book. All other scientific discussions are included only because, in the end, they throw light on these (in my view) most immediate human questions. These pages are meant to offer *a philosophy of freedom*."

—RUDOLF STEINER (*Intuitive Thinking as a Spiritual Path*, pp. 256–257)

WORLD TRANSITS 2000–2020: AN OVERVIEW

Richard Tarnas

There are few frames of reference more illuminating of individual and collective archetypal dynamics and psychological conditions than an archetypally informed knowledge of current planetary positions. In the following pages I would like to set out an overview of the major world transits of the outer planets that I believe are most relevant for understanding our current historical moment. In particular, I want to review both the most significant longer-term planetary alignments leading up to this era and, more recent, those that have unfolded since *Cosmos and Psyche* was completed five years ago, in 2005. On that basis, we can deepen and extend that book's brief anticipatory analysis of the extraordinary convergence of planetary configurations of the 2008–2012 period. This article is therefore continuous with the chapter "Observations on Future Planetary Alignments," from the final section of *Cosmos and Psyche*.[1]

The Outer-Planet Conjunction Series: The Presence of the Past

If we can, for a moment, adjust our archetypal telescope and zoom out to a wide-angle historical perspective, we can see that our moment in history is taking place in the aftermath of three great conjunctions involving the three intersecting cycles of the outer planets Uranus, Neptune, and Pluto—the "ambassadors of the galaxy," as Dane Rudhyar evocatively described them. We are, of course, living in a time when new celestial bodies at the outskirts of our solar system are being discovered at a rapid pace, as are extrasolar planets in other systems. These discoveries and revisions are challenging long-established astronomical assumptions and transforming the old planetary classifications and definitions. As a new body of

evidence, they represent a peculiarly apt astronomical development for our postmodern age, with its pervading awareness of the complex multiplicity and fluid indeterminacy of reality and the radically interpretive, provisional nature of our knowledge. They are also making more permeable the boundary between our solar system and the encompassing galaxy. That being said, Uranus, Neptune, and Pluto are currently the only celestial bodies in our solar system discovered in the modern era for which we have virtually universal consensus in the contemporary astrological research community concerning their archetypal significance and, equally important, for which we have such an extensive body of historical and biographical correlations empirically supporting those archetypal identifications.

The three great outer-planet conjunctions that immediately preceded and, archetypally speaking, still permeate our age are the following:

Neptune–Pluto conjunction   1880–1905
Uranus–Pluto conjunction   1960–1972
Uranus–Neptune conjunction   1985–2001

Each of these periods set in motion tremendous cultural transformations that continue to inform and impel the current age, each doing so in ways that closely reflect the specific archetypal principles associated with the particular planets involved. The years given in each case reflect a 15° orb, which the body of evidence summarized in *Cosmos and Psyche* points to as the approximate archetypally operative orb for outer-planet axial world transits, that is, the conjunctions and oppositions.[2]

The first of these great conjunctions, the **Neptune–Pluto Ψ Ψ** conjunction of 1880–

1905, represented the completion of the 500-year Neptune–Pluto cycle that had begun at the turn of the fifteenth century and that saw the voyages of global discovery and conquest and the emergence of the modern era in the West—the Renaissance, the Reformation, the Copernican and Scientific Revolutions, the Enlightenment, the democratic and industrial revolutions, the European people's colonization of most of the world, the ascendancy of the West as a global power—and the emergence of what Morin and Kelly have called the Planetary Era: "a new era…that involved an unparalleled increase and stabilization of communication and exchange between inhabitants of all of the world's continents."[3] The 1880–1905 period of this most recent Neptune–Pluto conjunction that began the next 500-year cycle in the late nineteenth and early twentieth centuries, the well-named *fin de siècle*, ushered in that profound cultural and historical metamorphosis in the collective modern psyche— from Nietzsche's "death of God," the discovery of the unconscious, and the first world parliament of religions to the emergence of quantum-relativistic physics, the similarly radical transformation of the arts, and global multicultural demographic and social shifts—which began the historical process that ultimately "wiped away the horizon," to use Nietzsche's phrase, of Western civilization's metaphysical universe.[4] At a deep psychological level, one can recognize here the beginning of the descent of the modern Western ego that had first been constellated and then followed its solar trajectory over the preceding five centuries.[5] As with other Neptune–Pluto axial alignments that coincided with the often subterranean destruction and seeding of great cultural world views, as at the end of the Roman Empire and start of the Middle Ages, the period of this conjunction essentially brought into being the underlying matrix of a new cultural epoch: in this case, the radically more complex, relativistic, indeterminate, multicultural and multiperspectival postmodern age. (All this can be seen as having been given a kind of electrically charged surge in revolutionary impact and historical visibility when one takes into account the additional major world transit of

Uranus moving into opposition with both Pluto and Neptune at the turn of the twentieth century, which began during the later stages of this Neptune-Pluto conjunction.)

The second of the great outer-planet conjunctions immediately preceding our era, the **Uranus–Pluto ♅ ♇** conjunction of the 1960s and early 1970s, coincided with that volcanic eruption of revolutionary and emancipatory impulses, accelerated historical change, social and political turmoil, and heightened creativity and innovation in all spheres of human activity that has shaped the global zeitgeist ever since. Much like past axial alignments in the Uranus–Pluto cycle, such as the French Revolutionary epoch of 1787–1998, though in this most recent case with greater global extent and intensity, the 1960–1972 period brought an overwhelming and often violent collective drive to make the world radically new. The worldwide anti-colonial independence movements, the Chinese Cultural Revolution, the civil rights and black power movements in the U.S. and South Africa, the sexual revolution, feminism and the women's movement, the empowerment of youth and the counterculture, the student and antiwar movements, the gay liberation movement, the environmental movement, the space race and computer revolution, the global agricultural revolution, the widespread radically secularizing and liberalizing religious impulses, the psychedelic revolution, the creative revolutions in virtually all the arts and sciences, social mores, fashion, language: there was scarcely any field of human experience that did not undergo rapid and radical change during that era, a decisive shift that has continued to shape the subsequent decades up to the present moment.

Finally, the **Uranus–Neptune ♅ ♆** conjunction of the 1985–2001 period coincided with a different, generally more subtle though pervasive cultural shift, growing from the preceding transformations but adding its own particular character—the global dissolving of boundaries, "revolution by dissolution." This epochal change began at the geopolitical level with *glasnost*, *perestroika*, and the nonviolent revolutions that took down the Berlin Wall and ended the Cold War, and extended into the new millennium with the planet-wide transformation of human experience produced by the personal computer, digital, and Internet revolutions, with incalculable effects on global culture, commerce, politics, the arts, and social mores. To mention only a few of the major social and technological changes during these years that reflected the distinctive themes of the Uranus–Neptune complex: the rapid multiplication and interpenetration of information sources and communication media, the extreme acceleration of computer processing and of fiber-optic and satellite connectivity, the ubiquitous dissemination of mobile phones and email, search engines and social networks, downloads and DVDs, the enormous multiplication of cable television stations, the opening of radically new cosmic vistas and understandings through the Hubble telescope and its continuing flood of images, the advances in and proliferation of photographic manipulation and music sampling, the extreme rapidity of shifting images and narratives in television and film, and the 24/7 digital world that now permeates, mesmerizes, and interconnects the lives of millions as never before. So also the biotechnology and pharmacology revolutions, with the immensely complex ramifications these advances have produced in the environmental context as well as subjective human experience, health, and ethics, from the psychopharmacological medication of children, youths, and adults and performance-enhancing drugs for athletes and elders to new possibilities of genetic manipulation and cloning in plants and animals, including human subjects.

The late twentieth-century era of the Uranus-Neptune conjunction also saw the full emergence of postmodernity in the public consciousness, with the widespread dissolution of old epistemological certainties and cultural assumptions, and the increased fluid complexification of personal identity with a new sense of multiple realities, multiple selves, multiple religious and philosophical commitments, multiple online personas, and so forth. Public awareness of various esoteric, mystical, meditative, gnostic, mythic, archetypal, and imaginative discourses entered more pervasively into the collective psyche, disseminated by the popular media (for example, the Harry Potter series, *The Da Vinci Code*, *The Lord of the Rings* film trilogy) and widely viewed television programs (the Joseph Campbell interviews with Bill Moyers), as well as by scholarly writings, conferences, and academic programs. A common theme during this period was the growing recognition of an *anima mundi* and the soul dimension of human life, often connected with a new transpersonal consciousness of the collective human psyche and of a Gaian planetary being. Countless books, symposia, and workshops reflected a general impulse toward the spiritualization and re-enchantment of everyday life, of science, of nature and the cosmos. An intensification of diverse spiritual impulses and religious movements was evident throughout the world, ranging from rapidly spreading mass Pentecostal revivals, heightened Islamic religiosity, and widespread popular interest in Buddhist meditative disciplines to large-scale Ecstasy raves, phantasmagoric collective ritual festivals such as Burning Man, and the international spread of South American ayahuasca rituals. In general, the collective psyche during these decades was permeated with an unprecedented ambience of global multiculturalism, metaphysical pluralism and flexibility, the rise of holistic, participatory paradigms in many fields from physics and medicine to psychology and philosophy, and the spread of a greater empathic consciousness of global interconnectedness with the diversity of humanity and the entire Earth community.

◆ ◆ ◆

We can readily observe today how almost every significant trend set in motion during these three previous transformational epochs remains vividly alive and consequential in our own time. This cumulative presence of the past, with the influx and integration of successive archetypal wave forms entering collective human experience, is a continuing reminder to us that the conventional astrological tendency to analyze history or individual lives in more punctuated or atomistic terms, with exact planetary aspects seen as marking discrete periods of a particular character that begin and end in the manner of light switches being turned on and off, is profoundly inadequate. Alfred North Whitehead's process philosophy is perhaps the best theoretical frame of reference for understanding the ways in which each era, each event, and each individual represents a creative concrescence or composition of the entire past experience of the human community and of the cosmos into a new concrete particular actuality—which in turn becomes part of the continuing and ever-evolving basis for the next novel concrescence, as shaped and inflected by the next convergence of archetypal wave forms and complexes then being constellated. C. G. Jung's theory of the collective unconscious of course provides an initial psychological framework for better understanding these historical and cultural developments, especially when combined with Stanislav Grof's transpersonal psychology and its radically expanded cartography of the unconscious. Rupert Sheldrake's theory of morphic fields and Ervin Laszlo's theory of the A-field provide further helpful frameworks that draw on the natural sciences, while additional crucial insights are provided by Christopher Bache's theory of the species mind and Jorge Ferrer's theory of participatory enactment.[6]

As a simple thought experiment for discerning the cumulative presence of the past relative to the sequence of these three most recent outer-planet conjunctions, one merely has to consider a typical popular film of the past few years—filled with special effects and computer simulations, multiple and virtual realities, multiple and virtual identities, metaphysical indeterminacy, multicultural references and contexts, magical and mythical themes, the frequent rendering of non-ordinary states of consciousness and mystical and otherworldly realms, the general ethos of emancipation and transgressive excitement, freedom of sexual expression and language, sudden eruptions of violence and manifestations of the underworld, the ubiquitous role played by technical innovation and instant electronic communications and sources of information, the high value placed on rapidly shifting imagery and disjunctive montage, narrative unpredictability, and ambiguous, disruptive recontextualizing of plot and character—to recognize how much the cultural phenomena that specifically emerged during these preceding conjunctions (including the emergence of the powerful collective maya-creating film medium itself during the Neptune-Pluto conjunction of 1880–1905) permeate and constitute the present moment. A similar thought experiment can be conducted with regards to the daily life experience of anyone reading these words in 2010, how much each day's activities, communications, and states of consciousness have been shaped, at once liberated and colonized, by the personal computer, the Internet, and the mobile phone; how much the current ideas, ideals, and range of existential options have been informed by the cultural impulses and social movements of the 1960s; and how much the deeper metaphysical, psychological, scientific, artistic, technological, and geocultural substrate of our current moment dates to the turn of the twentieth century.

The Saturn Opposition Series: The Immediate Context

In the wake of these major cyclical beginnings and archetypal waves leading up to the turn of the millennium, the first decade of the twenty-first century has been marked by a rapid sequence of three consecutive Saturn opposition alignments to these same three planets:

Saturn opposite Pluto	2000–2004
Saturn opposite Neptune	2004–2008
Saturn opposite Uranus	2007–2012

Since the end of 2000 and especially from September 2001 to the present, there has been a sustained tangible intensification of Saturnian qualities in the global zeitgeist, a pervading atmosphere of gravity, adversity, stress and tension, crisis and conflict, conservative reaction, contraction and limitation, necessity and finality, the bottom line, deficit, depression, failure, the weighty consequences of error, conditions that press things to their conclusion and define them in their finitude. In each case, these underlying Saturnian motifs have been given both greater collective significance and specific qualitative inflections by the respective presence of each of the outer three planetary archetypes in sequence.

Thus we can discern during this decade certain common themes taking different forms, with Saturn—the principle of hard reality, challenge, and crisis—expressing itself at a heightened level more or less continuously but in different modes depending on which outer planet it then opposed: very generally, with Saturn–Pluto in 2000–2004, a sustained crisis of power and violence; with Saturn–Neptune in 2004–2008, a sustained crisis of vision and disillusionment; and with Saturn–Uranus in 2007–2012, a sustained crisis of change and destabilization. We might also recognize in each case the distinctive presence of the relevant elemental domains associated with the same three outer planetary archetypes—during Saturn–Pluto, crises involving fire (the fiery devastation of September 11 and the World Trade Center, the "shock and awe" invasion of Iraq, terrorist bombings throughout the world from Bali to Madrid); during Saturn–Neptune, crises involving water (the Asian tsunami, Hurricane Katrina and New Orleans, melting polar ice caps, rising sea levels, record floods and droughts, oceanic dead zones, sharply increased awareness of the emerging global water crisis); and during Saturn-Uranus, crises involving air, space, and electricity (the epidemic of major airliner, military jet, and helicopter accidents, space travel and satellite accidents, widespread telecommunication breakdowns, massive electrical outages and power plant explosions, the emergence of long-term electricity crises in many countries along with pressures to restructure electrical grids and transmissions on a global scale, mass lightning strikes like the enormous storm of simultaneous lightning strikes across California in June 2008 that caused over a thousand wildfires). Of course, these simple correlative patterns belie a much more richly multivalent expression of each archetypal complex. And here as well we can recognize how much the current global situation in 2010 is a direct outgrowth of the archetypally relevant events that took place during the first two of these three Saturn alignments, with Pluto and then with Neptune, just preceding the present time during the third of these alignments, Saturn with Uranus.

• • •

The widespread empowerment of conservative, reactionary, and repressive forces during the 2000–2004 **Saturn–Pluto ♄ ♇** period was central in defining the background of the current intensely conflictual zeitgeist and geopolitical atmosphere, beginning with the Bush–Cheney administration in the U.S. produced by the Supreme Court fiat in late 2000, the election of Vladimir Putin in the same year in Russia, and the role played by Osama bin Laden and Al-Qaeda in shaping events from 2001 on. The organized use of terror and violence by fundamentalist and reactionary forces on both sides of major conflicts throughout the world; the resulting collective trauma, devastation, and mass death; the scapegoating and vengeance, splitting and projections that rigidly divided the world into simplistic good versus evil categories; and the systematic use of torture, mass imprisonment, and extreme, often Orwellian policies in the name of national security—all constitute continuing legacies that directly or indirectly shape the present moment.

On the individual level, one merely has to consider what is taken for granted today as permanent standard, highly restrictive and time-consuming airport security measures when flying from any airport in the world to another, compared with air travel at any time in the twentieth century—that is, at any time prior to 2001 and the Saturn–Pluto opposition—to discern the continuing tangible presence of that powerful complex. Similarly, the enormous complex of secret national security operations in the U.S. initiated by the Bush–Cheney administration in the wake of 9/11, now involving more than 3,000 government organizations and private companies in 10,000 locations, continue to operate in 2010 undiminished and without oversight.[7] In terms of the duration of these alignments, the major wars and international conflicts which have so regularly begun in close coincidence with Saturn–Pluto quadrature aspects—World War I, World War II, the Cold War, the Arab–Israeli wars, the India–Pakistan conflict, the Vietnam War, the Iran–Iraq War, and most recently the wars in Afghanistan, Iraq, and the "War on Terror" itself—generally continue long after the initial coinciding alignment is over. So also the distinctive Saturn–Pluto theme of the "end of an era," the widespread sense that history has undergone a kind of traumatic contraction, an encounter with immensely grave events and mortal dangers that ended an age of relative security, innocence, or naïveté. During this 2000–2004 period an atmosphere of grim *realpolitik* in the face of ineluctable historical forces of conflict and peril established itself in a way that did not loosen its grip after the alignment ended.

Yet, balancing out the many shadow manifestations of the Saturn–Pluto complex were deep positive changes in the collective psyche: a more grounded and experienced realism in the face of an intensely challenging world, a decisive strengthening of focus on matters of depth and gravity, a maturation of sensibility from an earlier condition of relative self-indulgence, decadence, and inflation; existential courage and force of will in facing danger and death, moral courage and depth of insight in facing the shadow within one's own national psyche and behavior, or confronting the shadow within one's own religion or within the civilization as a whole; the widespread increase in awareness of human environmental devastation and the mass extinction of species; individual and collective determination to shoulder major historical tasks, undergo necessary hard labors, and forge enduring structures and foundations. In these positive respects and others, the consequences of the enormous influx of the Saturn-Pluto complex into history and the collective psyche during the 2000–2004 alignment have not ceased.

◆ ◆ ◆

The shift of archetypal emphasis from this period into the 2004–2008 **Saturn–Neptune ♄ Ψ** opposition was conspicuous from the moment Saturn first reached and stationed at 15° before exact alignment in November 2004. The Saturnian atmosphere of the decade continued but metamorphosed from the Plutonic intensities and concerns of the immediate post-9/11 years into a more diffuse and subtle, less tangible form, often more passive, and more concerned with matters of vision, hope, trust, deception, and illusion.

The widespread global reaction of incredulity and disillusionment in the wake of George W. Bush's reelection in the U.S. in that month, and the bitter disappointment and dazed depression that overcame approximately half of the American population, marked a clear beginning of the general mood of social malaise that pervaded the next several years. The following months brought the Asian tsunami with its tidal wave of tragedy and anguish, followed by Hurricane Katrina and the catastrophic flooding of New Orleans with a similar gestalt of death and loss through water, floating corpses and contaminated water, globally transmitted images of suffering, helplessness, spiritual anguish, and government paralysis—along with, in both cases, an outpouring of private compassion, aid, and charity for those in need—all highly characteristic expressions of the Saturn–Neptune complex.

The widespread crisis of public confidence and diffuse malaise in the U.S. that characterized these years was redolent of the public mood during the Carter administration when Saturn and Neptune were in square alignment during the 1978–1980 period—an historical precedent that was frequently alluded to during the second Bush term. Another diachronic pattern was visible with the characteristic sense of collective psychological and often physical exhaustion and debilitation, disillusionment, and low morale that accompanied these years of the Iraq War (2004–2008)—of being caught in a quagmire, with a seemingly never-ending sorrowful daily-news dirge of innocent lives lost, families devastated, soldiers physically maimed and psychologically traumatized, because of a wrongful war begun under false pretenses—all strikingly similar to the collective mood during the later years of the Vietnam War during the exactly preceding Saturn-Neptune opposition of 1970–1973, or that during the Korean War in 1951–1953 during the Saturn–Neptune conjunction before that, or in Europe during the later years of World War I in 1916–1919 during the Saturn-Neptune conjunction prior to that.

These diachronic patterns in history were matched by various synchronic manifestations of the same complex during this period, as a mood of profound public discontent and loss of faith in government, accompanied by a sense of collective detachment and skepticism with a generally passive collective response, was widely reported as permeating the social and political mood of many other nations as well, such as the United Kingdom, France, Germany, Italy, the Ukraine, Canada, Mexico, and India. A characteristic summation within the American context was David Brooks's December 1, 2005, *New York Times* article, "The Age of Skepticism," with its insightful discussion of the public mood of disillusionment, weariness, disbelief, cynicism, pessimism, and crisis of confidence.[8]

Another major cultural theme of the 2004–2008 period was the distinctive Saturn–Neptune polarization between religion and secularism—"faith-based and reality-based" cultural views, creationism and evolution, intensified fundamentalist belief and intensified rationalist skepticism (overlapping the division, in the American political context, between "red states" and "blue states," a major news topic during precisely these four years). Here the dialectic between the two archetypal principles can be seen in its characteristic multivalence: Saturn bringing rigidity, division, and conflict to the Neptunian dimension of vision, belief, and the metaphysical imagination; Saturn and Neptune combining on each side of the conflict to constellate conservative religiosity on the one hand and metaphysically constrained scientism on the other; and finally Saturn and Neptune sharply polarizing with one side of the conflict associated with characteristic expressions of Saturn and the other side with characteristic expressions of Neptune, with Saturn as concrete reality, empirical science, and skeptical judgment versus Neptune as spirituality, religion, metaphysical realities, and illusion, with each side viewing the other side as living in a delusional world of their own construction. A flood of influential and widely discussed critiques of religion emerged during the years of this transit: Richard Dawkins's *The God Delusion* (published in 2006), Daniel Dennett's *Breaking the Spell* (2006), Sam Harris's *Letter to a Christian Nation* (2006), Christopher Hitchens's *God Is Not Great: How Religion Poisons Everything* (2007), and Bill Maher's film *Religulous* (produced in 2007–2008). These works continued the Saturn-Neptune skeptical tradition of Hume, Darwin, Marx, Nietzsche, Freud, Weber, Bertrand Russell, Virginia Woolf, Foucault, and others.

The distinctive positive Saturn–Neptune motif of confronting illusion and unmasking deception was evidenced during the 2004–2008 period in the many news reports and the growing public recognition throughout the second Bush–Cheney administration in the U.S. and the Blair administration in the U.K. that the Iraq War had been started under false pretenses, with deliberate deception, disinformation, and distortion of the available data having been deployed to sway public opinion concerning "weapons of mass destruction" in the buildup to the premeditated war. Similarly typical of this complex was the widespread skepticism and public awareness of "credibility gaps" mediated by increased irony and satire in the public media, continuing the tradition of major satirical masters of the past born with Saturn-Neptune aspects like Jonathan Swift and Mark Twain. This was visible in the American context with the influential role played in public life by *The Daily Show* with Jon Stewart and the *Colbert Report* with Stephen Colbert. The basic impulse at work was to reveal the sharp contrast between image and reality, between the carefully constructed appearance, whether by political or corporate spin, and the darker actuality this appearance attempted to conceal. This trend reached a memorable climax with Stephen Colbert's illusion-shattering performance at the White House Correspondents' Dinner on April 29, 2006, in the presence of President Bush and over 2,500 journalists and government officials, and later viewed by millions of people via the Internet.[9]

Many other characteristic Saturn–Neptune themes, both negative and positive, were evident during this period (including the positive fact of disclosing and confronting the negative symptoms of the complex, as also happened during the Saturn–Pluto period just discussed), involving issues of truth and deception, drugs, water contamination, and pollution, viral epidemics and vaccines, widespread fear and anxiety often involving invisible or intangible threats, and so forth. Fraud and plagiarism in scientific research, journalism, and nonfiction publishing such as histories and memoirs were discovered and became major topics of public concern, as for example the case of James Frey, whose memoir *A Million Little Pieces* was exposed in January 2006 as fraudulent by *A Smoking Gun* and who was then confronted by his previous supporter Oprah Winfrey on her widely viewed program.[10] International anxieties were prominent concerning the avian flu epidemic, the contamination of various products from China such as infant milk formula and toys, and epidemics of food poisoning such as salmonella outbreaks. Similarly dominant topics of public concern were the methamphetamine and prescription drug abuse epidemics, the disclosure of negative side effects and deaths caused by widely prescribed drugs, fraudulent marketing by pharmaceutical companies, and numerous athletic drug scandals and the consequent tainting of athletic performances at the highest level such as the Olympics, the Tour de France, and American major league baseball, causing an unprecedented degree of public distrust in athletic achievement along with a sharp increase in drug testing and anti-doping initiatives. A study by the U.S. Substance Abuse Administration and Mental Health Services Administration and the Center for Disease Control found that between 2004 and 2008 there was a 111 percent increase in emergency room visits involving prescription drug abuse.[11] Here, too, can be mentioned the poisoning of political candidates and enemies both literally (presidential candidate in the Ukraine, Russian dissident in London) and by deceptive political advertisements (Swift Boat Veterans for Truth).

The intensified public awareness of increasing ocean pollution, widespread media attention to the dangerously high levels of air pollution in Beijing prior to and during the 2008 Olympics, and more generally the sharply increased awareness of the emerging global water crisis and unprecedentedly widespread shortages of clean water, is similarly reflective of the Saturn–Neptune complex. The international airport security prohibition of liquids as potentially dangerous weapons, instituted in the summer of 2006, reflects this same complex. So also the disclosure of and widespread negative public response to plastic-bottled water's misleading marketing and harmful environmental impact. Other typical Saturn–Neptune themes were visible in the many widely discussed books and articles on such topics as health and illness, hospitals and medical care, psychotherapy and psychopathology, euthanasia and hospice care, the rising prevalence, prevention, or treatment of depression, insomnia, chronic fatigue syndrome, suicide, psychological trauma in returning Iraq War veterans, Gulf War syndrome, and so forth.

In addition to the pragmatic and compassionate response to these and other such conditions, this period saw many of the major positive Saturn–Neptune themes we recognize in the biographies of those born with or undergoing transits involving this planetary combination: a strengthened collective impulse to confront without illusion the gap between the ideal and the actual, seeking to transform institutions and cultural practices to better reflect one's spiritual and moral aspirations, quiet and modest service and sacrifice on behalf of others and of higher ideals, the practice of engaged spirituality, a renewed affirmation of spiritual and religious traditions and practices that foster compassionate action in the world, and the undergoing of dark nights of the soul out of which is forged a more self-transcending spirituality and grounded commitment to the greater good. Here too could be mentioned the large number of books, films, and television and radio programs during this period devoted to the lives and contributions of individuals born with these planets in major aspect who exemplified many of the themes cited above (in America, for example, Robert Kennedy and Abraham Lincoln being especially conspicuous in both scholarship and the media at this time, and specifically with respect to their having undergone sustained psychological suffering and disillusionment that played a critical role in their subsequent service to history and embodiment of spiritual ideals).[12]

• • •

The last of the three consecutive Saturn oppositions to the outer planets during the first decade of the new millennium is **Saturn opposite Uranus ♄ ♅** from the fall of 2007 to the fall of 2011, with a final station just within the 15° orb in the summer of 2012. The distinctive themes of the Saturn–Uranus complex, especially in hard aspect, have been intensely, almost overwhelmingly prominent during what has so far elapsed of this period (I am writing in the spring and summer of 2010, about midway through the transit): sudden unexpected problematic events, crises and schisms, accidents and errors, structural breakdowns and collapses, crashes of stock markets and airliners, technological and electronic breakdowns, a pervasive atmosphere of crisis management and mindset of crisis prevention; and more generally, a taut conflict between the conservative and the liberal or progressive, the reactionary and the radical, authority and rebellion, stability and disruption, change and the resistance to change, freedom and repression, the old and the young, the status quo and the new, with highly polarized societies and politics, protests, strikes, crackdowns, and civil unrest. And this brings us to the T-square with Pluto.

The Saturn–Uranus–Pluto T-square of 2007–2012: The Convergence of Three Planetary Cycles

The extreme intensity of the various characteristic Saturn–Uranus phenomena during this particular alignment is undoubtedly connected to the fact that the current Saturn–Uranus opposition is taking place in a T-square alignment with Pluto, a more rare three-planet configuration whose historical correlations consistently involve events of markedly greater transformative, destabilizing, and often destructive power. This Saturn–Uranus alignment has coincided with the beginning of the longer Uranus–Pluto square which also began in 2007 (10° orb for the square) and which will extend until 2020; and also, in the shorter term, with the Saturn–Pluto square which began in the fall of 2008 and will last through most of 2011. The convergence of these three cycles in the 2007–2012 period represents the dominant archetypal

dynamic of the current moment. Because the longest lasting of these alignments is the Uranus–Pluto square, we will address its significance and correlations before we explore in more detail the Saturn–Uranus opposition, the Saturn–Pluto square, and finally the full T-square configuration.

Uranus square Pluto	2007–2020
Saturn opposite Uranus	2007–2012
Saturn square Pluto	2008–2011

• • •

The **Uranus–Pluto ♅ ♇** square of 2007–2020 is the first major hard-aspect or dynamic alignment of the Uranus–Pluto cycle since the conjunction of the 1960s. While this transit is still at an early stage, we can see already many of the most distinctive manifestations of the Uranus–Pluto archetypal complex in current events: the intense acceleration of the pace of change, the intensified cultural ferment, the increased social and political turmoil internationally, the empowerment of emancipatory and revolutionary movements, the political activation of youth, the empowerment of women, the empowerment of ethnic minorities, the radicalization of political movements and ideologies across the spectrum, the activation of a collective will to power in various forms, the new sexual revolution, the increase in "extreme" and "radical" impulses in various phenomena (from extreme sports and extreme oil drilling to radicalized political expresses itself in several different movements), the unleashing of the elemental forces of nature in various senses (the tangible increase in signs of extreme climate change, volcanoes and earthquakes, tornadoes and hurricanes, tsunamis and floods, undersea oil eruptions, mining disasters, the return of nuclear power and the heightened danger of proliferating nuclear weaponry); and sharply accelerated technological and scientific advance with major social and environmental repercussions.

All these phenomena reflect the mutual activation of the two relevant archetypes: first, Pluto→ Uranus, that is, Pluto acting on Uranus, with the Plutonic principle empowering, compelling, intensifying from the depths and on a mass scale the Promethean principle of change, liberation, rebellion, innovation, creativity, the sudden and unexpected, speed and instantaneity, technology and technological breakthrough, cultural paradigm shift; and conversely, Uranus→Pluto, Uranus acting on Pluto, with the Promethean principle awakening, liberating, in sudden, unexpected ways, often technologically mediated, the Plutonic–Dionysian principle of nature's depths, of elemental and evolutionary transformative energies both destructive and regenerative, the underworld of the instincts, the libido, the will to power, chaos, birth and death.

As is usual with the diachronic patterns of correlation observed for outer-planet cycles, most of the specific manifestations and trends already visible early in the current Uranus–Pluto alignment are closely connected, both in their shared archetypal qualities and in their historical development, to events of the 1960–1972 period during the last Uranus-Pluto conjunction. A paradigmatic example is the unprecedented historical phenomenon that took place in 2008 during the first U.S. presidential election to occur during this alignment, in which the two leading candidates during the election's primary season were a woman and an African American, Hillary Clinton and Barack Obama. The tremendous groundswell of popular support for these two candidates directly reflected the unprecedented advances made during the 1960s by the feminist and civil rights movements, two of the most significant social movements of that decade. The election of Obama in November 2008 was of course a profoundly revolutionary development, allowing the U.S. to in some sense reclaim its nobler inheritance of evolving freedom, and owed its reality to the struggles and achievements of the civil rights movement decades earlier. We can also see in this election another important motif of Uranus–Pluto periods and of the 1960s in particular, and this was the decisive political activation and empowerment of youth, who played a crucial role in Obama's election. (One can compare this with the relative quiescence of younger voters in every previous U.S. election since the elections of 1972 and 1968, during the last Uranus–Pluto conjunction, when young people were highly active in the campaigns

of Eugene McCarthy, Robert Kennedy, and George McGovern.) The situation in Iran in 2008–2010 illustrates the same dynamic in a very different context, with the sharply increased political activism on the streets of young people and particularly of young women, who played a leading and courageous role in massive protest demonstrations there.

Historically, during Uranus–Pluto alignments of past centuries, the French in Paris have tended to be at the forefront—and more specifically at the barricades—of revolutionary activity (1968, 1848, 1789, 1648). Remarkably, in the months after Uranus and Pluto had first moved within 12° of exact square alignment in 2005 during the opening penumbral period of the transit, there was indeed a sudden explosion of massive urban rioting throughout France by immigrant youths, with the burning of thousands of vehicles and attacks on police stations, violent disturbances that eventually spread to all the major urban areas of the country and caused the declaration of a national state of emergency. During the following spring in France large demonstrations by many left-wing and progressive organizations occurred in support of immigrant rights, while simultaneously in the U.S. there took place enormous Hispanic demonstrations across the country also on behalf of immigrant rights, some as large as the March on Washington in 1963, with many describing the phenomenon as "a new civil rights movement."

These events turned out to be early outliers of the global wave of political and social protest and turmoil that now characterizes the daily news reports from countries around the world, much as in the 1960s, as demonstrations, riots, strikes, and violent eruptions of mass protest have taken place and continue to do so in country after country, from Tibet, China, India, Burma, and Thailand to Iran, Kyrgyzstan, Kenya, and Greece. A far more turbulent atmosphere of widespread political unrest with strident demands for change and reform pervades the international landscape than existed a few years earlier. It brings to mind again the zeitgeist of the late 1960s reflected in the Rolling Stones' "Street-Fighting Man" of 1968:

Everywhere I hear the sound of marching charging feet, boy.
Cause summer's here and the time is right for fighting in the street, boy.

On a more elemental level, we can see the sudden eruption and awakening of the Plutonic underworld in the increase in global climatic disturbances, and in the extraordinary wave of catastrophic earthquakes (Haiti, Chile, Mexico, Japan, Tibet, Sichuan China), volcanoes (Iceland), monsoons (Pakistan), mudslides with mass fatalities (China), and unusually destructive hurricanes, tornadoes, and storms (Louisiana, Mississippi, Texas, Alabama, Oklahoma, Tennessee, Massachusetts), destructively rising sea levels and glacier melting, as well as the catastrophic deep-water oil-rig explosion with its long-unstoppable gushing of crude oil into the Gulf of Mexico. We can also recognize the theme of human-directed unleashing of the forces of nature in the sudden resurgence of the nuclear power industry, which had stopped expanding after its period of power plant proliferation during the conjunction of the 1960s and early 1970s, and also in the increasing spread and development of technologies utilizing other sources of energy such as wind, water, and solar.

We see, too, the resurgence of another diachronic Uranus-Pluto theme from previous alignments, the awakening of the voice of nature (Uranus→Pluto) through the ecology movement and heightened ecological activism (from Thoreau's writings during the 1845–56 Uranus–Pluto conjunction to the birth of the environmental movement during the following conjunction of 1960–1972 with Rachel Carson's *Silent Spring*, the passage of unprecedented environmental and endangered species legislation, the first Earth Day, and the rise of both deep ecology and radical ecology all during that period).

In yet another expression of Plutonic-Dionysian liberation, we can mention here the ongoing emergence of what has been called "the new sexual revolution," which is taking many forms including the rise of the hook-up culture among the young, "sexting," anonymous sex, the significantly earlier entrance into sexual activity by very young adolescents, Internet-facilitated sexual disinhibition, the rise of polyamory, and the significant increase in sexual activity among elders. In many of these phenomena, much as in the 1960s sexual revolution, there is a recursive mutual activation of the two planetary archetypes: on the one hand, the Promethean (and often technologically mediated) liberation of the Dionysian, awakening the libidinal forces of nature (Uranus→Pluto); and on the other, the Plutonic empowerment of the Promethean forces of change, youth, novelty and innovation, technology, rebellion, and emancipation (Pluto→Uranus), each vector catalyzing the other in a recursive loop.

While the current Uranus-Pluto alignment is the first major-aspect alignment to occur since the conjunction of the 1960s, it is the first square to occur since the 1930s (the square of 1928–1937 being the closing square of the cycle that ended with the 1960s' conjunction). The intrinsic nature of the square alignment seems to intensify a quality correlated with destabilizing stresses, jarring events, power struggles, and increased concretizing, crisis-producing tendencies. In this respect, the 2007–2020 period can be said to resemble a combination of the 1960s and the 1930s in the constellated archetypal energies involved, but in the ecological, cultural, and political context of the twenty-first century. Given the length of this transit and the historical record of previous correlations, we would seem to be looking at a period of more than a decade and a half of worldwide intensified emancipatory and transformative activity, sustained social and political ferment and turmoil, environmental upheaval, heightened cultural and technological innovation, accelerated social change, and so forth, through and beyond the year 2020. But in the shorter term, through 2012, all these phenomena are profoundly affected by the additional heightened presence of the Saturn principle in direct multivalent interaction with the Uranus-Pluto complex.

For example, in the American context, which continues to have such far-reaching effects on the rest of the world, the tremendous energies of change and reform that were so prominent and widely celebrated at the time of the election of

Barack Obama to the presidency were from the beginning sharply constrained by the intractable exigencies of the 2008–2009 financial collapse and deepening recession, the continuing reality of two wars, and the consequent lack of sufficient money or political resources to support the investments in energy, the environment, health care reform, education, and the overall revolution in values that Obama sought to enact. Similarly, there has been increased public interest in and planning of major new space exploration, in a diachronic reactivation of the great age of space exploration during the Uranus–Pluto conjunction of 1960–1972: new plans have been announced by NASA and the Obama administration for developing the rocket capability to bring astronauts to an asteroid by 2025 and then on to Mars a decade later. But the financial constraints of the present time limit the speed with which the plan can be implemented, and require the grounding of the space shuttle fleet, which have caused a firestorm of controversy. Similarly, the development of high-speed trains in the U.S., reflecting Uranus-Pluto's association with powerful technologies and extreme speed, is being delayed by financial obstacles as well as entrenched corporate and political resistance. The same dialectic between Uranus–Pluto on the one hand and Saturn on the other is currently visible in the increased drive in the gay liberation movement in support of same-sex marriage, and the increased resistance to this among more conservative and older Americans, with gains and setbacks happening almost simultaneously in the 2008–2010 period.

Especially reflective of the intensely activated Saturn principle is the extent to which virtually all of Obama's policy initiatives, despite his decisive election victory, have been stridently opposed and obstructed from the first month of his presidency by conservative and more extreme right-wing forces, as well as by forces of entrenched corporate and political power such as powerful lobbying groups, the insurance industry, the oil industry, the coal industry, the automobile industry, the banking industry, the Republican party, the Tea Party movement, Fox News commentators, and

such anti-democratic procedural traditions as the Senate filibuster rule which essentially permits an obstinate minority party to block the passage of all significant legislation. In its first two years the Obama administration has in many ways been in a state of "Prometheus Bound." This externally imposed political constraint has been enforced by the daily reality of the administration's being in a state of constant crisis management, obliged to deal as level-headedly as possible with one acutely critical situation after another—crises that were usually the consequence of decisions and actions that took place during previous administrations, and that are often overwhelmingly challenging, even intractable, and unpredictable in their outcome. Essentially the same dynamic exists in countries, communities, and individual lives throughout the world. And this brings us to the Saturn–Uranus opposition and the Saturn–Pluto square. [See "Note" on the following page.]

· · ·

To many of us observing current events and the long unfolding of human history, the great archetypal cycles of history appear to be embedded in and informed by an evolutionary dynamic and *telos*, one that I believe is visible in the evidence recounted above and, in a more substantial way, in *Cosmos and Psyche*.[13] The discoveries of Uranus, Neptune, and Pluto in the eighteenth, nineteenth, and twentieth centuries, and the emerging understanding of their profound archetypal significance and historical correlations, mirror this long, now accelerating evolutionary drama of humanity's awakening to new cosmic horizons and archetypal dimensions.[14] Transformative evolutionary forces are fully in play now, energies that we can participate in but that are far more powerful than we can control or predict. The past and the future seem to be converging in our time with extraordinary intensity. Clearly some form of creative intelligence informs the whole, yet just as clearly the human future is radically uncertain, contingent both on human choices and on larger forces beyond our power, beyond our awareness. An old age of the world is passing away, and a new one is struggling to be born.

NOTE: For the remainder of this article, see *Archai: The Journal of Archetypal Cosmology*, vol. 2 (fall 2010), pp. 167–212. The whole article can be downloaded as a PDF from http://www .archaijournal.org/currentissue.html.

NOTES

1. Richard Tarnas, *Cosmos and Psyche: Intimations of a New World View* (New York: Viking, 2006), pp. 465–483.

2. For axial alignments of the outer planets, a penumbral area between approximately 15° and 20° before and after exact alignment is also suggested by the evidence, reflecting the larger wave pattern of the corresponding archetypal complex as it is constellated in the collective psyche and reflected in relevant cultural and historical phenomena. See also Tarnas, *Cosmos and Psyche*, p. 148, reprinted below in Appendix I: Orbs for World Transits of the Outer Planets.

3. Sean Kelly, *Coming Home: The Birth and Transformation of the Planetary Era* (Great Barrington, MA: Lindisfarne Books, 2010), vii. See also Edgar Morin, *Homeland Earth: A Manifesto for a New Millennium*, tr. S. Kelly and R. Lapointe (Kreskill, NJ: Hampton Press, 1999), pp. 5 ff.

4. Friedrich Nietzsche, *The Gay Science* (1882), trans. Walter Kaufmann (New York: Random House, 1974), p. 181.

5. See Tarnas, *Cosmos and Psyche*, 43–45.

6. Stanislav Grof, *Psychology of the Future* (Albany, NY: State University of New York Press, 2001); Rupert Sheldrake, *The Presence of the Past* (New York: Crown, 1988); Ervin Laszlo, *Science and the Akashic Field* (Rochester, VT: Inner Traditions, 2004); Christopher Bache, *Dark Night, Early Dawn* (Albany, NY: State University of New York Press, 2000); Jorge Ferrer: *Re-Visioning Transpersonal Theory* (Albany, NY: State University of New York Press, 2001).

7. See Hendrik Hertzberg's summary in the *Washington Post's* three-part series "Top Secret America" (http://www.newyorker.com/talk/comment /2010/08/02/100802taco_talk_hertzberg).

8. David Brooks, "The Age of Skepticism," *New York Times* (http://select.nytimes.com/2005/12/01/opinion/01brooks.html), Dec. 1, 2005.

9. Stephen Colbert's performance, White House Correspondents' Dinner, April 29, 2006, recorded by C-SPAN. Colbert's speech was at its core a Saturn-Neptune phenomenon, both in its basic comic stance of ironic praise for Bush—pretending to be a right-wing commentator who saw Bush as his hero and agreed with the administration's philosophy—and in its direct confrontation of the Bush administration's spin and propaganda: that is, employing illusion to reveal a delusion. The speech was filled with Saturn–Neptune themes and metaphors: the president celebrated for never letting reality affect his views, "reality has a well-known liberal bias," the "No Fact Zone" philosophy; the Bush administration described as the sinking Titanic, with further metaphors like the half-empty glass with undrinkable water and global warming's melting glaciers; the press praised for not covering depressing reality of these years and urged instead to write a novel about a courageous reporter who stands up to the administration ("you know—fiction!"); narrow religiosity ("I believe there are infinite paths to accepting Jesus Christ as your personal savior"); and America in crisis after crisis rebounding to show it was capable of "the most powerfully staged photo ops in the world."

The Colbert performance, with President Bush visible sitting a few feet away, many hundreds of powerful Washington politicians and journalists in the audience, and many thousands of overjoyed Internet viewers in the days immediately afterward, was widely credited as having played a major role in the 2006 mid-term elections that took Congress from the Republicans. The New York Times columnist Frank Rich called the speech a "cultural primary," the "defining moment" of the election ("Throw the Truthiness Bums Out," *The New York Times*, Nov. 5, 2006), while journalist Dan Savage described it as "one of the things that kept people like me sane during the darkest days of the Bush years"—using characteristic Saturn–Neptune themes of darkness and sanity to make his point (interview, Oct. 21, 2009, *The Stranger*). The speech seemed to many to have been the first major instance in the public consciousness that someone had successfully penetrated the Bush administration's bubble of denial, delusion, and spin. Here we see the Saturn–Neptune complex on both sides of the gestalt—on the one hand, the rigidly defended state of deluded belief and propaganda, obsessively filtering out potentially intrusive information that might intrude on the idealized quasi-religious self-image in sharp contrast to the actual events and consequences visible to the rest of the world (Saturn's rigid boundaries deployed to protect the Neptunian delusion); and on the other hand, the sane, grounded Saturnian confrontation of hard reality and factual information against the Neptunian illusion and deception, bringing the critical eye for shadow, the ironic judgment that reveals the darker reality behind the superficial, deceptive image.

10. Characteristic of the public response, and of both the negative and positive aspects of the Saturn-Neptune era it occurred in, was the reaction of *New York Times* columnist Maureen Dowd, herself born with the Saturn-Neptune conjunction: "It was a huge relief, after our long national slide into untruth and no consequences, into Swift boating and swift bucks, into W.'s delusion and denial, to see the Empress of Empathy icily hold someone accountable for lying." "Oprah's Bunk Club," *The New York Times*, Jan. 28, 2006.

11. Julie Steenhuysen, "Pain Drugs Abuse Requires Urgent Action: CDC," *Reuters* (http://www.reuters.com/), June 17, 2010.

12. The 2004–2008 Saturn-Neptune opposition provides an interesting test case for the issue of world transit orbs. In mundane astrology, the general tendency has long been to assume a small orb for outer-planet alignments, no more than 5°, and to mainly emphasize the year or years that the alignment was exact. For example, the Uranus–Pluto conjunction was exact in 1965–1966, whereas it was within a 15° orb from 1960 to 1972. The historical record of the era of the 1960s and early 1970s suggests how inadequate such a narrow orb is for comprehending the archetypally relevant events. We can see this easily in retrospect, as with the many other waves of archetypally relevant synchronic events during other outer-planet alignments discussed in *Cosmos and Psyche*.

But the analysis of this Saturn-Neptune opposition of 2004–2008 that appears near the end of *Cosmos and Psyche*, which summarized the early correlations that had taken place as of that moment, was written in Jan. 2005, just two months after the alignment had first reached 15°, with three additional paragraphs written in the first week of Sept. 2005 when the manuscript was in final galleys, when the alignment had first

reached 10°. If one reads now that ten-page section of *Cosmos and Psyche* (pp. 469–478), it is clear in retrospect that most of the major Saturn-Neptune themes were already visible in the immediate aftermath of the first 15° station in Nov. 2004 with Bush's second election and the Asian tsunami in Dec. 2004, and of Hurricane Katrina in Aug.–Sept. 2005 just as the alignment reached 10°.

In essence, everything in *Cosmos and Psyche* concerning this Saturn-Neptune opposition was written about events that occurred before that opposition had even begun according to the conventional assumptions of mundane astrology, and a full year before it first reached exact alignment. I believe this wider 10°–15° orb for the outer-planet alignments reflects the nature of archetypal wave patterns emerging in the collective psyche—ebbing and flowing, cumulatively concrescing—rather than the more atomistic and punctuated activation assumed in much conventional astrological theory and practice.

For further detail on the Saturn-Neptune complex, see my two-part article "The Ideal and the Real" in volume 1 of *Archai: The Journal of Archetypal Cosmology* (pp. 137–158) and in vol. 2 of *Archai* (pp. 105–128).

13. This point has been brilliantly developed by Sean Kelly, in the final pages of his just published *Coming Home: The Birth and Transformation of the Planetary Era* (Great Barrington, MA: Lindisfarne Books, 2010), pp. 165–178.

14. See Dane Rudhyar, *The Sun Is Also a Star: The Galactic Dimension of Astrology* (New York: Dutton, 1975); and *Birth Patterns for a New Humanity* (1969), reissued online as *Astrological Timing: The Transition to the New Age* (2001) at http://www.khaldea.com/rudhyar/at/at_tcpv.shtml. Gerry Goddard further developed this perspective in his essay "Uranus, Neptune, Pluto: Our Contemporary Evolutionary Challenge," published online by *Centre Universitaire de Recherche en Astrologie* (http://cura.free.fr/xxv/25god2.html).

MY PATH TO ASTROSOPHY

An interview with Robert Schiappacasse
by David Tresemer and William Bento

Robert Schiappacasse has worked as an administrator of Waldorf schools for decades. He has also pursued an interest in the wisdom of the stars. In one job interview, when asked about his interest in astrology, he said, "Everyone has a hobby about which they're passionate. Astrology is my hobby." Here we see how that passion began. The interviewers (Q) were David Tresemer and William Bento.

Q: *Most people look at the ground or the desk in front of them. They look down. At some point, you chose to look up. How did that come about?*

RS: When I was nineteen, I met a man who was an astrologer who introduced me to the study of human destiny in his workshop in West Virginia. He introduced me to the science of destiny in a room filled with star charts, star globes, and astronomical paraphernalia. He connected for me, for the first time, the starry world and human destiny. He said, "Let's draw up your chart of birth." It must have taken an hour for the mathematical calculations for ascendant, house structure, planets.... At the end I turned to him and asked him, "But what does this all mean?" He looked at me and said, "I can't tell you that—you'll have to figure it out for yourself." My first contact with astrology was not someone telling me about my life. Rather, he told me astrology is a matter for study and self-knowledge. He suggested some books and wished me well. I had to become very active to understand this new language of the stars and human destiny

Q: *The catalyst of looking up turned you to look in.*

RS: Yes, I began to ask questions of myself and began an inward-looking reflective process that has accompanied me throughout my life. It would be many years before I could break through the veil of the astrology of our time, as found in ephemerides and books—and begin to pay attention to the actual starry heavens.

Q: *You mean the movement from tropical to sidereal astrology?*

RS: Yes. Tropical astrology was detached from the sky. You couldn't see Mars where the books told you Mars was. It was 25° different. It didn't seem necessary to look up. It was more necessary to do the math and generate the pictures—Mars in Leo [tropically calculated] for example, and what that meant.

Q: *How did you make that transition from tropical to sidereal?*

RS: I had been a student of astrology since that time in my late teens. I studied astrology through Dane Rudhyar, who was awakening astrologers to the humanistic basis of astrology, and especially through Marc Edmund Jones, both of them coming out of a theosophical orientation to astrology. They didn't have a relationship to the sidereal zodiac. So, I learned to read astrological charts based on the tropical zodiac. At that time, when I read a chart I tended to put less emphasis on the zodiacal location and more emphasis on the natal and transiting planets and their angular relationships, in relation to a person's biographical experiences, looking for the microcosmic and macrocosmic correspondences. It wasn't until I began reading Rudolf Steiner and studying with Willi Sucher that I began to think that the tropical zodiac wasn't the true zodiac. I met Robert Powell in the early 1980s and found out about the authentic equal division sidereal zodiac of the Babylonians from him. It took another eight years of study, research, and practice to be convinced that this was the authentic zodiac that had been lost. I had been reading charts based on the "tropical zodiac" for over twenty years. I had to summon up the courage to overcome my "habit body" and follow my insight, experience, and conviction. After reading hundreds of horoscopes based on the tropical zodiac, switching to the sidereal orientation was a major transition. One often reads charts for individuals who have a mental picture of themselves based on the tropical Sun sign at birth. An individual can become attached to seeing him- or herself as a Leo, when in fact the Sun at the person's birth stood in the starry constellation of Cancer, the Crab. I began to suggest a new way of exploring an individual's karma and destiny, which was counter to the prevailing astrological world. This was not always successful. Changing to sidereal meant standing apart from 99 percent of the astrological practitioners and letting go of the majority of the astrological literature I had studied and relied upon. Yet, I persevered because I found that the equal division sidereal constellations opened up a deeper insight into human destiny.

Q: You studied with Marc Edmund Jones and Dane Rudhyar. Who are the other teachers whom you met in astrology?

RS: The teacher who first changed my understanding of astrology was Willi Sucher.[1] I found out about Willi through meeting William Bento in Berkeley, California in 1975. William was the first person that I met who was reading the writings of Rudolf Steiner and Willi Sucher. I remember a conversation in 1976, when I was dissatisfied with the superficial nature of much of Western astrology, where William suggested reading Steiner and Sucher. Before long, I met Willi Sucher and experienced him speaking on the spiritual foundations of the zodiac and human destiny. He spoke a different

language from the leading astrologers I had met. His research came from a different source, Anthroposophy, which I had been reading intensively. Thereafter I began to study with Willi Sucher on a regular basis in Meadow Vista, California. He was the first person to introduce me to the (unequal) sidereal zodiac, as well as to the heliocentric view. I have also learned a great deal through friends who were astrologers who encountered Rudolf Steiner's cosmology and spiritual worldview. At that time in the late 1970s, I was in regular contact with William Bento on a variety of topics and research questions. I also met William Lonsdale at that time, who studied with Willi Sucher as well. I heard about Robert Powell through this circle and read the "Mercury Star Journal," which he edited. I first met Robert in 1982 when he came to California to spend time with Willi Sucher. I met Brian Gray at Rudolf Steiner College, where he was studying with René Querido and also teaching. Later in 1983, with Brian Gray, Willie Bento, and Leita McDowell, we formed an astrosophy research group called *Starfire*. Willi Sucher came to work with our group at an internal conference at Rudolf Steiner College that same year. We explored and discussed Steiner's cosmological writings, Willi Sucher's research, and studied typescripts of Elizabeth Vreede's letters, not yet available in book form. Out of this co-working the original Starfire group held a number of public conferences. We addressed contemporary star events, such as Halley's Comet, or the Harmonic Convergence, at Rudolf Steiner College and elsewhere, beginning in the mid-1980s. This association called Starfire, which expanded in the mid-90s to include David Tresemer and Robert Powell, was the beginning of a colleagueship that continues to provide a basis for profound study, conversation, research, and practice. In 1985, when I was studying at the Seminary of the Christian Community in Stuttgart, Germany I spent time with Robert Powell, who lived in Stuttgart and was working on his zodiacal research and the *Hermetic Astrology* series. I saw the final draft of *Hermetic Astrology,* volume 1 at that time when I happened to be living in a house with Peter Treadgold, with whom I also became acquainted.

---

1 Willi Sucher's biography can be found on-line at the site of the Astrosophy Research Center, http://astrosophycenter.com/inv/bio.htm.

Peter later created the *Astrofire* computer program, which makes it possible to calculate a sidereal chart easily in the geocentric and heliocentric perspectives. Robert Powell's *Hermetic Astrology,* volumes 1, 2, and 3, started coming out in 1987, with a focus on renewing astrology based on Rudolf Steiner's spiritual research. He articulates in this series the foundations of a new star wisdom beginning with its emergence in the Egyptian, Babylonian, and Greek cultures. These books explore new ground with research into the origin and efficacy of the sidereal zodiac, the heliocentrically based Tychonic, or Hermetic, chart as an image of the free potential of an individual, and the pre-natal or conception chart based on the hermetic rule. The third volume of *Hermetic Astrology—The Star of the Magi and the Life of Christ*—introduces the initial fruit of his dating of the life of Christ, providing the opportunity to contemplate His teaching, healing, and deeds in relationship to the constellations of the heavens. In all, the *Hermetic Astrology* series offers a sweeping overview of significant esoteric foundations of the arcane science in the light of Rudolf Steiner's spiritual research. I have learned a lot from Robert Powell. His *Hermetic Astrology* series and other books have had, and continue to have, a major impact on my grasp and practice of astrology.

Q: About the transition from the tropical to sidereal zodiac, it seems an important research project for you at that time was the nature of the 360° of the zodiac.

RS: I remember in the late 1970s drawing up with some friends almost a thousand nativities that Marc Edmund Jones had researched, and studying them in a variety of ways, but particularly via the *Sabian Symbols*, images he received for each degree of the zodiac, arrived at by working with the psychic, Elsie Wheeler. These characterizations for each degree of the zodiac were used to stimulate helpful interpretive insights. Working with the Sabian Symbols,[2] and knowing about Willi Sucher's

interest in finding the historical dates of Christ's life, William Bento and I became very interested in the possibilities for identifying images from the life of Christ for each degree of the zodiac. If the life of Christ could be accurately dated, the position of, for example, the Sun against the background of the zodiac could be seen in parallel to a historical, divine-human event for each degrees of the zodiac. An accurate dating of the life of Christ would provide secure and genuine images of each degree of the zodiac, based on the position of the Sun (and planets) in relationship to Christ's teaching and actions in the course of his life. This would be a powerful tool for self-development and for chart interpretation. This possibility was imagined based on Rudolf Steiner's statement that Christ Jesus always acted in harmony with the collective being of the starry worlds.[3] We imagined how insightful and helpful it would be to know where the Sun was when Christ performed a healing miracle, or the raising of Lazarus, for example. These historical events would give us secure imaginations—not luciferic fantasies—of the quality of each of the 360° of the zodiac, based on Christ's undeniable spiritual authority. We sensed that the dating of Christ's life and activity as a human being on earth could bring to light a transformed understanding of the twelve signs of the zodiac: a powerful renewed imagination of the ancient hermetic maxim, "As above, so below." In this regard, the question of the authentic zodiac was naturally very important. I first had the opportunity to talk to Robert Powell about his research on the sidereal zodiac, in contrast to the tropical zodiac—which he called the tropical "calendar"—when I was living in Stuttgart. At that time in 1985 there was not yet a prospect

---

2 The Sabian Symbols provide images for each degree of the zodiac and are used as an aid to the interpretation of a horoscope. http://www.sabian.org/sabian_symbols.php. Dane Rudhyar who helped to popularize the Sabian Symbols in his book titled *An Astrological Mandala: The Cycle of Transformations and Its 360*

Symbolic Phases, referred to the symbols as a contemporary American I CHING." http://www.sabian.org/sabian_symbols.php.

3 "In Palestine during the time that Jesus of Nazareth walked on earth as Jesus Christ –during the three years of his life, from his thirtieth to his thirty-third year— the entire being of the cosmic Christ stood always under the influence of the entire cosmos; he made no step without the collective being of the whole universe with whom the earth is in harmony, that all which Jesus Christ did took place." Rudolf Steiner, Spiritual Guidance of Man and Humanity, pg. 66.

of an accurate historical dating of the chronology of Christ's life. Willi Sucher had been trying to find correspondences through a Platonic imaginative approach—look at the life of Christ Jesus, and look in the heavens for significant gestures in the heavenly constellations that reflect these events, such as the healing miracles. Without a reliable dating, however, this approach could not provide the specificity of Christ events for each degree. In the early 1990s when I saw a draft of Robert's book, *Chronicle of the Living Christ*, I was extremely excited, as was Willie [Bento], that there might be a breakthrough in our lifetime that would allow us to study the life of Christ in relation to the planets and constellations in the starry heavens. The idea that occurred to us in the early '80s was beginning to crystallize in our midst as a genuine possibility. Great minds have busied themselves with dating the life of Christ. No less of a spirit than Johannes Kepler, the famous astronomer, published his research attempting to date the birth of Christ Jesus in the early 1600s. In Western culture, this question has been a great mystery seeking the light of day. When I read *Chronicle of the Living Christ*, and was able to investigate what Robert Powell had discovered, I felt that I was living in a significant time for the emergence and development of a Christ-centered star wisdom.

Q: How has that impacted upon your personal life?

RS: Recognizing the primacy of the sidereal zodiac, and having had the opportunity to study the life of Christ in relationship to the constellations in the heavens has deeply influenced the outer and inner course of my life. The shift from the tropical to sidereal perspective was for me the lifting of a veil. While growing to recognize the equal division sidereal zodiac, I gradually experienced a deep re-alignment of my biographical course. Rather than tropical Libra rising, indicating a destiny ruled by Venus, I learned that the star constellation of Mercury ruled Virgo influenced the ascendant of my birth chart. This manifested in my life through a mid-life career change where I transitioned out of work in the film industry to devote myself to the service of Waldorf schools. Shifting from the tropical to sidereal, I was able to "come to my senses"

in a way that also freed my imagination. Similarly, through studying the deeds of the divine human, Christ Jesus, in relationship to the constellations in the heavens throughout his life, new and deeper vistas open. Observing the rhythmic return of the Sun, Moon and planets to the location in the sky—where they were at the time Christ taught, healed, or acted—has opened up opportunities for contemplation of Christ's life within the course of my biography, stimulating helpful insight, practical counsel, and stimulus for action.

Q: Does the reading of another person's star configurations constrain them? Does it reduce their freedom?

RS: All of us who are students of Anthroposophy and astrology have to come to an understanding with respect to this question—that is, the nature and relationship of human destiny to our emerging capacity for freedom. Karma and destiny are a given, that provide the ground for our emerging free action. How can the starry script of the astrological chart be best brought to a human being so that it is a spur to reflection, self-knowledge, and free activity? It's all about the "how." If a person is told that such-and-such a thing will happen in her twenty-third year, such a statement could be a constraint on that person's freedom. On the other hand, to take an approach to counseling where one presents to another human being the pictures and imaginations that are there in the heavens at the time of their birth, or conception, and the time indications throughout the course of the life, is a powerful freeing opportunity—an opportunity to picture one's karmic foundations alongside the seeds of one's emergent spiritual autonomy. For example, I was looking at the chart of an individual who had the Sun at the 29th degree of the Virgin when she was born. Before I was able to describe to her what was pictured in her birth chart, she asked, "Robert, I have just one question for you: Will I be involved in the service of other people for the rest of my life?" I noticed that she had a medallion around her neck, an image of Mary–Sophia—a beautiful medallion given her by her mother. The 29th degree of the Virgin—the constellation of Mary–Sophia, known to the Egyptians as Isis–Sophia—is the zodiacal degree of the bright fixed star Spica. Based on a chronology of Christ from Robert Powell's research, this was the place of the Sun during the conversation between Jesus and the mother, before Jesus decided to undergo the Baptism in the Jordan, referred to in [Steiner's book] *The Fifth Gospel*. We learn in this depiction of the mother's remarkable gesture of silent and devoted listening to the struggles and challenges of Jesus as he wrestled with how humanity would find its way into the future over against the demonic forces that he experienced in religion and culture. It's a beautiful and profound story of Mary, her openness to the wisdom of the moment, fully engaged in loving service that is pictured cosmically when the Sun joined the fixed star Spica. With the Sun in this zodiacal position, we witness the archetype of loving service to another. Through this encounter, Jesus resolved to be baptized by John. The Christological background of this degree of the zodiac—where the Sun was at the moment of her birth—was a very powerful imagination for my friend to receive. It did not limit her freedom, but provided a remarkable confirmation of her deep impulse for service to others: service that she undertook with her family, her professional life, and her friends. It lifted the everyday view of her life experience to a powerful spiritual archetype that confirmed and ennobled what she was experiencing.

Q: How would you advise a novice in pursuing star wisdom?

RS: The foundations of a new Christ-centered star wisdom have emerged significantly over the past century, beginning with Rudolf Steiner's extraordinary teachings that reveal humanity's relationship to the stars. His extensive spiritual research describing the spiritual beings at work in stars and in the kingdoms of nature—along with his lectures on karma and reincarnation in relationship to the soul's journey through the heavenly worlds between death and rebirth—are largely available in English translation.[4] The astronomical letters of Elizabeth Vreede, who Rudolf Steiner selected

to collaborate with him in astrosophical research, recently became available through SteinerBooks and are an important continuation of Rudolf Seiner's impulse. The pioneering writings of Willi Sucher such as *Isis Sophia, an Outline of a New Star Wisdom*, provide a further important foundation. More recently, the research of Robert Powell, put forward in *Hermetic Astrology*, volumes 1 and 2, are a primary reference for a renewed astrology. His recent book with Kevin Dann, *The Astrological Revolution*, is an excellent summary of the core of Robert's contributions to a renewal of astrology. His *History of the Zodiac* goes into details concerning the recovery of the spiritual origins of the sidereal zodiac of the Babylonians. In addition, Robert Powell's books, *Chronicle of the Living Christ* and *Hermetic Astrology, Volume III: The Star of the Magi and the Life of Christ* bring the zodiac and the planets alive through the life of the divine man, Christ Jesus. These books enable us to see, for example, how the Sun, Mars, or Jupiter in a particular region of the zodiac manifest through the teaching, healing, and deeds of Christ.

Studying the landscape of the night sky is the first foundation for learning to read the starry script. I would especially encourage a student to become acquainted with the night sky throughout the course of the year, through regular observation and reflection. I would also add that when I encountered astrology in the early 1970s, the study of astrology didn't include a focus on one's own spiritual self-development. Self-education and self-development go hand in hand with any form of astrological research and practice. Hence, I would advise a student of new star wisdom to become acquainted not only with Rudolf Steiner's core spiritual research, his lectures on humanity's relationship to the cosmos, but also his indications for prayer and meditation.

Q: When you view a particular degree or particular planetary aspect, and you realize that Christ Jesus was involved in a particular kind of activity there, how do you take that into your own experience?

RS: The wish to take hold of these pictures from the life of Christ in relationship to the starry and

---

4   See William Bento's article in this edition of the *Journal for Star Wisdom*, "Ensouling Star Wisdom," for a list of key titles.

planetary world requires study, contemplation, and meditation. It's a matter of learning how to take the pictures in and make them come alive within oneself in a way that awakens the feeling life. One can then look at a birth or conception chart and explore the events from Christ's life that occurred in the degrees where planets are. Living with these pictures can be a tremendously uplifting source of help in the course of our lives, a profound source for discovering deeper levels of meaning in our own biographical experience. Suppose you were aware of the fact that one of the planets at the moment of your birth, perhaps the Sun, was at a place in the zodiac during the life of Christ, where, for example, the "Feeding of the Five Thousand" occurred—at 11° of the Waterman [Aquarius]. My approach is to enter as fully as possible into the details of the story, to imagine myself into the situation so that I have a felt-sense of the encounter with Christ. I have found that contemplating and meditating on a Christ event in this way, in relationship to a planet that is present in a zodiacal degree, can awaken biographical insight, gratitude, and a deep sense of wellbeing.

Q: You have spoken about Raphael and star wisdom on many occasions. What special importance does that hold for you?

RS: I am currently very interested in the life of Raphael as a great artistic light of the Renaissance, a historical period that Rudolf Steiner identified as the beginning of the cultural age of the consciousness soul. Raphael was a powerful originator of the modern aesthetic, our sense of beauty. Out of his soul's vision he was able to create beautiful paintings—paintings that are still considered to be the quintessence of beauty in Western culture and beyond. If you look at Raphael's birth chart, you will see that he has a Sun–Venus conjunction late in the constellation of the Fishes [Pisces]. So at his birth the Sun's vital life-giving power was united with Venus, the planet of grace and beauty. A modern scholar of the renaissance, Michele Prisco, wrote, "Raphael was so much the interpreter of an ideal of classical beauty, which passed into the taste of entire centuries of civilizations and merged with our ideal of beauty, that

we are almost unable to distinguish any longer between true beauty and the beauty of his art." Sun conjunct Venus in the Fishes (Pisces) at the moment of his birth confirms that it was Raphael's intention to originate a new aesthetic in his characterization of the human being. Knowing as we do that the individuality of Raphael was the reincarnation of the individuality that also appeared as John the Baptist—explored astrosophically and in terms of karmic biographies in Robert Powell's book *Elijah Come Again*—we can recognize that Raphael's creation of a new and deeper aesthetic has its origin in the light of the Christ impulse. Raphael said at one point, "The painter is obliged to portray things not as nature makes them but as she should have made them." The constellation of Pisces is the region of true humanism, where humanity may discover that it is evolving toward becoming the 10th hierarchy, in the footsteps of the angels. People on Raphael's canvasses appear as gods and goddesses walking the earth. It is as though his paintings effortlessly and enthusiastically proclaim the coming of a "divine humanism," out of a deep perception that human beings possess a spark of divinity. This is suggested by the art historian Michele Prisco when he wrote, "Raphael.... is the greatest venerator of the spirit and culture of Humanism..." In this sense, Raphael is a great forerunner of our age of individualism, confident in the divine spark in each individual, and an exemplar of cultural creativity that uplifts and inspires human beings to a deeper and fuller expression of selfhood.

William Bento: When the "Chronicle [of the Life of Christ]" came forward, it led to jubilation on the part of Robert and me. There was a resounding gift given to that work, which was the introduction to David Tresemer and the beginning of the work the three of us did together from 1996 on.

RS: I remember the three of us meeting in Boulder in 1996 just after Robert Powell's *Chronicle of the Living Christ* was published. I was becoming acquainted with David through weekly meetings and discussions. William was about to move to town. The recent publication of the *Chronicle* enthused us to explore the events of the 3½ years of Christ's ministry, which were living strongly in the etheric world during the last 3½ years of the twentieth century. We met weekly to share and contemplate pictures of the life of Christ being recapitulated at the end of the twentieth century. This work led to the publication of *Signs in the Heavens*, which explored two significant comets appearing in the sky at that time—Hyakutake and Hale-Bopp—and their meaning for humanity. I experienced great joy through our meetings and discoveries at that time. Later, as a result of our research and weekly conversations, David became interested in the qualities of each degree of the sidereal zodiac. Based on the dating of the life of Christ in Robert Powell's *Chronicle of the Living Christ,* he took up the task of formulating images of the degrees of the zodiac based on events in the life of Christ, and the corresponding position of the Sun in the sidereal zodiac. It is a substantial piece of work, still unpublished, called the *Solar Cross.* I was very fortunate to participate in the process as David explored and contemplated events from the life of Christ in relationship to the Sun's changing position in the constellations of the sidereal zodiac. David and I later worked together on the book, *Star Wisdom & Rudolf Steiner: A Life Seen through the Oracle of the Solar Cross,* where we applied these images from the Solar Cross to the life of Rudolf Steiner and others. This work is a significant flowering of the hope, the longing, and the imagination that William Bento and I had back in the early '80s through our association with Willi Sucher.

Q: Do you have a vision of where star wisdom needs to go to be more accessible or more effective as a pathway for the youth that have to live in these challenging times?

RS: Star wisdom lives in and through human beings who are devoted to deepening their understanding of it and sharing it. Over the years we've worked to make new star wisdom available to younger people as guidance for individual destiny, as well as insight into world history and contemporary culture. The Starfire group has worked through publications, conferences, workshops and classes, together and separately, to share these perspectives with a new generation. Still, the foundations of an anthroposophically based astrology, or hermetic astrology, are not well known or appreciated. How will we find those who are interested? Perhaps it will happen in the same way as my first encounter with the man in West Virginia who had studied the stars his whole life, who didn't know anything about the sidereal zodiac or about Rudolf Steiner, but was devotedly carrying his astrological studies and practice forward. Then he met me. How was he to know that I would spend the next forty years of my life striving to bring star wisdom alive in myself and to share it with other people? He couldn't have known that. I have the same hope—that study, research, and practice in the spirit of Astro-Sophia will speak in a living way to a younger generation who over time, will answer its call.

❦

"The mission to which his birth called him [the birth of the Old Testament patriarch Jacob] was revealed to him through the realm of the angels...conscious perception of the angels came to him.... The first stage...is attained when one enters conscious interaction with the beings of the angelic hierarchy.... [This] does not involve knowledge of universal laws, but entering conscious interaction with the beings who know the mysteries of birth. The true horoscope will not be reached by a path of calculation but through a path of interaction with suprasensory beings. What angels have imparted to humankind, that is the 'horoscope' in the true sense."
—Valentin Tomberg, *Christ and Sophia*, p. 47)

ANTHROPOSOPHIC FOUNDATIONS FOR A RENEWAL OF ASTROLOGY

Brian Gray

The author of this article—a student of Anthroposophy since 1976, and of astrology since 1966—teaches subjects related to Anthroposophy and star wisdom at Rudolf Steiner College. Rudolf Steiner spoke about the importance of finding new ways to work with the stars:

> It became clearer and clearer to me—as the outcome of many years of research—that in our epoch there is really something like a resurrection of the Astrology of the third epoch, but permeated now with the Christ Impulse. Today we must search among the stars in a way different from the old ways, but the stellar script must once more become something that speaks to us.[1]

Along with the sciences of *astrosophy* and *astronomy*, a renewed *astrology*—transformed by the light of Anthroposophy—is beginning to emerge to serve striving human beings in our time. More than ever, individuals search for meaningful relationships with each other and the Earth, the starry heavens, and the spiritual world. In addition to study, meditation, and biographical reflection, contemplating the birth chart can kindle deeper interest in the cosmic realities of the soul and spirit. Knowledge of the spiritual hierarchies and their relationship to human beings can awaken. Striving to understand our relationship to the cosmos and spiritual world can bridge the gulf between materialistic-determinist worldviews and the deeper science of "the wisdom of becoming human"—the profound worldview of Anthroposophy.

This article presents contemplations of the birth chart that emerge from studying the work

of Rudolf Steiner for over 35 years, and applying what has been learned from Anthroposophy to 45 years of astrological practice. The author owes a great deal to the work of others.

Gratitude for Pioneers in Developing New Star Wisdom

The author gratefully acknowledges the rich and diverse contributions to the development of star wisdom by pioneers and colleagues in astronomy, astrology, and astrosophy. Star wisdom is an evolving spiritual enterprise rooted in ancient mystery schools by great initiates. Zarathustra (later incarnated as Zoroaster), founder of the school of the Magi, is one of its greatest benefactors. The work of Hermes and his later disciples in Egypt and Greece blossomed in Hellenic Alexandria and India. Mystery schools prepared fertile ground for star wisdom, which continued with vitality right up to the time of Christ.

When the Christ event kindled the "I," new spiritual impulses were given to human beings and to the Earth. Initiates began to focus attention upon the moment of birth and the birth chart of individuals. Natal astrology was born in humanity with the coming of Christ. Star wisdom, and particularly natal astrology, is rooted in Christian esotericism. After the coming of Christ to Earth, astrology took a number of experimental turns. It continued to be developed in India and Arabia through the medieval period, while Europe went into its inward-turning spiral. Interest in astrology and star wisdom was reborn in European culture during the Renaissance. Johannes Kepler's work in astronomy was motivated by his desire to find the Star of the Magi. Kepler's discoveries, along with those of Copernicus, Tycho de Brahe, Giordano

---

1 Rudolf Steiner, *Christ and the Spiritual World—the Search for the Holy Grail,* lecture 5, January 1, 1914.

Bruno and Galileo, owe a great deal to the Christ event and evolution of "I" consciousness.

At the beginning of the twentieth century, Rudolf Steiner's profound studies in cosmology quickened interest in bringing star wisdom out of decline and decadence. A Sun initiate who brought the warmth and light of the Archangel Michael's cosmic intelligence into human culture, Rudolf Steiner's outpouring of books, lectures, articles and artistic activity constitutes his remarkable work, *Anthroposophy*. Rudolf Steiner found capable students of star wisdom in Elizabeth Vreede and Willi Sucher, who pioneered a new star wisdom based in Anthroposophy—*astrosophy*. Their insights and publications provide foundations for a new star wisdom.

Contemporary researchers in star wisdom based in Anthroposophy include my colleagues Robert Powell, William Bento, Robert Schiappacasse, and David Tresemer. Having collaborated with these gifted individuals for several decades, my work owes a great deal to them. Our gatherings feel overlighted and inspired by Astrosophia. Robert Powell, founder of the *Journal for Star Wisdom* and a prolific author, offers significant discoveries and contributions to renew and develop star wisdom and esoteric Christianity that will live on for centuries to come. William Bento's work in star wisdom and pyschology is blossoming, and his ongoing contributions and discoveries are very significant. Robert Schiappacasse and David Tresemer are brilliant researchers and innovators pursuing new approaches to star wisdom in relationship to the Christ events. David Tresemer is pioneering research through his work with the Solar Cross. Along with William Bento, Robert Schiappacasse, David Tresemer and Robert Powell are evolving various ways to work with birth charts and world affairs that can only be called *Christian Star Wisdom*. Claudia McClaren Lainson's profound commentaries in this Journal speak for themselves. This article strives to "renew" astrology out of Anthroposophy, and make it available to others. Part 1 elaborates the esoteric background of the birth chart; part 2 brings new insights about the astrological houses.

PART ONE:
CONTEMPLATING THE BIRTH CHART IN THE LIGHT OF ANTHROPOSOPHY

Is it valid to "read" a birth chart?

Working out of Anthroposophy and star wisdom leads one to ask: Is it valid to "read" a birth chart? Does a birth chart (a picture of the heavens at the exact moment of one's birth—sometimes called a "horoscope") hold any significance for a modern human being? Are the tools of astrology still useful, or are new understandings of the human being and different ways to contemplate the birth chart needed? Deep moral questions arise about reading birth charts:

1. Can a birth chart be "read" without interfering with the karma or freedom of an individual? (Brief answer: Yes, if one understands the real nature of karma and of individual human freedom, and works in the proper way out of this understanding.)

2. Can astrology call forth subtle egoism that retards one's spiritual development? (Brief answer: Very possibly, unless moral training and humility guide both astrologer and subject to seek proper spiritual balance. There are strong and subtle temptations—for both astrologer and subject—at work during a chart reading which should not be lightly dismissed.)

3. Is it possible to practice astrology without having developed Imagination, Inspiration and Intuitive levels of cognition? (Brief answer: Yes, but with reservations. As with striving pupils of any craft or profession, knowledgeable students of astrology can serve others while trying to develop their own higher faculties of cognition. Once again, egoism must continually be held in check and spiritual development actively pursued by the astrologer.)

4. Didn't the Christ event change the human being's relation to the stars, freeing human beings from fatalistic superstitions about "predicting the future with astrology"? (Brief answer: Yes, the Christ brought the

divine "I" from spiritual realms beyond the stars and kindled the "I" in every human being. A moral star wisdom recognizes and fully supports individual human freedom. Indications in the birth chart should never be "read" fatalistically or as given "facts." Love, creativity, and freedom from compulsion are attributable to the divine "I.")

Rightly understanding the pitfalls of decadent astrological practices and striving to avoid them, students of star wisdom can justifiably contemplate and "read" the birth chart out of their insights founded in Anthroposophy. Meditation, moral responsibility, discretion, compassion, humility, sincere interest in others, enthusiasm, patience, the ability to listen and communicate clearly, understanding of life experiences, and a broad sense of humor are necessary, as well.

Anthroposophy ("the wisdom of becoming human") offers profound insights—about the human being, the starry worlds, and the spiritual hierarchies—that today's astrologers desperately need in order to properly serve human beings. If astrologers are spiritually adrift, astrology becomes a pale ghost of its former glory and fails to meet the soul and spiritual needs of modern human beings. Astrology can be renewed—indeed, it must be renewed.

Anthroposophic Foundations for "Renewing" Astrology

Astrology begins to be renewed when astrologers encompass the rich spiritual insights of Anthroposophy and apply them to star wisdom. Astrology emerged from ancient mystery schools, but we no longer understand these mysteries. Today's astrology is shadowlike because only initiates can grasp astrology's esoteric origins. Anthroposophy provides foundations for new understanding of how the stars and spiritual beings are related to the human being, and the Christ impulse radiates new life, light, warmth and depth into astrology.

Below are some insights from Anthroposophy that shine light into astrology. These are certainly not "dogmas," but brief summaries of the living insights researched and beautifully elaborated by Rudolf Steiner in his writings and lectures on Anthroposophy.

- The human being consists of *body*, *soul*, and *spirit*. The human *body* is subject to the laws of *heredity*, the human *soul* is subject to the laws of *karma*, and the human *spirit* is subject to the laws of *reincarnation*.[2]

- The birth chart is an image of the heavenly garment imprinted into and "worn" by the human being from the moment of birth until the moment of death. Contemplating images of the birth chart can inspire insights into how the human spirit's prenatal intentions are interwoven with the soul and living body throughout life and expressed in human biography.

- The starry worlds we perceive with our senses are images of "heaven"—the spiritual world we inhabit between death and rebirth. Zodiac, stars, and planets reflect working realms of spiritual beings who shape the human being—as physical body (form), etheric body (life), and astral body (consciousness). These spiritual beings fashioned the human vessel up to the stage at which the divine-human self-conscious "I" (being) could be kindled on Earth.

- The kindling of the "I" in humanity was achieved by the Cosmic Christ, who united with all human beings and the Earth "at the turning-point of time."[3] The human being's relationship with the stars changed when Christ kindled the macrocosmic "I" in every human being.[4]

- Human beings develop the "I" through perceiving, thinking, feeling, and acting creatively on Earth. Our individual "I" expresses itself through attentive interest, focus, living thinking, discernment, devotion, compassion, self-sacrifice, love, intention, inventive creativity,

---

2 Rudolf Steiner, *Theosophy: An Introduction to the Suprasensory Knowledge of the World and the Destination of the Human Being*, Chapters 1 and 2.

3 Rudolf Steiner, *The Spiritual Hierarchies and the Physical World*; also, *Esoteric Science: An Outline*.

4 Rudolf Steiner, "Cosmic 'I' and Human 'I'" Munich, lecture of 9 January 1912, GA 130.

and steadfast will. The "I" experiences wonder, compassion, and conscience as it strives to deepen and freely unite with divine Will, becoming more truly human.

- An individual's task is to awaken to her/his prenatal intentions without compulsion, and to meet opportunities and challenges presented by life with equanimity, love, and initiative. The hierarchy of human beings strives to become Spirits of Freedom and Love.

- The birth chart does not *influence, compel, constrain,* or *define* the human being in any way. Rather, the individual human spirit chooses and freely "uses" the birth chart to meet life's challenges and opportunities, fulfilling its own intentions during life on Earth.[5]

- As "moral legacy" of one's previous incarnations, the birth chart is related to the death chart from one's former life on Earth.[6] Understanding the birth chart as "moral legacy" can gently help modern individuals remember their free intentions and awaken new, creative moral intuitions through contemplation, meditation and living thinking.

- Many correspondences can be found among one's biography, the stellar patterns formed between conception and birth, the birth chart, and movements of the planets following birth. These cosmic correspondences result from the lawful activity governed by the Sun Archangel Michael, who keeps human life on Earth attuned to cosmic rhythms in the starry heavens.[7]

What practical contributions does Anthroposophy offer to "renew" astrology? We discover new viewpoints about the birth chart, the conception chart, star events between conception and birth, and the death chart. Direct links and correspondences between these charts and events can be found with the charts from former incarnations, so that astrology becomes a science of reincarnation and karma.[8] Reading a birth chart with veneration can inspire both the subject and the astrologer, elevating spiritual awareness and offering insights about individual destiny and the timing of challenges and opportunities in life. New structural frameworks for understanding the birth chart arise through questioning and probing into astrology's traditions and practices, looking with fresh eyes from the rich perspectives of Anthroposophy. For this author, some practical results of such investigations include the following.

After using the "tropical zodiac" in my first 15 years of work in astrology, about 30 years ago I began to use the Babylonian sidereal zodiac. I highly recommend that tropical astrologers explore the Babylonian sidereal zodiac, as it incorporates deeper spiritual realities that cannot be fathomed with the tropical zodiac. Re-discovery of this authentic zodiac by astrologer Cyril Fagan 62 years ago—a zodiac of star constellations that one can see in the night sky, rather than that imperceptible abstraction, the "tropical zodiac"—is an invaluable contribution to renewing star wisdom. Robert Powell's research and publications confirms its significance.[9]

I have gained deeper appreciation for the roles played by the seven "visible" planets—their meanings and their ancient connections with the 12 signs of the zodiac. New insights have awakened concerning the living geometrical patterns of angular relationships between planets (astrological aspects) and their relationship with the human soul.

Most significantly, the "houses" of the birth chart have shifted, deepened and taken on new life and meaning for me. As we shall find in what follows, the astrological houses are most intimately related to the expression of our "I"— our *individuality.* The houses are also the most

5 Rudolf Steiner, *Spiritual Guidance of the Individual and Humanity,* chap. 3.

6 Rudolf Steiner, *Life Between Death and Rebirth,* lecture 5, Nov. 26, 1912.

7 Rudolf Steiner, *Anthroposophical Leading Thoughts,* "The Activity of Michael and the Future" Nov. 2, 1924.

8 Robert Powell and Kevin Dann, *The Astrological Revolution: Unveiling the Science of the Stars as a Science of Reincarnation and Karma.* Robert Powell, *Elijah Come Again.*

9 Cyril Fagan, *Zodiacs Old and New,* 1950; *Astrological Origins,* 1971. Robert Powell, *Hermetic Astrology,* vols. 1 and 2; *The History of the Zodiac; The Astrological Revolution.*

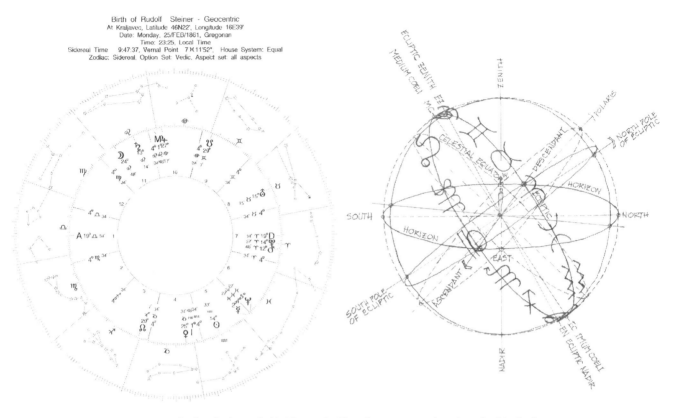

Figure 1. The birth chart (left); **Figure 2.** *Sky phenomena related to the birth chart*

deeply misunderstood and confusing framework in astrology, the topic of deepest disagreement among astrologers. Anthroposophy brings fresh viewpoints about the houses.

The architecture of the astrological "houses"—which organizes and structures the sacred "temple" of the birth chart—is presented in part 2 of this paper. Part 1 considers the birth chart as a whole, which places questions about the astrological houses into proper perspective.

The Birth Chart as Observable Earth/Sky Phenomena

What is a birth chart, and how is it related to the human being? The birth chart displays four basic phenomena. Understanding each of these phenomena is vitally important to renewing astrology:

1. the zodiac
2. the moving planets
3. the relationships between planets, termed "aspects"
4. the astrological houses, based on the relationship between the heavens and Earth

The geocentric birth chart is a picture of the Earth and sky seen by a viewer standing at the birthplace at the moment of birth. (See figures 1 and 2.) For consistency, most birth charts follow the convention of viewing the heavens as though the birth took place in the northern hemisphere, even if the birthplace is south of the equator.

A viewer is standing at the birthplace on the Earth's horizon in the center of the birth chart. Above the horizon (the upper half of the birth chart) span the visible arc of heavens; below the horizon (the lower half of the birth chart) the heavens are obscured by the plane of the Earth's horizon in the center of the birth chart. The viewer facing "southward" observes the spanning arc of the zodiac—thus we see the viewer's back. The eastern arc of the zodiac rises up above the horizon at the Ascendant (ASC) from the viewer's left, culminating southward above the viewer's head at the top of the birth chart and setting below the horizon to the viewer's right at the Descendant (DESC).

The zodiacal arc follows the plane of the *ecliptic*, the Sun's path over the course of the year. The ecliptic is the plane along which both Sun and Earth move. As the plane of the ecliptic is extended far outward beyond the Sun, it passes through the 12 constellations of the zodiac. All the planets move on orbital pathways lying fairly close to the ecliptic plane, the Sun's path through the zodiac as seen from Earth. The plane of the ecliptic is divided into 12 parts by the equal "signs" of the Babylonian sidereal zodiac, which form the outermost circle of the birth chart. The planets and all chart phenomena are displayed against the background of the zodiac.

Please note that *the plane of the birth chart is the circle of the zodiac.* This is too often forgotten.

The *horoscope* (*horoskopos*[10]) or *Ascendant* at the left side of the birth chart is the degree of the ecliptic rising along the plane of the eastern horizon. The Ascendant (also called the *horoscope* in this paper) is an extremely important point within the birth chart, and the exact time of birth is required to calculate this degree. For ancient astrologers, the most important point in the birth chart was the *horoscope* (Ascendant). Today, the entire birth chart is sometimes incorrectly referred to as the "horoscope." Opposite the Ascendant (*horoscope*) is the Descendant, the degree of the ecliptic setting along the western horizon at the right side of the chart.

Above the viewer's head, 90° between Ascendant and Descendant, is the Ecliptic Zenith (EZ)—the highest point on the zodiacal arc. Straight below the viewer's feet is the center of the Earth, and the plane passing through the center of the Earth

extends northward below the Earth's horizon to the Ecliptic Nadir (EN)—the lowest point on the zodiacal arc.[11]

It is helpful to sketch a viewer standing upright on the horizon in the center of the birth chart, particularly when "reading" the birth chart. We see the viewer's back, and map what the viewer sees onto the plane of the zodiac. *This is the "observable" birth chart.*

Some astrologers mistakenly think that the Earth is in the center of the birth chart. In reality, the *birth place on the horizon plane* is at the center of the chart—the place on the surface of the Earth where the child inhales its first breath and begins to incarnate. The Earth's center is at a right angle to the plane of the horizon, straight down below the viewer's feet toward the bottom of the chart. The upright viewer stands on the horizon bridging heaven and Earth.

A birth chart can be accurately "calculated" from the date, exact time and place of birth. This can be done even if no one viewed the sky at the birth moment, or if local viewing conditions at birth were poor. Most birth charts present the heavens as viewed from our Earth-centered (geocentric perspective). A birth chart can also present the view as it would be seen from the Sun (heliocentric perspective), or can combine views from both Earth and Sun (hermetic or tychonic perspectives). This paper will focus on the geocentric birth chart.

The birth chart as cosmic garment

The "observable birth chart" appears to be "outside" the human being. However, Rudolf Steiner describes the birth chart's *inner significance* for the human being in 1911:

> In a certain sense, we human beings are also cosmic beings. We live a dual life: a physical life in the physical body from birth until death, and a life in the spiritual worlds between death and rebirth. While we are incarnated

---

10 According to Cyril Fagan, "The Greek word *hora* meant not only 'hour' and 'season,' but also '*the degree of the zodiac ascending in a nativity.*' Hence, the Greek word *horoskopos* (horoscope) means literally 'an observation of the degree of the zodiac crossing the eastern horizon at any given moment.' In short, the words *Ascendant* and *Horoscope* are synonymous. Therefore, it is not possible to ascertain one's horoscope, unless the hour of birth to the nearest minute, as well as the date and place of birth, are known" (*Astrological Origins*, p. 168).

---

11 The author here uses the term *Ecliptic Zenith* (EZ) for what has been called the "nonagesimal," a vague designation for a point on the ecliptic 90° above the Ascendant. The author uses the term *Ecliptic Nadir* (EN) for greater clarity on the significance of this point.

in the physical body, we are dependent on the Earth...But once we have passed through the portal of death, we no longer belong to the forces of the Earth....

After death, we enter the realm of cosmic influences; for example, the planets affect us not only with gravity and other physical forces explained by physical astronomy but also with their spiritual forces. Indeed, we are connected with these cosmic spiritual forces after death, each of us in a particular way appropriate to our individuality. Just as a person born in Europe has a different relationship to temperature conditions and so on than a person born in Australia, so each of us similarly has a unique, individual relationship to the forces working on us during life after death. One person may have a closer relationship to the forces of Mars while another is more closely connected to those of Jupiter, and yet others may have a closer relationship to the forces of the entire galaxy, and so on. **These forces also lead us back to the earth to our new life. Thus, before our rebirth we are connected with the entire starry universe.**

The unique relationship of an individual to the cosmic system determines which forces lead her or him back to earth; they also determine to which **parents** and to which **locality** we are brought. The **impulse to incarnate in one place or another**, in this or that **family**, in this or that **nation**, at this or that **point in time**, is determined by the way the individual is integrated in the cosmos before birth.... [This description is significant when we address the "houses" in part 2.]

People who are knowledgeable about these things can "read" the forces that determine a person's path in her or his physical life; on this basis horoscopes are cast. Each of us is assigned a particular horoscope, in which the forces are revealed that have led us into this life. For example, if in a particular horoscope Mars is over Aries, this means that certain Aries forces cannot pass through Mars but are weakened instead.

Thus, **human beings on their way into physical existence can get their bearings through their horoscope.** Before ending this discussion...we should note that most of

what is presented today in this area is the purest dilettantism and pure superstition. As far as the world at large is concerned, the true science of these things has largely been lost. Therefore, the principles presented here should not be judged according to the claims of **modern astrology, which is highly questionable.**[12]

The active forces of the starry world push us into physical incarnation. Clairvoyant perception allows **us to see in a person's organization that she or he is indeed the result of the working together of such cosmic forces....** If we examined the structure of a person's brain clairvoyantly and could see that certain functions are located in certain places and give rise to certain processes, we would find that each person's brain is different. If we could take a picture of the entire brain with all its details visible, we would get a different picture for each person. **If we photographed a person's brain at the moment of birth and took a picture of the sky directly above her or his birthplace, the two pictures would be alike.** The stars in the photograph of the sky would be arranged in the same way as certain parts of the brain in the other picture. Thus, **our brain is really a picture of the heavens, and we each have a different picture depending on where and when we were born.** This indicates that we are born out of the entire universe....[13]

Allow me to use a comparison to make things clear. Imagine every person at birth as a spherical mirror reflecting everything around it. Were we to trace the outlines of the images in the mirror with a pencil, we could then take the mirror and carry the picture it represents with us wherever we went. Just so, **we carry a picture of the cosmos within us when we are born, and this one picture affects and influences us throughout our lives.**[14]

Rudolf Steiner's description here deepens our relationship to the birth chart. The birth chart is an image of the *spiritual "I"-organization*[15]

---

12 Rudolf Steiner, *Spiritual Guidance of the Individual and Humanity*, lecture 3, June 8, 1911, pp. 59–62.

13 Ibid., p. 62.

14 Ibid., p. 68.

15 See part 2 for a fuller description of the "I"-organi-

MEMBER OF THE FOURFOLD HUMAN BEING	FORMATIVE EXPRESSION	BIRTH CHART CORRESPONDENCE
Physical body	Echo of the zodiac (cosmic consonants)	Twelve sidereal constellations of the zodiac shaping twelve forms of the physical body in *space* and creating the twelve senses
Etheric body	Echo of the planetary movements (cosmic vowels)	Seven visible planets moving rhythmically in front of the zodiac through *time*; human life cycles as time-organism
Astral body	Experience of planetary movements (in thinking, feeling and willing)	Aspects between planets—geometric angles expressing dynamic inner relationships in human *consciousness*
"I," or Self	Perception of the echo of the zodiac	Twelve houses—earthly realms to unfold individual initiative through deeds on Earth, expressing individual human *being*

Table 1. *Correspondences between the Fourfold Human Being and the Birth Chart*

impressed into a person at the moment of birth, a spirit-soul organization that remains with the human being throughout life on Earth. As described, a "birth chart" is not a piece of paper, a display on a screen, nor what can be observed in the heavens. *The real "birth chart" is the image of an enduring cosmic garment (cosmic etheric body, astral body, "I"-organization and higher spiritual members) imprinted into and united with the human being's physical form and etheric body at the moment of the first breath.*[16]

Since the birth chart is a spiritual instrument through which the individual views the world between birth and death, it is *an image of the temple* for the human spirit, soul, and body. The architectural structure and organization of the birth chart as a *temple* is of key significance for each person. Patterns within the birth chart reveal dynamic interrelationships between the human spirit, soul, and body. Reading the birth chart properly from these viewpoints can help us understand expressions of the individual spirit working through a particular human personality, as well as the timing of events in one's biography, the nature of the *individuality's* karma, and her/his relationship with the cosmos and spiritual world—if we can lift ourselves into such understandings with the help of Anthroposophy.

The birth chart contains something of our cosmic *past*—karmic fruits of earlier incarnations, and results of our cosmic journey that followed our death from a previous life into birth for this incarnation. The birth chart is relevant to our earthly *present*—"this one picture affects and influences us throughout our lives." The birth chart also *sets the stage for—but never solely determines—our future.* The birth chart is used as an instrument by the human spirit seeking to express creativity, freedom, and love.

The Birth Chart and the Fourfold Nature of the Human Being

There is a remarkable relationship to be found between the fourfold nature of the human being and the four phenomena of the birth chart: zodiac, moving planets, aspects between planets, and astrological houses. Rudolf Steiner formulated the following in 1921.

It may be said that if a human being could look through herself/himself inwardly, she/ he would have to admit: I am an *etheric body*, in other words, I am the echo of cosmic vowels; I am a *physical body*, in other words, the echo of cosmic consonants. Because I stand here on the Earth, there sounds through my being an echo of all that is said by the signs of the Zodiac; and the life of this echo is my *physical body*. An echo is formed of all that is said by the planetary spheres and this echo is my *etheric body*.... [see table 1.]

---

zation.

16 See Rudolf Steiner, *Philosophy, Cosmology and Religion*, lecture 6, Sept. 11, 1922.

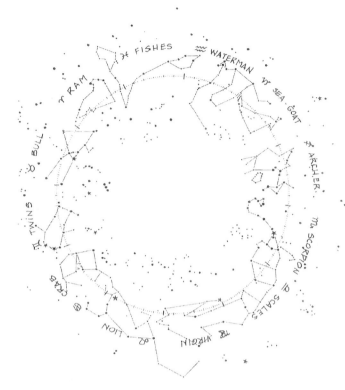

Figure 3. The Babylonian sidereal zodiac

If we want to speak in a real language, which can be learned from the mysteries of the cosmos, we would have to say: **The human being is constituted out of the echo of the heavens of the fixed stars, of the echo of the planetary movements, of what is experienced of the echo of the planetary movements, and of what knowingly experiences the echo of the fixed star heavens.** Then we would have expressed in real cosmic speech…we pass into concrete cosmic speech if we say: The human being consists of the echo of the Zodiac, of the echo of the planetary movements, of the experience of the impression of the planetary movements in thinking, feeling and willing, and in the perception of the echo of the Zodiac. The first is abstraction, the second reality.[17]

In table 1, we attempt to correlate Rudolf Steiner's cosmic picture of the four members of the human being with the four phenomena depicted in the birth chart mentioned above. These correspondences may seem surprising at first—particularly

that the "I" can be related to the twelve houses of the birth chart. The correspondences in table 1 bear careful consideration, as they provide secure foundations for understanding astrology and new ways to contemplate the deeper meanings within the birth chart from the insights of Anthroposophy.

We now briefly examine the correlations connecting the *physical body* to the zodiac, *the etheric body* to the moving planets, and the *astral body* to the dynamic angular aspects between the planets to complete part 1. Part 2 of this article addresses the question of the astrological houses and their mysterious relationship to the human "I" (the *individuality*).

Physical body: Echo of the zodiac

Esoteric tradition relates the 12 constellations of the zodiac to the human bodily form. (See table 2 and figure 3.) Rudolf Steiner states that members of the First Hierarchy—Seraphim, Cherubim, and Thrones—in service to the Father God, envision, create, and send forth forces to shape the 12 archetypal forms of the physical body. Members of the First Hierarchy—Seraphim (Spirits of Love), Cherubim (Spirits of the Harmonies), and Thrones (Spirits of Will)—establish and work from the *zodiac*. A group of Seraphim, Cherubim, and Thrones dwelling in the Ram provide formative forces to shape the human head, while other Seraphim, Cherubim and Thrones dwelling in the Bull send forces that fashion the throat and neck, and so on.[18] These same formative forces are available to human beings through the creative activity of speech. The zodiacal formative forces stemming from beings of the First Hierarchy are given expression through our human speech as *consonants*, which derive from the realms of the zodiac.

The human physical body was first created in a primal incarnation of our solar system called *Old Saturn*.[19] The physical body has *form*, and occupies *space*. Our physical body has been worked

17 Rudolf Steiner, "The Alphabet: An Expression of the Mystery of Man," Dornach, December 18, 1921.

18 Rudolf Steiner, *The Spiritual Hierarchies and the Physical World.*

19 Rudolf Steiner, *The Spiritual Hierarchies and the Physical World; An Outline of Esoteric Science; The Apocalypse of St. John, The Gospel of St. John;* and many other works.

SIGN OF ZODIAC [1]	PARTS OF HUMAN FORM [2]	SPIRITUAL HIERARCHY [3]	GESTURE [4]
Zodiac as whole sphere of 12 constellations	Entire human form of the physical body, with twelve senses	Father in the Heavens, working through the first hierarchy: Seraphim, Cherubim, Thrones	Human being in thinking, feeling, willing
♈ Ram Aries (*v, w*)	Upper head, upright posture	Lamb of God/ Logos/ Christ working through second hierarchy: Kyriotetes, Dynamis, Exusiai	The event
♉ Bull Taurus (*r*)	Throat, neck, mouth, ears, upward and forward orientation toward speech	Holy Spirit, working through the third hierarchy: Archai, Archangels and Angels	Limb system, will, deed
♊ Twins Gemini (*h*)	Symmetry of form allows body's equilibrium in space	Seraphim, Spirits of Love	Capacity for action
♋ Crab Cancer (*f*)	Rib cage, enclosing of interior organs with skin	Cherubim, Spirits of the Harmonies	Initiative
♌ Lion Leo (d, *t*)	Heart and lungs, dynamic enclosed organs of life	Thrones, Spirits of Will	Flaming enthusiasm
♍ Virgin Virgo (*b, p*)	Digestive system, interior organs of metabolism	Kyriotetes, Spirits of Wisdom	Soberness, inward turn
♎ Scales Libra (*ts*)	Pelvis, hips balance form between above and below	Dynamis, Spirits of Motion	Weighing the thought
♏ Eagle/Scorpion Scorpio (*s, z*)	Reproductive organs, sexual propagation of human form	Exusiai, Spirits of Form	Intellect, clear thought
♐ Archer Sagittarius (*g, k*)	Upper arms, thighs, largest bones and muscles	Archai, Spirits of Time and Personality	Resolve
♑ Sea-Goat Capricorn (*l*)	Elbows, knees, all joints in the body	Archangels, Spirits of Fire	Bring thoughts to the world
♒ Waterman Aquarius (*m*)	Forearms, lower legs, double bones of lower limbs	Angels, Sons of Life	Human being in balance
♓ Fishes Pisces (*n*)	Hands and feet, radiating bones connecting to Earth	Human Beings, Spirits of Freedom and Love	The event becomes destiny

Table 2. Physical Body: The Zodiac, parts of the Human Form, and the Spiritual Hierarchies

upon through four stages of cosmic evolution—Old Saturn, Old Sun, Old Moon, and present Earth. Since the spiritual *form* of the physical body has taken *matter* into itself, the body becomes both more complex and denser. During Earth evolution, our present physical body incorporates *fire*, *air*, *water*, and *earth*. It has become heavy and subject to forces of gravity. Earth is the densest planet in our solar system, and our dense human bodies are completely interwoven with the four kingdoms of nature—minerals, plants, animals, and human beings.

Our graceful *limbs* lift our bodies out of gravity into uprightness, allowing us to walk upright through *space*. Our radial limbs resemble the Earth's radius, in that our limbs stream out to connect center with the periphery. Our *chest* has arch-shaped ribs like the crescent Moon. Enclosing and protecting heart and lungs, our chest flexibly expands and contracts as we inhale and exhale rhythmically in *time*. Our *head* is like a sphere, similar to the dome of the heavens, resting high on its perch and passively observing the world through our nerve-sense activity, while most of the hard work is done within our chest and limbs. The rhythmic and circulatory systems are centered in the chest, while the metabolic system digests food and muscles move our limbs. Looked at artistically, the human body of 12 parts expresses itself in a threefold way: as *head*, *chest*, and *limbs*. The physical body is a beautifully crafted temple for the human being to dwell in, lovingly shaped by divine spiritual beings from the 12 realms of the zodiac.

In addition to the members of the First Hierarchy creating each realm of the zodiac, Rudolf Steiner describes how specific beings from each hierarchy work with particular strength from one or another zodiacal constellation. One can picture Seraphim, Cherubim and Thrones fashioning the zodiac of 12 heavenly "mansions," then offering each "sign of the zodiac" as a "home room" from which members of other spiritual hierarchies can also work upon the human being. The associations of certain hierarchies with specific "signs" of the zodiac provide keys for tracing Rudolf Steiner's descriptions of the sequential evolutionary stages through old Saturn, old Sun, old Moon, and the Earth.

Most of today's astrology knows nothing of these spiritual beings, their roles in shaping the temple of the human body, nor the contributions made from each realm of the zodiac toward human and cosmic evolution. Instead of considering the zodiac to be the working realm of mighty spiritual beings who form the beautiful temple of the human body, today's astrologer is more likely to associate "Leo" with personality traits of human arrogance and pride, or "Libra" with vacillating and wavering indecisiveness, and so on. It is tragic that abstract, superficial personality traits have displaced all esoteric astrological understanding of the lofty zodiacal spiritual beings who give human beings our form. Ancient star wisdom has certainly fallen into decadence in modern times. No wonder Rudolf Steiner said in 1911 that contemporary astrology is "purest dilettantism and pure superstition…highly questionable."

The human form is a temple *made in the image of the gods* (Gen. 1:26–27). The physical body is a glorious work of art, carefully fashioned over many stages of cosmic evolution as a microcosm reflecting the macrocosmic zodiac and the spiritual beings dwelling there. We shall further consider the human form as we consider other aspects of the fourfold human being.

Which Is the "Correct" Zodiac to Use with Birth Charts?

Now the zodiac question arises: Which zodiac should one use for birth charts? The "tropical zodiac" based on the solar calendar of equinoxes and solstices? The "astronomical" maps that divide the ecliptic into star constellations of unequal sizes? Or the "Babylonian sidereal" zodiac of twelve equal star constellations, measured from the "Bull's eye" (the bright star Aldebaran) located exactly in the middle of Taurus, the Bull? Let me share some of my experiences.

When the author began studying Western astrology forty-five years ago, the "tropical zodiac" was the standard framework for learning about the birth chart. My astrological study from books was very abstract, requiring calculation from ephemerides and tables of houses but no direct observing of the night sky. City lights or overcast skies limited opportunities for stargazing until I moved to California in 1979. In 1980, my friend Friedemann Schwarzkopf first showed me the stars of the zodiac in the night sky. I then gratefully witnessed the three beautiful Jupiter–Saturn conjunctions of 1980-81. While the "tropical ephemeris" listed these conjunctions in the tropical sign of Libra, in the night sky Jupiter and Saturn slowly and majestically moved back and forth in front of the stars of the Virgin. No longer could I defend my ignorance about the night sky, nor justify using the "tropical zodiac" without investigating the sidereal (star) zodiac more carefully and giving it a "chance" in my considerations of astrology.

So, one summer 30 years ago I carefully and accurately mapped each star of the zodiac onto radial graph paper during the day. At all hours of night, I observed the stars. Were the zodiacal constellations distinctive? Did they easily divide into 12 equal signs, or vary in size? I was not sure how the entire zodiac revealed its star forms. Observing the night sky and all its wonders, and mapping the zodiac star by star, reassured me that my quest was not in vain.

Viewers of the night sky are always rewarded with beautiful insights. For the first time, I could actually *see* the Lion, the Scorpion, the Archer, the Goat, with my own eyes! I "saw" no tropical signs of the zodiac in the heavens. The "tropical zodiac" is a calculated abstraction, with no identifying stars in the night sky. But the sidereal (*sidereal = star*) zodiac presents beautiful star patterns that can be seen, mapped, named, and recognized as familiar friends. The zodiac modestly revealed its forms. I carefully drew my own "zodiac map" (see figure 3) and in doing so gradually came to embrace the equal 30-degree divisions of the Babylonian sidereal as "authentic." Centered on the "Bull's eye," Aldebaran, as the midpoint of Taurus, the 12 equal constellations of the Babylonian zodiac are ordered into a beautiful, comprehensible unity.

For the past 30 years, the truth and authenticity of the Babylonian sidereal zodiac has never failed me. I highly recommend it for all work with birth charts and research into star wisdom. The work of Cyril Fagan[20] is revelatory, and Robert Powell's[21] numerous articles and publications on the origin and validity of the Babylonian sidereal zodiac, particularly its reliable consistency for reincarnation research, are tremendously helpful in clearing up the confusion between the "tropical calendar" and the "sidereal zodiac." A "tropical" astrologer may have to surrender some dearly held concepts and associations and be open to embrace the deeper spiritual realities of the "sidereal" zodiac, but what is gained thereby is of inestimable value.

Etheric body:
Echo of the movements of the planets

The etheric body is a tremendous mystery to us, since we can't directly perceive it with our senses but only notice its working effects. The etheric body (life body, body of formative forces) is only perceptible to spiritual sight. The etheric body animates, sustains, and maintains the physical body throughout our lives. Here Rudolf Steiner describes the etheric body:

> Now the etheric body does not consist of the same forms as those that make up the physical body.... For what is this etheric body? It is the vehicle of the forces of growth; it contains within it all those forces bound up with the processes of nourishment, and also those forces connected with the power of memory. The inner nature of the human being, in so far as this is expressed in the etheric body, is impressed into the air when we speak. When we put sounds together, words arise. When we put together the whole alphabet from beginning to end, there arises a very complicated *word*. This word contains every possibility of word-formation. It also contains at the same time the human being in his etheric nature. Before the human being appeared on the Earth as a physical being he already existed as an etheric being. For the etheric human being underlies the physical human being. How then may the etheric human being be described? The etheric human being is the Word that contains within it the entire alphabet.

> Thus when we are able to speak of the formation of this primeval Word, which existed from the beginning before physical human came into being, we find that what arises in connection with speech may indeed be called a birth—a birth of the whole etheric human being when the alphabet is spoken aloud.[22]

The human etheric body—which was added to the physical body during the Old Sun evolution—is the dynamic, formative activity bearing the power of the primeval Word. This etheric activity permeates the human being's seven vital organs, seven inner movements, seven life processes and the seven *vowels* in speech. The human body *lives* through the etheric body's vital activity.

The macrocosmic expression of etheric formative forces can be seen in the dynamic patterns being formed as each of the seven visible planets move through space over time, as viewed from the Earth. The Greek-derived word "planets" actually means "wanderers," or "wandering stars,"

---

20 Cyril Fagan, *Zodiacs Old and New; Astrological Origins.*

21 Robert Powell, *Hermetic Astrology,* vols. 1 and 2; *The History of the Zodiac; The Astrological Revolution.*

22 Rudolf Steiner, *Eurythmy as Visible Speech,* lecture 1, June 24, 1924.

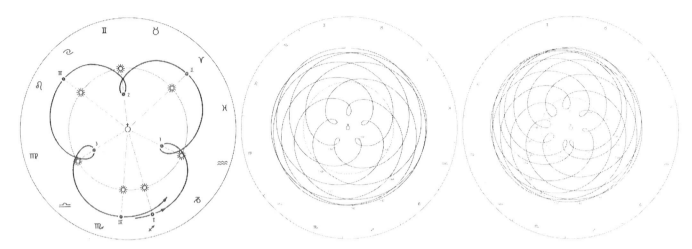

Figure 4. Etheric Body: Geocentric patterns of Mercury-Sun, Venus-Sun, and Mars-Sun

as opposed to the "fixed stars" of the zodiac and such star constellations as Orion or the Great Bear. Since Sun and Moon also "move" against the fixed star background of the zodiac as viewed from the Earth, they too can be considered as "planets."

We are used to seeing planets as objects moving slowly through space. However, if we imagine watching the planets from far above the Earth, each planet's movements create remarkable formative patterns. These geocentric planetary patterns arise when we imagine the Earth as our stable viewing point and watch each planet's movements around the moving Sun. (See figure 4 and table 3.) The movements of the planets take place in dynamic recurring cycles of time and form distinct patterns. When we observe the moving planets through their recurring cycles of time within, we find these planetary movements to be *rhythmic*. Joachim Schultz expresses this in his classic astronomical work, *Movements and Rhythms of the Stars*:

> The rhythms [of the planetary movements], appearing through the interplay of time and space, are the ordering, formative principle of all spatial and temporal cycles.[23]

The geocentric formative patterns formed by the movements of three visible planets with the Sun are illustrated in figure 4. In each of these figures,

the Earth is placed at the center of the form. The Sun appears to move in a circular orbit around the Earth, and each planet forms a distinctive pattern as it orbits the Sun and Earth over time. Mercury's pattern is formed by the six conjunctions Mercury makes with the Sun in the course of 348 days. Venus makes its beautiful pattern of five superior conjunctions (beyond the Sun) and five inferior conjunctions (between the Sun and Earth) in the course of eight years. Mars makes the more erratic dynamic pattern of eight conjunctions with the Sun and eight oppositions with the Sun over the course of 17 years.

Just as these dynamic macrocosmic etheric forms are made by the moving planets, we can imagine the formative power of these planets moving within the microcosm of our etheric body. Our etheric body permeates our vital organs and unfolds its activity over cycles of our life. There is a great deal to be discovered about the rhythmic movements of planets in human life cycles. Human biography tends to unfold in rhythms of seven-year cycles. Rudolf Steiner describes the significance of Saturn's orbit in relation to four seven-year cycles:

> As may be read in the little book, *Education of the Child*, epochs can be distinguished in the life of the individual: from birth to the change of teeth, from then to puberty, then the years up to 21 and again from 21 to 28, i.e. seven-year periods clearly different in character and

23 Joachim Schultz, *Movements and Rhythms of the Stars*, p. 16.

PLANET, VOWEL,[1] CYCLE OF LIFE	SIDEREAL PERIOD/ SYNODIC PERIOD	MOVEMENT[2]	LIFE PROCESS[3]	VITAL ORGAN
Saturn (*u*) 56–63 years	29.5 years/378 days (1 yr 13 days)	Movement into upright posture	Breathing	Spleen
Jupiter (*o*) 49–56 years	11.86 years/399 days (1 yr 33 days)	Movement of thinking	Warming	Liver
Mars (*e*) 42–49 years	2.14 years/780 days (2 yr 49 days)	Movement of speaking	Nourishing	Gall bladder
Sun (*au*) 21–42 years	365.25 days (1 yr)	Movement of the blood	Circulating	Heart
Venus (*a*) 14–21 years	584 days (1yr 219 days)	Movement of the glands	Growing and maturing	Kidneys
Mercury (*i*) 7–14 years	116 days	Movement of the breath	Maintaining	Lungs
Moon (*ei*) Birth–7 years	27.3 days/29.53 days	Movement of reproduction	Reproducing	Brain, sexual organs

Table 3. Etheric Body: The seven visible planets, seven vowels, seven human life cycles, periods of revolution, seven movements, seven life processes and seven vital organs.

after which new kinds of faculties are present. If we know how to investigate these things we shall find clear evidence of a rhythmic stream in human life that can be found again in the starry heavens. Strikingly enough, if life is observed from this point of view—but such observation must be calm and balanced, without the fanaticism of the opposition—it will be found that round about the twenty-eighth year something in the life of soul indicates, in many cases, a culmination of what has come into being after four periods of seven years each. Four times seven years, 28 years, although the figure is not absolutely exact, this is the approximate time of one revolution of Saturn.[24]

Elsewhere, Rudolf Steiner describes the experiences of an esoteric pupil who is able to perceive the weaving forces in her or his own etheric body:

The pupil comes to understand that she or he has grown out of our planetary system, and that the planets as physical celestial bodies are governed by planetary spirits, and that the human being is only able to lift the body into uprightness because the spirit of Saturn is at work within.... The pupil knows that all these spirits work with and through one another.

They have their main seat, their active base, in the human being, and one kind of movement works on another.... In the allocation of signs to the various elements we are already touching *the fundamental principle of all genuine astrology*...which has its source in nothing else than in the great and significant fact that *the human being is born out of the cosmos, that the human being is an essence, an extract of the whole cosmos.*[25]

Looking once again at the patterns in figure 4, an ordering, formative activity moves each of the planets through space in rhythmic pulses of time.[26] This formative activity in the heavens is the invisible macrocosmic "etheric" organism of our solar system, whose microcosmic counterpart is our human etheric body. Just as the formative forces move the seven planets through *space* in rhythms of *time*, the human etheric body expresses rhythmic life processes of activity within our vital organs unfolding over time. The *life* within our seven vital organs is the microcosmic etheric counterpart to the cosmic etheric forces moving the seven visible planets through space.

24 Rudolf Steiner, *Prophecy: Its Nature and Meaning,* Nov. 9, 1911.

25 Rudolf Steiner, *Man In the Light of Occultism, Theosophy and Philosophy,* June 7 & 11, 1912.

26 Adapted from Joachim Schultz, *Movements and Rhythms of the Stars,* pp. 141, 121, 173.

PLANET, CHAKRA [1]	SPIRITUAL HIERARCHY PLANETARY SPHERE [2]	SPIRITUAL INDIVIDUALITIES [3]	HUMAN SOUL TYPE [4]	HUMAN SOUL GESTURE [5]
Saturn 1,000-petalled lotus crown chakra	Thrones, Spirits of Will	Memory-bearers of cosmic system, devoted to the past	Self-conscious	Deep inward contemplation, conscience
Jupiter 2-petalled lotus brow chakra	Kyriotetes, Spirits of Wisdom	Expansive thinkers, benefactors of wisdom in the present	Dominant	Activity arising out of wisdom
Mars 16-petalled lotus throat chakra	Dynamis, Spirits of Movement	Persuasive talkers, orators, agitators in the cosmic system	Aggressive, assertive	Aggressive element, initiative
Sun 12-petalled lotus heart chakra	Exusiai, Spirits of Form	Transformers of destiny and freedom in warmth and light	Radiant	Human being harmonizing all soul qualities
Venus 10-petalled lotus solar plexus	Archai, Spirits of Time	Virginal lovers of Earth, reflector of secrets in dreams	Aesthetic	Loving sacrifice
Mercury 6-petalled lotus second chakra	Archangels, Spirits of Fire	Active combinative thinkers, capacity for intellect	Agile, Mobile	Self-expression, egoism
Moon 4-petalled lotus base chakra	Angels, Sons of Life	Ancient teachers of mysteries, hereditary reproductive forces	Romantic	Capacity for creation

Table 4. Astral Body: The seven visible planets, seven chakras, spiritual hierarchies in planetary spheres, seven spiritual individualites, soul types, and soul gestures

Table 3 displays some relationships between the moving planets and the etheric body. The human etheric body lives in rhythmic movements penetrating and animating our physical bodies with vitality through seven distinct life processes. We only notice the *effects* of our etheric body by observing certain life processes that recur rhythmically, such as our heartbeat and breathing. Within the human organism there is a normal "rhythm" of one breath (inhalation/exhalation) to four pulses of our heart. This rhythm provides the basis for our musical sensibilities. We perceive cosmic rhythms—the cycle of day and night, the waxing and waning Moon over 29½ days, the four seasons within the greater cycle of the year. Just as our human bodies are permeated with cooperative life processes that sustain our bodily existence, planet Earth, our solar system and galaxy all cooperate as a macrocosmic living organism through the ordering formative principles governed and regulated by spiritual beings.

We compare "rhythmic cycles" of patterned movements to a stable benchmark. For general stargazing, the diurnal *clockwise* movements of the celestial sphere and slowly shifting planets inform the unfolding of day and night. In natal astrology, however, the stable reference point is the moment of birth and the "birth chart" configuration—the planets and zodiac standing above the place of birth when the child inhales its first breath. With its first breath, the child "inhales" the astral body and "I" into the etheric and physical bodies and is imprinted by the stars.

The macrocosmic "I" and astral body begin to incarnate into the microcosmic etheric and physical body at the moment of birth. The position of stars and planets in the birth chart serve as the stable "benchmark" for measuring the phases of our life. A "birthday" celebrates the Sun's movement through the zodiac and rhythmic return to the same position where it was at the moment of one's birth. This annual motion is *counterclockwise*, progressing from the Crab to the Lion to the

PLANETS	FORMS	ANGULAR DIVISIONS IN DEGREES	QUALITIES OF THE ASPECTS	COLORS OF ASPECTS
Mars–Sun, Moon–Sun	8-sided double square, single square	90° square 135° sesquisquare 180° opposition	Mars-like; aggressive, conflicting, talkative, persuasive, insistent, stimulates waking-up	Red
Venus–Sun	5-pointed star	72° quintile 144° biquintile	Venus-like; loving sacrifice, aesthetic sensitivity, dreamy, gifted, idealistic	Green
Mercury–Sun, Jupiter–Uranus	6-pointed star	0° conjunction 30° semi-sextile 60° sextile 120° trine	Mercurial, Jupiterian, Uranian; creative thinking, inventive, stirs clear communcation	Blue
Sun as coordinator of 6 visible planets	7-pointed star	51.4° septile 102.8° bi-septile 154.2° tri-septile	Solar; initially challenging, stimulates inventiveness, creative originality	Purple

Table 5. *Astral Body: Planetary Aspects as Experience of the Movements of the Planets*

Virgin and so on through the 12 constellations of the zodiac. Both the *clockwise* diurnal motions, and the slower but distinctive *counterclockwise* moving of planets through all 12 constellations of the zodiac over cycles of time, are very important to understand and to distinguish. We will return to these different phenomena when discussing the astrological houses in part 2 of this paper.

Through this discussion, we find that the human etheric body is an extract of the cosmic movements of the planets. The etheric body achieves its vital activities within the human being without our conscious participation. So far as human consciousness extends, the human being is *sleeping* in the etheric body. How are these movements in the etheric body related to our *waking* experiences of them, which require the activity of the astral body?

Astral Body: Experiences of the Planetary Movements in Thinking, Feeling, and Willing

During the old Moon stage of cosmic evolution, the human "astral body" was added to the physical and etheric bodies. The "old Moon" separated from a central Sun, which shone upon it from "outside," giving the basis for an "inside—outside" polarity in *consciousness* to appear.

Since the human astral body still provides "inner experiences" that reflect events happening "outside" the human being, the astral body extends waking consciousness into the "outer" world while also opening up our own private "inner world." When we go to sleep, our astral body and "I" loosen their connections with the physical body and etheric body. At night, the astral body partially expands into the astral world, whose physical reflections we see in the "stars." The sleeping human being loses awareness of the sense world and of the inner sensations, feelings, passions and desires that occur when awake. When the astral body re-connects to the etheric and physical bodies, we "wake up" into a world of sensations provided through the 12 senses of the physical body. Sensations, feelings, and desires live in the "inner" astral body of the human being. The astral body is thus the body of "consciousness." Our astral body provides inner experiences by reflecting the world that would otherwise seem to remain outside the human being. The astral body's inner activity begins with sensation, and also inner experiences of feelings of pleasure and pain, longings such as hunger and thirst, desires and passions. Rudolf Steiner describes the astral body in this way:

> On awakening, the human being's conscious powers well up from the unconsciousness of sleep as if from mysteries and hidden springs. It is the *same* consciousness which sinks into dark depths when the human being falls asleep, and then arises again when she or he awakens. To the science of the suprasensory, what rouses

life again and again from the unconscious state is the third member of the human being. It may be called the Astral Body.[27]

A higher ordering principle shapes and works within the astral body, just as higher formative powers work through and shape the etheric body and physical body. This higher ordering principle creates seven astral organs of perception within the astral body, although they are only partially formed in undeveloped human beings. Rudolf Steiner describes exercises in concentration, contemplation and meditation to properly form these organs in *How to Know Higher Worlds*. These seven organs of perception are sometimes called "chakras" or lotus flowers, which are microcosmic expressions of the movements of the seven visible planets. The seven chakras are organs of perception that provide insights into the inner nature of reality (see table 4).

Just as each of the seven visible planets has its own *form* (physical body) and *patterns of movement* (etheric body), each planet is a complex expression of the *consciousness* of various spiritual beings who dwell in the planetary spheres and give each planet its own character and expression in the "astral" world. Each planet radiates diverse characteristics that are reflected in the human astral body as our inner capacities of thinking, feeling, and willing. These are experienced in our inner sensations, feelings, passions, and desires. Table 4 displays several characteristics of the human astral body in relation to the seven visible planets, the spiritual hierarchy operating within the surrounding planetary sphere, the spiritual individualities of each of the seven visible planets, the seven human soul gestures, and the seven human soul types personified within the human astral body.

Rudolf Steiner states that the human astral body is our *experience of the planetary movements in thinking, feeling, and willing*. How do we inwardly experience the planetary movements?

---

27 Rudolf Steiner, *An Outline of Esoteric Science*, chapter 2.

Astral Body: Aspects between Planets in the Birth Chart

This riddle can be solved by noticing that our experience of planetary movements is heightened when two planets form certain angular spatial relationships with each other. For instance, a conjunction of the Sun and Moon (New Moon) or an opposition of Sun and Moon (Full Moon) are vivid events that we experience. We notice the first quarter Moon and third quarter Moon—when exactly one-half the Moon's disc is brightly lit, and the other half of the Moon's disc is dark. These four events of relational movement between Sun and Moon—conjunction (0°), waxing square (90°), opposition (180°), and waning square (270° or 90°)—form *outer impressions* that affect our *inner experiences* within our astral body.

Our *experience of the planetary movements* happens when planets form particular angular relationships with one another, as viewed from the Earth. These angular relationships between planets are called *aspects* in astrology. Aspects can be designated on the birth chart by drawing connecting colored lines between two planets. I use four different colored pencil lines to designate specific angular aspects on a birth chart, as suggested on table 5.

Four distinct geometric patterns express the dynamic qualities of the astral body that form the astrological aspects. Some astrological traditions limit the geometry of planetary aspects to divisions of 12, based on the zodiac. However, specific geometrical patterns of aspects formed by planets with one another, or with the Sun—as viewed from the geocentric perspective—accurately characterize the dynamic qualities of the planets and their aspects. This is a more fruitful approach than limiting angular aspects between planets to divisions of 12.

A division of the circle by 4 would yield sequences of 90° aspects. However, the phases of the Moon in time and space are not exact intervals of 90°, because both Sun and Moon are progressing along the ecliptic. But for the purposes of seeking "archetypal aspects," we could certainly consider 90° aspects as a fourfold division of the ecliptic.

Are there other planetary pairs that form patterns of four? On figure 4, we find that Mars makes 8 conjunctions and 8 oppositions with the Sun over the course of 17 years. Although the 8 divisions of the ecliptic made by Mars are of varying angular sizes (due to the erratic orbit of Mars), we can consider the eightfold division of the ecliptic to be an "archetypal pattern" belonging to "Mars." A division of the ecliptic by 8 form aspects of 45°, 90°, 135°, and 180°. Any two planets separated by these angles have relationships whose qualities are "Mars-like." The qualities of the eight-pointed star formed by Mars–Sun—aggression, assertiveness—inform us that any two planets connected by *Mars aspects* are in some kind of conflict with each other. Assertive Mars configurations in one's birth chart are carried within the cosmic garment of the birth chart, bestowed at the moment of birth. We find a symbol for *Mars aspects* on figure 5.

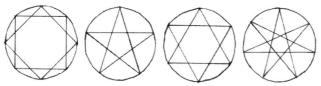

Figure 5. Astral Body: Shapes of planetary aspects among Mars–Sun (8), Venus–Sun (5), Mercury–Sun/ Jupiter–Uranus (6), and Solar (7)

Venus makes two beautiful pentagrams in its alignments with the Sun over the course of 8 years, as shown on figure 4. The angles between points of a five-pointed star are 72° and 144°. Hence any two planets related by angles of 72° or 144° can be considered as having "Venus-like" relationships. The qualities arising from Venus–Sun—loving sacrifice, social graciousness, affection and aesthetic appreciation—inform us that any two planets connected by *Venus aspects* are lovingly harmonized and emotionally supportive of one another. Venus aspects in one's birth chart will be expressed accordingly in the consciousness of one's astral body.

Mercury nearly forms a six-pointed star with the Sun in the course of a year, as shown on figure 4. The angles between points of a six-pointed star are 60° and 120°. Since the nature of Mercury is coordination and communication, the conjunction angle of 0° seems to belong to Mercurial aspects, and the author often includes a 30° angle as a Mercury aspect as well. *Mercury aspects* between any two planets—that is 0°, 30°, 60°, or 120°—inform us that the soul qualities of each planet easily and clearly communicate with each other in the birth chart.

Jupiter and Uranus also form a distinctive six-pointed star, forming seven conjunctions along the ecliptic over the course of 84 years. This further strengthens the validity of using sixfold aspects that we could expand to call *Mercury/ Jupiter/Uranus aspects.* Just as Mercury is connected with associative thinking and intellect, Jupiter's nature is expansive, active thinking. Uranus has not yet been discussed, since going into the nature of Uranus, Neptune and Pluto is beyond the scope of this present paper. Nonetheless, astrological associations of Uranus with an expanded, liberated consciousness and originality of viewpoint further justifies using six-pointed star aspects, whose quality is clarity, communication, and coordination.

Finally, the Sun lies at the center of the 7 visible planets. Three planets come between the Sun and Earth—Moon, Venus, and Mercury—and three planets always move beyond the Sun—Mars, Jupiter and Saturn. Since the Sun is related to the human heart, we can justifiably consider that the Sun plus its 6 visible planets equals 7. While there is not a sevenfold geometrical pattern formed by the Sun with other planets, there are 7 planets weaving along the ecliptic. Hence it is worth considering a seven-pointed star as the basis for yet another kind of planetary aspect. If we divide the ecliptic of 360° into 7 equal parts, the angles of 51.4°, 102.8°, and 154.2° are aspects forming a seven-pointed star. Since the Sun is the master star of our solar system it seems justified to consider the sevenfold aspects as *Solar aspects.*

These four kinds of planetary aspects are summarized on table 5. Their stellar patterns are symbolically indicated on figure 5.

PART TWO: A FRESH LOOK AT THE ASTROLOGICAL HOUSES

In part 1, "Contemplating the Birth Chart in the Light of Anthroposophy," we found clear relationships between the zodiac and the physical body, the moving planets and the etheric body, as well as between the experience of planetary movements and the astral body. We now have a foundation for understanding the birth chart as a whole, and a context to examine the most controversial topic in astrology—the astrological houses and their relationship to the "I." Can Anthroposophy offer insights to solve the riddles of the houses?

As suggested on table 1 in part 1, the "I" or "self" corresponds to the *perception of the echo of the zodiac.* The astrological counterpart of the "I" is the realm of the 12 houses of the birth chart. The 12 houses set the stage for the "I" to unfold initiatives and to perform deeds on Earth. However, we must learn how to "build" and structure this temple of the houses to make it worthy of the activity of the "I," the divine human being. Who is this "I"? What preparations have been made to provide the human spirit with the opportunity to live on the Earth, and to perform deeds out of freedom and love? Once we understand how the human "I" dwells in the temple of the human organism, we will know how to structure the temple of the 12 houses.

Riddles of the "I," or "Self"

The human "I," or "Self," is perhaps our deepest riddle. Each human being has the same name— we each refer to our "self" by the word "I" (or its equivalent in other languages). Yet when one speaks the word "I," only the speaker is being addressed. The name "I" never refers to another person; it refers only to the one who is speaking. "I" can address "you." But when *you* use the name "I" you are not addressing *me*, but rather *yourself.* Then, who am "I"? Where do "I" come from? How am "I" related to the "I" of another? How am "I" related to the Word?

Rudolf Steiner perceived that our "I" is part of our human spirit—the part that is always becoming more present, but never incarnating completely.

Our inner experiences suggest that the "I" dwells within our body, but these inner experiences of self are but small reflections of our fuller "I" dwelling in the surrounding world. Our fullest "I" never completely touches into us, though we refer to its "touching into us" as a "moral intuition."[28] Only part of our individual "I" lives within us; most of it lives in the great world around us. Our "I" continually presents itself anew as we walk through the world and through life. Each of us can say: "I am much more than my conscious self-experience." In 1906 Rudolf Steiner gave this meditative verse:

> In purest out-poured light
> Shimmers the Godhead of the world.
> In purest love toward all that is
> Out-pours the godhood of my soul.
> I rest within the Godhead of the world;
> There shall I find myself
> Within the Godhead of the World.[29]

The last three lines are revelatory. Our conscious "I" merely reflects our greater spiritual "I." Our task on the Earth is to unite our conscious microcosmic "I" with our greater macrocosmic "I" dwelling in the Godhead of the world. Our "I" lives for the most part in the periphery—in other people, in the landscape of stones, plants, and animals, in what "happens to us" in life, in the starry realms and in the soul and spiritual worlds *beyond the stars.* Our task is gradually to incorporate our *peripheral, greater "I"* into our physical body, etheric body, and astral body.

> When you say "I," what is that exactly? Now just imagine someone had planted trees in a beautifully artistic order. Each individual tree can be seen. However at a distance all the trees resolve into a single point. Take all the individual things—all that resounds from the Zodiac in the way of world consonants, then go far enough away: Everything that is formed as inward sound, in the most manifold way, is compressed within you to the single point "I."
>
> It is an actual fact that this name ["I"] which the human being gives one's self is really

---

28 Rudolf Steiner, *Intuitive Thinking as a Spiritual Path.*
29 Rudolf Steiner, *Guidance in Esoteric Training,* "Main Exercise," October 1906.

only an expression for *what we perceive in the measureless spaces of the universe.* Everywhere it is necessary to go back to what, as reflection, as echo, appears here upon Earth…[30]

For this incorporation of the human "I" into the nature of the human being is the whole mission of the Earth evolution. So we have, as it were, two intermingling evolutionary streams, in that we must go through the Earth evolution, following that of Saturn, Sun, and Moon, *and* that as Earth humanity we bring to development especially this fourth member, the "I", and join this "I" to the other principal members of human nature, upon which preparatory work was done earlier: namely, the physical body, the etheric body, and the astral body.[31]

Spiritual beings devote their creative activity toward humanity and the cosmos, refining the temple of the human being in evolutionary stages through Old Saturn, Old Sun, Old Moon and Earth. Rudolf Steiner even states "The human being is the religion of the gods":

The gods had a vision of *the ideal human being*; the reality of this is not the physical human being as she or he is today, but a state of development where the life of the human soul and spirit reaches its highest level in a physical human being whose potential is fully realized.

Thus the gods have *the image of the human being* before them as their highest ideal, their religion. In their mind's eye they see, as if on the far shore of divine existence, *the temple which is their supreme work of art, representing the human as the image of the divine being.* When human beings are in the spirit land between death and a new birth, their further development consists in making themselves more and more ready to behold *the temple which is the ideal of humanity.*…[32]

The Riddle of the "I"-organization and the Word

Just as spiritual beings creatively envision and build "the temple which is the ideal of humanity," human beings build the "temple of 12 houses to fulfill our ideals through our creative activity on Earth." We can align ourselves with the Word, the great spiritual formative power creating and sustaining—the physical body in harmony with the zodiac, the etheric body in harmony with the movements of the planets, and the astral body in harmony with the experience of planetary movements. The greater formative power of the Word ordering and working into the astral body, etheric body, and physical body is the "I"-organization:

Still more difficult to understand is the *"I" organization.* For this one needs to grasp the meaning of the first verse of the Gospel of St. John: "In the beginning was the Word." "The Word" is meant there to be understood in a concrete sense, not abstractly, as commentators of the Gospels usually present it. If this is applied concretely to the real human being, it provides an explanation of *how the "I" organization penetrates the human physical body.*[33]

The "I"-organization penetrating the human physical body is the formative power of the "Word" or "Logos" or "Christ" expressed in the first line of the Gospel of St. John: "In the beginning was the Word" (or "In the beginning was the Logos"). On table 2 in part 1, we saw that the Lamb of God–Logos, or Word–Christ, is the second member of the Trinity. Just as Aries or the Lamb of God creates the form of the human head, Christ dwells at the head of the spiritual hierarchies—as the sacrificial Lamb who performs the will of the Father through loving, divine creative deeds.

On table 1, we saw that the physical body is the "Echo of the zodiac," and that the "I" is the "Perception of the echo of the zodiac." Let's state this like an equation:

If: the echo of the zodiac = the physical body;
and: "I" = the perception of the echo of the zodiac;

---

30 Rudolf Steiner, "The Alphabet," Dec. 18, 1921.

31 Rudolf Steiner, "Esoteric Studies: Cosmic Ego and Human Ego—The Nature of Chist, the Resurrected" (New York: Anthroposophic Press, 1941) Jan. 9, 1912.

32 Rudolf Steiner, "The Vision of the Ideal Human Being," lecture 4, *The Inner Nature of Man: And Our Life between Death and Rebirth,* April 10, 1914.

---

33 Rudolf Steiner, *Broken Vessels: The Spiritual Structure of Human Frailty,* lecture 2, Sept. 9, 1924.

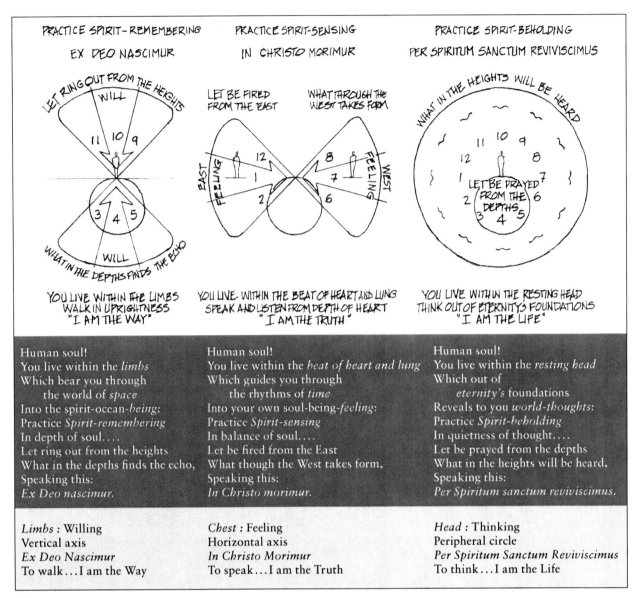

Figure 6: *Threefold expression of the human physical body and soul qualities of the "I"*
From "The Foundation Stone Meditation" by Rudolf Steiner (trans. Dorit Winter, René Querido, and Brian Gray)

then: "I" = the perception of the physical body = 12 houses of the birth chart.

Our physical body is a spiritual form created by the Word that has taken on matter and allows individual self-consciousness—the "I"—to awaken. In the same way, *the temple of 12 houses is a spiritual form aligned with the Word* that makes it possible for the human "I" to become a Spirit of Freedom and Love while living on Earth. The formative power shaping the physical body into the temple of the human "I" is the *"I"-organization* of the Word, or Logos (the Christ). Thus the "I"-organization of the Word or Logos (the Christ) will order the 12 houses of the birth chart.

The Human Form and the Birth Chart as Organized by the Word

Our human form is easily distinguished from the forms of animals, plants, and minerals. In the human form, the Word or Logos (the Christ) works as the "I"-organization. As we become clear about the human being's divine form, we can envision a "temple of 12 houses" worthy to express the human being's divine potential. We perceive a threefold structure in the human form: head, chest, and limbs. Let us contemplate how the child's will activity on the Earth advances upward from limbs to chest to head (see figure 6).

The physical body of a newborn baby lies in the horizontal plane, subject to the forces of gravity. But the child, seeing other human beings standing upright, strives to emulate them by achieving *uprightness*. During the first year of life the child works to lift its body up into the *vertical axis*. The child gradually learns to balance its body in space and *to walk upright* on the Earth. Just as the metabolic-limb activity of walking requires exertion of powerful will forces, one can say that beginning with the first year of life we strive to align our bodies with the Will of the Father in the heavens: *Ex Deo Nascimur* (*Out of God we are born*). Christ's "I"-organizing power gives us the capacity to use our limbs *to walk* on Earth: *I am the Way*. The Logos power working in the human form builds a vertical bridge between the Father in the heavens and Mother Earth in the depths: *Let ring out from the heights what in the depths finds the echo.*

The human body is also organized *to speak and to listen*. This activity begins within the heart as a feeling-longing for others, and speech is expressed through breathing. With deep feeling the child absorbs what lives in the souls of others, and during the second year of life the child is able to convey her or his own soul life to others through speech and gesture. Listening to others speak allows Christ's "I"-organizing power to work through the 'genius of language,' forming the child's larynx into an organ for speaking the mother tongue. Listening and speaking allows one soul to commune with another along the *horizontal axis* of interpersonal communication.

"Speaking" is an assertive activity that requires a "listener." The listener must temporarily suspend her or his opinions and "surrender" to receive the strongly felt words spoken by the other. Conversation is a kind of "dying and becoming" process; the listener briefly "dies" into the speaker, and then listener and speaker trade roles in *dia-logos*.

This "dying and becoming" is the loving communal gesture of the Christ who lives "in between" two or three or more: *In Christo Morimur* (*In Christ we die*, or *In Christ death becomes life*). In the birth chart, one's "I" flows from the horoscope/Ascendant in the east to the "other" in the west: *Let be fired from the East what through the West takes form.*

Through *thinking*, human beings gradually order their affairs and give direction to their lives. During the third year, a child begins formulating independent thoughts about the world. The activity of thinking is universal; every human being performs the activity of thinking in the same way. But the content of what a person thinks (the thoughts) depends upon the person's point of view, feelings, and previous experiences. When two or three individuals can lift their souls together into the pure revelatory activity of *living thinking*, they awaken in the spirit and build new worlds of understanding: Let be prayed from the depths what in the heights will be heard.... *Per spiritum sanctum reviviscimus*" (Through the Holy Spirit we reawake). The Holy Spirit can descend like Whitsun flames above our enlightened heads, and a new *circle of human community* is born of living intuitions: *I am the life.*

Finally, in the fourth year of life the child awakens to *its first and most important moral intuition*: "*I am.*" This magical experience of self-consciousness grows and begins to work more and more deeply into the child's soul from that moment forward. Biographical memories can usually be traced back to the dawning of the "I"-concept between 3 and 4 years of age.

The temple of 12 houses structuring the configuration of the birth chart will need to reveal these four key stages of spiritual development—*walking upright, speaking and listening, thinking,* and *coming to self-consciousness*—in its architectural form. We seek to build temple of 12 houses that fully expresses the image of the Divine Human Being. What form will this temple take?

Exploring Whole-Sign Houses:
The Oldest House System

We begin by investigating the "original" house system that arose around the time of the birth of Christ. This original house system may not be fully suited to our present stage of evolution, but once we understand the origin of the 12 houses, we can make adjustments for human evolutionary changes that have happened over the past 2,000 years.

The "original" house system was directly tied to the signs of the zodiac, and to the Earth's horizon at the point of the "*horoscope*" or Ascendant. In some ways this ancient system confounds us. The oldest recorded birth charts with 12 houses date back to the period when Jesus was born. According to Deborah Houlding, "Firm evidence for the use of houses in chart judgments has been dated to 22 BC, with the earliest extant book to describe their meaning being the *Astronomica* of Manilius, written in Latin around AD 10." [34]

Robert Hand concurs, stating that the oldest true "house system" was the signs of the zodiac themselves:

After several years of research into the oldest texts of our astrological tradition we now know what the earliest house system was. And in a way it was not a house system at all as we understand house systems. Rather, it was the signs of the zodiac, themselves, used as a house system. In this system the rising degree of the zodiac marks the sign it is located in as the 1st house. The rising sign itself thus becomes the 1st house, as we would refer to it, from its very beginning to its end, regardless of where in the sign the rising degree may fall. The next sign to rise after the rising sign becomes the 2nd house, the next sign the 3rd house, and so forth.

Actually, to understand this properly, one has to know that it is not that the signs were used as houses so much as *there were no houses at all,* merely the signs of the zodiac used as we would use houses, with no, second, separate, twelvefold division of the chart at all. This has several important consequences:

- As stated, wherever the rising degree falls in its sign, that entire, or whole, sign is the 1st house.
- Therefore, the beginning of a house is always 0° of a sign and the end of a house is always 30° of a sign.
- The culminating degree, or Midheaven, may or may not fall in the 10th sign from the rising sign.
- There are not intercepted signs because every complete sign is a house.
- And last, but most subtle, the entire house system is based on the **ecliptic** and not on some other circle such as the equator, horizon, or prime vertical, to say nothing of the even more exotic methods of the Placidus house system. [35]

Robert Hand's reflections on the whole-sign houses are very helpful for us to understand, for many of these original features of the 12 houses have been completely lost and need to be re-introduced to achieve a true house system.

It is important to note that the houses in the original house system were *numbered counter-clockwise,* corresponding to the movements of the planets through the signs of the zodiac. The clockwise diurnal rotation of the heavens is accounted for by the role of the *horoscope* (Ascendant), which views each succeeding degree of the zodiac as it rises after birth. Since the *horoscope* was *the key reference point for the original birth charts,* as the day progresses and the heavens turn clockwise, the *horoscope* continues to view the zodiac as each later degree of the ecliptic rises along the eastern horizon. Thus the houses are always numbered in counter-clockwise sequence from the viewpoint of the *horoscope.* Gauquelin's and Dorsan's idea that house systems should be numbered clockwise arises from ignoring the significance of the *horoscope as the key viewpoint for the entire birth chart.* We find even deeper reasons for the original house system being numbered counterclockwise from Robert Powell's research.

34 Houlding, *The Houses: Temples of the Sky,* p. 7.

35 Hand, *Whole Sign Houses:* , p. 1.

The Ancient Hermetic System of Houses: Another Name for Whole-Sign Houses

Robert Powell calls the whole-sign houses—the oldest known horoscopes with 12 houses—the *ancient hermetic system* of houses. He beautifully explains the origin of the houses in relation to *the horoscope of conception*, as expressed by the ancient rule of Hermes:

One of the earliest references to the houses is that found on four demotic horoscopes, drawn up on four ostraca from Medinet Habu in Egypt. The horoscopes are dated AD 13, 17, 18 and 35. These horoscopes reveal an early definition of the houses, as originated in Egypt in the hermetic astrology of antiquity. In this early definition each house is simply equated with a sign of the sidereal zodiac: the first house with the rising sign, the second house with the next sign, and so on. The houses in this original definition were therefore each 30° long, identical with the zodiacal signs. The first house in this early definition of the houses was the house containing the Ascendant, i.e. the zodiacal sign rising on the eastern horizon at the moment of birth.[36]

Before considering the meanings traditionally associated with the twelve houses, it is important to grasp the origin of the houses.... The origin of the house system, in fact, can only be understood against the background of *the horoscope of conception*, as determined by the rule of Hermes. The hermetic rule specifies that the Moon at the moment of conception indicates the place of the Ascendant—or its opposite, the Descendant—at birth.... during the Moon's orbits of the zodiac between conception and birth the entire course of destiny for the spiral of life is elaborated, whereby each lunar orbit of the sidereal zodiac corresponds to seven years of life.[37]

The goal of the incarnating human being is the birth configuration, whereby the moment of conception is an important point of transition.... at the moment of conception, as determined by the hermetic rule, the imprint of the image begins to work into the building up of the physical body (embryo), and at the same time the etheric body begins to be formed through the orbits of the Moon around the sidereal zodiac. Simultaneously...the karma for the coming life on Earth is woven into the etheric body reflecting the planetary movements taking place during the embryonic period. Thus the planetary movements between conception and birth indicate the weaving of destiny into the etheric body, and the formation of the etheric body itself—concurrent with the Moon's orbits of the zodiac—occurs in such a way that *one lunar orbit of the sidereal zodiac corresponds to seven years of life.*[38]

Here we find the deeper spiritual reasons why the world's oldest house system numbered the houses *counterclockwise* from the Ascendant (*horoscope*). The Moon's position at conception becomes the Ascendant/Descendant horizon at birth, and the counterclockwise motion of the Moon, Sun and planets through the signs of the zodiac in the period between conception and birth patterns the interweaving of individual destiny for the coming life. The motion of planets through the signs of the zodiac is *counterclockwise*, agreeing with the sequence of how the signs of the zodiac rise at the Ascendant (*horoscope*) following the moment of birth. This deeper wisdom at work in the original house system has been lost in recent times.

Structural Advantages of the Whole-Sign House System

As a structural solution to the problem of calculating cusp positions of houses, the ancient hermetic house system or whole-sign house[39] system is truly elegant. Since "houses" are identical with the 12 signs of the zodiac as measured along the ecliptic, no further calculation is needed to locate the "cusps" or division points between houses. The whole-sign house system can be consistently applied to births taking place anywhere on the Earth, because the 12 signs of the zodiac are divided on the plane of the ecliptic. "Domification" of the 12 sidereal signs of the zodiac (each sign considered as a house) is achieved by tracing the position of the signs of the zodiac as they appear at the birth place back *along*

---

36 Powell, *History of the Houses*, p. 3.
37 Powell, *Hermetic Astrology*, vol. 2, p. 248.

38 Ibid., pp. 253–254.
39 Robert Hand prefers the title "Whole Sign Houses" for this system.

ecliptic meridian lines to the north and south poles of the ecliptic plane.

Please remember that the birth chart is mapped on *the plane of the ecliptic*, the Sun's path through the sidereal zodiac. We must distinguish between two different systems in the birth chart: 1) the ecliptic system of the zodiac, and 2) the Earth's equatorial rotational axis system (see figure 2).

The equatorial rotational axis system identifies the MC/ IC along the north-south rotational meridian (lines of longitude extending from North Pole to South Pole). The *MC*, *Medium Coeli* or *midheaven* is the intersection of the ecliptic with the longitudinal meridian plane extending through the birth place from the North Pole and South Pole. The Earth's rotational axis at the North Pole extends out to the celestial sphere to a point near the star Polaris, in present times.

In contrast to the North rotational pole pointing toward Polaris, the celestial *north pole of the ecliptic* is centered in the constellation of Draco, at a point 23½° away from Polaris. Meridians radiating from *the north pole of the ecliptic* provide *equal divisions of the ecliptic*, forming the boundaries between signs of the zodiac at right angles to the ecliptic plane.

Since the rotational Midheaven (MC) is *not* a "house cusp" in whole-sign houses—the MC can fall in the 8th, 9th, 10th, or 11th house in Whole-Sign Houses—there is no need to divide the ecliptic into four quadrants.

Quadrant division of the ecliptic, and further subdivision into houses, arose centuries later than the original whole-sign house system of 12 equal houses. The introduction of quadrant divisions into the equal-house system usurped its original elegance and simplicity. Dividing the circle of the ecliptic into four unequal parts by the Asc-Desc axis and the MC-IC axis, then subdividing each quadrant into 3 houses, *played no part at all in the oldest/ original house system.*

Quadrant-division houses arose out of attempts to incorporate *both* the diurnal movement of the Earth along its rotational axis (through North and South Poles) *and* the ecliptic circle of the zodiac (which is tilted 23.5° off the equator) into a system of house division. Quadrant division as the basis for house division violates *the original idea that houses are equal divisions of the ecliptic—as the 12 signs of the zodiac.* For the past 1800 years, many ingenious attempts have been made to combine quadrant division (an unequal division of the ecliptic) with a house division of equal sizes. *Every attempt* to conflate these two disparate astronomical phenomena—that of the Sun, Moon and planets moving along the ecliptic divided into 12 equal-sized constellations of the zodiac *and* that of the rotational movement of the Earth along its rotational axis—*has led to confusion and failure.* Nonetheless, quadrant house systems are often still championed today.

Note that the original whole-sign houses are identical with the 12 signs of the zodiac, and share with the zodiac the *north pole and south pole of the ecliptic* as axial centers. The whole-sign houses allow easy and direct "domification," since the boundaries between each sign of the zodiac are meridians passing through the poles of the ecliptic.

An advantage of whole-sign houses is that they are an equal division of the ecliptic into twelve signs of the zodiac. Whole-sign houses nearly align with Rudolf Steiner's picture of the "I" being related to "the perception of the echo of the zodiac." However, they are not yet the *perception* of the echo of the zodiac, since the whole-sign houses *are equivalent with* the signs the zodiac. One further step is required for the whole-sign houses to fulfill the quality of being "the *perception* of the echo of the zodiac"—that is, the "perception of the physical body."

The Earth-Centered Equal-House System: In the Image of the Divine Human Being

This next step naturally leads to 12 equal houses that maintain their relationship to the ecliptic poles but are centered on the horizon and the Earth, that is the *horoscope* or Ascendant. See figure 7.

The Earth-centered equal-house system maintains all the advantages of the whole-sign houses system, in that it is *based in equal divisions of the ecliptic*, as are the signs of the zodiac. The divisions between houses are meridians at right angles to the ecliptic plane, centered at the ecliptic poles. The "top" of the chart is not the MC but

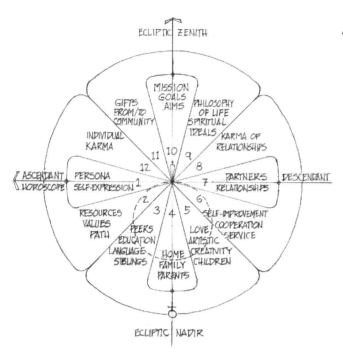

Figure 7. *Earth-centered equal-house system: In the Image of the Divine Human Being*

the Ecliptic Zenith (EZ), and the "bottom" of the chart is not the IC but the Ecliptic Nadir (EN).

However, the Earth-centered equal-house system has some distinct advantages over the whole-sign house system. In the Earth-centered equal-house system, the Ascendant (the *horoscope*) is always at the *center of the first house*, rather than in an earlier or later degree of a sign of the zodiac straddling the Ascendant. In the Earth-centered equal-house system, the Earth's center is always marked beneath the viewer's feet at the bottom of the chart in the middle of the 4th house, aligned with the plane of the ecliptic nadir and ecliptic zenith at 90° angles from the Ascendant–Descendant horizon.

Another clear advantage of the Earth-centered equal-house system is that it expresses the "I"-organization of the threefold human being shown in figure 6. The Earth-centered equal-house system maintains the spiritual formative integrity of the Logos or Christ working into human stature, as discussed above.

The Earth-centered equal-house system was not invented by the author. A form of it has been used in Vedic astrology for many centuries, and

it was apparently (re-)introduced in Europe as the "Vehlow Equal House" system in the nineteenth century by German astrologer Johannes Vehlow. Robert Powell reports that a French astrologer, Maurice Nouvel, wrote a book (in French) about this house system that justifies its use from Nouvel's perspectives.[40]

The author "rediscovered" this elegant house system over 30 years ago by naively pondering where to place the "Earth point" within the birth chart. The center of the Earth must be straight down beneath the viewer's feet, at a 90° angle from the horizon plane intersecting the ecliptic at Ascendant and Descendant. With the Earth centered directly "underfoot" (not at the IC), the meanings and clustering of the 12 houses become startlingly evident. See figure 7 and 8. To the left are the seven-year biographical stages of development and their corresponding planet. To the right are the 12 houses and their abbreviated "meanings."

Understanding the 12 Houses in the Earth-centered Equal-House System

Let us briefly contemplate figures 6, 7 and 8 in relation to the 7-year cycles unfolding in human biography. Wonderful interactions between houses, phases of life, and the interplay between the 12 houses and the 7 planets begin to reveal themselves.

The **4th house**, centered on the Earth, is "traditionally" home, family, and foundations of the physical body. A human being, standing upright, places both feet on either side of the vertical axis between the heavens and the depths of the Earth. The 4th house, the "foundation stone" of the birth chart, expresses the conditions of home and family life from birth to age 7, as well as one's future living situations and families in adulthood. A higher instinctive spiritual wisdom that forms and maintains the *physical body* also draws a person toward a specific family, hereditary stream, and place of birth (4th house). The *Moon* rules over the years from birth to 7 years of age.

"Traditionally" the **3rd house** refers to siblings, neighbors, friends, primary school education, and basic language and communication

---

40 Nouvel, *La vraie domification en astrologie.*

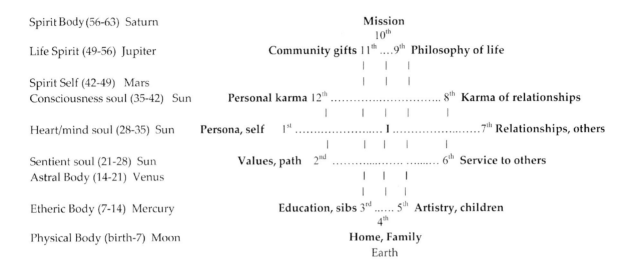

Figure 8. *Clustering of the 12 Houses around the Four Angles of the Birth Chart*

skills. The **5th house** reveals artistry and creative activity, love, playfulness, and children. The 3rd and 5th houses both refer to rhythmic, repetitive activity expressing the *etheric body's* movements through *cycles of time. Mercury* rules over the years from 7 to 14. Rhythmic movements are key to healthy education, and to social and artistic activities. Between ages 7 to 14, the child weaves back and forth between home and family (4th house), attending school (3rd), and artistic activity and play (5th). These three houses cluster at the foot of the birth chart and provide "foundations" for the first 14 years of life.

The **2nd, 1st,** and **12th** houses cluster along the eastern sector, and the **6th, 7th** and **8th** along the western sector of the birth chart, pointing to *body and soul* interactions between *self* and *others*.

In the **2nd house** one's *astral body* (desires) and *sentient soul* (motives to satisfy one's needs through sense experiences) touch, overlap and intermingle between age 14 to 21 and 21 to 28. The 2nd house expresses the person's moral character, values, level of commitment to follow a path through to a goal, and one's ability to be resourceful. Many 14 to 21 year-old adolescents (under the influence of *Venus*) can be very resourceful in finding ways to satisfy their desires and cravings, including earning money and gathering resources

needed to achieve their goals. Self-seeking activity becomes more refined between 21 and 28, as the "I" tempers and refines desires with motives that express one's moral orientation. The *Sun* provides this balance and moral tempering during the entire period from ages 21 to 42.

The **1st house,** centered on the Ascendant or horoscope, reveals the individual's "persona" and mode of self-expression. The Sun-like "I" shining in at ages 3, 9, 12, 18 and from 21 to 28 within the sentient soul, continues to ripen and go through existential crises between ages 28 to 35, the period of ripening of the *heart and mind soul.* The Saturn return between ages 29 to 30, and the Christ years from 30 to 33, provide the "I" with ample opportunities for deep philosophical musings and moral judgments requiring greater maturity. All these arise within the *Sun* years, and the **1st house** can become the focus for all life events from 21 to 42 years of age.

From early stages in life, an individual's *free intentions* and *karmic necessities* have been streaming into the soul from the **12th house** realm of the *consciousness soul* and *spirit self. Free intentions* include new gifts and capacities acquired in the spiritual world before birth. *Karmic necessities* are one's requests (from former incarnations) to return to activities or situations and continue work already begun. During the period from 35 to

42, the *consciousness soul* provides insights affirming that one is an immortal spiritual being living in a temporal body. Within the consciousness soul, the individual becomes more deeply *aware of what is true and good* and can strive to align her or his actions accordingly. At the same time, *individual karma*—in the form of free intentions and karmic necessities—can make the last third of the *Sun* phase (35-42) a challenging time. The full weight of what has yet to be accomplished begins to burden the *consciousness soul*; at the same time, the vision of what might be done is glimpsed.

From 42 to 49, new initiatives from *Mars* encourage one *to act out of the true and the good* that lives embryonically in the *spirit self.* The spirit self can shine in more clearly from the **12th house**. Rekindling youthful initiatives often happens during the *Mars* phase, with a renewed interest in maintaining a healthy relationship to body and soul. The positive side of individual karma is that one can begin to accomplish goals and initiate activity with others that might become very productive and fruitful. The "I" is shining ever brighter.

The cluster of three eastern houses we have just outlined (**2nd, 1st,** and **12th**) focus on developing **one's sense of self.** They are complimented by activities in **6th, 7th,** and **8th** houses opposite in the western sector of the birth chart, which have to do with forming and maintaining healthy **relationships with others.** The 6th, 7th, and 8th houses cluster together.

The **6th house** shows one's willingness to serve, assist, work with and heal others, often requiring personal sacrifice, self-improvement and unselfish cooperation. The qualities of loving sacrifice that can be expressed through the 6th house reveal the true nature of *Venus.* Community service opportunities can arise from 14 to 21 years of age, when adolescents learn to serve others and place *interest in others* above *self-interest.* Apprenticing and learning to work for others allows one to develop practical abilities and social skills, including appreciation for colleagues and co-workers and making oneself "presentable." The 6th house periods from 14 to 21 and 21 to 28 are important stages in preparing relationships for later life.

During the *Sun* phase of the **6th house** period from 21 to 28, the "I" finds further opportunities to work toward healthy relationships. One is tested over and over through relationships—with others at work, with friends and with romantic partners. Sensory enjoyments shared with others in social settings can continue to be a major focus and outlet for many people.

Appreciating others and offering up one's best leads in the **7th house** to forming committed relationships, which often become somewhat challenging from 28 to 35. One must be willing to "die" into others, and to be reborn as one's true "I" in a more generous and loving form. Self-transformation is needed to sustain relationships. Because relationships are of major concern throughout the period from 21 to 42, and because the 7th house of partnerships is also a *Sun* realm, the **7th house** can also be the focal point during this entire 21-year period of life.

Overlighting all relationships is the **8th house,** which holds insights into the *karma of relationships.* The 8th house reveals karmic connections with others from past lives, and as well the 8th house receives the fruits of the future karma being formed through one's relationships in this life. The karma of one's relationships has been shining in from early childhood, but relationship karma may come more fully to conscious expression during the last third of the *Sun* phase, from 35 to 42.

During the *Mars* phase from 42 to 49, another aspect of the **8th house** can emerge. New initiatives and fresh vitality can arise through forming active relationships with others. Because the astral body is "blooming" once again during the Mars phase, relationships with younger people also take on new levels of activity and importance. The individual hopefully has found her/his authentic "voice" in the world, and is able to lead others and take initiative. The positive fruits of the karma of relationships can come to the fore.

"Atop" the birth chart cluster the **9th, 10th,** and **11th** houses, which express one's **mission in life.** The **9th house** is the individual's spiritual ideals, higher educational striving, and overall philosophy of life. The 9th house experiences expand through travel and explorations into various realms of body/soul/ spirit. As one's wisdom grows, teaching, writing and publishing become 9th house activities. *Jupiter's* wisdom shines forth through the 9th house.

The **11th house** reveals spiritual and material contributions given by members of the greater community to support the individual's achievements. The 11th house also shows what the community hopes to receive as the fruit of the individual's achievements. Along with the 9th house, the 11th house comes under the influence of *Jupiter*, the planet of expansive wisdom arising out of experience, benevolence, optimism, vision, living thinking, and future orientation. While the 9th and 11th house realms of spirit shine into all phases of life, the expansive phase of life from 49 to 56 is particularly highlighted by Jupiter.

The highest realm of life mission is shown at the ecliptic zenith (EZ) in the **10th house**, which reveals one's spiritual goals, aims, and mission in life. The 10th house has the nature of *Saturn*; it reveals the full stature of what one resolves to accomplish. Here, one holds one's self spiritually accountable for what one strives to achieve during this life. An individual's *moral intuitions* are the only valid yardstick by which her or his accomplishments can be justly measured.

This brief tour of the houses reveals that *each house has meaning because of its position in relationship to the image of the divine human being living on Earth.* The three northern houses (3rd house, 4th house, and 5th house) establish **home and family life**, answering the question, "*What are my foundations?*" The three eastern houses (12th house, 1st house, and 2nd house) express one's **sense of self**, answering the question, "*Who am I?*" The three western houses (6th house, 7th house, and 8th house) establish one's **relationships with others**, answering the question, "*Who are my partners?*" The three southern houses (9th house, 10th house, 11th house) establish one's **goals in life**, answering the question, "*What is my mission?*"

Some astrologers mistakenly think that house meanings are derived from each sign of the zodiac, as direct mirrors. In that view, the 1st house is Aries, the 2nd house is Taurus, the 3rd house is Gemini, and so forth. Such was not the case with the whole-sign house system, and such is not the case in the Earth-centered equal-house system. To conflate the meanings of signs of the zodiac and houses confuses and demeans both realms. The meanings of the houses are derived from the spiritual realities formed by the "I"-organization—the power of the Word or the Christ—expressing itself through the architectural temple of the 12 houses.

Some Dynamics between Houses in the Earth-centered Equal-House System

It should be apparent that all 12 houses are "active" during each life phase. For example, while achievements in the upper houses ripen more fully in later life, an individual's goals, aims and mission play into and shape her/his biography from the moment of birth.

If we consider the four "angular" houses (**1st, 4th, 7th,** and **10th**), the opposite houses (180° apart) express complementary realms of activity. On the other hand, activities in each angular house are supported by activities one performs in the houses 120° (or four houses) away. The dynamics between houses that form equilateral triangles are very revealing.

For instance, consider the **4th house** of home, parents, family members. The angular 4th house is supported by the **12th house** and **8th house**, both *houses of karma*. We are drawn to incarnate at the particular place and to the particular parents and family that best serves our "picking up" threads of our personal karma (12th house) and of our relationship karma (8th house). Our home and family setting offers immediate opportunities in early life to continue our work within a very important karmic circle. Our family plays a major role in establishing our foundations.

12th house	8th house
personal karma	karma of relationships

Home, family 4th

In similar fashion, an individual's angular **1st house** of self/ persona is enhanced and supported by activities from the **5th house** of creativity, love and children, and from the **9th house** of philosophy of life/ spiritual ideals. Our talents, creative skills, and love for what we do help to shape our philosophy of life and spiritual outlook. Together, all these experiences strengthen our sense of self in the 1st house and help shape the expression of our personality.

9th house: philosophy of life

1st house: persona, self <

5th house: artistry, children

The angular **7th house** of committed relationships and partnerships with others is complemented and supported from the **3rd house** of education, siblings, language skills and communication, and also from the **11th house** of community gifts and friendships. The committed adult relationships we form in our thirties are usually with a different karmic circle of friends than the circle of family and friends from early life. This second circle of relationships carries us into later life.

11th house: community gifts

> 7th house: relationships, others

3rd house: education, siblings

Finally, the angular **10th house** of an individual's mission is complemented and supported by her or his efforts from the **2nd house** of moral values, resources, and commitment to follow a path through to its goal, and from the **6th house** of service to others, cooperation and self-improvement.

Mission 10th house

/ \

2nd: values, path   6th: service to others

The elegance of the Earth-centered Equal-House system

The Earth-centered House system is a ridiculously straightforward and simple temple to "build." Once the *horoscope* or Ascendant has been calculated for the exact time and place of birth, the houses center themselves on the horizon and the center of the Earth without further ado. The boundaries of the 1st house lie on the ecliptic plane 15° to either side of the Ascendant and all 12 houses are 30° in size. The "ruling point" of each house is the center point of that

house (such as the Ascendant), not the boundary or "cusp" between houses.

To the mathematician and spherical trigonometer, the Earth-centered equal-house system might seem primitively simple in comparison with the elaborate calculations required to erect the house systems of Placidus or Koch, for example. Most house divisions today begin with the division of the ecliptic into quadrants formed by the horizon and midheaven planes, which are rarely exactly 90° apart. Having worked with quadrant division house systems for many years, the author is painfully aware of their shortcomings. The houses are never equal in size, and two or more signs of the zodiac are often "intercepted"—considered to be "muted" in the birth chart. Defending such irrational house division when reading a birth chart often requires great ingenuity and "hand-waving dismissals" by the astrologer. Unequal houses are clumsy, nonsensical and spiritually barren of meaning and rationale. They are as indefensible as dividing of the zodiac into signs of unequal sizes. The Earth-centered equal-house system overcomes the aberrations arising from the faulty assumptions of quadrant division, re-establishing order and coherence and bringing new valid insights to the birth chart.

The beauty of the Earth-centered equal-house system, like that of the whole-sign house system, is that both are *true equal divisions of the ecliptic plane*—the plane of the zodiac, which is the plane of reference for the entire birth chart. Both house systems have meridians at right angles to the ecliptic plane that cross at the *north and south poles of the ecliptic*. On the celestial sphere, the *north pole of the ecliptic* always passes through a point on the Arctic Circle, and the *south pole of the ecliptic* always passes through a point the Antarctic Circle, since the plane of the ecliptic is tilted 23½° off the plane of the equator. The Earth-centered equal-house system and the whole-sign house system can both be erected anywhere on the surface of the Earth with consistency—which is not astronomically true for nearly all quadrant division house systems.

Reflections on the Gauquelin "Plus Zones" and Dorsan's "clockwise houses"

Interpreting the significance of planets placed in the original "house" system of the birth chart —the whole-sign house (or ancient hermetic house system)—had two different functions for the original natal astrologers. These two functions of a planet's position in the birth chart were initially kept distinctly separate when interpreting the chart:

1) First, a planet placed within a "house" signifies *the department of life* in which that planet plays a contributing role. For instance, Saturn's placement in the 1st house signifies that Saturn influences and colors the expression of one's personality (1st house). In similar fashion, Saturn's placement in the 9th house (counted counterclockwise from the 1st house) signifies that Saturn influences the person's philosophy of life and spiritual ideals (9th house).

2) Second, the "strength," or "intensity," of a planet in the birth chart was gauged by whether or not the planet was positioned near the four "angles" of the birth chart. The positioning of a planet near the four angles is called a planet's "angularity." In the whole-sign house system, this means that planets in the 1st house (the whole sign on the Ascendant), or planets in the 4th house, 7th house, and 10th house have greater strength or intensity of expression in the birth chart than planets not so positioned.

Originally these two functions of planetary placement: 1) a planet's position in a particular "house" or department of life, and 2) a planet's proximity to the four "angles" of the birth chart— were considered separately when 'reading' a birth chart, at least until the sixth century AD. They are two very different ways of gauging a planet's role and contribution to the birth chart.

However, over the centuries these two distinct functions gradually became confused and merged. The resultant "blurring" was increased by the excellent research of French statistician, Michel Gauquelin. Gauquelin exhaustively analyzed the positions of planets in thousands of birth charts. Gauquelin's research proves that "angularity"— certain planets positioned near the four angles of the birth chart—can be a significant indicator of a person's profession. Gauquelin summarized his research by identifying what are called "Gauquelin Plus Zones," spatial sectors of the birth chart near the four angles that emphasize the strength and intensity of certain planets.

In fact, what Gauquelin "proved" along with *angularity* was the validity of the whole-sign house system and Earth Centered equal-house systems, in which the four "angles" of the chart lie *inside* the 1st house, 4th house, 7th house, and 10th house. These four houses *straddle* the Ascendant –Descendant horizon and the Ecliptic Zenith-Ecliptic Nadir vertical plane. Gauquelin was only familiar with quadrant house divisions that were introduced later into astrology, and that "slipped" the 1st house *below* the Ascendant, rather than extending *the 1st house as the sector both above and below the Ascendant.*

Bolstered by statistical evidence of the ancient tenet of "angularity" as an indicator of a planet's strength and intensity in the birth chart, Michel Gauquelin and his widow (also a remarkable statistician) unfortunately strongly suggested that the houses of the birth chart should be numbered "clockwise" rather than counterclockwise. Gauquelin's idea completely obscures the ancient distinction between 1) a planet's position in the house as *contributing to a particular department of life,* and 2) *angularity as an expression of a planet's strength* in the birth chart. As a result, those two functions now seem to be "merged" in the minds of many astrologers, leading to more confusion and unclarity about the original astrological houses.

Gauquelin's idea of "clockwise houses" was pursued by Jacques Dorsan, a French sidereal astrologer, whose entertaining and provocative book, *The Clockwise House System,* has just been published in English by SteinerBooks. Dorsan's book was edited by Wain Farrants and Robert Powell, star colleagues who endorse it and who produce birth charts using clockwise houses. Wain Farrants employs Dorsan's house interpretations in his articles published in *Journal for Star Wisdom 2011* and in *Journal for Star Wisdom 2012.* Dorsan's "cookbook" approach to interpreting the meanings of planets placed in the various houses uses the Placidus house system—a quadrant system that divides the houses into unequal sizes. The houses are numbered clockwise, starting the 1st house as the realm just above the Ascendant, and so forth.

Dorsan's book is certainly interesting, and this author applauds Dorsan's "audacity" to challenge astrological tradition and look with fresh eyes at the astrological houses. One should always question and challenge traditions to seek fresh viewpoints. Dorsan's theory will either prove itself in practice and clockwise houses will find greater usage by astrologers, or not. The clockwise house system is worth researching and testing. But this author has deep reservations.

Dorsan's theory arose from misunderstanding how the counterclockwise house division originated within the World's Oldest House system. He confuses different ways of linking the birth chart to life cycles as supporting the idea of clockwise numbering. Dorsan's clockwise interpretations of houses are not more accurate than counterclockwise interpretations, nor do his descriptions of houses contribute to the ennobling of the "I." In light of this present paper, Dorsan's theory falls short on several accounts:

Clockwise houses fail to account for the Moon's cyclic movement through the zodiac between conception and birth in counterclockwise motion— that is, through the signs of the zodiac from Aries to Taurus to Gemini and so forth. The Sun and planets follow the same counterclockwise movement through the zodiac.

Clockwise houses overlook the role of the *horoscope* or Ascendant as the most significant point in the chart. The *horoscope* or Ascendant links the birth chart to the chart of conception. The original reason houses are numbered counterclockwise expresses the fact that the *horoscope* or Ascendant *always views what is appearing "new" on the eastern horizon*, while the heavens appear to turn "clockwise" by diurnal (daily) motion. Confusing clockwise diurnal motion of the heavens with what is being experienced at the *horoscope*

or Ascendant (counterclockwise in sequence) leads to the error of numbering houses clockwise.

Dorsan's clockwise houses are based on the *quadrant division system* of Placidus. As discussed, quadrant division as the basis for house subdivision was unfortunately later introduced into the practice of natal astrology that originally used the twelve equal signs of the zodiac as the twelve whole-sign houses. Quadrant division systems all attempt (and fail) to combine two incommensurable astronomical phenomena, confusing the meaning of the houses and requiring mathematical complexities that detract from the elegance and truthfulness of the whole-sign houses and of the Earth-centered equal-house systems.

Dorsan's attempt to embrace Gauquelin's "angularity" by numbering houses clockwise is not necessary. The Earth-centered equal-house system places the "angular" houses where they always belonged—*straddling the four true angles of the birth chart*. The Earth-centered equal-house system fully embodies "angularity" in its very structure.

Finally, Dorsan's "definitions" of the 12 houses are derived from mundane misinterpretations of the twelve signs of the zodiac that one finds in most house systems. The only difference is that Dorsan applies these mundane house interpretations in clockwise fashion. The meanings of the twelve houses are not, nor should they be, trivialized versions of the twelve signs of the zodiac. The twelve signs of the zodiac are the dwellings of the lofty spiritual beings who form the physical body of the human being, and the twelve houses are the human being's perception of the upright human form, expressing itself as the temple of the human soul—the "I."

For the above reasons, the author of this paper deeply questions the significance of Dorsan's clockwise house system. Only time will tell whether it will thrive or fade in astrological practice.

What constitutes a successful house system?
A great deal more could be said about the merits and fruitfulness of the Earth-centered, equal-house system. When combined with the

Babylonian sidereal zodiac, and the understandings presented in part 1 of this paper, this house system has consistently and repeatedly proven its value to the author for more than thirty years of employing it to "read" birth charts.

Because a wide variety of house systems have arisen over the past two millennia, today's astrologer has many choices available. There are at least twenty-four distinct house systems and as many as forty different combinations, each with their supporters and detractors. Having worked with a number of house systems over the past forty-five years, some systems have proven to be more or less useful in reading birth charts. Here is my current checklist for comparing one house system to another; anyone who uses it can decide which house system is most "successful."

1. The house system of the birth chart structures a true relationship to the incarnating human being, revealing at a glance archetypes of "I"-organization that relate astronomical phenomena with the divine human form living on Earth.

2. The house system is straightforward and easily applicable as an equal division of the ecliptic but centered on the Earth, expressing itself as the "perception of the echo of the zodiac."

3. The house system maintains astronomical integrity that can be applied consistently to births taking place anywhere on Earth.

4. The house system meaningfully and accurately reveals the twelve dynamic departments of life through which the "I" unfolds its activities on Earth in relation to body, soul, and spirit.

5. The house system reflects relative strengths of planets as they manifest in the individual's biography, including the "Gauquelin Plus Zones" that reflect angularity as one expression of planetary strength.

6. The house system organizes and interweaves the twelve departments of life with the sevenfold and ninefold nature of the human being, unfolding "I" activity through the seven major phases of life ruled by the seven planets.

7. The house system aligns with and expresses the sequence of unfolding astronomical events from conception to birth, centering on the *horoscope* or Ascendant. Thus the houses are numbered counterclockwise.

This checklist consists of the features encompassed by the Earth-centered equal-house system. I leave it to you, dear reader, to test other house systems against this list, and to decide for yourself the merit or validity of each one. I hope you will give the Earth-centered equal-house system a try. When combined with the Babylonian sidereal zodiac and with the insights presented in part 1, you will find it an excellent temple of houses to explore. This paper is offered as one contribution toward a healthy renewal of astrology based upon the foundations of Anthroposophy.

۞

> *To starry realms,*
> *To the dwelling places of Gods,*
> *Turns the Spirit gaze of my soul.*
>
> *From starry realms,*
> *From the dwelling places of Gods,*
> *Streams Spirit power into my soul.*
>
> *For starry realms,*
> *For the dwelling places of Gods,*
> *Lives my Spirit heart through my soul.*
>
> —RUDOLF STEINER

THE TWO BECOME ONE:
POSSESSION OR ENLIGHTENMENT?
A CHRIST EVENT IN 2012

Claudia McLaren Lainson

With startling frequency, young children have been coming to me in my private therapeutic practice, and they tell me they don't want to be here anymore. Others willingly share the horrific scenes from the video games they are playing, ashamed of how afraid they were at first. Yet they assure me that as they got used to the images, they no longer feared the dark, or had nightmares. Still others are so taken over by their aggression, anger, or addictions to technology, that they have lost command of their self-hood. Parents approach me expressing their utter despair over the loss of their authority with their children. They express their feelings of helplessness when confronted by their children's dependency on technology and the resultant argumentative behavior. Then there are the children who, if challenged in any way, seem to turn to ice as a dark presence simultaneously eclipses their natural gaze and something foreign looks out at me from behind their eyes. When I settle what has upset them, I watch as that "something" leaves and the child's normal gaze returns. These are examples of patterns that are increasing in the children and adults I am seeing. There are even occasions when I meet children who tell me about a being who lives in their head and who tells them what to do.

I have come to understand that possession manifests in many forms and that technology is not only intricately connected with the increase in degenerative symptoms, but also contributes to the apathy and hopelessness that is the result of too many indigestible bits of information and images that are congesting the human psyche. We are being consumed by living in a world of ubiquitous noise and incessant screen-time in one form or another, without practicing the balance such activities require if we are to preserve our wholeness. Through encountering the tragedy of young children who know something is terribly wrong and whose last recourse is a wish to leave the Earth, and by reading the headlines on almost any given day, it becomes painfully obvious that we are to wake up—and find a new road forward. All this makes the theme of two becoming one a phenomenon that urgently needs our attention.

Rudolf Steiner himself foretold, in his lectures to the priests, that before the end of the twentieth century the Sun Demon would show himself by manifesting in many humans as the being by whom they are possessed. It has become clear that there are possessed humans working in positions of great worldly power, but it never dawned on me, when reading this prophecy long ago, that I would be seeing possessing forces in children. Many of these children are being raised by parents who have likewise been raised on technology. It is only in the older generations that we can still find those who were raised without these influences. Those who experienced life before technology remember playing in nature and making games out of thin air. There was no such thing as being entertained; we were responsible for entertaining ourselves. What a difference it made when a child's toys were the woods, fields, and lakes, and where time unfolded before us as an endless stream of open possibility!

When we delve into the mystery of *Two Becoming One*, we are delving into mysteries that are specific to our present time on Earth and even more specific to the year 2012. Spiritless, mechanistic activities empower materialistic ideologies. Virtual socializing gives way to a type of tyrannical self-interest. Drone wars remove us from the killing reality. Virtual war games make war a hero's journey. Good against evil, right? So how bad could that be? It is as bad as it gets and we are blind to what we are doing, which is my primary point of astonishment. I recently came across the following quote, which I found uniquely applicable in explaining such profound lack of awareness [Italics mine]:

> Intensive engagement with and study of the most incisive occult problems of our time is still largely *suppressed* and *avoided* in today's anthroposophic movement. Likewise the equally significant and striking utterances by Steiner about the mystery of the reappearance of the etheric Christ and the impulse of his adversary, the anti-Christ, in the twentieth and twenty-first centuries, are only seldom examined, illumined or cited, although the drastic nature of these comments, along with the radical form in which they were expressed, ought to place every student of Anthroposophy on the highest alert. In perception of and engagement with this highly topical phenomenon of our times, a scarcely explicable kind of *paralysis* seems to have *taken hold* of human spirits. There seems no other way to explain this paralysis than as the *latent effect of the power of the anti-Christ himself.*[1]

This passage names the numbness that has come over humanity, explaining a state of denial toward the effects of the fast-paced world we have created and the beings who stand behind these creations. We must wake up to the effect adversarial forces are having upon our children and our culture. I realize that it is uncomfortable to speak of unpleasant things, but it is a truism of Anthroposophy as I experience it, that knowledge of evil calls forth the good. This is the way of the Grail Knights—to confront and overcome evil—and the urgencies of our time are calling for the re-awakening of this knighthood.

The good news is the commemoration this year celebrates. The Union in the Temple between the two Jesus children is a union of enlightenment. The unions I reference above are unions born of the inversion to what this year commemorates: the inversion of possession. The fact that this event in the biography of Christ is this year sounding into time, offers us a moment to pause and contemplate what meaning it may have for human life on Earth. In the Union between the two Jesus children (see glossary), a pure and innocent human being was united with a wise, experienced, great leader of humanity. The pure and innocent human being was the child described in the Luke Gospel, the "Nathan Jesus"—a child with a paradisiacal immaculate soul. Moreover, the wise human being described in the Matthew Gospel was the "Solomon Jesus" child, who in earlier incarnations had been one of the great leaders of humanity. The indwelling of two in one may be difficult for our earthly minds to comprehend, yet this Union in the Temple in Jerusalem was as necessary for the accomplishment of the deed of Christ on the hill of Golgotha as was the Baptism in the Jordan that occurred seventeen years after this event. And the being who 2012 years ago was Jesus, is the same being who can now enlighten us as we become one with our spiritual potential.

Two becoming one can herald a tendency toward either possession or enlightenment. The former is increasing. Only through our connection to higher worlds can we find the balance between the adversaries against humanity that are openly working in the world in our times, and more highly developed beings who seek to assist our development. The statue that Rudolf Steiner carved out of wood, the Representative of Humanity, is an imagination for our "right standing" in the world in this time of the consciousness soul, when the confrontation with evil has become part and parcel of our daily work.

The Union in the Temple was a union between two for the purpose of enlightenment. This collaboration between two beings of very special standing at the Turning Point of Time, can be contemplated as a call to spirit-remembering in this year, whereby we open our souls to receive imaginations, inspirations, and intuitions flowing

---

1   Von Halle, *Descent Into the Depths of the Earth on the Anthroposophic Path of Schooling*, p. 49.

from our higher "I." Rudolf Steiner refers to this higher "I" as manas consciousness (see glossary), a consciousness that develops the capacity to see into the etheric, and perceive the forces working behind world events. This year's memory of the union between the two is not limited to only a union between two different individualities that become one, but can be mirrored by a single individuality opening to receive forces descending from one's higher self. It is exactly these higher faculties that can act as ballast for the "weight" of materialism pulling humanity into subhuman realms. When one's higher and lower "I"-beings are in resonance, one is able to stand in the place where Michaelic truth can be found; and from this "free space" of balance one can find strength to endure trials, and rightly travel the path one's angel has set before oneself. In the event that we fail to recognize adversaries now working openly, this union could also manifest as an inversion of the Union in the Temple, whereby ahrimanic powers may unite with a prepared human being, or perhaps with an unprepared and unconscious human being, through whom evil can manifest. Rudolf Steiner prophesied that Ahriman would incarnate shortly after the beginning of the twentieth century. Indeed we live in a time that is shortly after the beginning of the twenty-first century.

In his lecture seris *The Fifth Gospel*, Rudolf Steiner addresses the Union in the Temple. Here it is explained how the two Jesus children came into the world as representatives of two of the sacred posts of Israel: King and Priest. In the Matthew Gospel we hear of the birth of the Solomon Jesus, descended from the kingly line of David. To this Jesus came the three wise men bearing gifts. In the Luke Gospel we hear of the Nathan Jesus, descended from the priestly line of David. It was he who was visited by the shepherds. The Solomon Jesus was the older of the two, having been born four years and nine months before the Nathan Jesus. This Solomon Jesus was the reincarnated Zarathustra, called "radiant star"—a very high initiate of great wisdom, who had frequently incarnated on Earth. The younger Jesus, the Nathan Jesus of Luke, was a paradisiacal

immaculate soul who was filled with love, but did not have earthly experience. It was in the temple in Jerusalem, during the Feast of the Passover in AD 12, that the union between these two Jesus children took place. The Zarathustra being departed from his body and united with the immaculate soul of the Nathan Jesus, who was twelve years of age at the time. This marked the joining together of the two lineages of priest and king. Two months after this union the Solomon Jesus child was put to rest—meaning he had completely excarnated from his physical body. It would not be correct to say that he died, for his being (encompassing great wisdom) lived on in the immaculate soul of the Nathan Jesus.

The very next day after this union, the now-transformed Nathan Jesus was seen in various rabbinical schools in Jerusalem, discoursing with the doctors and scribes, astounding them with his knowledge. It was in one of these schools that his parents found him, and were in wonder at the change that had come over their child. Later he returned to Nazareth with his parents. From that time onward he became a teacher among his companions. This union between the two Jesus children was the union of wisdom with love—a powerful combination that was completely necessary for the accomplishment of the incarnation of Christ that lay ahead. In like manner the collaboration between our higher and lower "I" is necessary to experience Christ as he is now manifesting in the etheric realms surrounding the Earth.

The Two Become One

This is a theme not only for the month of January (January 2 is the exact date of the commemoration) but also for the entire year and beyond; and when such commemorations are working from the etheric realms surrounding the Earth, they sound into history and become reflected in human lives and historic events. It has been over one hundred years since Christ began working in this way, and it has been thirty-three years since the last commemoration of this event. The etheric activity of Christ began in 1899 with what Rudolf Steiner referred to as the beginning of a New Age. We can look back through the last century and make note of events that formed on Earth as this commemoration "pulsed through time" three times before this year's fourth commemoration. These preceding commemorations were in the years 1911, 1945, and 1978. We can look at gestures in history peculiar to these years to help us understand what this year's commemoration may bring.

In 1911 the leadership of the Theosophical Society at Adyar established a new organization called the *Order of the Star in the East* (OSE). A young man named Krishnamurti was heralded as the leader of this order. The leaders of the Theosophical Society at that time, Charles Webster Leadbeater and Annie Besant, believed Krishnamurti to be the likely vehicle for a messianic entity called the World Teacher. On the anniversary of the Earth's biographical memory of the Union in the Temple, when the Zarathustra being entered into union with the immaculate Jesus being, another young man became exalted as the vehicle into which would come a World Teacher. Besant and Leadbeater became the "false prophets" who caused all to worship the person who was revered, in error, as the Messiah reappearing in a physical body and—simultaneously—as the Maitreya Bodhisattva (see glossary). This went against everything Rudolf Steiner was trying to prepare. In 1899 Steiner had encountered Christ in the etheric realm of the Earth, and in 1910 he had already begun to speak publicly about these matters in their true light.

The Krishnamurti affair was a *pretense* of two becoming one that was set up by Leadbeater and Besant. They became false prophets for a mistaken union that fortunately was revealed by Krishnamurti himself. Other false prophets have appeared throughout history. Two additional examples in the twentieth century are Adolf Hitler and Joseph Stalin. Both of these individuals were possessed by adversarial beings and both carried out intentions of adversarial powers, accomplishing an unbelievable amount of evil in their lives, particularly after the year 1933, a year when Rudolf Steiner proclaimed the beast would rise. In the twenty-first century the false prophets that show up will also be possessed by powers

gained from adversaries, but what will be new is the plethora of technological tools that will be at their fingertips. These tools were not available to Hitler or Stalin. However, technology provides a perfect medium for false prophets and their puppets to reach the masses. This makes the false prophets of the twenty-first century considerably better equipped than the false prophets that have come before them to create images that are capable of causing the masses to worship beasts. Krishnamurti was seen as a vehicle into which a World Teacher would work. This year's commemoration, one hundred years after the Krishnamurti affair, finds us in a world where we seem to be whirling toward not a World Teacher, but perhaps a World Ruler. What is the difference between a World Ruler—a Hitler or a Stalin—and the true Union we are commemorating this year?

The Union in the Temple between the two Jesus children was not a *possession* but rather an *enlightenment* born of spiritual guidance and obedience. The union that occurs under the influence of "false prophets" is a union that takes over the individuality; and through this individuality they are able to directly inspire the one possessed, such as a Hitler or a Stalin. This is not an enlightenment but rather a possession backed by the most powerful enemy of Christ—the one Rudolf Steiner called the Antichrist. Through enlightenment the innate individuality is not used, but rather there is a willing and conscious collaboration out of free will. In possession the situation is the opposite—the individuality *is* used, and may be unaware that there has been a possession of one's free will. In possession, directives from subearthly realms are followed for the pursuit of power *over* others, seeded with a hatred of one kind or another—though this hatred is often the last attribute of the one possessed to become obvious to those observing. This is antithetical to the enlightened collaboration of the spiritually decreed Union that this year is commemorating, which seeks strength *with* others, and increases one's love of one's fellow humanity and the Earth.

After 1911, the next commemoration of the Union in the Temple during the twentieth century began to show its fruits as Hitler began his rise to power in Germany, becoming a false prophet for the "rights" of the German people. This personality was obviously in union with very dark forces of hatred. It was indeed this dark personality who started World War II by invading Poland in 1939, using lies and propaganda to win the support of his people. In August of 1945, 33⅓ years after the Krishnamurti affair, the second commemoration of the Union in the Temple was marked by the United States conducting two atomic bombings against the Japanese cities of Hiroshima and Nagasaki. This can be seen as an opening of the gates of hell, for the Earth's crust was cracked, and the gates of the underworld were opened for the first time through a physical phenomenon. The possessed madman acquired access to demonic powers, and the United States, through nuclear weapons, found solutions based on anti-life measures that are emblematic of demonically inspired intervention.

With the unleashing of atomic power we entered into a new theater of war. Not just a war against other nations, but also a war against the foundational spiritual origin of our species—Divine Life. With the fracturing of the mantle of the Earth it was as if subearthly forces could more freely affect human beings, bringing possessive forces directly into the cultural sphere. It is not as if possession then began. Possession was well known in Biblical times and before. The change that was occurring with the opening of the gates of hell was a change that would only later show itself through its manifestation in the use of electricity, magnetism, and nuclear energies. These subearthly forces would create fields of influences little understood, and the ensuing inventions even less understood—as to their effects physically, culturally, and spiritually. As we began to mechanize our world more and more, we gave little thought to the balance this development would demand for the subtle bodies of the spiritual human being. As subearthly forces were increasingly used, church attendance began to fall, creation stories came under attack, fairy tales became childish, elemental beings became fantasy, and spiritual perceptivity and sensitivity

became taboo. So much of what would assist human beings in learning how to perceive Christ in the etheric realm was forgotten, thrown out, or cynically denied. False prophets proclaimed the value of progressive new products from pesticides to white bread, Agent Orange to growth hormones, terminator seeds to psycho-pharmaceuticals, cloning to the heinous idea of lab-grown meat. Science in ignorance of the spiritual origin and destiny of the Earth and humanity was more and more left open for immoral inspirations born of destructive beings working against a Christ-filled evolution. These immoral inspirations have gone hand in hand with an alarming increase of open indecency within the culture. This indecency results in destructive practices against the world of the elementals and the world of childhood. Indecency can become so systemic that it is no longer even noticed.

As the third and final commemoration of the Union in the Temple during the twentieth century approached, biotechnology was closing in on the creation of the first genetically modified plant cell, and enormous amounts of spiritual energy were being spent creating new and far-reaching technologies. In the year of 1978, 33⅓ years after the opening of the gates of hell, Digital Equipment Corporation gained the ability to address massive amounts of virtual memory, providing hundreds of times the capacity of most minicomputers. The race was on, from personal computer ingenuity to satellite technology. Rudolf Steiner was well aware of how human beings would gradually be severed from Cosmic Thoughts, as we now witness with the grid of personal opinion and fast-track technologies spinning ever-denser webs around both individuals and the planet. This grid is not unlike the thorn hedge that surrounded Sleeping Beauty's castle. The knights that drew their swords against the hedge, trying to reach the Sleeping Beauty, died in the hedge. The last knight, before whom the hedge simply parted, found reunion with Sleeping Beauty. In like manner, we all stand before this hedge. We are not to fight it, but rather develop the capacity to penetrate through in order to reunite with the

Sleeping Beauty—Sophia, the World Soul. As we learn to perceive etherically, which is the fruit of the collaboration between the human being and higher worlds, we will more easily understand how the "adversaries" are working to achieve their manifold and far-reaching agendas. Those who thus prepare etherically to see into these realms, will be those who are on a Grail quest. The Knights of the Grail were trained to confront evil. This is the task of our age, the age of the consciousness soul: to meet evil and do the good.

We could say that the knights, who sought to force their way through the hedge, brought the dead thoughts of the past. The successful knight brought forces from the future, forces we could liken to the etheric forces that Christ is bestowing in our times. With these forces the hedge simply parts to reveal the World Soul. The hedge has no power against the Michaelic truth of Christ. It is through Sophia that Michaelic truths become understandable. Without the Sleeping Beauty, world-thoughts remain cold. The more we develop our subtle bodies, the greater will be our ability to free ourselves from the deadening forces of abstraction and materialism. This capacity, then, will deliver us into realms where we awaken to the realizations that there *is* spiritual support from higher beings waiting to assist us. This recognition of what we can look up to will help us wrest ourselves free from powerful attachments to falsehoods born of materialism. Through spiritual deepening, human beings learn the art of becoming empty so as to become vessels into which spiritual knowledge will find us as we need it. What does this mean?

To counter the forces that have gained so much strength throughout the past century, we must return to spiritual knowledge. If we are to free ourselves from the captivating forces of illusion and manipulation that have spawned sinister traps that threaten the viability of our culture, we must engage in practices that fortify the etheric body. Immersion in the peace, beauty, and stillness of nature is one such practice. Further, on the one hand artistic activity such as painting, music, eurythmy, and so on are conducive to strengthening the etheric body; and on the other

hand spiritual practices such as meditation and prayer are most helpful. As we center ourselves through such pursuits we become willing vessels for angelic inspiration. Angels cannot come to the self-satisfied, nor to those filled with personal certainty—but they come instead to those who are aware of spiritual hunger and spiritual emptiness. This emptiness is found through the above practices, which when done in the light of love result in harmonious collaboration among all beings. The first beatitude can be our guide: *Blessed are the poor in spirit for theirs is the kingdom of heaven.*

Along with declining morals and increasing "genius" inspired from adversarial forces, and in addition to the changes in agriculture and technology, there are also the false prophets of marketing and advertising who continue to lead humanity to "buy into" what is best for the money-changers, in blatant disregard for what is best for human beings and the Earth. What does all this mean for the commemoration of the Union in the Temple?

We have looked at a few of the precedents that accompanied the three preceding times in history when this event in the biography of Christ has sounded into time. There is a story that can be traced through the past that reveals the necessity of spiritual awakening. If this awakening goes about unnoticed, disturbing issues will become all the more overwhelming from the year of 2012 onward. There is growing evidence that the generations being raised on technology and engineered foods will more easily be prey for possessing forces, and those possessed (or dumbed down) will not have the discrimination necessary to discern a "false prophet" from a super hero. We can remember that in 1911, even those who were spiritually striving were fooled by the promise of a messianic union. Then it was the proclamation of a "World Teacher." Now it might be—with the hundredth anniversary of this event—that a false prophet may proclaim and pave the way for a false, seriously possessed "World Ruler."

What deserves our attention is how the three preceding events set up precedents that could play out again in our time. The first commemoration remembers false prophets, making way for a mistaken union with a divine being. The second commemoration remembers someone possessed by the will-to-power, whose rule came to an end shortly before the gates of hell were opened through the detonation of the two atomic bombs. The third commemoration remembers the advancement of technologies with profit margins, rather than moral considerations held as sacrosanct. Putting the three together we could say that there may be false prophets proclaiming new messiahs possessed by the will-to-power, and that these individuals now have advanced technologies at their fingertips with which they can influence great masses of people with their agendas, lies, and propaganda. Hitler could only have dreamed of such channels of persuasion! In the meantime, the masses have been dumbed down by exactly the technologies that have been brought to them under the guise of the advancement of knowledge. Depth of thinking has been marginalized, as thinking fractures into bits and twitters. To work with Michaelic Cosmic Thoughts, one must have the power of concentration and the restfulness of contemplation. These are just a few of the attributes that technologies most successfully annihilate—and the mad trend of multi-tasking is a signature for the demise of wisdom-filled thinking.

The twenty-first century witnesses power concentrating to a smaller and smaller group of elites who hold most of the money. This does not reflect the collaborative culture that enlightenment brings, but rather it reflects the greed culture that possession entreats. It is perhaps time to stand before the thorn hedge and practice the new arts of etheric deepening as an antidote to the growing threat of toxic climates in the realms of thinking, feeling and willing—where we increasingly witness dead thoughts and obsessive/repetitive egoism, which breed animalistic instincts in mechanized bodies that eat lab meat and foods grown from pathologically suicidal seeds. It is time to stop moving so fast—it is time to slow down, and then move more purposefully. Hurry seems to be one of the signs of the influence of the beast (see chapter 13

of Revelation). We have to remember that thinking is a contemplative art in collaboration with higher beings, guided by Michael, and warmed by Sophia. Feeling is a heart-born experience of two or more creating (in person) a place for a third—Christ. Moreover, willing is to be placed in service to the mission and purpose of the whole evolution of the Earth—the mission that our planet may become a planet of love. If food continues to be extracted from its living archetypes—away from the Word of God who created all things—this will be the death knell for spiritual remembrance.

How many little children need come through the doors of therapists and say "I don't want to be here anymore" before we sound the alarm? How much longer will we turn a blind eye to *"entertainment"* that is seeding violence and debauchery as familiar and therefore tolerable? How many teens and young adults need come into the headlines as suicides, or addicts before we regard possession as a cultural pathology? How many adults need to commit mass murders or kill their families and children, or enact animalistic sexual deviations before we wake up to the presence of a beast among us? How indecent does the culture need to become before we notice how far we have fallen? Are technological media suitable teachers for our children—or has technology become the false World Teacher that was only hinted at in 1911 and has become realized in the twenty-first century through the terminal medium of virtual reality?

Technology is not bad in and of itself. It is a tool. Unfortunately it has become much more than the tool it is. It has become the fashioner of ideas, the source of indescribable indecency; and its promoters have become the false prophets of an educational promise that may be disguising a wolf in sheep's clothing. We have—to a greater or lesser extent—become possessed by the tool! Virtual toys, games, and applications are contributing to a type of possession that endlessly seeks to increase itself, swallowing reality in its wake and taking in victim after victim. This all sounds as though a disease is being characterized, not the marvelous new "World Teacher" of the virtual world. The three tempters of the twentieth century, now in the twenty-first century, have coalesced their efforts and now work together on behalf of a fourth tempter—a demon against the Sun and the very "I" of humanity. This year we celebrate the fourth commemoration of *Two Becoming One* in order to advance the purpose of love. Now, over one hundred years after the beginning of a New Age, we may face the danger of our "one" individuality fracturing—becoming two, becoming none—not through enlightenment, but through possession and its eventual consequence, which is the destruction of the "I." That is not what the holy Union in the Temple is sounding: that is an inversion of what this union is sounding.

The resounding of the Union in the Temple in 2012 provides an opportunity to find our connection with our higher self through reclaiming our collaboration with Cosmic thinking and the angelic worlds that await our turning to them. Through illumined thinking we will see the battle for the human soul raging around us, and the correct 'naming' of this divine phenomenon will reveal the part we are to play on behalf of spiritual worlds—revealing our tasks as players in this battle. By willfully uniting ourselves with Christ-imbued Love and the wisdom of Sophia, we will develop the intuition to unmask any false prophets that may be leading astray those who are sleeping. We will develop the consciousness to recognize any possessed beasts using lies and propaganda. We will develop the awareness to see the hidden dimensions behind all technologies that are deadening the capacities for human beings to connect with their higher spiritual member—manas, or spirit self.

It will take effort to name the forces that are working against what is humanity's spiritual potential, against what is decent, and against what is true. These efforts will bring to birth new cultural impulses that will assist us in protectively parenting against wolves in sheep's clothing, and will help us accurately perceive when and where lies are being spread through a great propaganda machine whose reach is the entire world. We are to become filled with knowledge of higher worlds: this is the Grail path! Moreover, as we collectively cross the threshold (see glossary), we are to arm ourselves with the love of truth that will set us free from the illusions our culture has "bought" into.

May this year's Union in the Temple be a union that ennobles us, and encourages us to help others. The Constitution of the Iroquois Nations states:

> We place at the top of the Tree of the Long Leaves [the tree of peace that bound the five nations together] an Eagle who is able to see afar. If he sees in the distance any evil approaching or any danger threatening he will at once warn the people of the Confederacy.[2]

There is a great binding law that we once remembered when we were connected to the eternal spirits. This is the law of peace. Peace is the natural state of being for children of God. May we increase peace through this coming year and learn to see like the Eagle. Danger is approaching! It is just this danger that, if recognized, will be the stimulus for our awakening. May we find our spiritual brothers and sisters and play our parts to bring forth the good, the beautiful and the true. I know our children's angels are praying that we do this—for the children come to me, and they tell me that they don't want to be here anymore.

---

2   See http://www.constitution.org/cons/iroquois.htm.

WORKING WITH THE STAR CALENDER IN THE *JOURNAL FOR STAR WISDOM*

Robert Powell, Ph.D.

In taking note of the astronomical events listed in the Star Calendar of the *Journal for Star Wisdom* (*JSW*), it is important to distinguish between long- and short-term astronomical events. Long-term astronomical events—for example, Pluto transiting a particular degree of the zodiac—will have a longer period of meditation than would the five days advocated for short-term astronomical events such as the new and Full Moon. The following describes, in relation to meditating on the Full Moon, a meditative process extending over a five-day period.

Sanctification of the Full Moon

As a preliminary remark, let us remind ourselves that the great sacrifice of Christ on the Cross—the Mystery of Golgotha—took place at Full Moon. As Christ's sacrifice took place when the Moon was full in the middle of the sidereal sign of Libra, the Libra Full Moon assumes special significance in the sequence of twelve (or thirteen) Full Moons taking place during the cycle of the year. In following this sequence, the Mystery of Golgotha serves as an archetype for *every* Full Moon, since each Full Moon imparts a particular spiritual blessing. Hence the practice described here of *Sanctification of the Full Moon* applies to every Full Moon. Similarly, there is also the practice of *Sanctification of the New Moon*, as described in *Hermetic Astrology, Volume 2: Astrological Biography,* chapter 10.

During the two days prior to the Full Moon, we can consider the focus of one's meditation to extend over these two days as *preparatory days* immediately preceding the day of the Full Moon. These two days can be dedicated to spiritual reflection and detachment from everyday concerns, as one prepares to become a vessel for the in-streaming light and love one will receive at the Full Moon, something that one can then impart

further—for example, to help people in need, or to support Mother Earth in times of catastrophe. During these two days, it is helpful to hold an attitude of dedication and service and try to assume an attitude of receptivity that opens to what one's soul will receive and subsequently impart—an attitude conducive to making one a true *servant of the spirit.*

The day of the Full Moon is itself a day of *holding the sacred space.* In doing so, one endeavors to cultivate inner peace and silence, during which one attempts to contact and consciously hold the in-streaming blessing of the Full Moon for the rest of humanity. One can heighten this silent meditation by visualizing the zodiacal constellation/sidereal sign in which the Moon becomes full, since the Moon serves to reflect the starry background against which it appears.

If the Moon is full in Virgo, for example, it reminds us of the night of the birth of the Jesus child visited by the three magi, as described in the Gospel of St. Matthew. That birth occurred at the Full Moon in the middle of the sidereal sign of Virgo, and the three magi, who gazed up that evening to behold the Full Moon against the background of the stars of the Virgin, witnessed the soul of Jesus emerge from the disk of the Full Moon and descend toward Earth. They participated from afar, via the starry heavens, in the Grail Mystery of the holy birth.

In meditating upon the Full Moon and opening oneself to receive the in-streaming blessing from the starry heavens, we can exercise restraint by avoiding the formulation of what will happen or what one might receive from the Full Moon. Moreover, we can also refrain from seeking tangible results or effects connected with our attunement to the Full Moon. Even if we observe only the date but not the exact moment when the Moon is full, it is helpful to find quiet time to reflect alone or to use the opportunity for deep meditation on the day of the full moon.

We can think of the two days following the full moon as a *time of imparting* what we have received from the in-streaming of the full disk of the Moon against the background of the stars. It is now possible to turn our attention toward humanity and the world and endeavor to pass on any spiritual blessing we have received from the starry heavens. Thereby we can assist in the work of the spiritual world by transforming what we have received into goodwill and allowing it to flow wherever the greatest need exists.

It is a matter of *holding a sacred space* throughout the day of the full moon. This is an important time to still the mind and maintain inner peace. It is a time of spiritual retreat and contact with the spiritual world, of holding in one's consciousness the archetype of the Mystery of Golgotha as a great outpouring of Divine Love that bridges Heaven and Earth. Prior to the day of the full moon, the two preceding days prepare the sacred space as a vessel to receive the heavenly blessing. The two days following the day of the full moon are a time to assimilate and distribute the spiritual transmission received into the sacred space we have prepared.

One can apply the process described here as a meditative practice in relation to the full moon to any of the astronomical events listed in the *JSW,* especially as most of these *remember* significant Christ Events. Take note, however, whether an event is long-term or short-term and adjust the period of meditative practice accordingly.

☙

"The shadow intellect that is characteristic of all modern culture has fettered human beings to the Earth. They have eyes only for earthly things, particularly when they allow themselves to be influenced by the claims of modern science. In our age it never occurs to someone that their being belongs not to the Earth alone but to the cosmos beyond the Earth. Knowledge of our connection with the cosmos beyond the Earth—that is what we need above all to make our own.... When someone says 'I' to themselves, they experience a force that is working within, and the [ancient] Greek, in feeling the working of this inner force, related it to the Sun; ... the Sun and the 'I' are the outer and inner aspects of one being. The Sun out there in space is the cosmic 'I.' What lives within me is the human 'I'.... Human beings are not primarily a creation of Earth. Human beings receive their shape and form from the cosmos. The human being is an offspring of the world of stars, above all of the Sun and Moon.... The Moon forces stream out from a center in the metabolic system.... [The] Moon stimulates reproduction.... Saturn works chiefly in the upper part of the astral body.... Jupiter has to do with thinking...Mars [has] to do with speech.... The Mercury forces work in the part of the human organism that lies below the region of the heart...in the breathing and circulatory functions.... Venus works preeminently in the etheric body of the human being."

—RUDOLF STEINER, *Offspring of the World of Stars*, May 5, 1921

SYMBOLS USED IN CHARTS

PLANETS		ZODIACAL SIGNS		ASPECTS	
⊕	Earth	♈	Aries (Ram)	☌	Conjunction 0°
☉	Sun	♉	Taurus (Bull)	✳	Sextile 60°
☽	Moon	♊	Gemini (Twins)	◻	Square 90°
☿	Mercury	♋	Cancer (Crab)	△	Trine 120°
♀	Venus	♌	Leo (Lion)	☍	Opposition 180°
♂	Mars	♍	Virgo (Virgin)		
♃	Jupiter	♎	Libra (Scales)		
♄	Saturn	♏	Scorpio (Scorpion)		
♅	Uranus	♐	Sagittarius (Archer)		
♆	Neptune	♑	Capricorn (Goat)		
♇	Pluto	♒	Aquarius (Water Carrier)		
		♓	Pisces (Fishes)		

OTHER			
☊	Ascending (North) Node	☌	Sun Eclipse
☋	Descending (South) Node	☍	Moon Eclipse
P	Perihelion/Perigee	☿	Inferior Conjunction
A	Aphelion/Apogee	☿	Superior Conjunction
N	Maximum Latitude	⚷	Chiron
S	Minimum Latitude		

TIME

The information relating to daily geocentric and heliocentric planetary positions in the sidereal zodiac is tabulated in the form of an ephemeris for each month, where the planetary positions are given at 0 hours universal time (UT) each day. Beneath the geocentric and heliocentric ephemeris for each month, the information relating to planetary aspects is given in the form of an aspectarian, listing the most important aspects—geocentric and heliocentric/hermetic—between the planets for the month in question. The day and the time of occurrence of the aspect on that day are indicated, all times being given in universal time, which is identical to Greenwich Mean Time (GMT). For example, zero hours universal time is midnight GMT. This time system applies in Britain; however, when summer time is in use, one hour has to be added to all times.

In other countries, the time has to be adjusted according to whether it is ahead of or behind Britain. For example, in Germany, where the time is one hour ahead of British time, one hour has to be added and, when summer time is in use in Germany, two hours have to be added to all times.

Using the calendar in the US, do the following subtraction from all time indications according to time zone: Pacific time subtract 8 hours (7 hours for daylight saving time); mountain time subtract 7 hours (6 hours for daylight saving time); central time subtract 6 hours (5 hours for daylight saving time); eastern time subtract 5 hours (4 hours for daylight saving time).

This subtraction will often change the date of an astronomical occurrence, shifting it back one day. On this account, since most of the readers of this calendar live on the American Continent, astronomical occurrences during the early hours of day x are listed as occurring on days $x-1/x$. For example, an eclipse occurring at 03:00 UT on the 12th is listed as occurring on the 11/12th since in America it takes place on the 11th.

See *General Introduction to the Christian Star Calendar: A Key to Understanding* for an in-depth clarification of the features of the calendar in the *Journal for Star Wisdom,* including indications as to how to work with it.

COMMENTARIES AND EPHEMERIDES
JANUARY–DECEMBER 2012
Claudia McLaren Lainson and Sally Nurney

The commentaries to the ephemerides of the *Journal for Star Wisdom* offer a practical approach for the study of Astrosophy. William Bento, in his article in this *Journal*, has outlined The Three Pillars of Star Wisdom as: Astrology, Anthroposophical Cosmology, and Esoteric Cosmic Christianity. The commentaries are a combination of these three pillars for the purpose of deepening into the life of Christ through the teachings of Rudolf Steiner, Valentin Tomberg, Robert Powell, and others. They offer meditative studies upon the deeds of Christ during his life on Earth, and they also invite us to participate in the presence of Christ here and now, as he is working in the etheric realms surrounding the Earth.

Connecting to the presence of Christ in the etheric is the task of our Age—the Age of the consciousness soul. Another task of our Age is to awaken to the presence of forces opposed to the working of Christ. Like the Grail Knights before us, we are to confront evil and bring forth the good. Knowledge of evil calls forth the good! This is a truth known to anyone who has studied the Grail legends, Anthroposophy, or the wisdom of Fairy Tales. Wisdom from ancient times is returning, now Christianized, to assist us on the quest of bringing forth new cultural impulses that will seed the founding of a peace-filled world.

Though the commentaries refer to specific events in *time*, the information they contain is based on the guidance of the Great Teachers of humanity, and is therefore *timeless*. They take us through the movements of the stars as they align with the events in Christ's life. Christ is teaching through these events now and forever. In connecting to Christ we are entering the School of the Greater Guardian of the Threshold—who is Christ. It is of great significance when the stars align with events in the life of Christ. What then sounds into time has a forming, sculpting force that will affect events on Earth for better or for worse. This all depends on our willingness to move in harmony with the great Beings of the stars, for to move against them will deliver us into trials of escalating intensity.

The etheric sphere surrounding the Earth holds the memories of the perfect biography of Jesus Christ. This realm holds the eternal book of life that we are all gradually learning to read. We can imagine that these biographical memories are portals through which the stars above and human beings below communicate, thus fulfilling the hermetic axiom: As above, so also below. Materialistic thinking, on the other hand, creates another sphere around the Earth. We can liken that sphere to the thorn hedge surrounding Sleeping Beauty's castle. It strives to prevent humanity form accessing the Christological memories of the perfect biography. Sophia, the World Soul, wears a mantle comprising all the stars in the heavens. She is the Sleeping Beauty, and each human soul is a droplet from her pure substance. Our souls awaken to her wisdom as we part the thorn hedge and remember how to read her stories, which she speaks through the movements of the stars.

We live in a wilderness of materialism. This wilderness will receive greater degrees of cosmic light as we move through this year of 2012 and beyond. It is just this light that will protect and strengthen those on a Christological, Sun-centric path, and this same light will create dread in the hearts of those who believe not in the spiritual world or its beings. A division is gradually occurring. A choice is being made by humanity. We can follow the call of spirit—the call of the Grail—as read through the stars, or we can continue to move with selfish agendas and fall even further from our divine potential.

As we follow the stars through this significant year, we are offered glimpses into forces moving and working behind world events. As we look to our world leaders we can bear witness to their deeds, for we shall know them by their fruits. It is incumbent on us all to better understand our times, and the beings of the stars are our guides. Just as Christ was in continual resonance with the stars throughout his entire ministry, so too will we, in a similar way, find resonance with the stars as we awaken to their stories. May our journeys this year be filled with light and love!

CONTRIBUTORS AND COMMENTS

Three people contributed to the commentaries. Sally Nurney wrote the astronomical Skywatch. This Skywatch tells us where to see the stars in the sky, and gives an overview of prominent monthly astronomical events. Richard Bloedon served as editor for the commentaries, for which we are deeply grateful. Claudia McLaren Lainson wrote the twelve months of commentaries, with specific attention to the significance of the year 2012 and the stellar events that highlight the challenges and hope for our work throughout this year. Some of the German has been re-translated by Richard Bloedon for use in the commentaries.

It is recommended that the whole sequence of commentaries first be read like a book, in order to gain an overview of the themes highlighted for the year 2012. Having this overview will assist one in deepening into the daily readings of the commentaries as they play out in time through the next twelve months.

The following is a list of abbreviations for books used frequently throughout the commentaries:

- *CHA*: Refers to Robert Powell's book, *Christian Hermetic Astrology*
- *Chron.*: Refers to Robert Powell's book, *Chronicles of the Living Christ*
- *ACE:* Refers to Anne Catherine Emmerich
- *LBVM*: Refers to the *Life of the Blessed Virgin Mary*, by ACE
- *LJC*: Refers to the Life of Jesus Christ, by ACE

JANUARY 2012

We begin the year with the Sun in the middle of the Archer (Sagittarius) and moving into Capricorn on the 15th. Venus begins 2012 as a brilliant evening star in Capricorn, and continues to shine after sunset until June of this year. Jupiter is visible in the night sky now and will be until the end of March. (July brings it back to view, but only in the predawn hours.) The waning Moon joins Jupiter on the 2nd, visible to the south at sunset, in 1° Aries (The Ram). Jupiter will become easier to see as the night darkens.

The "Quandrantids" meteor shower begins on the 1st and peak the 3rd–4th. Look to the northeast, below the Big Dipper after dark for a grand show of up to 40 meteors per hour! The Moon appears Full on the 9th. Mid-month, late nighters can see Mars rising with the Moon around midnight against the "tail end" of the Lion (Leo) and the beginning stars of the Virgin (Virgo). After midnight Saturn will rise behind Mars and Moon in 1° of the Scales (Libra), just past the bright star of Spica at 29° of Virgo. The New Moon is on the 23rd. The new crescent that emerges after sunset will shine with the evening star of Venus on the 26th; try to look westward as the light wanes this night. By the 30th, the growing Moon will have caught back up with Jupiter again.

Jan. 1: Sun 16° Sagittarius. Today is the 2012th anniversary of the birth of the Nathan Jesus. This is a being who is part angel and part human being. The Nathan Jesus received the Christ into his bodily sheaths at the Baptism in the Jordan, and his entire life of 33⅓-years lives eternally in the Earth's etheric aura—which is referred to by Rudolf Steiner as the "Eternal, or Fifth Gospel." The healthy evolution of humanity will depend on the human being's capacity to rise, through the consciousness soul, into these life-filled realms of the etheric, in order to receive the nourishment of life-filled forces that Christ alone can bestow, and *is now* bestowing, in union with this angel-human.

There is also a *night-side* to the biography of this immaculate soul in whom Christ indwelled on Earth, and this night-side is called the "Eternal

Apocalypse." The writer of the Apocalypse, the John Being, is guardian of these mysteries, and these mysteries are held in the starry realms surrounding the Earth. Through opening to the manas cognition that the angel Jesus is offering to humanity, one can find the way into these night mysteries that John guards. These are the mysteries of Sophia's inspirations, and these inspirations are part of the mysteries of the Holy Grail. Rudolf Steiner gives us indications of this truth:

> And we should keep in mind that continuation of the Parsifal saga, which says that when the Grail became invisible in Europe, it was carried to the realm of Presbyter John, who had his kingdom on the far side of the lands reached by the Crusaders. In the time of the Crusades the kingdom of Presbyter John, the successor of Parsifal, was still honored, and from the way in which search was made for it we must say: If all this were expressed in terms of strict earthly geography, it would show that the place of Presbyter John is not to be found on Earth.[1]

Where is this place? It is the place we visit each night to commune with the beings of the Moon, the Sun and Planets, and with the beings of the Stars. It is into these realms that the Grail has been taken. We reach these realms by lifting our "I" consciousness into the Christ-imbued etheric realms where the Nathan Jesus fills us with angel-thoughts. These angel-thoughts are the manna from heaven that give us the strength to begin a Grail Quest; and a Grail Quest will lead us to John, whose realm lies hidden in the depths of Sophia's night.

The Jesus being and Christ, the John being and Sophia: these are Grail Mysteries shepherding humanity into new realms of understanding. The year begins with our contemplation of this pure soul, a soul who carried to Earth the immaculate purity that belonged to human beings before the event of the Fall. And through this same being, humanity will find its way home.

ASPECT: Heliocentric conjunction between Venus and Uranus, 8°43' Pisces. Under this same aspect (although in Leo), two momentous events

occurred in the life of Lazarus: he united with John the Baptist while in the spiritual world, and he was then resurrected by Christ. Thereafter he was known as Lazarus-John in the mysteries, and he was known as Presbyter John after he went to live in Ephesus. The Venus mysteries are the mysteries of the purified etheric body—a body filled with peace and harmony—and Uranus brings startling images from the future that find a resting place in the peace-filled waters of our Venus nature. The conjunction of these two planets perfectly exemplified the miracle of the raising of Lazarus, when Lazarus-John received a new, Christ-imbued etheric body, and it is this same being who later wrote the startling Book of Revelation.

On this day of commemoration of the birth of the angelic Nathan Jesus, (under the influence of Venus conjunct Uranus) we may pray that through our communion with higher worlds we too will be raised from the deadening afflictions of materialism in this coming year.

January 2: Sun 17° Sagittarius: Conception of the Virgin Mary (8 Dec 22 BC). The Virgin Mary, in a previous incarnation, walked the Earth as the Queen from the South, the Queen of Sheba. She is mentioned in the Gospels: "The queen of the South will rise at the judgment with this generation and condemn it, for she came from the ends of the Earth to hear the wisdom of Solomon, and behold, something greater than Solomon is here" (Matt.12:42).

The Virgin Mary was illuminated by Sophia at the Holy Whitsun Festival, and she waits for each of us to find Sophia's illumination within the eternal silence of our own heart.

Event: The Union in the Temple. The Mystery of Two becoming One is remembered today. See the opening article to the commentaries: *The Two Become One*, in this issue of the *Journal for Star Wisdom*. Jesus Christ lived on Earth for 33⅓ years. Still today, 2012 years after his death and resurrection, the living pictures of his life on Earth continue to weave into evolution on Earth. These pictures unfold in rhythms of 33⅓-year cycles. We are currently in the 61st cycle of the 33⅓-year rhythm of Christ in the etheric. The last cycle ended on

---

1   Steiner, *Christ and the Spiritual World*, p. 139.

SIDEREAL GEOCENTRIC LONGITUDES : JANUARY 2012 Gregorian at 0 hours UT

DAY		☉	☽	☊	☿	♀	♂	♃	♄	♅	♆	♇
1	SU	15 ♐ 3	12 ♓ 13	19 ♏ 4R	24 ♏ 56	18 ♑ 56	25 ♌ 12	5 ♈ 31	3 ♎ 23	5 ♓ 56	3 ♒ 59	12 ♐ 25
2	MO	16 5	24 7	19 4D	26 17	20 9	25 27	5 33	3 27	5 57	4 1	12 27
3	TU	17 6	5 ♈ 57	19 5	27 39	21 23	25 40	5 34	3 30	5 59	4 3	12 29
4	WE	18 7	17 48	19 7	29 2	22 36	25 54	5 36	3 34	6 0	4 5	12 32
5	TH	19 8	29 43	19 9	0 ♐ 26	23 50	26 6	5 38	3 37	6 1	4 6	12 34
6	FR	20 9	11 ♉ 48	19 10	1 51	25 3	26 18	5 40	3 41	6 2	4 8	12 36
7	SA	21 10	24 5	19 10R	3 16	26 16	26 30	5 43	3 44	6 4	4 10	12 38
8	SU	22 11	6 ♊ 38	19 9	4 43	27 30	26 41	5 45	3 47	6 5	4 12	12 40
9	MO	23 13	19 28	19 6	6 9	28 43	26 51	5 48	3 50	6 7	4 13	12 42
10	TU	24 14	2 ♋ 34	19 1	7 37	29 56	27 1	5 51	3 53	6 8	4 15	12 44
11	WE	25 15	15 56	18 55	9 5	1 ♒ 9	27 11	5 54	3 56	6 10	4 17	12 46
12	TH	26 16	29 32	18 49	10 34	2 22	27 19	5 58	3 59	6 11	4 19	12 49
13	FR	27 17	13 ♌ 19	18 43	12 3	3 36	27 27	6 1	4 2	6 13	4 21	12 51
14	SA	28 18	27 14	18 38	13 33	4 48	27 35	6 5	4 4	6 15	4 23	12 53
15	SU	29 19	11 ♍ 16	18 34	15 4	6 1	27 41	6 9	4 7	6 17	4 25	12 55
16	MO	0 ♑ 20	25 21	18 33	16 35	7 14	27 48	6 13	4 9	6 18	4 27	12 57
17	TU	1 21	9 ♎ 29	18 33D	18 6	8 27	27 53	6 17	4 12	6 20	4 29	12 59
18	WE	2 23	23 38	18 34	19 39	9 40	27 58	6 22	4 14	6 22	4 31	13 1
19	TH	3 24	7 ♏ 46	18 35	21 11	10 52	28 2	6 27	4 16	6 24	4 33	13 3
20	FR	4 25	21 51	18 36R	22 44	12 5	28 5	6 32	4 18	6 26	4 35	13 5
21	SA	5 26	5 ♐ 52	18 34	24 18	13 18	28 8	6 37	4 20	6 28	4 37	13 7
22	SU	6 27	19 46	18 30	25 52	14 30	28 10	6 42	4 22	6 30	4 39	13 9
23	MO	7 28	3 ♑ 28	18 24	27 27	15 42	28 11	6 47	4 23	6 32	4 41	13 11
24	TU	8 29	16 56	18 16	29 3	16 55	28 11	6 53	4 25	6 34	4 43	13 13
25	WE	9 30	0 ♒ 8	18 6	0 ♑ 38	18 7	28 11R	6 59	4 26	6 36	4 45	13 15
26	TH	10 31	13 1	17 57	2 15	19 19	28 10	7 5	4 28	6 39	4 47	13 17
27	FR	11 32	25 36	17 48	3 52	20 31	28 8	7 11	4 29	6 41	4 49	13 19
28	SA	12 33	7 ♓ 55	17 40	5 30	21 43	28 5	7 17	4 30	6 43	4 51	13 21
29	SU	13 34	20 0	17 35	7 9	22 55	28 2	7 24	4 31	6 46	4 54	13 23
30	MO	14 35	1 ♈ 54	17 32	8 48	24 7	27 57	7 30	4 32	6 48	4 56	13 25
31	TU	15 36	13 44	17 31	10 27	25 19	27 52	7 37	4 33	6 50	4 58	13 27

INGRESSES :

2	☽ → ♈ 11:54	20	☽ → ♐ 13:55
4	☿ → ♐ 16:36	22	☽ → ♑ 17:53
5	☽ → ♉ 0:33	24	☿ → ♑ 14:23
7	☽ → ♊ 11:21		☽ → ♒ 23:45
9	☽ → ♋ 19:20	27	☽ → ♓ 8:30
10	♀ → ♒ 1:14	29	☽ → ♈ 20: 8
12	☽ → ♌ 0:49		
14	☽ → ♍ 4:44		
15	☉ → ♑ 16: 0		
16	☽ → ♎ 7:53		
18	☽ → ♏ 10:48		

ASPECTS & ECLIPSES :

1	☿ □ ♂ 5:54		☽ ☍ ♆ 8:23		☉ □ ♄ 21:12		☽ ☌ ♅ 21:38
	☉ □ ☽ 6:14	13	☽ ☊ ☊ 9:15	21	☽ ☌ ♇ 12:30	28	☉ □ ♇ 18:37
2	☽ ☍ ♄ 19: 0		☿ ☌ ♇ 12:54	22	☉ □ ♃ 6:29	29	☿ □ ♃ 3:57
	☽ ☌ A 20: 1		♀ ☌ ♆ 15:18		☽ ☌ ☿ 12: 2	30	☽ ☍ ♄ 5:20
	☽ ☌ ♃ 23:13	14	☽ ☌ ♂ 0:35	23	☉ ☌ ☽ 7:39		☽ ☌ ♃ 11:28
6	☽ ☌ ☋ 14:27		☽ ☍ ♅ 15:27	24	♀ □ ☊ 23:50		☽ ☌ A 17:27
7	☽ ☍ ☿ 19:52	16	☉ □ ☽ 9: 7	25	☽ ☌ ♆ 8:33	31	☉ □ ☽ 4: 9
8	☽ ☍ ♇ 11:22		☽ ☌ ♄ 14:59	26	☽ ☋ ☊ 9:12		
	☿ □ ♅ 23:13		☽ ☍ ♃ 18:33		☽ ☌ ♀ 13:12		
9	☉ ☍ ☽ 7:29	17	☽ ☌ P 21: 4	27	☽ ☍ ♂ 4:51		
12	☽ ☍ ♀ 5:27	19	☽ ☌ ☊ 18:26		☿ □ ♄ 9: 7		

SIDEREAL HELIOCENTRIC LONGITUDES : JANUARY 2012 Gregorian at 0 hours UT

DAY		Sid. Time	☿	♀	⊕	♂	♃	♄	♅	♆	♇	Vernal Point
1	SU	6:40:14	2 ♎ 23	8 ♓ 0	15 ♊ 3	21 ♋ 13	16 ♈ 12	27 ♍ 51	8 ♓ 42	5 ♒ 24	12 ♐ 20	5 ♓ 5'33"
2	MO	6:44:11	5 38	9 36	16 4	21 40	16 17	27 53	8 43	5 25	12 20	5 ♓ 5'33"
3	TU	6:48: 8	8 49	11 11	17 5	22 6	16 23	27 55	8 44	5 25	12 21	5 ♓ 5'33"
4	WE	6:52: 4	11 56	12 47	18 7	22 33	16 28	27 57	8 44	5 25	12 21	5 ♓ 5'33"
5	TH	6:56: 1	15 0	14 22	19 8	22 59	16 34	27 59	8 45	5 26	12 21	5 ♓ 5'33"
6	FR	6:59:57	18 1	15 58	20 9	23 26	16 39	28 1	8 45	5 26	12 22	5 ♓ 5'33"
7	SA	7: 3:54	20 59	17 33	21 10	23 52	16 44	28 3	8 46	5 26	12 22	5 ♓ 5'33"
8	SU	7: 7:50	23 55	19 9	22 11	24 19	16 50	28 5	8 47	5 27	12 22	5 ♓ 5'32"
9	MO	7:11:47	26 49	20 45	23 12	24 45	16 55	28 6	8 47	5 27	12 23	5 ♓ 5'32"
10	TU	7:15:43	29 41	22 20	24 13	25 11	17 1	28 8	8 48	5 27	12 23	5 ♓ 5'32"
11	WE	7:19:40	2 ♏ 31	23 56	25 14	25 38	17 6	28 10	8 49	5 28	12 23	5 ♓ 5'32"
12	TH	7:23:37	5 20	25 32	26 16	26 4	17 12	28 12	8 49	5 28	12 24	5 ♓ 5'32"
13	FR	7:27:33	8 7	27 7	27 17	26 31	17 17	28 14	8 50	5 29	12 24	5 ♓ 5'32"
14	SA	7:31:30	10 54	28 43	28 18	26 57	17 23	28 16	8 51	5 29	12 24	5 ♓ 5'32"
15	SU	7:35:26	13 39	0 ♈ 19	29 19	27 23	17 28	28 18	8 51	5 29	12 25	5 ♓ 5'32"
16	MO	7:39:23	16 24	1 55	0 ♋ 20	27 50	17 34	28 20	8 52	5 30	12 25	5 ♓ 5'31"
17	TU	7:43:19	19 9	3 31	1 21	28 16	17 39	28 22	8 53	5 30	12 25	5 ♓ 5'31"
18	WE	7:47:16	21 54	5 7	2 22	28 42	17 44	28 24	8 53	5 30	12 26	5 ♓ 5'31"
19	TH	7:51:12	24 39	6 42	3 23	29 9	17 50	28 26	8 54	5 31	12 26	5 ♓ 5'31"
20	FR	7:55: 9	27 24	8 18	4 24	29 35	17 55	28 28	8 54	5 31	12 26	5 ♓ 5'31"
21	SA	7:59: 6	0 ♐ 9	9 54	5 26	0 ♌ 1	18 1	28 30	8 55	5 31	12 27	5 ♓ 5'31"
22	SU	8: 3: 2	2 55	11 30	6 27	0 28	18 6	28 32	8 56	5 32	12 27	5 ♓ 5'31"
23	MO	8: 6:59	5 42	13 6	7 28	0 54	18 12	28 34	8 56	5 32	12 27	5 ♓ 5'30"
24	TU	8:10:55	8 30	14 42	8 29	1 20	18 17	28 36	8 57	5 32	12 28	5 ♓ 5'30"
25	WE	8:14:52	11 19	16 18	9 30	1 46	18 23	28 38	8 58	5 33	12 28	5 ♓ 5'30"
26	TH	8:18:48	14 10	17 54	10 31	2 13	18 28	28 39	8 58	5 33	12 28	5 ♓ 5'30"
27	FR	8:22:45	17 3	19 31	11 32	2 39	18 33	28 41	8 59	5 34	12 29	5 ♓ 5'30"
28	SA	8:26:41	19 57	21 7	12 33	3 5	18 39	28 43	9 0	5 34	12 29	5 ♓ 5'30"
29	SU	8:30:38	22 54	22 43	13 34	3 31	18 44	28 45	9 0	5 34	12 29	5 ♓ 5'30"
30	MO	8:34:35	25 53	24 19	14 35	3 58	18 50	28 47	9 1	5 35	12 30	5 ♓ 5'29"
31	TU	8:38:31	28 55	25 55	15 36	4 24	18 55	28 49	9 2	5 35	12 30	5 ♓ 5'29"

INGRESSES :

10	☿ → ♏ 2:42
14	♀ → ♈ 19:13
15	⊕ → ♋ 16: 7
20	☿ → ♐ 22:41
	♂ → ♌ 22:49
31	☿ → ♑ 8:29

ASPECTS (HELIOCENTRIC +MOON(TYCHONIC)) :

1	♀ ☌ ♅ 10:39		☿ ☌ ☋ 21: 5		⊕ □ ♄ 23:19	21	☽ ☌ ♇ 11:19		☿ △ ♀ 20:44
	☿ △ ♆ 22:20	8	☿ □ ♂ 3:47	14	☽ ☍ ♅ 19:52	22	♀ △ ♇ 14:14	29	☽ ☍ ♄ 17:40
2	⊕ ✶ ♃ 5:34		☽ ☍ ♇ 10:48	16	☽ ☌ ♄ 5: 4		☿ ✶ ♆ 22:34	30	☿ □ ♄ 23:13
	☽ ☍ ♄ 7:38		♂ ☋ ☊ 23:38		☽ ☍ ♀ 12:34	24	☿ □ ♅ 3:51	31	☽ ☌ ♃ 10:37
3	☽ ☍ ☿ 7:53	11	☽ ☌ ♂ 17:43	17	♂ ✶ ♄ 5:53		⊕ △ ♅ 11:15		
	♀ □ ♇ 17:32	12	☿ □ ♆ 1:13		☽ ☍ ♃ 13:56	25	☽ ☍ ♂ 3: 8		
	☽ ☌ ♃ 21:18		☽ ☍ ♆ 10:22	18	♀ ✶ ♆ 5:57		☿ ☌ ♇ 9:42		
4	⊕ ☌ P 2:58		♀ △ ♂ 11:13		☿ ☌ A 7:19		☽ ☌ ♆ 10: 1		
	☿ ✶ ♇ 3:15	13	☿ △ ♅ 6:11	20	☿ ✶ ♄ 9:26	26	♀ ☌ ♃ 8:51		
5	☿ ☍ ♃ 12:44		♀ □ ⊕ 6:24		☽ ☌ ☿ 11:46	27	☿ △ ♃ 12:54		
7	☿ △ ⊕ 2:13		♀ ☍ ♄ 17: 4		☿ △ ♂ 22:40	28	☽ ☌ ♅ 2: 7		

Sept 4/5, 1999—at which time the onset of the 61st cycle began. Within this current rhythm, today remembers the Union in the Temple. The Union in the Temple occurred twelve years after the birth of Jesus, hence the commemoration in this year, which is twelve years after the 60th commemoration of the birth of Jesus late in 1999.

In the years after this Union in the Temple, the Nathan Jesus being became ever more isolated from others, in preparation for his coming mission. He bore witness to the depravity into which humanity had fallen, and saw what no one on Earth had ever seen before him. *It burned his soul* (Rudolf Steiner, *The Fifth Gospel*, lecture 4). This same type of isolation may be reflected for today's Disciples of Christ in the increasing density of materialism, where so many are blind to what is truly happening in our midst. To be aware is often accompanied by a feeling of loneliness and separateness, and this is what prepares us for our new mission—the mission of applying cosmic intelligence as the blade that cuts through the jargon and foolishness of deceit now permeating life on Earth so we may work with new cultural impulses to create new paradigms of collaboration.

The next significant event in this 61st unfolding of Christ's biography will be in the year 2029 when the commemoration of the Baptism in the Jordan will sound into time.

January 3: ASPECT: Heliocentric Venus, 21° Pisces, square Pluto 21°21' Sagittarius: (2 Feb 31) This same aspect occurred when Jesus was interrupted in his teachings of the "Bread of Life" by the question, "How can you call yourself the bread of life come down from heaven, since everyone knows where you come from?" Jesus replied: "I am the life-giving bread that came down from heaven. Whoever eats of this bread will live forever. This bread is my flesh, which I will give for the life of the world" (John 6:51). Christ here tells us that with his sacrifice, the Earth and all her substances will be transformed. Not only shall we eat of the fruits of the Earth as they live in Nature, but new forces will find us through these fruits of the Earth as we deepen into understanding his sacrifice. These new forces are the etheric forces of renewal (Venus) that

will become available to humanity through Christ in his Second Coming. Counter to this is the grave matter of genetic manipulations (Pluto–Hades) of our physical sustenance, which sever bread from life. Let this day be a reminder to us to open to the presence of etheric renewal by honoring not only our food, but also our families—who gather together for both physical and spiritual nourishment. The dinner table can become the church of the family. Inversely we may stand "dumb" before the sacredness of food and blind to the suffering of Nature when her fruits are debased. The Last Supper is the antidote to the third temptation in the wilderness (turning stones to bread)—in that it is a promise given to humanity that the Logos will forever be the sustenance for those who choose spiritual nourishment. What is the bread of life? Valentin Tomberg offers this wisdom:

> The sacrament of the Last Supper is not simply a symbolic ritual expressing a religious and moral content; rather, it is a real process having profound effects within the human organization. The result of these effects is primarily that the body becomes spiritualized. In the body an inner change takes place, bringing it nearer to the moral spiritual world. By means of a sacred use of nourishment in the Last Supper, the metabolic processes of the body are spiritualized. This works against the hardening of the body. The body becomes inwardly more mobile, transparent to spirit.[2]

To "take in" all sustenance, in consciousness of the interweaving between heaven and Earth, is to make sacred our daily bread. This is true for daily meals as well as for high rituals of communion. When Venus and Pluto are squared, a tension between the heights and the depths may make itself evident. Such a squaring calls us to consciousness. Do we know the content and origin of our daily bread?

January 8: Moon opposite Pluto 12°40 Sagittarius.

Jesus and the Disciples take a walk with seven (formerly pagan) philosophers who had received baptism. The latter asked him about

---

2 Tomberg, *Russian Spirituality & other Essays*, p. 145.

the Persian King Djemschid, who had received a golden blade from God with which he had divided many lands and shed blessings everywhere (See David Tresemer's article in this *Journal for Star Wisdom*). Jesus replied that Djemschid had been a leader who was wise and intelligent in things of the sense world. He spoke of Djemschid as a false type of Melchizedek, whereas the actual Melchizedek was truly a priest and a king to whom they should turn their attention. The sacrifice of bread and wine, which Melchizedek offered, would be fulfilled and perfected and would endure until the end of the world. (*Chron.* p. 297)

The Master Jesus taught that the time for looking deeper into the sense world had come to an end. The Turning Point of Time was at hand. The forces in the physical world were exhausted. As time turned, through the deed of Christ, so too will the source of nourishment turn; the time of humanity's endless "taking" from nature will turn to humanity's eternal "giving" to nature. The new blade is the blade that cuts through the falsehoods of maya in order to reveal the new sacraments that will nourish the human being until the end of time. The origin of this nourishment is Christ. Rudolf Steiner addresses this turning point:

> Those who understood something of the Hebrew secret teachings did not regard what happened after the Mystery of Golgotha, in the destruction of Jerusalem, as an external event brought about by the Romans. The Romans were merely the accomplices of the spiritual powers, carrying out on their behalf what was entirely the plan of these spiritual powers. The idea they had was that the old way of gathering ingredients from the Earth in order to build the human body as a house had come to an end. With Jerusalem's attainment of its full greatness the substance, the material from the Earth that could be used in building the human body as a house, was exhausted.[3]

Where are the sacraments of the new communion with Christ to be found in our daily life? With the Moon waxing to its fullness and opposite Pluto an image of the human etheric body (Moon),

"taking in" the nourishment of Divine Love (Phanes—higher Pluto) is beautifully portrayed as preparation for tomorrow's Full Moon. Inversely, the "taking in" of debased nature (Hades—lower Pluto) is an indecency for the soul.

January 9: Full Moon: Sun 23° Sagitarrius opposite Moon 23° Gemini. The Moon was here, and just past its fullness, when Jesus healed ten lepers (*Chron.* p. 313). The disease of leprosy has a connection with hatred of the physical body. This comes about through the illusion that enlightenment is gained by ignoring the physical temple bestowed upon humanity via the sublime workings of the twelve beings of the zodiac. At this healing, Christ saw through the leprous disease and loved such people just as they were. Only one of the ten healed of leprosy came after Jesus to thank him (Luke 17:11–19).

We can remember today to care lovingly for our physical bodies, and also remember to take every opportunity to give thanks for the little miracles in everyday life. In the nineteenth arcanum of the book *Meditations on the Tarot*, The Sun, the anonymous author speaks of the accomplished union between intelligence and spontaneous wisdom—the cooperation between these two is intuition. During this Full Moon in Gemini, we stand under the hermetic teachings bestowing wisdom into intelligence:

> Now, the teaching-impulse called "Gemini" can be expressed by paraphrasing a little the first statement of the Emerald Table of Hermes: May that which is below be as that which is above, and may that which is above be as that which is below to accomplish the miracles of one thing.[4]

The miracle of one thing is the miracle of intuition—the experience of spiritual touch. This can be contemplated with today's Full Moon. Do we love the physical in all its expressions as the divine reflection of the above in the below? Can we seek to unite our intelligence with the spontaneous wisdom found so naturally in the young child? This is a Moon that calls us to

3 Steiner, *The Book of Revelation*, p. 130.

4 Anon. Meditations on the Tarot, Arcanum 19.

give ourselves over to the joy of life as children of God. "Oh Sun life, endure!"[5]

January 10: Venus enters Aquarius. Venus in Aquarius remembers the death of John the Baptist. Aquarius brings the fruit of pneumatism—spiritual perceptions. The loss of John's spiritual vision for his future contributed to his death. John did not will to live longer:

> As far as he was concerned, he had already fulfilled his mission, having recognized and baptized the Messiah. He had said, with respect to the Messiah, "He must increase, and I must decrease," Here, already, he had renounced the deeper will to live. The Angels and higher spiritual beings, who had helped him up until the baptism, were obliged gradually to withdraw. Thus John the Baptist was already "spiritually beheaded" before he became actually beheaded. (CHA, *The Ministry up to the Beheading of John the Baptist*)

As the loss of John's angelic support withdrew, he lost his certainty that Jesus was the Messiah. The loss of John's vision for his future, contributed to his death. Yet all this was as it was to be, for John was to become the guardian soul of the Disciples of Christ. With Venus in Aquarius, we are strengthened in our efforts to pass through the density of material thinking in order to find the spiritual guidance that empowers us to imagine a benevolent future and apply ourselves to forming group affiliations (Venus) that serve not only our personally intended future, but also the future intended for the whole of humanity.

January 13: Sun 27° Sagittarius: Death of Thomas (18 Dec 72). Thomas, the doubting one, was taken into the spiritual world as a true believer. This is a day to notice our doubts and bring them to light, that they may be faced and overcome.

ASPECT: Mercury conjunct Pluto 12° Sagittarius: This same aspect in this same degree of the zodiac occurred at the second conversion of Mary Magdalene (26 Dec 30). In this second conversion, Jesus cleansed the demons from the seven lotus flowers (chakras) of Mary Magdalene.

Seven weeks after the encounter with Jesus at Gabara, on December 26, 30, Martha again managed to persuade Mary Magdalene to come and hear Jesus speak, this time in a place called Azanoth, a few miles northwest of Gabara. On this occasion Jesus cast out all seven demons, as described in great detail by Sister Emmerich, and as is referred to briefly also in the Gospel: "Mary, called Magdalene, from whom *seven demons* had gone out" (Luke 8:2). This was a kind of initiation. It was a freeing and opening of all seven of Mary Magdalene's chakras. Through this initiation, she became the first fully redeemed soul.[6]

This redemption of Mary Magdalene is what made way for her becoming the "Apostle to the Apostles." For it was Magdalene who first saw the Risen One on Easter *morning,* (though the Virgin Mary had already encountered the Risen One earlier in the *night* of Holy Saturday) and she was given the task of being the messenger who bore the news of the Resurrection to the other Disciples of Christ. What were then called *demons* we could also call the "dead." The dead are psychological complexes of attachment, which have entered us over the course of our past incarnations and are still at work. The dead create darkened places within the seven lotus organs—stemming from thoughts, feelings or will impulses that are not aligned with truth. Today's aspect of Mercury and Pluto in conjunction exemplifies the healing forces of Mercury working through Christ from the realm of the Father (Higher Pluto—Phanes).

The upper three chakras are organs of knowledge and wisdom; the lower three are organs of revelation. We may each consciously work on uniting our seven centers of knowledge and revelation toward Christ, thus bringing forth goodness. The heart stands between the two as the uniting force between knowledge and revelation. The chakras are the organs wherein negative forces strive to dwell. We are subject to both our individual possession by our personal "dead," and culturally we are subjected to the collective "dead" of all humanity. The spiritual attention human beings

---

5 Steiner, *Twelve Moods of the Zodiac* (n/p).

6 Powell, *The Mystery, Biography, and Destiny of Mary Magdalene*, pp. 10–11.

have given over to sub-earthly kingdoms will work back destructively through nature:

> People talk of mysterious manifestations; the whole divine revelation of spring, summer, autumn, and winter is mixed up. Chaos is setting in, and this comes not from Heaven, but from the interior of the Earth. People think that these are merely climate changes, but this is not the case.[7]

Indeed, it is our thinking (Mercury) that must change. We are called to overcome doubt and confront our "dead." With Mercury conjunct Pluto and the Sun remembering the death of Thomas, we can strive to courageously face our doubt, and our "dead," so that human thinking can work to heal the chaos now afflicting all of nature. Can we radiate the light of spiritualized thinking to illumine the good and cast out the darkened lies of materialism?

ASPECT: Venus conjunct Neptune 4° Aquarius: This same aspect (though in Capricorn) also occurred at the conversion of Magdalene mentioned above. The combination of overcoming the doubt of Thomas, and the two aspects of today (Mercury–Pluto and Venus–Neptune), provides a strong memory of conversion. Venus in consort with Neptune can bring new clairaudience (from the inspiration of Neptune) to the degree to which she (Venus) quiets inner agitation—in order to listen carefully in all interpersonal relationships. This includes one's relationship to one's own heart, where discernment of the forces working behind world events can be penetrated. With Venus and Neptune in Aquarius, consciousness is quickened for spiritual receptivity.

January 15: Sun enters Capricorn: "May the future rest upon the past" (Rudolf Steiner, *Twelve Moods of the Zodiac*). Capricorn, the Goat, the symbol of sacrificial death and the sign of atonement. Aquila the Eagle extends above the first decan of Capricorn, the main star of Aquila (Altair), being located at 7° Capricorn. The first decan of Capricorn is ruled by Jupiter (Zeus), to whom the Eagle was sacred. Capricorn signifies a special opportunity: Courage becomes the power to redeem, the power to develop conscience, and the insight to know what is right.

January 19: ASPECT: Sun 4° Capricorn square Saturn 4° Libra. This same aspect occurred at the Adoration of the Magi (26 Dec 6 BC), with Saturn opposite today's position. With the Sun in Capricorn square Saturn in Libra—the constellation of relationships—we are wise to remain awake to what kinds of relationships are forming in the world. Libra is the constellation that seeks to bring relationships into balance, and in this balance the fulcrum becomes the absolute still-point between two things. At this still-point, Michaelic Cosmic Intelligence can be experienced as a formidable power of certainty between two things; this certainty is founded in objective truth. The kings who visited the newly born Jesus found this certainty of truth. They came to adore the Jesus child with Saturn in Aries. Aries is the sign of new leadership; and the kings, in all certainty, recognized the being of Christ, who would become the savior for all of humanity. Saturn is now opposite Aries, in Libra, and we are asked to carefully rethink our relationships and make certain we do not adore false prophets. This is inclusive of all our relationships—not only our personal ones, but also those with technology, economics, politics, science, medicine, animal husbandry, and agriculture. Do our relationships reflect what is best for the progress of humanity as spiritual beings? May we be encouraged to find the absolute fulcrum between two things, so as to experience the truth of Michaelic intelligence. With Saturn in Libra for most of this year, this is a task that continues for months.

January 21: Sun 6° Capricorn: The Adoration of the Magi (26 Dec 6 BC).

And the **Second Conversion of Mary Magdalene** (26 Dec 30). The magi were those who continued the Chaldean astrological tradition inaugurated in Babylon by Zoroaster in the sixth century BC. They were instructed to wait for the signs in heaven and follow this sign (the Star of the Magi) to the birthplace of the new king. This star was the radiant astral sheath of their great teacher—"Radiant

---

7 Tomberg, *Christ and Sophia*, pp. 399–400.

Star"—who had now come again into incarnation, as was the prophecy of ancient Babylon. This sign in the heavens was the Great Conjunction in 7 BC of Jupiter and Saturn in Pisces. The Babylonians knew when (the Great Conjunction), and the Jewish people knew where (Bethlehem). These two streams—the line of Abraham filled with the prophecy of the Messiah who would be born in Bethlehem into the line of David, and the ancient mystery traditions of Babylonian star gazers who knew of the future time of their teacher's reincarnation—came together during the Babylonian Captivity.

> During the Babylonian captivity, the Yahweh current of the Israelites met the school of Zoroaster. That meeting was one of the most significant events in human spiritual history. Not only was it a physical meeting of the representatives of two currents, but, more important, the current of Israel's *revelation* encountered the current of the *perceptive knowledge* of the Zoroaster mysteries. This was the preparation for the union of Nathan Jesus with Solomon Jesus—the innocent sister soul of Adam meeting the individuality of the great Zoroaster. (Valentin Tomberg, *Christ and Sophia*, p. 127)

This intersecting of streams, 500 years before Christ, prepared the ground for the event of the birth of the Solomon Jesus as preparation for the Turning Point of Time. It was into the kingly line of David that the Solomon Jesus, the reincarnated Zarathustra, would incarnate; the time of this incarnation was indicated by the Great conjunction, and the place was known through the messianic prophecies within the lineage of Abraham.

On the anniversary of this great event, decades later, Mary Magdalene experienced her second and last conversion. Magdalene, as the Apostle to the Apostles, was in mystical union with her teacher—and from this point onward she was therefore not spared from experiencing the trials of the God-Man in her heart. And, like the kings before her, Magdalene most certainly recognized Christ as the true king, one whose kingdom was not of this world.

The events of the Adoration and the Conversion, both occurring at this Sun degree, foretell how

necessary is spiritual navigation in these times of materialistic entrenchment. Humanity, too, is called to actively unite the stream of *perceptive knowledge* (School of Zoroaster) with *revelation* (Yahweh current of Israelites).

Today commemorates both the star and the casting out of demons. It is through the Star above each of our heads that we are led to redeem our lower natures, and this redemption gives us the clarity to perceive the true King.

The Sun was square Jupiter at Magdalene's conversion, as it is today. Our innermost self, our Sun heart, may experience a tension between its ideal and that which stands in the way of accomplishing this ideal. This can be experienced individually as well as collectively in the unfolding drama of history.

In this election year it is noteworthy to remember the Supreme Court decision in 2010—at this same Sun degree—that allowed corporations to spend money without limit in political campaigns. This decision will most assuredly influence the putting in place of the individual chosen by the powers of this world for us to adore as our leader and chief. Also, in 2010, Pluto crossed 9 degree of Sagittarius three times. This degree remembers the third temptation in the desert (to turn stones to bread), which has everything to do with the power of money. As we move into the next few years, we shall see the power of money as an increasing source of oppression.

January 22/23: New Moon 7° Capricorn: The Miracle of the Wedding at Cana. Moon and Sun are in close conjunction with the star Altair in the constellation of Aquila, the Eagle. This New Moon is within a degree of where the Sun was when Christ turned water into wine at the Wedding at Cana. This miracle reveals itself through a series of pictures: the exhaustion of the old wine, the filling of the empty vessels with water, and the turning of the water into new wine. In the exhaustion of the old wine, we see that the Yahweh function in the blood had been spent. Heredity alone would no longer represent the ties within a community; something more was needed. Through Christ's first miracle, community born of spirit came into being—the horizontal stream of heredity was raised into the vertical stream of Christ's light. In the filling of the vessels with water, we see the wine that stirs the blood being replaced by the clear, cool element that reflects what is above. With the water humanity is freed from the stirring forces in the blood and awakened to what lives beyond the confines of heredity—as new forces from eternity.

In the changing of the water into wine we see that the water is imbued with a force of pure love, which created a new wine—the wine of spirit descending into time—in contrast to the wine of ancestry, which had perpetuated itself to exhaustion. Through this miracle, humanity was given the capacity to form community based on spiritual blood—in contrast to being bound to hereditary blood. Thus Christ healed the future. From the stream of time moving toward us from the future, the radiant stream of descending eternal light will gradually transfigure our blood, freeing our soul for union with its higher self. This sacred union is to be mirrored in marriages—as the source of the new wine of karmic recognition and respect toward the mission of each one.

Just as Christ would later sacrifice his body on the cross of Golgotha, so at Cana was the human bloodline put on the cross between heredity/past and eternity/future. Christ will hold the cross until each of us has suffered the way home. This New Moon calls us to the still-point in time, between the past and the future. This is the portal between worlds. It is the crossing point in the heart; the place where that which worked and weaved between Mary and Jesus in Cana, begins to work and weave within our own soul and in the soul of our communities. Do our relationships honor the spirit?

January 25: Sun 10° Capricorn in conjunction with the megastar 9 Sagittae in the Arrow, above the Goat. Heliocentric Mercury was in conjunction with this megastar at the Resurrection. The Sun enters the second decan of Capricorn. Sagitta the Arrow extends above most of this decan, which is ruled by Mars.

January 27: Mercury 4½° Capricorn square Saturn 4½° Libra: Mercury and Saturn were square to each other at the Baptism in the River Jordan. This aspect illumines this event; the event of the conception of Christ, the most powerful teacher (Mercury) ever to incarnate on the Earth. His teachings would bring change to all teachings that had preceded him, and this change would call forth new laws (Saturn). Change is most often accompanied by tension (square). The phenomena of hermeticism was revealed at the Baptism, not simply as a teaching, but as an event. Today with this square in Capricorn and Libra, the Hermetic teacher is to be remembered through our courage (Capricorn) to redeem all that causes ill will in our relationships (Libra).

January 28, Mercury 7° Libra square Jupiter 7° Aries: Healing of the Paralyzed Man at the Pool of Bethesda (*Chron.* p. 273). In today's sky, this aspect is in the same degree as it was when this miraculous healing by Christ occurred. In this case, the man's paralysis was the result of an excess of personality in a previous life. Therefore, in his next incarnation, he became dependent on the mercy of other personalities. Our personality is the lens through which our "I" expresses itself in the world. If our "I" is filled with a sense of the power of the self, it forfeits its relationship with the higher self. This will eventually become a paralysis of movement (Mercury); for the "I" that is closed to Christ will become sclerotic, and this sclerosis will eventually become paralysis, and this paralysis will eventually become possession. It is incumbent on us to make way the narrow road that leads to union with the eternal "I" of Christ.

January 29: Sun 14° Capricorn: Death of John the Baptist. John the Baptist is the great individuality of whom Rudolf Steiner foretold that he would be with us again at the end of the twentieth century, to lead humanity past the great crisis it would then be facing. As John was there to behold the Light at the First Coming, so is this individuality here again to meet those witnessing the true Light of the Second Coming. John was united with Lazarus when Lazarus was raised from the dead. The

Lazarus–John being now prepares us to meet and withstand the meeting with our individual shadow nature; he prepares us as well for the meeting with the collective shadow nature of all humanity. After his beheading, John became the guardian of the circle of Christ's Disciples. In like manner is John now the guardian of the communities working with Michael and Sophia in the name of Christ. The Sun is in the middle of the constellation of Capricorn, the constellation that empowers us to transform darkness into light—to steadfastly meet resistance from rigid thought forms that are holding onto the past. This is our work: to transform the limitations of the brain-bound intellect into heart forces. The heart will lead us into our intended future. The disciples of John are now forming communities that can be recognized in the fact that they love one another. Can we live into the redeeming presence of spiritual guidance? Can we trust what is not seen?

FEBRUARY 2012:

The Sun begins in Capricorn (The SeaGoat) and moves into Aquarius (The WaterHuman) on the 14th. The Full Moon is on the 7th and the New Moon is on the 21st.

Jupiter continues to be visible in the southwest at sunset in front of the Ram (Aries) until the closing days of March, when it disappears into the Sun's glow. The waning Moon joins Mars on the 9th, rising in the late evening. The Moon may be too bright to spot Mars directly above it, but the 10th should offer a good view of the red planet. Mars will continue to be visible in the night sky until the first weeks of November. Saturn stations retrograde this month and on the 8th Saturn ceased moving forward and will appear to travel backward until turning direct in the end of June later this year. The 12th brings the Moon in conjunction with Saturn in Libra (the Scales). The end of February offers lovely sunset opportunities with the emerging new crescent Moon held between the beautiful evening star of Venus to the right and bright Jupiter to the left from about the 25th–27th.

February 1: ASPECT: Venus 27° Aquarius opposite Mars 27° Leo: Heliocentric Mars was conjunct today's Venus, when, on July 23, AD 32, Jesus reproached the Disciples for being impatient with him because he had delayed so long in going to Bethany, where Lazarus lay in "sleep." "Jesus said that he was like a person who could not give an account of his views and actions, because they would not be understood" (*Chron.* p. 316). With Venus remembering these words of Christ, who "could not give an account," a warning sounds to all karmic groups, for the situation is similar with initiates in our time. They must remain silent until they have been recognized. The failure to recognize spiritual messengers can thwart even the best laid spiritual plans and intentions. Venus in Aquarius quickens spiritual antennae for new ways of perceiving the subtle, allowing greater recognition of karmic brothers and sisters; and with this recognition, a community can awaken to meet its destined task. The jealous, rivalrous nature of lower Venus, or simply being led astray by incorrect external research, can thwart the recognition that is prerequisite for revelation. Rudolf Steiner was led astray by exoteric scholarship and for a while had thereby missed the path leading to Kyot as a real being in the Grail Mystery, as well as to recognition of his own role in the Grail family (as Schionatulander):

> He [Kyot] acquired a book by Flegetanis in Spain—an astrological book. No doubt about it, one may say: Kyot is the man who, stimulated by Flegetanis—whom he calls Flegetanis and in whom lives a certain knowledge of the stellar script—Kyot is the man who, stimulated by this revived astrology, see the thing called the Grail. Then I knew that Kyot is not to be given up; I knew that he discloses an important clue if one is searching in the sense of Spiritual Science: he at least has seen the Grail.[8]

The path that leads to recognition of spiritual teachers and ideas needs to be grounded in exoteric research, and at the same time be completely

---

8 Steiner, *Christ and the Spiritual World*, p. 110; see also the article by Ellen Schalk, "Kyot and the Stellar Script of Parsifal" (www.sophiafoundation.org).

SIDEREAL GEOCENTRIC LONGITUDES : FEBRUARY 2012 Gregorian at 0 hours UT

DAY	☉	☽	☊	☿	♀	♂	♃	♄	♅	♆	♇
1 WE	16 ♑ 37	25 ♈ 33	17 ♏ 31	12 ♑ 8	26 ♒ 30	27 ♌ 47R	7 ♈ 44	4 ♎ 34	6 ♓ 53	5 ♒ 0	13 ♐ 28
2 TH	17 38	7 ♉ 28	17 32	13 49	27 42	27 40	7 51	4 34	6 55	5 2	13 30
3 FR	18 39	19 34	17 33R	15 31	28 53	27 33	7 59	4 35	6 58	5 4	13 32
4 SA	19 40	1 ♊ 56	17 31	17 14	0 ♓ 4	27 25	8 6	4 35	7 0	5 7	13 34
5 SU	20 40	14 37	17 28	18 57	1 15	27 16	8 14	4 36	7 3	5 9	13 36
6 MO	21 41	27 39	17 22	20 41	2 26	27 6	8 21	4 36	7 5	5 11	13 38
7 TU	22 42	11 ♋ 5	17 13	22 26	3 37	26 55	8 29	4 36	7 8	5 13	13 39
8 WE	23 43	24 51	17 3	24 11	4 48	26 44	8 37	4 36R	7 11	5 16	13 41
9 TH	24 44	8 ♌ 55	16 51	25 58	5 59	26 32	8 46	4 36	7 14	5 18	13 43
10 FR	25 44	23 11	16 40	27 45	7 9	26 19	8 54	4 36	7 16	5 20	13 44
11 SA	26 45	7 ♍ 33	16 31	29 32	8 20	26 6	9 2	4 35	7 19	5 22	13 46
12 SU	27 46	21 57	16 24	1 ♒ 20	9 30	25 51	9 11	4 35	7 22	5 25	13 48
13 MO	28 46	6 ♎ 17	16 19	3 9	10 40	25 36	9 20	4 34	7 25	5 27	13 49
14 TU	29 47	20 29	16 18	4 59	11 50	25 21	9 29	4 34	7 28	5 29	13 51
15 WE	0 ♒ 48	4 ♏ 33	16 17D	6 49	13 0	25 4	9 38	4 33	7 30	5 31	13 53
16 TH	1 48	18 28	16 18R	8 39	14 10	24 47	9 47	4 32	7 33	5 34	13 54
17 FR	2 49	2 ♐ 13	16 17	10 30	15 20	24 29	9 56	4 31	7 36	5 36	13 56
18 SA	3 49	15 50	16 14	12 21	16 29	24 11	10 5	4 30	7 39	5 38	13 57
19 SU	4 50	29 17	16 8	14 11	17 38	23 52	10 15	4 29	7 42	5 40	13 59
20 MO	5 50	12 ♑ 34	15 59	16 2	18 48	23 32	10 25	4 28	7 45	5 43	14 0
21 TU	6 51	25 40	15 48	17 52	19 57	23 12	10 34	4 26	7 48	5 45	14 2
22 WE	7 51	8 ♒ 33	15 34	19 41	21 5	22 51	10 44	4 25	7 51	5 47	14 3
23 TH	8 52	21 14	15 20	21 30	22 14	22 30	10 54	4 23	7 54	5 50	14 5
24 FR	9 52	3 ♓ 40	15 7	23 17	23 23	22 9	11 4	4 22	7 58	5 52	14 6
25 SA	10 53	15 53	14 55	25 2	24 31	21 47	11 15	4 20	8 1	5 54	14 7
26 SU	11 53	27 55	14 46	26 45	25 39	21 24	11 25	4 18	8 4	5 56	14 9
27 MO	12 53	9 ♈ 48	14 40	28 25	26 47	21 2	11 36	4 16	8 7	5 59	14 10
28 TU	13 54	21 36	14 37	0 ♓ 2	27 55	20 39	11 46	4 14	8 10	6 1	14 11
29 WE	14 54	3 ♉ 24	14 36	1 35	29 2	20 15	11 57	4 12	8 13	6 3	14 13

INGRESSES :

1 ☽ → ♉ 8:58	19 ☽ → ♑ 1:17
3 ☽ → ♊ 20:17	21 ☽ → ♒ 8: 1
♀ → ♓ 22:33	23 ☽ → ♓ 16:52
6 ☽ → ♋ 4:14	26 ☽ → ♈ 4:12
8 ☽ → ♌ 8:50	27 ☿ → ♓ 23:33
10 ☽ → ♍ 11:23	28 ☽ → ♉ 17: 6
11 ☿ → ♒ 6:10	29 ♀ → ♈ 20:30
12 ☽ → ♎ 13:27	
14 ☉ → ♒ 5: 9	
☽ → ♏ 16:12	
16 ☽ → ♐ 20: 6	

ASPECTS & ECLIPSES :

1 ♀ ☍ ♂ 23:31	11 ☽ ☍ ♀ 1:24	21 ☽ ☌ ♆ 18:47	28 ☉ □ ☊ 16:42
2 ☽ ☌ ☋ 20: 0	☽ ☌ P 17:57	☉ ☌ ☽ 22:34	29 ☽ ☌ ☋ 22:36
4 ☽ ☍ ♇ 22: 6	12 ☽ ☌ ♄ 21: 8	22 ☽ ⊓N ☊ 12:59	
7 ☉ ☋ ☿ 8:45	13 ☽ ☍ ♃ 5:11	23 ☽ ☌ ☿ 0:36	
☉ ☍ ☽ 21:53	14 ☿ ☌ ♆ 6:44	☽ ☍ ♂ 2:22	
☽ ☍ ☿ 22:42	☉ □ ☽ 17: 3	☿ ☍ ♂ 11:15	
8 ☽ ☍ ♆ 17:51	15 ♀ □ ♇ 18:25	24 ☽ ☌ ♅ 8:25	
9 ☽ ⊔S ☊ 13:13	☽ ☌ ☊ 20:14	25 ☽ ☌ ♀ 18:59	
10 ♀ ☌ ♅ 2:24	17 ☽ ☌ ♇ 20:40	26 ☽ ☍ ♄ 12:50	
☽ ☌ ♂ 5:10	19 ☉ ☌ ♆ 20:49	27 ☽ ☌ ♃ 3:42	
☽ ☍ ♅ 23:35	☿ □ ☊ 23:25	☽ ☌ A 13:49	

SIDEREAL HELIOCENTRIC LONGITUDES : FEBRUARY 2012 Gregorian at 0 hours UT

DAY	Sid. Time	☿	♀	⊕	♂	♃	♄	♅	♆	♇	Vernal Point
1 WE	8:42:28	2 ♑ 0	27 ♈ 32	16 ♋ 37	4 ♌ 50	19 ♈ 1	28 ♍ 51	9 ♓ 2	5 ♒ 35	12 ♐ 30	5 ♓ 5'29"
2 TH	8:46:24	5 8	29 8	17 38	5 16	19 6	28 53	9 3	5 36	12 31	5 ♓ 5'29"
3 FR	8:50:21	8 19	0 ♉ 44	18 38	5 43	19 11	28 55	9 4	5 36	12 31	5 ♓ 5'29"
4 SA	8:54:17	11 35	2 20	19 39	6 9	19 17	28 57	9 4	5 36	12 31	5 ♓ 5'29"
5 SU	8:58:14	14 54	3 57	20 40	6 35	19 22	28 59	9 5	5 37	12 32	5 ♓ 5'29"
6 MO	9: 2:10	18 18	5 33	21 41	7 1	19 28	29 1	9 5	5 37	12 32	5 ♓ 5'29"
7 TU	9: 6: 7	21 47	7 10	22 42	7 28	19 33	29 3	9 6	5 38	12 32	5 ♓ 5'28"
8 WE	9:10: 4	25 20	8 46	23 42	7 54	19 39	29 5	9 7	5 38	12 33	5 ♓ 5'28"
9 TH	9:14: 0	28 59	10 23	24 43	8 20	19 44	29 7	9 7	5 38	12 33	5 ♓ 5'28"
10 FR	9:17:57	2 ♒ 44	11 59	25 44	8 46	19 50	29 9	9 8	5 39	12 33	5 ♓ 5'28"
11 SA	9:21:53	6 35	13 36	26 45	9 12	19 55	29 10	9 9	5 39	12 34	5 ♓ 5'28"
12 SU	9:25:50	10 33	15 12	27 45	9 39	20 0	29 12	9 9	5 39	12 34	5 ♓ 5'28"
13 MO	9:29:46	14 37	16 49	28 46	10 5	20 6	29 14	9 10	5 40	12 34	5 ♓ 5'28"
14 TU	9:33:43	18 49	18 25	29 47	10 31	20 11	29 16	9 11	5 40	12 35	5 ♓ 5'27"
15 WE	9:37:39	23 9	20 2	0 ♌ 47	10 57	20 17	29 18	9 11	5 40	12 35	5 ♓ 5'27"
16 TH	9:41:36	27 36	21 39	1 48	11 23	20 22	29 20	9 12	5 41	12 35	5 ♓ 5'27"
17 FR	9:45:33	2 ♓ 12	23 16	2 49	11 50	20 28	29 22	9 13	5 41	12 36	5 ♓ 5'27"
18 SA	9:49:29	6 56	24 52	3 49	12 16	20 33	29 24	9 13	5 41	12 36	5 ♓ 5'27"
19 SU	9:53:26	11 50	26 29	4 50	12 42	20 38	29 26	9 14	5 42	12 36	5 ♓ 5'27"
20 MO	9:57:22	16 52	28 6	5 50	13 8	20 44	29 28	9 14	5 42	12 37	5 ♓ 5'27"
21 TU	10: 1:19	22 3	29 43	6 51	13 34	20 49	29 30	9 15	5 43	12 37	5 ♓ 5'26"
22 WE	10: 5:15	27 24	1 ♊ 20	7 51	14 1	20 55	29 32	9 16	5 43	12 37	5 ♓ 5'26"
23 TH	10: 9:12	2 ♈ 54	2 57	8 52	14 27	21 0	29 34	9 16	5 43	12 38	5 ♓ 5'26"
24 FR	10:13: 8	8 32	4 33	9 52	14 53	21 6	29 36	9 17	5 44	12 38	5 ♓ 5'26"
25 SA	10:17: 5	14 18	6 10	10 52	15 19	21 11	29 38	9 18	5 44	12 38	5 ♓ 5'26"
26 SU	10:21: 2	20 13	7 47	11 53	15 45	21 16	29 40	9 18	5 44	12 39	5 ♓ 5'26"
27 MO	10:24:58	26 14	9 24	12 53	16 12	21 22	29 41	9 19	5 45	12 39	5 ♓ 5'26"
28 TU	10:28:55	2 ♉ 22	11 1	13 53	16 38	21 27	29 43	9 20	5 45	12 39	5 ♓ 5'25"
29 WE	10:32:51	8 34	12 39	14 54	17 4	21 33	29 45	9 20	5 45	12 40	5 ♓ 5'25"

INGRESSES :

2 ♀ → ♉ 12:59
9 ☿ → ♒ 6:32
14 ⊕ → ♌ 5:16
16 ☿ → ♓ 12:36
21 ♀ → ♊ 4:16
22 ☿ → ♈ 11:26
27 ☿ → ♉ 14:47

ASPECTS (HELIOCENTRIC +MOON(TYCHONIC)) :

1 ☽ ☌ ♀ 4:36	8 ☽ ☍ ☿ 1: 8	☿ □ ♀ 20:23	20 ♀ △ ♄ 20:44	26 ☽ ☍ ♄ 3:31
♄ ⊓N ☊ 8:32	♀ ⚹ ♅ 5: 9	☽ ☍ ♃ 23:29	21 ☽ ☌ ♆ 18:40	☿ ☌ ♃ 4:19
2 ♂ ☍ ♆ 17:53	☽ ☍ ♆ 18:27	14 ☿ ⚹ ♃ 7:49	22 ☿ ☍ ♄ 9:26	☿ ☌ ☊ 13:24
3 ☿ ⚹ ♅ 5:29	☽ ☌ ♂ 22:59	15 ♂ ☌ A 23:12	☽ ☍ ♂ 10:38	⊕ △ ♇ 18:22
⊕ □ ♃ 14:19	9 ☿ △ ♄ 0:47	16 ♀ ☌ ☊ 3:27	23 ☿ ⚹ ♀ 0:18	♀ □ ♅ 22:38
4 ☽ ☍ ♇ 20: 6	10 ☿ ☌ ♆ 18:12	☽ ☍ ♀ 6:15	☿ ⚹ ♆ 12: 8	27 ☽ ☌ ♃ 23:42
6 ♀ □ ♆ 0:58	11 ☽ ☍ ♅ 2:38	17 ☽ ☌ ♇ 18:16	24 ☿ △ ⊕ 6:48	28 ☿ □ ♆ 13: 9
☿ □ ♃ 8:19	☿ ☍ ♂ 17:53	18 ☿ ☌ ♅ 11:18	☽ ☌ ♅ 10:59	29 ♀ ☍ ♇ 0:18
7 ♀ □ ♂ 6: 5	12 ☿ ⚹ ♇ 11:59	♂ △ ♇ 18:55	☿ △ ♇ 17: 7	☿ ⚹ ♅ 2:58
☿ ☍ ⊕ 8:45	☽ ☌ ♄ 12: 9	19 ☿ □ ♇ 3:45	♀ △ ♆ 17:26	☽ ☌ ☿ 22: 5
☿ ⊔S ☊ 12: 8	13 ⊕ ⚹ ♄ 11:34	⊕ ☍ ♆ 20:49	25 ☿ △ ♂ 4:29	

free from *personal* convictions. The failure of karmic groups to recognize the presence of an initiate in their midst, is a tragedy for both the higher worlds and humanity. We are to form communities of karmic affiliations (Venus) through which the living word (Mars) can be delivered by initiates, thus ensuring the continuation of the spiritual guidance of humanity. With Venus opposed Mars in Leo, the possibility opens for the heart to hear what the head cannot. For there are those who "cannot give accounts" due to the inattentiveness in their sisters and brothers.

February 4: Venus enters Pisces: "In winning may gain be lost" (Rudolf Steiner, *Twelve Moods of the Zodiac*). Venus was in Pisces for several of the healing miracles and throughout the entire Passion of Christ, through the Resurrection. Pisces is the constellation that bears the fruits of Love, through the magnanimity born of the humble willingness to love others.

ASPECT: Moon 13° Gemini opposite Pluto 13° Sagittarius: This same aspect, in this same degree occurred when Peter received the keys (19 Mar 31). Jesus was surrounded by the twelve when he asked: "Who do people say the Son of Man is?" They replied, "Some say John the Baptist; others say Elijah; and still others, Jeremiah or one of the prophets" (Matt. 16:13–14). Then Jesus asked again: "But what about you?" he asked. "Who do you say I am?" Simon Peter answered, "You are the Messiah, the Son of the living God" (Matt. 16:16).

> At this very moment, the Sun was rising, and Jesus spoke the words recorded in Matthew 17:17–20. He told the Disciples that he was the promised Messiah, applying all the relevant passages from the prophets to himself. He announced that now the time had come for them to journey to Jerusalem for the Passover. Traveling through the day, that evening they arrived at Bethulia. Here Lazarus was waiting for Jesus. (*Chron.* p. 285)

Pluto (as Phanes—Divine Love of the Father) challenges each of us to witness the true event of our time: the event of Christ's work in our very midst. We begin our recognition of Christ through recognizing the true Name of others. The Name is inscribed in the star that rests above each of our heads. Our Name is given to us by the Father. If we can thus witness this higher aspect in others, we will come to know it in ourselves as well. This witnessing of the higher aspect is synonymous with faithfulness to Our Father who is in Heaven, whose name we hallow as the Father of Divine Love. This is the highest octave of Pluto, and we find our way to the Father through the Son. When Peter made his proclamation, the Sun was rising. It "dawned" on Peter who it was before whom he stood, for he had transcended the limitations of his personal will (Moon). He goes before us as an example of how we can allow the Sun to rise in the depths of our own heart, so as to understand the presence of Christ in each individuality.

> Christ is the mighty, divine individuality who appeared once in the flesh of Jesus of Nazareth, who once set us the example of an incarnation to which all searching, striving human souls can aspire—as to the great model and ideal of individual endeavor. Only once did Christ appear in the flesh! But he will appear again on Earth! He will appear in a spiritual body and those people who have become sufficiently spiritualized through their soul-striving, will be able to recognize him in his spiritual body and be able to live with him.[9]

Peter recognized Christ and received the keys to the kingdom. He goes before us to exemplify the fact that Christ indwells us all.

As Venus enters Pisces, remembering the Passion of Christ, and the Pluto–Moon opposition remembers Peter, we can ask if our *personal* will (Moon) is obedient to the will of our higher self. If not, it may not *dawn* on us who it is that walks among us as the bearer of Divine Love (Phanes—higher Pluto).

February 5: Sun enters the third decan of Capricorn ruled by the Sun, associated with the constellation of the Dolphin.

Saturn stations 4°36' Libra: Saturn will rest at this degree until the 10th of February. Opposite to this degree:

---

9 Steiner, *Freemasonry and Ritual Work*, p. 422.

Jesus said that he and the Father were one (John 10:30) and that he would be going to the Father. The Disciples asked why, if he and the Father were one, did he need to go to the Father? Jesus spoke of his mission, saying that he would withdraw from humanity, from the flesh, and that whoever—with him, through him, and in him—separated himself from his own fallen nature, would at the same time commend himself to the Father. (*Chron.* p. 345)

This was ten days before he would sacrifice himself on the Cross of Golgotha. Due to this sacrifice, Christ would become the "narrow way" to the Father in the heights. A new relationship to spirit was to be born. No longer would the Father of the Hebrew people, Abraham, be found through the physical line of heredity, but through the spirit, as a consequence of the deed of Christ. As Saturn is stationed opposite the memory of this discourse, we remember the words of Rudolf Steiner:

> Today we must find the same depth of soul and inner mood [as did the Hebrews looking to Abraham] as we look up to what comes from the heights of the spirit to quicken us in the spirit—to the Christ. If we ascribe all our abilities, everything we are able to do that makes us truly human beings, not to any earthly power but to the Christ, we shall gain a living relationship to the Christ.[10]

Saturn in the constellation of relationships (Libra) makes this a fertile time to penetrate the meaning of "separating ourselves from our fallen nature in order to find the Father, through Christ." We are challenged to find Hermetic discourse with Christ as a power greater than all others in the earthly world. And, as Christ is continually bringing new thoughts into evolution, it would behoove each of us to vigilantly guard against rigidifying beliefs that have outlived their time. These become "graven images" that block the emanations from Christ that "make all things new."

February 7: Full Moon: Sun 22° Capricorn opposite Moon 22° Cancer: The Sun was 22° Cancer when Lazarus died on 15 Jul 32. Upon receiving the news Jesus spoke the words: "Our friend Lazarus has fallen asleep" (John 11:17-13). It was also the time of a Full Moon when, twice before, Jesus had resurrected both the daughter of the Essene, Jairus (7 Feb 30), and the seven-year-old daughter of the shepherd (12 Jun 32). This latter event was six weeks prior to the Raising of Lazarus. "This alignment, which occurs at New Moon as well as Full Moon, facilitates the incarnation of the soul coming from the Moon sphere down to the Earth, whereby the Moon can be regarded as a kind of portal—a gateway from the cosmos to the earthly realm" (Robert Powell, *CHA,The Raising of Lazarus*). This Full Moon remembers the Sun at the death of Lazarus, and a Full Moon in Cancer works with catharsis. Rudolf Steiner gave this constellation the mantram: "Selflessness becomes Catharsis." Inversely, self-absorption and willfulness would lead away from catharsis. Catharsis is a Greek work meaning "cleansing" or "purging." This indicates the content for meditative work during this Full Moon. First we purge, and then we are raised from the dead.

ASPECT: Superior conjunction of the Sun and Mercury 22° Capricorn. Mercury was conjunct the Sun at this degree on 10 Jan 33, when Jesus returned from a five-month journey to the pagans—through Chaldea and Egypt—without his Disciples. During this time he had visited the two remaining kings in their tent city on the western border of Chaldea. Upon returning to his homeland, during this conjunction, he taught in a large synagogue in Beersheba, on the southern border of Israel. Here he formally declared who he was and he spoke of his approaching end. This was less than three months before his impending death (*Chron.* p. 333). With Sun conjunct Mercury in Capricorn, the winged-footed messenger delivers the fluid living currents of cosmic thought—the highest teachings—and reveals these to the heart (Sun). In this manner new thoughts break through the confines of old assumptions. In this last conjunction between Mercury and the Sun before his death on the cross, Christ was declaring his Heavenly origins and his Earthly mission. This teaching was given in the same city to which Elijah fled

---

10 Steiner, *The Fifth Gospel*, p. 172.

when he was escaping the vengeful Jezebel after her husband Ahab had killed all the prophets with the sword. This was what Jezebel's murderous heart wanted for Elijah, too. We are encouraged to open our minds and hearts to those bearing the new revelations—the Elijahs of our time. On the other hand, the Jezebels of our time are decadent practitioners possessed with power that they wield *over* others. They tend to attack and criticize those who are bringing the new revelations, and Mercury is the planet that carries to Earth the metamorphosis of thought that brings us into the future. We are not to be persuaded by the fear-based convictions of the Jezebels of our time. The mind is at its best when, in stillness of thought, it opens to behold cosmic thoughts—redeeming thoughts from the mighty beings of Capricorn. This stillness is impossible for the Jezebels, for the pursuit of power separates them from truth. Where may we be unconsciously aligned with the Jezebels of our time who seek to slay the new prophets?

February 9: ASPECT: Venus conjunct Uranus 7° Pisces. Venus and Uranus were in conjunction at both the Raising of Lazarus and at the conception of the Virgin Mary. Both of these events tell of the spiritual love that signified the life of these two great souls. Today, with this conjunction occurring in Pisces, there is a magnification of the spiritual love that human beings can experience toward each other. In less than three months (Venus–Sun conjunction of June 2012), Venus will bring to the Sun the new imaginations which she gathers during this conjunction with Uranus. This is a day to open to these new imaginations that foster higher ideals born of Love, in contrast to the jealousy and strife of the lower personality. Uranus indicates the thought life, and when it is in connection with the "will to power" it is electrifying and polemical, discharging "lightening bolts" of distorted truth. When in connection to Cosmic Intelligence, Uranus brings perfect clarity of light-illumined thought representing the eternal Divine Mind. In both cases Uranus brings imaginations, from either above or from below. In the realm of Imagination, unity is the operative principle. In the realm of egotism, division is the operating principle. Let all our works today reflect our unified love for the Earth and humanity!

February 10: Sun 26° Capricorn: The Presentation in the Temple (15 Jan 1 BC). According to the Jewish Law, the sanctification of the firstborn should take place traditionally upon the fortieth day after birth. This was also a naming day for the infant. The Holy Family traveled to Jerusalem and stayed in the outskirts of town. The following day they set off for the temple. It was still dark when Mary and Joseph arrived with their infant son. Simeon, the old priest of the temple, had been told in a dream the previous night that the first child presented that morning would be the Messiah. When Simeon saw the infant Jesus he was taken up in rapturous joy. Rudolf Steiner tells us that Simeon was the reincarnation of Asita, who was a sage at the time of Buddha. Asita wept when he saw the little Bodhisattva who was to become Buddha, for he knew he would not live to see the day when the Bodhisattva would walk the Earth as Buddha. But now, in his incarnation as Simeon, he was granted witness to the Buddha. The astral sheath of the Nathan Jesus was filled with the presence of the Buddha. In the words of Rudolf Steiner: "When the Buddha appeared to the shepherds in the image of the "heavenly hosts," he was present not in a physical body, but in an astral body through which he continued to influence the Earth" (Rudolf Steiner, *According to Luke*, p. 77).

Thus, Simeon saw the further stages of development of his beloved little Bodhisattva when he blessed the Jesus child in the temple. The next day Simeon died in peace. On this naming day in 1 BC, the name of he who would bear the One was pronounced. Now this name lives in each of us. Christ is in us. Hallowed be Thy Name! May this serve as a reminder to hold respectfully each name in the community and see the One in each other.

ASPECT: Moon 7/8° Virgo opposite Venus and Uranus 7/8° Pisces. Venus was here when the Pharisees cried out: "How can he give us his body (flesh) to eat?" (*Chron.* p. 277). Here we come into the mystery of the Transubstantiation: a mystery that cannot be comprehended if Christ is not recognized. It is the Son, who *was* and *is* free from the effects of the physical body, and who can lift the human being from the old doctrine of the Father principle—which lives in the heredity stream—into the new freedom of self-determination. This gift of the new freedom has potential far greater in scope than any influence coming out of the horizontal stream of heredity. Without the Son, the Father's laws in the physical body of the hereditary stream continue without change. It is the second member of the Trinity—the Son—who brings the transubstantiation of substance and of karma. This was not understood by the Pharisees. It is actually the goal of the opponent of Christ that the transubstantiation be eradicated, which would leave the human being unfree—with only the determinism of rigid doctrine.

> As human beings, we become human only by taking hold of ourselves by making Christ alive within; we become human only when we are adapted to the spiritual order in realms of spirit that are entirely free of nature. We do not become human by regressing into a view that reckons solely with the Father God.[11]

Becoming free is directly tied to being human, and freedom in Christ holds the mystery of Transubstantiation. Human freedom is under the greatest duress in our time due to the possessing forces of materialism. With Venus–Uranus opposite Moon, we are encouraged to open to new imaginations that fill us with the love of Christ in his eternal presence as the bearer of freedom. The beast that arose in 666 was invisible to all but the initiates, and his long-term goal is the utter destruction of the possibility of Transubstantiation. This beast has been more successful than would first appear. In 1998 the beast rose again, and with it came a flooding force of technological entrapments. We are now to see where and how the beast works; this will set us free. It is imperative that we understand just how we can find Transubstantiation—through communion with Christ the Living Word—and through the Transubstantiation of matter into spirit we will find our way toward serving the renewal of the Earth and humanity.

11 Steiner, *The Book of Revelation*, p. 103.

As we remember the Presentation in the Temple and the mysteries of Transubstantiation we can fill ourselves with the One so as to become willing collaborators in the healing of all life. Can we name the "beasts" moving among us in order to fill ourselves with spiritual strength? Knowledge of evil calls forth the good!

February 13: ASPECT: Mercury conjunct Neptune 5½° Aquarius: Mercury was here and close to conjunction with Neptune on 3 Feb 31, when Jesus taught in the temple concerning the sixth and seventh petitions of the Lord's Prayer: *Lead us not into temptation, but deliver us from evil.* He also taught the first Beatitude: *Blessed are the poor in spirit for theirs is the kingdom of heaven.* Jesus then predicted his coming persecution, his desertion by faithful Disciples, and how he would be put to death.

> As he was leaving the synagogue, the Pharisees and certain disloyal Disciples tried to detain him with further questions, but the Apostles and loyal Disciples surrounded him and escorted him from the synagogue amid much noise, shouting, and confusion." (*Chron.* p. 277)

After this trouble, they all withdrew to the end of town and here Jesus revealed that one among them was a devil—meaning Judas Iscariot. Christ, the great teacher (Mercury), in conjunction with Neptune's inspirations, here revealed the mysteries of temptation, of evil, and of the necessity for becoming "poor in spirit." If we are to be delivered from temptation and led away from evil, we must become poor in spirit. It is the inflamed egotism of entitlement, rights, and privilege that tempts us into the evil snares of the false power, rich though this power may appear in just these entitlements and privileges. Judas could not become poor in spirit—but instead his personal will lead him astray. Jesus knew, two years before the actual betrayal, that Judas would become a door for evil to enter his inner circle. "Here we can draw a great lesson. If one does not keep alert, the powers of evil will always find a way to gain entrance. They seek continually for the weakest point, the point of attack. But if one remains alert and takes care, the powers of evil are unable to enter" (*CHA, The Ministry up to the Beheading of John the Baptist*). Inspiration and alertness of mind (Mercury) are teachings under this conjunction, lest we unwittingly become a door. Are we loyal to our loved ones and our principles?

February 14: Sun enters Aquarius: "May the limited yield to the unlimited" (Rudolf Steiner, *Twelve Moods of the Zodiac*). Discretion becomes silence, becomes meditative force, and becomes power. The first decan of Aquarius is ruled by Mercury, the planet of movement, and is associated with the Southern Fish, whose main star Fomalhaut is 9° Aquarius.

February 14: Sun 0½° Aquarius: Healing of the Paralyzed Man at the Pool of Bethesda (19 Jan 31). The Sun is conjunct the megastar Sadr (Gamma Cygni) at 0° Aquarius. This is the third of the seven archetypal healings by Christ. At this healing the Sun was in conjunction with the megastar Sadr, marking the breast of the Swan (the center of the Northern Cross). A man had lain at the pool of Bethesda for 38 years, a pool whose waters could heal the sick. This miracle is connected to the third chakra—the solar plexus—the chakra that guards consciousness and governs movement.

> "I"-consciousness of the past, which preserves its activity from the previous incarnation and in which many human beings live and act, is called consciousness of the "dead" in the Gospels, and those who live under the "I" impulse of the past are simply called "the dead." Thus, healing the paralyzed man involved more than merely the present "I"; the "dead," in particular, heard the "voice of the son" and experienced a conversion in his past consciousness.[12]

The paralyzed man had used excessive personal force in his past incarnation, ignoring both others and the angels. Now, in the time of Christ's ministry, he was ignored both by others, and by the angel at the pool of Bethesda. He had lain there for 38 years, asking for help, but to no avail, until Christ visited this pool and asked: "Wilt thou be made whole?" This question was directed to his

12 Tomberg, *Christ and Sophia*, p. 251.

faith, not to his desire to be healed. Christ was asking if, even after 38 years, he still had enough strength and humility to believe that mercy could come to him. The paralyzed man's answer (John 5:7) showed that he would not forsake his faith, whether in the spirit or in human beings, despite the many years of waiting. Then he was healed by Christ, the one who represents both the world of angels and the world of human beings. The "dead" paralyze us in body, mind, and soul. They rigidify mobility and create obstacles in our ability to correctly perceive the present moment.

Today we may ask if we are free from the "dead" in our thinking, our feeling, and our willing. We can offer up the prayer that constrictions be revealed and healed.

February 15: ASPECT: Venus 13° 53' Pisces square Pluto 13° 53' Sagittarius. At the start of the forty days in the wilderness (21 Oct 29), heliocentric Venus was in square to Pluto, as it is today. Jesus entered the wilderness almost one month after his Baptism, which was when the Christ was conceived into his bodily sheaths. Jesus was led into the wilderness by the same spirit that was represented by the dove at the Baptism. In the wilderness the Jesus being fasted. This has a deeper meaning than just going without food. Fasting, in this case, is an imagination for the immense trial undergone by Jesus. With the conception of Christ into his physical being, he had to recreate, out of the resources of the Christ spirit which now indwelled him, all the elements that had previously supported him. From this moment onward Jesus Christ was in the process of building up the resurrection body. No longer could he find support from the merely physical elements arising from nature. He had to forge a relationship to the spirit—to the world of stars—and this new relationship was incredibly transfiguring for the elements of physical nature that sustained the physical body of Jesus, in whom Christ dwelled. By casting out the fallen aspects of the physical, Christ created the ground upon which he could stand. This is an imagination of fasting: refraining from taking in the coarse material world, until, through aligning with the stars, he could imprint all substance with a force that was free of all material influence that had gradually become interwoven with Lucifer and Ahriman. Christ indwelling Jesus imbued the elements with a descending source of nourishment built from the powers of the spiritual world. This marked the beginning of the transition of the Father Principle from the horizontal to the vertical. In casting out all the elements in which Lucifer or Ahriman could possibly dwell, he cast Lucifer and Ahriman out as well. Then, he met what he had cast out as they objectively approached him from without, tempting him in his time of greatest vulnerability through the three temptations in the wilderness. This is a picture of building the New Jerusalem—creating bodies free from material elemental influences. Because Christ had been taken into the body of Jesus, it was Jesus Christ who could overcome the tempters, and model for all human beings the task of overcoming temptation. The entire future of humanity was dependent on his success. With Venus square Pluto, an image arises of these forty days in the wilderness, and of how each of us must find this descending nourishment of spirit through which the tempters are overcome.

> He said to them, "I have food to eat that you know nothing about."
>
> Then his disciples said to each other, "Could someone have brought him food?"
>
> "My food," said Jesus, "is to do the will of him who sent me and to finish his work." (John 4:32–34)

With Venus square Pluto we may ask: From where do I find my sustenance?

Feb. 21 New Moon 7° Aquarius. Jesus heals a man with a withered hand (26 Jan 31), and a blind and dumb man who was possessed by a demon. The Pharisees were in an uproar over these healings and accused Jesus of being in league with the devil:

> Make a tree good and its fruit will be good, or make a tree bad and its fruit will be bad, for a tree is recognized by its fruit. You brood of vipers, how can you who are evil say anything good? For the mouth speaks what the heart is full of. (Matt. 12:33–34)

In the discretion gained through the practice of meditative silence, the fruit being offered will show itself in its true light. This meditative silence is a contemplation for a New Moon in Aquarius. Silence brings us into right awareness of spiritual thoughts and beings. Our hand withers if not serving the heart, and we are possessed by lower forces when our personal will seeks power, thus rendering us blind and speechless before the Living Word. This New Moon calls us to give from our hearts, see what is real, and speak what is true, in order to bring forth fruit that is good.

February 23: Sun conjunct Fomalhaut 9° Aquarius, one of the four Royal Stars of Persia.

> The zodiac is the circle of stars which embraces the movements of the Sun, Moon and planets. It is divided into twelve starry regions of space, each named in accordance with the animal or human figure corresponding to the cosmic power that radiates from that region. It has existed since time immemorial. But let me now refer to one, an Elder Brother of humanity, who more than any other mortal has been able to penetrate the mystery of the zodiac. I mean he who long ago bore the name Zarathustra. I look to him as a spiritual father; and from him I have learnt much concerning the zodiac and the mysteries of the stars. Long ago in ancient Persia Zarathustra was initiated by the sublime Being of the Sun Ahura Mazda, who elevated him to knowledge of the cosmos. Zarathustra was shown the mystery of the Father and the Son—the Father, Zervana Akarana, meaning "Infinite Time," and the Son, Ahura Mazda, meaning "Aura of Light." He beheld the radiant "Aura of the Light" surrounding and indwelling the Sun. And above and beyond the Sun, he beheld the mighty circle of stars, the zodiac, as the outer manifestation of Zervana Akarana, the Heavenly Father, father of both Ahura Mazda and Ahriman, the Evil Twin. Already then in ancient Persia Zarathustra spoke of the four royal stars as the four "foundation stones" of the zodiac—Aldebaran, the Bull's eye, the central star of the Bull; Regulus, the Lion's heart, shining from the breast of the Lion; Antares, the red-glowing Scorpion's heart, the central star of the Scorpion; and

bright Fomalhaut in the mouth of the Southern Fish, beneath the stream of water flowing from the urn of the Waterman. These four stars form a cross in cosmic space from the four signs of the zodiac. (CHA, *The Mystery of the Zodiac*)

Today the Sun quickens this cosmic cross. Fomalhaut, which is 21° south of the ecliptic, is called the *Watcher in the South.*

February 24: The Sun at 10° Aquarius enters the second decan of Aquarius, ruled by Venus and associated with the Swan (sacred to Venus). Sun at 10½° Aquarius is conjunct the megastar Deneb, marking the tail of the Swan (the head of the Northern Cross). The Sun was conjunct Deneb at the Feeding of the Five Thousand.

Feeding of the Five Thousand and the Walking on Water: These two miracles signify a day side (Feeding of the Five Thousand), and a night side (Walking on Water). Christ feeds five thousand with moral-sensory impressions, and these impressions echo into the night for the twelve Disciples.

Rudolf Steiner frequently spoke of spiritualizing sensory impressions; "moral impressions" was the term he gave to sensory impressions of moral and spiritual phenomena. Christ, whose heart was connected with the twelve constellations of the zodiac, filled the twelve senses[13] of the multitude with moral impressions. This satisfied their hunger. They sought to crown him king in this world, whereby they could continue to passively receive spiritual nourishment. His Disciples, on the other hand, bore witness to his spiritual kingliness when, later that *night*, he approached their boat as he walked on water, saying, "It is I; do not be afraid" (John 6:20). These worlds contain the revelation of Christ's kingly nature.

[This kingly nature] does not call the Christ to govern (as the five thousand wished), but bestows on the human beings the spiritual force of self-determination. The kingly nature of the Christ is his capacity not only to give humankind freedom, but also to give the needed strength to assert that freedom. In the

spiritual-moral sense, it would be proper to say that the royal nature of Christ involves giving kingly dignity to human beings.[14]

In the night comes the recognition of the kingly dignity that Christ gives to human beings. His words ("It is I; be not afraid") remind us of who it is that brings us certainty when the winds of change and the waves of uncertainty threaten our equilibrium. We are also reminded of the different natures of sense impressions. Moral impressions echo into the higher hierarchies by night, strengthening the human "I." Immoral impressions, impressions man-made to *imitate* creation, echo into the sphere of materialism by night, thereby capturing the ego in its *maya*. What is taken in by day determines which school we enter at night—the school of the Greater Guardian who is Christ, or the school of materialism that is ruled by the tempters. This is a good day to ponder the quality of impressions we place before our senses and, more importantly, the quality of impressions we allow to enter our children's senses. For the nature of these impressions by day will determine who, or what, it is they will meet in the night.

February 25: Venus conjunct Moon 24° Pisces: Venus was at this exact degree throughout the Passion and Resurrection of Christ.

February 28: Sun 14° Aquarius: Jesus taught on the same theme as the Sermon on the Mount: the Beatitudes and the Lord's Prayer (Matt. 5:3–12; 6:9–13).

Both Rudolf Steiner and Valentin Tomberg gave close attention to the Lord's Prayer and the Beatitudes. It is significant that both of these great teachers of humanity were born with the Sun at exactly 14½° Aquarius. This is a star language that indicates two individualities with a common mission who receive spiritual guidance from the same source. As true initiates all work together, coming into incarnation in various cultures at various times in order to continue the work of spiritually guiding humanity, it would follow that one of the tasks of an initiate is to assure his successor is recognized. Rudolf Steiner fulfilled this task, without

---

13 On the twelve senses, see Rudolf Steiner, *Anthroposophy (A fragment)*, "The Human Being as a Sensory Organism."

14 Tomberg, *Christ and Sophia*, p. 254.

trespassing upon the freedom of his successor, who was still under the age of 33 at the time of Steiner's death. (Before this age an individuality may not as yet have accepted the responsibility of a foreordained mission.) Rudolf Steiner said the individuality in the process of becoming the next Buddha was born in 1900 and would begin teaching in the 1930s.

It was more discreetly, and without putting a particular person in the limelight as candidate, that Dr. Rudolf Steiner, founder of the Anthroposophical Society predicted the manifestation—again in the first half of the twentieth century—not of the new Maitreya Buddha or Kalki Avatar, but rather of the Bodhisattva, i.e. the individuality in the process of becoming the next Buddha, whose field of activity he hoped the Anthroposophical Society would serve.[15]

Aquarius is future-oriented and brings something new into the present. Aquarian teachers bear witness to the future. Aquarius is leading us into the next zodiacal age (beginning in 2375), during which the Slavic cultural epoch will open new possibilities for *manas* cognition. We are on the doorstep to this Aquarian Age. Both of these great teachers brought change based on the traditions of the past, but not limited by these traditions. For to be limited is to become rigidified. The sanctity of humanity's freedom allows each of us to discern for ourselves whom we recognize as bearers of revelation. Error occurs when those in positions of authority misuse their positions by imposing personal opinions as objective truths, thereby transgressing upon the freedom of others.

MARCH 2012

March continues the pretty sunsets we observed at the end of February, for while the Moon continues her harried pace around the zodiac, Venus and Jupiter will remain in the setting western sky, coming closer until Venus is just above Jupiter on the 13th. Once Venus has passed over Jupiter, the Moon joins these two again from the 24th–26th, in a reversal of what we saw in February: now the setting tableau offers Venus–Moon–Jupiter. The Sun begins March in Aquarius, moving into Pisces on the 15th. The 8th brings the Full Moon with Mars shining above its illuminated disc in Leo (the Lion). Late in the evening of the 10th the waning Moon rises with Saturn in Libra (the Scales). The Moon will disappear to view by the 21st, with the New Moon on the 22nd in Aquarius. Mercury stations retrograde on the 13th, in Pisces (the Fishes) and stations direct next month, on April 5th.

March 1: Venus enters Aries. "Take hold of growth's being" (Rudolf Steiner, *Twelve Moods of the Zodiac*). Venus was in Aries at both the Ascension and Pentecost.

March 3: Sun 18° Aquarius opposite Mars 18° Leo: Heliocentric Mars was here at the Baptism in the Jordan, when the Word became flesh. At this event, heliocentric Mars was conjunct the Moon in Leo: a perfect picture of the Son of God—the Logos—descending into the physical body of Jesus of Nazareth. Witnessing the Baptism were Saturnin (a young Greek of royal blood from the city of Patras), Nicodemus, Obed, John Mark, Joseph of Arimathea and Lazarus. All witnessed the voice of thunder that spoke the words, "This is my beloved Son in whom I am well pleased," and Jesus became transparent with radiant light (*Chron.* p. 200).

MARCH 4: Sun 19° Aquarius: Raising an Essene girl from the dead (*Chron.* p. 219). The Sun is aligned with the megastar 68 Cygnus in the Swan—the second most luminous star visible to us.
ASPECT: Venus 4° Aries opposite Saturn 4° Libra: Jesus was journeying in pagan lands.

This path started in Ur, the town of Abraham, and led to Egypt, where the people of Israel remained until the Exodus. On this journey Jesus Christ took into himself the entire history of the people of Israel and bore this within him as he returned to Israel for the last three months of his ministry, leading up to the death on the cross. (*CHA, The Journey of Jesus Christ to the Pagans*)

---

15 Anon. Meditations on the Tarot, p. 614.

Just past the Venus–Saturn opposition (Cancer–Capricorn), on December 7/8, the pagan idols were shattering throughout Chaldea. This was approximately three months after Jesus had visited the three kings in their tent city, and about seven weeks after the prophecy Jesus had given to the adversarial pagan chiefs, whom he had reproached for their idol worship. Jesus had told them that on the anniversary of the night on which the star had appeared to the three kings, the idols would all break, and this would be proof of the truth of his words. Anne Catherine Emmerich had a vision:

> Everywhere, she saw idols broken and animal idols crying out. Historically (in AD 32) this was probably the night of December 7/8, the anniversary of the immaculate conception of the Virgin Mary, on which night the three kings had first seen the star, fifteen years before the birth of Jesus. (*Chron.* p. 331)

In this last Venus–Saturn opposition before the June 2012 Venus–Sun transit of this year, this shattering of idols is remembered. In fulfillment of the Sophia Age now being prepared, idols must shatter: the idols of money, power, greed, scarcity, fear and tyranny. As these old idols shatter, new paradigms will be birthed through the karmic groups (Venus) that are now making preparations for this New Age—an age in harmony with the new relationships (Libra) humanity must create, relationships of balance where the ideals of abundance, collaboration, and cooperation work to bring healing to both the Earth and humanity. Inversely, Venus, the planet of desire, may inspire the tyrants of idolatry to escalate their possessed enforcement of the old paradigm.

March 5: ASPECT: Mercury conjunct Uranus, 8° Pisces. Mercury was opposite today's Mercury, coming into opposition with Uranus, at the conception of John the Baptist. A Mercury–Uranus aspect is a signature for John's incredible capacity to receive the crystal clear Imaginations of Cosmic Intelligence, and through this means John was able to bear witness to the "Light" that had come into the world. Jesus said of John: "Not one among those born of women is greater than John the Baptist." This statement refers to the passing on of capacities through the hereditary stream. According to Rudolf Steiner, John was the last individual who had still been able to develop higher faculties on the basis of heredity. He was the "greatest of those born of women." Since the time of Christ's ministry, these abilities must come from beyond the Earth.

> We must no longer look merely to the Earth and find the Earth's god in the Christ, but we have to be aware in our souls that the Christ comes from the heavens. This is what Christ Jesus was referring to when he spoke of John the Baptist as one of the greatest "born of women." That is, people who have abilities that can be directly inherited.[16]

Clearly the inheritance of abilities that used to be connected with the hereditary stream, if not raised to Christ, are now the inheritance of abilities born more and more of sub-earthly realms. John raised his inherited capacities to the Light of the World.

With Mercury conjunct Uranus there is a quickening in the receptivity of illumined thinking—the thinking that permeated John. Inversely, there is a possibility for abstract thinking to "build towers of Babel" and to venerate false light-bearers. This conjunction of Mercury–Uranus heightens perception in one way or another. The stars remember the conception of John. May we feel the presence of this great individuality.

March 6: Sun enters third decan of Aquarius, ruled by the Moon. This decan is associated with Pegasus, the Winged Horse.

March 7/8: Full Moon: Sun 22° Aquarius opposite Moon 22° Leo: The Sun was at 22° Aquarius (where it is today) when the Pharisees again reproached Jesus on account of the irregular mode of the Disciples' fasting. Jesus retorted by charging them with their avarice and want of mercy. After this, Jesus and the Disciples went to Dan, called also Lais, or Leschem (10 Feb 31).

---

16 Steiner, *The Fifth Gospel*, p. 167.

SIDEREAL GEOCENTRIC LONGITUDES : MARCH 2012 Gregorian at 0 hours UT

DAY	☉	☽	☊	☿	♀	♂	♃	♄	♅	♆	♇
1 TH	15 ♒ 54	15 ♉ 17	14 ♏ 35R	3 ♓ 4	0 ♈ 10	19 ♌ 52R	12 ♈ 8	4 ♎ 10R	8 ♓ 17	6 ♒ 5	14 ♐ 14
2 FR	16 54	27 21	14 35	4 27	1 17	19 28	12 19	4 7	8 20	6 8	14 15
3 SA	17 55	9 ♊ 41	14 34	5 45	2 24	19 5	12 30	4 5	8 23	6 10	14 16
4 SU	18 55	22 23	14 30	6 57	3 31	18 41	12 41	4 3	8 26	6 12	14 17
5 MO	19 55	5 ♋ 30	14 24	8 2	4 37	18 17	12 52	4 0	8 30	6 14	14 18
6 TU	20 55	19 3	14 15	9 0	5 43	17 53	13 3	3 57	8 33	6 17	14 20
7 WE	21 55	3 ♌ 3	14 4	9 50	6 49	17 30	13 14	3 55	8 36	6 19	14 21
8 TH	22 55	17 27	13 52	10 33	7 55	17 6	13 26	3 52	8 40	6 21	14 22
9 FR	23 55	2 ♍ 7	13 41	11 6	9 0	16 43	13 38	3 49	8 43	6 23	14 23
10 SA	24 55	16 57	13 30	11 31	10 6	16 20	13 49	3 46	8 46	6 25	14 24
11 SU	25 55	1 ♎ 46	13 22	11 47	11 11	15 57	14 1	3 43	8 50	6 28	14 25
12 MO	26 55	16 29	13 17	11 54	12 15	15 34	14 13	3 40	8 53	6 30	14 25
13 TU	27 55	0 ♏ 59	13 15	11 53R	13 20	15 12	14 25	3 36	8 56	6 32	14 26
14 WE	28 54	15 13	13 15	11 43	14 24	14 50	14 37	3 33	9 0	6 34	14 27
15 TH	29 54	29 9	13 15	11 24	15 28	14 28	14 49	3 30	9 3	6 36	14 28
16 FR	0 ♓ 54	12 ♐ 48	13 15	10 59	16 31	14 7	15 1	3 26	9 6	6 38	14 29
17 SA	1 54	26 12	13 12	10 26	17 34	13 47	15 13	3 23	9 10	6 40	14 30
18 SU	2 53	9 ♑ 21	13 8	9 47	18 37	13 26	15 25	3 19	9 13	6 43	14 30
19 MO	3 53	22 18	13 0	9 3	19 40	13 7	15 38	3 15	9 17	6 45	14 31
20 TU	4 53	5 ♒ 3	12 50	8 14	20 42	12 48	15 50	3 12	9 20	6 47	14 32
21 WE	5 52	17 37	12 38	7 23	21 44	12 29	16 3	3 8	9 24	6 49	14 32
22 TH	6 52	0 ♓ 1	12 25	6 29	22 45	12 11	16 15	3 4	9 27	6 51	14 33
23 FR	7 51	12 14	12 13	5 35	23 46	11 54	16 28	3 0	9 30	6 53	14 34
24 SA	8 51	24 18	12 3	4 41	24 47	11 38	16 41	2 56	9 34	6 55	14 34
25 SU	9 51	6 ♈ 13	11 54	3 49	25 47	11 22	16 53	2 52	9 37	6 57	14 35
26 MO	10 50	18 3	11 49	2 59	26 47	11 7	17 6	2 48	9 41	6 59	14 35
27 TU	11 49	29 50	11 46	2 13	27 47	10 53	17 19	2 44	9 44	7 1	14 36
28 WE	12 49	11 ♉ 38	11 45	1 30	28 46	10 39	17 32	2 40	9 48	7 3	14 36
29 TH	13 48	23 30	11 46D	0 52	29 45	10 26	17 45	2 36	9 51	7 5	14 37
30 FR	14 47	5 ♊ 33	11 46	0 19	0 ♉ 43	10 14	17 58	2 31	9 54	7 7	14 37
31 SA	15 47	17 50	11 47R	29 ♒ 51	1 40	10 3	18 11	2 27	9 58	7 8	14 37

INGRESSES :

2 ☽ → ♊ 5:12	24 ☽ → ♈ 11:26	
4 ☽ → ♋ 14: 2	27 ☽ → ♉ 0:20	
6 ☽ → ♌ 18:49	29 ♀ → ♉ 6:22	
8 ☽ → ♍ 20:33	☽ → ♊ 13: 0	
10 ☽ → ♎ 21: 7	30 ☿ → ♒ 15:51	
12 ☽ → ♏ 22:21	31 ☽ → ♋ 23: 6	
15 ☽ → ♐ 1:28		
☉ → ♓ 2:20		
17 ☽ → ♑ 6:53		
19 ☽ → ♒ 14:26		
21 ☽ → ♓ 23:59		

ASPECTS & ECLIPSES :

1 ☉ □ ☽ 1:21	10 ☽ ☌ P 9:44	☽ ☍ ♂ 14:23	28 ☽ ☌ ☋ 0:15	
3 ☽ ☍ ♇ 8:45	11 ☽ ☌ ♄ 3: 8	☽ N ☊ 14:34	29 ☉ □ ♇ 19:43	
☉ ☍ ♂ 20: 1	☽ ☍ ♀ 16:31	21 ☉ i☌ ☿ 19:12	30 ☽ ☍ ♇ 17:46	
4 ♀ ☍ ♄ 11: 7	☽ ☍ ♃ 20:13	22 ☽ ☌ ☿ 11:48	☉ □ ☽ 19:40	
5 ☿ ☌ ♅ 11:34	13 ☽ ☌ ☊ 20:38	☉ ☌ ☽ 14:36		
7 ☽ ☍ ♆ 5:30	14 ♀ ☌ ♃ 5:56	☽ ☌ ♅ 18:36		
☽ S ☊ 18:10	15 ☉ □ ☽ 1:24	24 ☽ ☍ ♄ 17:15		
☽ ☌ ♂ 23:27	16 ☽ ☌ ♇ 2:59	☉ ☌ ♅ 18:19		
8 ☉ ☍ ☽ 9:39	18 ☿ ☌ ♅ 17: 6	25 ☽ ☌ ♃ 22: 1		
9 ☽ ☍ ♅ 10:44	19 ♂ □ ☊ 18:14	26 ☽ ☌ A 5:48		
☽ ☍ ☿ 15: 0	20 ☽ ☌ ♆ 3:17	☽ ☌ ♀ 19:25		

SIDEREAL HELIOCENTRIC LONGITUDES : MARCH 2012 Gregorian at 0 hours UT

DAY	Sid. Time	☿	♀	⊕	♂	♃	♄	♅	♆	♇	Vernal Point
1 TH	10:36:48	14 ♉ 50	14 ♊ 16	15 ♌ 54	17 ♌ 30	21 ♈ 38	29 ♍ 47	9 ♓ 21	5 ♒ 46	12 ♐ 40	5 ♓ 5'25"
2 FR	10:40:44	21 9	15 53	16 54	17 56	21 44	29 49	9 22	5 46	12 40	5 ♓ 5'25"
3 SA	10:44:41	27 28	17 30	17 54	18 23	21 49	29 51	9 22	5 47	12 41	5 ♓ 5'25"
4 SU	10:48:37	3 ♊ 47	19 7	18 55	18 49	21 54	29 53	9 23	5 47	12 41	5 ♓ 5'25"
5 MO	10:52:34	10 3	20 44	19 55	19 15	22 0	29 55	9 23	5 47	12 41	5 ♓ 5'25"
6 TU	10:56:31	16 16	22 21	20 55	19 41	22 5	29 57	9 24	5 48	12 42	5 ♓ 5'25"
7 WE	11: 0:27	22 24	23 59	21 55	20 8	22 11	29 59	9 25	5 48	12 42	5 ♓ 5'24"
8 TH	11: 4:24	28 26	25 36	22 55	20 34	22 16	0 ♎ 1	9 25	5 48	12 42	5 ♓ 5'24"
9 FR	11: 8:20	4 ♋ 20	27 13	23 55	21 0	22 22	0 3	9 26	5 49	12 43	5 ♓ 5'24"
10 SA	11:12:17	10 7	28 51	24 55	21 26	22 27	0 5	9 27	5 49	12 43	5 ♓ 5'24"
11 SU	11:16:13	15 44	0 ♋ 28	25 55	21 53	22 32	0 7	9 27	5 49	12 43	5 ♓ 5'24"
12 MO	11:20:10	21 13	2 5	26 54	22 19	22 38	0 9	9 28	5 50	12 44	5 ♓ 5'24"
13 TU	11:24: 6	26 32	3 43	27 54	22 45	22 43	0 10	9 29	5 50	12 44	5 ♓ 5'24"
14 WE	11:28: 3	1 ♌ 41	5 20	28 54	23 12	22 49	0 12	9 29	5 51	12 44	5 ♓ 5'23"
15 TH	11:32: 0	6 41	6 57	29 54	23 38	22 54	0 14	9 30	5 51	12 45	5 ♓ 5'23"
16 FR	11:35:56	11 31	8 35	0 ♍ 54	24 4	23 0	0 16	9 31	5 51	12 45	5 ♓ 5'23"
17 SA	11:39:53	16 11	10 12	1 53	24 31	23 5	0 18	9 31	5 52	12 45	5 ♓ 5'23"
18 SU	11:43:49	20 43	11 50	2 53	24 57	23 10	0 20	9 32	5 52	12 46	5 ♓ 5'23"
19 MO	11:47:46	25 6	13 27	3 53	25 23	23 16	0 22	9 32	5 52	12 46	5 ♓ 5'23"
20 TU	11:51:42	29 21	15 5	4 52	25 50	23 21	0 24	9 33	5 53	12 46	5 ♓ 5'23"
21 WE	11:55:39	3 ♍ 28	16 42	5 52	26 16	23 27	0 26	9 34	5 53	12 47	5 ♓ 5'22"
22 TH	11:59:35	7 27	18 20	6 52	26 42	23 32	0 28	9 34	5 53	12 47	5 ♓ 5'22"
23 FR	12: 3:32	11 19	19 57	7 51	27 9	23 37	0 30	9 35	5 54	12 47	5 ♓ 5'22"
24 SA	12: 7:29	15 5	21 35	8 51	27 35	23 43	0 32	9 36	5 54	12 48	5 ♓ 5'22"
25 SU	12:11:25	18 45	23 12	9 50	28 2	23 48	0 34	9 36	5 54	12 48	5 ♓ 5'22"
26 MO	12:15:22	22 18	24 50	10 50	28 28	23 54	0 36	9 37	5 55	12 48	5 ♓ 5'22"
27 TU	12:19:18	25 47	26 27	11 49	28 54	23 59	0 38	9 38	5 55	12 49	5 ♓ 5'22"
28 WE	12:23:15	29 10	28 5	12 48	29 21	24 5	0 39	9 38	5 56	12 49	5 ♓ 5'21"
29 TH	12:27:11	2 ♎ 29	29 42	13 48	29 47	24 10	0 41	9 39	5 56	12 49	5 ♓ 5'21"
30 FR	12:31: 8	5 44	1 ♌ 20	14 47	0 ♍ 14	24 15	0 43	9 40	5 56	12 50	5 ♓ 5'21"
31 SA	12:35: 4	8 55	2 57	15 46	0 40	24 21	0 45	9 40	5 57	12 50	5 ♓ 5'21"

INGRESSES :

3 ☿ → ♊ 9:37	
7 ♄ → ♎ 14:15	
8 ☿ → ♋ 6:20	
10 ♀ → ♋ 17: 6	
13 ☿ → ♌ 16: 4	
15 ⊕ → ♍ 2:27	
20 ☿ → ♍ 3:45	
28 ☿ → ♎ 5:56	
29 ♀ → ♌ 4:20	
♂ → ♍ 11:27	

ASPECTS (HELIOCENTRIC +MOON(TYCHONIC)) :

1 ☿ □ ⊕ 4:49	5 ☿ ☍ ♇ 10:10	☿ △ ♅ 21:11	♀ △ ♅ 13:47	23 ☿ □ ♇ 9:18
☿ □ ♂ 10:55	♀ ✶ ♃ 19:46	10 ♀ □ ♄ 18:37	18 ☽ ☍ ♀ 5:12	24 ☽ ☍ ♄ 12:32
2 ☿ ☌ P 6: 2	6 ☿ ✶ ♂ 14:22	☽ ☌ ♄ 21:17	☿ △ ♃ 13:37	⊕ ☍ ♅ 18:19
3 ☽ ☍ ♇ 5:43	☿ ✶ ⊕ 21:42	12 ☿ □ ♃ 6:26	19 ☿ ☌ ♂ 1:46	25 ♀ □ ♃ 9:24
☿ △ ♄ 9: 6	☿ ✶ ♃ 23: 7	☽ ☍ ♃ 10:11	20 ☽ ☌ ♆ 1:34	26 ☽ ☌ ♃ 11:59
♀ ✶ ⊕ 15:52	7 ☽ ☍ ♆ 4:37	☿ N ☊ 10:31	21 ♀ ☌ P 1:47	27 ☿ ✶ ♀ 9: 2
☽ ☌ ♀ 17: 0	⊕ △ ♃ 7: 2	♂ △ ♃ 21:40	☽ ☍ ♂ 17:19	28 ⊕ □ ♇ 0:15
♀ ✶ ♂ 17:51	☿ ☌ ♀ 8:31	13 ☿ ✶ ♄ 17: 0	☿ ☌ ⊕ 19:12	☿ ☌ ♄ 10:47
⊕ ☌ ♂ 20: 1	8 ☽ ☌ ♂ 5:17	14 ☿ ☍ ♆ 19:57	22 ☿ ☍ ♅ 13: 6	29 ♀ ✶ ♄ 14:49
4 ☿ △ ♆ 7:39	☿ □ ♄ 6:25	15 ☽ ☌ ♇ 23:54	☽ ☌ ♅ 18:46	30 ☿ △ ♆ 1:33
☿ □ ♅ 21:27	9 ☽ ☍ ♅ 11:52	16 ☿ △ ♇ 6:18	☽ ☍ ☿ 21:23	☽ ☍ ♇ 14:18

On the way, Jesus instructed his followers—his subject always being prayer. He explained the *Our Father.* He told them that in the past they had not prayed worthily, but like Esau had asked for the fat of the Earth; but now, like Jacob, they should petition for the dew of Heaven, for spiritual gifts, for the blessing of spiritual illumination, for the Kingdom according to the will of God, and not for one in accordance with their own ideas. (ACE, *Vol. 3,* p. 232)

Sister Emmerich continues to describe the city of Dan, situated at the base of a high mountain range, that covered a wide extent owing to the fact that every one of its houses was surrounded by a garden; but in spite of the fertility of this region, there were many who were sick. Jesus told them that the swellings that afflicted many were from little mildew insects that were blown through the air, in clouds like chimney smoke. Jesus pointed out another insect, which was to be crushed and applied to the bite of these mildew insects in order to effect a cure (ACE, *Vol. 3,* p. 232).

With this Full Moon, we see reproaches from the decadent Pharisee authority figures, instructions regarding the *Our Father,* communities of gardens, illness from airborne afflictions, and the healing of this affliction. Perhaps the stars are telling us we are to win back our freedom from decadent thoughts, deepen into the profundity of the *Our Father* (and *Our Mother*) prayers, and through these measures find our way to healing the afflictions born of materialism and the insects of dis-ease this materialism has created—both physically and spiritually. In this way our gardens—including the gardens of our subtle bodies of life energy—will bring forth the "dew of heaven" as nourishment for the Earth and humanity. To have the proper earthly forms is not enough: the spiritual worlds must be actively brought into these forms to nourish our earthly gardens. With the Full Moon in Leo, hearts are strengthened to receive the "dew of Heaven." And, with the light of the Sun in Aquarius illuminating this Moon, we can imagine the spiritually permeated airwaves (Aquarius) being healed from the suffocating effect of air-born insects of materialistic thinking, through the power of Michaelic Cosmic Thoughts.

Can we pray not for what we want, but for what is needed for the healing of the Earth and humanity? Can we find protection from air-born disease through the power of Christ?

March 10: Sun 24° Aquarius: Healing of the Syrophoenician Woman (12 Feb 31). Here Jesus is approached by a crippled woman who begs him to come and heal her daughter who is possessed. Concerned about giving offense, Jesus cannot heal the woman's pagan daughter before he heals the Jews. Later that day Jesus exorcises the unclean spirit from the daughter (Matt 15:21–28). Jesus also heals the crippled woman:

> Jesus asked her whether she herself wished to be healed, but the Syrophoenician woman replied that she was not worthy, and that she asked only for her daughter's cure. Then Jesus laid one hand upon her head, the other on her side, and said: "Straighten up! May it be done to you as you also will it to be done!" (*Chron.* p. 279).

This is a story about faith and one's willingness to be healed. The shepherding hand of our angel rests upon our head, and the guiding hand of destiny gently rests upon our side, leading us forward. Feeling into the presence of Christ-imbued spiritual forces makes faith a fact. Our willingness to be healed is foreshadowed by our courage to know what forces have entrapped us. This is the trial of our times. Where are we harboring a lack of faith in the truth of Love and its power to heal? This is a good day to bring healing love to another.

MARCH 13: Venus conjunct Jupiter 14° Aries: Jupiter and Venus are conjunct where the Sun was at the time of the Mystery of Golgotha. This place in the heavens holds the eternal inscription of the most profound event in the entire history of the Earth. This Venus–Jupiter conjunction also has ties to miracles involving cosmic nutrition, for heliocentric Venus was conjunct Jupiter at the Feeding of the Five Thousand; and at the Feeding of the Four Thousand, heliocentric Jupiter was within 5° of conjunction with Venus. Both times in Aries. These two miracles represent the spiritual progression of *physical Earthly evolution* and the *spiritual evolution of human consciousness*. Both the evolution of the Earth and the evolution of human consciousness are dependent on nutrition from cosmic worlds. We hear from John in Revelation: "I am the Alpha and the Omega, thus speaks the Lord, our God, who is and who was and who is coming, the divine ruler of the world" (Rev. 1:8). This is Christ, the Alpha and Omega, who holds the seven stars and the seven spirits. The stars and the spirits are cosmic sources of nutrition that lead humanity and the Earth toward future stages of evolution.

> To the angel of the church in Sardis write: These are the words of him who holds the seven spirits of God and the seven stars. I know your deeds; you have a reputation of being alive, but you are dead. (Rev. 3:1)

The letter to Sardis is the letter to our Age—the age of the consciousness soul. We are each a spark from the living being of Christ, who was born when the Sun was at today's degree; and this spark represents our eternal Name. To draw from the founts of cosmic wisdom awakens us to our eternal Name—"the name of a living being." When we ignore these nourishing spiritual realms "we are dead." During this Venus–Jupiter conjunction our remembrance of the Mystery of Golgotha and the life-bestowing sustenance of spirit, enlivens us to receive the Love of Christ (Venus) in equal measure to the Wisdom of Sophia (Jupiter). Today Love and Wisdom are streaming from the starry heavens, and our ability to bring harmony and love into our communities is potentized. We can look for what is missing, and joyfully seek there to serve.

March 15: Sun enters Pisces: "In losing may loss be found" (Rudolf Steiner, *Twelve Moods of the Zodiac*). Above the first decan is the Square of Pegasus, hence the association of this decan with the body of Pegasus, the Winged Horse, also called the Horse of the Fountain. This decan is ruled by Saturn. Pisces bestows Magnanimity born of Love. The challenge is to stay grounded in reality in the inclination toward the mystical.

March 18: Mercury conjunct Uranus 9°13' Pisces: Uranus was here at the Birth of the Solomon Jesus (5 Mar 6 BC), whose birth Sun is commemorated at the end of this month. Mercury, from one perspective, represents human intelligence. When human intelligence works with Michael's cosmic intelligence, good comes into being. When human intelligence works independently it tends to come in its own name. The former is uniting; the latter divisive.

With Mercury and Uranus conjunct today at the place of the birth of the Solomon Jesus, we have the possibility to lift our thinking on the wings of Cosmic Intelligence, or to plunge into thought-fields of electrified lies and half-truths. One path leads us to the love the constellation of the Fishes bestows, the other to the superficiality that craves personal recognition, and fragments love into competitiveness.

There is also the possibility that we may witness a heightened tension between egotistic thinking and spiritual thinking. When these two work together, perception is brightened and ordinary thinking is illuminated. When they strive against each other, unrest is felt in the surrounding atmosphere of Earth and in the depths of inner Earth. A good practice toward the higher unity of Mercury and Uranus is the third Beatitude: *Blessed are the meek for they shall inherit the Earth*. In meekness one's personal thinking comes to stillness, so that cosmic thoughts may be revealed. Meekness allows one to penetrate through what is, to see what is striving to become. May we find stillness.

March 22 New Moon 7° Pisces. Jesus returned to the place of his baptism (1 Dec 29). After completing his 40-day period of continual temptation in the wilderness, Jesus descended from the cave on Mount Attarus, and traveled through the night until, at daybreak, he reached the river Jordan (*Chron.* pp. 207–8). John the Baptist beheld Jesus on the opposite side of the river and spoke to those assembled to hear him: "Behold the Lamb of God!" This Moon remembers the True Light. Can we see, to the other side of the river, where Christ stands? Can we see the presence of something pure and sacred, as did John? This purity is an elixir for the burning thirst of materialism.

March 25: Sun enters the second decan of Pisces, ruled by Jupiter. This decan is associated with Cepheus, the Crowned King, located high above, whose head is surrounded and illuminated by the Milky Way.

March 29: Sun 13° Pisces: Flight into Egypt (2 Mar 5 BC). The Solomon Jesus' parents fled to Egypt after an angel appeared to Joseph and instructed him to flee with his family into Egypt. That same night, of March 2/3, 5 BC, the Holy Family left Nazareth with their one-year-old son. "Subsequently the murder of the innocent children of Bethlehem took place, which marked the culmination of Herod's evil deeds" (*CHA*, p. 41).

ASPECT: Sun 14°37' Pisces square Pluto 14°37' Sagittarius: At the Flight into Egypt, when the Sun was coming into opposition with Pluto, the murderous threat of hatred from Herod was overcome due to the intervention of an angel. "It fills me with sadness to speak of Herod the Great. He was a king, an earthly king. But spiritually he was also a kingly soul—a bright star fallen from heaven! In his case we have a tragic warning of what may befall even a great soul, when seized with the will to power. Thereby Herod opened himself to the powers of evil and became an instrument in the endeavor to thwart the good. How he fell from lofty heights and degenerated! Thus he came to represent the lower self of man, open to the working of evil, in opposition to the true Self, the Christ Self" (*CHA, The Journey of the Three Kings, and the Flight of the Holy Family to Egypt*).

Today Sun is square Pluto at the memory of the Flight into Egypt. Pluto in square to the Sun-Self creates tension—a tension of choice: The will to power of Hades, or the the will of Divine Love from Phanes. The Sun-filled heart will hear the guidance of angels just as did Joseph long ago. Following this guidance can be a path of initiation—an initiation into the inner sanctuary of the heart. Likewise, a will to power will drive a restless heart to murderous acts.

MARCH 30: Sun 15° Pisces: Birth of Solomon Jesus (5 Mar 6 BC). The reincarnation of the great teacher, Zarathustra, who was visited by the Three Kings. The kings brought the wisdom gathered by initiates in the three preceding cultural ages: Myrrh from Ancient India, Frankincense from Ancient Persia, and Gold from Ancient Egypt. The influence of this great teacher, the Master Jesus, is always present on Earth. It takes discernment to hear his teachings through the cacophony of distractions, but he is always here. There is always an initiate who is working with him, even if he himself is not physically incarnated. The ideal of Pisces, the Sun sign at this birth, is "Not I, but Christ in me."

ASPECT: Venus enters Taurus. "Feel growth's power" (Rudolf Steiner, *Twelve Moods of the Zodiac*). Venus was in Taurus at the Transfiguration, the Visitation, and the Union in the Temple.

MARCH 31: Sun 16° Pisces: Conception of the Nathan Jesus (6 Mar 2 BC). The Nathan Jesus is the immaculate soul who incarnated for the first time as Jesus of Nazareth. It is profound that the birth of the Solomon Jesus and the conception of the Nathan Jesus were so beautifully interwoven in the stars, just as was their interweaving upon the Earth.

APRIL 2012

The Sun begins the month in front of the Fishes (Pisces) moving into Aries on April 14th. Saturn, Mars and Mercury begin the month retrograde, though Mercury stations direct quickly, on April 5th and Mars on the 15th. Saturn becomes visible in the early night sky mid-month, rising around sunset on about the 18th. It will remain easily visible to star gazers until the middle of September when it begins to disappear into the Sun's predawn glow. Pluto stations retrograde on the 11th. The Full Moon is on the 6th (Sun in Pisces and Moon in Virgo) and the New Moon in Aries is on the 21st. The tiny crescent Moon of the 24th reflects the Sun's light from beneath Venus, (who is also reflecting the light of the Sun); it should be a beautiful sight!

The Lyrids meteor shower reaches its peak on the 21st to 22nd promising as many as twenty meteors an hour; look up toward the east into the constellation of Lyra after midnight or in the pre-dawn dark.

April 3: ASPECT: Moon 7° Leo opposite Neptune 7° Aquarius: Jesus disturbs the Pharisees (April 19, 31). The Moon was at today's position, and one day past opposition with Neptune, when the Pharisees proclaimed Jesus a "disturber of the peace," saying "that they had the Sabbath, the festival days, and their own teaching, and that they did not need the innovations of this *upstart*. They threatened to complain to Herod—who would certainly put a stop to Jesus' activities" (*Chron.* p. 293). Later this day, Jesus received the news that John's head had been retrieved from Herod's castle. For occult reasons this was most likely very necessary. "It was Joanna Chuza who, together with Veronica and Mary of Hebron, a niece of Elisabeth, went to Herod Antipas's castle at Machaerus to retrieve the head of Elisabeth's son, John the baptist, after he had been beheaded."[17]

John was murdered by Herod but this gave Herod no peace. "Herod feels that, though the physical personality of John had gone away he is now all the more present! He feels that his atmosphere, his spirituality—which was none other than the spirituality of Elijah, is still there. His tormented conscience causes him to be aware that John the Baptist, that is, Elijah, is still there."[18]

John created the spiritual atmosphere around the Disciples through which he aided Jesus in his teachings. The "upstart"—Jesus Christ—on the other hand, would create a spiritual atmosphere around the entire globe of the Earth, through which all the Great Teachers of humanity would be aided. As humanity matures, new teachers will not be received as threats, but as collaborators, for they will be seen through the new capacities that a mature humanity will have developed.

April 5: The Sun enters the third decan of Pisces, the Mars decan, associated with the constellation Andromeda, the Chained Woman, who—threatened by the sea monster Cetus from below—was rescued by Perseus.

April 6: Today is Good Friday—Commemoration of Christ's Passion and Death on the Cross. The stars and planets, which bore witness to the events of this day, show us the interconnectedness between Heaven and Earth: As the Sun rose that morning, judgement was passed on the Son of Man. As Mars rose he was scourged. Jupiter rose as he was crowned with thorns, and as Saturn rose he was carrying the cross up Mt. Calvary. As the Cross was raised upon the hill of Golgotha, Leo was rising—the Lion of Judah, out of unfathomable love and courage, was hung on a cross between two criminals. It is the star beings working from the constellation of Leo that form the heart as conception begins in a mother's womb. At the crucifixion of Christ, it was the cosmic heart that was being formed—a heart of eternal love and forgiveness. The forces of Divine Love rayed forth from the heart of Christ, the Son of God, and the Earth was illumined with grace.

Hanging there on the holy cross, the crucified Jesus Christ signified the new Tree of Life, raised up for the first time on Earth since the expulsion of man from Paradise. The blood flowed from his wounds for the regeneration of the Earth and Humankind, for the restoration of a new paradise, the heavenly Jerusalem—in place of the earthly city of Jerusalem—away from which, facing northwest, his gaze was now directed. Thus he could say to the repentant criminal crucified to his right: "Today you will be with me in Paradise." For, on that Good Friday the new Paradise began, a new afterlife for all who unite themselves with Christ. And the repentant criminal was the first human being to die in proximity to Christ, to be taken up by Christ, since the New Era denoted by the Mystery of Golgotha began. (*CHA*, p. 228)

17 Powell, "The Holy Women at Christ's Death and Resurrection," *Starlight*, spring 2011.
18 Steiner, *The Gospel of St. Mark*, p. 45.

The Moon was full as Christ hung on the cross, and was taunted, mocked, and rejected by those he came to redeem. On this Good Friday the Moon is full in the constellation of Virgo, opposite the Sun in Pisces. He who fed humanity with loaves (Virgo) and fishes (Pisces) dies that we may find the eternal nourishment of Heaven. It was fulfilled!

Full Moon 21° Virgo: The Last Anointing (1 APR 33). On this Good Friday and Full Moon the stars remember the Wednesday before Christ's death. Jesus was at the home of Lazarus in Bethany with about sixty others. He spoke of his approaching death, saying that one of them would betray him for money. Mary Magdalene, who was also present, was unspeakably sad. At the end of their meal, Magdalene walked in bearing a costly ointment, and cast herself down at Jesus' feet, weeping bitterly. She anointed his feet, wiping them with her hair, and then she anointed his head. This interruption was not welcome by the Disciples and they muttered among themselves. As she was leaving, Judas blocked her way and scolded her for her shameless waste of money. Jesus said that "wherever the Gospel would be taught, her deed and also the Disciples' muttering would be remembered" (Matt. 26:13).

For the furious Judas, this anointing sealed his intention. "It was dark, but he did not stumble. In Jerusalem the hight priests and Pharisees were gathered together. Judas went to them and said that he wanted to give Jesus over into their hands. He asked how much they would give him and he was offered thirty pieces of silver" (*Chron.* p. 349). On this day the ahrimanic spirit engulfed Judas. A few days later, at the Last Supper, Ahriman would fully enter into the being of Judas.

On this Good Friday, under a Full Moon, the Wednesday before the death of Jesus is remembered. The restlessness that drove Judas to betray Jesus stands in opposition to the devotion of Mary Magdalene's soul. Together they represents a soul's choice—restlessness or devotion. As Good Friday is celebrated throughout Christendom, the indefatigable devotion of Magdalene is remembered.

April 7: Holy Saturday—Commemoration of Christ's Descent into Hell. The descent of Christ to the Mother in the heart of the earthly realm, was for the redemption of Nature and the Mother. In Paradise the kingdom of the Father and the realm of the Mother were interpenetrated. After the Fall, the two kingdoms fell further and further from each other. Christ descended into the depths of the inner Earth and planted his spirit as a seed in the womb of the Earth—as he began his descent, Virgo was rising in the East. This is the constellation connected to the womb, and to the sowing of seeds that will birth new impulses into the womb of all creation (See *CHA, The Mystery of Golgotha*).

The descent into Hell fulfilled the sixth stage of the Passion. In Hell Christ encountered the Antichrist:

> The power of the Antichrist is, or is almost, equal to that of Christ. The feather that tips the balance is the powerlessness Christ voluntarily takes upon himself in his self-sacrificing deed; and this powerlessness, of which the Antichrist is incapable, ultimately leads to the hair's breadth more power which Christ possesses.[19]

It is incumbent upon each of us to render the Antichrist powerless through *recognizing* and *resisting* his presence in the world—for if left unnamed, this presence causes fear and uncertainty, and leads people to seek worldly power and worldly things in a vain attempt to assuage fear. Avoidance does not work, rather it divides people and sets each against the other through wars and other inequities. In "powerlessness" we stand together with Christ, and bring the strength of love and courage to take up the place of fear.

ASPECT: Venus 9° Taurus square Mars 9° Leo. Venus and Mars were coming into conjunction close to where Venus is today when the enmity of the Pharisees erupted during Jesus' teachings. The Pharisees charged Jesus with healing on the Sabbath, which was prohibited by law. "The Pharisees asked scornfully whether he—the prophet—would do them the honor of eating the paschal lamb with them. Jesus replied: 'The Son of Man is himself a sacrifice for your sins!' In the end, as

---

19 Von Halle, *Descent into the Depths of the Earth*, p. 108.

SIDEREAL GEOCENTRIC LONGITUDES : APRIL 2012 Gregorian at 0 hours UT

DAY	☉	☽	☊	☿	♀	♂	♃	♄	♅	♆	♇
1 SU	16 ♓ 46	0 ♋ 29	11 ♏ 46R	29 ♒ 29R	2 ♉ 37	9 ♌ 52R	18 ♈ 25	2 ♎ 23R	10 ♓ 1	7 ♒ 10	14 ♐ 38
2 MO	17 45	13 32	11 43	29 13	3 34	9 42	18 38	2 18	10 5	7 12	14 38
3 TU	18 44	27 3	11 38	29 2	4 30	9 33	18 51	2 14	10 8	7 14	14 38
4 WE	19 43	11 ♌ 4	11 31	28 57	5 26	9 25	19 4	2 9	10 11	7 16	14 38
5 TH	20 42	25 32	11 23	28 57D	6 21	9 18	19 18	2 5	10 15	7 17	14 38
6 FR	21 41	10 ♍ 22	11 15	29 3	7 15	9 11	19 31	2 1	10 18	7 19	14 39
7 SA	22 40	25 26	11 8	29 14	8 9	9 6	19 45	1 56	10 22	7 21	14 39
8 SU	23 39	10 ♎ 36	11 3	29 30	9 2	9 0	19 58	1 52	10 25	7 23	14 39
9 MO	24 38	25 40	11 0	29 51	9 54	8 56	20 12	1 47	10 28	7 24	14 39
10 TU	25 37	10 ♏ 30	10 59	0 ♓ 17	10 46	8 53	20 25	1 42	10 32	7 26	14 39
11 WE	26 36	25 1	10 59D	0 47	11 37	8 50	20 39	1 38	10 35	7 28	14 39R
12 TH	27 35	9 ♐ 10	11 1	1 21	12 27	8 48	20 53	1 33	10 38	7 29	14 39
13 FR	28 34	22 55	11 2	1 59	13 17	8 47	21 6	1 29	10 42	7 31	14 39
14 SA	29 33	6 ♑ 19	11 2R	2 41	14 5	8 46	21 20	1 24	10 45	7 33	14 39
15 SU	0 ♈ 31	19 22	11 0	3 27	14 53	8 47D	21 34	1 19	10 48	7 34	14 39
16 MO	1 30	2 ♒ 8	10 56	4 16	15 40	8 47	21 48	1 15	10 51	7 36	14 38
17 TU	2 29	14 40	10 51	5 9	16 26	8 49	22 2	1 10	10 55	7 37	14 38
18 WE	3 27	26 59	10 45	6 4	17 12	8 52	22 15	1 6	10 58	7 39	14 38
19 TH	4 26	9 ♓ 8	10 38	7 2	17 56	8 55	22 29	1 1	11 1	7 40	14 38
20 FR	5 25	21 10	10 32	8 4	18 39	8 59	22 43	0 56	11 4	7 41	14 37
21 SA	6 23	3 ♈ 5	10 26	9 8	19 22	9 3	22 57	0 52	11 7	7 43	14 37
22 SU	7 22	14 55	10 22	10 14	20 3	9 8	23 11	0 47	11 11	7 44	14 37
23 MO	8 20	26 42	10 19	11 24	20 43	9 14	23 25	0 43	11 14	7 46	14 36
24 TU	9 19	8 ♉ 30	10 18	12 35	21 22	9 21	23 39	0 38	11 17	7 47	14 36
25 WE	10 17	20 19	10 19D	13 49	22 0	9 28	23 53	0 34	11 20	7 48	14 36
26 TH	11 16	2 ♊ 15	10 20	15 5	22 37	9 36	24 7	0 29	11 23	7 49	14 35
27 FR	12 14	14 19	10 22	16 24	23 12	9 44	24 22	0 25	11 26	7 51	14 35
28 SA	13 12	26 38	10 23	17 44	23 46	9 53	24 36	0 20	11 29	7 52	14 34
29 SU	14 11	9 ♋ 15	10 24	19 7	24 19	10 3	24 50	0 16	11 32	7 53	14 34
30 MO	15 9	22 14	10 24R	20 32	24 50	10 13	25 4	0 11	11 35	7 54	14 33

INGRESSES :

3 ☽ → ♌ 5: 7	23 ☽ → ♉ 6:42
5 ☽ → ♍ 7:17	25 ☽ → ♊ 19:30
7 ☽ → ♎ 7:13	28 ☽ → ♋ 6:28
9 ☽ → ♏ 6:58	30 ☽ → ♌ 14: 0
☿ → ♓ 8:44	
11 ☽ → ♐ 8:22	
13 ☽ → ♑ 12:36	
14 ☉ → ♈ 11:11	
15 ☽ → ♒ 19:56	
18 ☽ → ♓ 5:55	
20 ☽ → ♈ 17:47	

ASPECTS & ECLIPSES :

3 ☽ ☍ ♆ 17:33	10 ☽ ☍ ♀ 0:26	20 ☽ ☍ ♄ 19:33
☽ ☌ ♂ 21:15	☽ ☌ ☊ 0:46	21 ☉ ☌ ☽ 7:18
4 ☽ S ☊ 0:44	♀ ☍ ☊ 6: 9	22 ☽ ☌ A 13:38
5 ☽ ☍ ☿ 5:36	12 ☽ ☌ ♇ 9:28	☽ ☌ ♃ 17:10
☽ ☍ ♅ 23:53	13 ☉ □ ☽ 10:49	☿ ☌ ♅ 20:26
6 ♀ □ ♆ 2: 0	15 ☉ ☍ ♄ 18:12	24 ☽ ☌ ☋ 3:40
☉ ☍ ☽ 19:18	16 ☽ ☌ ♆ 10:25	25 ☽ ☌ ♀ 3:35
7 ☽ ☌ ♄ 10:13	☽ ☍ ♂ 12:43	☿ □ ♇ 14:37
☽ ☌ P 17: 2	☽ N ☊ 16:42	27 ☽ ☍ ♇ 0:30
♀ □ ♂ 23:30	18 ☽ ☌ ☿ 19:27	29 ☉ □ ☽ 9:57
8 ☽ ☍ ♃ 15: 7	19 ☽ ☌ ♅ 3:44	30 ♂ □ ☊ 22:31

SIDEREAL HELIOCENTRIC LONGITUDES : APRIL 2012 Gregorian at 0 hours UT

DAY	Sid. Time	☿	♀	⊕	♂	♃	♄	♅	♆	♇	Vernal Point
1 SU	12:39: 1	12 ♎ 2	4 ♌ 35	16 ♍ 46	1 ♍ 7	24 ♈ 26	0 ♎ 47	9 ♓ 41	5 ♒ 57	12 ♐ 50	5 ♓ 5'21"
2 MO	12:42:58	15 6	6 12	17 45	1 33	24 32	0 49	9 41	5 57	12 51	5 ♓ 5'21"
3 TU	12:46:54	18 7	7 50	18 44	2 0	24 37	0 51	9 42	5 58	12 51	5 ♓ 5'21"
4 WE	12:50:51	21 5	9 27	19 43	2 26	24 42	0 53	9 43	5 58	12 51	5 ♓ 5'21"
5 TH	12:54:47	24 1	11 5	20 42	2 53	24 48	0 55	9 43	5 58	12 52	5 ♓ 5'20"
6 FR	12:58:44	26 54	12 42	21 41	3 20	24 53	0 57	9 44	5 59	12 52	5 ♓ 5'20"
7 SA	13: 2:40	29 46	14 20	22 40	3 46	24 59	0 59	9 45	5 59	12 52	5 ♓ 5'20"
8 SU	13: 6:37	2 ♏ 36	15 57	23 39	4 13	25 4	1 1	9 45	6 0	12 53	5 ♓ 5'20"
9 MO	13:10:33	5 25	17 35	24 38	4 39	25 10	1 3	9 46	6 0	12 53	5 ♓ 5'20"
10 TU	13:14:30	8 12	19 12	25 37	5 6	25 15	1 5	9 47	6 0	12 53	5 ♓ 5'20"
11 WE	13:18:27	10 59	20 49	26 36	5 33	25 20	1 6	9 47	6 1	12 54	5 ♓ 5'20"
12 TH	13:22:23	13 44	22 27	27 35	5 59	25 26	1 8	9 48	6 1	12 54	5 ♓ 5'19"
13 FR	13:26:20	16 30	24 4	28 34	6 26	25 31	1 10	9 49	6 1	12 54	5 ♓ 5'19"
14 SA	13:30:16	19 14	25 42	29 32	6 53	25 37	1 12	9 49	6 2	12 55	5 ♓ 5'19"
15 SU	13:34:13	21 59	27 19	0 ♎ 31	7 19	25 42	1 14	9 50	6 2	12 55	5 ♓ 5'19"
16 MO	13:38: 9	24 44	28 56	1 30	7 46	25 47	1 16	9 50	6 2	12 55	5 ♓ 5'19"
17 TU	13:42: 6	27 29	0 ♍ 33	2 29	8 13	25 53	1 18	9 51	6 3	12 56	5 ♓ 5'19"
18 WE	13:46: 2	0 ♐ 14	2 11	3 27	8 40	25 58	1 20	9 52	6 3	12 56	5 ♓ 5'19"
19 TH	13:49:59	3 0	3 48	4 26	9 7	26 4	1 22	9 52	6 3	12 56	5 ♓ 5'18"
20 FR	13:53:56	5 47	5 25	5 24	9 33	26 9	1 24	9 53	6 4	12 57	5 ♓ 5'18"
21 SA	13:57:52	8 35	7 2	6 23	10 0	26 14	1 26	9 54	6 4	12 57	5 ♓ 5'18"
22 SU	14: 1:49	11 25	8 39	7 22	10 27	26 20	1 28	9 54	6 5	12 57	5 ♓ 5'18"
23 MO	14: 5:45	14 15	10 16	8 20	10 54	26 25	1 30	9 55	6 5	12 58	5 ♓ 5'18"
24 TU	14: 9:42	17 8	11 53	9 19	11 21	26 31	1 32	9 56	6 5	12 58	5 ♓ 5'18"
25 WE	14:13:38	20 3	13 30	10 17	11 48	26 36	1 33	9 56	6 6	12 58	5 ♓ 5'18"
26 TH	14:17:35	22 59	15 7	11 16	12 15	26 41	1 35	9 57	6 6	12 59	5 ♓ 5'17"
27 FR	14:21:31	25 59	16 44	12 14	12 42	26 47	1 37	9 58	6 6	12 59	5 ♓ 5'17"
28 SA	14:25:28	29 1	18 21	13 12	13 9	26 52	1 39	9 58	6 7	12 59	5 ♓ 5'17"
29 SU	14:29:25	2 ♑ 6	19 58	14 11	13 36	26 58	1 41	9 59	6 7	13 0	5 ♓ 5'17"
30 MO	14:33:21	5 14	21 35	15 9	14 3	27 3	1 43	9 59	6 7	13 0	5 ♓ 5'17"

INGRESSES :

7 ☿ → ♏ 1:57
14 ⊕ → ♎ 11:17
16 ♀ → ♍ 15:45
17 ☿ → ♐ 21:57
28 ☿ → ♑ 7:44

ASPECTS (HELIOCENTRIC +MOON(TYCHONIC)) :

1 ☿ ⚹ ♇ 6:19	☽ ☍ ♃ 23:11	☽ ☍ ♀ 11:46	22 ☿ ☌ ♇ 13: 5
♀ ☍ ♆ 20:16	9 ☿ □ ♆ 5: 1	☽ ☍ ♂ 23:56	♀ ☍ ♅ 18:42
3 ☽ ☍ ♆ 15:21	☽ ☌ ☿ 19:22	19 ☽ ☌ ♅ 1:27	☽ ☌ ♃ 23:24
☽ ☌ ♀ 20:56	10 ☿ △ ♅ 13:38	☿ □ ♀ 16:24	23 ♀ ☌ ♂ 12:54
4 ☿ ☌ ☋ 20:20	11 ♀ N ☊ 15:35	☿ ⚹ ⊕ 18:59	24 ♀ □ ♇ 16: 5
5 ☿ ☍ ♃ 6:43	12 ☽ ☌ ♇ 6:27	20 ☿ ⚹ ♆ 2:23	26 ☽ ☍ ♇ 21:21
☽ ☌ ♂ 12:19	13 ♀ △ ♃ 22:42	⊕ △ ♆ 16:13	27 ☿ △ ♃ 6:34
☽ ☍ ♅ 22:59	15 ☿ ☌ A 6:35	♂ ☍ ♅ 18: 1	♂ □ ♇ 15:39
6 ♀ △ ♇ 2:24	⊕ ☌ ♄ 18:12	☽ ☍ ♄ 20:39	⊕ ⚹ ♇ 18:41
7 ☽ ☌ ♄ 8:47	16 ☽ ☌ ♆ 7:26	21 ☿ □ ♅ 11:11	28 ☽ ☍ ☿ 6: 3
8 ☿ ⚹ ♂ 16:18	18 ☿ ⚹ ♄ 9:38	☿ □ ♂ 14:20	☿ □ ♄ 20:49

Jesus continued teaching, the Pharisees became so exasperated that they raised a great commotion. But Jesus managed to slip away and disappear into the crowd, returning to Bethany where preparations were underway for the feast of the following day" (*Chron.* p. 287).

With Venus square Mars today, either a tension or a harmony can be felt within karmic groups with the spoken word. It is far too easy to misunderstand the words of others and get tangled in the lower realm of personalities. This causes great commotion where none need exist. If the words of others cause a reaction, we are being led to tangles in our own personality. The example Jesus gives is to speak the truth without compromise, while all the while remaining compassionately above the level of the personality.

April 8: Easter Sunday—Commemoration of Christ's Resurrection: The spiritual worlds held their breath at the descent of Christ into Hell. A world unknown to the higher hierarchies was being penetrated by Jesus Christ.

> The "gardener" who appeared to the woman made clairvoyant by grief was not a "gardener" from only *her* perspective. In a deeper sense, he was *truly* a gardener, because he had acquired the power to cause the Earth's soil to produce the fruits of goodness. From that time forward, the highest human initiates have likewise become "gardeners"; they work for the well-being of humanity—and not just the direct concerns of humanity, but also those that reach indirectly through nature and Earth's soil.[20]

What now occurred was the Resurrection of our Savior and this takes place as a real rhythm of the Earth and as a spiritual power, creating substance every Sunday anew in every single human being. At this moment the Savior of the world revealed the whole immeasurable grandeur of his love to the world with which he had completely united himself, as well as with the human beings living on it. At this moment, as the Christ Spirit arises from the grave in the first Resurrection body, he merges into the innermost heart of every human

soul. It is now up to us in humility, in devotion and in joy, to celebrate daily this inner core of holiness by becoming aware that we ourselves bear him—the highest and most precious—in us (Judith von Halle, *And If He Had Not Been Raised*, p. 127).

Today we celebrate the Risen One and the work of his "gardeners," as we remember the sabbath and keep it holy—for the sabbath Sunday is a day to rest from the toil of daily life, in memory of spiritual worlds and spiritual beings. The fact that materialistic culture has intruded upon this holy day of rest does not mean we need comply.

April 10: Sun 25° Pisces: Feeding of the Four Thousand (Matt. 15:32–39; *Chron.* 284). At the Feeding of the Four Thousand, seven loaves of bread and seven fish were multiplied. After all had eaten their fill, seven baskets full of bread were gathered. Seven indicates communion taking place in the course of time, as distinct from the Feeding of the Five Thousand, which depicted communion taking place with cosmic realms of space, where twelve baskets of bread are used.

In the Feeding of the Four Thousand we see our union with the *temporal* aspect of evolution connected with the seven days of existence—each day representing one of the seven pillars of Sophia's Temple (from ancient Saturn to future Vulcan). Seven signifies evolution taking place in time and the unfolding of our sevenfold nature: physical, etheric, astral, "I," spirit self, life spirit, and spirit body. Human beings develop over the course of *time*. As we purify our bodies, our chakras awaken as organs of perception—they become solarized through communion with Christ. As this occurs, we require less nourishment *from* the elemental world and, instead, become sources of nourishment *for* the elemental world. As we move forward through evolution we will reach ever-higher levels of purity. Sophia's Temple has seven pillars, and we are currently working with the fourth, Earth. Earth evolution is focused toward the development of the "I." This "I," given to humanity at the Turning Point of Time, is to reach ever higher into spiritual realms so as to be nourished by spiritual manna. This is a picture of overcoming the third temptation—"Man

20 Tomberg, *Christ and Sophia*, p. 299.

JOURNAL FOR STAR WISDOM 2011

does not live by bread alone, but by every word that issues forth from the Word of God."

Today remembers this miracle of honoring the unfolding of Sophia's Temple in time. The beings of nature and all the fruits of Mother Earth are sacred sources of nourishment, and they become sacraments through the human being's communion with Christ. It is what is living that leads humanity to spiritual nourishment. Ahriman said to Christ in the wilderness, at the third temptation:

> Look at the dead earthly phenomena, the stones; they can come to life as bread if you only command them to do so. They will become as bread because, from the Earth's interior, I can supply a lifelike force to all dead matter. You must simply will what is dead to live.[21]

Christ rejected the temptation by pointing to the Word of God as the other source of life—the true life that gives both nature and humanity the ability to move with evolution toward future stages of existence. Today remembers this miracle and the anti-life that is threatening humanity from sub-earthly realms—a threat to the unfolding of Sophia's Temple, and a treacherous debasing of her Mother in the depths of the Earthly realm. Which will it be—the bread of life, or the stones of materialism and all the entrapments caused by virtual realities and genetic manipulations? We are surrounded by that which is dead masquerading as the living. May we find the holiness of Life this day, and open our eyes to the usurper, who causes what is dead to appear as if living.

April 11: ASPECT: Pluto stations 14°39' Sagittarius. Pluto will remain at this exact degree until the 15th of this month, when the Sun enters Aries. At this degree Jesus blessed the children and addressed the rich youth. "And Jesus said to his Disciples, 'Yes, I tell you, whoever is rich will not easily find access to the kingdom of the heavens. Again I tell you: A camel will more easily go through the eye of a needle than a rich man will enter the kingdom of God'" (Matt. 19:23–25). Attachment to any power or authority that comes from any kind of material wealth, will obstruct

humanity from receiving the blessings of heaven. But children, and those like them, are blessed—because the kingdom of heaven is meant for them.

April 12: Sun 28° Pisces: Peter receives the keys (March 19, 31). Four days after the Feeding of the Four Thousand, Jesus and the Disciples had withdrawn to a mountain. At dawn, Jesus went to them and asked, "Who do you say I am?" Simon Peter answered, "You are the Messiah, the Son of the living God." Jesus replied:

> Blessed are you, Simon son of Jonah, for this was not revealed to you by flesh and blood, but by my Father in heaven. And I tell you that you are Peter, and on this rock I will build my church, and the gates of Hades will not overcome it. I will give you the keys of the kingdom of heaven; whatever you bind on Earth will be bound in heaven, and whatever you loose on Earth will be loosed in heaven. (Matt. 16:15–20)

We can only wonder about what has been loosed on Earth because of humanity's failure to hold the gates of Hell in check. In April of 2010, oil was pouring into the waters of the Gulf of Mexico; in April of 2011, radiation from the Fukushima meltdown was pouring into the ocean off the eastern shores of Japan. The keys to the kingdom of Heaven signify the power, drawn from the kingdom of the Father, to be able to hold in check the forces of the underworld arising through the gates of Hell. This realm of Hell is guarded by the "gate" of the first chakra, the Moon chakra.

> The two keys laid one over the other form a cross, and it is precisely the sign of the cross to which the Father had lent power to banish the evil forces back into the underworld. This can be achieved only in purity and in faith, qualities which Peter had." (CHA, p. 149)

It is time to become like Peter and restore our faith in Christ so that we can hold in check the forces of the underworld. First we face our inner underworld, then we are ennobled to serve the collective underworld whose tentacles weave through our culture. Guard the gate!

---

21 Ibid., p. 174.

April 13: Sun 29° Pisces: Triumphant entry into Jerusalem (19 Mar 33). Exactly two years after Peter is given the keys to guard the gates of Hell, he who would pass through the gates of hell for the salvation of all humanity, entered Jerusalem as the sacrificial lamb. This was two weeks before his Passion and death.

April 14: Sun enters Aries. "Arise, O shining light" (Rudolf Steiner, *Twelve Moods of the Zodiac*). Aries and "The Bride of the Lamb"—the process of spiritualization (Christ) and interiorization (Sophia). The teachings of Hermes in ancient Egypt contained a pre-Christian understanding of the relationship between the *Lamb and his Bride* through the mystery teachings of Isis and Osiris. The first decan is ruled by Mars and is associated with the Girdle of Andromeda, symbolizing the power of unity and purity worn by the Mystic Woman representing the soul of humanity.

April 15: Sun 1°19' Aries opposite Saturn 1°19' Libra: Saturn is where the Sun was at the Baptism in the Jordan. The Father spirit in the heights bears witness to the presence of his Son and all the human beings enlightened through his Son's presence on Earth. What is our relationship to the presence of Christ? Can we open to new possibilities?

April 19: Sun 4° Aries: Woe Upon the Pharisees (24 Mar 33). In this address to the crowds and Disciples, Jesus Christ threw down the gauntlet before the Pharisees (Matthew 23:2–39). Powerful words echo from this "woe" into our own time. The powerful princes of the material world have nothing but loathing for anything spiritual, and these words from Matthew are words to all that is vainglorious. Jesus, before the Pharisees had gathered around him, had been teaching his Disciples of humility, giving these instructions: "They should never boast, 'I have driven out devils in your name!' or 'I have done this and that!' Also, they should not carry out their work publicly" (*Chron.* p. 345). The moment we forget humility we are vulnerable to inflation, as were the Pharisees. In the seventh Arcanam of *Meditations on the Tarot*, the Chariot, the unknown author speaks of the

danger of the fourth temptation—the temptation to come in one's own name—which is the most subtle temptation of all. He calls this "inflation"—a condition fraught with risk. "Here, then, are the principal dangers of inflation: exaggerated importance attached to oneself, superiority complex tending toward obsession and, lastly, megalomania. The first degree signifies a practical *task* for work upon oneself; the second degree is a serious *trial*; whilst the third is a *catastrophe*."[22]

Today we can focus on humility, which from one perspective can be summarized as being all that we *are* and nothing that we *are not*.

April 20/21: New Moon 6° Aries. Jesus speaks of his Second Coming (26 Mar 33). "See that no one leads you onto a wrong path. Many will come and make use of my name. They will say:

"I am the Christ." And they will lead many astray. You will become aware of the tumult of war and the cries of battle; see that you do not fail in inner courage. It is necessary that all this should happen, but that is not yet the fulfillment of the aim.

One part of humanity will rise against another, one kingdom against the other. Everywhere there will be famines and earthquakes; and yet these are just the birth-pangs of the new world.

Many will appear who will make themselves mouthpieces for deceiving spirits; they will lead many astray. And as the chaos grows ever worse, the capacity for love will grow cold in many." (Matt. 24:4–12)

The position of the New Moon at 6° Aries, forms a cardinal cross between three other points on the zodiacal wheel: 6° Capricorn, 6° Libra, and 6° Cancer—marking four star memories. Today 6° Aries remembers the King of Kings speaking of his Second Coming. In 6° Libra remembers Christ healing one of the three kings, 6° Capricorn remembers the adoration of the three kings, and 6° Cancer remembers the July 2009 eclipse with Pluto marking the place of the Baptism in the Jordan. Four memories today quicken each other: King of kings, healing of kings, arrival of kings,

---

22 Anon. *Meditations on the Tarot*, p. 153.

eclipse of kings. This New Moon remembers kings and the possibility of a false king. Strong contemplations for today.

April 24: Sun enters the second decan of Aries, ruled by the Sun. This decan is associated with Cassiopeia, the Enthroned Woman, a figure of matchless beauty called "the daughter of splendor" or the "glorified woman clothed with the Sun."

April 24: Sun 10° Aries: The Visitation (March 30, 2 BC). The Nathan Mary, pregnant with Jesus, visited her cousin Elizabeth, who was pregnant with John the Baptist. During that meeting all four of them were filled with holy awe as the Old Adam, John the Baptist in Elizabeth's womb, was quickened by the presence of the New Adam, the Jesus child in Mary's womb. Rudolf Steiner describes how an "I" like that of John's was directly guided by the great mother lodge of humanity, the center of spiritual life on Earth. The John-I and the soul of the Luke Jesus both originated in this mystery center, although the qualities Jesus received were not yet pervaded by the egotistic "I"—that is, the being guided toward incarnation as the reborn Adam was a young soul.

> The reality of this situation, strange as it may seem, was that the great mother lodge sent out a soul unaccompanied by an actual developed "I," for the same "I" that was reserved for the Jesus of the Luke Gospel was bestowed on the body of John the Baptist, and these two elements—the soul being that lived in the Luke Jesus and the "I" that lived in the Baptist—were intimately related from the very beginning.[23]

The great mystery of the Visitation is the mystery of how the old Adam—who fell from Paradise—is visited by the New Adam, the being holding the forces of purity and love held back at the time of the Fall. The celestial part of John approached him from without, as the child in Mary's womb. Through the immaculate Jesus being, John was enabled to take hold of his incarnation in spite of the conditions on Earth at that time. Through the Jesus child he was quickened to take up his destiny as the forerunner of Christ. This Visitation points

us to the fact of heredity becoming subservient to destiny forces in-streaming from Christ. What John experienced at the Visitation is now possible for each human being. Our higher Christ-imbued self shall quicken as we turn to its splendor. The Sun today remembers the union between the lower and higher self.

This is a good day to remember our perfect self and devote ourselves to serving the perfection of all beings.

April 26: Sun 12° Aries: The Last Anointing (April 1, 33). Mary Magdalene's last anointing of Christ set the betrayal by Judas in motion. "Truly, I say to you, wherever this gospel is proclaimed in the whole world, what she has done will also be told in memory of her" (Matt 26:13). Magdalene's devotional understanding, stands in opposition to Judas' inability to see what was right before him—Christ. It takes courage to represent the new in the face of those muttering against its possibility, as Judas muttered against Magdalene. Now Christ is present in the etheric realms surrounding the Earth; he is with us. Will we know him? Are we Judas—or Magdalene?

April 27: Sun 13° Aries: The Last Supper through the Nailing on the Cross (April 2–3, 33). The Sun today remembers the most wretched moments of the life of Christ up to his final victory on the hill of Golgotha. All that Christ then experienced *from* humanity, allows him to give *to* humanity now. The deeds done to him during the Passion created the karmic field that allows him to touch us spiritually in this time of the Second Coming. Christ gives all his love to humanity, as humanity once gave all of its hatred to him. Each step of the way must be contemplated as the greatest mystery of Earth evolution. The Passion of Christ is the path of the initiate. We may pray for the strength to willingly carry the cross of our own burdens, for this lightens the Cross of Christ. In the words of Judith von Halle:

> Spiritual pupils cannot imagine, let alone wish to embark on a path of knowledge tht is broad and well-trodden—in other words, easily or effortlessly accessible. The path they pursue

---

23 Steiner, *According to Luke*, p. 112.

is their own, and by definition, therefore, no one has ever trodden it before. It is true to say that this path does not exist at the start of the jorney, when they form their resolve. The task is to forge it themselves, penetrating the undergrowth of their soul drives, guiding one's "I" through the "soul-void of space," through the "time-destroying stream."[24]

The sacred freedom that Christ brought to all humanity is a force of guidance directing all individuals to find their own way, upon their own untrodden path, to realize their own initiation. Sobering sanctification for the preservation of free impulses as intended by Rudolf Steiner.

April 29: Sun 14° Aries: The Death of Jesus on the Cross (April 3, 33). This death marks the birth of Christ into the Earth. This birth was his descent into Hell—a time when the spiritual world held its breath, wondering if the Son of God would ever emerge again from the darkness of the Earth. Yet, as the blood spilled from the sword thrust into him on the cross, the entire Earth was surrounded in radiant light. The Sun was at this same degree during the Transfiguration (4 Apr 31) two years earlier. This is a star language. The path to purification and ascent is through the descent. Christ's descent was not for his being, but for the whole of humanity and the spiritual world. The John being's painting of the Transfiguration is an imagination for our future. Raphael sketched the Transfiguration, and before his death painted the light-filled upper half. His Disciples finished the lower (dark) half of the painting, based on Raphael's sketches. This lower half shows the picture of the boy possessed. We, as disciples of John, are called to work on this masterpiece by meeting the possessions in our own souls. There comes a time when it is as if our hands and feet are nailed down, as the narrow way of redemption opens before us.

---

24 Von Halle, *The Descent into the Depths of the Earth*, pp. 19–20 (trans. revised).

MAY 2012

As we begin May, the Sun is in Aries, entering the Bull (Taurus) on the 15th. The first few days of the month offer the waxing Moon to the left of Mars in the southern night sky on the 1st and passing by Saturn on the 4th. The evening sky just after the setting of the Sun continues to show us Venus, the evening star, in the west, Mars to the south and Saturn to the southeast. The Full Moon is on the 5th, and the New Moon is on the 20th; it will be an Annular Solar eclipse in front of the Pleiades at 5° Taurus. During the 2nd half of the month, the Sun hides much in its glow: Mercury and Jupiter close by, and the sliver of Moon with Venus to the south as the Sun sets. Let us observe with wonder and senses other than our eyes, to benefit from all that the Sun magnifies each day, including the 30th, when the Sun will be in front of the star Aldebaran (the "Eye of the Bull" and a Royal Star of Persia). What emanates from this star?

May 1: Sun 15° Aries: Resurrection of Christ (5 Apr 33). The depths of this mystery hold the promise that each human being may become a Christ Bearer. The words of the Risen Christ, to Mary Magdalene, sound throughout time:

> Do not hold on to me, for I have not yet ascended to the Father. Go instead to my brothers and tell them, "I am ascending to my Father and your Father, to my God and your God." (John 20:17)

These words contain the powerful fact that Christ, following his descent to the Mother on Holy Saturday, would then, following the Resurrection, ascend to his Father, thereby restoring the unity between the Mother in the depths and the Father in the heights. It was a deed that would also unite fallen humanity with its divine archetype—an archetype sacrificed at the time of the Fall. From the moment of the Resurrection onward he has been within us. This eternal oneness with Christ interconnects the whole of humanity into brother—and sisterhood. The actual awakening of the Disciples to the reality of this oneness came only later at the Holy Whitsun Festival. During the forty days between the Resurrection and the Ascension, the Disciples were in a kind of sleep. Images from their daily life with Christ during his three and one half years on Earth rose into their consciousness (etheric images). These images helped them understand the cosmic teachings Christ was giving during these forty days after the Resurrection.

It is just these cosmic teachings that were culled from Christianity, and these cosmic teaching are resurrecting in this time of the Second Coming.

The forty days between the Resurrection and the Ascension are potent days to work with etheric after-images. If we hold silence after a conversation, after an event, or at day's end as we go into sleep, we may experience after-echoes sounding forth from our daily events. These are etheric responses, from angelic realms, inspiring and informing us of hidden dimensions working and weaving through our lives. During the time from May 1 through June 8th—which is two days after the Venus–Sun transit on the 5/6—the stars remember the forty days of Christ's cosmic teachings after his Resurrection.

ASPECT: Moon Conjunct Mars 10° Leo: Birth of the Nathan Mary (17 July 17 BC). At this birth, Moon and Mars were conjunct in the heart of Leo, (5°) conjunct Regulus. Considering Rudolf Steiner's communications concerning the Nathan Mary,

> it is clear that this Mary had a deep affinity with the Nathan Jesus, who was the *sister soul* of Adam, and whose sole historical manifestation (though not in a physical incarnation) was as Krishna. She was connected with the spiritual stream of love and compassion that attained its high point in Hinduism with Krishna, and in Buddhism with Gautama Buddha. She was a deeply loving and compassionate soul, who had developed the capacity for love and self-sacrifice to a high degree. Not long after the event in the Temple [Union in the Temple] at the Passover of AD 12, she died. Rudolf Steiner described how seventeen years later, at the Baptism in the Jordan, the Nathan Mary was spiritually united with the Solomon Mary. (*Chron.* p. 116)

The vessel for the Word (Mars), created in Mary's womb (Moon), is today remembered. With today remembering both the Resurrection of Christ and the birth of the Nathan Mary, a perfect picture

arises of the potential communion between every human being and Christ. This occurs as we purify our astral bodies (Mars), take command our emotional life (Moon), and learn how to speak from the heart (Leo). The content of our words will today reveal the degree to which we are free, and a free human being is filled with compassion.

May 3: Sun 17° Aries: Appearance in Emmaus (6 April 33). These days, following the Resurrection, specifically mark the communion of the Disciples and holy women with the resurrection body of Christ. There are several kinds of communion with Christ, four of which are primary: 1) *Communion with Christ's physical body*, Bread (resurrection body–forty days); 2) Communion with Christ's "I," Wine (descent into hell); 3) *Communion with Christ's etheric body*, the Eternal Gospel (Life Tableau of Christ); and 4), *Communion with Christ's astral body*, the Eternal Apocalpse of which the Book of Revelation is a fragment (*CHA*, p. 241).

The day after the Resurrection, Luke and Cleophas were traveling to Emmaus when a third person joined them. That evening the three went to a guesthouse, where they were served food. The third person took the bread, blessed it and broke it into small pieces. Through this act the Disciples recognized their traveling companion, who was Christ.

The bread communion is communion with the resurrection body of Christ, given to Luke and Cleophas and accompanied by Christ's words: "I am the bread of life." This bread of life is the substance of the Word of God living in all pure nourishment, as the antidote to destructive manipulation of the Mother's archetypes in seeds. Christ throughout the forty days was ministering the bread of life to his Disciples. Through his wounds and from his mouth flowed pure light, giving them the power to forgive sins, to baptize, to heal, and to lay on hands. As communion with the resurrection body was the forty days between the Resurrection and the Ascension, so is communion with the Self of Christ, the wine communion, connected to Christ's descent into Hell. It was the "I," the self of Christ that descended after Jesus died on the cross. Christ descended all the way to the heart of

SIDEREAL GEOCENTRIC LONGITUDES : MAY 2012 Gregorian at 0 hours UT

DAY	☉	☽	☊	☿	♀	♂	♃	♄	♅	♆	♇
1 TU	16 ♈ 7	5 ♌ 39	10 ♏ 23R	21 ♓ 59	25 ♉ 20	10 ♌ 24	25 ♈ 18	0 ♎ 7R	11 ♓ 38	7 ♒ 55	14 ♐ 32R
2 WE	17 6	19 31	10 21	23 27	25 48	10 35	25 32	0 3	11 41	7 56	14 32
3 TH	18 4	3 ♍ 51	10 18	24 58	26 14	10 47	25 46	29 ♍ 58	11 44	7 57	14 31
4 FR	19 2	18 35	10 15	26 31	26 39	11 0	26 1	29 54	11 47	7 58	14 30
5 SA	20 0	3 ♎ 38	10 13	28 5	27 2	11 13	26 15	29 50	11 50	7 59	14 30
6 SU	20 58	18 50	10 11	29 42	27 23	11 26	26 29	29 46	11 53	8 0	14 29
7 MO	21 56	4 ♏ 3	10 11	1 ♈ 21	27 43	11 40	26 43	29 42	11 55	8 1	14 28
8 TU	22 54	19 7	10 11D	3 1	28 0	11 55	26 57	29 38	11 58	8 2	14 28
9 WE	23 52	3 ♐ 53	10 11	4 43	28 16	12 10	27 12	29 34	12 1	8 3	14 27
10 TH	24 50	18 16	10 13	6 28	28 29	12 25	27 26	29 30	12 4	8 4	14 26
11 FR	25 48	2 ♑ 13	10 14	8 14	28 41	12 41	27 40	29 26	12 6	8 5	14 25
12 SA	26 46	15 44	10 14	10 2	28 50	12 57	27 54	29 22	12 9	8 6	14 24
13 SU	27 44	28 51	10 14R	11 53	28 57	13 14	28 9	29 18	12 12	8 6	14 23
14 MO	28 42	11 ♒ 35	10 14	13 45	29 2	13 32	28 23	29 15	12 14	8 7	14 22
15 TU	29 40	24 2	10 13	15 39	29 4	13 49	28 37	29 11	12 17	8 8	14 21
16 WE	0 ♉ 38	6 ♓ 14	10 12	17 35	29 5R	14 7	28 51	29 7	12 19	8 8	14 20
17 TH	1 35	18 15	10 11	19 33	29 2	14 26	29 5	29 4	12 22	8 9	14 19
18 FR	2 33	0 ♈ 8	10 9	21 32	28 58	14 45	29 20	29 0	12 24	8 10	14 18
19 SA	3 31	11 57	10 9	23 34	28 51	15 4	29 34	28 57	12 27	8 10	14 17
20 SU	4 29	23 45	10 8	25 37	28 42	15 24	29 48	28 54	12 29	8 11	14 16
21 MO	5 27	5 ♉ 33	10 8	27 42	28 30	15 44	0 ♉ 2	28 50	12 32	8 11	14 15
22 TU	6 24	17 23	10 8D	29 49	28 16	16 5	0 16	28 47	12 34	8 12	14 14
23 WE	7 22	29 19	10 8	1 ♉ 57	27 59	16 26	0 31	28 44	12 36	8 12	14 13
24 TH	8 20	11 ♊ 23	10 8	4 6	27 40	16 47	0 45	28 41	12 39	8 12	14 12
25 FR	9 17	23 36	10 9	6 16	27 19	17 9	0 59	28 38	12 41	8 13	14 11
26 SA	10 15	6 ♋ 2	10 9R	8 27	26 56	17 31	1 13	28 35	12 43	8 13	14 9
27 SU	11 13	18 44	10 9	10 38	26 30	17 53	1 27	28 32	12 45	8 13	14 8
28 MO	12 10	1 ♌ 44	10 9	12 50	26 3	18 16	1 41	28 30	12 47	8 14	14 7
29 TU	13 8	15 5	10 8	15 2	25 33	18 39	1 55	28 27	12 49	8 14	14 6
30 WE	14 5	28 49	10 8D	17 14	25 2	19 2	2 9	28 25	12 51	8 14	14 4
31 TH	15 3	12 ♍ 56	10 9	19 25	24 30	19 26	2 23	28 22	12 53	8 14	14 3

INGRESSES :

2 ♄ → ♍ 15: 5	20 ☽ → ♉ 12:44
☽ → ♍ 17:37	♃ → ♉ 20:19
4 ☽ → ♎ 18:14	22 ☿ → ♉ 2: 7
6 ☿ → ♈ 4:25	23 ☽ → ♊ 1:21
☽ → ♏ 17:35	25 ☽ → ♋ 12:23
8 ☽ → ♐ 17:38	27 ☽ → ♌ 20:49
10 ☽ → ♑ 20: 7	30 ☽ → ♍ 2: 2
13 ☽ → ♒ 2: 9	
15 ☉ → ♉ 8:22	
☽ → ♓ 11:41	
17 ☽ → ♈ 23:43	

ASPECTS & ECLIPSES :

1 ☽ ☍ ♆ 4: 0	8 ☽ ☍ ♀ 14:38	☽ ☌ ♃ 12:34	27 ☉ S☌ ☿ 11: 5
☽ S ☊ 8:16	9 ☽ ☌ ♇ 17:32	☉ ☌ ☽ 23:46	28 ☽ ☍ ♆ 11:45
☽ ☌ ♂ 8:25	12 ☉ □ ☽ 21:46	☉ ● A 23:52	☽ S ☊ 15:11
3 ☽ ☍ ♅ 12:57	13 ☉ ☌ ♃ 13:27	21 ☽ ☌ ☋ 9:18	☉ □ ☽ 20:15
4 ☽ ☍ ☿ 14:10	☽ ☌ ♆ 17:23	22 ☿ ☌ ♃ 5:51	29 ☽ ☌ ♂ 6:28
☽ ☌ ♄ 18: 0	☽ N ☊ 21:25	☽ ☌ ♀ 21:23	30 ☽ ☍ ♅ 23:55
6 ☿ ☍ ♄ 0:54	14 ☽ ☍ ♂ 3:47	23 ☉ □ ♆ 20:55	31 ☿ □ ♂ 0: 8
☉ ☍ ☽ 3:34	16 ☽ ☌ ♅ 12:10	24 ☽ ☍ ♇ 5:32	
☽ ☌ P 3:35	17 ☽ ☍ ♄ 21:43	25 ☉ ☍ ☊ 21:21	
☽ ☍ ♃ 12:13	19 ☽ ☌ A 16: 0	☿ □ ♆ 21:29	
7 ☽ ☌ ☊ 9:42	20 ☽ ☌ ☿ 4:38	26 ☿ ☍ ☊ 18:35	

SIDEREAL HELIOCENTRIC LONGITUDES : MAY 2012 Gregorian at 0 hours UT

DAY	Sid. Time	☿	♀	⊕	♂	♃	♄	♅	♆	♇	Vernal Point
1 TU	14:37:18	8 ♑ 25	23 ♍ 11	16 ♎ 7	14 ♍ 30	27 ♈ 8	1 ♎ 45	10 ♓ 0	6 ♒ 8	13 ♐ 0	5 ♓ 5'17"
2 WE	14:41:14	11 41	24 48	17 5	14 57	27 14	1 47	10 1	6 8	13 1	5 ♓ 5'17"
3 TH	14:45:11	15 0	26 25	18 3	15 24	27 19	1 49	10 1	6 9	13 1	5 ♓ 5'17"
4 FR	14:49: 7	18 24	28 1	19 2	15 51	27 25	1 51	10 2	6 9	13 1	5 ♓ 5'16"
5 SA	14:53: 4	21 53	29 38	20 0	16 18	27 30	1 53	10 3	6 9	13 2	5 ♓ 5'16"
6 SU	14:57: 0	25 27	1 ♎ 15	20 58	16 45	27 35	1 55	10 3	6 10	13 2	5 ♓ 5'16"
7 MO	15: 0:57	29 6	2 51	21 56	17 13	27 41	1 57	10 4	6 10	13 2	5 ♓ 5'16"
8 TU	15: 4:54	2 ♒ 51	4 28	22 54	17 40	27 46	1 59	10 5	6 10	13 3	5 ♓ 5'16"
9 WE	15: 8:50	6 43	6 4	23 52	18 7	27 52	2 0	10 5	6 11	13 3	5 ♓ 5'16"
10 TH	15:12:47	10 40	7 40	24 50	18 34	27 57	2 2	10 6	6 11	13 3	5 ♓ 5'16"
11 FR	15:16:43	14 45	9 17	25 48	19 2	28 2	2 4	10 7	6 11	13 4	5 ♓ 5'15"
12 SA	15:20:40	18 57	10 53	26 46	19 29	28 8	2 6	10 7	6 12	13 4	5 ♓ 5'15"
13 SU	15:24:36	23 17	12 29	27 44	19 56	28 13	2 8	10 8	6 12	13 4	5 ♓ 5'15"
14 MO	15:28:33	27 45	14 5	28 42	20 24	28 19	2 10	10 8	6 12	13 5	5 ♓ 5'15"
15 TU	15:32:29	2 ♓ 21	15 41	29 40	20 51	28 24	2 12	10 9	6 13	13 5	5 ♓ 5'15"
16 WE	15:36:26	7 5	17 18	0 ♏ 37	21 19	28 29	2 14	10 10	6 13	13 5	5 ♓ 5'15"
17 TH	15:40:23	11 59	18 54	1 35	21 46	28 35	2 16	10 10	6 14	13 6	5 ♓ 5'15"
18 FR	15:44:19	17 1	20 30	2 33	22 14	28 40	2 18	10 11	6 14	13 6	5 ♓ 5'14"
19 SA	15:48:16	22 13	22 6	3 31	22 41	28 46	2 20	10 12	6 14	13 6	5 ♓ 5'14"
20 SU	15:52:12	27 34	23 41	4 29	23 9	28 51	2 22	10 12	6 15	13 7	5 ♓ 5'14"
21 MO	15:56: 9	3 ♈ 4	25 17	5 26	23 36	28 56	2 24	10 13	6 15	13 7	5 ♓ 5'14"
22 TU	16: 0: 5	8 42	26 53	6 24	24 4	29 2	2 26	10 14	6 15	13 7	5 ♓ 5'14"
23 WE	16: 4: 2	14 29	28 29	7 22	24 32	29 7	2 27	10 14	6 16	13 8	5 ♓ 5'14"
24 TH	16: 7:58	20 24	0 ♏ 5	8 20	24 59	29 13	2 29	10 15	6 16	13 8	5 ♓ 5'14"
25 FR	16:11:55	26 25	1 40	9 17	25 27	29 18	2 31	10 16	6 16	13 8	5 ♓ 5'14"
26 SA	16:15:52	2 ♉ 33	3 16	10 15	25 55	29 23	2 33	10 16	6 17	13 9	5 ♓ 5'13"
27 SU	16:19:48	8 46	4 52	11 12	26 22	29 29	2 35	10 17	6 17	13 9	5 ♓ 5'13"
28 MO	16:23:45	15 2	6 27	12 10	26 50	29 34	2 37	10 18	6 18	13 9	5 ♓ 5'13"
29 TU	16:27:41	21 20	8 3	13 8	27 18	29 39	2 39	10 18	6 18	13 10	5 ♓ 5'13"
30 WE	16:31:38	27 40	9 38	14 5	27 46	29 45	2 41	10 19	6 18	13 10	5 ♓ 5'13"
31 TH	16:35:34	3 ♊ 58	11 14	15 3	28 14	29 50	2 43	10 19	6 19	13 10	5 ♓ 5'13"

INGRESSES :

5 ♀ → ♎ 5:27
7 ☿ → ♒ 5:47
14 ☿ → ♓ 11:51
15 ⊕ → ♏ 8:28
20 ☿ → ♈ 10:42
23 ♀ → ♏ 22:50
25 ☿ → ♉ 14: 3
30 ☿ → ♊ 8:53

ASPECTS (HELIOCENTRIC +MOON(TYCHONIC)) :

1 ☽ ☍ ♆ 0:51	☿ □ ♃ 14:30	☿ △ ⊕ 6:22	21 ☿ ⚹ ♆ 13:38	☿ ☍ ⊕ 11: 5
☿ ⚹ ♅ 11:44	7 ☿ △ ♄ 18:23	16 ☽ ☌ ☿ 2:51	⊕ □ ♆ 20:20	♀ □ ♆ 21:34
3 ☿ △ ♂ 3:14	8 ☿ △ ♀ 17:14	☽ ☌ ♅ 7:50	22 ☿ △ ♇ 18:24	28 ☽ ☍ ♆ 8:16
☽ ☍ ♅ 10: 8	☿ ☌ ♆ 20:43	☿ ☌ ♅ 15:11	23 ♀ ☍ ♃ 10: 9	29 ☿ ☌ P 5:18
☽ ☌ ♂ 19:27	9 ♀ △ ♆ 1:41	17 ☿ □ ♇ 5:22	24 ☽ ☍ ♇ 3:27	30 ☿ △ ♂ 0:25
4 ☿ □ ⊕ 6: 1	☽ ☌ ♇ 15:13	☽ ☍ ♂ 7:22	☿ ☌ ☊ 12:40	♀ △ ♅ 10:16
☽ ☌ ♀ 16:54	10 ☿ ⚹ ♇ 14: 7	18 ☽ ☍ ♄ 4:23	25 ☿ ☌ ♃ 11:28	☿ △ ♄ 19:11
☽ ☌ ♄ 21:13	13 ♀ ⚹ ♇ 8:50	19 ☿ ☍ ♂ 2:19	26 ⊕ △ ♅ 0:35	☽ ☍ ♅ 19:36
5 ☿ S ☊ 11:23	⊕ ☍ ♃ 13:27	☽ ☍ ♀ 23:52	☿ ☍ ♀ 3:44	31 ☿ △ ♆ 8:56
6 ♀ ☌ ♄ 10:11	☽ ☌ ♆ 13:47	20 ☽ ☌ ♃ 10:28	☿ □ ♆ 14:27	
☽ ☍ ♃ 13:52	14 ☿ ⚹ ♃ 3: 3	☿ ☍ ♄ 21: 5	27 ☿ ⚹ ♅ 5:51	

the Mother at the Earth's center. And it was from communion with the Self of Christ that the Grail Knights were schooled to develop the courage to descend into Hell, meet evil, confront and overcome this evil. Parsifal took up this battle with evil for the sake of human beings and the Mother Earth. He is the human being of the future: the future Jupiter human being.

The Self of Christ follows the 12-year rhythm of Jupiter. In 1945 Christ began his penetration of the sub-earthly layers of the Earth on behalf of the Mother in the heart of the Earthly realm. Christ is currently working in the seventh interior sphere, the Earth Mirror (July 23, 2004 - June 3, 2016), connected with the manas cognition of the spirit self (see Robert Powell, *The Christ Mystery*). The Beatitude that is the antidote to the evil of this sphere is *Blessed are the peacemakers for they shall be called the Children of God*. Valentin Tomberg speaks of the peacemakers:

If the consciousness soul is filled with consciousness of the guilt and need of earthly life, it lifts it like a cup, interceding for the need of Earth. It can then encounter a current descending from above, one that absorbs the darkness of guilt and need into its own clear light, carried upward by the consciousness soul. It may happen then that the ascending darkness and the descending light unite, which leads to a "rainbow" of reconciliation between the two worlds. For example, Goethe, in his soul, carried knowledge of this process of reconciliation and peace between the two worlds. Such knowledge became not only the basis of his theory of color, but also of his fairytale, *The Green Snake and the Beautiful Lily*.[25]

The fruition of Earth evolution is the ripening of the consciousness soul to receive into itself the angelic sphere. We reach this fruition through partaking in communion with Christ as did the Disciples Luke and Cleophas. If Christ, or an ambassador of Christ, were among us–would we know this? Or, would we persecute such a one in this Second Coming as we did in the first? This is food for thought during these days, remembering the

forty days of Christ's cosmic teachings. In remembrance of Christ's appearance in Emmaus, can we open our awareness to sense unseen beings moving among us? We are not alone!

Of Note: The Moon at this appearance of Christ to Luke and Cleophas was 20° Scorpio—directly opposite the position in the heavens of the Venus–Sun transit next month. We can imagine that the cosmic teachings of Christ are quickening for human beings of good will upon the Earth.

Sun 18° Aries: Death of Silent Mary (8 Apr 30).

Silent Mary was gifted with clairvoyance and beheld in advance the coming persecution and trials of Jesus, which was more than she could bear. She died in the face of the burden of suffering that she beheld was in store for the Messiah. An arrow of grief pierced through her heart and she was called back to the realm of the Father." (CHA, *Jesus' First Visit to Jerusalem since the Baptism*)

May 4: Sun 19° Aries: Conversation with the Pharisee Nicodemus (9 April 30). "The wind blows where it wills, and you hear the sound of it, but you do not know whence it comes or whither it goes; so it is with everyone who is born of the Spirit" (John 3:8). In the second arcanum of *Meditations on the Tarot*, The High Priestess, the unknown author describes the *"pure act of intelligence"*: Like the wind, "the pure act in itself cannot be grasped; it is only its reflection which renders it perceptible, comparable and understandable or, in other words, it is by virtue of the reflection that we become conscious of it" (*Meditations on the Tarot*, p. 30). This seems to fit the *nighttime* conversations between Jesus and Nicodemus. Three times or more it is reported in the *Bible* that Nicodemus comes to Jesus in the *night*. Rudolf Steiner says this:

"By night" means nothing else than that this meeting between Jesus and Nicodemus occurred in the astral world: in the spiritual world, not in the world that surrounds us in our ordinary day consciousness. This means that Christ could converse with Nicodemus outside the physical body—by night, when the physical body is not

---

25 Tomberg, *Christ and Sophia*, page 220.

present, when the astral body is outside the physical and etheric bodies.[26]

Jesus approaches Nicodemus in the night. The original forces of the world are living in Jesus—he is bringing not only new teachings, but a kind of teaching that comes from his astral body into the consciousness of others who are prepared to receive these teachings. Jesus makes the preparation for receiving these cosmic teachings clear: "Truly, truly, I say to you, unless one is born of Water and the Spirit, [one] cannot enter the Kingdom of God" (John 3:5).

The "pure act of intelligence" comes like the wind—no one knows whence it comes or whither it goes. It is the spirit of Jesus' teaching in the night. Nicodemus is able to receive these teachings as reflections, and through the reflections he can grasp the wind that blows where it will as the cosmic teachings of Christ. Nicodemus was born of Water and of Spirit, as was John—they entered the kingdom of God by letting go of the lower human being and reviving the higher human being. This is the second birth—to be born into spirit consciousness. This is to be "born of Water and the Spirit."

This day calls forth the memory of Nicodemus who communed with Christ's astral body in the night, when the Sun was in the constellation of Aries—whose virtue is devotion—dedicated to the higher ideals that all are striving toward knowingly or unknowingly. What material attachments bind us from receiving the wind of spirit?

May 4: Sun enters third decan of Aries, ruled by Mercury and associated with Cassiopeia's outstretched legs seated on her throne, so that this decan is sometimes known as Cassiopeia's Throne or Cassiopeia's Chair.

May 5: ASPECT: Mercury 29° Pisces opposite Saturn 29° Virgo. This degree marks the place of the first magnitude star Spica (29° Virgo). Saturn, now retrograde, revisits the constellation of the Virgin, and stands today at Spica, and will remain very near this star until mid-August of this year. At the

conversation between Jesus and the Virgin Mary, before the Baptism in the Jordan River, the Sun was at this degree. Saturn is remembering this conversation, when the Zarathustra "I" poured into the Blessed Virgin. This is also where Mercury was at Mary's birth, making her receptivity to the despair of the Master Jesus intimately understandable. Virgo was seen by the ancient clairvoyants as a young woman holding an ear of corn or shaft of wheat—which is marked by the star Spica. In this earth sign of Virgo, representing the harvest, what has been sown must now be reaped.[27]

Saturn marks the portal to the kingdom of the Father. With Mercury standing opposite Saturn at Spica, the wing-footed messenger is receiving from the Father the harvest to be reaped on behalf of the Mother Earth, for Virgo relates to the Earth, to the very heart of the Mother Earth, and to the womb or bowels of the Earth, and she is dying to be heard.

May our mind (Mercury) find stillness so that it may receive the resolves of the Father (Saturn). A mind that receives spirit becomes a collaborator with spiritual beings; a mind shut off from spirit feels itself a victim of the harvest now to be reaped.

Full Moon: Sun 20° Aries opposite Moon 20° Libra. This Full Moon remembers the Theophany (28 March 31). Theophany refers to the appearance of a deity to a human or other being, or to a divine disclosure. On this day the Pharisees were again putting challenges to Jesus about healing on the Sabbath.

> [Jesus] recounted the parable of the sick man and poor Lazarus. This so outraged the Pharisees that they pressed around and sent for the temple guards to take Jesus into custody. At the height of the uproar, it suddenly grew dark. Jesus looked up to heaven and said: "Father, render testimony to thy Son!" A loud noise like thunder resounded and a heavenly voice proclaimed: "This is my beloved son in whom I am well pleased!" Jesus' enemies were terrified. The Disciples then escorted Jesus from the temple to safety. (*Chron.* p. 288)

---

26 Steiner, *The Gospel of John in Its Relation to the Other Three Gospels,* pp. 195–196.

27 See Paul and Powell, *Cosmic Dances of the Zodiac.*

With the Sun and Moon remembering the Aries–Libra Full Moon during the Crucifixion of Christ (Moon 14° Libra), the Words from the cross can be contemplated as a healing practice concentrated on our chakras:

7th: Father, into your hands I commend my spirit.

6th My God, my God, why have you forsaken me?

5th: I thirst.

4th: Today you will be with me in Paradise.

3rd: Father, forgive them, for they do not know what they do.

2nd: Behold your son; behold your Mother.

1st: It is fulfilled.

May 11: Sun 25° Aries: The appearance of the Risen One to the seven Disciples. This occurred at the northeast end of the Sea of Galilee (John 21:1-23). Here Peter is bid three times to "Feed my Sheep." He is given the task to be the spiritual leader of the Church, to ensure that the sacraments, above all Holy Communion, continue to be celebrated for all time. Peter asks what will become of John, and the Risen One answers: "If it is my will that he remain until I come, what is that to you?" Implicit here is the task of the Church of John to wait until the Second Coming of Christ in the etheric realm. The Church of Peter has the task to lead human beings to the threshold of the spiritual world, and the Church of John has the task of leading them across the threshold *into* the spiritual world. John and Peter work together, united in their service to Christ and Sophia. The Church of John is centered in the heart, and those who choose to join this Church are summoned by the call of the Grail. Corresponding to the Mass in the exoteric church is the Grail Mystery in the esoteric church. Grail communion is communion with the Beings of the stars, which requires a crossing of the threshold—which in turn requires a meeting with the fallen nature of the soul in the depths of the underworld. This is why it is the John being that Rudolf Steiner claims will be with us at the end of the century. For it was John who accompanied Lazarus through the underworld after his death, and before he was raised by Christ. We live now in the time of the Second Coming, a time when the Church of John is opening, and this is a time when humanity is both collectively and individually crossing the threshold. Moreover, we live in a time when star wisdom is being reborn as communion with the beings of the Heavens. With the Sun in Aries, the constellation of self-sacrifice, spiritual strength, and leadership, we may feel inspired to open to the vastness of the mysteries surrounding us in our everyday life. Alternatively we may find we are excessively caught up in the small story of our "little" biography. As our interest in others and in the vastness of other worlds that interact with us increases, new possibilities are revealed. We may ask ourselves: What about John? Where do I stand before the hermetic mysteries of the stars?

May 13: ASPECT: Sun conjunct Jupiter 28° Aries: Sun and Jupiter were conjunct, close to today's conjunction, at the Transfiguration on Mt. Tabor (4 Apr 31). Jesus climbed Mt. Tabor accompanied by Peter, James and John. He told them he was going to reveal himself in his full glory, so that they might keep their faith even when they should see him humiliated, mistreated and arrested like a criminal. Jesus began instructing them concerning the Lord's Prayer and other mysteries.

He spoke so inspiringly that the three Disciples were wholly transported by his words. The Sun set and it became dark, but the three did not notice it, so entranced were they by Jesus, whose whole appearance became brighter and brighter. He spoke further and shone with an ever-increasing transcendental splendor, becoming quite translucent. This glory reached its culmination at midnight—the shining of the midnight Christ-Sun—which was so intense that the Apostles covered their heads and prostrated themselves on the ground. A shining pathway of light reached down from heaven upon Jesus Christ, comprising the different choirs of Angelic beings in descending order from heaven down to the Earth. Among the shining figures that approached Jesus in the light were Moses and Elijah, to whom Jesus spoke of the sufferings that he had endured up until now and would endure in the future, including his Passion relating everything in detail. (*CHA, The Transfiguration*)

Peter, James and John bear witness to the transfiguring power of Divine Love that completely irradiated the human form of Jesus. Venus at the Transfiguration was 21° Taurus, very close to where Venus will be at the Venus–Sun transit in less than one month, and Sun and Jupiter were coming into conjunction at the Transfiguration as they are today. The star memory of the Transfiguration reminds us of the Great Teachers of Humanity—the twelve—who surrounded Christ on Mt. Tabor, and were reflected on Earth as the circle of twelve Disciples surrounding Jesus. Those who follow the guidance of the Great Teachers of humanity are most often charged with heresy. For the Great Teachers come to bring change; and change more often than not, is met with fear—which cries: Heretic!

NOTE: 28° Aries is the exact location of Jupiter and Saturn during the great conjunction in May of 2000. Today marks the Jupiter return of that conjunction. In 2010 and 2011 we experienced the *opposition* between Jupiter and Saturn—an opposition to what was founded at the conjunction ten years earlier. These oppositions foretell an alignment with the spirit's will, announced at the conjunction, or else give evidence to a defiance toward the spirit's will. What was the meaning of the conjunction in 2000?

The great conjunction of 2000 occurred approximately nine months after the beginning of a new cycle in the rhythmic unfolding of the life of Christ in the etheric realms surrounding the Earth (September 1999), when a new 33⅓-year cycle commenced. The beginning of a cycle impregnates the Earth with new life forces. Jupiter and Saturn conjoining nine months after this new cycle, in the constellation of Aries, tells a star story. This story speaks of new leadership (Aries) coming into form (Saturn) through communities receiving new wisdom teachings (Jupiter). These new communities are to form under what can be called "Grail laws"—laws that honor each individual, creating collaborative cultures that are willing to confront evil.[28]

It is now twelve years later and Jupiter has returned to this exact position in the heavens—remembering this great conjunction that began the new millennium. One may ask: Among contemporary events what gives evidence as to how humanity is faring with its custodianship of Natura, and the forming of new leadership? Two main events addressing the question of Natura were the BP oil spill in 2010, and the Japanese nuclear meltdown of 2011—both occurred in relationship to the Jupiter–Saturn oppositions during those years, and both events were catastrophies for Natura. As for the question of new leadership, it is self-evident that the old leadership is pushing through with agendas antithetical to "Grail laws." We are perhaps too slowly waking up to a heinous ignorance toward our Mother Earth and all her elemental beings, as well as to the cost of a fear- and money-based culture. As long as the bottom line is money, moral decisions will evade us and keep us on a trajectory against protection of the Earth and humanity.

Jupiter revisits the wisdom she proclaimed in 2000 when she came into conjunction with Saturn. We are now waking up to manipulations of the etheric (the realm in which Christ is manifesting) through weather modification technology that is in ignorance of what the domino effect of this interference may portend. And, there are a great many other new technological advancements that make it clear how human intelligence may work in consort with ahrimanic powers.

The etheric is the realm where prayers multiply and grow in concordance with all the prayers from human beings who see through the actions of materialism to the event it seeks to obscure—the coming of a new culture. Pray, and know that many are praying with you! Jupiter's wisdom is today magnified by the Sun. Let us participate! Venus was at this exact degree (28° Aries) at the death of Novalis, who was an incarnation of John the Baptist (whose presence at the Transfiguration is mentioned in the commentary for May 13). John

---

28 See Robert Powell, "The Cosmic Beginnings of the New Millennium," *Christian Star Calendar 2000*). The article gives a clear account of what then occurred, so as to reveal the meaning behind world events that have unfolded since this time. A further signature of this great

conjunction in 2000 was an impregnation of new Christ-imbued life in all of Nature. These new forces arising in Natura called for human beings to work with her, protect her, and help her give birth to new possibilities.

is praying with us in love for Mother Earth and for her Daughter in the heavens above: Sophia.

May 15: Sun enters Taurus: "Become bright, radiant being" (Rudolf Steiner, *Twelve Moods of the Zodiac*). Inner Balance becomes progress. The work of transforming the will. The first decan is ruled by Venus and is associated with Perseus, who was helped by Athena to overcome the Medusa.

May 17: Sun 2° Taurus: The Virgin Mary receives her first communion (23 Apr 33). Shortly after midnight the Blessed Virgin Mary received the holy sacrament from Peter (three weeks after the Last Supper). During this communion, Jesus appeared to her. Later she retired to her room to pray, and toward dawn the Lord appeared to her again and gave her power over the Church, a protective force, such that light flowed from him into her. In this we see a stage in the preparation for the event of Pentecost coming in the weeks that follow. The Virgin Mary could listen to the presence of the Christ. Taurus shapes the larynx and Eustachian tubes, mirrored by the form of the stethoscope. Through the organ of the larynx and its connection to the Eustachian tubes, we can listen to the heart of God. This is the kind of listening of the Virgin Mary. The assault on hearing from constant noise tends to obliterate the periphery, thereby encapsulating the human being in the self, through hardening the sacred organ of hearing.

The sense of hearing is a spiritual sense. The highest expression of hearing is through creating the stillness of inner balance. In this balance, point and periphery commune. This is the stillness of Mary—the stillness that could commune with the Risen One from the very center of her heart. It was into this still-point of centeredness that Mary would receive the Holy Spirit at Pentecost. It is this inner stillness that is the antidote to a human being's enslavement within the self; thus it is this very stillness that "noise" seeks to destroy. The preciousness of the organ of hearing can today be contemplated—as well as the centeredness of holding inner silence.

Today is the Christian celebration of the Ascension of Christ.

May 20: New Moon Annular Eclipse 5° Taurus—the Pleiades. This eclipse will be visible from the Chinese coast, the south of Japan, and the western part of the US.[29] From one perspective, the New Moon/annular eclipse in the Pleiades may be a heavenly reminder that the time for forgetting the stars is over. (Osiris died when the Sun was setting, opposite the Pleiades in Scorpio). With the death of Osiris, a veil came down over the star wisdom of ancient Egypt—a darkness that occulted both Isis–Sophia and Osiris–Christ. Why is this eclipse significant? Because it may be a "heavenly sign" that Isis has truly resurrected Osiris, that his grave is no longer a secret, and that her cow horns are being replaced with the golden horns that hear the cosmic Word sounding from the place of the Pleiades. Perhaps it is Sophia that is rising. Perhaps it is Sophia who is guiding us to find the Risen Christ. Because this eclipse is opposite the Sun at Osiris' death, it can be seen as a heavenly sign of the resurrection of the ancient star wisdom of Egypt. In Egyptian mythology, Typhon killed his brother Osiris and dismembered him. His consort, Isis, cherished and cared for his dismembered body. After his death, Osiris caused a light to shine into Isis, whereby she conceived his son Horus. Horus is in the one who is in the process of becoming an Osiris—we are all Horus with the Christ–Osiris spark of divinity residing within our souls:

> For although the soul is initially connected to the transitory realm, it is destined to give birth to the eternal. Humanity may therefore be termed the tomb of Osiris; it is our lower nature—Typhon, or Set—that has killed him. The love that is present in his soul—Isis—must cherish and care for the members of his corpse, and then the higher nature or eternal soul—Horus—can be born, and in due course rise to the state of "being an Osiris."[30]

The god within us all is held down by our lower nature, which has become a grave; and from this grave our higher nature is to rise to a new life.

---

29 See Robert Powell's article "The Pleiades and 2012," in *Journal for Star Wisdom 2011* or in articles at www.sophiafoundation.org.

30 Steiner, *Christianity as Mystical Fact*, p. 89.

Does this eclipse point us to this rising from the grave of the abstract and dead, in order to find a new path filled with revelatory light and truth?

Rudolf Steiner mentioned that the Pleiades are significant, stating that this is the region where the whole solar system entered the Universe and that the next solar system will take place in the Pleiades, and that the whole solar system is moving toward the Pleiades. If we are not moving toward world harmony, as represented by the seven dancing sisters of the Pleiades, we may be moving toward global destruction. Is this eclipse the clarion call for peacemakers? As this eclipse is 16 days before the Venus–Sun transit and is occurring in the year 2012, we can imagine the harmony of the seven sisters of the Pleiades as an antidote to world strife. We can strive to replicate their harmony everywhere on Earth. In what great or subtle ways has disharmony led to an eclipse of the One who was represented by Osiris and is now rising in spite of the pall of materialism? Make peace!

When the Moon was conjunct the Pleiades, John the Baptist was buried at Juttah. We can pray that John will not be buried as we move forward into 2012, but rather that he be revealed as the guiding light for humanity in this time of the resurrection of Osiris–Christ by Isis–Sophia.

Jupiter enters Taurus: "In Thoughtful Revelation" (Rudolf Steiner, *Twelve Moods of the Zodiac*). Jupiter was in Taurus at the Flight into Egypt of the family of the Solomon Jesus. In the time of ancient Egypt the vernal equinox was in Taurus. Through thoughtful revelation these ancient Egyptian mysteries can be unlocked, thus reopening humanity to the wisdom (Jupiter) of the stars.

May 25: Sun enters the second decan of Taurus, ruled by the Moon and associated with the constellation of Eridanus the River.

May 27: Superior conjunction of Mercury and Sun 11° Taurus. A week after the annular eclipse, Mercury, the messenger of the Gods, receives Michaelic thoughts and unites them with the heart of the solar system—the Sun. The light that shines in as potential is always met by an opposing light

that seeks to thwart the true light. History exemplifies this struggle in the Life of Jesus, in the life of Mani, in the life of Valentin Tomberg, in the life of so many authentic light-bearers. This conjunction remembers August 29, AD 70—when Jerusalem fell to the Romans. The Romans were developing the intellectual soul; and when the intellectual soul is not illuminated by the consciousness soul, good comes in the wrong time. (Good in the wrong time is one of the signatures of evil.) It will take efforts of illumined consciousness (Mercury) to reclaim the rising promise of Osiris–Christ, through the wisdom of Isis–Sophia shining in our Sun-hearts (see May 20). "Become bright, radiant being."

Today is the Christian celebration of Pentecost.

May 30: Sun conjunct Aldebaran, the Bull's eye, known as the *Watcher in the East*.

ASPECT: Mercury 19° Taurus square Mars 19° Leo. Mars was close to this degree, conjunct Pluto at 18° Leo, at the birth of the Virgin Mary (7 Sept 21 BC). The Virgin Mary, since the time of her assumption, is known as the Queen of Heaven. With Mars remembering this birth, and square to Mercury, we can pray that our words (Mars) may be spoken from the heart—to firmly will existence from out of cosmic light (Mercury).

JUNE 2012

The Full Moon (Sun in Taurus and Moon in Scorpio) is on the 4th, a partial lunar eclipse. The Sun is in Taurus to begin the month, moving into Gemini (The Twins) on the 15th. Neptune stations before going retrograde on the 5th, returning to direct motion November 12th. Saturn stations direct on the 26th. The New Moon (Sun and Moon in Gemini) is on the 19th.

The 5th brings an important conjunction between the Sun and Venus, "visible" to our deeper senses; read David Tresemer's illuminating article in the pages of this journal. The evening sky continues to show us Mars and Saturn. Mars is in Leo (the Lion) and moves into the stars of Virgo (the Virgin) on the 23rd. Saturn is in Virgo

(The Virgin) through the month, with the Moon as partner to Mars on the 26th and Saturn on the 27th. Rising before the Sun, Jupiter becomes visible in the last week of the month; Venus as morning star beginning around the same time, visible as a shining diamond in the east in the pre-dawn glow. The waning Moon will join Jupiter in Taurus before sunrise on the 17th, Venus on the 18th. After the New Moon on the 19th, the Moon joins Mercury on the 21st though they may be still too close to the Sun to be seen, just after sunset.

June 1: Mercury conjunct Venus 23° Taurus: Eclipse of 2009. Venus stood at this degree during the longest eclipse of the twenty-first century on July 21/22, 2009, when Pluto was at the exact location where it was at the Baptism in the Jordan of Jesus. The year 2012 comes three years after this eclipse.

June 3/4: Full Moon and partial lunar eclipse: Sun 18° Taurus, Moon 18° Scorpio. This partial eclipse will be visible over east Asia, Australia, the Pacific, and the western Americas. This Full Moon and partial eclipse is in close opposition to the Venus–Sun transit occurring in two days at 20° Taurus.

The Moon was at this degree during the nighttime conversation between Nicodemus and Jesus (April 9, 30). In this nighttime conversation, Christ—in his astral body—was influencing Nicodemus during the time when Nicodemus was outside his body in suprasensory consciousness.

Thus, when you read of his meaningful conversation with Nicodemus during the night—a conversation that Rudolf Steiner said took place in suprasensory consciousness—you will find that in Nicodemus it illuminated his memory of a conversation with a being whose voice could be heard, but whose countenance could not be seen. That conversation was a "ray" from the nighttime activity of Christ reaching human consciousness. Christ faced Nicodemus and spoke to him of the need to be born of water and of the Spirit: "You are Israel's teacher," said Jesus, "and do you not understand these things?" (John 3:10). This question was both a reproof and instruction; it expresses

the activity of the Christ being that, during the night, was addressed to many.[31]

Nighttime dialogue with Christ is reached through the stage of inspiration; inspirational consciousness reaches into the region where the Eternal Apocalypse will remain for as long as the Earth survives. The Eternal Apocalypse is communion with Christ's astral body, and this communion is the meaning behind Christ's words: "Heaven and Earth shall pass away: but my words shall not pass away" (Luke 21:33).

Nicodemus was able to imprint this nighttime discourse into his etheric body, thus allowing memory of this encounter to pass from the night into his day-conscious memory. This tells us that Nicodemus had reached the stage of inspirational consciousness. Reading of the Gospels prepares us for communion with the Etheric Christ by day, and reading the Apocalypse prepares us for communion with Christ's astral body by night. During this Full Moon, meditation on right preparation for sleep—as well as on the cosmic dimensions of the Christ's teachings—are contemplations that help raise us to new possibilities streaming from out of the future.

ASPECT: Moon 22° Scorpio opposite Venus 22° Taurus: The Sun was at 22° Scorpio at the Raising of the Youth of Nain—where the Moon is today (13 Nov 30). At this raising, Moon and Venus were coming into conjunction. Who was this youth from Nain?

Apart from Charlemagne himself, who was the reincarnation of a great initiate, there was Parsifal who became Grail king, who had lived on Earth as a youth (the youth of Nain) and at the age of twelve was raised from the dead by Christ (Luke 7:11–16). According to Rudolf Steiner, the founding, the beginning of the Grail mysteries, the first appearance of Parsifal, was at the turn from the eighth to the ninth centuries—that is, during the reign of Charlemagne (Frankish king, 768–800; Romans emperor, 800–814). Parsifal received his initiation into the Grail mysteries through Titurel, the founder of these mysteries (Robert Powell, "Exploring the destinies of Lazarus, Mary

31 Tomberg, *Christ and Sophia*, pp. 389–390.

Magdalene and Martha in the First Century and the Grail stories of the Ninth Century leading to the Revelation of the Mystery of the Holy Grail," Pilgrimage to South of France, 1998, Sophia Foundation).

A day before the Venus–Sun transit of 2012, and just past the *exact* time of the Full Moon, the Moon–Venus opposition remembers Parsifal as the reincarnation of the Youth of Nain. Another incarnation, between these two of Nain and Parsifal, was that of Mani in the 3rd century AD. We may ask: Is there a star language in this that speaks of the return of this Mani–Parsifal being as part of the spiritual destiny of humanity in these times—when humanity is collectively facing the presence of evil? Nain, Mani, Parsifal. All three incarnations are connected with healing evil, and the Moon was in Scorpio during Christ's descent into the evil realms of Hell. Just before the last Venus–Sun transit of our lifetimes, Venus stands opposed to the hidden realms of Scorpio.

These aspects are preparatory. To view the goodness in others, in spite of what behavior may be active, is to prepare the ground that allows us to face our own darkness. The eurythmic gesture for Venus—with the right hand extended outward, cupped, and the left arm extended behind, in a stirring movement—shows us the way of both "offering" and "receiving," through faithful attendance to the good, the beautiful and the true. This is a healing for all disharmony our Venus nature in the second chakra may feel, when being opposed by the lunar forces of past karma.

June 5: Venus conjunct Sun 20° Taurus. This is the relatively rare event of Venus moving directly between the Sun and Earth. This alignment is rare, coming in pairs that are eight years apart but separated by over a century. This transit will not occur again until 2117 (see David Tresemer's article in this *Journal for Star Wisdom*).

As described in Hermetic Astrology, Volume II: "The planet Venus (referred to in Revelation as the "morning star") describes in its orbit around the Sun the sphere or globe of the next stage of evolution (sometimes called "Future Jupiter") spoken of in Revelation as the Heavenly Jerusalem. In saying,

"I will give you the morning star," the Risen One is pointing to the future abode of humanity after the present Earth evolution will have come to an end. And in the references to the Heavenly Jerusalem in the last two chapters of Revelation, it is indicated that the Bride of the Lamb, Divine Sophia, plays a central role: "Come, I will show you the Bride, the wife of the Lamb. And he carried me away in the Spirit to a mountain great and high, and showed me the Holy City, Jerusalem, coming down out of heaven from God" (Rev. 21:9–10).

As Sophia is the heart of the New Jerusalem—future Jupiter existence for humanity—she holds a key to understanding the orbit of Venus around the Sun. Venus calls us to the inspirations of Sophia, sounding in lyrical poetry as soul nourishment for those aspiring to the call of brotherly and sisterly love. Sophia's mission is to draw forth new expressions of creativity, and it is just this creativity that Venus–Sun transits call forth.

From one perspective the Venus transits can be seen as the opening and closing of a great cosmic door—a door that opens once in any given century. The door opens at the beginning of the transit and closes eight years later at the end of the transit. Some aspects of the renewal that the Venus–Sun transits invite, are the renewal of education, arts, religion, music, poetry, collaboration, peace, and familial love within communities. Many things have occurred in the stars these past eight years, most recently the Jupiter–Uranus conjunction of 2010–11, and the Jupiter–Saturn opposition of 2010–11 (See past issues of this *Journal*). Both of these events have been preparatory for creating new paradigms in community (Jupiter) that reflect healing impulses for both the Earth and human beings. Whatever the future holds, it will be the preparation thus gathered, and creativity enriched during this transit, that will help to sustain health and well-being in times of change. The stars have guided us to this moment, and now they pronounce that the time of preparation is over—the time of trial is beginning. Trial accompanies new birth. Through trial the new capacities are forged on the steel anvil of morality to test their worthiness. The past eight years have been the time of

SIDEREAL GEOCENTRIC LONGITUDES : JUNE 2012 Gregorian at 0 hours UT											
DAY	☉	☽	☊	☿	♀	♂	♃	♄	♅	♆	♇
1 FR	16 ♉ 0	27 ♍ 25	10 ♏ 9	21 ♉ 36	23 ♉ 55R	19 ♌ 50	2 ♉ 37	28 ♍ 20R	12 ♓ 55	8 ♒ 14	14 ♐ 2R
2 SA	16 58	12 ♎ 12	10 9	23 45	23 20	20 14	2 51	28 17	12 57	8 15	14 1
3 SU	17 55	27 13	10 10	25 53	22 44	20 39	3 5	28 15	12 59	8 15	13 59
4 MO	18 53	12 ♏ 18	10 10R	28 0	22 7	21 3	3 19	28 13	13 1	8 15	13 58
5 TU	19 50	27 20	10 10	0 ♊ 5	21 29	21 29	3 33	28 11	13 3	8 15R	13 57
6 WE	20 48	12 ♐ 9	10 9	2 9	20 52	21 54	3 47	28 9	13 4	8 15	13 55
7 TH	21 45	26 39	10 8	4 10	20 14	22 20	4 1	28 7	13 6	8 15	13 54
8 FR	22 42	10 ♑ 45	10 6	6 9	19 36	22 45	4 15	28 6	13 8	8 14	13 52
9 SA	23 40	24 24	10 5	8 6	18 59	23 12	4 28	28 4	13 9	8 14	13 51
10 SU	24 37	7 ♒ 37	10 4	10 1	18 23	23 38	4 42	28 3	13 11	8 14	13 50
11 MO	25 34	20 25	10 3	11 53	17 48	24 5	4 56	28 1	13 13	8 14	13 48
12 TU	26 32	2 ♓ 52	10 3D	13 43	17 14	24 32	5 9	28 0	13 14	8 14	13 47
13 WE	27 29	15 2	10 4	15 31	16 41	24 59	5 23	27 58	13 16	8 13	13 45
14 TH	28 26	27 1	10 5	17 16	16 10	25 26	5 37	27 57	13 17	8 13	13 44
15 FR	29 24	8 ♈ 51	10 6	18 58	15 40	25 54	5 50	27 56	13 18	8 13	13 42
16 SA	0 ♊ 21	20 38	10 8	20 38	15 13	26 22	6 4	27 55	13 20	8 13	13 41
17 SU	1 18	2 ♉ 26	10 9	22 16	14 47	26 50	6 17	27 54	13 21	8 12	13 40
18 MO	2 16	14 17	10 9R	23 51	14 23	27 18	6 31	27 54	13 22	8 12	13 38
19 TU	3 13	26 15	10 8	25 24	14 2	27 47	6 44	27 53	13 23	8 11	13 37
20 WE	4 10	8 ♊ 21	10 6	26 54	13 43	28 16	6 58	27 52	13 24	8 11	13 35
21 TH	5 8	20 38	10 3	28 21	13 26	28 45	7 11	27 52	13 26	8 10	13 34
22 FR	6 5	3 ♋ 6	9 59	29 46	13 12	29 14	7 24	27 52	13 27	8 10	13 32
23 SA	7 2	15 48	9 55	1 ♋ 8	13 0	29 44	7 37	27 51	13 28	8 9	13 31
24 SU	7 59	28 42	9 51	2 28	12 50	0 ♍ 13	7 51	27 51	13 29	8 9	13 29
25 MO	8 57	11 ♌ 52	9 48	3 44	12 42	0 43	8 4	27 51	13 29	8 8	13 27
26 TU	9 54	25 17	9 46	4 58	12 37	1 13	8 17	27 51D	13 30	8 7	13 26
27 WE	10 51	8 ♍ 58	9 45	6 9	12 35	1 43	8 30	27 51	13 31	8 7	13 24
28 TH	11 48	22 56	9 45D	7 18	12 35D	2 14	8 43	27 51	13 32	8 6	13 23
29 FR	12 45	7 ♎ 10	9 46	8 23	12 37	2 45	8 56	27 52	13 33	8 5	13 21
30 SA	13 43	21 38	9 47	9 25	12 41	3 15	9 8	27 52	13 33	8 4	13 20

INGRESSES :

1	☽ → ♎ 4:13	21	☽ → ♋ 18: 3
3	☽ → ♏ 4:26	22	☿ → ♋ 4: 3
4	☿ → ♊ 22:57	23	♂ → ♍ 13:16
5	☽ → ♐ 4:17	24	☽ → ♌ 2:22
7	☽ → ♑ 5:37	26	☽ → ♍ 8:19
9	☽ → ♒ 10: 4	28	☽ → ♎ 11:58
11	☽ → ♓ 18:25	30	☽ → ♏ 13:44
14	☽ → ♈ 6: 2		
15	☉ → ♊ 15: 9		
16	☽ → ♉ 19: 3		
19	☽ → ♊ 7:27		

ASPECTS & ECLIPSES :

1	☽ ☌ ♄ 1:29		☽ ☌ ♇ 2:52	17	☽ ☌ ♃ 7:58	26	☽ ☌ ♂ 10:52
	☿ ☌ ♀ 20:20	8	☉ □ ♂ 2:22		☽ ☌ ☋ 15:38	27	☉ □ ☽ 3:30
3	☽ ☍ ♃ 9:29	10	☽ ☌ ♆ 1: 8	18	☽ ☌ ♀ 0:11		☽ ☍ ♅ 7:52
	☽ ☌ P 13:18		☽ N ☊ 4:31	19	☉ ☌ ☽ 15: 1	28	☽ ☌ ♄ 8:21
	☽ ☌ ☊ 20:36	11	☽ ☍ ♂ 7:15	20	☽ ☍ ♇ 10:14	29	☉ ☍ ♇ 14:41
4	☽ ☍ P 11: 1		☉ □ ☽ 10:41		☿ □ ♄ 15:55		☉ □ ♅ 20: 0
	☉ ☍ ☽ 11:11		☿ □ ♅ 17:32	21	☽ ☌ ☿ 16:48		
	☽ ☍ ♀ 15: 1	12	☿ ☍ ♇ 0:48	24	♅ □ ♇ 4:26		
5	♀ □ ♂ 0:20		☽ ☌ ♅ 20:27		☽ ☍ ♆ 17:14		
	☽ ☍ ☿ 5: 8	14	☽ ☍ ♄ 1:54		☽ S ☊ 20:16		
6	☉ ☌ ♀ 1: 1	16	☽ ☌ A 1:12	25	♃ □ ♆ 7:30		

SIDEREAL HELIOCENTRIC LONGITUDES : JUNE 2012 Gregorian at 0 hours UT											
DAY	Sid. Time	☿	♀	⊕	♂	♃	♄	♅	♆	♇	Vernal Point
1 FR	16:39:31	10 ♊ 15	12 ♏ 49	16 ♏ 0	28 ♍ 42	29 ♈ 56	2 ♎ 45	10 ♓ 20	6 ♒ 19	13 ♐ 11	5 ♓ 5'13"
2 SA	16:43:27	16 27	14 24	16 58	29 10	0 ♉ 1	2 47	10 21	6 19	13 11	5 ♓ 5'12"
3 SU	16:47:24	22 35	16 0	17 55	29 38	0 6	2 49	10 21	6 20	13 11	5 ♓ 5'12"
4 MO	16:51:21	28 37	17 35	18 53	0 ♎ 6	0 12	2 51	10 22	6 20	13 12	5 ♓ 5'12"
5 TU	16:55:17	4 ♋ 31	19 10	19 50	0 34	0 17	2 52	10 23	6 20	13 12	5 ♓ 5'12"
6 WE	16:59:14	10 17	20 46	20 47	1 2	0 23	2 54	10 23	6 21	13 12	5 ♓ 5'12"
7 TH	17: 3:10	15 55	22 21	21 45	1 30	0 28	2 56	10 24	6 21	13 13	5 ♓ 5'12"
8 FR	17: 7: 7	21 23	23 56	22 42	1 58	0 33	2 58	10 25	6 22	13 13	5 ♓ 5'12"
9 SA	17:11: 3	26 41	25 31	23 39	2 26	0 39	3 0	10 25	6 22	13 13	5 ♓ 5'11"
10 SU	17:15: 0	1 ♌ 50	27 6	24 37	2 55	0 44	3 2	10 26	6 22	13 14	5 ♓ 5'11"
11 MO	17:18:56	6 50	28 42	25 34	3 23	0 49	3 4	10 27	6 23	13 14	5 ♓ 5'11"
12 TU	17:22:53	11 39	0 ♐ 17	26 32	3 51	0 55	3 6	10 27	6 23	13 14	5 ♓ 5'11"
13 WE	17:26:50	16 20	1 52	27 29	4 20	1 0	3 8	10 28	6 23	13 15	5 ♓ 5'11"
14 TH	17:30:46	20 51	3 27	28 26	4 48	1 6	3 10	10 28	6 24	13 15	5 ♓ 5'11"
15 FR	17:34:43	25 14	5 2	29 24	5 16	1 11	3 12	10 29	6 24	13 15	5 ♓ 5'11"
16 SA	17:38:39	29 29	6 37	0 ♐ 21	5 45	1 16	3 14	10 30	6 24	13 16	5 ♓ 5'10"
17 SU	17:42:36	3 ♍ 35	8 12	1 18	6 13	1 22	3 16	10 30	6 25	13 16	5 ♓ 5'10"
18 MO	17:46:32	7 34	9 47	2 15	6 42	1 27	3 17	10 31	6 25	13 16	5 ♓ 5'10"
19 TU	17:50:29	11 26	11 22	3 13	7 10	1 32	3 19	10 32	6 25	13 17	5 ♓ 5'10"
20 WE	17:54:25	15 12	12 57	4 10	7 39	1 38	3 21	10 32	6 26	13 17	5 ♓ 5'10"
21 TH	17:58:22	18 51	14 32	5 7	8 8	1 43	3 23	10 33	6 26	13 17	5 ♓ 5'10"
22 FR	18: 2:19	22 25	16 7	6 5	8 36	1 49	3 25	10 34	6 27	13 18	5 ♓ 5'10"
23 SA	18: 6:15	25 53	17 41	7 2	9 5	1 54	3 27	10 34	6 27	13 18	5 ♓ 5'10"
24 SU	18:10:12	29 17	19 16	7 59	9 34	1 59	3 29	10 35	6 27	13 18	5 ♓ 5' 9"
25 MO	18:14: 8	2 ♎ 35	20 51	8 56	10 3	2 5	3 31	10 36	6 28	13 19	5 ♓ 5' 9"
26 TU	18:18: 5	5 50	22 26	9 54	10 32	2 10	3 33	10 36	6 28	13 19	5 ♓ 5' 9"
27 WE	18:22: 1	9 0	24 1	10 51	11 0	2 15	3 35	10 37	6 28	13 19	5 ♓ 5' 9"
28 TH	18:25:58	12 7	25 36	11 48	11 29	2 21	3 37	10 37	6 29	13 20	5 ♓ 5' 9"
29 FR	18:29:54	15 11	27 11	12 45	11 58	2 26	3 39	10 38	6 29	13 20	5 ♓ 5' 9"
30 SA	18:33:51	18 12	28 46	13 42	12 27	2 32	3 41	10 39	6 29	13 20	5 ♓ 5' 9"

INGRESSES :

1	♃ → ♉ 19:35
3	♂ → ♎ 19: 4
4	☿ → ♋ 5:35
9	☿ → ♌ 15:20
11	♀ → ♐ 19:47
15	⊕ → ♐ 15:16
16	☿ → ♍ 3: 1
24	☿ → ♎ 5:12
30	♀ → ♑ 18:50

ASPECTS (HELIOCENTRIC +MOON(TYCHONIC)) :

1	☿ □ ♅ 0:20		☽ ☌ ♇ 1:43		☿ ☍ ♆ 21:47	17	♂ △ ♆ 9:42	25	☿ ☌ ♄ 6:53		☽ ☌ ☿ 16:52
	☽ ☌ ♂ 2:10		♀ ☌ ☋ 16:52	12	☿ △ ♇ 8: 2	18	♀ □ ♅ 11:15	26	☿ △ ♆ 4:46	30	☽ ☍ ♃ 17:58
	☽ ☌ ♄ 8:43	8	☿ △ ⊕ 7:11		☽ ☌ ♅ 14:54		☿ ☍ ♅ 18:15		⊕ □ ♅ 18: 4		
	☿ ☍ ♇ 11:18		☿ N ☊ 9:47	13	♀ ⚹ ♄ 19:36		☿ □ ♀ 23:10	27	☽ ☍ ♅ 2:51		
3	☽ ☍ ♃ 4:37		☿ △ ♀ 16:21	14	☽ ☍ ♄ 12:28	19	⊕ ⚹ ♄ 2:53		⊕ ⚹ ♂ 8:14		
4	☿ ⚹ ♃ 6:28	9	☽ ☍ ☿ 6:43		☽ ☍ ♂ 16:25		☿ □ ♇ 11:40		☿ ☌ ♂ 18:10		
	☿ □ ♂ 6:29		☿ □ ♃ 18:41	15	♀ ⚹ ♂ 5:15	20	♀ ☌ ♇ 5: 9		☿ ⚹ ⊕ 20:21		
	☽ ☌ ♀ 9:24		☽ ☌ ♆ 21:42		♀ ⚹ ♆ 20:50		☽ ☍ ♇ 9:40	28	☿ ⚹ ♇ 9:23		
	☿ □ ♄ 17:13	10	☿ ⚹ ♂ 5:36	16	☿ □ ⊕ 6:32		☽ ☍ ♀ 10:20		☽ ☌ ♄ 18: 5		
6	☿ △ ♅ 0:25		☿ ⚹ ♄ 5:42		☿ △ ♃ 10:37	22	⊕ ⚹ ♆ 9:16	29	☽ ☌ ♂ 8:17		
	♀ ☌ ⊕ 1: 1		♂ ☌ ♄ 6:46		☽ ☌ ♃ 21:48	24	☽ ☍ ♆ 14:11		⊕ ☌ ♇ 14:41		

placing "oil in the lamps"; and now the lamps are to shine into the darkness of material culture, thus to begin the work of serving the renewal of culture by means of what has been gained through collaboration with the dictums of the stars. Communities are now to be ready to serve!

As the Sun and Venus unite today at 20° Taurus, many beautiful and profound events are remembered (within 3°), that give color and meaning to today's event. Some of these are:

Venus 21 Taurus: Transfiguration on Mt. Tabor
Mars 20 Taurus: The Visitation of Elizabeth
    and Mary, and the enmity of the Pharisees.
Saturn 21 Taurus: The conception of John the
    Baptist
Uranus 20 Taurus: Death of the Solomon Jesus
Uranus 22 Taurus: Death of the Nathan Mary
Mars 18 Taurus: Birth of Raphael
North Node 22 Taurus: Union of two Jesus
    children in the temple
Heliocentric Mars 20 Taurus: Feeding of the
    Five Thousand and the Walking on Water
Sun 23 Taurus: The Ascension of Christ
Venus 23 Taurus: The 2009 eclipse
Uranus 22 Taurus: The bombing of Hiroshima
And, some events opposite today's transit:
20 Scorpio: Appearance to Luke and Cleophas
    the day after the resurrection.
Sun 22 Scorpio: Raising of the Youth of Nain
Mercury 19° Scorpio: The death of the hermetic
    messenger, Kepler.

What story are the stars telling us? They are saying that the new communities born of Sophia's love will work toward transfiguring human beings, and these transfigured human beings will sit in community as vessels into which visitations from angelic messengers can be heard. The stars further pronounce the presence of John the Baptist, as the guardian of Sophia communities, who will guide these new communities into new expressions of creativity—in faithfulness to the Master Jesus and his blessed Mother. These communities will unite with noble purpose, to find the spiritual nourishment promised by the Lamb and his Bride. And it is this nourishment that is preparing them to receive Christ in his Second Coming, as was promised at the Ascension so long ago:

> They were looking intently up into the sky as he was going, when suddenly two men dressed in white stood beside them. "Men of Galilee," they said, "why do you stand here looking into the sky? This same Jesus, who has been taken from you into heaven, will come back in the same way you have seen him go into heaven." (Acts 1:10–11)

Communities are now being prepared so that they can recognize Mani in his probable manifestation in the near future; and this is being accomplished through hermetic initiates, now incarnated, who are preparing Venus inspired communities to be able to hear this great leader of humanity when he begins his teachings. If the new teachers are eclipsed, humanity will bear the consequence.

The star stories have imprinted us over the past eight years, just as our parents imprint us through our childhood. What has been given is with us—we have breathed it into our soul and spirit. We simply need remember that the messages from star beings are alive in the air we breathe. The mantra of John is the mantra of Venus-born communities: "Love one another." The opposite of this love would be the destruction of all that is loved by God, through war and hatred—for these are actions of those who have severed themselves from the purpose of Earth evolution. What we don't know we fear, what we fear we hate, what we hate we destroy. It is the Earth we no longer know. With a Venus–Sun transit we are called to remember what we love, so that which loves us may find us.

Today Neptune stations at 8°15' Aquarius. The planet Neptune concentrates its energy, amplifying this position in the zodiac. Heliocentric Mercury was here on Nov. 15, 30: John, Heal the Blind. To truly see means opening our third eye. With Neptune stationed where John is instructed to heal the blind, we can meditate on our third eye and feel there the mighty presence of the "I."

June 5: Sun enters the third decan of Taurus, ruled by Saturn, associated with Orion below and Auriga above.

June 8: Sun 23° Taurus: The Ascension of Christ (14 May 33). Early in the morning of this day, Jesus presented the Blessed Virgin Mary to the Apostles and Disciples as their advocate and as the center of their community. Here we see another stage in preparation for the coming event of Pentecost— the preceding stage was when Mary received communion (see commentary of May 17). As the Sun climbed higher in the sky, Christ continued to the Mount of Olives and ascended to the top, all the while becoming increasingly radiant with light until he became more radiant than the mid-day Sun. Then he disappeared into this radiance. Two angels then appeared saying: "Men of Galilee, why do you stand looking into heaven? This Jesus, who was taken up from you into heaven, will come in the same way as you saw him go into heaven" (Acts 1:11 [ESV]).

The Angelic voice sounds again in our time as Christ's appearance in the etheric realm becomes increasingly self-evident. The Resurrection of Christ portrayed by Matthias Grunewald, in his painting of the Isenheim Altarpiece, clearly shows the wounds of Christ. These wounds are the new organs of the will streaming from the ascended Christ. Under the auspices of Taurus, a constellation working with the transformation of the will, this image of Christ with the wounds of Golgotha shows human beings the way toward their own passion and transformation. Through transforming our lower will, we will increasingly find the Christ-Will in the encircling round of Earth.

After the Ascension of Christ the Disciples were in abject misery.

> That day was the beginning of a sorrowful time for the Disciples; they felt forsaken and saddened. The world of imagery [bestowed on them through Christ during the forty days following the resurrection], having so much meaning, was blotted out, and their souls were plunged into silent darkness. Their grief during this time cannot really be compared to any pain we may experience in daily life. It was

not the result of affliction or trouble but the absence of all that enlivened and motivated their souls. In such situations, positive suffering actually brings alleviation. Sharp pain is certainly an experience, but when life is merely an aching emptiness it is not really an experience; rather it is a soul condition that feels like a void. The Disciples' experience of soul death preceded the event of Pentecost; it was a necessary preparation for it, since the resurrection of the soul during that event was an experience that could only follow the soul's death. That painful preparation for the Pentecost was alleviated, however, by one thing; the pain was shared by all of the Disciples.[32]

Tomberg goes on to describe how their mutual suffering bound them together, whereby the twelve created an organ of Pentecostal revelation.

The absence of Christ that caused such pain in the Disciples may be comparable to the pain and emptiness of so many souls today that have lost the Christ. As human beings learn how to join together, in the work of transforming their lower natures, they too may find the comfort of forming an organ to receive the fire of Divine Love.

June 11: ASPECT: Mercury 13°13' Gemini square Uranus 13°13' Pisces and Mercury opposite Pluto 13°48' Sagittarius. Together, these aspects (involving three planets) form three equal points on the zodiacal wheel, suggesting a cross at 13° of the mutable signs: Mercury in Gemini, Uranus in Pisces, and Pluto in Sagittarius. The fourth point that would complete this cross would be 13° Virgo. This place is left open today: no planets are in the middle of this constellation. We can imagine the three planets highlighting this vacancy in Virgo. This is where Mercury was at the Baptism in the Jordan. What is here pronounced?

In *Meditations on the Tarot*, the arcanam The Devil and the arcanam The Tower, can be seen as representing, respectively, Pluto and Uranus. These arcana speak of interference from enchainment to matter and inflated egotism. Mercury in Gemini, from the same standpoint, represents the fifth arcanam—the Pope: the guardian of the fifth

32 Tomberg, *Christ and Sophia*, pp. 302–303.

wound—the spear in the heart of Christ. Today, imaginatively, the Pope (Mercury) stands witness to the tension between the devil (Pluto) and the tower of destruction (Uranus). The Pope enters into the tension between humanity and adversarial forces. The open point in Virgo is representative of the 11th arcanam, Force—a suprasensory, feminine current that can penetrate all material substance. Today we can imagine ourselves standing with the Virgin in this open door, in service to the Pope and in opposition to adversaries. Human beings *are* being called to receive cosmic "force" and to bestow this suprasensory "force" on all the beings of Nature. This is the same "Force" through which Christ was birthed into Earthly existence. Today we are called to stand with Virgin-Sophia who *is* absent in the thoughts of so many. Through Sophia we find Christ, and she is highlighted in the stars today by her very absence in the cross the stars have scripted. Where can we radiate harmony as we go about our life today?

June 12: Sun 26° Taurus: Blessing of the Children (17 May 32). Jesus blesses a thousand children. This was a very important component in this land of milk and honey, streaming with the soul of Sophia. Sophia breathes familial love, creating deep bonds between mothers and children. Later this evening, Jesus dined with ten of the holy women, as he continued to teach. The women and the children! Are we blessing the feminine aspect of our nature and working to protect the innocence of our children?

June 15: Sun enters Gemini the Twins. "Reveal thyself, Sun life" (Rudolf Steiner, *Twelve Moods of the Zodiac*). The first decan is ruled by Jupiter and associated with Orion, whose bright star Betelgeuse is located at 4° Gemini.

June 18/19: New Moon 3° Gemini: Cosmic Pentecost (24 May 33). The Sun was 2½° Gemini at Pentecost, when the Holy Spirit descended into the Blessed Virgin Mary. At this degree, the Sun is directly opposite the Galactic Center (2° Sagittarius). The Galactic center, also known as the Central Sun, is the Divine Heart of the galaxy, which is the source of the Holy Spirit. The Blessed Virgin

Mary, who was presented by Jesus Christ (before the Ascension) as the center of the community, served here—at Pentecost—as this heart-center and as the bearer of Divine Sophia.

> Because of extremely complicated influences and experiences coming from the spiritual world, Mary had an astral body that was so purified it could receive the revelations of Sophia and pour them out again as *inspirations* of the soul. This faculty was the very reason why, at the time of Pentecostal revelation, the Virgin Mary occupied the central position in the circle of the twelve. Without her, the revelation would have been only spiritual; there would have been twelve *prophets,* united in the Holy Spirit as was ancient prophesy. Through the cooperation of Mary, however, something more could happen; the Disciples' *hearts* beat in harmony with hers while they experienced the Pentecostal revelation as personal human conviction. Through *this* experience, they became not prophets, but specifically Apostles.[33]

The difference between prophets and apostles is that prophets proclaim revelations impersonally, whereas apostles reveal the Holy Spirit *within* their own souls. This was possible only because the Virgin Mary transmitted *ensouled* revelation to the Disciples—through her, revelation became personal and yet maintained its objectivity.

From the moment of Pentecost onward, the silence imposed on Sophia through Lucifer's intervention in human destiny was released. Sophia became free to reach down into groups of earthly human beings. This was a great event for both the earthly and spiritual worlds.

The sparks of fire that issued from her blessed soul were the ensouled manifestation of Christ's cosmic I Am. The eternal "I" of the world, which was born into the Disciples through the immaculate heart of the divine Mary-Sophia, who was standing at the center of their community. Since that first Pentecost, the Christ spirit has lived within human souls on Earth. Pentecost was the awakening of Christ's Disciples from a dreamlike state, whereby they united with the principle of Christ's love as an

---

33 Tomberg, *Christ and Sophia*, p. 306.

experience *within* their own being. We also are to awaken from our dream-like sleep to meet the challenge of our time with hearts filled with love.

Emanations from the heart of the galaxy are increasing in our time, leading up to a Pentecost on a world scale.[34] In remembrance of this profound moment, which today quickens, we are encouraged to live into this New Moon as a Sophianic awakening to Christ. It is our "I" that receives the new Pentecostal revelation, and it is the sense of ego that is represented by the constellation of Gemini.

Can we find the strength of self to radiate from our center while all the while remaining open to the periphery?

June 23: Mars enters Virgo. "Work with powers of life."[35] Mars in Virgo gives voice to Sophia and all the mysteries of the Earth Mother. Mars was in Virgo at the start of the forty days in the wilderness when Christ was continually tempted. This is a picture of the Logos (Mars) working with the Demeter mysteries (Virgo) until August 15th when it then enters Libra.

June 25: Saturn stations at 27° Virgo. Opposite to this degree (Pisces) the birth of the Solomon Jesus is remembered—intensifying the cosmic memory of Christianized Star Wisdom.

June 26: Sun enters the second decan of Gemini, ruled by Mars and associated with the Greater Dog, Canis Major, whose leading star Sirius is at 19½° Gemini.

June 24: Celebration of St. John's Day.

June 28: Sun 12½° Gemini: Birth of John the Baptist (4 Jun 2 BC). John the Baptist was revealed by Christ to be the reincarnated Elijah, and later came to Earth as the Renaissance painter Raphael, and still later as Novalis. John fulfilled his mission when he baptized Christ in the Jordan River in the year AD 29, when he bore witness to the incarnation of Christ—the true Light of the World and the Lamb of God. After the fulfillment of this mission, his new mission began, which was in service to Sophia. Just as John was the guide and preparer for those who would recognize Christ, so too is he the preparer and guide for those working on behalf of Sophia. This is a day to open our eyes and ears to the truth ringing through the world—a truth enlightened by wisdom and born of love. John works in the apocalyptic realms where the Book of Revelation lives eternally. To know evil, is to bring forth the good. This is true of those following a Christ-centered Grail path. For those who do not know Christ, such knowledge is imprudent. John is the *bearer of strength* and works through the *power of the* Word. May we find the fulness of voice that proclaims the Light and cowers not in the shadows of fear!

JULY 2012

The Sun begins July in Gemini (the Twins), moving into Cancer (The Crab) on the 17th. Uranus stations before going retrograde on the 13th (remaining retrograde until December 14th). Mercury goes retrograde on the 16th, until August 9th. The Full Moon is on the 3rd (Sun in Gemini and Moon in Sagittarius). By the 15th, the waning Moon joins with Jupiter and Venus clustered around the "eye of the Bull," Aldebaran; an impressive pre-dawn show for several mornings! The New Moon in Gemini is on the 18th. On the 25th, the new crescent will hang between Saturn and Mars in the last degrees of Virgo (the Virgin). The 28th and 29th bring the peak of the annual Southern Delta Aquarid meteor showers; look to the constellation of Aquarius in the southwest, after midnight, while the half Moon sets in the west making for better viewing of the twenty meteors each hour.

July 1: Sun 14° Gemini: Death of the Solomon Jesus (5 June 12).

In the case of a highly developed individuality such as Zarathustra, who reincarnated as the Solomon Jesus, death signifies merely

---

34 See Robert Powell's article "World Pentecost," *Journal for Star Wisdom 2010*, or articles at www .sophiafoundation.org.

35 Steiner, *Twelve Moods of the Zodiac* (no pg no.).

a translation of activity from one realm to another. This individuality worked on, after the death of the body on June 5, AD 12, in union with the Nathan Jesus. Thus, the Solomon Jesus was active in preparing the way for the unfolding of the earthly mission of Jesus Christ—the mission which began with the Baptism in the Jordan and culminated in the death on the cross on Golgotha. (*Chron.* p. 91)

Today we are reminded of the presence of initiates working from behind the veil of sense existence. Faithfulness and perseverance (Gemini) are virtues that guide us to develop our "I." As our "I" develops we become more aware of the continuous interaction among all beings—inclusive of the beings of spiritual worlds. Today we can bring our attention to the weaving between worlds and between each other.

July 3: Full Moon: Sun 16° Gemini, opposite Moon 16° Sagittarius.
This Full Moon remembers "Jesus wandering in the fields east of Megiddo, teaching the workers who were busy sowing seeds (15 Nov 30). He taught them in parables. This was the time of a New Moon. As he was thus engaged, some disciples of John the Baptist arrived and accompanied Jesus into Megiddo" (*Chron.* p. 257). From prison, John had sent his disciples to ask Christ:

"Are you he who is to come, or are we to expect another?"...And Jesus answered them, "Go and tell John what you hear and what you see. The blind become seeing, the lame walk. Lepers are cleansed, the deaf hear, the dead are raised and those who have become poor receive the message of salvation. And all those are blessed who do not stumble over my Being." (Luke 7:20–23)

In less than two months time, John would be beheaded by Herod, through the instigation of his wife, Herodias. At the time of John's capture and imprisonment he felt he had already fulfilled his mission, having recognized and baptized the Messiah. As a consequence the angels and higher spiritual beings gradually withdrew from him.

Thus John the Baptist was already "spiritually beheaded" before he became actually beheaded.

That the higher spiritual beings had withdrawn is revealed by the fact that when John was in prison he no longer knew with certainty that Jesus was the Messiah, and so he sent some of his disciples to ask him: "'Are you the Christ?' That which previously, with the help of higher spiritual beings, he had known with certainty, he now began to doubt, as the protecting spiritual beings had withdrawn." (*CHA, The Ministry up to the Beheading of John the Baptist*)

This Full Moon recalls doubt, which can assail the spiritual seeker when in the presence of dark forces—as was John when destiny brought him into connection with Herod and Herodias. The fact that this Full Moon finds Jesus in Megiddo also speaks of dark forces, for this ancient city has been the scene of more battles than anywhere else on Earth. And yet, it was in this city that many were healed by Christ. This is a focus of this Full Moon—to understand that there is no darkness impenetrable to the healing power of Divine Light, and that faithfulness to our mission helps us overcome doubt.

Sun 16° Gemini: Conception of Solomon Jesus (7 June 7 BC).

The stellar configuration at *conception* relates more to the *body*, the formation of the physical embryo beginning at this moment, whereas the position of the stars at *birth* have to do more with the destiny of the *soul*, which begins unfolding at the moment of birth. The zodiacal position of the Sun at birth is connected with the spirit, signifying in the present case that the spirit of the Solomon Jesus chose to be born [nine months later] with the Sun in the middle of the constellation of Pisces, opposite the Full Moon in the middle of Virgo. Exactly four years later, the Sun was again in the middle of Pisces at the conception configuration of the Nathan Jesus. Moreover, it was the New Moon, so the Moon (connected especially with the life forces) was also in the middle of Pisces. Since the Sun and Moon at the *conception* of the Nathan Jesus were at the same point in the zodiac as the Sun at the *birth* of the Solomon Jesus, there is, astrologically speaking, a deep relationship between the spirit of the Solomon

Jesus and the body (including life forces) of the Nathan Jesus. This sheds a clear light on the event in the Temple in AD 12, when the spirit of the Solomon Jesus passed over into the body of the Nathan Jesus. (*Chron.* p. 72)

As this year is commemorating the Union in the Temple between the two Jesus children, it is helpful to see the connection between the spirit of the Solomon Jesus and the body of life forces of the Nathan Jesus. Through understanding this star language, we see the foreshadowing of the union that would follow approximately seventeen years later.

ASPECT: Moon conjunct Pluto 13° Sagittarius: Transfiguration on Mt. Tabor (4 Apr 31). Pluto stood at this exact degree at the Transfiguration, three days after a Full Moon. The Transfiguration revealed the glory of Christ transfigured through the solarization of his seven chakras. The Light of Divine Love rested in the Son of God who had become the Son of humankind. This is an imagination of the future potential for all humanity. With Moon–Pluto in Sagittarius we are called to exercise control of speech. The content of our speech will determine whether we are moving toward the light of transfiguration, or toward the darkness of Hades (Pluto).

Today the Full Moon remembers John's doubt, the Sun remembers the wisdom of Solomon Jesus, and Pluto remembers the Transfiguration. Perhaps the stars are saying that if we overcome doubt we will find the wisdom that leads us toward Transfiguration. Full Moon in Sagittarius asks us to practice control of speech.

July 6: Sun 19° Gemini. This position is aligned exactly with the most radiant star in our heavens, Sirius, known as the star of the Master Jesus and revered by the Egyptians as the star of Isis (a pre-Christian manifestation of Sophia). Today we celebrate Sun conjunct Sirius directly following the commemoration of the conception of the Master Jesus three days past. There is a mysterious connection between the star Sirius, our Sun, and Shambhala—the golden realm at the heart of the Earth, the Earth's heart chakra. When Sun aligns with Sirius we can imagine a conversation

amplifying between the Daughter in the heights and the Mother in the depths—through our Sun-heart. "Reveal thyself, Sun life."[36]

Sun enters third decan of Gemini, ruled by the Sun and associated with the constellation of the Lesser Dog, Canis Minor. The second star in this constellation, Gomeisa, signifying redemption, marks the neck of the dog at 27½° Gemini. The Lesser Dog was seen by the Egyptians in connection with Horus, just as the Greater Dog was seen to be the dwelling place of Isis, and Orion was seen as the cosmic abode of Osiris.

July 13: Uranus stations, 13½° Pisces. The term "station" refers to the point in a planet's retrograde cycle where it is standing still, and hence, concentrating its energies heavily on a single zodiacal position. Uranus stations today where it was at the "Flight into Egypt" by the family of the Solomon Jesus child. At this event the Sun was conjunct Uranus. What could a "Flight into Egypt" harken for our time?

Perhaps a "flight into Egypt" could herald a re-turning to the stars and to the beings who dwell there, as a remembering of the star wisdom practiced in ancient Egypt—but now this star wisdom is to be Christianized. It was under the tutelage of Hermes Trismegistus, around 2500 BC, that star wisdom flourished. What the stars then spoke was mirrored on Earth as mandates that guided human activity, henceforth the mantra: "As above, so also below." A re-turning to Egypt would be a "flight into the future"—an acceptance of the guiding influences of the stars, and a reawakening to new imaginations (Uranus). This is exactly the activity that is to resurrect in human consciousness. We are to unlock the mysteries of Egypt and lift the veil between the human soul and the World Soul—the soul of Isis–Sophia.

> When the individuality who once in the mystery places of Egypt raised the eyes of his soul up to the stars and sought to unravel their secrets in celestial space as in those days under the guidance of the Egyptian sages, lived again in our own epoch as Kepler, what had existed in another form in his Egyptian soul appeared

---

36 Steiner, *Twelve Moods of the Zodiac* (no pg no.).

SIDEREAL GEOCENTRIC LONGITUDES : JULY 2012 Gregorian at 0 hours UT

DAY	☉	☽	☊	☿	♀	♂	♃	♄	♅	♆	♇
1 SU	14 ♊ 40	6 ♏ 17	9 ♏ 48	10 ♋ 24	12 ♉ 47	3 ♍ 46	9 ♉ 21	27 ♍ 53	13 ♓ 34	8 ♒ 4R	13 ♐ 18R
2 MO	15 37	21 3	9 48R	11 20	12 56	4 18	9 34	27 53	13 34	8 3	13 17
3 TU	16 34	5 ♐ 48	9 46	12 13	13 7	4 49	9 47	27 54	13 35	8 2	13 15
4 WE	17 31	20 26	9 42	13 2	13 19	5 21	9 59	27 55	13 35	8 1	13 14
5 TH	18 29	4 ♑ 50	9 37	13 47	13 34	5 52	10 12	27 56	13 36	8 0	13 12
6 FR	19 26	18 55	9 31	14 29	13 51	6 24	10 24	27 57	13 36	7 59	13 11
7 SA	20 23	2 ♒ 35	9 25	15 7	14 10	6 56	10 37	27 58	13 37	7 58	13 9
8 SU	21 20	15 50	9 19	15 41	14 30	7 28	10 49	27 59	13 37	7 57	13 8
9 MO	22 17	28 41	9 15	16 11	14 52	8 1	11 1	28 0	13 37	7 56	13 6
10 TU	23 15	11 ♓ 11	9 13	16 37	15 16	8 33	11 14	28 2	13 37	7 55	13 5
11 WE	24 12	23 22	9 12	16 58	15 42	9 6	11 26	28 3	13 37	7 54	13 3
12 TH	25 9	5 ♈ 20	9 12D	17 15	16 9	9 39	11 38	28 5	13 37	7 53	13 2
13 FR	26 6	17 11	9 13	17 27	16 38	10 12	11 50	28 6	13 38	7 52	13 0
14 SA	27 3	28 58	9 15	17 35	17 8	10 45	12 2	28 8	13 37R	7 51	12 59
15 SU	28 1	10 ♉ 48	9 15R	17 38	17 39	11 18	12 14	28 10	13 37	7 50	12 57
16 MO	28 58	22 44	9 14	17 36R	18 12	11 52	12 25	28 12	13 37	7 49	12 56
17 TU	29 55	4 ♊ 50	9 11	17 29	18 47	12 25	12 37	28 14	13 37	7 47	12 55
18 WE	0 ♋ 52	17 8	9 6	17 17	19 22	12 59	12 49	28 16	13 37	7 46	12 53
19 TH	1 50	29 41	8 59	17 1	19 59	13 33	13 0	28 19	13 37	7 45	12 52
20 FR	2 47	12 ♋ 28	8 50	16 40	20 37	14 7	13 12	28 21	13 36	7 44	12 50
21 SA	3 44	25 30	8 41	16 15	21 16	14 41	13 23	28 23	13 36	7 42	12 49
22 SU	4 42	8 ♌ 46	8 32	15 45	21 56	15 16	13 34	28 26	13 36	7 41	12 47
23 MO	5 39	22 14	8 24	15 12	22 37	15 50	13 45	28 29	13 35	7 40	12 46
24 TU	6 36	5 ♍ 52	8 18	14 36	23 19	16 25	13 56	28 31	13 35	7 38	12 45
25 WE	7 33	19 41	8 15	13 57	24 2	16 59	14 7	28 34	13 34	7 37	12 43
26 TH	8 31	3 ♎ 38	8 13	13 15	24 46	17 34	14 18	28 37	13 34	7 36	12 42
27 FR	9 28	17 44	8 14D	12 33	25 31	18 9	14 29	28 40	13 33	7 34	12 41
28 SA	10 25	1 ♏ 57	8 14	11 49	26 16	18 45	14 40	28 43	13 32	7 33	12 39
29 SU	11 23	16 15	8 14R	11 5	27 3	19 20	14 50	28 46	13 32	7 31	12 38
30 MO	12 20	0 ♐ 37	8 12	10 22	27 50	19 55	15 1	28 50	13 31	7 30	12 37
31 TU	13 18	14 58	8 8	9 41	28 38	20 31	15 11	28 53	13 30	7 29	12 36

INGRESSES :

2 ☽ → ♐ 14:33	25 ☽ → ♎ 17:45
4 ☽ → ♑ 15:52	27 ☽ → ♏ 20:43
6 ☽ → ♒ 19:24	29 ☽ → ♐ 22:58
9 ☽ → ♓ 2:29	
11 ☽ → ♈ 13:15	
14 ☽ → ♉ 2: 5	
16 ☽ → ♊ 14:27	
17 ☉ → ♋ 2: 2	
19 ☽ → ♋ 0:36	
21 ☽ → ♌ 8:11	
23 ☽ → ♍ 13:42	

ASPECTS & ECLIPSES :

1 ☽ ☍ ♃ 5: 4	10 ☽ ☌ ♅ 4:46	☉ ☌ ☽ 4:23	29 ☽ ☌ P 8:35
☽ ☌ ☊ 5:43	11 ☉ □ ☽ 1:47	20 ☽ ☌ ☿ 7:32	☽ ☍ ♀ 19: 6
☽ ☍ ♀ 10:40	☽ ☍ ♄ 9:22	21 ☽ ☍ ♆ 22: 4	30 ☽ ☌ ♇ 20: 2
☽ ☌ P 18:19	13 ☽ ☌ A 16:26	☽ S ☊ 23:35	
2 ♃ ☍ ☊ 22:25	14 ☽ ☌ ☋ 20:52	24 ☽ ☍ ♅ 13:24	
3 ☽ ☌ ♇ 12: 9	15 ☽ ☌ ♃ 2:56	☽ ☌ ♂ 19: 8	
☉ ☍ ☽ 18:51	☉ □ ♄ 4: 7	25 ☽ ☌ ♄ 15:21	
5 ☽ ☍ ☿ 15:59	☽ ☌ ♀ 14:29	26 ☉ □ ☽ 8:55	
7 ☽ ☌ ♆ 9:38	17 ☽ ☍ ♇ 15:46	28 ☽ ☌ ☊ 10:34	
☽ N ☊ 12:10	♂ □ ♇ 19:55	☉ i☌ ☿ 19:49	
9 ☽ ☍ ♂ 18:40	19 ♂ ☍ ♅ 2:36	☽ ☍ ♃ 21:36	

SIDEREAL HELIOCENTRIC LONGITUDES : JULY 2012 Gregorian at 0 hours UT

DAY	Sid. Time	☿	♀	⊕	♂	♃	♄	♅	♆	♇	Vernal Point
1 SU	18:37:48	21 ♎ 10	0 ♑ 20	14 ♐ 40	12 ♎ 56	2 ♉ 37	3 ♎ 42	10 ♓ 39	6 ♒ 30	13 ♐ 21	5 ♓ 5' 8"
2 MO	18:41:44	24 6	1 55	15 37	13 26	2 42	3 44	10 40	6 30	13 21	5 ♓ 5' 8"
3 TU	18:45:41	27 0	3 30	16 34	13 55	2 48	3 46	10 41	6 31	13 21	5 ♓ 5' 8"
4 WE	18:49:37	29 51	5 5	17 31	14 24	2 53	3 48	10 41	6 31	13 22	5 ♓ 5' 8"
5 TH	18:53:34	2 ♏ 41	6 40	18 28	14 53	2 58	3 50	10 42	6 31	13 22	5 ♓ 5' 8"
6 FR	18:57:30	5 30	8 15	19 25	15 22	3 4	3 52	10 43	6 32	13 22	5 ♓ 5' 8"
7 SA	19: 1:27	8 17	9 50	20 23	15 52	3 9	3 54	10 43	6 32	13 23	5 ♓ 5' 8"
8 SU	19: 5:23	11 4	11 24	21 20	16 21	3 14	3 56	10 44	6 32	13 23	5 ♓ 5' 7"
9 MO	19: 9:20	13 50	12 59	22 17	16 50	3 20	3 58	10 45	6 33	13 23	5 ♓ 5' 7"
10 TU	19:13:17	16 35	14 34	23 14	17 20	3 25	4 0	10 45	6 33	13 24	5 ♓ 5' 7"
11 WE	19:17:13	19 19	16 9	24 11	17 49	3 31	4 2	10 46	6 33	13 24	5 ♓ 5' 7"
12 TH	19:21:10	22 4	17 44	25 9	18 19	3 36	4 4	10 46	6 34	13 24	5 ♓ 5' 7"
13 FR	19:25: 6	24 49	19 19	26 6	18 49	3 41	4 6	10 47	6 34	13 25	5 ♓ 5' 7"
14 SA	19:29: 3	27 34	20 54	27 3	19 18	3 47	4 7	10 48	6 34	13 25	5 ♓ 5' 7"
15 SU	19:32:59	0 ♐ 19	22 29	28 0	19 48	3 52	4 9	10 48	6 35	13 25	5 ♓ 5' 6"
16 MO	19:36:56	3 5	24 4	28 58	20 18	3 57	4 11	10 49	6 35	13 26	5 ♓ 5' 6"
17 TU	19:40:52	5 52	25 39	29 55	20 47	4 3	4 13	10 50	6 36	13 26	5 ♓ 5' 6"
18 WE	19:44:49	8 40	27 14	0 ♑ 52	21 17	4 8	4 15	10 50	6 36	13 26	5 ♓ 5' 6"
19 TH	19:48:46	11 30	28 48	1 49	21 47	4 13	4 17	10 51	6 36	13 27	5 ♓ 5' 6"
20 FR	19:52:42	14 21	0 ♒ 23	2 47	22 17	4 19	4 19	10 52	6 37	13 27	5 ♓ 5' 6"
21 SA	19:56:39	17 13	1 58	3 44	22 47	4 24	4 21	10 52	6 37	13 27	5 ♓ 5' 6"
22 SU	20: 0:35	20 8	3 33	4 41	23 17	4 30	4 23	10 53	6 37	13 28	5 ♓ 5' 6"
23 MO	20: 4:32	23 5	5 9	5 39	23 47	4 35	4 25	10 54	6 38	13 28	5 ♓ 5' 5"
24 TU	20: 8:28	26 4	6 44	6 36	24 17	4 40	4 27	10 54	6 38	13 28	5 ♓ 5' 5"
25 WE	20:12:25	29 6	8 19	7 33	24 47	4 46	4 29	10 55	6 38	13 29	5 ♓ 5' 5"
26 TH	20:16:21	2 ♑ 11	9 54	8 31	25 17	4 51	4 30	10 55	6 39	13 29	5 ♓ 5' 5"
27 FR	20:20:18	5 20	11 29	9 28	25 48	4 56	4 32	10 56	6 39	13 29	5 ♓ 5' 5"
28 SA	20:24:15	8 31	13 4	10 25	26 18	5 2	4 34	10 57	6 40	13 30	5 ♓ 5' 5"
29 SU	20:28:11	11 47	14 39	11 23	26 48	5 7	4 36	10 57	6 40	13 30	5 ♓ 5' 5"
30 MO	20:32: 8	15 7	16 14	12 20	27 19	5 12	4 38	10 58	6 40	13 30	5 ♓ 5' 4"
31 TU	20:36: 4	18 31	17 49	13 17	27 49	5 18	4 40	10 59	6 41	13 31	5 ♓ 5' 4"

INGRESSES :

4 ☿ → ♏ 1:13
14 ☿ → ♐ 21:12
17 ⊕ → ♑ 2: 9
19 ♀ → ♒ 18: 4
25 ☿ → ♑ 7: 0

ASPECTS (HELIOCENTRIC +MOON(TYCHONIC)) :

1 ☿ ☌ ☋ 19:35	☿ △ ♅ 21: 6	☿ ⚹ ♆ 6:11	♀ ☌ ♆ 22:36	☿ ☌ ⊕ 19:49
♂ ⚹ ♇ 20:11	8 ☿ ⚹ ♀ 6:57	☽ ☍ ♇ 16:50	24 ☽ ☍ ♅ 8:46	30 ☽ ☌ ♇ 21:33
2 ♀ △ ♃ 12:36	9 ☽ ☌ ♅ 23:10	18 ☿ □ ♅ 18:29	♂ ☌ ☋ 21:47	
3 ♀ □ ♄ 4:11	11 ♀ ☌ A 10:13	19 ☿ ☌ ♇ 16:27	26 ☽ ☌ ♄ 1:29	
☽ ☌ ♇ 12:21	☽ ☍ ♄ 21:25	21 ☽ ☍ ♀ 13:21	☿ □ ♄ 17:58	
4 ⊕ ☌ A 18: 6	12 ☿ ☌ A 5:50	⊕ □ ♄ 15:59	☿ △ ♃ 20:58	
5 ☿ ☍ ♃ 2:29	♀ □ ♂ 12:51	⊕ △ ♃ 18:33	27 ☽ ☌ ♂ 14: 8	
☽ ☌ ♀ 3:27	13 ☽ ☍ ♂ 3:27	☽ ☍ ♆ 20: 9	28 ☽ ☍ ♃ 5:13	
6 ☿ □ ♆ 8:50	14 ☽ ☌ ♃ 9:50	22 ♀ △ ♄ 12:42	♀ ⚹ ♇ 6:30	
7 ☽ ☌ ♆ 7: 4	16 ☿ ⚹ ♄ 9:36	♀ □ ♃ 14:59	⊕ ⚹ ♅ 13:22	
♀ ⚹ ♅ 13:40	17 ☽ ☍ ☿ 2:39	23 ☿ ⚹ ♂ 6:47	☿ ⚹ ♅ 17:57	

in a newer guise as the great laws of Kepler, which today are such an integral part of astrophysics. It happened also that within the soul of this man something arose that forced these words to be spoken—words that may be read in the writings of Kepler: "I have brought the sacred vessel out of the holy places of Egypt; I have transported it to the present time, so that people today may understand something of those influences that could affect even the most distant future."[37]

As Uranus "stations" at the flight into Egypt, we may ask: "Where is this Egypt today?" At the death of Johannes Kepler, the Moon stood at this same degree of the heavens—where Uranus is today. The being of Kepler was venerated by Rudolf Steiner, and was a kind of guide, from across the threshold, when Rudolf Steiner was seeking the Grail Family. Steiner recognized here the Kyot being, who previously was considered to be fictitious:

And then, when I was not in the least looking for it, I came upon a saying by Kyot... "He said, a thing was called the Grail." Now exoteric research itself tells us how Kyot came to these words. He acquired a book by Flegetanis in Spain—an astrological book. No doubt about it, one may say that Kyot is the man who, stimulated by Flegetanis (whom he calls Flegetanis and in whom lives a certain knowledge of the stellar script), Kyot is the man who, stimulated by the revived astrology, sees the thing called the Grail. Then I knew that Kyot is not to be given up. I knew that he discloses an important clue if one is searching in the sense of spiritual science; he at least has seen the Grail.[38]

Kyot was a key in Steiner's quest into the Grail mysteries, and the Grail mysteries are intimately connected with star wisdom:

It became clearer and clearer to me, as the result of many years of research, that in our epoch there is really something like a resurrection of the astrology of the third epoch, but permeated now with the Christ impulse. Today we must search among the stars in a

way different from the old ways; rather, the stellar script must once more become something that speaks to us.[39]

With Uranus stationing at "The Flight into Egypt," the Moon of Kepler, the guidance of Kyot, the resurrection of Christianized star wisdom, and a "thing called the Grail," we are led to the kind of imaginations Uranus today is amplifying. Steiner states that the Grail time was a Saturn time—Sun and Saturn stood together in Cancer. With Saturn in Libra for the next few years we can imagine a tension between humanity and the Grail mysteries. This next week the memory of the Flight into Egypt will be magnified.

July 17: Sun enters Cancer: "Thou resting, glowing light" (Rudolf Steiner, *Twelve Moods of the Zodiac*). Selflessness becomes Catharsis. The instinct to purify oneself is amplified. The Cathars were the "pure ones." The first decan is ruled by Mercury and is associated with the constellation of Argo the Ship in which, according to Greek mythology, Jason and the Argonauts recovered the Golden Fleece.

ASPECT: Moon 12°55' Gemini opposite Pluto 12° 55' Sagittarius: Jesus teaches about the Bread of Life (2 Feb 31). Jesus speaks of himself as the Bread of Life 113 weeks before he will offer himself for the redemption of the Earth and humanity. The transubstantiation of substance is a mystery we are able to practice every day; from ordinary blessings before meals, to the high rituals of sacramental communion.

We could also say: through matter from the outer world, the human body becomes material; by its own structure it is not so, but this nonmaterial body structure as an invisible form is materialized in that it is filled out with matter from the outer world. This happens through food. Food is the door through which the material outer world penetrates into the human organism to stimulate it to material activity. If, however, a substance were to enter though the same door that would stimulate it not to material but to spiritual activity, then we would have the process of the Last Supper.

---

37 Steiner and Schuré. *The East in the Light of the West–Children of Lucifer*, pp. 162–163.

38 Steiner, *Christ and the Spiritual World*, p. 110.

39 Steiner, *Christ and the Spiritual World*, p. 106.

There, subconscious will processes instead of metabolic processes are activated; or more exactly, the effect of the Last Supper is the transformation of metabolic processes into will processes. In nutrition the projection of the material part of the outer world into the human being takes place. Through the effect of the Last Supper, however, the union—the communion—of the subconscious human will with the spirit-being of the outer world takes place. Spiritual being enters into [the human being] during Communion.[40]

Materialism will increase the density of the human being in body, soul and spirit. In density the human being will become more animal, more susceptible to sub-earthly influences. The greater this materialization becomes the more impossible it will be to understand past lives, and the transubstantiation of substance. This is the goal of those working against Christ—to eradicate the very possibility of humanity receiving Christ, the Bread of Life. With Moon opposite Pluto we invite Divine Love into our inner depths to increase our spiritual foundation; or, like the Pharisees, we can reject such a possibility and decide instead in favor of Hades, and the gradual path of being turned to stone in our physical foundation. As the Sun enters Cancer today we can contemplate purification and the living bread of life.

July 18: New Moon 1° Cancer, aligned with Procyon (redeemed or redeeming) in the Lesser Dog. This is where the Sun was when Jesus taught the need to be awake to the signs of the times (*Chron.* 305). In this discourse Christ spoke of the fire he is bringing and that it will be a fire that divides one person from another. Is this the division between the house of the serpent and the house of the Lamb and his Bride? Christ went on to speak of the signs the people cannot read:

> When you see a cloud rising in the west, you say at once: It is going to rain; and it happens. And when you notice that the south wind is blowing, you say: It is going to be hot; and that also happens. Your hearts and minds are all awry! You know how to interpret the appearance of the

Earth and sky; but the signs of our times, why do you not interpret them? (Luke 12:47–48)

What would be said to humanity in our times regarding the reading of the signs of the times? Two of the most reliable indicators of the health of a culture are the well-being of the children and the well-being of the elemental beings. Both children and elementals are harbingers of the future: the future the children will found, and the future the Earth's ecosystem will create. When the will of spirit, proclaimed through the movements of the stars above, are mirrored in human activity below, there is harmony.

If the children and the elemental beings are healthy, and the hermetic laws are in order, a culture is blessed. On the other hand, if the children and the elemental beings are found wanting, and hermetic laws are ignored, the signs of the times pass by unnoticed—and the culture is in decline!

This New Moon invites us to awaken as healers and peace-keepers, that we may extend a helping hand to children and elemental beings, in whatever small or large measure, and in the spirit of selflessness (Cancer).

ASPECT: Mars 13° Virgo, opposite Uranus 13° Pisces: Demise of the Cathars (16 Mar 1244). At the death of the Cathars, the "pure ones," the Sun was in the Fishes and heliocentrically (perspective from the Sun) the Earth was seen in front of the constellation of Virgo—both at 12½°, and Mars was square Uranus. Today's opposition between Mars in Virgo, and Uranus in Pisces, remembers when the Cathars met their demise. In the words of Robert Powell:

> It is my conviction that the Manichaeans—at least some of them—reincarnated several hundred years later as Cathars. For, allowing for differences in cultural milieu, there is a remarkable similarity between Manichaeism and Catharism, as has been pointed out and substantiated by a leading Cathar researcher, Deodat Roche. In other words, the spirit of Manichaeism lived on in the Cathar religion not in the sense of cultural transmission but through the reincarnation of certain Manichaeans as Cathars. This would also explain

---

40 Tomberg, *Russian Spirituality and Other Essays,* pg. 145.

the persecution of the Cathars (as a continuation of the persecution of the Manichaeans).

Montsegur was one of the last Cathar strongholds until March 16, 1244, when over two hundred Cathars—after a lengthy siege of their castle on the summit of the holy mountain—surrendered themselves to die in the flames of the bonfire lit for them by the crusaders against the "Cathar heresy." An unknown hand wrote the following epigraph for the Cathars: "After seven hundred years the laurel will blossom again upon the ashes of the martyrs." Some have interpreted this to mean that the Cathars knew they would reincarnate in the twentieth century, seven hundred years after their martyrdom. The question is: What is the connection of the Cathars to the Grail stream?[41]

This mysterious quote, regarding the laurel's blossoming seven hundred years after the demise of the Cathars, is interesting in that it suggests the return of the Cathars from the mid-twentieth century on. As both the Cathars and Manichaeans were healing streams, we can see how their presence now would assist humanity in opening to the healing ministrations of Christ in his Second Coming. Also, we may keep in mind that Rudolf Steiner once suggested Mani's reincarnation would be in the beginning of the twenty-first century—if conditions were right. As Christ "Turned Time" in his first coming, we can understand how "Time will Turn" again at this time of his Second Coming. Just as there was a confluence of great initiates at the first Turning Point of Time, so too can we expect a great confluence now.

As Mars opposes Uranus today, the march of the allegedly heretical "pure ones" into the fires of purification sounds from the stars. As the New Moon is conjunct Procyon in Cancer, the constellation of catharsis, this conjunction may foretell a persecution (Mars) toward those bearing new imaginations (Uranus), who are found to be heretical by keepers of the status quo; or, inversely, this opposition may bring an opportunity to experience

the "catharsis" that leads to communion with new revelations.

What is the connection of the Cathars to the Gail stream? Perhaps this rests with John. For Rudolf Steiner referred to John as the successor of Parsifal—this tells how closely John is working with the Grail mysteries—and the Grail mysteries have much to do with Revelation. Study of the Book of Revelation brings one into communion with the astral body of Christ, and in reading the apocalypse in the school of the night, one is working with John and Sophia in the light of the Holy Grail.

And we should keep in mind that continuation of the Parsifal saga which says that when the Grail became invisible in Europe, it was carried to the realm of Presbyter John, who had his kingdom on the far side of the lands reached by the Crusaders. In the time of the Crusades the kingdom of Presbyter John, the successor of Parsifal, was still honored, and from the way in which search was made for it we must say: If all this were expressed in terms of strict earthly geography, it would show that the place of Presbyter John is not to be found on Earth.[42]

July 20: Sun 3/4° Cancer: Jesus teaches the significance of the word *Amen* (*Chron.* p. 306). This is also where the Sun was at the July 2009 eclipse, when Pluto stood exactly where it was at the Baptism of Christ, and where Venus stood very close to where she was at the Venus–Sun transit last month. The Sun at this degree remembers the Amen as the antidote to world illness. Valentin Tomberg addresses the *Amen*:

The *a* sound leads to understanding the "risen head," or the current of relationship to the cosmic heights. The *m* sound reveals the "risen hands," or the current in cosmic space. The *e* sound leads to the inner life of the resurrection body, and the *n* sound reveals the force of its denial of evil.[43]

And further: "The words of the Amen, the faithful and true witness, the beginning of God's creation" (Rev. 3:14). Meditation on this verse brings us into contact with the mystery of the resurrection

41 Powell, during 1998 Pilgrimage to the South of France (http://www.Sophiafoundation.org).

42 Steiner, *Christ and the Spiritual World*, p.139.
43 Tomberg, *Christ and Sophia*, p. 301.

body. *Putting on the resurrection body* (This is a term used by St. Paul, who recognized immortality as *"putting on the resurrection body"*) is the goal of all humanity.

The head of the Amen is the Kingdom of stars in the heavens; *the heart of the Amen* is the Power of the radiant cross of Sun's light, and *the limbs of the Amen* are the rainbow of Glory when matter is permeated by spirit. The Kingdom, the Power, and the Glory of the Amen stand as the antidote to the adversarial forces confronting humanity today.

The Amen is Christ in his cosmic robes. This is a day to experience the presence of the Amen and the strength of the *N* as "No" to forces rising from the abyss. This is the gesture for the constellation of Pisces, making this the gesture of the entire Age of the Consciousness Soul.

July 28: Inferior conjunction of Mercury and Sun: 11° Cancer: Theophany (28 Mar 31). A beautiful imagination of Mercury–Sun is placed before us in this Theophany: Jesus had outraged the Pharisees and at the height of the uproar, it suddenly grew dark. "Jesus looked up to heaven and said, 'Father, render testimony to thy Son!' A loud noise like thunder resounded and a heavenly voice proclaimed, 'This is my beloved son in whom I am well pleased!'" (*Chron.* p. 288).

As the healing messages from Mercury reach our hearts (Sun) we remember the true light. This is a day to practice penetrating to the light, no matter the uproar or darkness that may approach with illusory powers.

July 27: Sun enters second decan of Cancer, ruled by Venus. This decan contains the star cluster Praesepe, the Beehive (12½° Cancer), and according to Rudolf Steiner, bees are completely open to the influence of Venus and develop a life of love throughout the entire bee colony.[44] This decan is associated with the neck of the Lesser Bear, Ursa Minor.

Praesepe, the beehive, is at the center of the spiraling arms of Cancer, the heart of the crab. It was through this gateway that the Greeks believed human souls entered earthly incarnation in order to gather the golden nectar of earthly experience to take back to Sophia, the Queen of the cosmic realm. Cancer marks a point of decision in our yearly journey through the zodiac: Development or envelopment? The spiraling arms of Cancer invite us to breathe in the Light and to move forward with the evolution of life and consciousness. The opposite is envelopment, whereby we are arrested in our progress and are thus relegated to the dark corridors of rigidified convention.

July 30: Moon conjunct Pluto 12° 37' Sagittarius: Raising of Nazor (1 Sept 32). With Moon conjunct Pluto at this same degree, Jesus went to the field in which Nazor had died, and he prayed there. Returning to the house, Jesus and his followers found Nazor sitting upright in his coffin. Nazor was raised from a distance. Christ went to where his soul and spirit lingered over the field of his death. This is similar to how thoughts and words linger over locations in which they were expressed. We live in times when it is prudent to surround oneself with a protective sheath born of one's conscious attention. This can be likened to wrapping oneself in Sophia's (Virgo) protection— the "B" gesture in eurythmy. As we become more skilled at this ownership of our personal "field," we are protected from corrupt thoughts, feelings and deeds in our environment. Into such conscientiously tended space, the voice of spiritual guidance is more easily heard. We are guided to know when certain spaces and beings need to be cleared of ill will. By cleansing our environments, we help raise from the dead that which is fallen. This can be done while in the location or even from a distance, as was the case in this healing of Nazor. These hygienic healing capacities are awakening as gifts from Sophia. Nazor was instructed, after his raising, to be kinder to his servants. We can remember to be kinder in our words, thoughts and deeds, so as to preserve the environments of this kingdom: the kingdom of our Mother. Elemental beings are longing to serve the good. Today we can be particularly attentive to elemental beings. The constellation of Sagittarius, in which today's aspect occurs, asks us to control our speech. This is the right

---

44 Steiner, *Bees*, p. 2.

use of speech in order to bless the Earth and others with our words.

AUGUST 2012

The month begins with the Sun in the Crab (Cancer) and a full Moon on the 1st (Moon in Capricorn). The Sun moves into the Lion (Leo) on the 17th. We'll observe a 2nd full Moon this month, on the 31st with Sun in Leo and Moon in Aquarius. Uranus, Neptune and Pluto continue to be retrograde in August, while Mercury turns direct on the 9th in Cancer. The New Moon is the 17th this month, (Sun and Moon in Cancer) which will allow excellent viewing of the Perseid Meteor Showers' peak, on August 13/14. With as many as 60 meteors per hour and sweet summer evenings, this is THE time to lie upon the Earth, gazing to the northeast and watch the show. Jupiter and Venus continue to offer the pre-dawn sights, in the east before the Sun's rise; the waning Moon joins them on the 12th so perhaps an all-night sleep-out away from city lights is in order! Mars and Saturn finally come together on the 15th, upon the sacred star of Spica at 29° Virgo; the sheaf of wheat in the hand of the Divine Mother of the stars (Virgo, the Virgin). The new crescent Moon joins them on the 21st; look to the southwest as the light wanes at twilight.

August 1: Full Moon: Sun 15° Cancer opposite Moon 15° Capricorn: This Full Moon opposes the Sun within 3° of Preasepe—the beehive—the center of the spiraling arms of Cancer. Preasepe marks the decision point: development or envelopment? We choose development through the cathartic fires of purification. Today's Moon remembers the place of the Moon during the Adoration of the Magi. This was when the three kings visited the Solomon Jesus bearing gifts for the one they recognized as the true King. It is incumbent upon each of us to actively pursue transformation of thinking (Capricorn) in order to wrench ourselves from the systemic entrapments of materialistic thoughts. The "L" gesture in eurythmy accompanies the constellation of Capricorn, gesturing the living waters that carry us into the currents of the future. This takes courage! Courage to see the anti-Grail forces working to deaden humanity. To climb the mountain with this Full Moon and see the bigger picture can spare us the soul agony of being fooled by false prophets and indecent motives.

"May the past bear the future."[45]

August 1: Venus enters Gemini: "Set repose in movement."[46] Venus was in Gemini at the death of both the Solomon Jesus and the Nathan Mary. These two high initiates representing the pillars of Wisdom and Love, carried out missions of faithful service to the Christ—the Sun Being: "Cor Jesu, Rex et centrum omnium cordium." ("Heart of Jesus, King and centre of all hearts"—Litany of the Sacred Heart)

August 6: ASPECT: Moon conjunct Uranus 13° Pisces: The Stilling of the Storm and the Flight into Egypt. The Moon at this location remembers Christ's Stilling of the Storm, and Uranus at this location remembers the Flight into Egypt by the family of the Solomon Jesus child. In bringing together these two remembrances, an image arises of a mystery teaching for our times.

At the stilling of the storm (21 Nov 30), Christ raises his hand to still the upheaval of wind and waves threatening the disciples in their little boat on the Sea of Galilee:

> When the party put out from shore the weather was clam and beautiful, but they had scarcely reached the middle of the lake before a violent tempest arose. I thought it very strange that, although the sky was shrouded in darkness, the stars were to be seen. The wind blew in a hurricane and the waves dashed over the boat, the sails of which had been furled. I saw from time to time a brilliant light glancing over the troubled waters. It must have been lightning. The danger was imminent, and the disciples were in great anxiety when they awoke Jesus with the worlds: "Master! Hast Thou no care for us? We are sinking!" (*ACE*, vol. 3, pp. 46–47)

---

45 Steiner, *Twelve Moods of the Zodiac* (no pg no.).
46 Ibid.

In this scene, as described by Sister Emmerich, a battle of the soul is imaged: The lightning flashes of new imaginations (Uranus) agitate the airs of false light in our astral bodies, as well as the swelling waves of false power in our etheric bodies, causing wind and waves to surge within the soul. Though the storm raged, the stars were visible above (reminding us of the guiding star wisdom of Egypt). Jesus calmed the storm and instructed the disciples to row back to Chorazin, named thus on account of the town Great Chorazin—a city Jesus cursed.

He began to speak reproachful words about the towns where most of his spiritual deeds had taken place and which had not found the way to a change of heart and mind: "Woe to you, Chorazin, woe to you, Bethsaida! If the deeds done in you had been done in Tyre and Sidon, they would long ago have signified their change of heart and mind with mourning garments and ashes" (Luke 10:13).

The cities Chorazin, Capernaum, and Bethsaida formed what is called the "Evangelical Triangle," the small area where most of Jesus' miracles were accomplished (Matt. 11:20). Yet, in spite of bearing witness to the power of Christ, this had little effect in the lives of these people. In the temple of Chorazin, there is what is called the "Moses seat." Jesus saw the people bowing to the laws of Moses, and to the pharisees who hypocritically held up these laws and laid the burdens of these laws on the shoulders of their followers; and yet as the long-awaited Messiah worked in their midst, they knew him not.

As Moon and Uranus come into conjunction today, we are reminded that falsehoods in our inner depths will cause storms of wind and waves, and that lightning flashes of new imaginations (Uranus) can be a shock to the soul, but the stars shine in spite of the raging storms; it is to the stars we turn to find the keel of spiritual guidance in times of change. The Solomon Jesus child spent almost seven years in Egypt, thus gaining initiation into this wisdom stream that understood the language of the stars.

The old gods of competition, exploitation, and scarcity will wreak havoc until we make the turn to collaboration, reverence, and abundance.

The descendants of the people of Chorazin, after the time of Christ, allowed a Medusa to be built right into their synagogue wall. This is the fate of those who do not change: they are turned to stone.

Winds, waves, disturbances—and the stars above and within as keels in times of uncertainty. The silence of the heart can be our inner Egypt; our place of initiation!

August 7: Sun 20° Cancer: Sun enters third decan of Cancer, ruled by the Moon and associated with the flank of the Great Bear (Ursa Major).

ASPECT: Moon conjunct Saturn 29° Virgo. Spica rests in the tip of the shaft of wheat carried by the Virgin. This star represents the power of feminine wisdom. The Sun was conjunct Spica at the conversation between the Master Jesus and the Virgin Mary before the Baptism in the Jordan River, and also when Jesus visited the two remaining kings in their tent city on September of 32. Saturn and Moon today remember these significant events in the life of Jesus Christ. Will the resolves of spirit-necessity (Saturn) find receptivity in the lunar depths of human beings?

A day to ponder the freedom inherent in emptiness. Practice non-attachment.

August 10: Sun 22° Cancer: Death of Lazarus (15 July 32). The Temple Legend is intrinsic to our understanding of the mystery of the death and resurrection of Lazarus, for Lazarus was the reincarnated Hiram Abiff—the master builder of Solomon's Temple. After the division into sexes, during the Lemurian evolution, karma began to develop within single human beings. Along with humanity's incarnations over long periods of time, the karma of the individual became ever more concentrated as human beings confronted the outside world more and more. The "I" learned to discriminate between the outside world and the self. After a time, humans began to forget they were part of the outside world and instead confronted this world as their enemy (Cain kills his brother Abel). Humanity developed a longing for possessions without piety. Piety brings the astral body into harmony, and this harmony give us the Master Word, which

SIDEREAL GEOCENTRIC LONGITUDES : AUGUST 2012 Gregorian at 0 hours UT

DAY	☉	☽	☊	☿	♀	♂	♃	♄	♅	♆	♇
1 WE	14 ♋ 15	29 ♐ 14	8 ♏ 1R	9 ♋ 2R	29 ♉ 27	21 ♍ 6	15 ♉ 22	28 ♍ 56	13 ♓ 29R	7 ♒ 27R	12 ♐ 34R
2 TH	15 12	13 ♑ 20	7 52	8 26	0 ♊ 17	21 42	15 32	29 0	13 28	7 26	12 33
3 FR	16 10	27 11	7 41	7 54	1 7	22 18	15 42	29 3	13 27	7 24	12 32
4 SA	17 7	10 ♒ 42	7 30	7 26	1 58	22 54	15 52	29 7	13 26	7 23	12 31
5 SU	18 5	23 53	7 20	7 4	2 50	23 30	16 2	29 11	13 25	7 21	12 30
6 MO	19 2	6 ♓ 41	7 12	6 47	3 42	24 7	16 11	29 15	13 24	7 20	12 28
7 TU	19 59	19 10	7 6	6 36	4 35	24 43	16 21	29 19	13 23	7 18	12 27
8 WE	20 57	1 ♈ 21	7 2	6 31	5 28	25 19	16 31	29 23	13 22	7 16	12 26
9 TH	21 54	13 19	7 0	6 33D	6 22	25 56	16 40	29 27	13 21	7 15	12 25
10 FR	22 52	25 10	7 0	6 41	7 17	26 33	16 49	29 31	13 19	7 13	12 24
11 SA	23 50	6 ♉ 58	7 0	6 57	8 12	27 10	16 59	29 35	13 18	7 12	12 23
12 SU	24 47	18 50	6 59	7 19	9 8	27 47	17 8	29 39	13 17	7 10	12 22
13 MO	25 45	0 ♊ 49	6 57	7 49	10 4	28 24	17 17	29 44	13 15	7 9	12 21
14 TU	26 42	13 1	6 52	8 25	11 0	29 1	17 25	29 48	13 14	7 7	12 20
15 WE	27 40	25 30	6 45	9 9	11 57	29 38	17 34	29 53	13 13	7 5	12 19
16 TH	28 38	8 ♋ 17	6 36	9 59	12 55	0 ♎ 16	17 43	29 57	13 11	7 4	12 18
17 FR	29 35	21 23	6 24	10 56	13 53	0 53	17 51	0 ♎ 2	13 10	7 2	12 17
18 SA	0 ♌ 33	4 ♌ 47	6 12	11 59	14 51	1 31	17 59	0 7	13 8	7 0	12 16
19 SU	1 31	18 27	6 0	13 9	15 50	2 9	18 7	0 11	13 6	6 59	12 15
20 MO	2 29	2 ♍ 19	5 50	14 24	16 49	2 47	18 15	0 16	13 5	6 57	12 15
21 TU	3 26	16 21	5 42	15 45	17 48	3 25	18 23	0 21	13 3	6 56	12 14
22 WE	4 24	0 ♎ 27	5 36	17 12	18 48	4 3	18 31	0 26	13 1	6 54	12 13
23 TH	5 22	14 35	5 34	18 43	19 49	4 41	18 39	0 31	13 0	6 52	12 12
24 FR	6 20	28 43	5 33	20 19	20 49	5 19	18 46	0 37	12 58	6 51	12 11
25 SA	7 18	12 ♏ 50	5 33	21 59	21 50	5 58	18 53	0 42	12 56	6 49	12 11
26 SU	8 16	26 55	5 32	23 42	22 51	6 36	19 1	0 47	12 54	6 47	12 10
27 MO	9 13	10 ♐ 57	5 30	25 29	23 53	7 15	19 8	0 52	12 52	6 46	12 9
28 TU	10 11	24 54	5 25	27 18	24 55	7 53	19 14	0 58	12 50	6 44	12 9
29 WE	11 9	8 ♑ 45	5 17	29 10	25 57	8 32	19 21	1 3	12 48	6 42	12 8
30 TH	12 7	22 26	5 7	1 ♌ 3	27 0	9 11	19 28	1 9	12 46	6 41	12 8
31 FR	13 5	5 ♒ 55	4 55	2 58	28 3	9 50	19 34	1 14	12 45	6 39	12 7

INGRESSES :

1 ☽ → ♑ 1:17
♀ → ♊ 15:52
3 ☽ → ♒ 4:57
5 ☽ → ♓ 11:23
7 ☽ → ♈ 21:19
10 ☽ → ♉ 9:49
12 ☽ → ♊ 22:22
15 ☽ → ♋ 8:31
♂ → ♎ 13:56
16 ♄ → ♎ 14:15
17 ☉ → ♌ 10:14
☽ → ♌ 15:29
19 ☽ → ♍ 19:59
21 ☽ → ♎ 23:14
24 ☽ → ♏ 2:10
26 ☽ → ♐ 5:16
28 ☽ → ♑ 8:48
29 ☿ → ♌ 10:43
30 ☽ → ♒ 13:24

ASPECTS & ECLIPSES :

1 ☽ ☍ ☿ 15:57
2 ☉ ☍ ☽ 3:27
3 ☽ ☌ ♆ 18: 2
☽ N ☊ 18:20
4 ♆ □ ☊ 21: 1
6 ☽ ☌ ♅ 12:49
7 ☽ ☍ ♂ 11:26
☽ ☍ ♄ 20: 3
9 ☉ □ ☽ 18:54
10 ☽ ☌ A 10:48
11 ☽ ☌ ☋ 0: 2
☽ ☌ ♃ 20:31
13 ☉ □ Π 7:13
☽ ☌ ♀ 19:44
☽ ☍ ♇ 22:39
15 ♀ ☍ ♇ 8:55
♂ ☌ ♄ 10:30
16 ☽ ☌ ☿ 3:23
♀ □ ♅ 6:35
17 ☉ ☌ ☽ 15:54
18 ☽ S ☊ 2:28
☽ ☍ ♆ 3:55
20 ☽ ☍ ♅ 18:23
21 ☽ ☌ ♄ 23:59
22 ☽ ☌ ♂ 6:24
23 ☉ □ ☊ 4:43
☽ ☌ P 19:12
24 ☽ ☌ ☊ 11:36
☉ ☍ ♆ 12:24
☉ □ ☽ 13:53
25 ☽ ☍ ♃ 10:24
27 ☽ ☌ ♇ 2: 4
28 ☽ ☍ ♀ 0: 1
☉ □ Π 12:51
30 ☽ ☍ ☿ 17:49
☽ N ☊ 22:12
31 ☽ ☌ ♆ 1:18
☉ ☍ ☽ 13:57
☿ □ ☊ 21:49

SIDEREAL HELIOCENTRIC LONGITUDES : AUGUST 2012 Gregorian at 0 hours UT

DAY	Sid. Time	☿	♀	⊕	♂	♃	♄	♅	♆	♇	Vernal Point
1 WE	20:40: 1	22 ♑ 0	19 ♒ 25	14 ♑ 15	28 ♎ 20	5 ♉ 23	4 ♎ 42	10 ♓ 59	6 ♒ 41	13 ♐ 31	5 ♓ 5' 4"
2 TH	20:43:57	25 34	21 0	15 12	28 50	5 28	4 44	11 0	6 41	13 31	5 ♓ 5' 4"
3 FR	20:47:54	29 13	22 35	16 9	29 21	5 34	4 46	11 1	6 42	13 32	5 ♓ 5' 4"
4 SA	20:51:50	2 ♒ 58	24 10	17 7	29 51	5 39	4 48	11 1	6 42	13 32	5 ♓ 5' 4"
5 SU	20:55:47	6 50	25 46	18 4	0 ♏ 22	5 44	4 50	11 2	6 42	13 32	5 ♓ 5' 4"
6 MO	20:59:44	10 48	27 21	19 2	0 53	5 50	4 52	11 3	6 43	13 33	5 ♓ 5' 3"
7 TU	21: 3:40	14 53	28 56	19 59	1 24	5 55	4 54	11 3	6 43	13 33	5 ♓ 5' 3"
8 WE	21: 7:37	19 5	0 ♓ 32	20 57	1 54	6 0	4 55	11 4	6 44	13 33	5 ♓ 5' 3"
9 TH	21:11:33	23 25	2 7	21 54	2 25	6 6	4 57	11 4	6 44	13 34	5 ♓ 5' 3"
10 FR	21:15:30	27 53	3 42	22 52	2 56	6 11	4 59	11 5	6 44	13 34	5 ♓ 5' 3"
11 SA	21:19:26	2 ♓ 29	5 18	23 49	3 27	6 17	5 1	11 6	6 45	13 34	5 ♓ 5' 3"
12 SU	21:23:23	7 14	6 53	24 47	3 58	6 22	5 3	11 6	6 45	13 35	5 ♓ 5' 3"
13 MO	21:27:19	12 8	8 29	25 44	4 30	6 27	5 5	11 7	6 45	13 35	5 ♓ 5' 2"
14 TU	21:31:16	17 11	10 4	26 42	5 1	6 33	5 7	11 8	6 46	13 35	5 ♓ 5' 2"
15 WE	21:35:13	22 23	11 40	27 40	5 32	6 38	5 9	11 8	6 46	13 36	5 ♓ 5' 2"
16 TH	21:39: 9	27 44	13 15	28 37	6 3	6 43	5 11	11 9	6 46	13 36	5 ♓ 5' 2"
17 FR	21:43: 6	3 ♈ 14	14 51	29 35	6 34	6 49	5 13	11 10	6 47	13 36	5 ♓ 5' 2"
18 SA	21:47: 2	8 53	16 26	0 ♒ 33	7 6	6 54	5 15	11 10	6 47	13 37	5 ♓ 5' 2"
19 SU	21:50:59	14 40	18 2	1 31	7 37	6 59	5 17	11 11	6 47	13 37	5 ♓ 5' 2"
20 MO	21:54:55	20 35	19 37	2 28	8 9	7 5	5 18	11 12	6 48	13 37	5 ♓ 5' 2"
21 TU	21:58:52	26 37	21 13	3 26	8 40	7 10	5 20	11 12	6 48	13 38	5 ♓ 5' 1"
22 WE	22: 2:48	2 ♉ 44	22 49	4 24	9 12	7 15	5 22	11 13	6 49	13 38	5 ♓ 5' 1"
23 TH	22: 6:45	8 57	24 24	5 22	9 44	7 21	5 24	11 14	6 49	13 38	5 ♓ 5' 1"
24 FR	22:10:42	15 13	26 0	6 20	10 15	7 26	5 26	11 14	6 49	13 39	5 ♓ 5' 1"
25 SA	22:14:38	21 32	27 36	7 17	10 47	7 31	5 28	11 15	6 50	13 39	5 ♓ 5' 1"
26 SU	22:18:35	27 51	29 12	8 15	11 19	7 37	5 30	11 15	6 50	13 39	5 ♓ 5' 1"
27 MO	22:22:31	4 ♊ 10	0 ♈ 47	9 13	11 51	7 42	5 32	11 16	6 50	13 40	5 ♓ 5' 1"
28 TU	22:26:28	10 26	2 23	10 11	12 23	7 47	5 34	11 17	6 51	13 40	5 ♓ 5' 0"
29 WE	22:30:24	16 39	3 59	11 9	12 55	7 53	5 36	11 17	6 51	13 40	5 ♓ 5' 0"
30 TH	22:34:21	22 46	5 35	12 7	13 27	7 58	5 38	11 18	6 51	13 41	5 ♓ 5' 0"
31 FR	22:38:17	28 48	7 11	13 5	13 59	8 3	5 39	11 19	6 52	13 41	5 ♓ 5' 0"

INGRESSES :

3 ☿ → ♒ 5: 3
4 ♂ → ♏ 6:45
7 ♀ → ♓ 16: 4
10 ☿ → ♓ 11: 7
16 ☿ → ♈ 9:57
17 ⊕ → ♒ 10:21
21 ☿ → ♉ 13:18
26 ☿ → ♊ 8: 8
♀ → ♈ 12: 7
31 ☿ → ♋ 4:51

ASPECTS (HELIOCENTRIC +MOON(TYCHONIC)) :

1 ☿ S ☊ 10:39
2 ♀ S ☊ 13:19
3 ☿ □ ♂ 0:57
☽ ☌ ☿ 4:55
☽ ☌ ♆ 16:49
4 ☿ △ ♄ 11:31
☿ □ ♃ 17: 8
☿ ☌ ♆ 23:14
5 ☽ ☌ ♀ 3:58
6 ☽ ☌ ♅ 8:19
☿ ⚹ ♇ 16:14
8 ☽ ☍ ♄ 7: 8
9 ♀ △ ♂ 6:53
10 ☽ ☍ ♂ 16:31
☽ ☌ ♃ 22:34
11 ☿ △ ♂ 5:33
♀ ⚹ ♃ 15:40
☿ ⚹ ♃ 19:33
☿ ☌ ♀ 21:22
12 ☿ ☌ ♅ 19: 3
13 ☿ □ ♇ 6:57
14 ☽ ☍ ♇ 1: 6
♀ ☌ ♅ 16: 6
16 ☿ ⚹ ⊕ 4:45
♀ □ ♇ 5:15
♃ □ ♆ 15: 8
17 ☿ ☍ ♄ 8:30
♂ □ ♆ 9:29
♂ ☍ ♃ 12:59
☿ ⚹ ♆ 15: 8
18 ☽ ☍ ♆ 3:32
☿ △ ♇ 19:40
20 ☿ ☌ ☊ 11:55
☽ ☍ ♅ 15:13
21 ☽ ☍ ♀ 9:22
22 ☿ □ ⊕ 7:37
☽ ☌ ♄ 8:23
☿ □ ♆ 15:46
☿ ☌ ♃ 17:43
23 ⊕ △ ♄ 1: 3
☿ ☍ ♂ 3:14
☿ ⚹ ♅ 8:44
24 ⊕ ☌ ♆ 12:24
☽ ☍ ♃ 14:54
☽ ☌ ♂ 20:22
25 ☿ ☌ P 4:34
⊕ □ ♃ 6:20
♂ △ ♅ 21:21
26 ☽ ☍ ☿ 2:54
☿ ⚹ ♀ 6:48
27 ☽ ☌ ♇ 4:39
☿ △ ♄ 5:14
☿ △ ♆ 10:13
☿ △ ⊕ 22:51
28 ☿ □ ♅ 3:14
☿ ☍ ♇ 12:26
30 ♀ ☍ ♄ 0:40
♀ ⚹ ♆ 19:13
31 ☽ ☌ ♆ 1:41
⊕ ⚹ ♇ 14:54

is wisdom, and with this wisdom we can transform the etheric body into something eternal.

> We had to dive down completely into longing and desire and then emerge from it again like Hiram Abiff, bringing with him the Golden Triangle, which denotes the higher powers. Only then, after having converted our passions into piety and outwardly our soul-fire into beauty, would we be able to unite the pillars Jachin and Boaz. That is to say, we could raise ourselves up to wisdom and strength—buddhi and atman—because we had worked upon our karma spiritually.[47]

Lazarus had come to the borderline of the highest initiation in his previous incarnation as Hiram; and as Lazarus, during his time in the underworld between his death and his raising from the dead, he united with John the Baptist, and prepared himself to become the first initiated by Christ. Thus he crossed the borderline and entered an even higher stage of initiation.

In these days between now and the Sun remembrance of the Raising of Lazarus (August 22), we can imagine the powers of wisdom and strength, born through piety, that allow each of us passage through the underworld of our own soul. And, we can remember to receive the outer world as part of the inner world and take to heart the mutual healing now required of both the inner and outer worlds of the Earth and humanity. These are days to discover special reverence for our brothers and sisters indwelling Natura, and to engage in the work of catharsis—the purification that the beings of the constellation of Cancer call forth.

August 12: Sun 25½° Cancer: Birth of the Nathan Mary (17 July 17 BC). The Nathan Mary bore the vessel for the Logos. Purity and gentleness are remembered today. At this birth, Venus, Mars and Moon were all conjunct Regulus, the heart of the Lion, providing us a beautiful contemplation for the purity of heart we are all striving to attain.

August 14: ASPECT: Mars conjunct Saturn 29° Virgo. Saturn here remembers the first crusades, when Raymond of Toulouse led the crusaders

from Antioch to Jerusalem. There they scaled the walls and took the Holy City from the Fatimids. Aggressive forces (Mars) battled for Jerusalem as Saturn left Virgo and moved into Libra. Saturn will be in Libra for the remainder of this year, and Mars will be in Libra through September of this year. With both Mars and Saturn passing through Libra, the scales, we can pray for peace as the eternal balance between opposing points of view. Libra calls us to find equanimity as the fulcrum point through which Michaelic thoughts can find us. The taking of Jerusalem in our time is not an event in the physical world, but an event in the spiritual world whereby we remember (Saturn) the lofty heights from which we have fallen, due to the unruly forces within our astral (Mars) bodies.

ASPECT: Venus 12° Gemini, opposite Pluto 12° 19' Sagittarius: Venus remembers Jesus' teachings of three parables: the lost sheep (Luke 15:3–7), the lost coin (Luke 15:8-10), and the ten virgins (Matt. 25:1–13; *Chron.* p. 293).

> "The Lost Sheep": The great joy in the spiritual world toward those who have changed their heart and mind, over the ninety-nine righteous persons who think they need not change.
> "The Lost Coin": The great joy in the household of one who has recovered a missing piece of silver.
> "The Ten Virgins": The preparedness of soul necessary for the unknowable hour when Christ may appear.

These three parables remind us to be humbly mindful of our shortcomings, so that the one looking for us can find us; to rejoice when we discover lost treasures in our soul, for these make us whole; and to practice spiritual discipline, so if times of trial come, we have the fortitude to remain faithful.

Love seeks us, we seek our wholeness, and Love comes to unite with those practicing Love. Today Venus, the planet of love, stands across the sky from Divine Love (higher Pluto)—she is fully revealed to Phanes (higher Pluto). If we are too certain of our selves, if we do not seek lost parts of our soul or are wasteful with our soul's energy, and if we are lazy toward our spiritual practice,

---

47 Steiner, *Freemasonry and Ritual Work*, pp. 414–446.

we may find ourselves ill-prepared, disillusioned, and fragmented and it will be Hades (lower Pluto) who will knock upon our door.

Today with Mars conjunct Saturn and Venus opposite Pluto, we may find hidden treasures long lost that strengthen us in our pilgrimage toward the New Jerusalem—the peace-filled city of love.

August 15: ASPECT: Mars conjunct Saturn 29° Virgo. Opposite to today's conjunction (in Pisces) Saturn remembers the death of the prophetess Anna, and Mars remembers the death of John the Baptist. This conjunction foretells the necessity of learning how to perceive revelations in order to understand the work of John in our time. John is working to reveal the Sophia mysteries.

Mars enters Libra. Mars was in Libra during the three temptations in the wilderness through the end of the forty days. The constellation of Libra seeks what is real! Its virtue is equanimity. In equanimity the fulcrum is found. And it is the fulcrum that holds the balance between opposing forces. Through the fulcrum point, Michael speaks! The Word (Mars) made flesh, in the wilderness of temptation, held this fulcrum point by never once looking at the tempters, but rather did he keep his eyes on his Father in Heaven. This exemplifies the path before us as we are all collectively being tempted with the "false power and glory" that approaches ever more aggressively through the prince of this material world. "And being effects being."[48]

August 16: Saturn enters Libra. "In world enjoyment reposing" (Rudolf Steiner, *Twelve Moods of the Zodiac*). Saturn was in Libra at the conception and birth of the Solomon Mary. This is the Mary, referred to as the Virgin Mary, who in a previous life was the Queen of Sheba—she who was wiser even than Solomon. Saturn in Libra is square to where it was in the ninth century at the time of the Grail. Parsifal was to unite wisdom and love in order to gain entrance into the castle of the Grail, and it was through the pain of trials that he developed his wisdom:

What sort of time was it when Parsifal entered the Castle, where Amfortas lay wounded and on

Parsifal's arrival suffered unceasing pain from his wound? What was this time? The saga itself tells us—it was a Saturn time [when the forces of Saturn are especially strong]. Saturn and the Sun stood together in Cancer, approaching culmination.[49]

With Saturn entering Libra, our time is a time that is square to the Grail time. It is a time when the truth of wisdom creates tension in the world of materialism, and—simultaneously—balance and harmony are created in the souls of those seeking entrance into the mystery of the Grail.

August 17: New Moon 29° Cancer. The Moon was here when Jesus returned to Bethany the day before he raised Lazarus from the dead (25 July 32). Mary Solome, who was traveling with Jesus and the disciples, ran ahead to tell Martha and Mary Magdalene that Jesus was approaching. Jesus spoke to Martha:

"I Am the resurrection and the life. Whoever fills himself with my power through faith, he will live even when he dies; and whoever takes me into himself as his life, he is set free from the might of death in all earthly cycles of time. Do you feel the truth of these words?" And she said, "Yes, Lord. With my heart I have recognized that you are the Christ, the Son of God, who is coming into the world. (John 11:25–27)

The spiritual light of Christ filled Martha with faith and love. Martha was an empty vessel who served selflessly, and into her empty vessel (Moon) she received the light of Christ. This is a mighty contemplation for this New Moon in Cancer (selflessness). As the Sun and Moon leave Cancer, catharsis thus achieved becomes, in Leo, freedom.

August 17: Sun enters Leo: "Irradiate with senses' might" (Rudolf Steiner, *Twelve Moods of the Zodiac*). The first decan, ruled by Saturn, is associated with the faint constellation of Leo Minor, the Lesser Lion, above Leo and below the Great Bear. The virtue: Compassion becomes Freedom. This freedom is the foundation of the spiritualized "I."

---

48 Steiner, *Twelve Moods of the Zodiac* (no pg no.).

49 Steiner, *Christ and the Spiritual World*, p. 128.

August 21: Sun 2° Leo: Conversation at Jacob's Well (26 July 30). The zodiacal sign of Leo corresponds to the human heart. At this conversation the Samaritan woman's heart opened to receive Christ—he who was, is, and ever shall be the living waters of eternal life.

> Everyone who drinks of this water will become thirsty again, but whoever drinks of the water that I give him, his thirst shall be quenched during this aeon of time. The water that I give him will become in him a spring of the water flowing into true life. (John 4:13–14)

This woman, who was converted at the time of her conversation with Jesus at Jacob's Well, is named Dina the Samaritan, referred to in John 4:4–42. After her conversion, Dina joined the circle of holy women around the Blessed Virgin Mary and was one of the most industrious helpers in the community. Her two sons were later among the seventy-two disciples of Christ.[50]

As the Sun crests to its heart point (5° Leo—the star Regulus), we remember Dina, whose conscience was troubled owing to the dissolute life she had lived in Damascus earlier in her biography. The star beings of Leo tell us that "compassion becomes freedom." As we learn compassion our attention is freed from encapsulation within the self, and is transformed into the freedom to compassionately serve others.

August 22: Sun 3° Leo: The Raising of Lazarus (26 July 32).

> The raising of Lazarus was an archetypal event for humanity, demonstrating the possibility in the future, following Golgotha, for the human being to receive the breath of life from the creative source of the living Word, received as an initiatory breath from the etheric life-body of Christ Jesus. This was the octave of the baptism in the Jordan, wherein a new consciousness was to be born of water, understanding water as the physical agent of cleansing and the faithful bearer of vibratory imprint.
>
> The importance of the desert experience for the Israelites was a movement forward away from the Egyptian mystery tradition where the spiritual aspirant left the physical body during the three-day temple sleep to unite with the spiritual world, which could be born as an imprinting thereafter as a source of inspiration throughout life. In contrast the Israelite's mission under the guidance of Yahweh was to make a step forward, undertaking the work of calling down the spiritual world into the physical body—with the goal of bringing an imprint of the spiritual world into the "I" of the individual."[51]

Powell goes on to explain how the miracle of raising Lazarus was a "baptism by air," denoting a rebirth, after which the transformed consciousness of the one initiated develops the ability to work with conscience (a bestowal from the beings of Saturn), which is working with the spiritual world. How does this apply to us?

The miracle of raising Lazarus works irrespective of time and place, where what is forgotten is remembered, where what sleeps is awakened, and where what is dead is brought to life.

This is a day to listen for the world call to awaken from our sleep in the increasingly ominous illusions of materialism. Are we willing to be called from the grave of our entombment?

August 23: Sun 5° Regulus, the Lion's Heart. Regulus is one of the four Royal Stars of Persia.

> Already then in ancient Persia, Zarathustra spoke of the four royal stars as the four "foundation stones" of the zodiac—*Aldebaran*, the Bull's eye, the central star of the Bull; *Regulus*, the Lion's heart, shining from the breast of the Lion; *Antares*, the red-glowing Scorpion's heart, the central star of the Scorpion; and bright *Fomalhaut* in the mouth of the Southern Fish, beneath the stream of water flowing from the urn of the Waterman. (*CHA*, p. 16)

In the Foundation Stone meditation, given by Rudolf Steiner, the spirits of the elements in the East, West, North and South are to hear the prayer, and the beings in the cosmos above are "trigger points" for the directions mirrored upon the Earth below.

---

50 See Robert Powell, *Starlight*, spring 2011.

51 Powell, *Elijah Come Again*, p. 133.

Aldebaran: The Bull's eye is the watcher in the East—15° Taurus.

Antares: The Scorpion's heart is the watcher in the West—15 degree Scorpio.

Regulus: The Lion's heart is the watcher in the North—5° Leo.

Fomalhaut: The Southern Fish is the watcher in the South—9° Aquarius.

August 27: Sun enters the second decan of Leo, ruled by Jupiter and associated with the tail of the Great Bear, Ursa Major.

August 28: Sun 10½° Leo: The Healing of the Nobleman's Son (3 Aug 30) (John 4:46–54). In this second miracle of Christ, he healed the stream of heredity: The present worked back onto the past. Selathiel (the nobleman) had given himself to his king. He came to Christ to beg that his son Joel be healed. Joel had been adopted by his King, Zorobabel; even this he had given away. Selathiel was a kings-man. This meant he had to suppress his own "I" to serve his master's "I." This suppression weakens the "I." The weakness of the father's "I" created a physical weakness in the son's body. The boy's blood was too weak to carry an "I" and therefore his blood became inflamed. In his illness the boy constantly repeated: "Jesus, the prophet of Nazareth, alone can help me!" In desperation Selathiel rode to find Jesus. Jesus spoke: "Go, thy son liveth!" When Selathiel asked if this was really true, Jesus responded: "Believe me, in this very hour he has been cured." The nobleman's faith in Christ restored his "I" to uprightness, and healed his son. Jesus Christ gave the nobleman a new name. Instead of *basilikos* (King's man) he was called *pater* (father); he became "father of his own house." This fatherhood involves not only responsibility in the physical world, but also the appointment of being a spiritual authority in the home. This story teaches the absolute necessity of fathering children with spiritual authority. This healing reveals the fact of the power of the vertically aligned, Christ centered "I" over any horizontal influence in the hereditary stream. We may contemplate today where we may be compromising our true self with excuses born of some hereditary

story, or to gain favor with any powers of this world. Have we become a satellite of any person or bloodline, or collective body of thought? There is a great deal of reality being created by satellite-humans. Are we moons, or suns? Do we create, or are we puppets of another's creation? Are we taking up the responsibility of spiritually fathering our children?

August 30: ASPECT: Moon 1° Aquarius opposite Mercury 1° Leo: The Second Temptation in the Wilderness (28 Nov 29). Today's Moon remembers the second temptation, when Christ was tempted to plunge from the pinnacle of the temple. Mercury, the teacher and healer, asks that we not plunge, but rather esteem crystal clarity of mind and inbreathe spiritual light without any compromise of full consciousness.

August 31: Sun 12° Leo: Death of the Nathan Mary (5 Aug 12). "Not long after the event in the Temple at the Passover of AD 12, the Nathan Mary died. Rudolf Steiner describes how, seventeen years later, at the baptism in the Jordan, the Nathan Mary was spiritually united with the Solomon Mary" (*Chron.* p.116).

> At the moment when the baptism took place in the Jordan, the mother (the Solomon Mary), too, experienced something like the end of a transformation process. She felt—she was in her forty-fifth or forty-sixth year at the time—as if the soul of the mother of the Jesus child who had received the Zarathustra spirit in his twelfth year, the mother who had since died (the Nathan Mary), now entered her. The Christ spirit had come to Jesus of Nazareth, and the spirit of the other mother, who was then in the world of the spirit, had come to the stepmother with whom Jesus had the talk. From then on, she felt herself to be like the young mother who had borne the Jesus child of Luke's Gospel.[52]

The Nathan Mary comes as Grace for those who seek her.

ASPECT: Full Moon: Sun 13° Leo opposite Moon 13° Aquarius. This is the second Full Moon of this month, called a Blue Moon. This Moon

---

52 Steiner, *The Fifth Gospel*, p. 70.

falls very close to where the Sun was at the birth of Rudolf Steiner and Valentin Tomberg (14° Aquarius). The Sun opposite in the zodiac, at 13° Leo, remembers the death of the Nathan Mary referred to in the above commentary.

This Full Moon is cradled between Nathan Mary's death and the births of Rudolf Steiner and Valentin Tomberg—a cradle that rocks between innocent purity and great wisdom. We are led to find these qualities in ourselves, in others, and in the world of nature surrounding us all.

A Full Moon is a New Moon from the perspective of the angels. When full, the Moon is furthest from the Sun and empty of light from the cosmic perspective. During this time the angels are active in human dream life. The Full Moon works most strongly on the base of the spine, affecting the will and instinctual life in the subconscious.

This Blue Moon evokes the living stream of Anthroposophy and the birth of purified reflection: "The sign for Aquarius, which mirrors the etheric flow through the stars of the constellation, is represented by two undulating lines, one above the other—suggesting the early teachings of Hermes, "as above, so below," and the words given in the Lords Prayer, "On Earth as it is in Heaven," foretelling the birth of purified reflection" (Laquanna Paul and Robert Powell, *Cosmic Dances of the Zodiac*). With discretion and spiritual discernment we raise the "pleading cup" to the beings of the stars, seeking guidance through the perfected power of reflection. What thoughts may stand in the way of receiving this reflection?

SEPTEMBER 2012

The Sun begins in Leo and enters Virgo on the 17th. The waning Moon joins Jupiter in Taurus on the 8th and Venus on the 12th. The New Moon is on the 15th (Sun in Leo, Moon in Aquarius) and includes Mercury within the Sun's light. Two days later, the Moon catches up to Saturn and Mars the day after that—if they are not too close to the Sun to be seen—we'll see them in the western sky as the sunsets. Pluto stations

Direct on the 18th, retrograde since April. The Full Moon is on the 29th.

Sept. 1: Venus enters Cancer. "Create life warmth" (Rudolf Steiner, *Twelve Moods of the Zodiac*). Venus was in Cancer at the death of the Virgin Mary, at the conception of the Solomon Jesus, and at the birth of John the Baptist.

APSECT: Mercury 6° Leo, opposite Neptune 6° Aquarius: The Ascension of Christ. At this event heliocentric (perspective from the Sun) Mercury opposed Neptune very close to today's opposition. This aspect can cause a tremendous power of inspiration, as exemplified by the Ascension. At the Ascension, the inspiration of the Second Coming was enshrined into the spiritual atmosphere of the Earth as a promise for the future. This future has found us. May we find today the inspiration (Neptune) that brings healing forces (Mercury) to all whom we encounter, through the silence of meditative peace.

Sept. 2: ASPECT: Venus 1° Cancer, square Saturn 1° Libra: Heliocentric Venus was here at the Wedding of Cana (1 degree Cancer), and the Sun was here at the Baptism in the River Jordan (1 degree Libra). Bringing these star memories together, we could say that the "beautiful lady" Venus is imprinting human beings with the miracle of Divine Love, while Saturn remembers the One who brought this Love to Earth. In today's square, there may be a tension (individually or collectively) between the Christ-spirit of the Earth and the bond of Love weaving between all peoples. It is incumbent upon us to bring forth the highest manifestation of this square: conscious harmony within spiritual groups working toward the virtues of selflessness (Cancer) through equanimity (Libra).

Sept. 7: Sun enters third decan of Leo, ruled by Mars and associated with the constellation of the Hunting Dogs (Canes Venatici).

Sept. 8: Sun 20° Leo. Uranus was at 20° Leo at the conversion of Lucifer. Christ on the cross signified the Tree of Life, raised up for the first time on Earth since the expulsion of human beings from Paradise. God had set up his cross in the wilderness of the world, as the seed of redemption–a sign for all posterity. And it was this situation to which the planet Uranus (20° Leo) bore witness as it rose about two o'clock that afternoon. Lucifer, beholding the innocent Son of Man on the cross, was overcome by his guilt and underwent a profound conversion. This conversion can be conceived of as the beginning of the redemption of the Cosmic Lucifer (see *CHA*, "The Mystery of Golgotha"). Uranus brings lightning bolts to either illumine or destroy the works of human beings, depending upon their moral character.

> To arrive at Illumination, a subtle temptation must be met. Instead of thinking becoming a vehicle for divine truth, it can become "brilliant" and then "electrified." And there is a world of difference between an illumined person and a brilliant thinker. The brilliant thinker is able to combine thoughts to his own pleasing, to make everything conform to the way in which he wants to see things, whilst an illumined person is interested solely in divine truth, for which he sacrifices his personal viewpoints.[53]

The world is intricately woven with distortions of truth. Media is a vehicle through which brilliant thinkers can fashion mass opinion. When the truth is altered even just one degree, the arc of projection will cause it to miss its mark. This is a very good day to meditate on the uncompromising power of truth. How do we live it, and how do we protect our children from becoming pawns of the virtual world's brilliance? The heart is the great thinker and Uranus in Leo points us to this future potential. Negative Uranus works against this potential, luring human souls into virtual worlds sculpted by illusions. Can we sacrifice our attachment to our personal viewpoints so our minds can open to others as well as the mighty reality of Cosmic Thoughts?

Sept. 10: Sun 22° Leo: Death of the Virgin Mary (15 Aug 44). Anne Catherine's visions indicate that after the Ascension of Christ Jesus, Mary lived for three years in Jerusalem in a house on Mount Zion, and for another three years at the home of Lazarus in Bethany. After this she traveled with John the Evangelist to Ephesus. Under the cross Christ spoke to John: "Behold, your mother!" In the Gospel of John (19:27) we read: "And from that hour the Disciple took her to himself." Adhering to this command John stayed with the Blessed Virgin in Ephesus. Anne Catherine gives the following account:

> A short time before the Blessed Virgin's death, as she felt the approach of her reunion with her God, her Son, and her Redeemer, she prayed that there might be fulfilled what Jesus had promised to her in the house of Lazarus at Bethany on the day before his Ascension. It was shown to me in the spirit how at that time, when she begged him that she might not live for long in this vale of tears after he had ascended, Jesus told her in general what spiritual works she was to accomplish before her end on Earth. He told her, too, that in answer to her prayers the Apostles and several Disciples would be present at her death, and what she was to say to them and how she was to bless them...After the Blessed Virgin had prayed that the Apostles should come to her, I saw the call going forth to them in many different parts of the world....I saw all, the farthest as well as the nearest, being summoned by visions to come to the Blessed Virgin. (*LBVM*, pp. 363–364)

This is the great being who goes before us into future Jupiter evolution. She who was Eve, the mother of all, prepares the way. The Blessed Virgin helps all her children find their way home. We are encouraged to keep the light of goodness shining for all, and especially for the children. Today we remember to behold our common Mother—the Earth—and all her children, inclusive of her elemental beings.

ASPECT: Superior conjunction of Mercury with Sun, 22° Leo: Mercury was at this degree at the birth of the Nathan Mary, and the Sun was at this degree at the death of the Solomon Mary (Virgin Mary). The births and deaths of the Marys are today remembered, recalling the grace that befalls us when our wisdom is loving and our loving is filled with wisdom.

---

53 Powell, *Hermetic Astrology*, vol. 2, p. 312.

Sept. 15: New Moon 27° Leo: Jesus is healing and teaching in Capernaum.

> Just then a man in their synagogue who was possessed by an impure spirit cried out, "What do you want with us, Jesus of Nazareth? Have you come to destroy us? I know who you are—the Holy One of God!"
>
> "Be quiet!" said Jesus sternly. "Come out of him!" The impure spirit shook the man violently and came out of him with a shriek. (Mark 1: 23–26)

It may come to pass that an unclean spirit calls out against us from the soul of another. Then are we challenged with reaction in the place of response. Jesus *responds* with the conviction born of love. An unclean spirit calling out against us can only ruffle us if we too have an unclean spirit that draws in the uncleanliness of the other. With this scene unfolding at the degree of today's New Moon, we may reflect upon our reactive nature, and the beings behind reaction. When our spirits are clean we have the Moon under our feet: In the cosmic language of the soul, the Moon is underfoot at the time of the New Moon.

Sept. 17: Sun enters Virgo: "Behold Worlds, O soul!" (Rudolf Steiner, *Twelve Moods of the Zodiac*). The first decan ruled by the Sun, and associated with the constellation of the Cup (Crater): here we can think of the Grail chalice held by the Queen of Peace, represented by the Virgin. The virtue of Virgo: Courtesy becomes tactfulness of heart. The inner work of descent (Persephone) brings awareness of self-knowledge. Hydra "the Serpent" stretches its undulating life force throughout the entire region beneath Virgo.

Sun 0° 19' Virgo: The Moon (portal to both angels and demons) stood here at the beginning of the forty days in the wilderness. Anne Catherine describes how, during these forty days of temptation of Christ, he never once looked at his tempters. Instead he addressed himself directly to his Father in Heaven. This is a powerful example for humanity, who is now facing the united activity of the tempters on a global scale. May we remember to keep our attention on the in-streaming of

spiritual Light and Love! This is what guides us through the changes so very necessary in our time. What we attend will grow, and as the Sun enters Virgo, the sign of the Divine Sophia, we are to tend our garden gate. This means having proper boundaries. Our boundaries protect us and allow us to choose what shall enter and what shall leave. The "B" in eurythmy is the gesture for the constellation of Virgo. This gesture characterizes the forming of our essential cloak of protection. May we thus practice wrapping ourselves in the protecting mantle of Sophia. May we stand upon the serpent!

Sept. 18: Pluto stations at 12° Sagittarius 2: Pluto stands where it was at the death of John the Baptist. John (as the reincarnated Elijah) and Moses are the two witnesses to the Second Coming of Christ. John is considered as the second witness:

> The second witness, the reincarnated Elijah individuality serving now in a female form, as the *bearer of strength*, is bearing the strength of the feminine side of Christ. This can be understood in connection with Divine Sophia, as Sophia is the feminine counterpart of Christ.[54]

As John was the witness to the true light at the first coming, so also is John the witness to the true light at the Second Coming. Unlike the first coming, the Second Coming will be interwoven with the coming of Ahriman into physical incarnation:

> The important point is that at this time of the coming of the Antichrist,[55] Elijah, as one of the two witnesses, is incarnated and offers a powerful stream of inspiration to all who turn to her at this time. (Ibid., p. 187)

As Pluto stations at this point, amplifying this degree, we remember John's death. After his death he became the guardian of the Disciples of Christ, just as now this being is working as a kind of guardian for the disciples of Sophia.

ASPECT: Uranus 12° Pisces, square Pluto 12° Sagittarius 2: Uranus here remembers the Flight into Egypt. This "Flight" is a frequent star

---

54 Powell, *Elijah Come Again*, p. 187.

55 Note that the term *Antichrist* used in traditional Christianity is known as Ahriman–Satan in spiritual science.

SIDEREAL GEOCENTRIC LONGITUDES : SEPTEMBER 2012 Gregorian at 0 hours UT

DAY	☉	☽	☊	☿	♀	♂	♃	♄	♅	♆	♇
1 SA	14 ♌ 3	19 ♒ 9	4 ♏ 42R	4 ♌ 54	29 ♊ 6	10 ♎ 29	19 ♉ 40	1 ♎ 20	12 ♓ 42R	6 ♒ 37R	12 ♐ 6R
2 SU	15 1	2 ♓ 6	4 30	6 50	0 ♋ 9	11 9	19 46	1 26	12 40	6 36	12 6
3 MO	15 59	14 46	4 20	8 47	1 13	11 48	19 52	1 31	12 38	6 34	12 5
4 TU	16 58	27 8	4 13	10 44	2 17	12 27	19 58	1 37	12 36	6 33	12 5
5 WE	17 56	9 ♈ 16	4 8	12 41	3 21	13 7	20 4	1 43	12 34	6 31	12 5
6 TH	18 54	21 13	4 5	14 38	4 25	13 46	20 9	1 49	12 32	6 29	12 4
7 FR	19 52	3 ♉ 3	4 4	16 34	5 30	14 26	20 15	1 55	12 30	6 28	12 4
8 SA	20 50	14 51	4 5	18 30	6 35	15 6	20 20	2 1	12 28	6 26	12 4
9 SU	21 49	26 42	4 4	20 24	7 40	15 46	20 25	2 7	12 25	6 25	12 3
10 MO	22 47	8 ♊ 42	4 3	22 18	8 46	16 26	20 29	2 13	12 23	6 23	12 3
11 TU	23 45	20 57	4 0	24 11	9 52	17 6	20 34	2 19	12 21	6 22	12 3
12 WE	24 44	3 ♋ 30	3 54	26 3	10 58	17 46	20 38	2 26	12 19	6 20	12 3
13 TH	25 42	16 24	3 47	27 55	12 4	18 26	20 43	2 32	12 16	6 18	12 2
14 FR	26 40	29 43	3 37	29 45	13 10	19 7	20 47	2 38	12 14	6 17	12 2
15 SA	27 39	13 ♌ 24	3 26	1 ♍ 34	14 17	19 47	20 50	2 45	12 12	6 15	12 2
16 SU	28 37	27 26	3 16	3 22	15 23	20 28	20 54	2 51	12 10	6 14	12 2
17 MO	29 36	11 ♍ 43	3 7	5 9	16 30	21 8	20 58	2 57	12 7	6 12	12 2
18 TU	0 ♍ 35	26 10	3 0	6 55	17 37	21 49	21 1	3 4	12 5	6 11	12 2
19 WE	1 33	10 ♎ 41	2 55	8 39	18 45	22 30	21 4	3 10	12 2	6 10	12 2D
20 TH	2 32	25 9	2 53	10 23	19 52	23 11	21 7	3 17	12 0	6 8	12 2
21 FR	3 30	9 ♏ 32	2 53D	12 6	21 0	23 52	21 10	3 24	11 58	6 7	12 2
22 SA	4 29	23 45	2 53	13 48	22 8	24 33	21 12	3 30	11 55	6 5	12 2
23 SU	5 28	7 ♐ 48	2 54R	15 29	23 16	25 14	21 15	3 37	11 53	6 4	12 2
24 MO	6 27	21 40	2 53	17 8	24 24	25 55	21 17	3 44	11 51	6 3	12 3
25 TU	7 25	5 ♑ 21	2 50	18 47	25 32	26 37	21 19	3 50	11 48	6 1	12 3
26 WE	8 24	18 50	2 44	20 25	26 41	27 18	21 21	3 57	11 46	6 0	12 3
27 TH	9 23	2 ♒ 8	2 37	22 2	27 50	28 0	21 22	4 4	11 43	5 59	12 3
28 FR	10 22	15 13	2 28	23 38	28 58	28 41	21 24	4 11	11 41	5 57	12 4
29 SA	11 21	28 5	2 18	25 13	0 ♌ 8	29 23	21 25	4 18	11 38	5 56	12 4
30 SU	12 20	10 ♓ 44	2 9	26 48	1 17	0 ♏ 5	21 26	4 24	11 36	5 55	12 4

INGRESSES :

1 ☽ → ♓ 20: 4
♀ → ♋ 20:33
4 ☽ → ♈ 5:37
6 ☽ → ♉ 17:48
9 ☽ → ♊ 6:38
11 ☽ → ♋ 17:23
14 ☽ → ♌ 0:30
☿ → ♍ 3:21
16 ☽ → ♍ 4:20
17 ☉ → ♍ 9:51
18 ☽ → ♎ 6:20
20 ☽ → ♏ 8: 3
22 ☽ → ♐ 10:37
24 ☽ → ♑ 14:34
26 ☽ → ♒ 20: 7
28 ♀ → ♌ 21:23
29 ☽ → ♓ 3:35
♂ → ♏ 21:16

ASPECTS & ECLIPSES :

1 ☿ ☍ ♆ 21: 5
☉ □ ♇ 23: 7
2 ☽ ☌ ♅ 19:57
3 ♀ □ ♄ 7:43
4 ☽ ☍ ♄ 8:53
5 ☽ ☍ ♂ 8: 7
7 ☽ ☌ ☋ 2: 5
☽ ☌ A 5:57
☉ □ ♃ 10: 9
8 ☽ ☌ ♃ 11:12
☉ □ ☽ 13:14
9 ☿ □ ♃ 0: 2
10 ☽ ☍ ♇ 6:36
☉ ˢ♉ ☿ 12:28
12 ☽ ☌ ♀ 15:15
14 ☽ □ˢ ☊ 6:49
☽ ☍ ♆ 11:34
16 ☉ ☌ ☽ 2:10
☽ ☌ ☿ 11:26
17 ☽ ☍ ♅ 0:40
18 ☽ ☌ ♄ 11:29
19 ☽ ☌ P 2:45
♅ □ ♇ 4: 8
☽ ☌ ♂ 20:33
20 ☽ ☌ ☊ 12:51
☿ ☍ ♅ 22: 6
☿ □ ♇ 23: 6
21 ☽ ☍ ♃ 19:39
22 ☉ □ ☽ 19:40
23 ☽ ☌ ♇ 7:17
26 ☽ ☍ ♀ 15:26
27 ☽ ᴺ□ ☊ 0:51
☽ ☌ ♆ 6:59
♀ □ ♂ 8:51
29 ☉ ☍ ♅ 6:57
☉ □ ♇ 17:43
30 ☽ ☌ ♅ 1:39
☉ ☍ ☽ 3:18
♀ □ ☊ 16:25

SIDEREAL HELIOCENTRIC LONGITUDES : SEPTEMBER 2012 Gregorian at 0 hours UT

DAY	Sid. Time	☿	♀	⊕	♂	♃	♄	♅	♆	♇	Vernal Point
1 SA	22:42:14	4 ♋ 42	8 ♈ 47	14 ♒ 3	14 ♏ 31	8 ♉ 9	5 ♎ 41	11 ♓ 19	6 ♒ 52	13 ♐ 41	5 ♓ 5' 0"
2 SU	22:46:11	10 28	10 23	15 1	15 3	8 14	5 43	11 20	6 53	13 42	5 ♓ 5' 0"
3 MO	22:50: 7	16 5	11 59	15 59	15 35	8 19	5 45	11 21	6 53	13 42	5 ♓ 5' 0"
4 TU	22:54: 4	21 33	13 35	16 57	16 8	8 25	5 47	11 21	6 53	13 42	5 ♓ 4'59"
5 WE	22:58: 0	26 51	15 11	17 55	16 40	8 30	5 49	11 22	6 54	13 43	5 ♓ 4'59"
6 TH	23: 1:57	2 ♌ 0	16 47	18 54	17 13	8 35	5 51	11 23	6 54	13 43	5 ♓ 4'59"
7 FR	23: 5:53	6 59	18 23	19 52	17 45	8 41	5 53	11 23	6 54	13 43	5 ♓ 4'59"
8 SA	23: 9:50	11 48	19 59	20 50	18 18	8 46	5 55	11 24	6 55	13 44	5 ♓ 4'59"
9 SU	23:13:46	16 28	21 35	21 48	18 50	8 51	5 57	11 24	6 55	13 44	5 ♓ 4'59"
10 MO	23:17:43	20 59	23 11	22 47	19 23	8 57	5 59	11 25	6 55	13 44	5 ♓ 4'59"
11 TU	23:21:40	25 22	24 47	23 45	19 56	9 2	6 1	11 26	6 56	13 45	5 ♓ 4'59"
12 WE	23:25:36	29 36	26 24	24 43	20 28	9 7	6 2	11 26	6 56	13 45	5 ♓ 4'58"
13 TH	23:29:33	3 ♍ 43	28 0	25 42	21 1	9 13	6 4	11 27	6 56	13 45	5 ♓ 4'58"
14 FR	23:33:29	7 41	29 36	26 40	21 34	9 18	6 6	11 28	6 57	13 46	5 ♓ 4'58"
15 SA	23:37:26	11 33	1 ♉ 13	27 39	22 7	9 23	6 8	11 28	6 57	13 46	5 ♓ 4'58"
16 SU	23:41:22	15 19	2 49	28 37	22 40	9 29	6 10	11 29	6 58	13 46	5 ♓ 4'58"
17 MO	23:45:19	18 58	4 25	29 36	23 13	9 34	6 12	11 30	6 58	13 46	5 ♓ 4'58"
18 TU	23:49:15	22 31	6 2	0 ♓ 34	23 46	9 39	6 14	11 30	6 58	13 47	5 ♓ 4'58"
19 WE	23:53:12	25 59	7 38	1 33	24 19	9 45	6 16	11 31	6 59	13 47	5 ♓ 4'57"
20 TH	23:57: 9	29 23	9 15	2 31	24 53	9 50	6 18	11 32	6 59	13 47	5 ♓ 4'57"
21 FR	0: 1: 5	2 ♎ 41	10 51	3 30	25 26	9 55	6 20	11 32	6 59	13 48	5 ♓ 4'57"
22 SA	0: 5: 2	5 56	12 28	4 29	25 59	10 1	6 22	11 33	7 0	13 48	5 ♓ 4'57"
23 SU	0: 8:58	9 6	14 4	5 28	26 33	10 6	6 24	11 33	7 0	13 48	5 ♓ 4'57"
24 MO	0:12:55	12 13	15 41	6 26	27 6	10 11	6 25	11 34	7 0	13 49	5 ♓ 4'57"
25 TU	0:16:51	15 17	17 17	7 25	27 40	10 16	6 27	11 35	7 1	13 49	5 ♓ 4'57"
26 WE	0:20:48	18 18	18 54	8 24	28 13	10 22	6 29	11 35	7 1	13 49	5 ♓ 4'56"
27 TH	0:24:44	21 16	20 31	9 23	28 47	10 27	6 31	11 36	7 2	13 50	5 ♓ 4'56"
28 FR	0:28:41	24 11	22 7	10 22	29 20	10 32	6 33	11 37	7 2	13 50	5 ♓ 4'56"
29 SA	0:32:38	27 5	23 44	11 20	29 54	10 38	6 35	11 37	7 2	13 50	5 ♓ 4'56"
30 SU	0:36:34	29 57	25 21	12 19	0 ♐ 28	10 43	6 37	11 38	7 3	13 51	5 ♓ 4'56"

INGRESSES :

5 ☿ → ♌ 14:36
12 ☿ → ♍ 2:17
14 ♀ → ♉ 5:55
17 ⊕ → ♓ 9:57
20 ☿ → ♎ 4:28
29 ♂ → ♐ 4: 6
30 ☿ → ♏ 0:29

ASPECTS (HELIOCENTRIC +MOON(TYCHONIC)) :

1 ☿ □ ♄ 4: 6
☿ ⚹ ♃ 14:30
☿ □ ♀ 23:30
2 ⊕ □ ♂ 1:53
☿ △ ♅ 3:40
☽ ☌ ♅ 17:27
☿ △ ♂ 21:38
4 ♀ △ ♇ 1:53
☿ ᴺ□ ☊ 9: 2
☽ ☍ ♄ 17: 6
5 ☽ ☌ ♀ 13:39
6 ☿ ⚹ ♄ 18:36
☿ ☍ ♆ 23:38
7 ☿ □ ♃ 8:31
☽ ☌ ♃ 11:32
8 ☽ ☍ ♂ 7:20
☿ △ ♇ 9:47
9 ♀ ⚹ ⊕ 8:21
☿ □ ♂ 14: 9
10 ☽ ☍ ♇ 9:56
☿ ☍ ⊕ 12:28
☿ △ ♀ 18:55
14 ☿ △ ♃ 10: 7
☽ ☍ ♆ 12:46
☿ ☍ ♅ 23:28
15 ☿ □ ♇ 14: 2
16 ☽ ☍ ♅ 23:37
17 ☽ ☌ ☿ 16: 1
18 ☿ ⚹ ♂ 10:10
♀ □ ♆ 14: 8
☽ ☌ ♄ 16:41
20 ♀ ☌ ♃ 9:17
21 ☽ ☍ ♃ 0:39
☽ ☍ ♀ 2:29
♀ ⚹ ♅ 10:17
22 ☿ ☌ ♄ 3:16
☽ ☌ ♂ 3:56
☿ △ ♆ 8: 1
23 ☽ ☌ ♇ 10:21
24 ☿ ⚹ ♇ 12:28
27 ☽ ☌ ♆ 8:55
☿ ☌ ☋ 18:51
♀ ☌ ☊ 20:21
28 ⊕ ⚹ ♃ 4:52
29 ⊕ ☌ ♅ 6:57
30 ☽ ☌ ♅ 1:43

memory this year. With Pluto amplifying the death of John the Baptist, and Uranus remembering the "Flight," an intensity may be brewing between the future stream of the John being—speaking through the starry worlds of Wisdom Sophia—and the materialistic intentions of Hades (lower Pluto), who would want John's revelatory stream to be "beheaded" in favor of dogmatism, cynicism, and intellectualism. The opportunity before us is to overcome the lower Uranus nature in order to become illumined through the mysteries of John in our time. As noted previously:

> To arrive at Illumination, a subtle temptation must be met. Instead of thinking becoming a vehicle for divine truth, it can become "brilliant" and then "electrified." And there is a world of difference between an illumined person and a brilliant thinker. The brilliant thinker is able to combine thoughts to his own pleasing, to make everything conform to the way in which he wants to see things, whilst an illumined person is interested solely in divine truth, for which he sacrifices his personal viewpoints.[56]

Today illuminations are brought to consciousness through tension, as Pluto stalls at John's death. We can be like Herod and behead John, or we can be like the Disciples and open our hearts to the teachings of John working and weaving between us.

Sept. 20: ASPECT: Mercury 12° Virgo, opposite Uranus 12° Pisces: Mercury is where it was at the Baptism of Christ. Mercury now stands opposed to Uranus. Mercury, the messenger of the gods, is "grailing" for the true Intelligence of the Cosmos (Uranus), whose outer aspect comes to manifestation in the light of the starry heavens—and this light of the starry heavens is the dwelling place of what Orphic cosmology calls Ouranos. Just as Jesus received the Light of the World at the Baptism, so today does Mercury face Uranus with the objective of longing to be permeated with the light of Cosmic Intelligence. Inversely, Mercury attuned to the brain-bound intellect is a robber and thief

of all that is holy and otherworldly. Practice an open mind.

Sept. 26: Sun 9° Virgo: The Raising of Nazor (1 Sept 32). See commentary for July 30, where the significance of this raising is brought into practical application for the work of our time.

Sept. 27: ASPECT: Venus 28° Cancer, square Mars 28° Libra: Venus and Mars were squared during the temptations in the wilderness. During this time Christ spoke to his Father in Heaven through a language that was inwardly deepened and full of soul. This is an aspect of Mars and Venus squared: Words (Mars) are deepened and filled with soul (Venus). This can be practiced today under this influence. Inversely, words can be filled with fallen soul qualities, thus bringing harm to the soul through misuse of the word. With this aspect we seek equanimity (Libra) in our words, and purity (Cancer) in our hearts.

Sept. 28: Sun enters the second decan of Virgo, ruled by Mercury and associated with the constellation of Corvus the Raven, the messenger of Apollo and the bird that fed the prophet Elijah (I Kings 17:3).

Venus enters Leo. "Existing grounds of worlds."[57] Venus was in Leo at both the birth of the Virgin Mary and the Nathan Mary, and at the raising of Lazarus.

Sept. 29: Sun 12° Virgo: Healing of Mara the Suphanite (4 Sept 30).

> She was converted through her encounter with Jesus Christ in the town of Ainon. She was wealthy and came from the region of Supha in the land of the Moabites, who were descendants of Lot. Because she was from the region of Supha, she was called the Suphanite. Her Jewish husband, who lived in Damascus, had rejected her because she had had four lovers, one after the other. Through these liaisons she had given birth to three children—a son and two daughters, all born out of wedlock. Filled with remorse and anguish, she had lived in Ainon for some time. She tried to live

---

56 Powell, *Hermetic Astrology*, vol. 2, p. 312.

57 Steiner, *Twelve Moods of the Zodiac* (n/p).

an exemplary life. Hearing the preaching of John the Baptist against adultery had intensified her sense of wanting to do penance. Nevertheless, she became possessed from time to time, as was the case when Jesus arrived in Ainon. He freed her of the demonic influence and blessed her three illegitimate children. Following Mara's conversion Dina and Seraphia (Veronica) welcomed her warmly into the circle of holy women.[58]

ASPECT: Full Moon: Sun 12° Virgo opposite Moon 12° Pisces: This Full Moon remembers the conception of the Nathan Jesus (6 Mar 2 BC). Anne Catherine Emmerich describes the scene as Mary stood before the Angel Gabriel who filled the room with an infusion of light. Mary, in her awe and wonder said to the angel: "Behold, I am the handmaid of the Lord; let it be done to me according to your word" (Luke 1:38). This Annunciation to Mary, by the Angel Gabriel, accompanied the conception of the Nathan Jesus child.

The Annunciation came unto Mary, for she was empty, having given herself over to the will of the Lord. Into her pure womb came the spiritual essence of the Jesus child. This Full Moon asks us to ponder where our personal will may be blocking the gifts our angels long to bestow. With the Moon in Pisces, the Queen of the night will be shining the light of love into open human hearts. The day before, the day of, and the day after the Full Moon are times to empty ourselves through giving; and in this emptiness we may pray to be touched by an angel.

ASPECT: Mars enters Scorpio. "In growth activity persists."[59] Mars was in Scorpio at the birth of the Nathan Jesus, the wedding at Cana, and the flight into Egypt.

OCTOBER 2012

The Sun begins in Leo and enters Virgo on the 17th. The waning Moon joins Jupiter in Taurus

on the 8th and Venus on the 12th. The New Moon is on the 15th and includes Mercury within the Sun's light. Two days later, the Moon catches up to Saturn and Mars the day after that; if they are not too close to the Sun to be seen, we'll see them in the western sky as the Sun sets. The Full Moon is on the 29th.

October 3: Sun 16° Virgo: Birth of Solomon Mary (7 Sept 21BC). The Solomon Mary is the one referred to as the Blessed Virgin Mary, who is the mother of the Master Jesus (the reincarnated Zarathustra individuality). This Mary can be considered the mother of humanity who once incarnated as the Queen of Sheba. This is the one referred to in Matthew 12:42: "The Queen of the South will rise at the judgment with this generation and condemn it; for she came from the ends of the Earth to listen to Solomon's wisdom, and now one greater than Solomon is here." The "Queen of the South" refers to the Queen of Sheba—Queen of the Sabian star gazing people—that is today the region called Yemen. The judgement in which she shall participate, according to the above passage, will not be the judgment from the spiritual world upon the generations, but rather will it be the self-imposed judgment of those who cannot stand before the light of spirit and therefore turn away due to the burden of their own guilt. In remembrance of the Blessed Virgin Mary we may contemplate our willingness to stand in the light and be seen, as well as our willingness to remember the living beings of the stars, as was the practice of the Queen from the South so long ago. The Virgin Mary and Sophia (Virgo) patiently wait as the dawning of lost star wisdom now awakens—Christianized—as our guide into the Light of spiritual remembrance. May we stand in honest self-reflection.

ASPECT: Venus 5° Leo opposite Neptune 5° Aquarius. Venus is conjunct the heart of the Lion (Leo). Venus and Neptune were in opposition (close to today's degree) at the attempted murder of Jesus:

At the close of the Sabbath, when Jesus came out of the synagogue, he was immediately surrounded by about twenty Pharisees. They began to lead him out of the town toward a nearby hill, for they intended to cast him down from

---

58 Powell, "The Holy Women at Christ's Death and Resurrection," *Starlight*, spring 2011.
59 Steiner, *Twelve Moods of the Zodiac* (n/p).

the brow of the hill. Suddenly, however, Jesus stopped, stood still, and with the help of angelic beings passed–as if invisible–through the midst of the crowd to his escape. (*Chron.* p. 241)

The sphere of Venus holds the beings of the Archai—the Time Spirits, who stand guard over the harmony of great evolutionary cycles. There are fallen archai beings who fight against the natural course of evolution and seek to destroy harmony through introducing violence and degenerate sexuality into a culture. Neptune is the sphere of inspiration where the Cosmic Soul is able to inspire the human soul in order to bring harmony into the personal feeling nature. Inversely, negative Neptune creates a magnetic field of hatred for all that is good, noble, charitable, and loving, and this magnetic field holds a sucking force of sympathy toward all that is egoistical in human nature. With Venus in Leo opposite Neptune in Aquarius, we find Venus asking if we have a peaceful heart (Leo), and Neptune asking if the source of our inspiration is the angelic realm of the Holy Spirit (Aquarius). We stand as witnesses before a culture that has adjusted itself to violence and sexuality as if it were caught in a magnetic field of attraction. What can we do today that serves the loving nature of Venus working on behalf of the World Soul, Sophia, in the light of the Holy Spirit?

As today remembers the birth of the Blessed Virgin Mary and the attempted murder of Jesus, we are offered eyes to see what is working in the world that stems from fallen realms. If we allow the murder of decency, we will become burdened with our own guilt in the silent depths of our soul, and may turn from the spiritual world's gaze in self-hatred that renders us feeling unworthy of love. The truth is that we are loved just as we are and we need shake off any illusion to the contrary.

October 4: Son 17° Virgo: Conception of John the Baptist (9 Sept 3 BC). This is a day to celebrate the presence of the John being in our time, as the guide and protector of those seeking to awaken to the apocalyptic challenges we are facing. Just as John came before Herod and was beheaded, so too are we facing a type of Herod in the collective

activity of a world-wide, power-based, dominating system—a system that fragments the spiritual capacities of the human nerve/sense system—resulting in a kind of beheading of our individuality. This means that the personality loses its hold on itself and sinks down rather than lifting itself into spiritual worlds. Rudolf Steiner saw how the third temptation (related to money) would play out in the future through the economic sphere:

This may be illustrated by the most mundane things. I could prove it to you, for example, in the details of the development of the banking system in the second half of the nineteenth century. Perhaps it is only for future historians to show clearly that a fundamental change then came about, which we may describe by saying that in banking affairs the personality was gradually shattered. I should have to draw your attention to the time when the four Rothschilds went out into the world from Frankfurt, one to Vienna, another to Naples, the third to London, the fourth to Paris. The whole banking system was then brought into a personal sphere by the personal talent directed to it. The personality immersed itself in finance. Today you see banking affairs becoming impersonal. Capital is passing into the hands of joint stock companies; it is no longer managed by the individual personality. Capital is beginning to control itself.

Now the personality may save itself and ascend again. It can save itself, for example, by really learning to strengthen its inner soul-forces and depend upon itself and make itself independent of the objective forces of capital. But the personality may also throw itself into these forces; it may in a certain way sail into and plunge into the abyss by allowing itself to be ensnared by the forces active in capital.[60]

Astonishing insight was delivered by Steiner in 1908. Consider how one hundred years later, in 2008, the banking system began to crash. Where do we turn? We may turn to the John stream working in the world in collaboration with the Grail stream—as a source for strengthening our inner soul-forces. There is a new culture coming into being and we are to align with John as servants of

---

60 Steiner, *The Apocalypse of St. John*, p. 123.

these new cultural impulses. We are not to become beheaded, as was John, but rather are we to lift our thoughts into spiritual heights. Are we free from the "objective forces of capital"? This question has everything to do with the third temptation in the wilderness—the temptation to turn stones into bread. This is a very real and practical question to be pondered. With the Sun remembering John's conception in Virgo, we can surround ourselves with the protective "B" gesture that in eurythmy accompanies the constellation of the Virgin, and from this place of inner peace we may open ourselves to receive guidance. Are we free from the beings who works through greed and fear?

October 5: Mercury conjunct Saturn 5° Libra: The healing of the blind youth Manahem (6 Oct 30). Heliocentric Mercury remembers the youth, Manahem, who had the gift of prophecy. "Human souls living in paradise prior to the Fall saw spiritually beholding the world as a revelation of God. But with the Fall a transformation of humanity's seeing took place, whereby the eyes of human beings were opened, and henceforth they saw the "bare facts" of the world without the illumination of God. They no longer saw the world as an expression of God, which is spiritual seeing, but for its own sake, estranged from God, which is ordinary seeing. Manahem did not want to see this God-estranged world, and by being born blind he retained spiritual seeing. For, generally, either the external world is seen in an illusory way, which is the tendency of the left eye, or in a God-less way, which is the tendency of the right eye, or in the case of blindness the outer world is not seen at all, which gives the possibility of seeing with the third eye, the spiritual organ located in the region of the forehead between the right and left eye. Manahem's blindness meant he saw only with the third eye" (CHA, *The Sun Chronicle in the Life of the Messiah*).

If, like Manahem, we were willing to see the world through our third eye, we would see the world united with its archetypes, and this would reveal all truth. With Mercury conjunct Saturn at the place of this healing, our conscience (Saturn) may be stirred to see the world in its true light. As we evolve we will accomplish this seeing, and we

will find the illusions of the power-mongers deflate before the glory of the Light of the World. Today is a good day to practice seeing God in all things, through the God-like seed in us. Who is looking through my eyes?

October 7: Sun enters third decan of Virgo, ruled by Venus and associated with Hydra the Serpent. Here it is the tail of the Serpent, and the Biblical image is of the Woman standing upon the serpent (Gen. 3:15). Likewise, the Chinese goddess of mercy Kwan-Yin is depicted riding upon a dragon. For the Chinese, Sophia is Kwan-Yin.

ASPECT: Mars 5° 46' Scorpio square Neptune 5° 46' Aquarius: The Wedding at Cana (28 Dec 29). Mars is where it was at this wedding, when the Divine Love of the Father descended, through the Son, for the renewal of humanity's union with spirit—a marriage between heaven and Earth, between one heart and another, regardless of race, religion, or creed. With Mars square to Neptune we are called to govern the temptation to fall into the illusion of separateness based on egoism. Our words (Mars) will reveal our inner state of harmony (Neptune). May we speak words that create peace. May we stand upon the serpent!

October 10: Sun 23° Virgo: The Little Transfiguration (16 Sept 29). Here we find Jesus walking with Eliud, who was one of the best-instructed of the Essenians. "Around midnight, Jesus said to Eliud that he would reveal himself, and—turning toward heaven—he prayed. A cloud of light enveloped them both and Jesus became radiantly transfigured. Eliud stood still, utterly entranced. After a while, the light melted away, and Jesus resumed his steps, followed by Eliud, who was speechless at what he had beheld" (*Chron.* pp. 197–198).

In this "Little Transfiguration" Jesus reveals himself to his friend and confident, Eliud, who did not live to see the Crucifixion. The light encompasses Eliud as well as Christ. Perhaps there is a story here for us. Perhaps we are encouraged to be Eliuds ourselves, and walk with Christ. With the Sun in Virgo, the constellation representing Sophia, we may contemplate our willingness to trust our intuitive nature, and practice our "tactfulness

SIDEREAL GEOCENTRIC LONGITUDES : OCTOBER 2012 Gregorian at 0 hours UT

DAY	☉	☽	☊	☿	♀	♂	♃	♄	♅	♆	♇
1 MO	13 ♍ 19	23 ♓ 10	2 ♏ 2R	28 ♍ 21	2 ♌ 26	0 ♏ 47	21 ♉ 27	4 ♎ 31	11 ♓ 34R	5 ♒ 53R	12 ♐ 5
2 TU	14 18	5 ♈ 22	1 56	29 54	3 35	1 29	21 27	4 38	11 31	5 52	12 5
3 WE	15 17	17 24	1 53	1 ♎ 25	4 45	2 11	21 28	4 45	11 29	5 51	12 6
4 TH	16 16	29 18	1 52	2 56	5 55	2 53	21 28	4 52	11 26	5 50	12 6
5 FR	17 15	11 ♉ 6	1 52D	4 26	7 5	3 35	21 28R	4 59	11 24	5 49	12 6
6 SA	18 14	22 52	1 54	5 55	8 15	4 17	21 28	5 6	11 22	5 48	12 7
7 SU	19 13	4 ♊ 43	1 55	7 24	9 25	5 0	21 27	5 13	11 19	5 47	12 8
8 MO	20 12	16 42	1 56	8 51	10 35	5 42	21 27	5 21	11 17	5 46	12 8
9 TU	21 11	28 55	1 56R	10 18	11 46	6 24	21 26	5 28	11 14	5 44	12 9
10 WE	22 11	11 ♋ 26	1 54	11 44	12 56	7 7	21 25	5 35	11 12	5 43	12 9
11 TH	23 10	24 21	1 50	13 9	14 7	7 50	21 24	5 42	11 10	5 42	12 10
12 FR	24 9	7 ♌ 41	1 46	14 33	15 18	8 33	21 22	5 49	11 7	5 42	12 11
13 SA	25 9	21 28	1 40	15 56	16 29	9 15	21 21	5 56	11 5	5 41	12 12
14 SU	26 8	5 ♍ 40	1 34	17 18	17 40	9 58	21 19	6 3	11 3	5 40	12 12
15 MO	27 8	20 14	1 29	18 39	18 51	10 41	21 17	6 11	11 0	5 39	12 13
16 TU	28 7	5 ♎ 2	1 26	19 59	20 3	11 24	21 14	6 18	10 58	5 38	12 14
17 WE	29 7	19 56	1 24	21 17	21 14	12 8	21 12	6 25	10 56	5 37	12 15
18 TH	0 ♎ 6	4 ♏ 50	1 23D	22 35	22 25	12 51	21 9	6 32	10 54	5 36	12 16
19 FR	1 6	19 34	1 24	23 51	23 37	13 34	21 7	6 39	10 51	5 36	12 17
20 SA	2 6	4 ♐ 5	1 25	25 6	24 49	14 18	21 4	6 47	10 49	5 35	12 18
21 SU	3 5	18 18	1 26	26 19	26 1	15 1	21 0	6 54	10 47	5 34	12 19
22 MO	4 5	2 ♑ 13	1 27	27 31	27 13	15 45	20 57	7 1	10 45	5 33	12 20
23 TU	5 5	15 48	1 27R	28 41	28 25	16 28	20 53	7 8	10 43	5 33	12 21
24 WE	6 4	29 6	1 25	29 49	29 37	17 12	20 50	7 16	10 41	5 32	12 22
25 TH	7 4	12 ♒ 6	1 22	0 ♏ 55	0 ♍ 49	17 56	20 46	7 23	10 38	5 32	12 23
26 FR	8 4	24 52	1 19	1 58	2 1	18 39	20 42	7 30	10 36	5 31	12 24
27 SA	9 4	7 ♓ 25	1 15	2 59	3 13	19 23	20 37	7 38	10 34	5 31	12 25
28 SU	10 4	19 46	1 11	3 57	4 26	20 7	20 33	7 45	10 32	5 30	12 26
29 MO	11 4	1 ♈ 56	1 9	4 51	5 38	20 51	20 28	7 52	10 30	5 30	12 28
30 TU	12 4	13 58	1 7	5 42	6 51	21 35	20 23	7 59	10 28	5 29	12 29
31 WE	13 3	25 53	1 6	6 29	8 4	22 20	20 18	8 6	10 26	5 29	12 30

INGRESSES :

1	☽ → ♈	13:23	21	☽ → ♑	20: 8
2	☿ → ♎	1:40	24	☽ → ♒	1:39
4	☽ → ♉	1:26		☿ → ♏	3:57
6	☽ → ♊	14:28		♀ → ♍	7:45
9	☽ → ♋	2: 6	26	☽ → ♓	9:45
11	☽ → ♌	10:16	28	☽ → ♈	20: 9
13	☽ → ♍	14:29	31	☽ → ♉	8:20
15	☽ → ♎	15:52			
17	☽ → ♏	16:12			
	☉ → ♎	21:25			
19	☽ → ♐	17:12			

ASPECTS & ECLIPSES :

1	☽ ☍ ☿	11:37		☉ □ ☽	7:33	18	☽ ☌ ♂	13:41	29	☽ ☍ ♄	11:54
	☽ ☍ ♄	22:31	11	☽ S ☊	13:30	19	☽ ☍ ♃	2:31		☿ □ ♆	17:38
2	♂ ☌ ☊	14:37		☽ ☍ ♆	20:27	20	☽ ☌ ♇	13:48		☉ ☍ ☽	19:49
3	♀ ☍ ♆	22:19	12	☽ ☌ ♀	14:36	22	☉ □ ☽	3:31	31	☽ ☌ ☋	10:33
4	☽ ☌ ☋	5:13	14	☽ ☍ ♅	8:53	24	☽ N ☊	4:14		☽ ☍ ☿	22:54
	☽ ☍ ♂	7:44	15	☉ ☌ ☽	12: 2		☽ ☌ ♆	11:48			
5	☽ ☌ A	0:39	16	☽ ☌ ♄	2: 3	25	☉ ☌ ♄	8:34			
	☿ ☌ ♄	9:39		♀ □ ♃	23:22		☿ ☌ ☊	9:45			
	☽ ☌ ♃	21: 7	17	☽ ☌ P	0:49	26	☽ ☍ ♀	15: 4			
7	☽ ☍ ♇	14:53		☽ ☌ ☿	2:23	27	☽ ☌ ♅	6: 4			
8	♂ □ ♆	1:58		☽ ☌ ☊	18:26	28	♂ ☍ ♃	12:34			

SIDEREAL HELIOCENTRIC LONGITUDES : OCTOBER 2012 Gregorian at 0 hours UT

DAY	Sid. Time	☿	♀	⊕	♂	♃	♄	♅	♆	♇	Vernal Point
1 MO	0:40:31	2 ♏ 47	26 ♉ 58	13 ♓ 18	1 ♐ 2	10 ♉ 48	6 ♎ 39	11 ♓ 39	7 ♒ 3	13 ♐ 51	5 ♓ 4'56"
2 TU	0:44:27	5 35	28 34	14 17	1 36	10 54	6 41	11 39	7 3	13 51	5 ♓ 4'56"
3 WE	0:48:24	8 22	0 ♊ 11	15 16	2 10	10 59	6 43	11 40	7 4	13 52	5 ♓ 4'55"
4 TH	0:52:20	11 9	1 48	16 15	2 44	11 4	6 45	11 41	7 4	13 52	5 ♓ 4'55"
5 FR	0:56:17	13 55	3 25	17 14	3 18	11 10	6 46	11 41	7 4	13 52	5 ♓ 4'55"
6 SA	1: 0:13	16 40	5 2	18 14	3 52	11 15	6 48	11 42	7 5	13 53	5 ♓ 4'55"
7 SU	1: 4:10	19 24	6 39	19 13	4 26	11 20	6 50	11 42	7 5	13 53	5 ♓ 4'55"
8 MO	1: 8: 7	22 9	8 16	20 12	5 1	11 26	6 52	11 43	7 5	13 53	5 ♓ 4'55"
9 TU	1:12: 3	24 54	9 53	21 11	5 35	11 31	6 54	11 44	7 6	13 54	5 ♓ 4'55"
10 WE	1:16: 0	27 39	11 30	22 11	6 9	11 36	6 56	11 44	7 6	13 54	5 ♓ 4'55"
11 TH	1:19:56	0 ♐ 24	13 7	23 10	6 44	11 41	6 58	11 45	7 7	13 54	5 ♓ 4'54"
12 FR	1:23:53	3 10	14 44	24 9	7 18	11 47	7 0	11 46	7 7	13 55	5 ♓ 4'54"
13 SA	1:27:49	5 57	16 21	25 9	7 53	11 52	7 2	11 46	7 7	13 55	5 ♓ 4'54"
14 SU	1:31:46	8 46	17 59	26 8	8 27	11 57	7 4	11 47	7 8	13 55	5 ♓ 4'54"
15 MO	1:35:42	11 35	19 36	27 8	9 2	12 3	7 6	11 48	7 8	13 56	5 ♓ 4'54"
16 TU	1:39:39	14 26	21 13	28 7	9 37	12 8	7 7	11 48	7 8	13 56	5 ♓ 4'54"
17 WE	1:43:36	17 19	22 50	29 7	10 11	12 13	7 9	11 49	7 9	13 56	5 ♓ 4'54"
18 TH	1:47:32	20 14	24 27	0 ♈ 6	10 46	12 19	7 11	11 50	7 9	13 57	5 ♓ 4'53"
19 FR	1:51:29	23 10	26 5	1 6	11 21	12 24	7 13	11 50	7 9	13 57	5 ♓ 4'53"
20 SA	1:55:25	26 10	27 42	2 5	11 56	12 29	7 15	11 51	7 10	13 57	5 ♓ 4'53"
21 SU	1:59:22	29 12	29 19	3 5	12 31	12 35	7 17	11 51	7 10	13 58	5 ♓ 4'53"
22 MO	2: 3:18	2 ♑ 17	0 ♋ 57	4 5	13 6	12 40	7 19	11 52	7 11	13 58	5 ♓ 4'53"
23 TU	2: 7:15	5 25	2 34	5 4	13 41	12 45	7 21	11 53	7 11	13 58	5 ♓ 4'53"
24 WE	2:11:11	8 37	4 11	6 4	14 16	12 50	7 23	11 53	7 11	13 59	5 ♓ 4'53"
25 TH	2:15: 8	11 53	5 49	7 4	14 52	12 56	7 25	11 54	7 12	13 59	5 ♓ 4'52"
26 FR	2:19: 5	15 13	7 26	8 4	15 27	13 1	7 27	11 55	7 12	13 59	5 ♓ 4'52"
27 SA	2:23: 1	18 37	9 4	9 4	16 2	13 6	7 28	11 55	7 12	14 0	5 ♓ 4'52"
28 SU	2:26:58	22 6	10 41	10 3	16 37	13 12	7 30	11 56	7 13	14 0	5 ♓ 4'52"
29 MO	2:30:54	25 40	12 19	11 3	17 13	13 17	7 32	11 57	7 13	14 0	5 ♓ 4'52"
30 TU	2:34:51	29 20	13 56	12 3	17 48	13 22	7 34	11 57	7 13	14 1	5 ♓ 4'52"
31 WE	2:38:47	3 ♒ 5	15 34	13 3	18 24	13 28	7 36	11 58	7 14	14 1	5 ♓ 4'52"

INGRESSES :

2	♀ → ♊	21:12
10	☿ → ♐	20:28
17	⊕ → ♈	21:31
21	☿ → ♑	6:16
	♀ → ♋	10: 1
30	☿ → ♒	4:19

ASPECTS (HELIOCENTRIC +MOON(TYCHONIC)) :

1	⊕ □ ♇	13:26		☽ ☌ ♀	4:30		☿ ⚹ ♆	10: 0	21	☿ ☍ ♀	2: 3	26	♀ □ ♄	0: 4
2	☽ ☍ ♄	2:35		♀ △ ♆	6:29		☿ ☌ ♂	20:42		☽ ☍ ♀	21:29		♀ □ ⊕	23:56
	☿ □ ♆	12:39		☽ ☍ ♇	18:24	14	☽ ☍ ♅	10: 8	22	☽ ☌ ☿	0: 9	27	☽ ☌ ♅	8:43
3	☿ ☍ ♃	23:18	8	☿ ☌ A	5: 6	15	☿ □ ♅	1:46		☿ □ ⊕	20: 8	28	☿ S ☊	9:54
4	☿ △ ♅	4:35	10	♀ □ ♅	3:34		☿ ☌ ♇	19:48	23	♂ ☌ ♇	11:52		♀ △ ♅	18:32
	♀ ☍ ♂	21:15	11	♂ ⚹ ♄	10:31	16	☽ ☌ ♄	3:23		☿ □ ♄	14:38	29	☽ ☍ ♄	11: 9
5	☽ ☌ ♃	0: 8		♀ ☍ ♇	11:43		♄ △ ♆	13:47	24	☽ ☌ ♆	14:52		♀ ⚹ ♃	15:10
	☽ ☍ ☿	7:29		♂ ⚹ ♆	16: 7	18	☽ ☍ ♃	12:13	25	☿ ⚹ ♅	0: 8	31	♀ ☌ P	18:40
6	☿ △ ⊕	21:20		♃ ⚹ ♅	18:18	19	♂ □ ♅	20:21		⊕ ⚹ ♆	3: 4		⊕ △ ♇	23:13
	☽ ☍ ♂	23:24		☽ ☍ ♆	22:59	20	☽ ☌ ♂	13:44		☿ △ ♃	7:48			
7	♀ △ ♄	2:51	13	☿ ⚹ ♄	9:17		☽ ☌ ♇	16:36		⊕ ☍ ♄	8:34			

of heart": a virtue of Virgo. These qualities will assist us in finding new depths, and greater effectiveness. We may find a light dawning from deep within that is guiding us to our true strength. May we be embraced in light!

October 14: Moon 22° Virgo: Laying of the Foundation stone of the Rosicrucian Temple at Malsch, near Karlsruhe, Germany (5 Apr 1909). On this day, one day before the New Moon in Virgo, we remember Rudolf Steiner laying this Rosicrucian foundation stone on the evening of the Full Moon in Virgo. At this event he spoke the following words:

> We want to sink the foundation stone of this temple into the womb of our Mother Earth, beneath the rays of the Full Moon shining down upon us here, surrounded by the greenness of nature enveloping the building. And just as the Moon reflects the bright light of the Sun, so do we seek to mirror the light of the divine-spiritual beings. Full of trust we turn toward our great Mother Earth, who bears us and protects us so lovingly.... In pain and suffering our Mother Earth has become hardened. It is our mission to spiritualize her again, to redeem her, in that through the power of our hands we reshape her to become a spirit-filled work of art. May this stone be a first foundation stone for the redemption and transformation of our Planet Earth, and may the power of this stone multiply itself a thousandfold.[61]

In remembrance of our Mother Earth we may contemplate this prelude to tomorrow's New Moon, and find a practice that is our part in her redemption. She will hear our prayers, witness our resolves, and bless our every step toward achieving this sacred task of restoring her to the work of art that is her true being. Thus can the foundation stone of the Rosicrucian Temple "multiply a thousandfold" through us!

October 15: New Moon: 27° Virgo: The death of John the Baptist (4 Jan 31).

> That night, during the festivities to celebrate Herod's birthday at Machaerus, John the Baptist was beheaded at the request of Herodias'

daughter, Salome. After witnessing the spectacle of Salome dancing before him, Herod had said to her, "Ask what you will, and I will give it to you. Yes, I swear, even if you ask for half my kingdom, I shall give it to you." Salome hurriedly conferred with her mother, who told her to ask for the head of John the Baptist on a dish. (*Chron.* p. 270)

Even after the death of John, Herod was uneasy, for he could still feel the mighty spirit of John and this gave him great dis-ease.

This Moon remembers Herod and the power of the desire nature which has the ability to completely overwhelm us. If this were to happen, we would be given "half of Herod's kingdom" as was offered to Salome. This is not the kingdom we are seeking. With the Moon and Sun in Virgo we can cast the knowing glance to the cunning of the serpent, Hydra, that stretches his undulating forces beneath this constellation. Crater—"the Cup" and a Grail symbol—is balanced on the serpent's back along with Corvus—"the Raven" and a symbol for intuitive feminine wisdom. This Moon calls forth the Cup and the Raven: the Grail quest seeks the cup, and the Raven leads the Grail seeker to the mysterious and holy Castle of the Grail. It is in the realms where John is working that the Grail is preserved. John leads us to the Grail. Perhaps he speaks through the Raven. Inversely, Hydra can lead us into the dark castle of Klingsor, and once in his realm it is hard to get out—as exemplified with Herod and Herodias. We can pay particular attention to the phenomena (Virgo) of nature in our surroundings and read the story the Mother is always telling.

October 16: Sun 29° Virgo conjunct the star Spica: The ancient clairvoyants saw Virgo as a young woman holding an ear of corn or shaft of wheat. The tip of the shaft of wheat marks the star Spica. This heavenly virgin holds the mysteries of feminine wisdom and the star Spica blesses us with the grace and love of this wisdom. Beneath the feet of this woman we find the body of Hydra–"the Serpent"—stretching its undulating life force throughout the entire region beneath Virgo. To find the blessing of the wheat, the daily bread, we

---

61 Rudolf Steiner, in Powell, *The Christ Mystery*, p. 31.

must overcome the temptation of the serpent. This is a day that calls our attention to the awakening of the Divine Feminine within and without, in nature, in the depths of the Earth and in the heights of Heaven.

The Sun was conjunct Spica at the conversation between Master Jesus and the Virgin Mary just before the Baptism in the Jordan, and when Jesus visited the two remaining kings in their tent city (21 Sept 32). Mysterious esotericism surrounds both of these events. Sophia, Divine Wisdom, works and weaves to bring the light of higher worlds into the imaginative understanding of human beings. This is a day to attend her presence in all the subtleties of natural phenomena.

ASPECT: Venus 20° Leo square Jupiter 20° Taurus: Venus and Leo were square close to today's transit when Jesus taught of the need to be awake at the coming of the Son of Man.

> Be dressed, ready for service, and keep your lamps burning, like servants waiting for their master to return from a wedding banquet, so that when he comes and knocks they can immediately open the door for him. It will be good for those servants whose master finds them watching when he comes. Truly I tell you, he will dress himself to serve, will have them recline at the table and will come and wait on them. It will be good for those servants whose master finds them ready, even if he comes in the middle of the night or toward daybreak. But understand this: If the owner of the house had known at what hour the thief was coming, he would not have let his house be broken into. You also must be ready, because the Son of Man will come at an hour when you do not expect him. (Luke 12:35–40)

With Venus square Jupiter, our personalities (Venus) may feel a tension between what we would like to do and what wisdom (Jupiter) would ask us to do. This tension can be likened to contractions that accompany any birth. To hold the ideal in spite of personal desire is a transformative experience. Inversely, to compromise the ideal to make the desire nature comfortable will leave us unprepared for the meeting with Christ that will come at some unknown hour. Without the vigilance of

earnest preparation, robbers can enter our house and lead us away from the One we are waiting for. This One is in each of us! We are the ones as Christ lives in us. There is no one coming to save us. We must rise to save ourselves through a courageous heart (Leo) and a strong will (Taurus). Venus in Leo asks us to open our hearts and suffer our discomfort, as Jupiter in Taurus asks us to believe the ideal and suffer its presence against the background of materialism. The work before us is the work of continual preparedness in order to birth a new future.

October 17: Sun enters Libra. "Worlds sustain worlds" (Rudolf Steiner, *Twelve Moods of the Zodiac*). The first decan is ruled by the Moon and associated with the constellation of Bootes the Ploughman. The deeper meaning of Bootes has to do with the Hebrew "Bo," which means *coming*; hence Bootes is the *Coming One*. How appropriate that the Baptism of the Coming One, the Messiah, took place when the Sun entered this decan! Libra calls for balanced thought, which becomes balanced action, and a certain standard of uprightness that requires an alignment with higher consciousness. In Libra contentment becomes equanimity.

Sun 0° 50' Libra: The Baptism in the Jordan (23 Sept 29). Jesus, having become an empty vessel, makes his way to the Jordan accompanied by Lazarus. At the moment of the Baptism a voice of thunder sounds from the heavens: "This is my beloved Son; today I have begotten thee!" Christ, the Great Spirit of the Sun, entered into the vessel vacated by the Master Jesus through his conversation with the Virgin Mary directly preceding his walk to the Jordan River. At the Baptism the Son of God was conceived within a human being. Anne Catherine speaks of how perfectly transparent, entirely penetrated by light, the Jesus being became. She also sees:

> But off at some distance on the waters of the Jordan, I saw Satan, a dark, black figure, as if in a cloud, and myriads of horrible black reptiles and vermin swarming around him. It was as if all the wickedness, all the sins, all the poison of the whole region took a visible form at

the outpouring of the Holy Ghost, and fled into that dark figure as into their original source. (ACE, *LJC*, pp. 441–142)

This is a profound day to meditate on the Divine Light that came into the world at this Baptism and how the equal opposite to the light witnessed the event from the opposite shore of the Jordan. As the dark being Anne Catherine saw spreads his poisons so blatantly in our time, right before our very eyes, it is clear who is the antidote. It has always been clear. This is a day to meditate on the presence of Christ. At the threshold into Libra stands the Michaelic figure of Arcturus, whose name means "the Watcher" (or Guardian). Christ, the Greater Guardian of the threshold, was born this day. Emblazoned in the stars is the story of Michael (Arcturus), Sophia (Spica), in nomine Christi (in the name of Christ).

October 23: Sun 6° Libra: The healing of Theokeno (28 Sept 32). Theokeno was one of the three kings who visited the birth of the Solomon Jesus child. He was the king known as Caspar whose name means "born of God," and it was Theokeno who brought frankincense to the newborn child. The three kings had been pupils of Zoroaster in their previous incarnations in Babylon, and Theokeno was, in that incarnation, famed for his reverence and piety as a mighty Persian king. His gift of frankincense was an offering from the Persian wisdom stream. The three kings reincarnated again in the eighth to ninth centuries AD as collaborators in the spiritual stream of the Holy Grail.

At this healing we find the Sun exactly square to where it was when the kings came to adore Jesus thirty-seven years earlier (6° Capricorn). Jesus took Mensor and visited Theokeno in his tent where he was confined to his bed. Jesus took Theokeno by the hand and raised him up. After this Theokeno was no longer bedridden. Then the three went to the temple where Jesus taught (*Chron.* p. 328–329).

He explained that when the good angels withdraw, Satan takes possession of a temple service. He said that they should remove the various animal idols and teach love and compassion and give thanks to the Father in Heaven. Jesus now

took bread and wine, which had been prepared beforehand. Having consecrated the bread and wine, he placed them upon a small altar. He prayed and blessed everyone. Mensor, Theokeno, and the four priests knelt before him with their hands folded across their chests. (Ibid.)

Satan not only takes possession of a temple service but also of human beings if they allow animal instinct to rule in the temple of the human body. From the time of Christ forward, the "I" is to govern the animal forces in the astral body. Those who have animals on their altars will not attract good angels. It is no longer animals we offer for sacrifice but our lower human passions. Christ now works in the "I." The "I" that governs the animal nature, in turn shows compassion toward the animal kingdoms. The "I" enmeshed in the human animalistic nature will be deaf to the suffering of animals. Our hearts are the altars in our human temple, and upon this altar we give thanks, and partake in communion with the spiritual world. Human beings are now to rise from their beds of contentment and work for the salvation of the Earth and humanity. This will attract the good angels.

The square of the Sun's position between the Adoration of the Magi and Christ's visit to the kings thirty-seven years later, exemplifies the awakening to a new relationship (Libra) in the mystery traditions—a relationship founded on a new covenant—a covenant with the Sun mysteries. May we rise from our contentment and ease in order to forge Michaelic resonances of truth into a world going deaf.

October 27: Sun enters the second decan of Libra, ruled by Saturn and associated with the constellations of Corona the Crown (above) and Crux the Southern Cross (below), representing the "crown of life" (Rev. 2:10) bestowed on those who "take up the cross" (Matt. 10:38) and follow the Anointed One, remaining "faithful unto death" (Rev. 2:10).

October 28: ASPECT: Mars 20° Scorpio opposite Jupiter 20° Taurus: Mars stands opposite where it was at the Visitation between the Nathan Mary and her cousin Elizabeth, where Jupiter stands today. Jupiter remembers the Visitation, and Mars stands as a witness to this memory. The Nathan Mary, pregnant with Jesus, visited her cousin Elizabeth, who was pregnant with John the Baptist. During that meeting all four of them were filled with holy awe as the Old Adam, John the Baptist in Elizabeth's womb, was quickened by the presence of the New Adam, the Nathan Jesus in Mary's womb. The Adam that experienced the Fall (John the Baptist) was reunited with the paradisical substance held back from him at the time of the Fall. This pure substance was present in the Jesus child.

When something falls, something else simultaneously rises. In Paradise the pure substance rose from Adam and was guarded in the lodge of the Sun as the Adam being fell from these etheric realms of Eden into physical incarnation. This chaste and virgin substance of the first Adam was brought into physical incarnation for the first time through this pure Nathan soul. Through the Mystery of Golgotha the tragedy of this necessary duality was overcome once and for all.

> John the Baptist and Jesus of Nazareth—through the sharing of the original "I" forces of the first Adam—John receiving the portion of the "I" of the Adam who lived and walked upon the Earth and Jesus of Nazareth, who received the portion of the divine prototype of humanity, the purified substance that had been held back, never having incarnated upon the Earth until the birth of the Nathan Jesus, whose destiny it was to become the "New Adam."[62]

It is a wonder to behold how the Buddha worked with both John and the Nathan Jesus:

> John's "I" was further removed from the spiritual world and closer to the Earth than the beings who had previously guided Elijah [a former incarnation of the John being]. (Rudolf Steiner, *According to Luke*, p. 130)

The Buddha's influence shaped John's "I" instead of inducing inspiration as had happened to Elijah, so that John's preaching at the Jordan is a revival of Buddha's sermon at Benares.

---

62 Powell, *Elijah Come Again*, p. 124.

> It is important to purify yourself through your own personal forces.... The Buddha's words seem to flow from John's mouth....

> From the mouth of John the Baptist, we hear what the Buddha had to say six hundred years after the end of his final life in a physical body. Such is the unity of all religions.... Refusing to hear the Buddha in John the Baptist is like coming back to a blooming rosebush after having seen it in bud and refusing to believe that the flowers emerged from those buds. (Ibid., 132–133)

The Word (Mars) stands opposite Wisdom (Jupiter), reminding us to fill our words with wisdom and work collaboratively to form unity out of diversity. Inversely, with Mars in Scorpio words can have a sting. Our words reveal the forces that govern our soul and spirit. With the visitation, the fact of Christ's deed—as the one who united the higher and lower aspects of humanity's "I"—can lead us to speak from our higher "I" so as to ennoble our self and contribute to the ennoblement of the world. May we speak wisely!

October 29: Full Moon: Sun 11° Libra opposite Moon 11° Aries: This Full Moon stands opposite to the Full Moon in April AD 33, when Christ carried the cross to Golgotha and was there nailed upon it (Moon 11° Libra: Sun 13° Aries). Moments later Leo rose in the eastern sky as the "Lion of Judah" hung upon the cross.

In contemplating the path through materialism we may feel that our hands and feet are tied down—so narrow is the way. This Moon invites us to open to what is streaming toward us, and to the spiritual help that surrounds us. Thus may we carry the burdens of our personal karma and meet the collective burdens of humanity's karma, as the catalyst for awakening—for bringing change. The light of the Libra Sun, shining from the Aries Moon, can harmonize the will to serve the ideals (Aries) that are beckoning us into a new future.

ASPECT: Mercury 5° Scorpio square Neptune 5° Aquarius: When Mercury was 5° Taurus (square to today's position) two events occurred that give the gesture of this aspect: The conversation between Nicodemus and Jesus (8 Apr 30) and the cleansing of the temple (6 Apr 30). During this square, we remember the apocalyptic messages we can receive from the Cosmic Christ (conversations with Nicodemus). Thus may commence the cleansing of the decadence of materialism from the citadels of all that is Holy. At the cleansing of the temple:

Vendors had again erected tables to sell their wares, and Jesus demanded that they withdraw. When they refused, he drew a cord of twisted reeds from the folds of his robe. With this in hand he overturned their tables and drove the vendors back, assisted by the Disciples. Jesus said: "Take these things away; you shall not make my Father's house a house of trade." They replied: "What sign have you to show us for doing this?" Jesus answered them: "Destroy this temple, and in three days I will raise it up." They said: "It has taken forty-six years to build this temple, and you will raise it up in three days?" But he spoke of the temple of his body (John 2:13–21; *Chron.* p. 229).

A square between Mercury and Neptune brings forth a tension that can serve to awaken consciousness, or a tension that breaks forth with aggression as a means of denying what consciousness is striving to awaken. In the temple the later broke forth. The presence of Jesus drove the people to an awakening they did not seek. The negative forces of Neptune held them transfixed in the "rightness" of their actions—in the illusion that blinded them to the ahrimanic principles working through them wanting to "sweep all that is holy into a pool of filth."

How appropriate are these images in our time! The mind (Mercury) that has forgotten what is holy will compromise without disturbing the conscience. And having so compromised, it will choose the illusion (lower Neptune) of worldly gain over the inspiration (higher Neptune) of spiritual guidance.

As we contemplate this square today in Scorpio and Aquarius, we can be mindful that the sting of death (Scorpio) can be the harbinger of an apocalyptic awakening to new life, and the call of the Holy Spirit (Aquarius) is heard when we are willing to die—and in letting something lower die we become something higher! The temple would

be raised in three days: the Resurrection is proclaimed! What do we need to let die in order to receive penetrating insight into hidden dynamics we could otherwise ignore?

The Golgotha Full Moon and this Mercury–Neptune aspect make this a fine day to face our own underworld in order to bring forward our highest purpose. When facing our inner darkness we may feel as if our hands and feet are tied down, but when facing this with Christ we are given the keys to hold the underworld in check.

NOVEMBER 2012

The Sun begins in Libra, and moves into Scorpio on the 17/18th. Neptune stations Direct on the 12th in Aquarius (the WaterHuman) retrograde since June. Mercury stations before moving retrograde in Scorpio on the 7th (and stations direct on the 27th).

The large but waning Moon joins Jupiter in Taurus on the 1st, rising in the east together about 2 hours after sunset. The New Moon in Libra is on the 13th and is a total solar eclipse. The day before, the Moon conjoins Venus and Saturn in Libra, invisible behind the Sun's glow. Mercury is also hidden here, and is exactly conjunct the Sun during the Leonid Meteor shower peak; this annual shower reaches its peak on the 17th-18th. Look to (you guessed it!) the constellation of Leo in the east after midnight for up to 40 meteors an hour. Venus and Saturn come together on the 27th in Libra, ahead of the Sun's path but likely too close to be seen before dawn. The next day brings us the Full Moon, and a penumbral lunar eclipse. The month closes as it began; the large but waning Moon with Jupiter in Taurus.

November 1: Sun 13° Libra: Healing the blind (6 Oct 30 and 6 Oct 31). According to Valentin Tomberg (*Christ and Sophia*, chapter 8) Cain and Abel represent two thought streams, one stream (Abel) running vertically, and the other (Cain) running horizontally. Each of us has both a Cain and an Abel side. From this perspective, the ascending vertical stream is more feminine in nature, connected to subtle spiritual guidance, and is too often killed by the horizontal stream, which is more overt and masculine in nature. This masculine stream is too often filled with egoistical self-interest and is often hostile toward the Abel side of human nature. World events make it clear that Cain is still killing Abel. In the time of Christ these streams manifested as two different types of human beings. One type is born blind but with a sensitive capacity for hearing the spiritual Word (Homer is an example). The other type has sight but is deaf to the spiritual Word.[63]

These eyewitnesses and ministers of the word, spoken of at the beginning of the Gospel of Luke, were united by Christ. The sheep (Abel) are those who hear the Word, and the goats (Cain-vagabonds) are those who subjectively see. In the healing of the man born blind, Christ uses earth and saliva. This union of earth and water balanced the "I" between these two differing streams, thereby restoring equilibrium (Libra).

Saliva is in the process of becoming a moral substance. In the future, hate will increasingly produce poisonous saliva and love will increasingly produce healing saliva. Christ's saliva was filled with the healing power of love. The earth element in this healing represents the moral composition of the body and its effect on the Earth after death. A moral body serves the resurrection promise of the entire Earth, whereas a corrupt body serves Earth's degeneration. Together earth and spittle—morality and love—heal.

The state of blindness (and deafness) of humanity today tells us how far we are from the equilibrium of the center point, where these two streams are united. The man born blind incarnated specifically to develop the capacity to hear the words of the "Good Shepherd," and having heard these words his sight could be restored.

"For judgment I am come into this world, that they which see not, might see; and that they which see might be made blind" (John 9:39). These words ring through the world with escalating urgency.

The virtual light can steal our sight (imagination) and virtual sound can steal our hearing (inspiration). A blind and deaf humanity is the intentional goal of destructive beings working against what is moral (earth) and loving (spittle). We find the place of balance between these two streams of horizontality and verticality (between sight and hearing) in our third eye. This is the cavity in the forehead that harbors "I" initiative; it is the seat of concentration and initiation of thought.

Valentin Tomberg speaks of how in Paradise human beings had one eye vertically above the other. Since the Fall we have horizontally placed eyes. There is an inherent obligation with technological forces—the obligation to balance time spent with the virtual through time spent in nature, the arts, and all manner of sacred endeavors. Take a moment and sit in meditation with the chakra in the region of your brow. Feel its currents. Celebrate the gift of insightful understanding that this chakra bestows. When Cain serves Abel we have eyes to see and ears to hear. This is a day to see with our eyes shut, and hear in absolute silence. There is a great deal the eyes of spirit need to see in this world.

ASPECT: Venus 10° Virgo opposite Uranus 10° Pisces: Venus was at this degree at the conception of John the Baptist. It is interesting that the imaginations streaming to us from out of the future are connected to the apocalyptic work of the John stream. These new imaginations can be shocking (Uranus) to the status quo, but with Uranus in Pisces they carry a loving intention. Venus in Virgo loves the Earth and loves humanity; she seeks to create harmony in both the natural and human worlds. Venus welcomes new imaginations and seeks karmic groups that are mature enough to use these revelations for the good.

Venus in her negative manifestation can be jealous and rivalrous. The lightning bolts of illumination guiding humanity forward can be seized and bent to the obedience of personal wills that have been captured in the allure of power. But, this can only be a temporary event. All that has been built into the culture that is based on greed and power will eventually fall, as all of history has shown us.

---

63 "You will be a restless wanderer on the Earth" (Gen. 4:12).

Today, with Venus facing Uranus remembering the conception of John, and the Sun remembering the healing of the blind, we are encouraged to open our spiritual eyes to something entirely new, and work with any jealousy or rivalry that entraps us in the eternal repetition of false power. Catch a new thought today, and apply it to something earthly. It is John's conception that Venus today remembers, and it was John who *saw the light of the world*.

November 3: ASPECT: Venus 12° Virgo square Pluto 12° Sagittarius: Venus in Pisces was square Pluto close to this degree at both the Feeding of the Five Thousand (28 Jan 31), and the Walking on the Water (29 Jan 31). Pluto can be seen as the source of Divine Love, called Phanes in Orphic Mythology, as well as the realm of Hades, god of the underworld. When Venus is squared Pluto, the personality can rise to new heights of consciousness or plunge into lower realms of materialism. Both of the miracles mentioned above are imaginations wherein the planet of Love (Venus) called forth the loftiest truths from both the heights and the depths.

From the heights the twelvefold nature of the zodiac streamed into Christ's heart and that day he nourished five thousand through the source of Divine Love (Higher Pluto—Phanes). This miracle established a new communion between human beings on Earth and the cosmic world above.

From the depths the life-filled forces of the Mother held Christ up while that night he walked upon the waters of human error without sinking. This represents communion with the Mother forces in the interior of the Earth—with Demeter. The sinless one holds nothing in his being that can separate him from his Mother in the depths.

The tension of the square was felt by the multitudes, during the feeding of the five thousand, who wanted to crown Christ a king in this world, thereby relieving themselves of finding their way to divinity out of their own efforts. This tension was also felt by the Disciples, at the walking on the water, as Peter experienced his faith faltering when faced with the murky depths of his subconscious—he found he could not yet commune with the interior forces of the Earth.

Pluto takes 248 years to make one orbit. That means Pluto is in a given sign for approximately 20 years. All through the life of Christ, Pluto was in Sagittarius: 6° Sagittarius at the Baptism in the Jordan, through 17° Sagittarius at Pentecost. This corresponds in our time to the period from the year 2009, when Pluto was at 6° Sagittarius, to approximately the year 2014 when Pluto will reach 17° Sagittarius. These five years mirror the position of Pluto during the life of Christ.

The longest eclipse of the twenty-first century occurred in 2009 when Pluto was exactly at the same position as it was at the Baptism. If it is true that Ahriman will incarnate shortly after the beginning of the twenty-first century, it could be that this will occur within the time that Pluto is remembering the life of Christ. **The god of the underworld, it would seem, would most certainly be working against the reappearance of Christ in the etheric during the potency of the time that Pluto is remembering Christ's life on Earth.**

Today we can live into the tension between Venus—our personality, and Pluto—representative of the highest and the lowest. We can receive cosmic nutrition by focusing on communion with Divine Love, and we can walk on the waters of our human error by focusing on the Mother and her life-giving warmth, as we continue the work of our redemption.

Can we humble ourselves before our blessed imperfection?

November 6: Sun enters third decan of Libra, ruled by Jupiter and associated with the constellation of Centaurus the Centaur. The most famous centaur was Chiron, to whom was ascribed great wisdom.

November 10: Mars enters Sagittarius: "In life's active force of will."[64] Mars was in Sagittarius at the start of the forty days in the wilderness and at the raising of the daughter of Jairus.

November 12: Neptune stations before going direct 5° 27' Aquarius: Heliocentric (viewed from the Sun) Mercury was here at the first temptation in the wilderness (27 Nov 29), when Christ

---

64 Steiner, *Twelve Moods of the Zodiac* (n/p).

SIDEREAL GEOCENTRIC LONGITUDES : NOVEMBER 2012 Gregorian at 0 hours UT

DAY	☉	☽	☊	☿	♀	♂	♃	♄	♅	♆	♇
1 TH	14 ♎ 3	7 ♉ 43	1 ♏ 6	7 ♏ 12	9 ♍ 17	23 ♏ 4	20 ♉ 13R	8 ♎ 14	10 ♓ 25R	5 ♒ 28R	12 ♐ 31
2 FR	15 4	19 30	1 7	7 50	10 30	23 48	20 8	8 21	10 23	5 28	12 33
3 SA	16 4	1 ♊ 17	1 8	8 22	11 42	24 32	20 2	8 28	10 21	5 28	12 34
4 SU	17 4	13 8	1 9	8 48	12 56	25 17	19 56	8 35	10 19	5 28	12 35
5 MO	18 4	25 8	1 11	9 7	14 9	26 1	19 51	8 43	10 17	5 27	12 37
6 TU	19 4	7 ♋ 19	1 11	9 19	15 22	26 46	19 45	8 50	10 16	5 27	12 38
7 WE	20 4	19 47	1 12	9 23R	16 35	27 31	19 39	8 57	10 14	5 27	12 40
8 TH	21 4	2 ♌ 36	1 11R	9 18	17 48	28 15	19 32	9 4	10 12	5 27	12 41
9 FR	22 5	15 49	1 11	9 4	19 2	29 0	19 26	9 11	10 11	5 27	12 43
10 SA	23 5	29 30	1 10	8 40	20 15	29 45	19 19	9 18	10 9	5 27	12 44
11 SU	24 5	13 ♍ 38	1 9	8 6	21 29	0 ♐ 30	19 13	9 26	10 7	5 27	12 46
12 MO	25 6	28 11	1 8	7 22	22 42	1 15	19 6	9 33	10 6	5 27D	12 47
13 TU	26 6	13 ♎ 6	1 8	6 29	23 56	2 0	18 59	9 40	10 4	5 27	12 49
14 WE	27 6	28 13	1 8	5 26	25 10	2 45	18 52	9 47	10 3	5 27	12 50
15 TH	28 7	13 ♏ 24	1 8D	4 16	26 24	3 30	18 45	9 54	10 2	5 27	12 52
16 FR	29 7	28 30	1 8	3 0	27 37	4 15	18 37	10 1	10 0	5 27	12 54
17 SA	0 ♏ 8	13 ♐ 21	1 8	1 40	28 51	5 1	18 30	10 8	9 59	5 27	12 55
18 SU	1 8	27 53	1 8R	0 19	0 ♎ 5	5 46	18 23	10 15	9 58	5 27	12 57
19 MO	2 9	12 ♑ 0	1 8	28 ♎ 59	1 19	6 31	18 15	10 22	9 57	5 28	12 59
20 TU	3 9	25 41	1 8	27 44	2 33	7 17	18 7	10 29	9 55	5 28	13 0
21 WE	4 10	8 ♒ 58	1 8D	26 35	3 47	8 2	18 0	10 35	9 54	5 28	13 2
22 TH	5 11	21 53	1 8	25 34	5 1	8 48	17 52	10 42	9 53	5 29	13 4
23 FR	6 11	4 ♓ 28	1 9	24 44	6 15	9 33	17 44	10 49	9 52	5 29	13 6
24 SA	7 12	16 48	1 9	24 4	7 30	10 19	17 36	10 56	9 51	5 30	13 7
25 SU	8 13	28 56	1 10	23 36	8 44	11 5	17 28	11 3	9 50	5 30	13 9
26 MO	9 13	10 ♈ 55	1 11	23 20	9 58	11 50	17 20	11 9	9 49	5 30	13 11
27 TU	10 14	22 47	1 11	23 15D	11 12	12 36	17 12	11 16	9 48	5 31	13 13
28 WE	11 15	4 ♉ 37	1 11R	23 21	12 27	13 22	17 4	11 23	9 48	5 32	13 15
29 TH	12 15	16 24	1 11	23 37	13 41	14 8	16 56	11 29	9 47	5 32	13 17
30 FR	13 16	28 13	1 10	24 2	14 56	14 54	16 48	11 36	9 46	5 33	13 19

INGRESSES :

2 ☽ → ♊ 21:23	☿ → ♎ 5:41
5 ☽ → ♋ 9:39	20 ☽ → ♒ 7:42
7 ☽ → ♌ 19:11	22 ☽ → ♓ 15:25
10 ☽ → ♍ 0:51	25 ☽ → ♈ 2: 7
♂ → ♐ 8: 4	27 ☽ → ♉ 14:37
12 ☽ → ♎ 2:56	30 ☽ → ♊ 3:36
14 ☽ → ♏ 2:49	
16 ☽ → ♐ 2:24	
☉ → ♏ 20:53	
17 ♀ → ♎ 22:18	
18 ☽ → ♑ 3:33	

ASPECTS & ECLIPSES :

1 ☽ ☌ A 15:47	12 ☽ ☌ ♄ 18:28	☉ ʖ ☿ 15:38	♀ ☌ ♄ 1:14
♀ ☍ ♅ 21:47	13 ☉ ☌ ☽ 22: 7	☉ ☌ ☊ 23:57	☽ ☌ ☋ 17: 3
2 ☽ ☌ ♃ 1:16	☉ ● T 22:10	20 ☽ N ☊ 9:45	♂ ☌ ♇ 20: 3
☽ ☍ ♂ 9:21	☿ □ ♆ 23:48	☉ □ ☽ 14:31	28 ☽ ☍ PN14:33
3 ♀ □ ♇ 17:16	14 ☽ ☌ ☊ 4:36	☽ ☌ ♆ 17:36	☉ ☍ ☽ 14:45
☽ ☍ ♇ 22:53	☽ ☌ P 10:12	22 ☉ □ ♆ 7:11	☽ ☌ A 19:47
7 ☉ □ ☽ 0:35	☽ ☌ ☿ 10:37	23 ♂ □ ♅ 9:40	29 ☽ ☌ ♃ 1: 2
☽ S ☊ 21:23	15 ☽ ☍ ♃ 8:23	☽ ☌ ♅ 10:26	
8 ☽ ☍ ♆ 5:14	16 ☽ ☌ ♂ 9:44	25 ☽ ☍ ♀ 21:53	
10 ☽ ☍ ♅ 18: 7	☽ ☌ ♇ 23:17	26 ☽ ☍ ♄ 0:29	
11 ☽ ☌ ♀ 14:12	17 ☿ ☌ ☊ 9:27	27 ☽ ☍ ☿ 0:56	

SIDEREAL HELIOCENTRIC LONGITUDES : NOVEMBER 2012 Gregorian at 0 hours UT

DAY	Sid. Time	☿	♀	⊕	♂	♃	♄	♅	♆	♇	Vernal Point
1 TH	2:42:44	6 ♒ 57	17 ♋ 11	14 ♈ 3	18 ♐ 59	13 ♉ 33	7 ♎ 38	11 ♓ 59	7 ♒ 14	14 ♐ 1	5 ♓ 4'51"
2 FR	2:46:40	10 55	18 49	15 3	19 35	13 38	7 40	11 59	7 15	14 2	5 ♓ 4'51"
3 SA	2:50:37	15 0	20 26	16 3	20 11	13 43	7 42	12 0	7 15	14 2	5 ♓ 4'51"
4 SU	2:54:34	19 13	22 4	17 3	20 46	13 49	7 44	12 1	7 15	14 2	5 ♓ 4'51"
5 MO	2:58:30	23 33	23 41	18 4	21 22	13 54	7 46	12 1	7 16	14 3	5 ♓ 4'51"
6 TU	3: 2:27	28 1	25 19	19 4	21 58	13 59	7 48	12 2	7 16	14 3	5 ♓ 4'51"
7 WE	3: 6:23	2 ♓ 38	26 56	20 4	22 34	14 5	7 49	12 2	7 16	14 3	5 ♓ 4'51"
8 TH	3:10:20	7 23	28 34	21 4	23 10	14 10	7 51	12 3	7 17	14 4	5 ♓ 4'51"
9 FR	3:14:16	12 17	0 ♌ 11	22 4	23 46	14 15	7 53	12 4	7 17	14 4	5 ♓ 4'50"
10 SA	3:18:13	17 20	1 49	23 5	24 22	14 20	7 55	12 4	7 17	14 4	5 ♓ 4'50"
11 SU	3:22: 9	22 33	3 26	24 5	24 58	14 26	7 57	12 5	7 18	14 5	5 ♓ 4'50"
12 MO	3:26: 6	27 54	5 4	25 5	25 34	14 31	7 59	12 6	7 18	14 5	5 ♓ 4'50"
13 TU	3:30: 3	3 ♈ 24	6 41	26 6	26 10	14 36	8 1	12 6	7 18	14 5	5 ♓ 4'50"
14 WE	3:33:59	9 3	8 19	27 6	26 47	14 42	8 3	12 7	7 19	14 6	5 ♓ 4'50"
15 TH	3:37:56	14 51	9 56	28 7	27 23	14 47	8 5	12 8	7 19	14 6	5 ♓ 4'50"
16 FR	3:41:52	20 46	11 34	29 7	27 59	14 52	8 7	12 8	7 20	14 6	5 ♓ 4'49"
17 SA	3:45:49	26 48	13 11	0 ♉ 8	28 36	14 57	8 9	12 9	7 20	14 7	5 ♓ 4'49"
18 SU	3:49:45	2 ♉ 56	14 49	1 8	29 12	15 3	8 10	12 10	7 20	14 7	5 ♓ 4'49"
19 MO	3:53:42	9 9	16 26	2 9	29 48	15 8	8 12	12 10	7 21	14 7	5 ♓ 4'49"
20 TU	3:57:38	15 25	18 4	3 9	0 ♑ 25	15 13	8 14	12 11	7 21	14 8	5 ♓ 4'49"
21 WE	4: 1:35	21 44	19 41	4 10	1 1	15 19	8 16	12 11	7 21	14 8	5 ♓ 4'49"
22 TH	4: 5:31	28 3	21 19	5 10	1 38	15 24	8 18	12 12	7 22	14 8	5 ♓ 4'49"
23 FR	4: 9:28	4 ♊ 21	22 56	6 11	2 15	15 29	8 20	12 13	7 22	14 9	5 ♓ 4'48"
24 SA	4:13:25	10 38	24 33	7 12	2 51	15 34	8 22	12 13	7 22	14 9	5 ♓ 4'48"
25 SU	4:17:21	16 50	26 11	8 12	3 28	15 40	8 24	12 14	7 23	14 9	5 ♓ 4'48"
26 MO	4:21:18	22 58	27 48	9 13	4 5	15 45	8 26	12 15	7 23	14 10	5 ♓ 4'48"
27 TU	4:25:14	28 59	29 25	10 14	4 42	15 50	8 28	12 15	7 24	14 10	5 ♓ 4'48"
28 WE	4:29:11	4 ♋ 53	1 ♍ 2	11 14	5 18	15 56	8 30	12 16	7 24	14 10	5 ♓ 4'48"
29 TH	4:33: 7	10 38	2 40	12 15	5 55	16 1	8 31	12 17	7 24	14 11	5 ♓ 4'48"
30 FR	4:37: 4	16 15	4 17	13 16	6 32	16 6	8 33	12 17	7 25	14 11	5 ♓ 4'47"

INGRESSES :

6 ☿ → ♓ 10:23
8 ♀ → ♌ 21:12
12 ☿ → ♈ 9:13
16 ⊕ → ♉ 20:58
17 ☿ → ♉ 12:34
19 ♂ → ♑ 7:39
22 ☿ → ♊ 7:25
27 ☿ → ♋ 4: 7
♀ → ♍ 8:35

ASPECTS (HELIOCENTRIC +MOON(TYCHONIC)) :

1 ☿ ☌ ♆ 1:45	☿ ☌ ♅ 22:54	☿ ☍ ♄ 19:43	☿ □ ♆ 17: 4	24 ⊕ □ ♆ 4:16	☿ ⚹ ♃ 23:20
☿ △ ♄ 4:13	9 ☿ □ ♇ 8:32	♀ ⚹ ♄ 19:57	19 ☿ ⚹ ♅ 11:37	☿ □ ♅ 6: 9	
☽ ☌ ♃ 11:58	☿ ⚹ ♃ 9:35	14 ☿ △ ♇ 20:55	☿ ☌ ♃ 23:15	☿ ☍ ♇ 13:35	
2 ☿ □ ♃ 16:22	10 ☽ ☍ ♅ 21:24	15 ☽ ☍ ♃ 2:12	20 ☿ □ ♀ 13:34	25 ☽ ☍ ♄ 18:59	
☿ ⚹ ♇ 18:20	11 ☿ □ ♂ 12:19	16 ☿ ☌ ☊ 11:11	☽ ☌ ♆ 21: 2	27 ☿ ⚹ ♀ 2:26	
3 ☿ ⚹ ⊕ 7:57	☽ ☍ ☿ 23:15	17 ☽ ☌ ♇ 1:13	21 ☿ ☌ P 3:50	28 ☿ ☍ ♂ 1:59	
4 ☽ ☍ ♇ 1:48	12 ☽ ☌ ♄ 15:51	☿ △ ♂ 7:50	☽ ☍ ♀ 22:46	☿ □ ♄ 15: 4	
☿ ⚹ ♂ 10: 6	13 ⊕ △ ♂ 4:29	♀ △ ♇ 13:38	22 ♀ N ☊ 8:23	☽ ☌ ♃ 23:11	
☽ ☍ ♂ 16: 7	♀ ☍ ♆ 9: 9	☿ ☌ ⊕ 15:38	23 ☿ △ ♆ 11:30	29 ⊕ ⚹ ♅ 0:33	
7 ☽ ☌ ♀ 15:26	☿ ⚹ ♆ 16:39	18 ☽ ☌ ♂ 2:18	☽ ☌ ♅ 15: 1	☿ △ ♅ 6:57	
8 ☽ ☍ ♆ 8:35	☿ △ ♀ 19:38	♀ □ ♃ 3:37	☿ △ ♄ 15:16	☿ ⚹ ⊕ 8:20	

was asked to bow to the prince of this world. He responded: "My kingdom is not of this world." These days from the 5th of November to the 19th of November offer introspection regarding our relationships with earthly powers over and above our relationship with Christ and Sophia. To whom do we turn and for what benefit?

November 13: New Moon 26° Libra and total solar eclipse: The total eclipse will be visible from northern Australia and the southern Pacific Ocean. The Sun was at this degree three days before Christ began his forty-day fast that would last throughout his period of temptation in the wilderness. As Christ was traveling and teaching in these last days before entering the wilderness, the Sun was at 26° Libra. Judas Iscariot was among the crowd of those who listened to his teachings. It would be one year before Judas would become a disciple.

With Neptune stationing at the first temptation (see commentary above) and today's eclipse remembering Christ's last days before the wilderness, where he taught in the presence of his future betrayer, we are encouraged to find the inner strength to meet whatever temptations are facing us both individually and collectively, in personal or worldly events. Powerful inspirations are streaming from Neptune, and from this New Moon, that stimulate us to find a new fulcrum of spiritual certainty (Libra), which can balance the scales between the betraying voice of "this-world-only Judases" on the one hand, and on the other hand from the world-weary sleep of contentment. We are to say "no" to Judas and "no" to the sleep of contentment. With the fulcrum pointing due north, nothing can eclipse the Sun-filled power of Christ in us. This New Moon and the solar eclipse herald an awaking of consciousness, no matter how inconvenient. In three days' time the Sun will enter Scorpio, which signals Christ's entrance into the wilderness. Jesus did not falter before the tempters, for he overcame all doubt. His certainty becomes our keel as we make our way through the convincing illusions of materialism. This is a Moon that asks us to prepare, find our center, and relinquish doubt.

November 16/17: Sun enters Scorpio: "Existence consumes being."[65] The first decan is ruled by Mars and is associated with the constellation of Lupus the Wolf. Sun entering Scorpio began the forty days in the wilderness. With Sun in Scorpio, we are asked to be patient in order to gain insight.

ASPECT: Superior conjunction Mercury and Sun 0° 8' Scorpio: The Sun was here just before Judas became a disciple (24 Oct 30). Three days ago, the New Moon solar eclipse remembered when Judas stood in the periphery around Christ, and the approaching Judas is again remembered with today's Sun.

With the Sun entering Scorpio we find two emblematic events: Jesus' arrival at Attarus—the place of the temptations, and one year later, Judas becoming a disciple. Today we may find our minds alert to what lies hidden (Scorpio). It is the hidden dynamic underlying events and within the souls of others that can be revealed with Mercury in Scorpio. The opposite of the betrayal by Judas, and the work of the tempters, is the mission of John. John took the place of Judas in the circle of twelve and held the place of the Scorpion, too. With John, however, the Scorpion became the eagle and soared into realms of insight and these profound insights became a book: the Book of Revelation! This is what we seek today. May what is hidden be revealed!

November 17: Venus enters Libra: "In being experience being."[66] Heliocentric Venus was in Libra throughout the Passion, death and Resurrection of Christ.

Sun 1° Scorpio: Summons of Judas (24 Oct 30). Venus and Sun had entered Scorpio just before Judas became a disciple. The twenty-five-year-old Judas had heard of the wealth and fame of Jesus and longed to satisfy his desires through becoming part of this group (Venus). Judas was introduced to Jesus by Bartholomew and Simon, saying: "Master, this is Judas of whom we have spoken." Jesus was most friendly toward Judas, but was filled with an indescribable sorrow. Judas bowed and said: "Master I pray that you may allow me

65 Ibid.
66 Ibid.

to take part in your teaching." Jesus replied most gently with the prophetic words: "You may take a place, unless you would prefer to leave it to another" (see CHA, *The Sun Chronicle in the Life of the Messiah*). How these words ring through time! The ennobled Venus nature serves the true "I," while the lower, desire aspect of Venus, wants to be served. In the latter condition the Judas principle is never far from the heart (Sun). This is a good day to reflect upon any hidden agendas (Scorpio) we may harbor that are dangerous to our loyalties. As we enter into the constellation of Scorpio we are mindful of how damaging hidden agendas can be. There is a bifurcating beast slinking through the world, searching in communities for the weak link. This beast delights in finding entrance, and through this weak link it can destroy circles, pitting one member against the other. This is what happened to Judas. He was the weak link in the circle of twelve due to the lower forces of his Venus nature working for self-gain in the Scorpionic underworlds. This is a day to review our loyalties. May we have the patience to curb our reactions and wait instead for the insight that shows us the pain in our own hearts!

November 18: Sun 2° Scorpio: Immaculate Conception of the Nathan Mary (24 Oct 18 BC). This is the Mary, born to Joachim and Anna, who bore a high degree of love and the ability for self-sacrifice. At an early age she married Joseph of Nazareth, and bore one child, the Nathan Jesus. This pure, loving soul died shortly after the Union in the Temple in AD 12.

November 19: Sun 3° Scorpio: Death of Johannes Kepler (5 Nov 1630). As the death horoscope is an expression of the fulfillment of an individuality's life, it is interesting to note Kepler's death horoscope with Sun, Mars, South Node, and Mercury in Scorpio. Kepler is one who penetrated into hidden realms to understand mysterious dynamics working in the movements of the planets and in the depths of the Earth. In his lecture cycle *Christ and the Spiritual World*, Rudolf Steiner spoke about Kyot, then wove in Kepler, and then he again wove back through the Grail, and then he wove into the hidden realms of Presbyter John, into whose realms the Grail has been taken—a realm beyond sense existence. Steiner called Kepler "a man in whom lived and pulsed the Christ-filled Astrology which draws after it, merely as its shadow, astrological superstition." The Kyot being led Steiner to "a thing called the Grail" and Kepler worked with forces that spring from the elemental world that maintain communication between the stars and the Earth, and as we follow the stars we find Presbyter John as the keeper of the Grail Mysteries. Such rich content to inbreathe! Mars was conjunct Kepler's death Sun in Scorpio at the birth of the Nathan Jesus, who later became Jesus Christ at the Baptism in the Jordan River. Jesus Christ is the highest manifestation of the work of reaching into realms of hidden dynamics, for it was he who descended into Hell. Steiner notes that the indications given by Kepler are spiritual revelations permeated by Christ.

Kepler did not view science and spirituality as mutually exclusive. His laws danced with the ancient Pythagorean concept of universal harmony. Today we can imagine the elemental beings rejoicing in the symphony of stars, and the stars rejoicing in the chorus of the elementals—and somewhere between the two we may find the mysteries of the Holy Grail. Kepler's music of the spheres is the music that sounds through heaven and Earth:

> The heavenly motions are nothing but a continuous song for several voices, perceived not by the ear but by the intellect, a figured music which sets landmarks in the immeasurable flow of time.[67]

The Grail Knight, Kyot, was trained to confront evil, as were all Grail Knights. These knights must be returning, for it is time to confront evil and unmask lies in order to restore harmony between Heaven and Earth. We can look into the eyes of the children we meet, and we may see that there are knights among them. This is a day to remember the harmony inherent in all archetypal life and to find the penetrating insight to notice forces

---

67 Kepler, *The Harmony of the World* (*Harmonices mundi*).

working against divinity, the Grail, and harmony. The human being, as mediator between the stars above and the elementals below, have a sovereign part to play in the drama of discord resounding throughout our world. What part can we play?

November 23: Mars 9° 52' Sagittarius square Uranus 9° 52' Pisces: Power on the Twelve (4 Dec 30). With Mars at this degree:

> Jesus continued the Sermon on the Mount near Bethsaida-Julias. He spoke on the fourth beatitude. Afterward, he went with the twelve to a place on the east shore of the lake. There he gave the twelve authority to cast out unclean spirits (Matthew 10:1–4). Jesus then sailed with the twelve and about five other Disciples to Magdala, where he exorcised some people who were possessed. Peter, Andrew, James, and John also cast out unclean spirits. Jesus and the Disciples then spent the night on board the boat. (*Chron.* p. 262)

The fourth beatitude is *"Blessed are they who hunger and thirst for righteousness, for they shall be filled."* It is related to the sentient feeling soul of human beings in connection with the astral body. In a culture where it seems the new religion is violence, this sense for righteousness is sorely needed. Mars calls forth the Word—the content of our speech measures the moral standing of our soul. With Mars (the Word) in Sagittarius, control of speech is to be practiced. With Mars square Uranus we may be surprised by what our words reveal.

Mars remembers the fourth beatitude and the exorcism of the possessed. We are surrounded by individuals who have become possessed by violence, greed, and self-centeredness—and who are often in leadership positions. Becoming animals is not our aim (Sagittarius). We are to set our sight on collaborative measures of brother- and sisterhood in order to transform the culture of violence into a culture of peace. Does our speech embolden egotism, or love? Does our thinking encompass the spiritual seeing of illumination (Uranus) or are we merely regurgitating the electrical thoughts of controversy? Choose words carefully today, and measure thoughts with the rule of love.

November 26: Sun enters the second decan of Scorpio, ruled by the Sun and associated with the constellation of Hercules, the Mighty Sun Hero.

November 27/28: ASPECT: Venus conjunct Saturn 11° Libra: Birth of the Virgin Mary. Heliocentric Saturn was here at the birth of Mary. With Venus and Saturn conjunct, the spiritual resolves we have made press to become realized through our karmic groups. This can be experienced as a burden or a blessing. It all depends on our relationship to our eternal mission and purpose (Saturn). The Moon was exactly at this degree as Christ carried the cross, was nailed to it and was raised upon it. The Michaelic figure of the Centaur stretches his starry body throughout the entire region of Libra, thereby bequeathing his etheric forces to this sign. The Centaur—half man, half animal—reminds us of Longinus, whose spear pierced the right side through to the heart of Jesus Christ. In balancing the scales of Libra we find equilibrium through standing in the fulcrum—the exact point where Michaelic truth arms us with the certainty of Cosmic Truths. Today we can search for the altar of truth that stands in the balance, as portrayed in Rudolf Steiner's statue, the Representative of Humanity. May we emulate this gesture, to discover the place of refuge in a culture that is increasingly tending more toward the animal-human than the Michaelic human. In remembrance of the Virgin Mary and the collective mission of humanity to rediscover her wisdom, may we find contentment with where we are, and determination to continue our journey.

ASPECT 2: Mars conjunct Pluto 13° Sagittarius: The Transfiguration of Christ (4 Apr 31). Pluto was at this exact degree during the Transfiguration of Christ. With Mars today conjunct this memory we are encouraged to govern our lower astral forces and invite the light into our lives. Orpheus described Phanes (higher Pluto) as an androgynous creator god, the source of the primal will, the fire of love that underlies the whole of existence.

> Phanes is the creator of all, from whom the world has its first origin... He is imagined

as marvelously beautiful, a figure of shining light.... He is of both sexes, since he is to create the race of gods unaided, "bearing within himself the honored seed of the gods" (Orphic Fragment 85).... He made an eternal home for the gods and was their first king.... Phanes bore a daughter, *Night*, whom he took as his partner and to whom he gave great power. She assisted him in the work of creation, and he finally handed over his sceptre to her, so that she became the next in order to the rulers of the universe.... Night bore to Phanes Gaia and Ouranos (Earth and Heaven).... To Ouranos Night handed over the supreme power.[68]

On the seventh day, God rested and gave to Sophia, the Mother, the work of developing the seven pillars of creation. As we accept the light, as did Christ during the transfiguration, we will find our way to the Great Mother in the heights (Sophia) and simultaneously, to the Great Mother in the depths—Our Mother who art in the darkness of the underworld. The primal will of Divine Love (higher Pluto), in conjunction with the force of the Word (Mars)—that underlies all creation—can be a contemplation for today.

November 28: Full Moon and penumbral lunar eclipse: Sun 11° Scorpio opposite Moon 11° Taurus: The shadow of the Earth can be divided into two distinctive parts: the umbra and the penumbra. Within the umbra, there is no direct solar radiation. However, as a result of the Sun's large angular size, solar illumination is only partially blocked in the outer portion of the Earth's shadow, which is given the name penumbra. The penumbra causes a subtle darkening of the Moon's surface. A penumbral eclipse occurs when the Moon passes through the Earth's penumbra (partially blocked solar radiation). Total penumbral eclipses are rare, and when these occur, that portion of the Moon which is closest to the umbra (no direct solar radiation) can appear somewhat darker than the rest of the Moon. A partial lunar eclipse occurs when only a portion of the Moon enters the umbra. When the Moon travels completely into the Earth's umbra, one observes a total lunar eclipse. Today's eclipse is a penumbral lunar eclipse, or a partial eclipse—as only part of the Moon enters the Earth's umbra. The region of visibility will be Europe, east Africa, Asia, Australia, Pacific, and North America. This is the second of two lunar eclipses in 2012.

The Moon was at this degree at the Raising of the Youth of Nain (13 Nov 30).

> At around nine in the morning, as Jesus and the Disciples were approaching Nain, they met a funeral procession emerging from the city gate. Jesus commanded the coffin bearers to stand still and set the coffin down. He raised his eyes to heaven and spoke the words recorded in Matthew 11:25–30. There then occurred the miraculous raising from the dead of the youth of Nain—the 12-year-old Martialis, son of the widow Maroni—described in Luke 7:11–17. (*Chron.* p. 257)

The Sun at this healing was 22° Scorpio, very close to opposition with the Venus–Sun transit of this past June. The Youth of Nain is the Mani–Parsifal individuality. It is this individuality that is one of the greatest ever to incarnate on the Earth (according to Rudolf Steiner). And, this individuality may be teaching in the near future. He may be the teacher who is preparing to meet the Grail Knights of the twenty-first century, whose task is the confrontation with evil. There are initiates who are preparing now for this incarnation, so that this great teacher can be recognized in his new incarnation.

Receive what is new, and penetrate through the veils between worlds so as not to be overcome by the powers of evil, but rather to pass through all trials in the light of Mani–Parsifal.

DECEMBER 2012

The Sun begins the month in the Scorpion, standing in front of the star Antares on the 2nd ("Heart of the Scorpion" and a Royal Star of Persia). The Sun moves into Sagittarius (The Archer) on the 17th. Uranus stations Direct on the 13th (retrograde since July), and Jupiter remains

---

68 Powell, *Hermetic Astrology,* vol. 2, p. 290–291.

retrograde. The waning Moon joins Saturn in Libra and Mercury in Scorpio as it approaches the New Moon on the 13th (Sun in Scorpio, Moon in Taurus), and joins Mars in Sagittarius as it begins its waxing cycle. The Geminids Meteor shower peaks on the 13th/14th and will be a great year for viewing with the Moon's light absent from the sky; look to constellation of Gemini in the south east in the early evening (about 7 o'clock) and to the south as the night deepens. The waxing Moon finds Jupiter in Taurus before opposing the Sun for a Full Moon on the 28th with the Sun in Sagittarius and the Moon in Gemini.

December 2: Today is the beginning of Advent.
ASPECT: Sun conjunct Antares.

December 3: Sun 17° Scorpio: First conversion of Mary Magdalene (8 Nov 30). Jesus arrived at the mountain beyond Gabara, and delivered a powerful discourse with the words: "Come! Come to me, all who are weary and laden with guilt! Come to me, O sinners! Do penance, believe, and share the kingdom with me!" (*Chron.* p. 256).

Magdalene was deeply moved inwardly by these words and experienced her first conversion. Later that evening, at a banquet with the Pharisees, Magdalene entered the room to anoint Jesus' head. This is a sure sign that she recognized him as a true King, and as the Messiah. It is astonishing, given the times, that Magdalene walked uninvited into a room where men were gathered. Women of those times were not allowed such privilege. The certainty of Magdalene is an example for us all. No matter where the old rules stultify, we are to walk in truth and without fear. This is a good day to contemplate where we may find ourselves limited or afraid in facing worn-out powers. Where do we fear to enter due to our weariness and guilt? Who is willing to receive us just as we are?

In this first Monday of Advent we may reflect upon our inner world and our openness for conversion.

December 6: Sun 19° Scorpio: Meeting with Maroni, the widow of Nain (10 Nov 30).

Today marks the place of the Sun when Jesus met Maroni (the Youth of Nain's mother) in the Valley of the Doves, south of Capernaum. She begged him to come and heal her twelve-year-old son. As Jesus taught in the synagogue when the Sabbath began, a possessed man ran in causing great commotion (*Chron.* p. 256). Images we can work with are: the Valley of the Doves, the widow, and the possessed man. The Holy Spirit (dove) can find us as we renew our relationship with the World "I" (mystical union), which grants us deliverance from possession by our lower nature (the Scorpion becomes the Eagle). As we begin to find Christ, as did Maroni, the dove of the Holy Spirit will lead us back to the Father—and we will be widows no longer. First we remember, then we awaken, then we are reborn. Where does our soul feel widowed from our spirit, or seek to find the ground of our being in false authorities of this world?

December 7: Sun enters the third decan of Scorpio, ruled by Mercury and associated with the constellation of Ophiucus the Serpent Holder. Ophiucus, sometimes also called Aesclepius, has a healing mission.

December 11: Mercury 5°42' Scorpio square Neptune 5°42' Aquarius: Mercury was square Neptune opposite (5° Taurus) today's position at the conversation with Nicodemus (9 Apr 30).

> Before daybreak, Jesus and Nicodemus went to Jerusalem to Lazarus' house on Mount Zion. Joseph of Arimathea joined them there. Later, a whole group of about thirty disciples came. Jesus gave instructions about what the disciples should do during the coming period." (*Chron.* p. 230)

Jesus and Nicodemus had talked all through the previous night. Just before this conversation, Silent Mary, the sister of Magdalene and Lazarus, had died in the presence of the Holy Virgin.

With Mercury standing opposite to this conversation between Jesus and Nicodemus, we remember Nicodemus' eagerness to learn (Mercury).

> The nightly conversation with Jesus was in fact an initiation of Nicodemus. The task is to be able to read the language spoken by the

movements of the heavenly bodies, to grasp their significance intuitively." (CHA, *Jesus' First Visit to Jerusalem Since the Baptism*)[69]

Great inspiration can be found when Mercury and Neptune are aspecting. On this Tuesday in the second week of Advent we may pray before going to sleep, that we can find the echo of today's stars in the night school of Sophia. What inspiration may we find as we awaken tomorrow morning?

December 13: New Moon 26° Scorpio: Jesus heals Lepers and meets opposition. The day after Jesus and his Disciples had left Megiddo, he was in Capernaum where he healed two lepers.

> The Pharisees protested loudly because he had healed on the Sabbath and questioned by what right he was able to forgive sins. Without uttering a word, Jesus passed through their midst. He went to his mother's house. After consoling his mother and the other women there, Jesus went out and spent the night in prayer. (*Chron.* p. 258)

This New Moon offers the contemplation of Jesus silently passing through the midst of his enemies. This is a skill of graciousness that can be used in the presence of our enemies as well. The "voice of silence" is a powerful voice, as it causes accusations to reflect back upon the accuser, and this allows for the angel's voice to be heard in the soul of the accuser—if the soul is willing. If we respond with protest or defensiveness, we contribute to disharmony and we block the angels. Remaining silent has a place and a very high purpose. Intentional silence creates sacred space, and into this space we find the comforter as we prepare to "spend the night in prayer"—for the other. This is a Moon in which we can offer our silence before our accusers. A key element is the movement that follows the silence. To stay can draw forth further aggression. To silently and graciously leave protects both the self and the other.

ASPECT: Uranus goes direct at its exact location during the Adoration of the Magi. This degree is magnified for the next five days.

---

69 See the entry to the commentaries for May 4, 2012.

December 14: Sun 27° Scorpio: First raising of the daughter of Jairus (18 Nov 30). Jesus was approached by Jairus, the chief of the synagogue. Jairus pleaded with Jesus to come and heal his daughter, Salome, who was on the point of death (Mark 5:21–24). Jesus agreed to go with Jairus, but on the way a messenger came to relate the news that Salome was already dead. Jesus, in his mercy, performed the miracle of raising Salome from the dead. Because of her parents' attitude toward Jesus, she was led again to her illness and death two weeks later (*Chron.* 258). The Bible refers to "the dead" as unconscious ego desires carried over from a previous life, and added to in the current life. Robert Powell notes that reincarnation shapes the soul; this is the "mother aspect." Destiny, however, is carried over by the stars; this is the "father aspect." In the soul of Salome the mother forces were shaping, and in her meeting with Christ the father aspect was brought as a gift of destiny. If we do not change our habits when the grace of destiny frees us from our enslavement to unconscious instincts, drives and desires from another life, we will fall again, as did Salome. Hereditary patterns are unconsciously imitated until penetrated (Scorpio) by our individuality. As we do this we find our willingness to be raised from the dead. We find Christ within. The Scorpion becomes the Eagle. May we find our willingness to redeem old habits shaped long ago.

December 16: Sun enters Sagittarius: "Growth attains power of existence" (Rudolf Steiner, *Twelve Moods of the Zodiac*). Control of Speech becomes Feeling for Truth. Blessed are the self-disciplined, for they shall know the truth.

ASPECT: Venus 5°47 Scorpio square Neptune 5°47' Aquarius: Peter receives the keys (19 Mar 31). With Venus opposite (5° Taurus) today's Venus we remember Peter being given the keys to the kingdom of heaven. The keys signify the power drawn from the kingdom of the Father to be able to hold in check the forces of the underworlds rising through the gates of Hell. This same day Jesus was informed of a revolt that would be led by Judas of Gamala, who had the support of a large number of Galileans. When Lazarus suggested Jesus hold back from going to the celebrations in Jerusalem, Jesus replied that this uprising would be the fore-runner of a far greater one that would take place at a later time. He was referring to his future trial and persecution (*Chron.* p. 286).

There are Karmic groups (Venus) that face persecution for standing up for their truth. There are other karmic groups that become intoxicated with illusions spawned from out of the gates of Hell, or from inflated realms of egoism.

> A key to understanding the magnetization of the feeling life is presented in the twenty-second arcanum of the Tarot, "The World," which depicts a woman holding a wand in her left hand and a philtre in the right. She is the personification of maya, the illusion presented by the appearance of the world that bewitches the human being. This underlies communist ideology, which teaches that all religion, spiritual philosophy, belief, and so on is merely an illusion, a "spiritual superstructure" imposed upon the real world. The personification of maya depicted on the Tarot card "The World" holds forth a philtre which, if the human being drinks from it, intoxicates him.[70]

The spirit of compromise has eroded the moral fiber of many cultures, and when the moral fiber erodes, it is easier to drink from the philtre that intoxicates. Intoxication leads to uprisings, fears, wars, terror, oppression, and to the murder of the innocent. Neptune represents the realms called Night in Orphic cosmology, and the twenty-second arcanam of the Tarot—The World. This is Sophia's world. When the keys that keep the underworld in check are compromised, it is not Sophia, but the antisophia who inspires karmic groups. Are the innocent being murdered in our world?

With Venus square Neptune there is a tension that awakens consciousness to perceive the forces of compromise and intoxication, as well as an awareness of the necessity to hold the gates of Hell shut. What greater uprisings are in the future, due to humanity's ignorance regarding adversarial powers? *Blessed are the Peacemakers!*

December 17: Sun 0°44' Sagittarius: Stilling of the Storm (21 Nov 30). In this miracle reported in the Gospel of Luke, (8:22–25), Jesus and his Disciples crossed a lake. While they were sailing he fell asleep and a great storm mounted, casting great waves that endangered the little boat. The Disciples awakened Jesus saying, "Master, Master, we are perishing!" Jesus rose up, raised his hand and a great calm ensued. The Disciples were amazed at his command over the elements. Powerful images are contained in this story.

In changing times much will be asked of human beings striving to keep their destiny communities (the boat) intact. Astral forces of wind and etheric forces of water will surge from the depths of both individual and collective human nature. Change requires that we decide between fear and conviction. The nature of one's conviction will determine the course of one's destiny. Unshakeable belief in Christ and Sophia calms the storms in both human and earthly kingdoms.

> The eurythmy gesture "G" (Sagittarius) uses the force of the upper arms to push away the forces of darkness, to open the veiled secrets and the curtains of deception, with an aim to reveal the light of clarity and to understand the truth.[71]

Solutions to complex world dilemmas become possible as we part the curtains. This is a day to remember and rekindle our willingness to aim our arrows (Sagittarius) with conviction toward solutions living beyond worldly possibilities. Storms of one sort or another always accompany change. It is rare that the nature of the change is perceived correctly as it is occurring. An example is this:

> People talk of mysterious manifestations; the whole divine revelation of spring, summer, autumn, and winter is mixed up. Chaos is setting in, and this comes not from Heaven but from the interior of the Earth. People think that these are merely climate changes, but this is not the case.[72]

Here is a great contemplation of the connection between the Earth's behavior and human thinking.

---

70 Powell, *Hermetic Astrology*, vol. 2, p. 320.

71 Paul and Powell, *Cosmic Dances of the Zodiac*, p. 74.

72 Valentin Tomberg, *Christ and Sophia*, p. 399–400.

SIDEREAL GEOCENTRIC LONGITUDES : DECEMBER 2012 Gregorian at 0 hours UT

DAY	☉	☽	☊	☿	♀	♂	♃	♄	♅	♆	♇
1 SA	14 ♏ 17	10 ♊ 5	1 ♏ 8R	24 ♎ 35	16 ♎ 10	15 ♐ 40	16 ♉ 39R	11 ♎ 42	9 ♓ 45R	5 ♒ 33	13 ♐ 20
2 SU	15 18	22 2	1 6	25 16	17 25	16 26	16 31	11 49	9 45	5 34	13 22
3 MO	16 19	4 ♋ 6	1 3	26 4	18 39	17 12	16 23	11 55	9 44	5 35	13 24
4 TU	17 19	16 21	1 1	26 57	19 54	17 58	16 15	12 2	9 44	5 36	13 26
5 WE	18 20	28 49	0 59	27 55	21 8	18 44	16 7	12 8	9 43	5 36	13 28
6 TH	19 21	11 ♌ 35	0 58	28 58	22 23	19 31	15 59	12 14	9 43	5 37	13 30
7 FR	20 22	24 41	0 58D	0 ♏ 4	23 38	20 17	15 50	12 20	9 43	5 38	13 32
8 SA	21 23	8 ♍ 10	0 59	1 14	24 52	21 3	15 42	12 27	9 42	5 39	13 34
9 SU	22 24	22 4	1 0	2 27	26 7	21 50	15 34	12 33	9 42	5 40	13 36
10 MO	23 25	6 ♎ 24	1 2	3 42	27 22	22 36	15 26	12 39	9 42	5 41	13 38
11 TU	24 26	21 6	1 3	5 0	28 37	23 22	15 18	12 45	9 42	5 42	13 40
12 WE	25 27	6 ♏ 7	1 3R	6 19	29 52	24 9	15 10	12 51	9 42	5 43	13 42
13 TH	26 28	21 19	1 2	7 40	1 ♏ 6	24 56	15 2	12 57	9 42	5 44	13 44
14 FR	27 29	6 ♐ 32	0 59	9 3	2 21	25 42	14 54	13 3	9 42D	5 45	13 46
15 SA	28 30	21 36	0 56	10 26	3 36	26 29	14 47	13 9	9 42	5 46	13 48
16 SU	29 31	6 ♑ 23	0 52	11 51	4 51	27 15	14 39	13 14	9 42	5 47	13 51
17 MO	0 ♐ 32	20 44	0 48	13 17	6 6	28 2	14 31	13 20	9 42	5 48	13 53
18 TU	1 33	4 ♒ 38	0 44	14 43	7 21	28 49	14 24	13 26	9 42	5 50	13 55
19 WE	2 34	18 2	0 42	16 10	8 36	29 36	14 16	13 31	9 42	5 51	13 57
20 TH	3 36	1 ♓ 0	0 40	17 38	9 51	0 ♑ 22	14 9	13 37	9 43	5 52	13 59
21 FR	4 37	13 35	0 41D	19 6	11 6	1 9	14 2	13 42	9 43	5 53	14 1
22 SA	5 38	25 50	0 42	20 35	12 21	1 56	13 55	13 48	9 43	5 55	14 3
23 SU	6 39	7 ♈ 52	0 44	22 4	13 36	2 43	13 48	13 53	9 44	5 56	14 5
24 MO	7 40	19 45	0 46	23 34	14 51	3 30	13 41	13 58	9 44	5 58	14 7
25 TU	8 41	1 ♉ 33	0 46R	25 4	16 6	4 17	13 34	14 3	9 45	5 59	14 9
26 WE	9 42	13 19	0 45	26 34	17 21	5 4	13 28	14 8	9 46	6 0	14 12
27 TH	10 43	25 8	0 42	28 5	18 36	5 51	13 21	14 14	9 46	6 2	14 14
28 FR	11 44	7 ♊ 1	0 37	29 36	19 51	6 38	13 15	14 19	9 47	6 3	14 16
29 SA	12 46	19 1	0 30	1 ♐ 8	21 6	7 25	13 9	14 23	9 48	6 5	14 18
30 SU	13 47	1 ♋ 8	0 22	2 39	22 21	8 12	13 3	14 28	9 49	6 6	14 20
31 MO	14 48	13 25	0 13	4 11	23 36	8 59	12 57	14 33	9 49	6 8	14 22

INGRESSES :

- 2 ☽ → ♋ 15:53
- 5 ☽ → ♌ 2:14
- 6 ☿ → ♏ 22:29
- 7 ☽ → ♍ 9:33
- 9 ☽ → ♎ 13:22
- 11 ☽ → ♏ 14:15
- 12 ♀ → ♏ 2:43
- 13 ☽ → ♐ 13:40
- 15 ☽ → ♑ 13:33
- 16 ☉ → ♐ 11:18
- 17 ☽ → ♒ 15:54
- 19 ♂ → ♑ 12:31
- ☽ → ♓ 22: 6
- 22 ☽ → ♈ 8:15
- 24 ☽ → ♉ 20:51
- 27 ☽ → ♊ 9:50
- 28 ☿ → ♐ 6:15
- 29 ☽ → ♋ 21:45

ASPECTS & ECLIPSES :

- 1 ☽ ☍ ♇ 6:35
- ☽ ☍ ♂ 12: 1
- 3 ☉ ☍ ♃ 1:33
- 5 ☽ [S] ☊ 4: 6
- ☽ ☍ ♆ 12:50
- 6 ☉ □ ☽ 15:31
- 7 ☿ ☌ ☊ 18:44
- 8 ☽ ☍ ♅ 2:41
- 10 ☽ ☌ ♄ 10:20
- 11 ☿ □ ♆ 12:55
- ☽ ☌ ♀ 13: 8
- ☽ ☌ ☊ 15:56
- 12 ☽ ☌ ☿ 0:20
- ☽ ☍ ♃ 14:11
- ♀ ☌ ☊ 22:34
- ☽ ☌ P 23:17
- 13 ☉ ☌ ☽ 8:41
- 14 ☽ ☌ ♇ 11:30
- 15 ☽ ☌ ♂ 8:17
- 16 ♀ □ ♆ 18:20
- 17 ☽ [N] ☊ 17:12
- ☿ ☍ ♃ 19: 8
- 18 ☽ ☌ ♆ 2: 6
- 20 ☉ □ ☽ 5:18
- ☽ ☌ ♅ 16:33
- 23 ♀ ☍ ♃ 3:34
- ☽ ☍ ♄ 12:12
- 24 ☽ ☌ ☋ 22:25
- 25 ☽ ☌ A 21:11
- 26 ☽ ☌ ♃ 0:16
- ☉ □ ♅ 1:21
- ☽ ☍ ♀ 9: 9
- 27 ☽ ☍ ☿ 6:50
- 28 ☉ ☍ ☽ 10:21
- ☽ ☍ ♇ 14:33
- 30 ☉ ☌ ♇ 13:35
- ☽ ☍ ♂ 14:47

SIDEREAL HELIOCENTRIC LONGITUDES : DECEMBER 2012 Gregorian at 0 hours UT

DAY	Sid. Time	☿	♀	⊕	♂	♃	♄	♅	♆	♇	Vernal Point
1 SA	4:41: 0	21 ♋ 43	5 ♍ 54	14 ♉ 17	7 ♑ 9	16 ♉ 11	8 ♎ 35	12 ♓ 18	7 ♒ 25	14 ♐ 11	5 ♓ 4'47"
2 SU	4:44:57	27 1	7 31	15 18	7 46	16 17	8 37	12 19	7 25	14 12	5 ♓ 4'47"
3 MO	4:48:54	2 ♌ 9	9 8	16 18	8 23	16 22	8 39	12 19	7 26	14 12	5 ♓ 4'47"
4 TU	4:52:50	7 8	10 45	17 19	9 0	16 27	8 41	12 20	7 26	14 12	5 ♓ 4'47"
5 WE	4:56:47	11 57	12 22	18 20	9 37	16 33	8 43	12 20	7 26	14 13	5 ♓ 4'47"
6 TH	5: 0:43	16 37	13 59	19 21	10 15	16 38	8 45	12 21	7 27	14 13	5 ♓ 4'47"
7 FR	5: 4:40	21 8	15 36	20 22	10 52	16 43	8 47	12 22	7 27	14 13	5 ♓ 4'47"
8 SA	5: 8:36	25 30	17 13	21 23	11 29	16 48	8 49	12 22	7 27	14 14	5 ♓ 4'46"
9 SU	5:12:33	29 44	18 50	22 24	12 6	16 54	8 51	12 23	7 28	14 14	5 ♓ 4'46"
10 MO	5:16:29	3 ♍ 50	20 27	23 25	12 44	16 59	8 52	12 24	7 28	14 14	5 ♓ 4'46"
11 TU	5:20:26	7 49	22 4	24 26	13 21	17 4	8 54	12 24	7 29	14 15	5 ♓ 4'46"
12 WE	5:24:23	11 40	23 40	25 27	13 58	17 9	8 56	12 25	7 29	14 15	5 ♓ 4'46"
13 TH	5:28:19	15 25	25 17	26 28	14 36	17 15	8 58	12 26	7 29	14 15	5 ♓ 4'46"
14 FR	5:32:16	19 5	26 54	27 29	15 13	17 20	9 0	12 26	7 30	14 16	5 ♓ 4'46"
15 SA	5:36:12	22 38	28 30	28 30	15 51	17 25	9 2	12 27	7 30	14 16	5 ♓ 4'45"
16 SU	5:40: 9	26 6	0 ♎ 7	29 31	16 28	17 31	9 4	12 28	7 30	14 16	5 ♓ 4'45"
17 MO	5:44: 5	29 29	1 44	0 ♊ 32	17 6	17 36	9 6	12 28	7 31	14 17	5 ♓ 4'45"
18 TU	5:48: 2	2 ♎ 47	3 20	1 33	17 43	17 41	9 8	12 29	7 31	14 17	5 ♓ 4'45"
19 WE	5:51:58	6 2	4 56	2 34	18 21	17 46	9 10	12 29	7 31	14 17	5 ♓ 4'45"
20 TH	5:55:55	9 12	6 33	3 35	18 58	17 52	9 11	12 30	7 32	14 18	5 ♓ 4'45"
21 FR	5:59:52	12 19	8 9	4 36	19 36	17 57	9 13	12 31	7 32	14 18	5 ♓ 4'45"
22 SA	6: 3:48	15 22	9 46	5 37	20 14	18 2	9 15	12 31	7 33	14 18	5 ♓ 4'44"
23 SU	6: 7:45	18 23	11 22	6 39	20 51	18 7	9 17	12 32	7 33	14 19	5 ♓ 4'44"
24 MO	6:11:41	21 21	12 58	7 40	21 29	18 13	9 19	12 33	7 33	14 19	5 ♓ 4'44"
25 TU	6:15:38	24 17	14 34	8 41	22 7	18 18	9 21	12 33	7 34	14 19	5 ♓ 4'44"
26 WE	6:19:34	27 10	16 10	9 42	22 44	18 23	9 23	12 34	7 34	14 19	5 ♓ 4'44"
27 TH	6:23:31	0 ♏ 2	17 46	10 43	23 22	18 28	9 25	12 35	7 34	14 20	5 ♓ 4'44"
28 FR	6:27:27	2 52	19 22	11 44	24 0	18 34	9 27	12 35	7 35	14 20	5 ♓ 4'44"
29 SA	6:31:24	5 40	20 58	12 45	24 38	18 39	9 29	12 36	7 35	14 20	5 ♓ 4'44"
30 SU	6:35:21	8 28	22 34	13 46	25 16	18 44	9 30	12 37	7 35	14 21	5 ♓ 4'43"
31 MO	6:39:17	11 14	24 10	14 48	25 53	18 49	9 32	12 37	7 36	14 21	5 ♓ 4'43"

INGRESSES :

- 2 ☿ → ♌ 13:52
- 9 ☿ → ♍ 1:33
- 15 ♀ → ♎ 22:15
- 16 ⊕ → ♊ 11:24
- 17 ☿ → ♎ 3:44
- 26 ☿ → ♏ 23:45

ASPECTS (HELIOCENTRIC +MOON(TYCHONIC)) :

- 1 ☽ ☍ ♇ 8:16
- ☿ [N] ☊ 8:18
- 2 ♀ △ ♂ 6: 0
- 3 ⊕ ☌ ♃ 1:33
- ☽ ☍ ♂ 8:53
- ♂ □ ♄ 10:47
- 4 ☿ ☍ ♆ 1:30
- ☿ ✶ ♄ 7:42
- ♀ ☍ ♅ 23:32
- 5 ☿ △ ♇ 11:33
- ☽ ☍ ♆ 16:16
- 6 ☿ □ ♃ 0: 5
- ♀ □ ♇ 3:22
- ☽ ☌ ☿ 14:14
- ☿ □ ⊕ 18:41
- 7 ♀ △ ♃ 17:29
- 8 ☽ ☍ ♅ 7:21
- ☽ ☌ ♀ 17:46
- 9 ♂ ✶ ♅ 10:59
- 10 ☽ ☌ ♄ 4: 5
- 12 ☿ ☍ ♅ 4:42
- ☿ □ ♇ 16:25
- ☽ ☍ ♃ 17:32
- ☿ △ ♂ 17:32
- 13 ☿ △ ♃ 12:10
- 14 ☽ ☌ ♇ 12:15
- ♀ △ ⊕ 23:38
- 16 ☽ ☌ ♂ 17:32
- 17 ☿ △ ⊕ 10:56
- ♂ △ ♃ 22:29
- 18 ☽ ☌ ♆ 5: 6
- ☿ ☌ ♀ 7:55
- 19 ☿ △ ♆ 11:17
- ☿ ☌ ♄ 23:56
- 20 ♀ △ ♆ 14:43
- ☽ ☌ ♅ 21:56
- 21 ☿ ✶ ♇ 15:32
- ♀ ☌ ♄ 16:17
- 23 ☽ ☍ ♄ 2:51
- ☽ ☍ ♀ 8: 8
- ⊕ △ ♆ 21:27
- 24 ☿ □ ♂ 1:20
- ☽ ☍ ☿ 4:20
- ☿ ☌ ☋ 18: 6
- ♀ ✶ ♇ 20:14
- 25 ⊕ △ ♄ 16:16
- 26 ☽ ☌ ♃ 10:22
- 28 ☽ ☍ ♇ 14:40
- ⊕ □ ♅ 20:17
- 29 ♂ [S] ☊ 4: 6
- ☿ □ ♆ 16:28
- 30 ⊕ ☍ ♇ 13:35
- 31 ☿ △ ♅ 12: 5

If we cannot part the curtains of deception, our thinking will remain shallow and the causes of change will be misinterpreted. When the winds of change threaten equilibrium, to whom would you turn?

December 19: Sun 2° Sagittarius conjunct the Galactic Center. The Archer's arrow aims at the Galactic Center: the heart of the Milky Way. This is opposite to where the Sun was at Pentecost.

December 21: Winter Solstice: Sun 4° Sagittarius. The classic Maya Long Count calendar covers a time period from approximately the year 3114 BC to AD 2012. The Maya culture flourished from about AD 250 to 900. An Age is a Yuga in Hindu chronology, encompassing a period of about 5,000 years. The last Age, or Yuga, is referred to as the *Kali Yuga*, or the *Iron Age* in Greek terminology. This is the Age the Maya Long Count calculates. According to Rudolf Steiner the transition in 1899 was from the Dark Age to the New Age of Light, which is accompanied by the appearance of Christ working into Earth evolution in a new way. The following are excerpts from an article by Robert Powell:

Nevertheless, the impulses of the Dark Age continue on into the present time. In other words, since 1899 we are living in a period of a great epic struggle between the forces of light, led by Christ, and forces of darkness, which are opposing the light of Christ. In the Christian tradition the Letters of John refer to the Antichrist as the force opposing Christ.

Let us now consider the difference between the end date of the Kali Yuga according to Rudolf Steiner, which is the year 1899, and the end date of the Maya calendar, which is the year 2012. What is this difference about? My understanding is that the Maya astronomers were aware, like the Hindu chronologists, that humanity entered into a dark age which would end around the present time. As discussed above, looking at the starting points of both the Maya calendar (in 3114 BC) and Kali Yuga (in 3102 BC), there is only a twelve year difference between these two starting dates. However, what the Maya astronomers seemed to

have grasped is that there would be a period of conflict between the forces of light and darkness before the real New Age would begin. That would explain why the Maya astronomers came to the year 2012 as the start of the New Age instead of the year 1899.

According to Rudolf Steiner the event of Pentecost, which took place nearly two thousand years ago, is to become a world event. He spoke of this as the coming World Pentecost. What does he mean by this? The World Pentecost is an event comparable to Pentecost two thousand years ago. However, it will be a world event, not just an event that impacts a relatively small group of people in a particular geographical location. At that time in AD 33 it was ... initially the twelve Disciples who became Apostles, who then went out onto the streets of Jerusalem, to the pool of Bethesda, and baptized three thousand people that day (and thousands more subsequently). In contrast, the World Pentecost will be an event of the outpouring of Divine Love for the whole of humanity. Will humanity be sufficiently prepared to receive this? And when is the World Pentecost going to happen? And, further, what might this foretell concerning our primary question regarding the significance of the year 2012?

Let us contemplate once again the movement of our Sun around the Central Sun. From the beginning of Kali Yuga or the Maya calendar, around 5,120 years ago, our Sun entered a part of the galaxy where there had previously been a constellation that had been destroyed long ago. Our Sun thus came into a region of cosmic debris that acted as a shield of cosmic dust so that our Sun—and consequently the entire solar system—was no longer receiving the full outpouring of the great wave of Divine Love from the Central Sun. While the spiritual beings undergoing their evolution upon our Sun are at such a high level of spirituality that they are still able to focus upon and receive the outpouring of Divine Love from the Central Sun, this is not the case for most human beings on the Earth, with the exception of a few highly evolved spiritual masters. The Hindu and Maya astronomer-chronologists evidently intuited that this shielding effect impeding the inflow of the great wave of Divine Love from the Central Sun would last for only a limited period of time, as in the analogy used earlier of being out on a walk and experiencing the Sun disappearing behind a cloud, knowing that the Sun will eventually reappear from behind the cloud. The date of the start of the New Age has been a matter of forecasting when the Sun would pass out of the shielding effect of cosmic dust belonging to this part of the galaxy, where there are the remnants of a constellation that was destroyed long ago through which our Sun has been passing for some 5,120 years. It is a matter of forecasting when our Sun will pass out from this galactic region of cosmic dust and debris to begin to receive again the great wave of Divine Love that is continually proceeding from the Central Sun. The prophecy of the Maya astronomers, who were attuned to the galactic level of existence, is that this will occur around the end of 2012. This is not so far away [this article was published in 2010]. According to the astrosophical research presented in this article, we are rapidly approaching the event of a galactic alignment at the winter solstice in 2012 through which humanity as a whole will receive a great wave of Divine Love—and this is precisely the event prophesied by Rudolf Steiner as the World Pentecost. Whether this event will occur exactly when the galactic alignment occurs on December 21, 2012, or whether it takes place at some later point in time, it is important that we consciously prepare for it.

In using the expression galactic alignment in relation to the year 2012, it has to be clarified that this galactic alignment is not with the Central Sun as at the historical event of Pentecost. Rather, it has to do with the Sun at the winter solstice crossing the Galactic Equator during the 36-year period from 1980 to 2016, as discussed in *Christ & the Maya Calendar* [by Robert Powell and Kevin Dann], where the expression "2012 Window" is used to denote this 36-year period.[73] In the voluminous literature concerning the date of the end of the Maya calendar, 2012 is well known as falling within the period 1980–2016 of the galactic alignment of the winter solstice Sun with the Galactic Equator. The new perspective offered in this article is that–if this date intuited by the Maya truly does denote the real start of the New Age–2012 marks the end of the (approximately) 5,120-year period of the Sun's passage through the local galactic region of cosmic dust and debris obscuring our solar system from the Central Sun, and that the exit of our Sun from this dust-filled local galactic region signifies the (re-)opening to the great wave of Divine Love proceeding from the Central Sun and that this is the World Pentecost.

Whether or not the onset of the great wave of Divine Love will be around December 21, 2012 remains to be seen. Apart from the Maya calendar, there are other prophecies that point to this time period as a time of transition…In the last analysis, however, it is difficult to pinpoint with any degree of accuracy the exact time when our solar system will exit the region of cosmic dust and debris in this local part of the galaxy which our Sun—on its path around the Central Sun—has been traversing now for some 5,120 years. However, that the World Pentecost will come, of this we can be sure. And it is essentially and intrinsically an inner event for which inner preparation is required.[74]

What this date will unfold will become apparent as we move up to it and go beyond. This date may indicate that cosmic influences will gradually begin to illumine the Earth—and perhaps already have been—bringing forth the best in those willing to face their shadow nature, and the worst in those (individually or as nations) who would wish to flee from such an encounter. For if the light is going to intensify, so also will our perceptions of the shadow. We could all probably agree that we are in a time of change. The end of an Age would call forth change. Our task is to awaken and find our part in bringing forth the good, the moral and the true.

Whatever may manifest this year or beyond, the truth of preparing for Cosmic Light endures. This is the task of all humanity.

73 In "Sun on the Galactic Center" (*Journal for Star Wisdom 2010*), David Tresemer points out that the galactic alignment of the winter solstice Sun with the Galactic Center will not take place until about 2230, which raises the question of whether this will be the time of the World Pentecost rather than 2012.

74 Powell, from articles in *Journal for Star Wisdom* 2010, 2012.

December 22: Venus 13° Scorpio opposite Jupiter 13° Taurus: Heliocentric Venus was at this degree when Christ appeared to the five hundred. As Peter was addressing the crowd, "The Risen One approached, as a radiant figure, and passed through the middle of the crowd. Peter moved aside, and the Lord took his place. He spoke of the persecution which would befall his followers, but also of the eternal reward in heaven" (CHA, *The Forty Days After the Mystery of Golgotha*).

With Venus remembering this appearance of Christ to the five thousand listeners, we can remember Peter moving aside and making way for something higher. As we do this, as did Peter, we too may find persecution from those who cannot understand the source of our inspiration. Venus is connected with the second chakra, which yearns to listen to the dictates of wisdom, and it is Jupiter, the representative of wisdom, that is opposite Venus today. May we make way for higher wisdom as we move through this day, as well as the coming year, with the goal of finding compassion toward those who would persecute our humble devotion toward something greater. Can we feel the presence of invisible beings?

December 24: Sun 7° Sagittarius: The First Temptation in the Wilderness. There are forces that transcend the human being; forces that originated in cosmic aeons prior to that of the human beings. Remnants of these forces live in densified forms within the interior of the Earth, and from here they work negatively against the human being. The remnants from previous aeons that work negatively with the will nature of human beings are those of "trapped life." Through the transformation of the will, whereby it becomes obedient to Divine Will, "trapped life" becomes united with cosmic love (Pluto–Phanes). The first temptation in the wilderness was the temptation to bow to the Prince of this World. This is the temptation to use the personal will in service of self-gain—a temptation that continues in our time through all forms of tyranny.

Humanity has the task to bring to realization that which Nature does not bring to realization. Nature becomes conscious in us and we have to create further. The kingdoms of Nature are beneath the human being. The ideal to strive for is the kingdom of God (*regnum Dei*)—as in the Lord's Prayer: "Thy kingdom come!" To bring this to realization—this is the task which the human being has to fulfill on Earth, following one's highest ideal. This world that is not yet there is what the human being has to learn to build.[75]

May we become the "handmaids of the Lord" so that our deeds reflect what is best for all of humanity and all of Earth's creatures, in our remembering of spirit.

December 25: Christian Celebration of the Birth of Christ. This day a seed is planted in the womb of our soul. May we believe in this gift and tend it through the coming months, until it quickens at Candlemas, and then sprouts, revealing its new life, at Easter. We can follow the flowering and fruiting as we move through the next nine months that lead us to Michaelmas. This is the seed of our future spiritual potential for the coming year. What in childhood came from without as gifts, as adults becomes our recognition of a new aspect of our eternal being that is born from the depths of winter's night.

Sun 8° Sagittarius: The Second Temptation in the Wilderness. Forces from past aeons that work negatively against the feeling nature of human beings can be called the forces in the inner Earth that work from "trapped sound" (Neptune–Night). Through the transformation of our heart, our feeling life becomes permeated with cosmic sound, whereby we hear spiritual beings working with us. The second temptation in the wilderness was the temptation to plunge from the pinnacle of the temple, with the assurance that angels would catch us. This is the temptation to fall from consciousness, forsaking the angels, and instead become pawns in magnetic attractions to fallen densified forces. This can result in terrible polarization in the feeling life, as happened with those who were behind the communist revolution of 1917 in Russia.

Circumstances are always influenced by the subconscious if the human being is not active. If he does not strive continually with respect to his

---

75 Tomberg, *Starlight*, vol. 10.

subconscious, he succumbs to some kind of inertia, which leads to a darkening of the subconscious. Thus, the human being can find himself in complete darkness. "The pinnacle of the temple" (Luke 4:11) is the superconscious. The temptation [of casting oneself from the pinnacle of the temple] of Jesus Christ in the wilderness is that of believing in the wisdom of the subconscious.[76]

May our heart beat as one with the hearts of others, in spirit awareness. May we reach for the true pinnacle of our temple.

December 26: Sun enters the second decan of Sagittarius, ruled by the Moon and associated with the constellation Corona Australis, the Southern Crown, forming a moon-like chalice beneath the central part of the Archer.

Sun 9° Sagittarius: The Third Temptation in the Wilderness. Forces from past aeons that work negatively against the thinking life of human beings can be called the forces in the inner Earth that work out of "trapped light" (Uranus–Ouranos). This can lead to a poverty of thought, whereby thinking is torn from cosmic thoughts. Through the transformation of our thinking we can become a vehicle for cosmic light. The third temptation in the wilderness was the temptation to turn stones to bread.

> The temptation of "turning stones to bread" is that of "producing" the living and organic from the dead and material. For example, one does precisely this if one conceives of thinking as a mechanical process in the brain. That is, if one supposes that the brain produces thoughts just as the glands produce secretion. Thus, the third temptation has to do with materialism, just as the second temptation has to do with the force of moral irresponsibility, and the first temptation with the will to power.[77]

May our thinking be illumined by truth, and our contemplation ennobled through spirit beholding.

December 27/28: Sun 11° Sagittarius: Second raising of the daughter of Jairus (1 Dec 30). Thirteen days after her first raising from the dead, Salome was again close to death. At this second raising

from the dead, Salome was deeply moved and shed tears. "Jesus exhorted the parents to receive God's mercy thankfully, to completely renounce vanity and worldly pleasure, to do penance, and to beware of again compromising their daughter's life, now restored for the second time. Jesus told Salome that in the future she should no longer live according to the dictates of her flesh and blood, but that she should eat the Bread of Life—the Word of God—and she should repent, believe, pray, and do good deeds. Salome's parents became inwardly transformed and expressed their determination to change their ways" (*CHA, The Raising of the Youth of Nain and of the Daughter of Jairus*).

As the year comes toward its end, we can contemplate how we may strive to change our ways to become more of who we truly are in the coming new year.

ASPECT: Full Moon: Sun 11° Sagittarius opposite Moon 11° Gemini: Woe upon the Pharisees (24 Mar 33). Just weeks before his death on the cross, Jesus proclaimed his woe upon the Pharisees. Earlier this day, with the Moon at 11° Gemini, Jesus taught his Disciples undisturbed, as the Pharisees had not yet come. "Jesus spoke of his mission, saying that he would withdraw from humanity and from the flesh, and that whoever—with him, through him, and in him—separated himself from his own fallen nature, would at the same time commend himself to the Father" (*Chron.* p. 345).

This Full Moon offers us the contemplation of raising ourselves from the dead habits that separate us from our spiritual potential—through uniting ourselves with Christ. Those who do not have ears to ear, or eyes to see are addressed in the woe, which is recorded in Matthew 23:2–39. May we find our inner lodge of peace and from this place radiate love to all our fellow human beings, as well as to all the beings of nature.

December 30: Sun 14° Sagittarius: The healing of two possessed youths from Gergesa (5 Dec 30). Jesus met two youths who were possessed by ahrimanic demons, inhabiting tombs beside a path. Because of the two, none could pass—owing to the demons' exceeding force. When they saw Jesus they cried out: "What have you to do with

76 Ibid.
77 Ibid.

us, O Son of God?" (Matt. 8:29). Jesus cast out the demons into a nearby heard of swine, whereon the whole heard of swine rushed down a steep bank into the sea.

In this healing, the relationship of Ahriman to the element of water becomes clear. The perceptive demons recognized the Son of God and experienced him as a direct threat to their activity. The demons called out from the possessed, asking to be thrown into the herd of swine. Cleverly, as Ahriman stood before Christ, he wished to be cast into the swine—so that through the people eating of the swine meat, the demons would find more than just two bodies to possess. It was known in ancient wisdom that Ahriman could enter the human lymph system (the fluid system) through the pinworms in pork. This was the knowledge behind the Jewish prohibition against eating pork. Those laws were disregarded in this region. When the people of Gergesa heard of the death of their swine, they asked Jesus to leave:

> The fact that the Gergesenes finally urged the Lord to leave their district, expresses the tragic aspect which the Christ impulse already bore at the dawn of the new era, and must always bear whenever it encounters evil. People had then degenerated to such an extent that they could not properly value the benefits of his deed, but, happy to violate the laws, were more interested in the profit and loss attached to their herd of swine than in their own healing and wellbeing.[78]

---

78 Von Halle, *Illness and Healing*, pp. 132–138.

As our year ends and we enter the year 2013, we may ask ourselves: Are we, too, happy to violate the laws, preferring to cast out Christ rather than serve the flame of Love? Motives for profit alone will continuously lead humanity astray from moral development and practices.

ASPECT: Sun conjunct Pluto 14°20' Sagittarius: Sun was conjunct Pluto during the temptations of Christ. This aspect asks us to choose between union with Hades or union with the Divine Love of the Father. Pluto was at this degree at the call of Zacchaeus the Tax Collector:

> A man was there by the name of Zacchaeus; he was a chief tax collector and was wealthy. He wanted to see who Jesus was, but because he was short he could not see over the crowd. So he ran ahead and climbed a sycamore-fig tree to see him, since Jesus was coming this way.
>
> When Jesus reached the spot, he looked up and said to him, "Zacchaeus, come down immediately. I must stay at your house today." So he came down at once and welcomed him gladly." (Luke 19:1–10)

We are all called to come down at once, for Christ Jesus must stay at our house today. Blessed are those who welcome him gladly!

❦

"When the Christ impulse entered the evolution of humanity in the way known to us, one result was that the chaotic forces of the sibyls were thrust back for a time, as when a stream disappears below ground and reappears later on. These forces were indeed to reappear in another form, a form purified by the Christ impulse.... Yes, a time is coming when the old astrology will live again in a new form, a Christ-filled form, and then, if one can practice it properly so that it will be permeated with the Christ impulse, one may venture to look up to the stars and question them about their spiritual script."

—RUDOLF STEINER (*Christ and the Spiritual World and the Search for the Holy Grail*, pp. 94, 122)

GLOSSARY

This glossary of entries relating to Esoteric Christianity lists only some of the specialized terms used in the articles and commentaries of the *Journal for Star Wisdom*. For reasons of space, the entries are very brief, and the reader is encouraged to read the works of Rudolf Steiner for a more complete understanding of these terms.

Ahriman: An adversarial being identified by the great prophet Zarathustra during the ancient Persian cultural epoch (5067–2907 BC) as an opponent to the Sun God, *Ahura Mazda,* or *Ahura Mazdao* (obs.), ("Aura of the Sun"). Some influences upon the human being of Ahriman's activity: limits human cognition to that which is derived from sense perception, hardens thinking (materialistic thoughts), attacks the etheric body by way of modern technology (electromagnetic radiation, etc.), hardens hearts (cold and calculating), cultivates egotism ("My will be done"). Also called Satan, Ahriman represents one aspect of the Dragon. Ahriman's influence leads to materialistic thinking devoid of feeling, empathy, and moral conscience. Ahriman helps inspire science and technology, and works through forces of sub-nature such as gravity, electricity, magnetism, radioactivity—forces that are antithetical to life.

ahrimanic beings: Spiritual beings who have become agents of Ahriman's influences.

Angel Jesus: A pure immaculate Angelic being who sacrifices himself so that the Christ may work through him. This Angelic being is actually of the status of an Archangel, who has descended to work on the Angelic level in order to be closer to human beings and to assist them on the path of confrontation with evil.

Ascension: An unfathomable process at the start of which, on May 14, AD 33, Christ united with the etheric realm which surrounds and permeates the earth with Cosmic Life. Thus began his cosmic ascent to the realm of the heavenly Father, with the goal of elevating the Earth spiritually and opening pathways between the Earth and the spiritual world for the future.

astral body: Part of the human being that is the bearer of consciousness, passion, and desires, as well as idealism and the longing for perfection.

Asuras: Fallen Archai (Time Spirits) from the time of Old Saturn, whose opposition to human evolution comes to expression through promoting debauched sexuality and senseless violence among human beings. So low is the regard that the Asuras have for the sacredness of human life, that as well as promoting extreme violence and debauchery (for example, through the film industry), they do not hold back from the destruction of the physical body of human beings. In particular, the activity of the Asuras retards the development of the consciousness soul.

bodhisattva: On the human level a bodhisattva is a human being far advanced on the spiritual path, a human being belonging to the circle of twelve great teachers surrounding the Cosmic Christ. One who incarnates periodically to further the evolution of the Earth and humanity, working on the level of an angelic, archangelic, or higher being in relation to the rest of humanity. Every 5,000 years one of these great teachers from the circle of bodhisattvas takes on a special mission, incarnating repeatedly to awaken a new human faculty and capacity. Once that capacity has been imparted through its human bearer, this Bodhisattva then incarnates upon the earth for the last time, ascending to the level of a Buddha in order to serve humankind from spirit realms. See also Maitreya Bodhisattva.

Central Sun: Heart of the Milky Way, also called the Galactic Center. Our Sun orbits this Central Sun over a period of approximately 225 million years.

chakra: One of seven astral organs of perception through which human beings develop higher levels of cognition such as clairvoyance, telepathy, and so on.

Christ: The eternal being who is the second member of the Trinity. Also called the *Divine I AM*, the Son of God, the Cosmic Christ, and the Logos/Word. Christ began to fully unite with the human vessel (Jesus) at the Baptism in the Jordan, and for 3½ years penetrated as the *Divine I AM* successively into the astral body, etheric body, and physical body of Jesus, spiritualizing each member. Through the Mystery of Golgotha Christ united with the Earth, kindling the spark of Christ consciousness (*Not I, but Christ in me*) in all human beings.

Christ Jesus: The Divine-Human being; the God-Man; the union of the Divine with the Human. The presence of the Cosmic Christ in the physical body of the human being called the Nathan Jesus during the 3½ years of the ministry.

consciousness soul: The portion of the human soul in which "I" consciousness is awakening not only to its own sense of individuality and to the individualities of others, but also to its higher self—spirit self (Sanskrit: *manas*). Within the consciousness soul, the "I" perceives truth, beauty, and goodness; within the spirit self, the "I" becomes truth, beauty, and goodness.

crossing the threshold: a term applicable to our time, as human beings are increasingly encountering the spiritual world—in so doing, crossing the threshold between the sense-perceptible realm and nonphysical realms of existence. To the extent that spiritual capacities have not been cultivated, this encounter with non-physical realms beyond the sense world signifies a descent into the subconscious (for example, through drugs) rather than an ascent to knowledge of higher worlds through the awakening of higher levels of consciousness.

Decan: The zodiac of 360 degrees is divided into twelve signs, each of thirty degrees. A decan is ten degrees, thus one third of one sign or 1/36th of the zodiac.

Devil: Another name for Lucifer.

Dragon: As used in the Apocalypse of John, there are different appearances of the dragon, each one representing an adversarial being opposed to Michael, Christ, and Sophia. For example, the great red dragon of chapter 12 opposes Sophia, the woman clothed with the Sun (Sophia is the pure Divine-Cosmic Feminine Soul of the World). The imagery from chapter 12 of Revelations depicts the woman clothed with the Sun as pregnant and that the great red dragon attempts to devour her child as soon as it is born. The child coming to birth from the woman clothed with the Sun represents the Divine-Cosmic "I AM" born through the assistance of the pure Divine Feminine Soul of the World. The dragon is cast down from the heavenly realm by the mighty Archangel Michael. Cast down to the Earth, the dragon continues with attempts to devour the cosmic child (the Divine-Cosmic "I AM") coming to birth among humankind.

Ego: The soul sheath through which the "I" begins to incarnate and to experience life on Earth (to be distinguished from the term *ego* used in Freudian and Jungian psychology—hence written capitalized "Ego" in order to make this distinction). The terms *Ego*, "*I*," and *soul* are often used interchangeably in spiritual science. The Ego maintains threads of integrity and continuity through memory, while experiencing new sensations and perceptions through observation and thinking, feeling, and willing. The Ego is capable of moral discernment and also experiences temptation. For this reason it is often stated that the "I" comprises a higher nature ("Ego") and a lower nature ("ego").

Emmerich, Anne Catherine (also "Sister Emmerich"): A Catholic stigmatist (1774–1824) whose visions depicted the daily life of Jesus, beginning some weeks before the event of the descent of Christ into the body of Jesus at the Baptism in the River Jordan and extending for a period of several weeks after the Crucifixion.

Ephesus: The area in Asia Minor (now Turkey) to which the Apostle John (also called John Zebedee, the brother of James the Greater) accompanied the Virgin Mary approximately three years after the death of Christ Jesus. Ephesus was a very significant ancient mystery center where cosmic mysteries of the East found their way into the West. Initiates at Ephesus were devoted to the goddess Artemis, known as "Artemis of Ephesus," whose qualities are more those of a Mother goddess than is the case with the Greek goddess Artemis, although there is a certain degree of overlap between Artemis and Artemis of Ephesus with regard to many of their respective characteristics. A magnificent Ionic mystery temple was built in honor of Artemis of Ephesus at a location close to the Aegean Sea. Mary's house, built by John, was located high up above, on the nearby hill known as Mount Nightingale, about six miles from the temple of Artemis at Ephesus.

etheric body: The body of life forces permeating and animating the physical body. The etheric body was formed during Ancient Sun evolution. The etheric body's activity is expressed in the seven life processes permeating the seven vital organs. The etheric body is related to the movements of the seven visible planets.

Fall, The: A fall from oneness with spiritual worlds. The Fall, which took place during the Lemurian period of Earth evolution, was a time of dramatic transition in human evolution when the soul descended from "Paradise" into earthly existence. Through the Fall the human soul began to incarnate into a physical body upon the earth and experience the world from "within" the body, perceiving through the senses.

Fifth Gospel: The writings and lectures of Rudolf Steiner based on new spiritual perceptions and insights into the mysteries of Christ's life on earth, including the second coming of Christ—his appearance in the etheric realm in our time, beginning in the twentieth century.

Golgotha, Mystery of: Rudolf Steiner's designation for the entire mystery of the coming of Christ to the Earth. Sometimes this term is used more specifically to refer to the events surrounding the Crucifixion and Resurrection, In particular, the Crucifixion—the sacrifice on the cross—marked the birth of Christ's union with the Earth. Also referred to as the "Turning Point of Time," whereby at the Crucifixion Christ descended from the sphere of the Sun and became the "Spirit of the Earth."

Grail: An etheric chalice into which Christ can work to transform earthly substance into spiritual substance. The term *Grail* has many deep levels of meaning and refers on the one hand to a spiritual stream in service of Christ, and on the other hand to the means by which the human "I" penetrates and transforms evil into good. The power of transubstantiation expresses something of this process of transformation of evil into good.

Grail Knights: Those trained to confront evil and transform it into something good, in service of Christ. Members of a spiritual stream that existed in the past and continues to exist—albeit in metamorphosed form—in the present. Every human being striving for the good can potentially become a Grail Knight.

I AM: One's true individuality, that—with few exceptions—never fully incarnates but works into the developing Ego and its lower bodies (astral, etheric, physical). The **Cosmic I AM** is the "I AM" of Christ, through which—on account of the Mystery of Golgotha—we are all graced with the possibility of receiving a divine spark therefrom.

Jesus (see Nathan Jesus and Solomon Jesus): The pure human being who received the Christ at the Baptism in the River Jordan.

Jesus Christ: See Christ Jesus.

Jesus of Nazareth: The name of the human being whose birth is celebrated in the Gospel of Luke, also referred to as the Nathan Jesus. When Jesus of Nazareth reached the age of twelve, the spirit of the Solomon Jesus (Gospel of Matthew) united with the body and sheaths of the pure Nathan Jesus. This union lasted for about 18 years, until the Baptism in the River Jordan. During these 18 years, Jesus of Nazareth was a composite being comprising the Nathan Jesus and the spirit ("I") of the Solomon Jesus. Just before the Baptism, the spirit of the Solomon Jesus withdrew, and at the Baptism Jesus became known as "Christ Jesus" through the union of Christ with the sheaths of Jesus.

Jezebel: Wife of King Ahab, approximately 900 BC, who worked through the powers of black magic against the prophet Elijah.

Kali Yuga: Yugas are ages of influence referred to in Hindu cosmography, each yuga lasting a certain numbers of years in length (always a multiple of 2500). The Kali Yuga is also known as the Dark Age, which began with the death of Krishna in 3102 BC (-3101). Kali Yuga lasted 5,000 years and ended in AD 1899.

Kingly Stream: Biblically, the line of heredity from King David into which the Solomon Jesus (Gospel of Matthew) was born. The kings (the three magi) were initiates who sought to bring the cosmic will of the heavenly Father to expression on the Earth through spiritual forces working from spiritual beings dwelling in the stars. The minds of the wise kings were enlightened by the coming of Christ Jesus.

Krishna: A cosmic-human being, the sister soul of Adam that overlighted Arjuna as described in the Bhagavad Gita. The overlighting by Krishna of Arjuna could be described as an incorporation of Krishna into Arjuna. An incorporation is a partial incarnation. The cosmic-human being known as Krishna later fully incarnated as Jesus of Nazareth (Nathan Jesus—Gospel of Luke).

Lazarus: The elder brother of Mary Magdalene, Martha, and Silent Mary. At his raising from the dead, Lazarus became the first human being to be fully initiated by Christ (see Lazarus–John).

Lazarus–John: At the raising of Lazarus from the dead by Christ, the spiritual being of John the Baptist united with Lazarus. The higher spiritual members of John (Spirit Body, Life Spirit, Spirit Self) entered into the members of Lazarus, which were developed to the level of the consciousness soul.

Lucifer: The name of a fallen spiritual being, also called the Light-Bearer, who acts as a retarding force within the human astral body and also in the sentient soul. Lucifer inflames egotism and pride within the human being, often inspiring genius and supreme artistry. Arrogance and self-importance are stimulated, without humility or sacrificial love. Lucifer stirs up forces of rebellion, but cannot deliver true freedom—just its illusion.

luciferic beings: Spiritual beings who have become agents of Lucifer's influences.

magi: Initiates in the mystery school of Zarathustra, the Bodhisattva who incarnated as Zoroaster (Zaratas, Nazaratos) in the sixth century BC and who, after he came to Babylon, became a teacher of the Chaldean priesthood. At the time of Jesus, the magi were still continuing the star-gazing tradition of the school of Zoroaster. The task of the magi was to recognize when their master would reincarnate. With their visit to the new-born Jesus child in Bethlehem (Gospel of Matthew), to this child who was the reincarnated Zarathustra/Zoroaster, they fulfilled their mission. The three magi are the "priest kings from the East" referred to in the Gospel of Matthew.

Maitreya Bodhisattva: The bodhisattva individuality that is preparing to become the successor of Gautama Buddha and will be known as the Bringer of the Good. This bodhisattva was incarnated in the second century BC as Jeshu ben Pandira, the teacher of the Essenes, who died about 100 BC. Rudolf Steiner indicated that Jeshu ben Pandira reincarnated at the beginning of the twentieth century as a great bodhisattva individuality in order to fulfill the lofty mission of proclaiming Christ's coming in the etheric realm, beginning around 1933: "He will be the actual herald of Christ in his etheric form" (lecture about Jeshu ben Pandira held in Leipzig on November 4, 1911). There are differing points of view as to who this individuality actually was in his twentieth century incarnation.

manas: Also called the Spirit Self; the purified astral body, lifted into full communion with truth and goodness by becoming the true and the good within the essence of the higher self of the human being. Manas is the spiritual source of the Ego ("I"), and as it is the eternal part of the human being that goes from life to life, Manas bears the human being's true "eternal name" through its union with the Holy Spirit. The "eternal name" expresses the human being's true mission from life to life.

Mani: The name of a lofty initiate who lived in Babylon in the third century AD. The founder of the Manichean stream, whose mission is the transformation of evil into goodness through compassion and love. Mani reincarnated as Parzival in the ninth century AD. Mani/Parzival is one of the leading initiates of our present age—the age of the consciousness soul (AD 1414 –3574). One of the highest beings ever to incarnate upon the earth, he will become the future Manu beginning in the astrological age of Sagittarius. This future Manu will oversee the spiritual evolution of a sequence of seven ages, comprising the seven cultural epochs of the Sixth Great Age of Earth evolution from the Age of Sagittarius to the Age of Gemini—lasting a total of 7 x 2,160 years (15,120 years), since each zodiacal age lasts 2,160 years.

Manu: Like the word Buddha, the word Manu is a title. A Manu has the task of spiritually overseeing one Great Age of Earth evolution, comprising seven astrological ages (seven cultural epochs)—lasting a total of 7 x 2,160 years (15,120 years), since each zodiacal age lasts 2,160 years. The present Age of Pisces AD 215–2,375—with its corresponding cultural epoch (AD 1414–3574)—is the fifth epoch during the Fifth Great Age of Earth evolution. (Lemuria was the Third Great Age, Atlantis the Fourth Great Age, and since the great flood that destroyed Atlantis, we are now in the Fifth Great Age). The present Manu is the exalted Sun-initiate who guided humanity out of Atlantis during the ancient flooding that destroyed the continent of Atlantis formerly in the region of the Atlantic Ocean—the Flood referred to in the Bible in connection with Noah. He is the overseer of the seven cultural epochs corresponding to the seven astrological ages from the Age of Cancer to the Age of Capricorn, following the sequence: Cancer, Gemini, Taurus, Aries, Pisces, Aquarius, Capricorn. The present Manu was the teacher of the Seven Holy Rishis who were the founders of the ancient Indian cultural epoch (7227–5067 BC) during the Age of Cancer. He is known in the Bible as Noah, and in the Flood story belonging to the Gilgamesh epic he is called Utnapishtim. Subsequently this Manu appeared to Abraham as Melchizedek and offered Abraham an agape ("love feast") of bread and wine. Jesus is designated as "high priest after the order of Melchizedek" (Hebrews 5:10).

Mary: Rudolf Steiner distinguishes between the Nathan Mary and the Solomon Mary (see corresponding entries). The expression "Virgin Mary" refers to the Solomon Mary, the mother of the child Jesus whose birth is described in the Gospel of Matthew.

Mary Magdalene: Sister of Lazarus, whose soul was transformed and purified as Christ cast out seven demons who had taken possession of her. Christ thus initiated Mary Magdalene. Later, she anointed Christ Jesus. And she was the first to behold the Risen Christ in the Garden of the Holy Sepulcher on the morning of his resurrection.

megastar: Stars with a luminosity greater than 10,000 times that of our Sun.

Nain, Youth of: Referred to in the Gospel of Luke as the son of the widow of Nain. The Youth of Nain—at the time he was 12 years old—was raised from the dead by Jesus. The Youth of Nain later reincarnated as the Prophet Mani (third century AD) and subsequently as the Grail King Parzival (ninth century AD).

Nathan Jesus: From the priestly line of David, as described in the Gospel of Luke. An immaculate and pure soul whose one and only physical incarnation was as Jesus of Nazareth (Nathan Jesus).

Nathan Mary: A pure being who was the mother of the Nathan Jesus. The Nathan Mary died in AD 12, but her spirit united with the Solomon Mary at the time of the Baptism of Jesus in the River Jordan. From this time on, the Solomon Mary—spiritually united with the Nathan Mary—was known as the Virgin Mary.

New Jerusalem: A spiritual condition denoting humanity's future existence that will come into being as human beings free themselves from the *maya* of the material world and work together to bring about a spiritualized Earth.

Osiris: Osiris and Isis are names given by the Egyptians to the preincarnatory forms of the spiritual beings who are now known as Christ and Sophia.

Parzival: Son of Gahmuret and Herzeloyde in the epic *Parzival* by Wolfram von Eschenbach. Although written in the thirteenth century, this work refers to actual people and events in the ninth century AD, one of whom (the central figure) bore the name Parzival. After living a life of dullness and doubt, Parzival's mission was to seek the Castle of the Grail and to ask the question "What ails thee?" of the Grail King, Anfortas—moreover, to ask the question without being bidden to do so. Parzival eventually became the new Grail King, the successor of Anfortas. Parzival was the reincarnated prophet Mani. In the incarnation preceding that of Mani, he was incarnated as the Youth of Nain (Luke 7:11-15). Parzival is a great initiate responsible for guiding humanity during the Age of Pisces, which has given birth to the cultural epoch of the development of the consciousness soul (AD 1414-3574).

Pentecost: Descent of the Holy Spirit fifty days after Easter, whereby the cosmic "I AM" was birthed among the disciples and those individuals close to Christ. They received the capacity to develop Manas or Spirit Self within the community of striving human individuals, whereby the birth of the Spirit Self is facilitated through the soul of the Virgin Mary. See also World Pentecost.

phantom body: The pure spiritual form of the human physical body, unhindered by matter. The far-distant future state of the human physical body when it has become purified and spiritualized into a body of transformed divine will.

Presbyter John: Refers to Lazarus-John who moved to Ephesus about twenty years after the Virgin Mary had died there. In Ephesus he became a bishop. He is the author of the Book of Revelations, the Gospel of St. John, and the Letters of John.

Risen One: The initial appearance of Christ in his phantom body (resurrection body), beginning with his appearance to Mary Magdalene on Easter Sunday morning. Christ frequently appeared to the disciples in his phantom body during the 40 days leading from Easter to Ascension.

Satan: The traditional Christian name for Ahriman.

Serpent: Another name for Lucifer, but sometimes naming a combination of Lucifer and Ahriman, as in Revelations 12:9: "And the great dragon was cast out, that old serpent, called the Devil, and Satan, which deceiveth the whole world...."

Shepherd Stream: Biblically, the genealogical line from David the shepherd through his son Nathan. It was into this line that the Nathan Jesus was born, whose birth is described in the Gospel of Luke. Rudolf Steiner describes the shepherds, who—according to Luke—came to pay homage to the new-born child, as those servants of pure heart who perceive the good will streaming up from Mother Earth. The hearts of the shepherd were kindled with the fire of Divine Love by the coming of the Christ. The shepherds can be regarded as precursors of the heart stream of humanity that now intuits the being of Christ as the spirit of the earth.

Solomon Jesus: Descended from the genealogical line from David through his son Solomon. This line of descent is described in the Gospel of Matthew. The Solomon Jesus was a reincarnation of Zoroaster (sixth century BC). In turn, Zoroaster was a reincarnation of Zarathustra (6000 BC), the great prophet and founder of the ancient Persian religion of Zoroastrianism. He was a Bodhisattva, who as the founder of this new religion that was focused upon the Sun Spirit Ahura Mazdao, helped prepare humanity for the subsequent descent into incarnation of Ahura Mazdao, the cosmic Sun Spirit, as Christ.

Solomon Mary: The wise mother of the Solomon Jesus, who adopted the Nathan Jesus after the death of the Nathan Mary. At the time of the Baptism of Jesus in the River Jordan, the spirit of the Nathan Mary united with the Solomon Mary.

Usually referred to as the Virgin Mary or Mother Mary, the Solomon Mary bore witness at the foot of the cross to the Mystery of Golgotha. She died in Ephesus eleven years after Christ's Ascension.

Sophia: Sophia is part of the Divine Feminine Trinity comprising the Mother (counterpart of the Father), the Daughter (counterpart of the Son), and the Holy Soul (counterpart of the Holy Spirit). Sophia, also known as the Bride of the Lamb, is the Daughter aspect of the threefold Divine Feminine Trinity. To the Egyptians Sophia was known as Isis, who was seen to belong to the starry realm surrounding the earth. In the Book of Proverbs, attributed to King Solomon, Sophia's temple has seven pillars (Proverbs 9:1). The seven pillars in Sophia's temple represent the seven great stages of Earth evolution (from Ancient Saturn to Future Vulcan).

Sorath: The great enemy of Christ who works against the "I" in the human being. Sorath is identified with the two-horned beast that rises up from the depths of earth, as described in the Apocalypse of St. John. Sorath is the Sun Demon, and is identified by Rudolf Steiner as the Antichrist. According to the Book of Revelations his number is 666.

Sun Demon: Another name for Sorath.

Transfiguration: The event on Mt. Tabor where Christ Jesus was illumined with Divine Light raying forth from the purified etheric body of Jesus, which the Divine "I AM" of Christ had penetrated. The Gospels of Matthew and Luke describe the Transfiguration. The sunlike radiance that shone forth from Christ Jesus on Mt. Tabor was an expression of the purified etheric body that had its origin during the Old Sun period of Earth evolution.

Transubstantiation: Sacramental transformation of physical substance—for example, the transubstantiation of bead and wine during the Mass to become the body and blood of Christ. During the Holy Eucharist the bread and wine are transformed in such a way that the substances of bread and wine are infused with the life force (body) and light (blood) of Christ. Thereby the bread and wine are re-united with their divine archetypes and are no longer "merely" physical substances, but are bearers on the physical level of a spiritual reality.

Turning Point of Time: Transition between involution and evolution, as marked by the Mystery of Golgotha. The descending stream of involution culminated with the Mystery of Golgotha. With the descent of the Cosmic Christ into earthly evolution, through his sacrifice on Golgotha an ascending stream of evolution began. This sacrifice of Christ was followed by the events of his Resurrection and Ascension, which in turn was followed by Whitsun (Pentecost)—all expressing the ascending stream of evolution. This path of ascent was also opened up to all human beings by way of the power of the divine "I AM" bestowed—at least, potentially—on all humanity by Christ through his sacrifice on the cross.

Union in the Temple: The event of the union of the spirit of the Solomon Jesus with the 12-year-old Nathan Jesus. This union of the two Jesus children signified the uniting of the priestly (Nathan) line and the kingly (Solomon) line—both lines descended from King David.

Whitsun: "White Sunday"; Pentecost.

World Pentecost is the gradual event of cosmic revelation becoming human revelation as a signature of the end of the Dark Age (Kali Yuga). Anthroposophy (spiritual science) is a language of spiritual truth that could awaken a community of striving human beings to the presence of the Holy Spirit and the founding of the New Jerusalem.

Zarathustra: The great teacher of the ancient Persians in the sixth millennium BC (around 6000 BC). In the sixth century BC, Zarathustra reincarnated as Zoroaster. He then reincarnated as the Solomon Jesus (6 BC–AD 12), whose birth is described in the Gospel of Matthew.

Zoroaster: An incarnation of Zarathustra. Zarathustra/Zoroaster was a Bodhisattva. Zoroaster lived in 6th century BC. He was a master of wisdom. Among his communications as a teacher of wisdom was his specification as to how the zodiac of living beings in the heavens comes to expression in relation to the stars comprising the twelve zodiacal constellations. Zoroaster subsequently incarnated as the Solomon Jesus, whose birth is described in the Gospel of Matthew, to whom the three magi came from the East bearing gifts of gold, frankincense, and myrrh.

REFERENCES

*See "Literature" on page 10 for an annotated list
of books on Astrosophy.*

Allen, Paul Marshall. *A Christian Rosenkreutz Anthology.*
Blauvelt, NY: Garber, 2000.

——. *Vladimir Soloviev: Russian Mystic.* Blauvelt, NY: Garber,
2008.

Andreev, Daniel. *Rosa Mira: Die Weltrose.* Frankeneck,
Germany: Vega, 2009.

——. *The Rose of the World.* Great Barrington, MA: Lindisfarne
Books, 1997.

Anonymous. *Meditations on the Tarot.* New York: Tarcher/
Putman, 2002.

——. *The Mysterious Story of X7.* Berkeley, CA: North Atlantic
Books, 2009.

Boardman, Terry. *Kaspar Hauser: Where Did He Come From?*
Stourbridge. UK: Wynstones Press, 2007.

Dorsan, Jacques. *The Clockwise House System: A True
Foundation for Sidereal and Tropical Astrology.* Great
Barrington, MA: Lindisfarne Books, 2011.

Fagan, Cyril. *Zodiacs Old and New; Astrological Origins.*
London: Anscombe, 1951.

Hand, Robert. *Whole Sign Houses: The Oldest House System:
An Ancient Method in Modern Application.* Bel Air, MD:
Arhat, 2000.

Houlding, Deborah. *The Houses: Temples of the Sky.*
Bournemouth, UK: Ascella, 2006.

Houser, Kaspar. *Kaspar Hauser Speaks For Himself; Kaspar's
Own Writings.* North Yorkshire, UK: Camphill Books,
1993.

König, Karl. *A Christmas Story.* North Yorkshire, UK:
Camphill Books, 1995.

Nouvel, Maurice. *La vraie domification en astrologie.* Puiseaux,
France: Pardés, 1991.

O'Leary, P. V. (ed.) *The Inner Life of the Earth: Exploring the
Mysteries of Nature. Subnature, and Supranature.* Great
Barrington, MA: SteinerBooks, 2008.

Powell, Robert. *The Christ Mystery.* Fair Oaks, CA: Rudolf
Steiner College, 1999.

——. *Elijah Come Again: A Prophet for Our Time: A Scientific
Approach to Reincarnation.* Great Barrington, MA:
Lindisfarne Books, 2009.

——. *Hermetic Astrology,* vols. 1 and 2. San Rafael, CA: Sophia
Foundation Press, 2006.

——. *History of the Zodiac.* San Rafael, CA: Sophia Academic
Press, 2007.

——. *The Most Holy Trinosophia: The New Revelation of the
Divine Feminine.* Great Barrington, MA: SteinerBooks,
2000.

——. *The Mystery, Biography, and Destiny of Mary Magdalene:
Sister of Lazarus John & Spiritual Sister of Jesus.* Great
Barrington, MA: Lindisfarne Books, 2008.

——. and Kevin Dann. *The Astrological Revolution: Unveiling
the Science of the Stars as a Science of Reincarnation and
Karma.* Great Barrington, MA: SteinerBooks, 2010.

——. *Christ and the Maya Calendar: 2012 & the Coming of the
Antichrist.* Great Barrington, MA: SteinerBooks, 2009.

Prokofieff, Sergei O. *Relating to Rudolf Steiner: And the
Mystery of the Laying of the Foundation Stone.* London:
Temple Lodge, 2008.

Schultz, Joachim. *Movements and Rhythms of the Stars: A
Guide to Naked-eye Observation of Sun, Moon and
Planets.* Edinburgh: Floris Books, 2008.

Steiner, Rudolf. *According to Luke: The Gospel of
Compassion and Love Revealed.* Great Barrington, MA:
SteinerBooks, 2006.

——. *According to Matthew: The Gospel of Christ's Humanity.*
Great Barrington, MA: SteinerBooks, 2006.

——. *Anthroposophical Leading Thoughts.* London: Rudolf
Steiner Press. 1985.

——. *Anthroposophy (A Fragment): A New Foundation for the
Study of Human Nature.* Hudson, NY: Anthroposophic
Press, 1996.

——. *The Apocalypse of St. John: Lectures on the Book of
Revelation.* Hudson, NY: Anthroposophic Press, 1993.

——. *Bees.* Hudson, NY: Anthroposophic Press, 1998.

——. *The Bhagavad Gita and the West: The Esoteric
Significance of the Bhagavad Gita and Its Relation to the
Epistles of Paul.* Great Barrington, MA: SteinerBooks,
2009.

——. *The Book of Revelation: And the Work of the Priest.*
London: Rudolf Steiner Press, 2008.

——. *Broken Vessels: The Spiritual Structure of Human Frailty.*
Great Barrington, MA: SteinerBooks, 2003.

——. *Calendar 1912–1913: Facsimile Edition.* Great Barrington,
MA: Steiner Books, 2003.

——. *Christ and the Spiritual World: And the Search for the
Holy Grail.* London: Rudolf Steiner Press, 2008.

——. *Christianity as Mystical Fact: And the Mysteries of
Antiquity.* Great Barrington, MA: SteinerBooks, 2006.

——. *Cosmosphy* vols. 1 and 2. Spring Valley, NY:
Anthroposophic Press, 1985.

——. *The Destinies of Individuals and of Nations.* London:
Rudolf Steiner Press, 1986.

——. *Egyptian Myths and Mysteries.* Hudson, NY:
Anthroposophic Press, 1971.

——. *Esoteric Christianity and the Mission of Christian Rosenkreutz*. London: Rudolf Steiner Press, 2000.

——. *Eurythmy as Visible Speech*. London: Rudolf Steiner Press, 1984.

——. *The Fifth Gospel: From the Akashic Record*. London: Rudolf Steiner Press, 1998.

——. *"Freemasonry" and Ritual Work: The Misraim Service*. Great Barrington, MA: SteinerBooks, 2007.

——. *From the History & Contents of the First Section of the Esoteric School 1904–1914*. Great Barrington, MA: SteinerBooks, 2010.

——. *From Sunspots to Strawberries… Answers to Questions*. London: Rudolf Steiner Press, 2002.

——. *From Symptom to Reality in Modern History*. London: Rudolf Steiner Press, 1976.

——. *The Gospel of John in Its Relation to the Other Three Gospels*. Spring Valley, NY: Anthroposophic Press, 1982.

——. *The Gospel of St. John*. New York: Anthroposophic Press, 1962.

——. *Guidance in Esoteric Training: From the Esoteric School*. London: Rudolf Steiner Press, 2001.

——. *How to Know Higher Worlds: A Modern Path of Initiation*. Hudson, NY: Anthroposophic Press, 1995.

——. *Human and Cosmic Thought*. London: Rudolf Steiner Press, 1991.

——. *Human Questions and Cosmic Answers: Man and his Relation to the Planets*. London: Anthroposophical Publishing, 1960.

——. *The Incarnation of Ahriman: The Embodiment of Evil on Earth*. London: Rudolf Steiner Press, 2006.

——. *The Inner Nature of Man: And Our Life between Death and Rebirth*. London: Rudolf Steiner Press, 1994.

——. *Intuitive Thinking as a Spiritual Path: A Philosophy of Freedom*. Hudson, NY: Anthroposophic Press, 1995.

——. *Isis Mary Sophia: Her Mission and Ours*. Great Barrington, MA: SteinerBooks, 2003.

——. *Karmic Relationships: Esoteric Studies*, vol. 4. London: Rudolf Steiner Press, 1997.

——. *Man and the World of Stars: The Spiritual Communion of Mankind*. NY: Anthroposophic Press, 1963.

——. *Man in the Light of Occultism, Theosophy, and Philosophy*. London: Rudolf Steiner Press, 1964.

——. *Mystery Knowledge and Mystery Centers*. London: Rudolf Steiner Press, 1973.

——. *Mystery of the Universe: The Human Being, Model of Creation*. London: Rudolf Steiner Press, 2001.

——. *An Outline of Esoteric Science*. Hudson, NY: Anthroposophic Press, 1997.

——. *Philosophy, Cosmology and Religion*. Spring Valley, NY: Anthroposophic Press, 1984.

——. *The Reappearance of Christ in the Etheric: A Collection of Lectures on the Second Coming of Christ*. Great Barrington, MA: SteinerBooks, 2003.

——. *Rosicrucian Christianity*. Spring Valley, NY: Mercury Press, 1989.

——. *Search for the New Isis, the Divine Sophia: The Quest for the Isis–Sophia*. Spring Valley, NY: Mercury Press, 1983.

——. *The Secret Stream: Christian Rosenkreutz & Rosicrucianism*. Hudson, NY: Anthroposophic Press 2000.

——. *Spiritual Beings in the Heavenly Bodies and in the Kingdoms of Nature*. Great Barrington, MA: SteinerBooks, 2011.

——. *The Spiritual Guidance of the Individual and Humanity: Some Results of Spiritual-Scientific Research into Human History and Development*. Hudson, NY: Anthroposophic Press, 1991.

——. *The Spiritual Hierarchies and the Physical World: Zodiac, Planets & Cosmos*. Great Barrington, MA: SteinerBooks, 2008.

——. *Theosophy: An Introduction to the Spiritual Processes in Human Life and in the Cosmos*. Hudson, NY: Anthroposophic Press, 1994.

——. *The True Nature of the Second Coming*. London: Rudolf Steiner Press, 1971.

——. *Turning Points in Spiritual History*. Great Barrington, MA: SteinerBooks, 2007.

——. *Twelve Moods of the Zodiac*. Eschborn, Germany: Verlag Gerhold, 1987.

——. *World History in the Light of Anthroposophy*. London: Rudolf Steiner Press, 1977.

——. and Edouard Schuré. *The East in the Light of the West/ Children of Lucifer: A Drama*. Blauvelt, NY: Garber, 1986.

Sucher, Willi. *Isis Sophia I: Introducing Astrosophy*. Meadow Vista, CA: Astrosophy Research Center, 1999.

——. *Isis Sophia II: An Outline of a New Star Wisdom*. Meadow Vista, CA: Astrosophy Research Center, 1985.

Tomberg, Valentin, *Christ and Sophia: Anthroposophic Meditations on the Old Testament, New Testament, and Apocalypse*. Great Barrington, MA: SteinerBooks, 2006.

——. *Russian Spirituality and other Essays: Mysteries of Our Time Seen through the Eyes of a Russian Esotericist*. Asheville, NC: Logosophia, 2010.

Tradowsky, Peter. *Kaspar Hauser: The Struggle for the Spirit*. London: Temple Lodge, 1997. Reprint expected by 2012.

Tresemer, Lila Sophia, and David Tresemer. *One Two ONE: A Guidebook to Conscious Partnerships, Weddings, and Rededication Ceremonies*. Brooklyn, NY: Lantern, 2009.

von Halle, Judith. *Descent into the Depths of the Earth on the Anthroposophic Path of Schooling*. London: Temple Lodge, 2011.

——. *Illness and Healing: And the Mystery Language of the Gospels*. London: Temple Lodge, 2008.

Vreede, Elisabeth. *Astronomy and Spiritual Science: The Astronomical Letters of Elizabeth Vreede*. Great Barrington, MA: SteinerBooks, 2001.

ABOUT THE CONTRIBUTORS

DANIEL ANDREEV (1906-1959) was born in Berlin. His father was the well-known Russian writer Leonid Andreev. His mother Alexandra Veligorsky died during childbirth. Daniel's father, overcome with grief, gave up Andreev to Alexandra's sister Elizabeth Dobrov, who lived in Moscow. It was a critical event in Daniel Andreev's life, for in contrast to many of the Russian intelligentsia at the time, the family maintained its Russian Orthodox faith. Daniel's childhood included contact with persons such as his godfather Maxim Gorky. Daniel was conscripted as a noncombatant in the Soviet Army in 1942, and after the war he returned to writing fiction and poetry. He was arrested in 1947, along with his wife and many of his relatives and friends, and sentenced to twenty-five years in prison, while his wife received twenty-five years of labor camp. All of his previous writings were destroyed. With the rise of Khrushchev, Andreev's case was reviewed and his sentence reduced to ten years. He was released to his waiting wife in 1957, his health ruined following a heart attack in prison. While in prison, he had written the first drafts of *The Rose of the World* and *Russian Gods* (a collection of poetry), as well as *The Iron Mystery,* a play in verse. Andreev spent the last two years of his life finishing these works. Andreev's wife Alla, realizing the negative reception the books would get from the Soviet authorities, hid them until the mid-1970s and did not publish them until Gorbachev and glasnost. The first edition of *The Rose of the World* (100,000 copies) quickly sold out, and since then several editions have been equally popular in Russia.

WILLIAM BENTO, Ph.D., has worked in the field of human development for more than thirty years. He is a recognized pioneer and a published author in psychosophy (soul wisdom) and astrosophy (star wisdom) and travels extensively as a speaker, teacher, and consultant. He currently resides in Citrus Heights, California. Dr. Bento is the Associate Dean of Academic Affairs at Rudolf Steiner College, Fair Oaks, California and works as a transpersonal clinical psychologist at the Center for Living Health in Gold River, California. His involvement in guiding social therapy seminars for Camphill Communities has been well received over the last two decades. He is coauthor of *Signs in the Heavens: A Message for Our Time* and author of *Lifting the Veil of Mental Illness: An Approach to Anthroposophical Psychology.* His forthcoming book is *Psychosophy: A Primer for an Extended Anthroposophical Psychology,* to be published by SteinerBooks.

WAIN FARRANTS discovered astrology (both tropical and sidereal) and Anthroposophy during his first years at the University of Toronto. After completing a B.Sc. in psychology and mathematics, he spent the next few years teaching math at a secondary school in Mochudi, Botswana. Later, he traveled to England and became a biodynamic gardener in a Camphill Community for disabled adults in the North York Moors National Park. After a few years there, he assumed responsibility for the Botton Village Bookshop. He has edited and coedited numerous books written by Karl König, Peter Roth, Baruch Urieli, Peter Tradowsky, and Andrea Damico Gibson. Wain has also contributed a number of articles to the *Christian Star Calendar*. He has considerable experience in a wide variety of orthodox, complementary medical, and alternative therapies, without which he would not have made his contribution to the *Journal*.

BRIAN GRAY trained as an architect. Since 1981, he has taught at Rudolf Steiner College in Fair Oaks, California. He teaches classes to aspiring Waldorf school teachers on topics such as the creation of the world and cosmic warmth from a spiritual perspective, sacred architecture, and the constitution of the human being. He teaches various aspects of Astrosophy related to biography, life cycles, karma and reincarnation, and astro-geographia. A student of astrology since 1967, Brian has interpreted astrological charts for thousands of people and offers regular classes in observation of the stars and in esoteric Christianity. He has discovered hidden astrological keys in several important works of literature, from the Parzival story of the Grail knights to parts of the Bible. Brian directs the Foundations in Anthroposophy Program at Rudolf Steiner College. His courses from January to May 2012 on "Deepening Anthroposophy," are a new venture at Rudolf Steiner College.

CLAUDIA MCLAREN LAINSON is a teacher and Therapeutic Educator. She has been working in the field of Anthroposophy since 1982, when she founded her first Waldorf program in Boulder, Colorado. She lectures nationally on various topics related to spiritual science, human development, the evolution of consciousness and the emerging Christ and Sophia mysteries of the twenty-first century. Claudia is the founder of Windrose Farm and Academy near Boulder. Windrose is a biodynamic farm and academy for collaborative work in anthroposophic courses, therapeutic education, cosmic and sacred dance and nature-based educational programs. Claudia most recently founded the School for the Sophia Mysteries at Windrose.

SALLY NURNEY has been interested in astrology all her life, beginning her research with her "Sun sign" in elementary school. After several years of travel and exploration, she arrived at The StarHouse in Boulder, Colorado, in 1997 and quickly transitioned to the Sidereal perspective of reading the stars. Along with her studies in the Path of the Ceremonial Arts, she has deepened her direct understanding of the stars through research with David Tresemer at The StarHouse and study with Brian Gray at the Rudolf Steiner College in Fair Oaks, California. She currently lives in the Rocky Mountain foothills near the StarHouse of Boulder.

ROBERT SCHIAPPACASSE has been a student of Rudolf Steiner's Anthroposophy for more than thirty years. He developed a deep interest in humanity's relationship to the world of the stars and, in 1977, began studies with Willi Sucher, a pioneer researcher in the field of Astrosophy, or star wisdom. He presents at conferences and workshops on star wisdom themes and other anthroposophic topics. He is coauthor with David Tresemer and William Bento of the book *Signs in the Heavens: A Message for our Time*, about the comets Hyakutake and Hale-Bopp and their crossing of the mysterious and ominous star Algol at the end of the twentieth century. Robert most recently worked with David Tresemer on the book *Star Wisdom and Rudolf Steiner: A life Seen through the Oracle of the Solar Cross*. He also coauthored with David Tresemer the articles "The Chain Reaction Experiment"; "The Signature of Saturn in Christ Jesus' Life"; and "The Signature of Pluto in the Events of Christ Jesus' Life."

ROBERT POWELL, Ph.D., is an internationally known lecturer, author, eurythmist, and movement therapist. He is founder of the Choreocosmos School of Cosmic and Sacred Dance, and cofounder of the Sophia Foundation of North America. He received his doctorate for his thesis *The History of the Zodiac*, available as a book from Sophia Academic Press. His published works include *The Sophia Teachings*, a six-tape series (Sounds True Recordings), as well as *Elijah Come Again: A Prophet for Our Time; The Mystery, Biography, and Destiny of Mary Magdalene; Divine Sophia—Holy Wisdom; The Most Holy Trinosophia and the New Revelation of the Divine Feminine; Chronicle of the Living Christ; Christian Hermetic Astrology; The Christ Mystery; The Sign of the Son of Man in the Heavens; The Morning Meditation in Eurythmy;* and the yearly *Journal for Star Wisdom* (previously *Christian Star Calendar*). He translated the spiritual classic *Meditations on the Tarot* and co-translated Valentin Tomberg's *Lazarus, Come Forth!* Robert is also coauthor with Kevin Dann of *The Astrological Revolution: Unveiling the Science of the Stars as a Science of Reincarnation and Karma* and *Christ & the Maya Calendar: 2012 & the Coming of the Antichrist;* and coauthor with Lacquanna Paul of *Cosmic Dances of the Zodiac* and *Cosmic Dances of the Planets*. He teaches a gentle form of healing movement: the sacred dance of eurythmy, as well as the cosmic dances of the planets and signs of the zodiac. Through the Sophia Grail Circle, Robert facilitates sacred celebrations dedicated to the Divine Feminine. He offers workshops in Europe, Australia, and North America, and with Karen Rivers, cofounder of the Sophia Foundation, leads pilgrimages to the world's sacred sites: Turkey, 1996; the Holy Land, 1997; France, 1998; Britain, 2000; Italy, 2002; Greece, 2004; Egypt, 2006; India, 2008; Turkey, 2009; and the Grand Canyon, 2010. Visit www.sophiafoundation.org and www.astrogeographia.org.

RICHARD TARNAS is a professor of philosophy and cultural history at the California Institute of Integral Studies in San Francisco, and the founding director of its graduate program in Philosophy, Cosmology, and Consciousness. He also lectures on archetypal studies and depth psychology at Pacifica Graduate Institute in Santa Barbara. A graduate of Harvard and formerly the director of programs at Esalen Institute, he is the author of *The Passion of the Western Mind*, a history of the Western world view from the ancient Greek to the postmodern that became both a bestseller and a required text in many universities. His most recent book, *Cosmos and Psyche: Intimations of a New World View*, received the Book of the Year Prize from the Scientific and Medical Network in the UK.

DAVID TRESEMER, Ph.D., has a doctorate in psychology. In 1990, he cofounded the StarHouse in Boulder, Colorado, for community gatherings and workshops (www.TheStarHouse.org) and cofounded, with his wife Lila, the Healing Dreams Retreat Centre in Australia (www.healingdreams.com.au). He has also founded the Star Wisdom website (www.StarWisdom.org), which offers readings from the Oracle of the Solar Crosses, an oracle relating to the heavenly imprint received on one's day of birth. Dr. Tresemer has written in many areas, including *The Scythe Book: Mowing Hay, Cutting Weeds, and Harvesting Small Grains with Hand Tools* and a book on mythic theater, *War in Heaven: Accessing Myth Through Drama*. With his wife, he also coauthored several plays produced in the U.S., including *My Magdalene* (winner of Moondance 2004, Best Script). With William Bento and Robert Schiappacasse, he wrote *Signs in the Heavens: A Message for Our Time*. He is also the author, with Robert Schiappacasse, of *Star Wisdom & Rudolf Steiner: A Life Seen through the Oracle of the Solar Cross*, and with his wife, the recent book, *One-Two-ONE: A Guidebook for Conscious Partnerships, Weddings, and Rededication Ceremonies*.

A star is above my head.
Christ speaks from the star:
"Let your soul be borne
Through my strong force.
I am with you.
I am in you.
I am for you.
I am your I."
—RUDOLF STEINER

Sophia Foundation
of North America

Earth Chakras
& the 2012
Venus Transit
at Mt. Shasta, California

Saturday, June 2 –
Wednesday, June 6, 2012

with Co-founders of the Sophia Foundation of N. A.

Robert Powell, PhD
internationally known author
and lecturer on cosmology and star wisdom

and **Karen Rivers, M.A.**
Director of the New Chartres School
Wisdom University Faculty

Featuring — observation of the Venus transit,
the new star wisdom of Astrosophy,
and the enlivening experience of Sacred Dance.

To the starry heavens above,
I direct my gaze.
Starlight penetrates into my heart.
The heart's power strengthens my eyes.
My eyes strengthen the inner light of my soul.
Peace streams into my soul.
—BASED ON A VERSE BY RUDOLF STEINER

Experience the stars, the dramatic occultation of Venus across the face of the Sun, from the holy ground of one of the earth's seven primary chakras. Mt. Shasta, the location of this event, is one of the earth's planetary chakras, corresponding to the seven visible planets. This most potent region of Mt. Shasta, one of the most powerful upon the planet has long been known to the Native Americans, who thought it to be the center of creation. The Modoc Indians taught that after the creation the Great Spirit dwelt upon Mt. Shasta.

During this time on Mt. Shasta we will focus upon Earth mysteries and the wisdom of the Stars, helping participants find a living relationship to the starry heavens through evening star-gazing, and to the Earth through sacred dance, song and silence, uniting with Divine Sophia. The culmination of the retreat will be the observation of the Venus transit, which starts around 3:30 pm on Tuesday, June 5 and lasts for about six hours. The Sun will set around 8:30 pm while Venus is still transiting. We will observe the transit through a specially prepared telescope, which will be set up by astronomer David Cooper. In the words of Rudolf Steiner: "Venus transits are very interesting because they take place only once every hundred years or so, and very significant things can be observed when Venus is passing in front of the Sun."

The movement of Venus before the face of the Sun occurs in pairs eight years apart with over a hundred years between the pairs. Venus orbits the Sun every 225 days. From the earth's point of view, Venus usually crosses the position of the Sun above or below the Sun's bright disc. In 1874 and 1882, Venus went across the Sun's face, and then again in 2004. The second of the pair will occur on June 5/6, 2012. The Venus eclipse of the Sun will not recur again until December 2117, in another pair eight years apart.

PROPHECY · PHENOMENA · HOPE
The Real Meaning of 2012
Christ & the Maya Calendar—An Update

Robert Powell

Robert Powell, explores what 2012 really means, updating the research presented in the ground-breaking book, *Christ & the Maya Calendar: 2012 and the Coming of the Antichrist* (coauthored with Kevin Dann). Here, Powell focuses on two significant prophecies by Rudolf Steiner. The first (from 1909) concerns the Second Coming of Christ, his appearance to humanity as the Etheric Christ. The second (from 1919) represents the shadow side of Christ's Second Coming—the incarnation in human form of Ahriman.

Powell points to the steady, multifaceted encroachment of ahrimanic forces today, especially as the harmful effects of modern technology on the etheric body. After looking into Steiner's prophetic remarks on the Book of Revelation, Powell looks into the prophecies of the Russian poet/mystic Daniel Andreev and examines the prophecy of the American clairvoyant Jeane Dixon concerning the human birth of the Antichrist. He also includes spiritual research by Judith von Halle regarding an earlier incarnation of Jospeh Stalin, as well as Andreev's indications relating to Stalin's earlier incarnations, which may be seen as preparation of this individuality for his role as "Mr. X," the human vessel for the incarnation of Ahriman.

Applying the astrological rules of reincarnation, Powell's research supports Jeane Dixon's prophecy, that Mr. X was born in 1962, a finding whose accuracy was also confirmed by Willi Sucher, Powell's mentor in Astrosophy. This finding, seen in relation to various contemporary phenomena, confirms Rudolf Steiner's prophetic statement that the incarnation of Ahriman into his human vessel would take place shortly after the year 2000.

Nonetheless, great hope for humankind is offered by the return of Christ in the etheric realm, an event to which human beings can connect, as humanity and the Earth pass through the great trials associated with 2012.

ISBN: 9781584201113 | 138 pages | pbk | $16.00

THE ASTROLOGICAL REVOLUTION
Unveiling the Science of the Stars as a Science of Reincarnation and Karma

Robert Powell & Kevin Dann

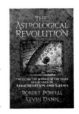

The reader is invited to question the basis of modern astrology—the tropical zodiac, which emerged through Greek astronomers from what was originally a calendar dividing the year into twelve solar months. Ninety-eight percent of Western astrologers use the tropical zodiac, meaning that it is based on a calendar system that no longer embodies the reality of the stars.

Astrology needs to be brought back into alignment with the stars in the heavens. The first step in this astrological revolution is to recognize the sidereal zodiac. In antiquity, the Babylonians, Egyptians, Greeks, Romans, and Hindus used the sidereal zodiac, and today Hindu (Vedic) astrologers still use the sidereal zodiac. Based on recognition—through the newly discovered rules of astrological reincarnation, that the sidereal zodiac presents an authentic astrological zodiac—a new practice of astrology is possible that offers tools to reestablish a wisdom-filled astrology in the modern world. This new astrology, based on the sidereal zodiac, is similar to the classic sidereal form but in a modern form, as that practiced by the three magi, who—prompted by the stars—journeyed to Bethlehem two thousand years ago.

Drawing on specific biographical examples, *The Astrological Revolution* reveals new understandings of how the starry heavens work into human destiny. The book points to the astrological significance of the entire celestial sphere, including all the stars and constellations beyond the twelve zodiacal signs. This discovery is revealed by studying the megastars, the most luminous stars of our galaxy, illustrating how megastars show up in an extraordinary way in Christ's healing miracles by aligning with the Sun at the time of those miraculous events.

KEVIN DANN, Ph.D., has taught history at SUNY Plattsburgh, the University of Vermont, and Rutgers University. He is also the coauthor of *Christ & the Maya Calendar* with Robert Powell.

ISBN: 9781584200833 | 254 pages | pbk | $25.00

THE CLOCKWISE HOUSE SYSTEM

A TRUE FOUNDATION
FOR SIDEREAL AND TROPICAL ASTROLOGY

Jacques Dorsan
Wain Farrants and Robert Powell, editors

Jacques Dorsan, a leading pioneer of sidereal astrology in France, uses more than eighty sidereal horoscopes to illustrate his clockwise house system. With charts from the original French edition and many added, this book embodies one of the most important astrological discoveries of twentieth and twenty-first centuries. Astrology normally views the twelve houses in astrology in a counterclockwise direction, the direction of the zodiac signs. According to Dorsan, however, we should view them in a clockwise direction.

By using this clockwise house system along with the sidereal zodiac, everything falls into place in a horoscope, unlocking the mystery of the horoscope. We are given access to a true form of astrology, enabling a giant leap forward in the practice of astrology. It allows us to recover the original astrology. Moreover, Rudolf Steiner's indications, as well as the research of the French statistician Michel Gauquelin, confirm that the astrological houses run in a clockwise direction.

This English translation includes more than eighty charts, both those in Dorsan's original work in French and more added by the editor of this edition.

JACQUES DORSAN was born December 22, 1912, in Orléans, France. In 1936, he moved to the Ivory Coast, where he drew his first horoscope. It was more than seven years before he began to do consultations. Fourteen years later, after intense practice in Brazil and before returning to France, he had become convinced that the houses actually move in the direction opposite the zodiacal signs. He put his idea to the test for more than twenty years before publishing the original version of this book *Le véritable sens des maisons astrologiques* (1984). Jacques Dorsan lived in Morocco, New York City, Monaco, Luxembourg, Belgium, Zaire, and New Caledonia. He died September 8, 2005, in Nice.

ISBN: 9781584200956 | 330 pages | pbk | $30.00

THE VENUS ECLIPSE OF THE SUN 2012

A RARE CELESTIAL EVENT:
GOING TO THE HEART OF TECHNOLOGY

David Tresemer, Ph.D.

"David Tresemer's acknowledgement of the School of Zarathustra is not only an affirming statement about the true origins of astrology. It is a sincere call to every star seeker to find his or her way back to an astrology informed by an imaginative communion with the stars. He demonstrates this way by penetrating a rare celestial event with his earnest painstaking research, his scholarship and his free-spirited pursuit of finding meaning in every story, image and event. From his Star Wisdom Credo to his last chapter, entitled 'Hands of the Heart,' David points out how the practical art of reading the signs in the Heavens can lead to making a difference in the world."
—**William Bento**, Ph.D., transpersonal psychologist; Associate Dean, Rudolf Steiner College

The hyperbole and inflated attention given to the supposed "end of the world" on December 21, 2012, has obscured an actual rare celestial event happening in June of 2012—the passage of Venus before the face of the Sun as seen from the Earth, which happens every 125 years. Although Venus is much smaller than the Sun, Tresemer calls this an eclipse because of the ways he expects it to affect world events. What impact will it have?

David Tresemer considers the dynamics of Sun, Earth, Venus, and the exact location in the heavens of this eclipse event, weaving a dramatic story about the heart of technology, its uses for good or for ill, and the direction in which to find one's power in "hands of the heart," actions based on warm feeling toward another.

Find out about the nature of "erotic phantasms" and how to work constructively with them and who will support us through these times.

ISBN: 9781584200741 | 172 pages | pbk | $15.00

CPSIA information can be obtained at www.ICGtesting.com
Printed in the USA
BVOW051314271111

276851BV00002B/1/P